UNSETTLED

VIKING
COMPASS

UNSETTLED

AN ANTHROPOLOGY OF THE JEWS

MELVIN KONNER

VIKING COMPASS

VIKING COMPASS
Published by the Penguin Group
Penguin Group (USA) Inc., 375 Hudson Street,
New York, New York 10014, U.S.A.
Penguin Books Ltd, 80 Strand,
London WC2R 0RL, England
Penguin Books Australia Ltd, 250 Camberwell Road, Camberwell,
Victoria 3124, Australia
Penguin Books Canada Ltd, 10 Alcorn Avenue,
Toronto, Ontario, Canada M4V 3B2
Penguin Books India (P) Ltd, 11 Community Centre, Panchsheel Park,
New Delhi–110 017, India
Penguin Books (N.Z.) Ltd, Cnr Rosedale and Airborne Roads, Albany,
Auckland, New Zealand
Penguin Books (South Africa) (Pty) Ltd, 24 Sturdee Avenue,
Rosebank, Johannesburg 2196, South Africa

Penguin Books Ltd, Registered Offices:
80 Strand, London WC2R 0RL, England

First published in 2003 by Viking Penguin,
a member of Penguin Group (USA) Inc.

1 3 5 7 9 10 8 6 4 2

Library of Congress Cataloging-in-Publication Data

Konner, Melvin
Unsettled : an anthropology of the Jews / Melvin Konner.
p.   cm.
Includes bibliographical references and index.
ISBN 0-670-03244-1
1. Jews—History. 2. Jews—Civilization. 3. Jews—Identity. I. Title.

DS116.K66 2003
909'.04924—dc21   2003050182

This book is printed on acid-free paper. ∞

Printed in the United States of America
Set in Granjon
Designed by Daniel Lagin

To three rabbis:

Bernard L. Berzon
Arnold M. Goodman
Herbert A. Friedman

with enduring gratitude

The Jews had light and gladness, joy and honor.
So let it be with us. . . .

—from the weekly service ending the Sabbath

ACKNOWLEDGMENTS

How can I thank all the people who have contributed to my knowledge of Judaism and Jewishness over more than half a century? I learned the Hebrew alphabet on the knee of my grandfather, Abraham Levin, from the *Daily Forward* and watched him sway in tallis and tefillin every morning. My parents were less religious but equally respectful, and they saw to it that I was in the local Orthodox synagogue, Ahavath Israel, almost every day between age eight and my mid-teens; it was truly my second home. The rabbi, Bernard L. Berzon, the teachers, and even the scoutmaster there gave me the foundation of knowledge and emotion that made this book possible. Conversations with my friend Gerard Glassman, a brilliant boy who came to Judaism late and with great intensity, sharpened my thinking on long walks through the Brooklyn night.

In college I was aloof, but Mervyn Verbit, then the Hillel director at Brooklyn College, argued with me enough to keep the spark alive. My years in Cambridge, Massachusetts, were not very Jewish, but raising a family in Atlanta brought me back into the fold, at least partly. Rabbi Arnold Goodman and others at the Ahavath Achim Conservative synagogue were tolerant of my odd relationship to Judaism and helped me revive and extend my childhood knowledge. Steven Weiss, the assistant rabbi, inspired me with his passion and depth, as did Rabbi Mark Kunis, then of Congregation Shearith Israel. Two of my faculty colleagues, Rabbi David Blumenthal and Dr. Deborah Lipstadt, have provided welcome friendship, guidance through their writings and other Jewish texts, and many hours of illuminating conversation. Rabbi Emanuel Feldman, the distinguished leader of the Atlanta Orthodox community for four decades, bridged a huge gap of faith and practice to befriend me, and I learned much from him.

Dr. Herbert and Hazel Karp generously took my young family under their wing, introducing us to the local Jewish community and inviting us to share Jewish festivals in their home several times a year, in Atlanta and Jerusalem, for two decades. Drs. Shlomit and David Finkelstein did the same, and their more secular perspective—we were as likely to discuss Buddhism or quantum physics as Judaism—taught me that Jewish practice does not require conventional faith. Steve and Gita Berman, two of the most dedicated members of the Atlanta Jewish world, have opened their hearts to me, and I am grateful for their warmth and humor. Dr. Joseph and Rachel Glazer often opened their home to me, as Joe advised me on the translation of Yiddish poetry. When my family faced tragedy, these friends were there. So were my brother, Lawrence Konner, and my friends Herbert Perluck, Joseph Beck, Sarah Steinhardt, Michael Cantor, Jerome and Melissa Walker, John Stone, Peter Brown, and many others, Jewish and not.

My first trip to Israel was supported by the American Jewish Committee, and the quite sophisticated tour was led by the late Yehuda Rosenman, a Jewish sociologist with broad knowledge and a twinkle in his eye. On that trip, my one meeting with the great Yiddish poet Avraham Sutzkever, conducted imperfectly in two or three languages—we both liked Robert Lowell, we discovered—inspired me to read and try to translate his work. I spent the following year at the Center for Advanced Study in the Behavioral Sciences, attached to Stanford University, and the friendship of John and Mary Felstiner, experts on different aspects of Jewish culture, was important both personally and professionally. In 1988 I began teaching a course on Jewish anthropology, and I am grateful to several hundred students over the years since for asking the right questions and forcing me to think more carefully than ever before about the answers. I thank my colleagues in the department of anthropology at Emory University, and President James Laney and Dean David Minter, for their open-minded support.

A real turning point for me came in 1989, when I was invited to join the Wexner Heritage Foundation seminar in Atlanta. This two-year series of tri-weekly four-hour classes and three weeklong retreats, one in Israel, built a second, new foundation of Jewish knowledge on the old one I had laid down in childhood. Wexner assembled people in midlife who had distinguished themselves in some way as Jewish leaders and brought the best scholars in Jewish studies, religious and secular, to teach them. As Rabbi Herbert Friedman, then president of the foundation—the seminar series was his brainchild, and it has now been held throughout the United States—once said, I was a maverick in this group. But whatever I had to offer, it had a lot to offer me. I made lasting friendships, gained great insight into the American Jewish community, and learned many new things about Judaism and Jewishness. In addition to Rabbi Friedman, I am grateful to Rabbi Nathan Laufer, his successor; to Rabbi Ramie Arian; to Lori Baron, the staff director; and to Leslie Wexner, whose ongoing generosity makes these seminars possible. I also thank Glenda and David Minkin, Toby Director Goldman, Michael Rosensweig, and other members of the seminar.

In the late nineties, Rabbi Arnold Goodman organized an interdenominational seminar on Genesis, and it helped me to understand the enduring fascination of those ancient stories. I am grateful to him, the Reverend Joanna Adams, the Reverend Jack Graham, Dr. Jonathan Lauter, Dr. Herbert Karp, and other members of the seminar.

I have now made seven trips to Israel and have been changed by them not once, but several times, in different ways. My friends the Selas—Michael, Pazit, and their three children (now grown), Nogah, Ayelet, and Yoni—have opened their home to me and my family many times and taught me about Israel, warts and all. Their exceptional warmth and hospitality have helped create my sense, partly fictional, that I belong there, and their sophisticated insights into Israeli life and history—Pazit is a clinical psychologist, Michael a software engineer, both combat veterans, both doves—have helped make whatever grasp I have of the complexities of Israel possible. Louis Williams, a former officer in the Israel Defense Forces Spokesman Bureau and author of a standard history of the IDF in English, and his wife, Dr. Susan Lourenço, are both now activists in the cause of Arab rights. They are also good friends who have helped in many ways. Others in Israel who have been generous with their hospitality, knowledge, and experience include Dr. Elli and Debbie Wertman and their family, David and Toba Frankel, Rabbi David and Dr. Malka Schaps, Dr. Eliyahu and Malka Regev, Esther Freiberg, Dr. Avi Nissan, and Sarah Willen.

On one of my visits my daughter Susanna took me to meet her friends in Ramallah, East Jerusalem, and Amman. Their generous hospitality across a great gap of possible enmity will never be forgotten. One of them, Walid Husseini, became a friend, and I am very grateful for his continuing insight into the bitter anguish of his tragically suffering people.

Judith Robertson has provided unstinting professional support for this project for years, doing library research, reconciling contradictions, tracking down pesky, hard-to-find references, managing my personal library, typing, applying for and securing permissions, and helping during a stressful and disorderly relocation. My agent, Elaine Markson, a friend for decades, believed in the project early on and found a wonderful editor, Janet Goldstein, who helped make it real. Janet's firm editorial hand shaped the book in countless positive ways. Assistant editors Susan O'Connor and Lucia Watson have been gracious and helpful, as has copyrights manager Tsuyako Uehara, and Bruce Giffords and his editorial production team helped me fix scores of errors and smooth over many rough places. The physical design of the book, by Daniel Lagin (interior) and Michelle Ishay (cover), achieves a level of elegance and beauty that I can only hope the text approaches.

Shlomit Finkelstein read the manuscript at a level of detail and with a breadth of knowledge that has saved me from many embarrassments and made the book immeasurably richer. Professor Ira Katznelson of Columbia

University also gave it especially close attention and made many valuable suggestions. Others who read it and provided helpful comments include Rabbi David Wolpe, the Reverend Peter Samuelson, and Dr. Leslie Rubin. Professor Isaac Jack Lévy gave meticulous attention to Chapter 8, "Spain and Beyond," and his expert knowledge of Sephardic Jewry improved it greatly. Alas, I cannot share with any of these colleagues the slightest responsibility for what is wrong with this book; that responsibility is only mine.

My late wife, the ethnographer Marjorie Shostak, was completely secular in origins and disposition, but she generously supported my increasingly frequent forays into Jewish practice and, more important, supported my commitment to raise Jewish children. I will always be grateful for that, and for her love and encouragement over three decades. Kathy Mote, our non-Jewish nanny for over fifteen years, has always done the same, and has made a point of learning a lot about Judaism. Her devotion saved our family during my wife's long illness and after her death. My life has now been joined to that of Ann Cale Kruger, who has brightened it beyond measure and helped heal the wounds of the past. But my greatest gratitude goes to my three children, Susanna, Adam, and Sarah, who were eighteen, fourteen, and nine when we lost their mother. Their resilience and love made it possible for me not just to survive but to face the future with new hopes and dreams. Many of mine are simply theirs, and I hope to help them realize those dreams.

This book is dedicated to three rabbis. Rabbi Bernard L. Berzon was the passionate voice—I can still hear it ringing from the pulpit—and wise leader of my childhood Orthodox synagogue, whose guidance helped form my consciousness. His collection of simple and forceful sermons, *Good Beginnings,* has just been brought back into print by Jonathan David Publishers. Rabbi Arnold M. Goodman is the emeritus spiritual leader of our family's Conservative synagogue in Atlanta, one of America's largest such congregations. Brilliant and insightful, he has worked for many years on the law committee of the Conservative movement, and our conversations over the years, on subjects ranging from Torah to the biology of sexual orientation, have never failed to bring me closer to an understanding of Judaism. Rabbi Herbert A. Friedman, president emeritus of the Wexner Heritage Foundation, left a Reform pulpit in Denver in 1945, joined the U.S. Army, went to Germany, and helped to save the remnant of Hitler's victims and get them to Israel. He indulged my strange approach to Judaism and Jewishness—a maverick, he once publicly called me—and, directly and through the seminars, taught me much about Jewish faith, Jewish practice, and the Jewish people. None of these deeply religious men could fully approve of my basically secular book, but I hope they would think it was good for the Jews, and useful to anyone who wants to understand them.

CONTENTS

INTRODUCTION

Who are the Jews and why are they still here? Other people have suffered greatly; others have survived. But the Jews seem to garner a kind of attention focused on no other people. They may be unique in their accomplishments and so have often been targets of envy. They may also be unique in their standoffishness and have also been feared and resented. But there is no doubt that they are unique in the amount of attention the world has given them, now perhaps more than ever. Why? That is the mystery at the heart of this work, and it took me, and will take us, through the grand sweep of Jewish cultures in time and space.

But this is no conventional Jewish history. It makes no claim to thorough coverage of events and leaders—the standard succession of wars and treaties, speeches and conventions, is not the point here. Rather, it is to understand the cultures of the Jews, from their origins to today and even perhaps tomorrow. Of course, some standard historical facts are needed as anchor points, but the interest of anthropologists is always drawn away from kings and ministers to ordinary people: How did or do they live? What do they believe in? What are their hopes and dreams? What do they worship? What do they teach their children? What entertains and uplifts them? What threatens their survival and how do they react? How do they see themselves in a wider human world?

This approach leads to some quite different emphases than those of conventional history. Here are some of the main points this book will make:

- Contrary to some claims, peoplehood—something quite different from religion—has been a part of Jewish identity from the beginning. It preceded by centuries Temple Judaism, the priestly religion of the ancient Holy Temple in Jerusalem, and, certainly, Torah Judaism, which the rabbis created after the Second Temple was destroyed, and it has figured in every phase of Jewish history.

Notwithstanding the power of Jewish religion ancient and modern, in every generation there have been substantial numbers of Jews who did not practice Judaism yet played important roles in Jewish life.

• The notion of the Jews as a studious, mild, ethical people who do not fight is a myth. Ancient Israel was born in violence, as were both Temple and Torah Judaism. It is true that the Jews did not have an army of their own for two millennia, but they have fought bravely and effectively in the armies of every nation they have ever lived in, even nations where they were bitterly persecuted and had to fight for the right to fight.

• The great Jewish gifts to the world—monotheism, the Ten Commandments, resistance against tyranny—were born in weakness in a group of tribes, then a kingdom, buffeted between great empires; nurtured in a series of bitter exiles; and annealed in genocide. This produced allegiance to a single all-powerful God who could protect them, a code of laws that maintained decency in the face of perversions of power, and a searing sense of injustice.

• The Jews did not come to Israel from anywhere else at any time. They have been there from time immemorial. They became a coherent people there, discovered God there, built a kingdom there, created the Torah there, and composed much of the Talmud there. Attempts to evict them partly succeeded, but their presence there has always been significant. Wherever they were in exile they longed to go back there, and in every generation some did. Their presence there is permanent, and future attempts to evict them will incur a huge cost.

• At least four times ancient Israel was devastated because of Jewish factionalism, extreme religious zealotry, and military overreach. This may happen again. Recent Jewish fanaticism, mass murder, assassination, splinter cults, and messianic dreams all eerily recall the patterns of the distant past. Indeed, if that past holds any lessons and current conditions continue, modern Israel, like its ancient counterpart, will be at least as threatened from within as from without.

• The Jews have suffered bitterly, but every generation has celebrated life every year. They have sung their warriors' praises in joy, circumcised their sons in joy, prepared for the Sabbath in joy, danced with the Torah in joy, learned and taught it in joy, settled throughout the world in joy, and returned to their dangerous homeland in joy. They have made jokes about themselves and others, told and written funny stories, and commented on their frequently painful daily lives with a thousand lighthearted quips and proverbs. The view of the Jews as always weeping and lamenting is another myth.

The Jews came onto the stage of history as a group of warlike tribes centered in the hill country of Judea. They were indigenous to the Jordan River region, and slowly developed from a collection of tribes into a kingdom. Like everything else in the ancient world, this involved great violence. What we call civilization was nourished by rivers of blood.

There is no evidence outside the Bible for any of the events described in it until quite late in the saga. The Creation, the Flood, the patriarchal family settling the land, the Exodus, the revelation on Mount Sinai, the wandering in the desert, or the conquest of Canaan, the Promised Land—all exist only in biblical texts. But the Bible is a document like any other. It has its own purposes and distortions, but as a wise archeologist once said, just because it is written in the Bible doesn't necessarily mean that it is wrong.

And of course, there are other kinds of truth. If the text of the Bible is the revealed word of God, or even the work of authors directly inspired by God, then its claims do not have to be held to any scientific or scholarly standard. I understand this kind of belief, I respect it, and I once subscribed to it myself. But it will not figure in any sense in this account of how the people of Israel lived, and how they became the Jews—except when there is independent corroborating evidence. With all due respect to believers, I write here as an anthropologist who does not believe anything that is not scientifically proven.

So what do we know? From the start the Israelites were in a buffer zone between empires, and this was formative. We can't grasp the origins of the Jews without understanding the weakness of their physical position. The hatred of domination by foreign powers was of the essence of Israelite culture. But the Israelites had their own emperor—the one God who trumped all earthly powers. They came late to the world stage, millennia after the rise of the Near Eastern civilizations, and were no more than a footnote to ancient history. But by adopting writing and making texts central to their culture, and by placing one God at the heart of religion and ethics, the Israelites changed the world.

The destruction of their first Temple in Jerusalem and the resulting first exile brought a new kind of Judaism into being. Texts, scribes, and interpreters became all-important, longing for Jerusalem became central, adaptations to host countries were created, weakness became strength—the strength of monotheism, ethics, and speaking truth to power—and a succession of prophets constantly reminded the people of these imperatives. The Temple and its priesthood were restored; but the new religion, centered on Torah interpretation as much as on animal sacrifice, developed in parallel. Idol worship continued to be a problem, and prophets arose to decry it, but also to hold Israel's rulers to account for their treatment of the poor. Despite the Temple's restored glory, this concern with the weak was now permanent.

Greek culture was more tempting than Babylon's, and the spectrum of adaptations from isolation to apostasy set the precedent for all future Jewish cultural encounters. But Greek anti-Semitism set limits on assimilation, and rabbinical Judaism was born. For the Jews at least, the ascent of Rome was a disaster, because Rome was the Stalinist Russia of its time. Severe oppression including thousands of crucifixions created seething rebellion, zealotry, messianism, and magic that gave rise to the mission of Jesus, as well as to two Jewish-Roman wars. Rome's genocidal response to those wars ended Temple Judaism and drove most of the Jews out of their land.

Rabbinical—talmudic—Judaism was now the religion of the Jews, as they spread over much of the civilized world. But as Christianity acquired political power Jews were increasingly defined as the enemies of Christ and were treated as such—humiliated, beaten, exiled, and murdered again and again. This now helped define their culture. Jews living under Islam were also considered inferior, but enjoyed much more tolerance. Islamic culture shaped the Jews, who participated in it at all levels, and who brought the benefits of this higher culture to their central European brethren. In Islamic Spain, the Jews wrote troubadour poetry in Hebrew, served as military leaders, and made great contributions to philosophy.

They also developed a mystical tradition in Spain and Israel, paralleled by folk beliefs about imps and demons. But the mainstream of Jewish thought went through rabbinical academies, where the best minds gathered, competed, were nurtured, and were married off in every generation, creating a kind of cult of the intellect. With the opening of European secular thought to Jews, these outsiders' contribution was way out of proportion to their numbers. They have continued to be overrepresented in every secular intellectual enterprise that humanity has turned its mind to.

Jews are not called wanderers for nothing, and their travels have reached the ends of the earth. Thriving and substantial Jewish communities existed for centuries in Arabia, Ethiopia, India, and China, while smaller numbers of Jews settled in the mountains of the Caucasus, on the island of Curaçao, and on the Alaskan frontier, to name just a few examples. Jewish communities have played a role beyond their numbers in Australia, South Africa, and Argentina. The common threads of these far-flung cultures tell us much about the essence of Jewishness. Exotic Jewish communities may not be the norm today, but they reflect the process that began Jewish life in every location outside of Israel.

Less exotically, Jews settled in central and eastern Europe, where they built the culture that dominates the Jewish world today. They created Yiddish, making it a language of everyday life as well as a literary language.

They developed a variety of rabbinical traditions, and reached the pinnacle of excellence in Torah and Talmud study. These Jews were largely murdered by the Nazis and their collaborators in all occupied countries. So were the Sephardic Jews of the northern Mediterranean. But enough survived to carry on most Jewish traditions. They fought against their oppressors in many ways, and they won important victories. Tempered in this crucible of death, many of the survivors were hardened fighters who would help create the state of Israel.

Jews, or at least *conversos,* may have come to the Americas with Columbus. By Washington's time there were several established communities, mainly Sephardic Jews, and they committed themselves to the Revolution with blood and treasure, as Jews have done in every other war the United States has fought. This was the greatest diaspora, and the one in which Jewish life would become most normal. The huge influx of Ashkenazic Jews in the nineteenth and early twentieth centuries transformed them and their new country both. Their (mainly temporary) involvement in organized crime, their immense contribution to entertainment and the arts, and their achievements in science, technology, and business brought respect. But it was their continual legal testing of America's stated ideals, both on their own behalf and that of others, that would be their greatest contribution.

Beginning in the nineteenth century the ages-old trickle of Jews back to Israel widened to a rivulet, then a stream, then a river. Legendary fights against swamps, malaria, and hostile Arabs marked several generations. The kibbutz, the world's most successful invented society, played a critical role in addressing these and other challenges. Hebrew was revived as a modern language, the only ancient language that has ever been reborn. A culture of sacrifice and militancy arose to protect this fragile entity from its far more numerous enemies. But great divisions created tensions and inequalities, not least with respect to whether and when the Palestinian people will have a state of their own.

Despite men's domination of Jewish life, women have emerged from the shadows since biblical times. They have led armies, defied kings, contributed to the Talmud, built multinational business empires, written memoirs and letters, resettled Israel, led it, given their lives in heroic actions against their enemies, helped end apartheid in South Africa and segregation in America, sat in the Senate and on the Supreme Court, and helped create the labor movement and the feminist revolution—all while producing the next generation of Jews. However, the history of Jewish women is in some ways just beginning.

Jewish life will survive future threats just as it has survived all past ones. Jews have suffered, but not lying down. They have a tradition of arguing with God, and have pursued social justice by arguing with kings. They will continue to be hated, to achieve great things for themselves and others, to defend their ancient homeland, and to face the world with the proud yet open-minded stance that has allowed them to survive for more than three millennia. There is every reason to believe that they will be here for the next.

⚭

While this is an anthropologist's view of Jewish culture and history, it is also inevitably a personal view, and so it seems wise to say who I am. I was born in Brooklyn and raised in a "modern Orthodox" family. I went to public schools where about a third of the students were Jewish, and I was in the local Orthodox synagogue—Ahavath Israel, Avenue K and East Twenty-ninth Street—every day of my life between ages eight and seventeen, five days a week for classes, the other days for services. The leader of that congregation, Rabbi Bernard L. Berzon, remains incandescent in my memory four decades later. Friday evenings in his home were almost as likely to include discussions of Shakespeare or Dostoyevsky as Talmud and Torah. But he glowed with a love for the Jewish people, the Jewish Torah, and the Jewish God.

I lost my faith at seventeen amid the rebellions of the sixties, a philosophy course in my first semester in college, and of course a great love. At the beginning of that semester I used to walk halfway across Brooklyn to see the young lady on Friday nights; at the end of it I no longer saw the meaning of God. I never regained my faith, and I was largely out of touch with anything Jewish for fifteen years. I had reconstructed a worldview based on science—evolution, anthropology, and behavioral biology would eventually explain my nature and that of every other human being. But unlike some nonbelievers, I considered my loss of faith precisely that—a loss.

Still, I maintained what I considered a strong inner Jewish identity. With my name, average looks, and nondistinctive voice I could easily have passed, but I always found an excuse to let people know that I was Jewish. During those years I read extensively about the Holocaust, married someone at least nominally Jewish, followed the novels of Bernard Malamud, Philip Roth, and Saul Bellow very faithfully, and ate bagels and lox. That was about it.

At seventeen, in the throes of the sixties, I may have thought that both sectarianism and God were on the way out, but at thirty I knew better. At thirty-two, when my first child was born, I was ready for some kind of Jewish reawakening. When she was eight days old I was walking around Harvard Yard with her in a Snugli and I noticed some music at Memorial Church. It was Yom Kippur, and I was amazed to find about 1,500 people in a Reform Jewish service there. I had been on the Harvard campus for twelve years and had never realized how large and active the Jewish community was. And this was not the largest service. The Conservative one in

Memorial Hall held 2,500, the Orthodox one 750, a Reconstructionist service and others many more. I had had no idea.

As Chanukah approached, I looked into my daughter's eyes and asked myself, "Are three thousand years of tradition going to end with me?" I lit Chanukah candles for the first time in fifteen years. So it went, as not faith, but Jewish practices reentered my life. Many required negotiations with my wife, who had grown up virtually devoid of them. When we had our son circumcised, it was a ritual in our home on the eighth day, and we read the passage where God commands Abraham to circumcise and seal the covenant. *And he who is not circumcised in the skin of his foreskin . . . that soul shall be cut off from his people.* This ominous shadow would not fall on our son, who now had a Jewish identity, Jewish anatomy, and Jewish vulnerability. After moving to Atlanta, and thanks in no small part to my wife's open-mindedness, we joined a synagogue and gave our three children a Jewish education. That way, as adults they would have a choice.

In 1985 I went to Israel for the first time with a group of college professors sponsored by the American Jewish Committee. To say that this had a major impact on me would be the understatement of that decade. It so happened that we arrived on Christmas Day, and as the bus took us from the airport through the streets of Tel Aviv, I realized I was looking at a normal working day, without decorations or Christian music, as people shopped or found their way home in the gathering dusk. For the first time in my life I was in a Jewish country, not a Christian one. I also felt shame that I had waited so long to make the pilgrimage, although as a child I had absorbed Zionist ideals. Near the end of that for me momentous trip, I was walking atop the Masada fortress when a fellow traveler asked me why I looked so pained. "This is the greatest adventure in Jewish history," I said—meaning modern Israel—"and I am not a part of it."

The six months after that trip were a daze of admiration and affection very much like being in love. I woke up and went to sleep thinking about Israel, feeling the pain of separation from the beloved, steeped in fantasies about moving there to be with her. My wife was feeling the pinch of jealousy, I think, when she asked at breakfast one morning, "Where is this going?" The answer turned out to be increased involvement in the Jewish community and the mounting of a course called "Anthropology of the Jews." This would be a stretch for me, since my expertise was in the biological basis of human behavior, but there was no course in Jewish anthropology at my university. I thought I could fill the gap, since I knew a lot about anthropology and a lot about the Jews.

It was much harder than that, but as I taught it for more than a decade, I learned what I needed to know, and then some. The end result was this book, motivated by personal involvement with Jews and Judaism but informed by an extensive literature. I was greatly aided in my adult education by two years in the Wexner Heritage Foundation seminars, which revived what I knew in childhood and added much more. I eventually made six more trips to Israel, talking extensively with people in three kibbutzim, three West Bank settlements, Tel Aviv, Haifa, and of course Jerusalem. My friendships with Israelis range across all walks of life and from one end of the political spectrum to the other, including an ultra-Orthodox rabbi with a long beard and a black coat, bronze-tanned pioneers, career warriors, and left-wing activists. Some of their views make me very uncomfortable, but I mainly listen. On one trip my eldest daughter—the one for whom I first lit the Chanukah candles—took me to meet her friends in Ramallah and Amman. It was bracing and important to hear, see, and feel their side of the story.

I also visited and studied many archeological sites and began to understand in a new way how this ancient people emerged from a rock-strewn, brown-and-green, sun-washed landscape and acquired the values that changed the world. I saw a good deal of the rest of the Jewish world as well, visiting synagogues in Edinburgh, Paris, Padua, Cairo, and other cities—some now just museums—and the heart of Jewish mysticism in Girona, Spain. I also visited the concentration camp at Dachau. This book may not be based on conventional research, but a great deal of lived experience went into it.

The most important of these experiences are not in travels though, but in the course of my own American-Jewish journey. I began as an Orthodox boy, became a skeptical uninvolved young man, and grew back into Jewishness as children entered my life. I can perhaps be fairly accused of practicing "pediatric Judaism," the contemptuous term some rabbis use for people who engage in Jewish activities through and for their children. But my favorite definition of a Jew is an unofficial one: someone who has Jewish children. By that definition as well as several others, I am certainly a Jew. Yet there is more to my holiday and Friday night observances than "for the children's sake." I love the forms, the ritual, the poetry, the haunting melodies that take me back to 1950s Brooklyn. On that first trip to Israel I went to the Western Wall several times, picked up a prayer book, and chanted the prayers I had said so many times as a boy. One day I heard Yehuda Rosenman, our fine guide on that trip, say to a colleague behind me, "There's Mel Konner again, praying to the God that he doesn't believe in."

This is very Jewish. The Torah tells us that when Moses offered God's Law to the Hebrew people, they said, "We will do and we will understand." This paradox of practice before understanding, practice leading to understanding, is characteristically Jewish. There is no leap of faith, no rebirth in the Jewish God. There are practices that lead to and confirm faith every day. As the rabbi of my childhood said when I asked him about my doubts—I can still see the intensity on his face—"If you lose your faith, it will be a terrible thing." He raised a finger in a characteristic gesture. "But don't stop coming to shul."

I did stop for a long time, and when I started again, not at all consistently, it may have been too late. Certainly I have not had my faith reawakened. But I have had my love for the tradition and my allegiance to the people who practice it reconfirmed beyond all measure. This has been immensely rewarding for me, both an emotional and an intellectual adventure. I hope that, in a small way, this book—the culmination of my search so far—may help other Jews to understand their Jewishness and their history. I hope too that the many non-Jewish friends of the Jews will find in it some answers to their questions about this people. And, perhaps quixotically, I hope that even some enemies of the Jews may find in it reasons to mitigate their enmity, or even to awaken their sympathy. The epigraph I chose for the book comes from the Havdalah service that ends the Sabbath. "So let it be with us" does not, in my mind, refer only to the Jews. It refers to all humanity. For surely the making of a decent, prosperous, peaceful world will help to ensure Jewish survival.

UNSETTLED

1

GENESIS

HOW THE JEWS WERE BORN IN ISRAEL

At first God crafted the skies and the land, but the land was tumble-bumble, dark hid the deep, and God's wind hissed at the face of the waters. But God said, "Light will be," and it was light. So it was dusk and it was dawn, Day One....

Whatever else we may or may not know about the Jews, it is likely that in their earliest generations as an identifiable people, they were already telling this story. By the time they had really become Jews they had written it down, and the pale, dried skin it was inked on was sacred to them. There can have been no time when there were Jews but no text, because text was of their essence. They belonged to it even more than it belonged to them. They very nearly worshiped it, and they surely believed that it reflected the mind of God, whom they called Elohim, or Yahweh.

Radically arrogant in their divine abstractions, they saw no distinction between God and their God. Yahweh was God. Anyone could worship Yahweh, perhaps, but he was theirs first. Eventually they would conclude that there could be no other. Thus did a group of paltry, poor hill-country tribes, relentlessly buffeted among huge warring states, dismiss with a small wave of its hand all the great gods of all those looming, mighty empires.

Or really, a wave of its mind. As soon as there were Jews, no doubt, they insisted upon abstractions. Where others built statues of gold, bronze, and marble, minimally fitting tributes to their feared, cherished gods, the Jews rejected all such concretions and all the deeply held beliefs that went along with them. Think of the passion and reverence of Achilles and Agamemnon, Penelope and Odysseus, Antigone and Creon, to get some sense of what the Jews rejected: ancient, comforting, tried-and-true, fiercely fought-for, deeply held beliefs about awesome gods and compassionate goddesses.

They spoke, instead, of God, and let the idea hang in the air among them. They prayed to God, and basked in the glow of the Thou thus envisioned. God was theirs, not just as a people but as individuals, and each and every one of them could become intimate with God. Some wrote of God in paroxysms or trances of inspiration, and others found the writing holy. In time, if not at once, they cast off the distinction between the abstraction of a God-inspired text and that of a text authored by God. God, the first writer. God, who existed because he wrote. God, who wrote his message down and gave it to his people and through them to the world. Still in the new millennium, Jews throughout the world raise that text aloft every Sabbath for all to see, and sing or chant the proclamation of what it is—just as Jews did in two earlier millennia, and for all the Sabbaths in between. Hear their proclamation:

> *And this is the Torah*
> *Moses set*
> *Before the children of Israel—*
> *From the mouth of God,*
> *In the hand of Moses.*

The God of Creation, the God of the Flood, the God of Abraham, Isaac, and Jacob, yes; but most of all the God of Moses. The writer-God who made Moses a vehicle for the text. The invisible God for whom abstractions were harder than stone. The whispering God whose message, delivered by Moses, felled an empire. The shapeless God who dwelled in fog or a column of flame. The God who dragged his people out of the muck of slavery to meet and exchange words with him in the wilderness. The God whose greatest prophet climbed to the top of a barren mountain to sit for forty days and nights taking dictation. The God for whom the most palpable embodiment would be, once and for all, the text.

Yahweh or Elohim? According to scientific Bible scholarship, the books we know as Genesis and Exodus were melded from two main sources, each set down by an earthly author who lived not much less than three thousand years ago. One of them called God Yahweh, the other Elohim, and they wrote parallel versions of the tales that shaped their lives. A later editor—likely a committee—folded together versions by the Elohist and the Yahwist. And that was just the beginning; at least two other authors had their contributions edited in before the Torah as we know it was canonized.

But the first two concern us here because they first tried to define this people. They contradict each other in places, but they record a common tradition. Perhaps they represented different factions in the courts of Israel's kings, or rival branches of the hereditary priesthood. Perhaps tribal loyalty was a factor, and the blended text we know helped make two related tribes a nation. It has even been suggested that the Yahweh author was a woman in the court of King David's grandson, composing an ironic text that gave women pivotal roles and made important men look like fools.[1]

We can't know, really, but it is interesting to think that Elohim was the Hebrews' first name for their distinctive, solitary God. In the Torah's grammar, *Elohim* is a singular proper noun, but it seems to have a plural ending. *El,* god; *Elohim* . . . gods? *Elohim* is a singular noun with a strange property: plurality contained in singularity. If this is so, the very idea of one God—the supreme idea of an idea-ridden people—is contained in what may have been God's first name. *Elohim* proclaims not only God's oneness but the oneness of God's comprehensive inclusiveness. In other words, God's name proclaims the impossibility and falsity of every other competing idea of God. Say "Elohim," and you declare that the gods of Achilles are just so many chunks of stone, so many vain and helpless dreams, all absorbed in the complex unity of the only God.

Still, the Torah can say what it will; for our purposes, there must be other evidence for nonfundamentalists to believe the tales it tells. Independently corroborating historical documents. Archeological excavations. Tombstones engraved with telltale symbols. Trade records etched in stone tablets. Ships loaded with wine casks at the bottom of the sea. Altars. Stories told in Ur or Egypt of a small tribal people on the banks of the Jordan River, conquered and enslaved or still peskily fighting back. Monuments to conquest. Bows and shields interred with slain princes. Scratches on limestone slabs. Something.

The fact is, there is no corroborating evidence that Abraham, Isaac, or Jacob ever existed. Except for the Torah text, there is no decisive proof that the Hebrews were slaves in Egypt, that they rebelled and walked away from the place, or that a leader such as Moses arose and took that people into the desert. There is no proof that they wandered for forty years; that they crossed the Jordan from the east; that they made assaults on Jericho and other towns in what is now Judea; that they arrived believing that they had been promised that land; that they conquered the Canaanites west of the Jordan and stood off the Philistines coming in from the coastal plain; that they came, desert nomads, to settle in a land in which they had spied out giants, a land in which their forefathers had met Yahweh face-to-face, a land flowing with milk and honey. There is not one single fact that requires us to accept one single miracle, and the voices of science are raised in unison against most of them.[2]

And yet, the Bible is a document. Like many ancient documents it is quirky and tendentious, inventive and mythological, dazzlingly poetic and craftily dramatized. It has designs on the mind of the reader that are often not compatible with historical or scientific truth. But it also contains historical facts that have been independently confirmed. And again, even for those that have not: just because it is written in the Bible doesn't necessarily mean that it is wrong.

But even leaving faith aside, there is yet another kind of truth, and that is literary truth. The Torah itself reveals great truths about human nature. But more important for our purposes, it yields enormous insight into the minds and hearts of the people who have carried this Torah with them in some form for nearly three thousand years, and who told one another some of the stories for centuries before they were written down. Obviously, it does not correspond to an account of their culture, only to some of their aspirations and beliefs. If the Jews, instead of making written words their lifeblood, were a nonliterate people, then anthropologists would be interviewing tribal elders. They would diligently record the rules of behavior, the punishments for misbehavior, the nature of God and people's relationship to God, the precise prescriptions governing festivals and rituals, the stratification of society, and the role of priests. They would learn about the expected behavior of men and women, the protocol of marriage and family, and the reckoning of kinship and its attendant responsibilities. And of course they would write down the great, old stories, the sagas of wise, strong, and charismatic men and women from a time beyond time, the adventure tales that carry people out of themselves and that somehow, circuitously—not just by positive or negative example, but by the compelling literary power that grabs people by the throat and shakes them to the core—make them feel something indelible, and teach them how to live. In this sense the Torah, indeed the whole Jewish Bible or "Old" Testament, is an anthropological document.

So the Torah, historically true or not, is where we begin our journey; but we will range far beyond it. Jews have lived in every corner of the world and have persisted for more than three millennia. They have had many different interpretations of the Torah, and some have abandoned it for secular pursuits. But none have escaped its influence, and as we trace their history and survey the great sweep of changing Jewish cultures, we will find the Torah everywhere, proclaiming as it does that there is one God, that God expects human beings to meet certain obligations, that God demands justice. We will have many other sources of information about the cultures of the Jews—diaries, letters, artifacts, literature, histories, and even the past century's conventional anthropological studies of still-extant Jewish cultures. But the Torah will inform us in every time and place, and before we can understand its meaning, we must understand the world that gave birth to it.

The roots of the Jews are lost in the deep, blood-soaked mud of ancient empire. For several centuries in the middle of the second millennium B.C.E.—before the common era—the time when the Hebrews should, according to legend, have been slaves unto Pharaoh in Egypt, there are repeated references in Egyptian letters to people called *apiru*. It is possible, just possible, that *apiru* means Hebrew. It is also possible that *apiru* is merely a word for servants or slaves. Conceivably both are true—the ancient Hebrews could have derived their very name from their status as the oppressed. This would befit a people destined to be victimized countless times, to be crushed, to survive, and to triumph, and to build a culture that endlessly celebrates liberation from slavery and transcends oppression.

But the sojourn in Egypt, the generations in the wilderness, the conquest against all odds—these are legends. They may be true, but all we know about them is what we read in the Bible. It isn't necessarily wrong, but neither is it necessarily right. Scientifically, it is conjecture. Not conjecture, though, is the people Israel. They are mentioned clearly in the year 1207 B.C.E., on a stone column called the Merneptah stela, after the Pharaoh who commissioned it and made this boastful declaration:

> The chiefs are thrown flat and say, "Peace!"
> Not one of them lifts his head among the border enemies.
> Libya is seized,
> Hatti is pacified,
> Gaza is plundered most grievously,
> Ashkelon is brought in,
> Gezer is captured,
> Yanoam is made nonexistent,
> Israel is stripped bare, wholly lacking seed,
> Hurru has become a widow, due to Egypt.
> All lands are together "at peace":
> Anyone who stirs is cut down,
> By the king of Upper and Lower Egypt, Merneptah.[3]

That's it. A footnote in a catalog of destruction. But note the irony: The first mention of Israel is meant to be its last—"Israel is stripped bare, wholly lacking seed." So Merneptah's boast becomes the first claim that this particular people has come to the end of its history. Three millennia later, after many similar pronouncements, the people is still here. Why don't we hear about Israel earlier? Because it was utterly insignificant. This was a tiny, offbeat group of tribes in a geographic backwater, on a piece of territory always at the crossroads of empires. When the Hittite empire gets to clashing with the Egyptian one, or push comes to shove between the Babylonians and the Assyrians, the stakes may well include that territory west of the Jordan. *(You call that a river? That's not a river. The Nile is a river. The Euphrates is a river. The Jordan is a stream between—what are those tribes called again? Well, next conquest!)*

At some point an adviser may say, *Those people west of the Jordan's stream, those villages that dot the hills of Judea and Samaria, they have no real gods. Let us give them our gods.* And an emperor may nod absently over his evening wine, wave the adviser away, and soon find himself in a very annoying struggle with people who, if they have no gods, must yet have some-thing in their heads that makes them lay down their lives and kill perfectly good soldiers in order to keep other gods out. So another adviser says, *They have this god that they talk about—or rather that they don't. They write about him. Or they wrote about him once. They dedicate burnt offerings on altars erected before . . . nothing! They chant and murmur and sing in what appear to be trances, eyes closed, minds wandering. They have a god without an image, with a name that they won't say. But this god and his laws are to them worth dy-ing for. My advice: Exact tribute, tax them into poverty, drag them off in chains into slavery, whatever. But don't mess with their drivel about their God. Trust me, it will be more trouble than it's worth.*

We know that the Egyptian empire existed for at least two thousand years before the Hebrews are supposed to have been slaves there. The Egyp-tians conquered what is now Israel repeatedly during that time. Since slavery was pervasive in the ancient world and one of the main goals of conquest was to garner masses of slaves—along with gold, copper, goats, lapis lazuli, and other assorted tribute—it would be odd indeed if the tribal peoples of the Jordan region had never been enslaved by the Egyptians. Since famine was common, it is also quite likely that starving, seminomadic Israelites at some time or other migrated down into the Sinai Peninsula and farther south into Goshen, the northeast corner of Egypt, in search of pas-ture for their flocks. If they did, they would sooner or later have been at the mercy of whoever held those lands. This generic process, which undoubt-edly happened more than once over the centuries of ancient Egyptian rule, could be the basis of the biblical saga.

Egypt was constantly fending off attempts by the Hittites—then the reigning force to the north—to encroach on that piece of land. The peoples between the Jordan and the Mediterranean served as a buffer against the Hittites. The Hittites, for their part, didn't want the Egyptians in their backyard either, and tried to bring the between tribes under their own in-fluence. But ideally Egypt wanted to rule the fringes without being there. It needed allies it could rely on, allies that were weak compared to Egypt but strong enough to fend off the Hittites.

In the three centuries before Merneptah's ill-timed arrogance, Egypt did indeed dominate Israel, during an epoch known as the New Kingdom.[4] Their initial violent conquest left a layer of destruction in every archeolog-ical excavation in ancient Israel. After this, the land between the Jordan and the sea was crossed by north-south highways, along which Egyptian out-posts guarded travel and trade. Hundreds of letters from Egypt's emissaries and local vassals addressed to a long succession of Pharaohs reveal their thorough dominance and disabling exploitation. Destructive taxes de-manded large shipments of goods and extensive forced labor, often amounting to indentured servitude. Caravans went south toward the Nile laden with gold, silver, turquoise, lapis lazuli, cattle, horses, sheep, goats, wheat, barley, and of course slaves. They came back with tax collectors and soldiers.

After the main wave of conquest, repeated further efforts were needed to reestablish Egyptian dominance. One battle at Megiddo, a large town in the fertile valley east of the Carmel Mountains, was typical. Pharaoh Thutmose III laid siege to the town from May to December in the year 1468 B.C.E. When the city fell, the local princes crawled on their bellies to kiss the Pharaoh's feet, and then they and their families were forced, along with other captives, to carry all their wealth to Egypt. Over and above what Pharaoh's army ate and used and took for themselves, the recorded plunder included 11,000 tons of wheat, 20,500 sheep, 1,929 cattle, 2,041 horses, 924 chariots (including a ceremonial one made of gold), 200 coats of leather mail, and 502 bows. Taking three towns farther north on the same campaign, Thutmose captured 1,796 slaves and their children, 235 pounds of unworked gold and silver discs, and a wealth of valuable, finely crafted furniture, bowls, utensils, clothing, and statuary.[5]

Such lists reveal the brutality of the New Kingdom, but they also tell us a lot about life in Israel at the time. The larger towns had accumulated great wealth, were ruled by elites, and were constantly prepared for war, while the smaller settlements around and between the towns were simple agricultural villages. The bases of life were grain for bread, olives for oil, grapes for wine, and a local spring or river for water. Sheep, goats, and some cattle provided milk and meat. If you were a successful farm family, you could work hard, produce this natural wealth, pay taxes and tribute but still live decently, build a substantial stone house among others in the settlement, furnish it, and even buy some jewelry and make some household idols. Then, periodically, an army led by Pharaoh, by one of his Asian enemies, or even just by a local warlord from over the next hill would sweep through your life and take it all away.

Details are important, and we will have more of them, but over and above them there are patterns. Historians usually say that there are no laws of history. But there are certainly regularities and consistencies, and some anthropologists think of them as laws of culture change. In the Yangtze Valley, as in the valleys of the Nile, the Tigris, and the Euphrates—and later, in the Indus Valley, and much later but completely independently on the broad central Mexican plain around Lake Texcoco, in the Yucatán, and in the highlands of Peru—populations of hunters and gatherers slowly turned to farming and from then on had to defend their land instead of moving wherever the game was. Birth rates rose, and in terms of population, rural people had their backs to the wall. They united voluntarily or submitted to brutal conquest and domination.

Towns emerged and in time became cities. If there is one law of collective human action it is that people move to cities; they have been doing it for ten thousand years, and decrying it for most of that time. Call it the lure of the bright lights or population pressure on agricultural land, it has happened over and over again. Cities need food, specialized nonfarm labor, bosses, servants, and organized defenders. They need political stability, at least on the order of decades. And because life is inherently unpredictable and perilous, they need gods to explain their good or bad fortune, with priests to explain the otherwise unfathomable thoughts, motives, and wishes of those gods.

By the time there were towns, eight or ten thousand years ago, the seeds of empire were already in place. Kinship, the main organizer of all small-scale societies, determined the succession of chieftains and then the divine right of kings. Divine, because the priests and the kings were tightly allied, except when they were one and the same. Also in this ostensibly holy alliance were engineers who could raise houses, watchtowers, temples, and palaces and bring water to parched land; tax collectors and record keepers who could impose tribute on a widening mass of ignorant farmers around those towns; bureaucrats who could distribute to nonfarmers, however unfairly, the mountains of grain exacted in tribute and piled high in the king's silos; and above all, an army.

An army with strong ties of wealth, blood, loyalty, and fear to the political pyramid of priests, kings, and princes. An army that, in tandem with the priests' incantations, could keep common people at just that pitch between fear and comfort that would make them slowly work themselves to death while grumblingly or acceptingly paying tribute. And an army of legends and heroes to defend the kingdom from other armies that would, if they invaded, make the lives of common people even worse.

Thus, the rise of civilization. It is a story of population density, fear, aggression, conquest, subjugation, tribute, priestly incantations, and increasing dependency on those stronger or smarter or better-connected than you for your livelihood, your future, and your life. Karl Marx said something of capitalism that may not be true of that system, but is demonstrably true of what we like to call civilization: Civilization arose from the mud—literally, the mud of irrigated farmland near prodigious waterways—with blood oozing from every pore—mainly, the blood of expendable commoners who were slaughtered, enslaved, dragged off in chains at spearpoint, and either literally or figuratively sacrificed to the physical and spiritual comfort of their "betters." The poems, plays, and art that we associate with civilization were largely incidental.

With the possible exception of the early civilization of the Indus Valley, in any case temporary, this is the true story of every spot in the world where ecological conditions favored the rise of intensive agriculture. The pattern is depressingly consistent. To historians these processes may not be laws, but to an anthropologist they are about as close to being laws as anything describing biological materials—not without exception, but very helpful indeed.

⟨⟩

The case of the Israelites, Hebrews, or Jews was not exceptional at first. They were nowhere near the center of the action, which four or five thousand years ago was on the upper Nile, around Thebes, and in the lush bottomland "between the rivers"—the literal meaning of Mesopotamia. These two vast green valleys gave rise to empires—"civilizations"—through the general process just described, and through innumerable battles like the one fought by Pharaoh Thutmose at Megiddo. Of course this too was action, on the edges, where empires relentlessly clashed.

As we have seen, Egypt and Hatti, as the Hittite empire was known, were the main rivals. Israel was a confederation of tribes, a handful among many, who happened to dwell on the fringe of Egyptian dominance instead of squarely belonging to either empire. There were other tribes, and possibly other confederations, in the Middle East at the time.

But the Merneptah carving only mentions Israel; the other names are all towns or states, and Israel is the only tribal group listed. Intriguingly, its mention makes it masculine, while all the other names are feminine. Israel was distinctive in the region—not for its religion, but for its rough-and-ready tribal power. If its tribes attacked towns and settlements, other tribes, or even, from time to time, each other, Egypt would not shed many tears. Divide and rule was the strategy: create a buffer zone of towns and tribes strong enough to keep the Hittites at bay, but too weak to challenge Egypt.

But Egypt's policy of devastating taxation and frequent brutal reconquest steadily eroded the population. An Egyptian text gives a clear view of what a village farmer could have expected from the empire in the way of taxation before Israelite independence:

The scribe arrives. He surveys the harvest. Attendants are behind him with staffs, Nubians with clubs. One says to him, "Give grain." "There is none." He is beaten savagely. He is bound, thrown in the well, submerged head down. His wife is bound in his presence. His children are in fetters. His neighbors abandon them and flee. When it's over, there's no grain left.

There were also countless demands for conscripted and slave labor. A chronicler would later say of the Romans, "They made a desert and called it peace." In effect the Egyptians made a desert and called it empire, and in time they paid the price. By the year of Merneptah's boast, Egyptian power over Israel was on the verge of collapse. Invaders from Europe and Turkey—the Philistines of biblical fame—had conquered and settled the Mediterranean coast. Phoenicians, those ancient seafarers and scribes, controlled the coast of Lebanon. Europeans had kept Hatti out, and in the resulting power vacuum the tribal confederation known to Merneptah as Israel became strong.

The next two centuries have been thought of as a golden age for tribal Israel, corresponding to the biblical period of Judges, and culminating in David's kingdom. There is no evidence that Israel at this time embodied any ideal traits, or indeed that it differed much from other tribal confederations, except in power.[6] But something encouraged rebellion against Egyptian tyranny and gave the resulting political entity the credibility to take root and grow.

At first the Israelites were clients of the Europeans, who used them as the Egyptians had but allowed them more freedom. They began a period of settlement, building, and expansion throughout the region once destroyed by Egyptian rule. Towns grew, hundreds of villages were founded, population increased, and Israel emerged as the key political and military force. The newest settlements and the greatest population growth took place in the hill country west of the Jordan River. This was the Early Iron Age. Because the Europeans held the lush coastal plain, the Israelites settled in the hills. They grew their villages, reoccupied hundreds of abandoned village sites, and built many new ones near permanent springs or, more densely, in river valleys. In wooded areas they cut down trees, burned scrub, and terraced hills, establishing fields, vineyards, orchards, and homes. This settlement period corresponds to what the Bible describes as the conquest of Canaan, and in a sense it was that, although not from outside. But in any case it provided the foundation for the Israelite kingdom to come.

For five centuries settlements increased. No doubt there were some groups that fit the classic idea of the Israelites as a tent-dwelling pastoral people following herds of goats and sheep, Bedouin-like, as they wandered in the desert. But many were settled in peasant villages, and the towns included a rich, armed, priest-ridden urban elite.

All these people ate bread, making it from grain grown by rain agriculture. Wheat grew best in the lowland plains and highland valleys, while barley tolerated the drier semideserts and arid hills. They dipped their bread in olive oil, which besides having needed calories served as ointment, cosmetic, and lamp fuel. Peas, beans, lentils, and chickpeas complemented the grains, largely meeting protein needs and restoring nitrogen to the soil. Vineyards produced wine and raisins, and orchards yielded dates, figs, apricots, pomegranates, carobs, almonds, walnuts, and pistachios. Milk from goats and sheep was made into cheese and yogurt, and the same animals supplied occasional meat. Dove, quail, antelope, wild plants, and honey came directly from the land.

We know the yearly rhythm of life from one of the oldest Israelite inscriptions, the Gezer calendar.[7] A sort of to-do list etched on a limestone slab the size of a handheld computer, it itemizes farmwork month by month. Its significance for us today is that it describes the foundation of the Jewish calendar used ever since. In China, Texas, or Ecuador many centuries later, Jews are still celebrating holidays and marking seasons according to the rhythm of Israelite peasant life three millennia ago. It is fundamental to Jewish culture.

"Two months: ingathering," the list begins, meaning the harvest of grapes and olives in late summer and early fall. This is the start of the traditional Jewish year, the harvest itself still marked by Sukkot, the Feast of Booths, when religious Jews eat in temporary wooden structures that recall the makeshift huts of the ancient autumn harvest. "Two months: sowing" meant late fall, when the rains began, and "Two months: late grass," the continued sowing of winter. A month of "cutting flax" followed around March, when seeds were gathered to eat or press into oil. Barley harvest came next, and then a month of "harvesting and measuring" wheat in May and June.

This was the most important harvest, the one described in the biblical book of Ruth and celebrated in the Jewish Feast of Weeks, Shavuot. The corners of the fields were left uncut by Torah law, so poor people like Ruth could eat. "Measuring" meant counting portions of grain on the threshing floor, vital for both businesslike farming and tax collecting. This same threshing floor was the site of Ruth's sweet seduction of Boaz, leading to the line of Davidic kings. "Two months: pruning" meant preparation of vines for harvest, and finally "One month: summer fruit," the harvest of figs and pomegranates, after which the cycle began again with grapes and olives.

We know a good deal about life in Israel at this time. Peasants lived in four-room houses built of limestone blocks cut from the rocky landscape. Pillars inside the entrance on one side held a thin wall separating the stable from the living area. The wall might have a built-in trough for livestock in stalls paved with stone. The rest of the house was the family's living space. The main room, often plastered, had a hearth, an oven, and cisterns. Pottery found in many of these houses—storage jars, cooking pots, oil lamps, dishes and bowls, and figurines—tells us the ethnic affinity of the inhabitants. Grain pits show that grain was the staff of life, specific to the period of settlement, with its small-scale, decentralized agriculture, unlike the silos and storehouses of kingdoms. The pits were up to ten feet wide and six deep, lined with stone, plaster, ash, clay, or dung, and bell- or bottle-shaped. They protected grain from rats, mice, dampness, and bacteria.

In the wake of Egyptian rule there could not be so brutal an exercise of power. There were still elites, but they were local, and they shared a common culture with the peasantry. Arable land was communally shared and rotated, and kin and clan ties tempered political power. Still, villagers were sometimes ravaged by extortionists, and depended on patrons, sheikhs, headmen, estate owners, and local lords for protection from enemies, access to vital resources, even propitiation of the gods that most people throughout the region believed in.

Who were these gods? A pantheon of strange and wondrous superhuman characters, some indigenous, others imported from Egypt or Mesopotamia, with its own shifting divine council, from time to time joined by the gods of conquered peoples.[8] El was a pastoral, nomadic, chieflike god in a class by himself, traversing wild paths of desert, mountain range, and sea, sometimes along with his consort, Asherah. Baal was a high god of war and governance, who had Anat and Astarte as his sexy, magical consorts. Reshep, friend of warriors in life, and Horon, who guarded them in the underworld after death, made a life of endless risk tolerable for fighters. And Shamash, the sun, the ultimate giver of life, delivered his daily pulse of light and warmth, never taken for granted.

These were the gods of official cults, elites, and power, but they were also the gods of the weak peasant households. Still, they had to live at least as well as kings and chieftains, so they were given large quantities of burned animal flesh, the most precious food. Their priests and wealthy human allies shared in it, of course, and these human friends of the gods needed jewels, gold goblets, silver breastplates, and the best imported, decorated garments so that they could converse with the gods in style. Poor homes were also full of imps, sprites, and spirits, household idols, local saints and witches, ghosts of ancestors dangerous and caring, and countless other ways of giving the world meaning.

Sometime during this era there arose the seemingly preposterous idea that there was only one god. We don't know when it appeared, who among the Israelites believed in it first, or why it made sense to them. But we know that the rest of the gods and spirits did not die quickly or quietly, and the story of Israel's priests and prophets is largely one of combating idol worship for the next thousand years. The oft-repeated biblical phrase "a stiff-necked people" referred in the first place to their tendency to backslide toward idols. Abraham may have smashed his father's gods, but the people he founded returned to them again and again.

Before the settlement period the whole pantheon must have seemed very much alive and real. The people were a collection of tribes—some pastoral wanderers, some settled villagers, some urban elites, some priests and warriors. Virtually all adults were married, had children, and, except for the elites, worked at farming, herding, or crafts from childhood to old age.

Feasts and festivals full of worship, saga, song, and dance marked the annual round. Women were subordinate to men, but as men were to their betters. Supernatural forces—God or gods, imps, sprites, and ghosts—were as real and present as the rock you stubbed your toe on or the unseen mouse scurrying in the grain pit.

But this static picture doesn't capture the dynamic, threatening course of life. Women died in childbirth, infants and young children were routinely lost to illness, and the specter of infectious disease clouded the whole of life. Fights, accidents, and drunkenness punctuated household calm. Overall, this was a less violent era than the brutal epoch of Egyptian exploitation. But peace, that sacred, hoped-for state, was invariably provisional, a pause between raids and wars. In fortunate times it might persist as much as a generation or two, but no one could have expected it to endure.

✺

Now consider the saga on its merits for a moment, as if there were no archeology or history and the Bible did in fact reveal a word-for-word truth. According to Torah, the first Jew, Abraham, was a wandering Aramean, a tribal chieftain who rebelled against his own father's idolatry, in one legend even smashing his father's idols. God—*the* God, the Jewish God, Yahweh, Elohim—told Abraham, then known by the less lofty "Abram," in no uncertain terms to leave home and head south, "to the land that I will show you."

Abram must have wondered if he'd heard right. Leave everyone and everything on the strength of a none-too-plausible vision? Trash your dad's dearly loved and perfectly serviceable gods because you hear some other kind of god—invisible, no less—talking to you inside your head? Walk away from your cozy corner of a vast, secure empire to be a vagabond, drifting through hostile territory until you come to "the land that I will show you"? And true to character, yes, Abram was just such a hero, like every founder first of all a leaver, a rejectionist, an explorer, a dreamer.

According to Jewish tradition, Abraham came to the Promised Land from elsewhere. His great-grandchildren, Joseph and his brothers, left it in time of famine to find food (and, in Joseph's case, worldly success) in Egypt. They stayed in Egypt for many generations, and although they bred and grew, their lot in life worsened until they were enslaved and savagely oppressed by a Pharaoh "who did not know Joseph." A new leader, Moses—Jewish by birth and destiny but not by upbringing, education, status, faith, or marriage—led this now numerous slave people out of Egypt, among signs and wonders, into the wilderness to worship an invisible, solitary God.

A pilgrimage that could have been made in a matter of weeks took forty years, as the scraggly column, wanderers descended from a wanderer, wended its way through the Sinai (with a stop at a certain sacred mountain), the Negev, and the land of Moab east of the Jordan, taking a route so circuitous as to make us ask if God might not have given them a map. But according to tradition, the meandering circuit allowed them to slough off slave habits, become ready for independence, and be tested in their devotion to God.

Now another leader, Joshua, stood at the head of a military force. This force, with God's help, could cross the Jordan and conquer the tribes and cities on the other side, where, according to Israel's spies, people were giants. Finally, after another two centuries of more or less continual war, a last great leader, David, arose. This talented warrior-chieftain unified Israel and Judah, two independent but related nations, and established the kingdom of Israel. Under him and his son Solomon this kingdom would have wider extent, greater unity, and more international credibility than it would have again for nearly three thousand years.

༄ﷻ༄

So the Bible says. But archeology cannot vouch for any of these claims. As we have hinted, what it suggests is quite different. During the millennia before the House of David, Israelites were residents of the territory they would later claim to have conquered from outside. The land that, according to their own tradition, was assigned to them by God, even though others already lived there, was in fact where *they* had lived for centuries at least. Excavations of towns and households leading up to what is clearly Jewish culture under Jewish priests and kings show no such discontinuity as the Joshua story requires.[9] On the contrary, it shows a people ensconced in a place, slowly but surely changing and creating their own history.

Now the Jews appear to have a problem. They can believe the account in their most sacred document, the Torah, and its sequels, the Prophets and Writings—what Jews call the Tanakh, and Christians the Old Testament. This has them taking the land away from others because God promised it to them. Or they can believe the archeological account, which has them in place on the land continuously—if not from time immemorial then at least from a time that precedes Moses and even Abraham. It would seem that the two accounts cannot both be true.

Or can they? The culture of David's kingdom and that of his heirs was an amalgam of styles and peoples. Some of them had farmed the hills of Judea for millennia, sharing them with other farming cultures. Others were pastoral nomads who had ranged over hotly contested pastures to the west and south. Still others had been dragged off into slavery in Egypt, or had gone there voluntarily and found themselves disadvantaged strangers in a strange land. And of course the centuries of Egyptian rule, with its brutal taxation and conscriptions, put the whole region into a kind of slavery, and the period of expansion under European protection must have been both literally and figuratively a liberation. No doubt there were Joshuas and Deborahs, Judiths and Sauls, because as in most of the ancient world there was more or less ceaseless war, and war produces heroes.

But at a certain point, perhaps eight or nine centuries before the common era, a unified culture composed a unified story: the kingdom of Israel; the House of David. This monarchy, David's line, comes into history's notice perhaps two centuries after the reign of David's son Solomon. It is in the form of a stone tablet inscribed with the words "House of David." That is all, but it is substantial. It tells us that by the eighth century before the common era there was a line of kings in Jerusalem descended from David. To many historians, including nonreligious ones, it fits with other evidence that a great tribal chieftain and gifted warrior unified the cultures that shared the monotheistic ideal, creating the first Jewish kingdom. He went up to what would sometimes be called the City of David but was literally Yerushalayim, Jerusalem: the City of Peace. Then as now it was a high point for miles around, looking down and off to the west into the Jordan River valley, to the north into Samaria, to the west toward the rich coastal plain, to the south toward the Salt Sea and the desert they had once, according to song and story, crossed generations before.

The City of Peace has been at war for most of the time since. So its name was presumably a prayer, an avowal of hope for the future, and a term for a temporary rest from war for a people who must have known war and its consequences as well as they knew anything. But when the invincible warlord who became King David decided to make Jerusalem his capital, it was not just to preserve the ancient custom of "going up" to become great. It was because the city of hoped-for peace stood just about in the heart of the sunrich, hill-pocked, sparsely watered region where the tribes known collectively as Israel had lived for centuries.

⁂

To summarize, it is increasingly clear that the people who became the Hebrews, the Israelites, and ultimately the Jews did not come from anywhere else, but were indigenous, aboriginal, intrinsic to the region west of the Jordan River. The tales of Abram's migration from what is now Turkey cannot be investigated except through the Bible. The sojourn in Egypt and reconquest of Israel are different kinds of questions, because much scientific evidence bears on them. Archeologists now agree that there was no major war of conquest in Canaan in which the conquerors were Israelites,[10] no replacement of Canaanite culture but rather the gradual growth of a new, Israelite culture in towns in the central highlands. As Robert Coote has said, "There was nothing mysterious about the origin of Israel and nothing miraculous about it, other than the mystery of vitality and enterprise in the face of oppression and the miracle of resistance to tyranny."[11]

Still, in a sense the Bible stories are true, as a sweeping depiction of Israel over centuries of change. As it slowly emerged it was under the rule of Egypt, which faced shifting alliances, external threats, rebellion, and internal discord. Wars shifted the border between the Egyptians and the Hittites; and client Canaanite peoples, including those becoming Israel, fluctuated in independence or loyalty.

We know that some Israelites were carried into slavery in Egypt during this long reign. Climate shifts and famines may have made some of the Israelites go down into Egypt as the patriarchs do in the Bible. Since the Pharaohs enlisted foreign talent, Abraham's advisory role and even Joseph's viceroylike position may have been part of the Israelites' Egyptian experience. Finally, the ebb and flow of dynasties produced some that ruled with a velvet glove and some with an iron fist. At times in Israel conditions were oppressive enough to have approached the unhappy state of slavery without the people even leaving home. At some times and places, there may even have been rebellion and exodus.

What is not plausible is that the Israelites as one coherent bloc went down into Egypt, became slaves there, left in a burst of miracles, wandered for forty years, and returned to claim their former land with a fierce army of conquest. This came down to us because it is a much grander story, and because those celebrating the power and glory of the kingdom of Israel, centuries after the tribes had unified and settled, told it in this dramatic, compelling, coherent way—truer than true and durable for at least three millennia.

2

KINGDOM COME

HOW THE ISRAELITES BECAME A NATION

We do not know for certain how and when the House of David began, but even correcting for the hero worship of hindsight, the Bible must have a piece of the truth. We know that there was enormous expansion of the Israelite population throughout the Jordan region toward the end of the second millennium, as bronze tools and weapons gave way to iron. A priesthood was joined to a centralized polity, represented by Samuel's anointing of King Saul. Its military arm was a force to contend with, as Egyptian power waned in the face of the Philistine threat. A more developed and settled Israel was linked in the south to Judah, a loose alliance of pastoral tribes with a few agricultural villages. Rival chieftains had long vied for supremacy in the Judean hills, making pacts in shifting power balances. But now one brilliant warlord, David, took advantage of the vacuum left by the Egyptians and their battered Canaanite enemies. From a base in Hebron, the Bible says, David expanded north and west, unifying the southern and central tribes and encompassing more and more settlements.

This much is easy to accept, but the Bible claims far more. By its account, David was able to leverage the power of the Philistines and Phoenicians, who had come from Europe and Turkey to settle the coast and bait the Egyptians. Shielded by the Sea Peoples' long diplomatic shadow, David carried his rule north to Israel and moved his capital to Jerusalem. The unified kingdom grew, and at its height ranged from the Mediterranean coast to the lands east of the Jordan, from what is now southern Lebanon to the Sinai.

The process was not pretty. When the Bible says that women sang, "Saul has slain his thousands but David his ten thousands," it may not be exaggerating much. It goes on to say that David's son Solomon consolidated the kingdom and built the first Temple in Jerusalem. As in all ancient states, an alliance of priests, a military hierarchy, a wealthy elite, and a system of taxation were the essence of rule. But the later heirs to David's line could not hold the kingdom together, and it broke into two parts: the northern kingdom of Israel, and the southern kingdom of Judah. Israel remained more settled, rich, and powerful, while Judah remained wilder and more free.

Current archeology suggests a more modest story.[1] David could have been a brilliant warlord, unifying Judah and centering it in Jerusalem, but he may not have ruled a larger unified kingdom. Solomon may have built impressive structures, but nothing like the monumental architecture the Bible gives him credit for. And the father and son ruling in Judah may have had little real influence over the northern kingdom of Israel, which was ecologically richer and far more advanced. Still, the two kingdoms shared a language, Hebrew; a national saga; a body of custom, law, and ritual; and a tendency—sometimes weak, always challenged—to worship one major God.

But of course, neither kingdom was strong enough to secure a place for long among the real empires of the region. The Assyrians, Babylonians, and, once again, the Egyptians had compelling interests along the Jordan and reaching west to the sea. These great powers had little patience for the pretensions of a fragmented Jewish kingdom—olive oil and wine notwithstanding—except to the extent that its princes were pliant vassals.

They often were. But it was not so easy for them to choose which empire to kowtow to at any given moment. Inevitably, first Israel in the north, then Judah in the south ran afoul of imperial plans. The Bible says the throne of Israel was taken away from David's line for his and Solomon's sins, but in any case the throne was hotly contested, a tragedy for any kingdom. After three false starts based on military rivalry, a new dynasty was established by an army commander, whose son Ahab ruled for twenty-two years. He and his queen, Jezebel, became two of the most famously evil characters in the Bible. In reality his was a brutal but brilliant reign that made Israel a regional power, from Damascus south to Bethel, near Jerusalem, and east over the Jordan to dominate the Moabites. Ahab even formed a military alliance with Judah; *he* had the regional power David could only dream of. But for the author of the Books of Kings, these achievements meant little. Two great prophets—Elijah and his disciple, Elisha—passed an indelible judgment on Ahab and his kin: They encouraged idol worship, greed, and social injustice, and so their lineage was doomed.

Indeed it was. Ahab was killed in the wars across the Jordan, and each of his two sons reigned only briefly. After an inconclusive rebellion, Elisha anointed Jehu, another army commander, as king of Israel. According to the Bible, Jehu killed the last king in Ahab's line, threw Jezebel from a high palace window, and left her corpse to the dogs. His army went on to slaughter seventy of the king's sons, piling their heads in public view at the city gate. The Bible approves all this because of Ahab and Jezebel's idolatry. The struggle between the monotheists, represented by the prophets, and the polytheistic pagans, encouraged or tolerated by the royal house, may have brought down the greatest worldly kingdom Israel would achieve. But as we will see, this story was told with the hindsight of a monotheistic kingdom centered in Judah a century later—both had continued in parallel—so it cast Israel's history in the light of religious struggle, seen from the viewpoint of the prophets and priests of Judah. And the wrath of Elijah, one of the most loved figures in all Jewish tradition, guaranteed Ahab's demonization.

Religious ideology may well have played a role in the fall of the kingdom, but perhaps Israel had simply overreached the bounds of a minor royal house in a new, small state between great empires. Ahab and his successors challenged their neighbors, and they are mentioned in monumental inscriptions left by those foreign powers. In the mid-ninth century B.C.E. even the Assyrians were turned back by Ahab's army. Archeologists see this as a golden age for the Israelite kings.

Israel in this era was the most densely settled kingdom in the region, ten times as populous as Judah.[2] Fortified citadels with stunning monumental architecture stood not only at Samaria, the capital, but at Dan, Megiddo, Hazor, Jezreel, and elsewhere in the lush Jordan region. Brilliant hydraulic-engineering projects brought water into large towns, underground, from nearby springs. Israel was enriched by a major revival of trade in the eastern Mediterranean, and it felt the cultural influence of the Phoenicians in architecture, pottery, and writing. Jezebel herself was a Phoenician princess. Ahab, cursed in the Books of Kings, held Assyria at bay; Jehu, praised as the hero of the one God, gave way to the Assyrians. He is shown very plausibly on one of their obelisks prostrate on the ground at the feet of their king.

At that time the Assyrians had more important concerns elsewhere, and they allowed their Aramean vassal state in Damascus to deal with Israel. It did so with great destruction around the year 835, occupying much of the upper Jordan for decades. Inscriptions show that parts of this region began to speak and write in the lingua franca of Aramaic. Closely related to Hebrew and written in Hebrew characters, Aramaic would later become an important Jewish language. But the Assyrians were not preoccupied for long, and—divide and conquer—they soon set Israel against Damascus again. It was up to the empire to determine who would win this contest, and around the year 800 a new golden age began for the Israelites. Unprecedented growth of olive oil production, winemaking, and other agricultural products drove population to an estimated 350,000.

Alas, this favored age was brief. The kingdom was known to outsiders for its military strength, especially its chariot brigades, but the reason we know about Israel's strength is from the Assyrians' boasts when they conquered it. And it was known to the prophets Amos and Hosea for its wealth, greed, corruption, and oppression of the poor:

Assuredly,
Because you impose a tax on the poor
And exact from him a levy of grain,
You have built houses of hewn stone,
But you shall not live in them;
You have planted delightful vineyards,
But shall not drink their wine.
For I have noted how many are your crimes,
And how countless your sins—
You enemies of the righteous,
You takers of bribes,
You who subvert in the gate
The cause of the needy![3]

This was just a salvo in a centuries-long war of words waged by the prophets against their errant kings. It is emblematic of the prophetic books to defend the one God of Israel against highborn idol worshipers and the poor against their oppressors.

Events seemed to vindicate the prophets. Assyrian forces repeatedly swept into Israel, besieging cities, destroying them, and imposing tribute. A new king came to power by assassinating his predecessor—a time-honored method—and carried arrogance to its ultimate conclusion.[4] Thinking he could bring a resurgent Egypt to his aid, he stopped paying tribute to Assyria. The emperor mounted a ruthless campaign, there was no help from Egypt, and in 722 the kingdom of Israel was destroyed. Its population dispersed into the Assyrian empire, and Israel was resettled by strangers.

But many of Israel's citizens fled south to Judah, where they had long had an alliance, and the refugees found a home where they understood the language, religion, and national saga.[5] To the Israelites, Judah must have seemed a backwater, an underdeveloped country whose small towns were filled with bumpkins and whose hinterlands were home to wild men, but beggars can't be choosers, and the Israelites were running for their lives. They had a profound effect on Judah—one might even say a civilizing effect. The hill country around Jerusalem grew in population and settlements, much as the northern kingdom had done earlier. Archeology shows that as the year 700 approached, there were around 120,000 people living in Judah—a fourfold increase—in three hundred towns, villages, and farmsteads. The new settlers brought state-level organization, monumental architecture, mass production of pottery and other crafts, and large-scale, centralized oil- and wine-pressing industries.

They also brought widespread literacy. Inscriptions on monuments, seals and their impressions, and thousands of shards of pottery inscribed with Hebrew writing—mercantile records, political messages, prayers and incantations—appear in Judah's archeological record for the first time. It is not that Judeans were illiterate before the Israelites arrived, but writing was limited to fewer people and played a smaller role. Judah prospered and grew for about a century, its ideological hallmark the consolidation of monotheism. The battle against idolatry had gone on for centuries. Kings and Chronicles tell stories from the viewpoint of prophets, and the prophetic books themselves speak even more strongly. Monarchs who stood firm against the cults of other gods were heroes, even if they lost the kingdom. Those who stabilized the state while allowing cults to flourish in the countryside—or, even more offensively, in Jerusalem—were cursed, as Ahab had been for his reign over Israel.

But for the scribes and prophets, monotheism was Judah's historic mission. Israel was far stronger than Judah in population, wealth, and military strength, but its kings led their people astray into idolatry. Israel's fall was therefore inevitable, and its vindicated prophets moved south away from the ruins—along with tens of thousands of other Israelites—to the pure, rural, high-minded realm of Judah, in the hills around Jerusalem, City of David. There they joined their more faithful brethren in the proper worship of one transcendent God.

⌘

At the heart of this epoch was the reign of Josiah, one of the most revered biblical kings. Josiah echoed the faith and strength of Moses and David in a later time, and those heroes' legends were shaped in Josiah's image. He seems to have allied himself with a rigorously monotheistic priesthood, destroying the "high places" throughout the countryside, showing no mercy to anyone who strayed after other gods: "He dealt with them just as he had done to Bethel: He slew on the altars all the priests of the shrines who were there, and he burned human bones on them."[6]

"Then," the text calmly continues, "he returned to Jerusalem." That Jerusalem was, perhaps for the first time, the great godly capital of a united Jewish kingdom, ruled by a rigorous but wise king in concert with priests and prophets who were all literally reading from the same page. That page was in the scroll Josiah discovered while renovating the Temple—a document that would change Jewish destiny.

Josiah's great-grandfather had known the prophet Isaiah. They had seen the dismal end of Israel's northern kingdom and were implacable enemies of idolatry. But two generations of idolatrous kings intervened, bringing strange gods into the Temple and encouraging idolatry in the countryside. Priests and prophets railed against these practices, but it was not until Josiah, a boy of eight, took the throne that they had a champion who could make One-Godliness the absolute law of the land.

They reared him to the task. At twenty-six, already in the eighteenth year of his reign, he weighed out large sums of silver for an army of masons and carpenters to renovate the Temple. During the work the high priest found an old scroll, which a scribe read to the king. "When the king heard the words of the scroll of the Teaching, he rent his clothes," anguished by his prior ignorance and sin. He sent the leading priests and scribes to find out more about what the scroll meant, and their search among the people led to Huldah the prophet. From her home in Jerusalem she sent harsh words to the king: Because of his fathers' idolatry, disaster would fall upon Judah. But he himself, being righteous, would not live to see it.

Josiah did not wait for Huldah's prophecy to unfold. He destroyed every trace of idolatry in the Temple, in Jerusalem, and in all the high places of the two errant kingdoms. But in the end, like so many Jewish kings bad or good, he was caught between clashing empires. An Egyptian Pharaoh campaigning against the Assyrians slew Josiah. According to Chronicles, Pharaoh did not want the fight, but Josiah confronted his archers and died in a hail of arrows. He left behind a monotheistic, unified Jewish kingdom under Egyptian dominance. But both would give way before the newly empowered empire of Babylon, built on the ashes of Mesopotamia. As in centuries past, Judah had to ally itself with one empire or another, while trying to maintain some independence. Repeatedly, it made the wrong choices.

Josiah's descendants reigned for two generations, each coming into conflict with the Babylonian king, and each meeting defeat and exile. The last in the line, Zedekiah, defied the Babylonians for the final time in 586 B.C.E. He was captured, his sons were killed before his eyes, his eyes were put out, and he was carried into captivity in Babylon, along with many of his enslaved, defeated people.

☙〜❦

The scroll Josiah discovered was a culmination of centuries of literary achievement, beginning with the first attempts to carve thoughts on stone. No one supposes that the Jews invented writing, but writing has been central in their history. If we can understand how this came about, we may gain understanding of Jewish origins. Writing began just over five thousand years ago in Mesopotamia and Egypt with pictographs or hieroglyphs— pictures or symbols representing words, as in the ideograms of modern China. Actually, China developed its symbols independently somewhat later—as did the Mayans, much later but also independently. The impulse to record existed, and writing was invented wherever there was an organized concentration of population and wealth.

But pictographs require mastery of hundreds or thousands of symbols just to write and read a basic vocabulary, so they were a specialty in the ancient world, restricted to scribes or elite groups with free time to study them. This changed with alphabetic scripts, which represented sounds, not words, and abruptly reduced the number of symbols to twenty or thirty. Almost anyone could remember thirty symbols and master the code to make words from them. But to go from pictographs to alphabetic script took almost two thousand years. By about 1500 B.C.E. some pictographs began to convey not just a word but also the sound or syllable at the outset of that word. An exquisite figurine found in the Sinai Peninsula between Egypt and Israel depicts the Canaanite goddess Asherah. And below the head of the goddess is an inscription now known to convey a series of consonants: *"lb'lt."* Many written languages of the region, including Hebrew and Aramaic, omitted most vowel sounds, and this Canaanite phrase was probably a devotional inscription: *"le-ba'alat"*—"For the Lady."

Within a few centuries, several alphabetic scripts were widely used throughout the Middle East. This included tribal Israel, soon to become the Israelite kingdom. Inscriptions were made at this time on a bronze dagger unearthed at Lachish, on a javelin blade near Bethlehem, and on many clay tablets in an archive at Ugarit on the Mediterranean coast. By the eleventh century the dominant script was the one developed by the Phoenicians, brilliant seagoing merchants who from a base in Lebanon moved goods along trade routes from Mesopotamia and Egypt as far as Carthage and Spain. What had been a back-and-forth pattern in the early script, alternating direction line by line, became in Phoenician hands a standard right-to-left pattern. At the same time the script's efficiency was streamlined. This led to the script for Hebrew and Aramaic, the two great languages of the Israelites.

Recall that most of the Israelites were not immigrants but were developing and expanding indigenous tribes on the west bank of the Jordan. They spoke Hebrew and took part in the evolving use of alphabetic scripts. Recall too the Gezer calendar around 900 B.C.E., which recorded the annual agricultural round in a transitional script resembling the Phoenician and Hebrew alphabets. By then the first great Israelite expansion was complete, and the first Hebrew inscription is an account of some of the wars of Israel's kings. Ironically, it is on a stone tablet carved for a king of Moab. These were the people who had already given the Israelites one of the Bible's most important characters: Ruth, the great-grandmother of King David. The Moabites had long been under the influence of Israel, and wrote their language in Hebrew characters. By this time, Hebrew was an established written language in which, in all likelihood, parts of the Bible had been set down.

☙❧

The evolution of alphabets and the questions of authorship are easy to understand, but what no one can explain is why the Bible was so good. For Orthodox Jews, the reason the *Torah* is so good is that it was dictated to Moses by

God. But the philosopher Benedict Spinoza pointed out in the seventeenth
century that the Torah contains the death of Moses, some events after his
death, and many internal contradictions; for this, among other efforts, Spinoza was excommunicated by the rabbis of Amsterdam. Thomas Hobbes had
a similar view that was largely ignored. But by the nineteenth century, "scientific" Bible criticism showed that the Torah alone had at least four different
authors, and this analytic tradition has matured in modern scholarship.[7]

The "J" author used the name Yahweh for God—Jahweh in German—
and wrote most of Genesis and large parts of Exodus.

The "E" author, who called God Elohim, also contributed much to
Genesis and Exodus.

The "P" or Priestly author wrote parts of Genesis and Exodus, most of
Leviticus, and the more ritualistic and legalistic parts of Numbers.

The "D" author, or Deuteronomist, wrote the last of the five books, com-
pleting the story of Moses and the end of the Israelites' desert wanderings.

A fifth author—"R" for Redactor, likely a committee rather than a
person—put all the pieces together to make the Five Books of Moses. Many
conundrums dissolve as soon as this is understood. For example, there are
two very different versions of human creation in Genesis. P, who wrote the
first chapter, says the man and the woman were created together simultaneously, but J says the man was put to sleep and a rib was removed from his
side to make his helpmeet. The two versions have very different implications for gender equality, and religious interpreters of the text might well
wonder just what God meant. But if there were two human authors who—
however inspired—meant different things, then of course they would tell
different stories.

Bolder scholars try to specify *when* various parts of the Bible were written. Some say the major work was done in the period after the Babylonian
exile, which would mean after the seventh century B.C.E. Others claim the
majority of the writing was done earlier, during the reign of King Josiah of
Judah, in the eighth century. One fascinating theory attributes the J text to
a woman writing in the court of King David's grandson, in the tenth century—a woman with a keen sense of irony and profound skepticism about
the wisdom of the patriarchy.[8] All the theories are based on the texts themselves, with no other historical or archeological evidence. There are no
manuscripts, inscriptions, or dates, just more or less plausible modern theories of how a particular author might have manipulated the story to the advantage of a particular party or faction vying for power.

J and E on the national narrative are examples. J, perhaps a woman, was
strongly identified with Judah. Her story emphasizes the patriarchs and
their relationship to God and the land. Their lives centered in Judah, especially in Hebron, which until David's time was Judah's capital. E, most
likely a Levite priest, concentrates on Moses and the Exodus. He empha-

sizes a covenant with God made long after the time of the patriarchs, at Sinai, a place far removed from Judah. This story ends with the conquest of Canaan, the urban core of which becomes Israel. Consistent with priestly authorship, the E text is more concerned with ritual and law.

These narratives may have incorporated centuries-old oral traditions, and they existed side by side for generations. But at a certain point it became useful to weave them together, probably in the service of national unity. Older scholarship suggested that this happened during the unified kingdom of David and Solomon; more recent work doubts the extent of such a kingdom and places the blending later, in Josiah's time. Either way, the intent of the separate narratives seems to have been to assert the primacy of Judah or Israel, while the melded saga serves the higher purpose of unity.

◔◍◍◑

Here is a plausible account of how the text evolved, based on modern biblical scholarship informed by archeology.

J and E were based on oral traditions and older written texts. E may have been first because of the more advanced state of Israel and its priests, but J did not need to wait for the full flowering of Judah to set down her own great saga. The two were probably joined after the fall of Israel, when the northern kingdom's remnant fled south and merged with Judah. Not long after this a third author, clearly a priest, wrote the P text as a substitute for the combined J-and-E saga. It reflected the official ideology of the Jerusalem priesthood, glorifying Aaron, the brother of Moses, because the priesthood reckoned its descent from him. There were also divisions within the priesthood. Over time, priests in several cities developed different practices, and some wrote their own accounts of ritual and story.

The Torah was probably completed under Josiah, who had already begun to restore the worship of one God when he found "the words of the scroll of the Teaching." The Hebrew is *"divray sefer ha-Torah,"* and an alternative translation would be "the words of the book of the Torah." No wonder Josiah rent his clothes: a major part of the Torah had been lost, and practice and faith had been on the wrong path. Biblical scholars and archeologists believe that the scroll was Deuteronomy, the book that became both the culmination of the Torah and the foundation of Judaism forever after.[9] The idea that Deuteronomy had a separate author is not new. Indeed, stylistic and religious continuities with the next few books of the Bible strongly suggest that D also wrote Judges, Samuel, and Kings. But this sweeping history of the two Jewish kingdoms begins in the desert outside the Promised Land: "These are the words Moses spoke to all Israel across the Jordan."

Here, despite its immense scope, the whole of Deuteronomy takes place. Moses restates the laws he has already given, including those of justice: "Hear out your fellow men, and decide justly between any man and a fellow Israelite or a stranger. You shall not be partial in judgment: hear out low and high alike. Fear no man, for judgment is God's."[10] He charges Joshua and the people to follow God's command by going into the Promised Land and conquering it in accord with Israel's destiny.

He repeats the Ten Commandments from the declaration of faith to the renunciation of coveting. He reminds the people of their many past transgressions, and he predicts that they will be tempted to sin the same way again, especially if they intermarry. "For they will turn your children away from Me to worship other gods, and the Lord's anger will blaze against you and He will promptly wipe you out. Instead . . . you shall tear down their altars, smash their pillars, cut down their sacred posts, and consign their images to the fire."[11]

This is remarkably like what Josiah was doing in his generation half a millennium later, so it is not surprising that some scholars think that D was a priest or scribe writing at that time—that the found scroll was really a new one. The author may even have been Huldah, the prophet the priests and scribes sought out when King Josiah needed to know what "the words of the scroll of the Teaching" meant. Perhaps she herself wrote it and even planted it to be found by Josiah's builders.

But it could also have been old when it was found. It describes the last acts and the death of Moses, so Moses cannot have written it. But it summarizes all of Moses' teachings and reviews the story of the Exodus, the miracles wrought by God, and how the Law was conveyed to Moses on a mountain in the wilderness. It repeats the dietary laws—the clean and unclean animals, and the prohibition against seething a kid in its mother's milk. Judicial process, laws of marriage, family, and inheritance, and punishment of criminals ("eye for eye, tooth for tooth") are all set down here. It also holds some of the most compassionate words in Hebrew scripture:

> For the Lord your God is God supreme . . . who shows no favor and takes no bribe, but upholds the cause of the fatherless and the widow, and befriends the stranger, providing him with food and clothing. You too must befriend the stranger, for you were strangers in the land of Egypt.[12]

> If, however, there is a needy person among you . . . do not harden your heart and shut your hand against your needy kinsman. Rather, you must open your hand and lend him sufficient for whatever he needs.[13]

> If a fellow Hebrew, man or woman, is sold to you, he shall serve you six years, and in the seventh year you shall set him free. When you set him free, do not let him go empty-handed: Furnish him out

of the flock, threshing floor, and vat, with which the Lord your God has blessed you. Bear in mind that you were slaves in the land of Egypt.[14]

When a man has taken a bride, he shall not go out with the army or be assigned to it for any purpose; he shall be exempt one year for the sake of his household, to give happiness to the woman he has married.[15]

You shall not abuse a needy and destitute laborer, whether a fellow countryman or a stranger in one of the communities of your land. You must pay him his wages on the same day, before the sun sets, for he is needy and urgently depends on it.[16]

Significantly for Josiah and his priests, Deuteronomy contains information about how the Levites must be supported by tithing, what sacrifices they must make at various festivals, and generally how they must conduct themselves and be treated. It would guide the Temple priesthood for centuries. Moses also teaches the people a prayer, which they are to recite when they "go to the place where the Lord your God will choose to establish His name"—to the Temple—to bring "every first fruit of the soil." It contains in a few sentences the core narrative of the Jewish people, and except for the last sentence it is recited still at every Passover seder:

You shall then recite as follows before the Lord your God: "My father was a fugitive Aramean. He went down to Egypt with meager numbers and sojourned there; but there he became a great and very populous nation. The Egyptians dealt harshly with us and oppressed us; they imposed heavy labor upon us. We cried to the Lord, the God of our fathers, and the Lord heard our plea and saw our plight, our misery, and our oppression. The Lord freed us from Egypt by a mighty hand, by an outstretched arm and awesome power, and by signs and portents. He brought us to this place and gave us this land, a land flowing with milk and honey. Wherefore I now bring the first fruits of the soil which You, O Lord, have given me."[17]

All this and more is set down as Moses' final ethical will. He recites a litany of curses for the Israelites if they are stiff-necked, a litany of blessings if they do God's will. He recites a beautiful long poem blessing Israel, and another blessing each tribe in turn. He is allowed to climb Mount Nebo to look into the Promised Land, but he dies in Moab and is buried in an unknown grave, perhaps by God himself.

But not before setting forth his last word on the Law. "When Moses had put down in writing the words of this Teaching to the very end, Moses charged the Levites . . . : Take this book of Teaching and place it beside the Ark of the Covenant of the Lord your God, and let it remain there as a witness against you. Well I know how defiant and stiff-necked you are: even now, while I am still alive in your midst, you have been defiant toward the Lord; how much more, then, when I am dead!"[18]

So the scroll was set beside the ark, which held the tablets of the Law given to Moses on Mount Sinai. And although the tablets were lost, the scroll of the Teaching was not. To this day, every Sabbath in synagogues throughout the world, the Torah scroll containing the Five Books of Moses is removed from what is still called the Holy Ark. All rise, the Ark is opened, and the congregation sings this song, evoking an ancient time and kindred rite: "And behold the Ark was brought out and Moses said, 'Arise, O Lord, and scatter your foes, and let those who hate you flee before you. For out of Zion shall the Law go forth, and the word of the Lord from Jerusalem.'"

☙

We have said that J, E, and P—writers of transcendent genius—drew on centuries-old oral traditions, some widely shared among the peoples of the region. For example, there is a flood in the great Gilgamesh epic of Babylon, and as in the book of Genesis it is a drama of human weakness and godly power. But the Gilgamesh flood and its heroic human survivor become forces in a struggle among the gods—as always in pagan narratives, a mirror of human struggles writ large.

In Genesis, in contrast, God is alone in the heavens, just as Noah is about to be left alone in the earthly world, stranded and silent on the surface of the sea. Noah, not yet a Jew but still the best man on earth, uniquely obeys God's will and so is chosen to be saved, to become a second Adam, to start the world over. The Genesis flood is no power struggle, because God's power is unique and unopposed, perfectly capable of ending the world. The Hebrew story is about right, not power, and out of it comes the first covenant, the first deal between God and us, sealed by a rainbow.

But God as yet is neither perfect nor complete. God grows in the story, coming to terms with human weakness. Noah, in keeping with deep Middle Eastern tradition, "built an altar to the Lord and, taking of every clean animal and of every clean bird, he offered burnt offerings on the altar. The Lord smelled the pleasing odor, and the Lord said to Himself: 'Never again will I doom the earth because of man, since the devisings of man's mind are evil from his youth; nor will I ever again destroy every living being, as I have done.'"[19] God may be alone and all-powerful, but he is also oddly human. Moved by the sweet smell of the sacrifices, God bends to the human dilemma. The Hebrew uses the word for "heart" twice in the passage: "and the Lord said to his heart, 'Never again will I curse the earth for man's sake, since the will of the heart of man is evil from his youth.'" This is drama; God is a feeling, changing character.

God learns from experience, even from people, especially Abraham. When God tells him he will destroy Sodom and Gomorrah, there follows the most astounding conversation in ancient literature. "And Abraham came forward and said, 'Will You sweep away the innocent along with the guilty? What if there should be fifty innocent within the city; will You then wipe out the place and not forgive it for the sake of the innocent fifty who are in it? Far be it from You to do such a thing. . . . Shall not the judge of all the earth deal justly?'"

God's paltry servant reminds God about justice? Ostensibly, Abraham is calling God back into character, but the reminder has the flavor of a reprimand, even of trying to teach. God concedes, but the servant isn't satisfied. "Abraham spoke up, saying, 'Here I venture to speak to my Lord, who am but dust and ashes: What if the fifty innocent should lack five? Will you destroy the whole city for want of the five?'" Now Abraham has entered the realm of sophistry. Through some sort of lawyer's trick, refusing to save the towns for forty-five becomes a quibble over five—as if God could not make the calculation. But God answers calmly, "I will not destroy if I find forty-five there." Yet it goes on, Abraham coming back and back with the same brazen bargaining. Forty? Thirty? Twenty? God gives in again and again. At last it stops at ten; yet the ten good people are not found, and Sodom and Gomorrah are destroyed.[20]

In the classic interpretation, God knows all this in advance, and the lesson is for Abraham. But there is another rabbinical commentary that places this argument at the heart of Jewishness. Why was Noah not the first Jew? Because when God says, in effect, "Build an ark and save yourself, I'm about to destroy the world," Noah just picks up a hammer. Abraham, in arguing, shows that his moral sense is internalized. He is not just following orders, even from God. Jacob, the grandson of Abraham and a chip off the old block, wrestles with an angel. "And a man wrestled with him until the break of dawn." The Hebrew word is *ish,* man, but this is no ordinary man. Although he has injured Jacob in the socket of his hip, he cannot prevail, and at dawn he asks to be released. In the King James Version, Jacob says: "I will not let thee go, except thou bless me."

The man asks his name, and then changes it from Jacob to Israel "because you have striven with beings divine and human, and have prevailed."[21] The King James says "with God and with men," which is a more straightforward way of translating *"im Elohim v'im anashim."* Although Jacob is not to know the being's name, he names the place Peniel—"face of God"— because he has seen God face-to-face. But it is Jacob's new name we must attend to. Yisra-El means "strove with God." But of course, it is not just Jacob who limps away, hurt, with a new name. It is all his descendants, destined, he has been told, to be as numerous as the stars. *Israel:* a whole nation of God wrestlers, striving and undaunted, hurt but not subdued.

☙

What are women doing while men seem to dominate the story? As we have seen, some recent scholarship outside the religious tradition has interpreted the Torah saga itself as hinging on women's acts at every major turning point.[22] In this view the author of major parts of the narrative was a woman who viewed the patriarchy with irony and gave women a critical role. While impossible to prove, it is a fascinating claim.

Consider some pivotal points in the saga. Eve may be made from Adam's rib, but it is she who begins the real human story by challenging God's dictum about the tree of knowledge. She, not Adam, can't stand not knowing; for good and ill, it is she who demands to know. Without Eve's boldness the human tale would never have started, and we would still be in boring Eden, our lives too dull to be worth a story.

When blind Isaac is about to bestow both blessing and inheritance on Esau, Rebecca tricks him into blessing Jacob instead and ensures the Jewish lineage forever. When, in Egypt, the Pharaoh condemns all newborn Jewish boys to death, it is two midwives who defy him, saving many. As for Moses—the one who will free the people, receive the Torah, and bring them to the brink of the Promised Land—he is saved by the decisiveness of his mother, Yocheved, who hides him; the boldness of his sister Miriam, who sets him afloat in a pitch-sealed basket in the Nile; and the tenderness of an Egyptian princess who, against all odds, finds him and takes him to her bosom.

And the strength of biblical women persists beyond the Torah. Deborah, in Judges, is renowned not only for wisdom and prophecy but for military prowess, and when she defeats the Canaanite army of King Jabin she sings a victory song celebrating herself:

> *The open land was gone in Israel,*
> *Gone until Deborah arose,*
> *Arose a mother in Israel. . . .*
> *Awake awake, O Deborah!*
> *Awake awake, let the song ring out!*[23]

The song also commemorates the pivotal role of Jael, who clinched the victory of Deborah's fellow general Barak. She entertained Sisera, the enemy general, and agreed to protect him after he lost a major battle. "Then Jael . . . took a tent pin and grasped the mallet. When he was fast asleep from exhaustion, she approached him stealthily and drove the pin through his temple until it went down to the ground."[24]

Although it is not in the canon, the apocryphal Book of Judith recounts another woman's heroism. A wealthy widow, she "was very lovely to behold. Her husband had left her gold and silver, men and women slaves, livestock, and field; and she maintained this estate. No one spoke ill of her, for she feared God with great devotion."[25] But her people had lost heart as they were overrun by a vast Assyrian army. She "took off her widow's garments, bathed her body with water, and anointed herself with precious ointment. She combed her hair, put on a tiara, and dressed herself. . . . She put sandals on her feet, and put on her anklets, bracelets, rings, earrings, and all her other jewelry. Thus she made herself very beautiful, to entice the eyes of all the men who might see her."[26]

Thus arrayed, she traveled with her servants across enemy lines and offered herself to Holofernes, head of the Assyrian army, as a willing spy and concubine. He was duly enamored, but on the night he tried to seduce her, he drank himself into a stupor, and Judith cut off his head with his sword. Finding his headless body, his officers lost heart, but when Judith presented the head to the Israelites, they revived, praised the Lord, and passed the ammunition.

These tales of powerful, brave women pervaded the consciousness of Jews living in Temple times. But whether the heroes are male or female, the Bible is not for the faint of heart. The men are violent, autocratic, stubborn, and abusive. The women are sly seductresses and bold deceivers, born to manipulate men and in turn to be hurt by them. And the men at least converse frequently with God, as if the eternal ruler of the universe were a character in a novel, evidently male, patriarchal, arrogant, arbitrary, and violent.

രാ

As much as the editors of classic Jewish texts tried to purge them of their pagan past, it cannot be denied. The God of the Hebrews started as one among many and then became paramount, long before the Jews were brazen enough to abolish all rivals. *"Mi khamokha ba'elim Adonai?"* is one of the most familiar lines in the modern Jewish liturgy. "Who is like You among the gods, Lord?" Among the *gods*? What gods? The standard interpretation is something like, "Who is like You among the gods others worship, but that we know are not real?"

Anthropologists studying "simple" societies, as well as more complex traditional ones, find a wide variety of religious faiths. Commonly, people believe in many gods and spirits and experience life as a constant fluid exchange between the spirit world and the tangible one. Searching for doctrine in small-scale societies is often a fool's errand, since people have private beliefs loosely connected to the more shared, public ones.

It is often said that the one God of the Jews is aboriginal, connected to their pastoral life. The image of a shepherd alone against the night sky fosters the kind of I-Thou relationship that leads to a single, overarching, abstract Other. Such a God would also be more portable than idols, statues being a burden to a nomadic pastoral people. Wherever you are, God is there. This is possible, and it would reach back before the Israelites came onto the stage of history, or would assume that the pastoralist subgroup had a disproportionate influence. The monotheistic thrust did come mainly from wilder, more pastoral Judah. It is also of course consistent with biblical narrative: Abraham, Isaac, Jacob, and Moses were all pastoralists, and David the shepherd became the warrior-king. Yet if pastoral life were the source of monotheism, then one would expect to see herders around the world worshiping one God. They don't, unless they have already felt the influence of a state-level monotheistic religion. But pastoral nomads are fiercely independent and doubt the claims of their settled agricultural neighbors. States are based on agriculture, and state religions are the ultimate spiritual imperialism—pantheons of cantankerous, powerful gods, as in Greece and Rome.

If belief in one God did not come from the pastoral life, where did it come from? Anthropologists associate monotheism with highly centralized states: one king, one God. But Greece and Rome, not to mention Egypt, Babylonia, and India, contradict this theory. Still, in all these cultures one god in the pantheon stands out above all others, ruling the heavens as a king rules his people. This worked well for an expanding empire. The favorite gods of conquered peoples could be absorbed into the pantheon, just as the new subjects took their lowly place in the empire. But in some times and places religious thinkers became skeptical that the one high god had competition or even company. This required a tremendous leap of faith. Gods who had been for centuries or millennia vividly associated with aspects of life—war, fertility, crafts, sea, wind, fire—had to be set aside, their ancient functions folded into the powers of one god who somehow did it all. Worse, this supreme and solitary god tended to be the most remote one in the pantheon, the one who stayed aloof from human affairs. It was not only implausible but dissonant and painful; attachment to the lesser gods was strong.

⚭

Particularly poignant was the loss of female gods. While there was not really a stage in human history when goddesses reigned everywhere, love and devotion to female gods were vital to ancient religions. Perhaps the female figurines of the Paleolithic, some over twenty thousand years old, were fertility idols, and certainly thousands of figurines found throughout the ancient Middle East were representations of goddesses. They tended to be wives and daughters of the male high god, but the goddesses had powers of their own, and they had devoted followers. This devotion is easy to understand. We see it in prayer to and longing for Mary, whose apparitions have moved some Christians for two millennia—even when opposed by church doctrine. Many find comfort in prayer to a mother figure, and in the sphere of fertility and family the logic of the goddess is compelling.

But as empires emerged, the high god was male, like the emperor. Goddesses had their place, as did female priests, cult leaders, and temple courtesans, but it was a subordinate place in a male-run world. Imperial expansion meant relentless war, and in this context few could doubt that the highest, strongest gods were male. Still, *eliminating* the goddesses was something else again, and monotheism required it. This was a lot to expect; life was hard enough without losing ancient sources of comfort. The prophets of Israel, then, who saw themselves as battling pure evil, were also tearing ordinary people away from some of their deepest beliefs and affections. Driving idols out of the Temple may have been a struggle for power, and perhaps even a struggle for truth, but taking idols out of the home was a struggle for yearning hearts and anxious minds. So "backsliding" to worship Asherah, the Canaanite fertility goddess—to take one example—was inevitable.

But then, the relationship between the God of the Israelites and the gods and goddesses of Canaan was always an intimate one. We know the Canaanite gods from a list found at Ugarit on the Mediterranean, over thirty of them, starting with Il.[27] Il or El was a common Semitic name for "god," and it became one way that the Jews spoke of their God. *El elyon*— "God most high"—remains in the liturgy. The Canaanite Il is male, the father of the gods and of humankind. He is seen as a bull, virile and powerful, yet also wise and beneficent.

Dagan, perhaps a grain god, is next on the list, followed by Baal. *Baal,* in Canaanite or Hebrew, means "lord" or "master," and his full name is "prince, lord of the earth." He is also called *aliy* or *aliyan*—"high one" or "most high." But where Il is remote and ethereal, Baal is immanent in the weather, the "rider of the clouds," seen in storms. And he has enemies, too: Yaam, the sea god; destructive desert "devourers"; and Mot, the god of death, who makes even gods mortal. The great goddess is Asherah, consort of Il and mother of gods, "the lady of the sea," who protects her sons and daughters. Anat, in contrast—"the maiden"—is a violent sexual goddess, young, beautiful, desired, and dangerous. She is Baal's consort or sister, and when they are depicted together she is naked and voluptuous, while Baal has his hand raised to smite his foes. But like Baal, Anat is *in* the flux and turmoil of the world, and is so aggressive that she defeats his enemy, death.

These are just a few of the known Canaanite gods. Others were linked with the sun, moon, and planets, or with craftsmanship, pestilence, flame, healing, music, and wet-nursing. Their personalities and roles would not be unfamiliar to other peoples throughout the Middle East and around the Mediterranean. Rather, the notion of *one* God is unfamiliar. So where did it come from? There are very few clues. The Torah itself says that Abraham, then called Abram, visited King Melchizedek of Shalem, "a priest of God most high," who proceeded to bless him:

> Blessed be Abram of God most high,
> Creator of heaven and earth.
> And blessed be God most high . . .[28]

This suggests both that Abram was a monotheist and that he was not alone in this. Thus, within Jewish tradition there is room for influence on or at least confirmation of monotheism by powerful people outside the patriarchal lineage.

Tradition aside, we know of a brief monotheistic phase in Egyptian religion, back in the second millennium. In the mid-fourteenth century one Pharaoh decided that the sun god, Aton, would be worshiped to the exclusion of other gods. He changed his name to Akhenaton, taught his followers to oppose the traditional pantheon, and incurred the anger of the temple priests. He also wrote or commissioned this famous hymn to Aton:

> How plentiful it is, what you have made, although they are hidden from view, sole god, without another beside you; you created the earth as you wished, when you were by yourself, before mankind, all cattle and kine, all beings on land, who fare upon their feet, and all beings in the air, who fly upon their wings. . . .
>
> All distant lands, you have made them live. . . . How efficient are your designs, Lord of eternity: a Nile in the sky for foreigners and all creatures that go upon their feet, a Nile coming back from the underworld for Egypt.[29]

The language is not unprecedented, but it is aggressively monotheistic, and it has echoes in Hebrew scripture and liturgy. There are only so many ways to say these things, but the parallels are still interesting. One theory says that the Hebrews were slaves in Egypt around the time of Akhenaton, and that monotheism flowed one way or the other. Akhenaton's reign did come while Egypt ruled Canaan and Israel, and he could have affected some Hebrew slaves or vassals. In this view, the idea of one God would have been around for at least five or six centuries before the conflicts over idols in the Israelite kingdom.

The only other prominent monotheism in the ancient Middle East was

Zoroastrianism.[30] Early in the first millennium, this dominant faith of Persia began to embrace one God: Ahura Masda, "the Wise Lord." But because Ahura Masda was good, an alternative force was invoked to explain evil, something like Satan in Western religions. Yet there is no evidence for contact with the Hebrews early enough to suggest influence.

What we know is that the idea of one God had an uphill fight. In Egypt it died with Akhenaton, lasting only a generation. Zoroastrian monism soon gave way to its dualist impulse, and within a few generations many gods had come back. And the struggle against other gods in Israel and Judah is one of the main themes of the Bible. The text confirms the polytheistic past, but it is hard to be sure what certain passages are saying.

Psalm 82, for instance. In the King James Version, it starts, "God standeth in the congregation of the mighty; he judgeth among the gods." But the most recent official Jewish translation goes, "God stands in the divine assembly; among the divine beings He pronounces judgment."[31] And a modern scholar emphasizing the pagan past of the Jewish God renders it this way:

> *Yahweh takes his stand in the Council of El*
> *to deliver judgments among the gods.*[32]

In this view Yahweh is actually confronting the council over which another god, El, "has presided from time immemorial."[33] In fact, the name *Yahweh* does not appear in the Hebrew, only *Elohim*. In this first passage *Elohim* appears twice, translated first as "God" and then as "gods" or "divine beings." To make matters worse, the same word, *Elohim,* appears a few passages later in an unmistakably plural form:

> *Amarti "Elohim atem"* . . .
> *I said, "You are gods"* . . .

These "gods" turn out to die as men do, but such holdovers from the Israelites' pagan past should be no surprise. The Bible is full to the brim with proof that fidelity to one sole God is no easy discipline. Moses works for forty days and nights on Mount Sinai taking God's dictation and comes down to find the people worshiping a golden calf—a classic symbol of pagan faith throughout the region. Centuries later Elijah, the greatest prophet after Moses, must set up a contest on Mount Carmel between God and Baal to prove God's power to an always doubtful people. Humiliating? Perhaps. Necessary? Clearly. When, and only when, Elijah's sacrifice bursts into flame, the people turn away from Baal. Centuries later Josiah, reading the scroll of the Teaching, must still destroy the altars of other gods and put their priests to death.

The tension lasted over a thousand years. From the mythic times of the patriarchs, when—according to legend—Abram smashed his father's idols, through the confrontation of Moses and Aaron with Pharaoh and his priests, to the long struggle of Israel's prophets not only with pagan empires but with the weak will and idolatry of their own "stiff-necked people," faith in one God had more enemies than friends. Egypt, Assyria, Babylonia, Greece, and Rome took their turns trying to tempt or force the Israelites—and the Jews they later became—away from the lone God their prophets allowed them. Yet, with the help of two religions based on it, the faith of the weak, scattered Jews would conquer the Middle East, Europe, and half the world.

3

BABYLON

HOW THE KINGDOM FELL
AND THE CULTURE CHANGED

The last thing the last king of Judah saw, before he was blinded and dragged into exile, was the execution of his sons. He did not see his house in Jerusalem burned, or those of his subjects, nor the smashing of the city's walls; but those things happened, and archeology proves it. Evidence of a vast fire is everywhere in the telltale layer of the ruin's excavations, just in the right historical period, and arrowheads are found in the houses and fortifications.[1] The Bible goes on to say that a remnant of the people stayed in the countryside not far from Jerusalem, along with the prophet Jeremiah. But they soon fell to fighting among themselves, provoked a Babylonian crackdown, and fled for their lives to Egypt. The rest had already gone to Babylon. The prophet Jeremiah tells the people to settle in, get married, be fruitful and multiply. They do this both in Babylon itself and in the countryside.

So the Bible reports. Archeology suggests that of the seventy-five thousand people in Judah before Jerusalem was destroyed, somewhere between five thousand and twenty thousand went to Babylon. Others, fleeing a burning Jerusalem, probably did disperse to Egypt and elsewhere. The Jewish community of Alexandria was founded around this time, and there may have been other, farther-flung destinations. Still, many thousands remained in the hills around Jerusalem, providing continuous occupancy of Bethel to the north, Bethlehem to the south, and scores of other towns and villages.[2]

But the elites of Judah's people—the priestly, scribal, and noble families—were probably largely carried away. Although there is little direct evidence, it is not difficult to guess what happened to them. We know they created the Book of Lamentations, expressing with exquisite anguish their loss in leaving their land. Deprived of everything they knew, including the Temple at the heart of their life, they "sat down by the waters of Babylon and wept, as they remembered Zion." They yearned toward it incessantly, and placed that longing at the center of their faith. And when they returned it was as a changed people with a new shape and intensity of belief.

To say that the Babylonian exile was a cultural watershed for the Jews is an understatement. Their cities were crushed, their Temple destroyed, their leaders killed or captured; and yet, as before and since, they found strength in weakness. New leaders and teachers arose in exile, and as much as the people longed for the Temple, they had to find a substitute for its priesthood and sacrificial ritual. What they found—what they created—was a new kind of religious life, a new spiritual strength born out of helpless yearning. The changed religion certainly included the memory of the Temple and the fond wish to return to Jerusalem to rebuild it. But Jews also needed a new way to worship in the absence of altar and sacrifice. And although they would rebuild their Temple and renew its ancient devotions, practicing them again for five centuries, they would never again depend on them so much. They turned to abstractions because they had no choice. And when in the end, for the second and last time, they had to leave the Temple behind—to turn their burdened backs on ritual sacrifice for good—they had a tradition they could rely on, because of what they had built in Babylon. Not walls or temples, altars or monuments, but structures of heart and mind that would outlast every concrete thing built by human hands.

The new faith-in-exile had to center on the Torah—"the words of the scroll of the Teaching" found by Josiah. A hundred years had passed, and a new commitment to law and text had set in even before the exile. The literary and spiritual power of Deuteronomy ensured that scribes and teachers would have a growing importance in the kingdom, creating a second religious center of gravity apart from the Temple priests. Such teachers revered the Temple yet may have had something to fear from the priests. In any case they took care to emphasize the Temple religion and provide the details of its practices. This emphasis grew as Deuteronomy was combined with the priestly text of Leviticus and the rest of the Five Books of Moses.

For Deuteronomy itself, the text states clearly what Moses intended:

> And Moses wrote down this Teaching and gave it to the priests . . . and to all the elders of Israel.
> And Moses instructed them as follows: Every seventh year . . . you shall read this Teaching aloud in the presence of all Israel. Gather the people—men, women, children, and the strangers in your communities—that they may hear and so learn to revere the Lord your God and to observe faithfully every word of this Teaching. Their children too, who have not had the experience, shall hear and learn.[3]

The passage prescribes a centralized reading, probably at the Temple, once in seven years, and a method that will transcend generations. But that was just the beginning. If a king rent his clothes in grief over what he hadn't known, there would obviously now be a need to study. Deuteronomy is clear on this, too, in one of its most famous passages:

> Hear, O Israel! The Lord is our God, the Lord is One.
>
> And thou shalt love the Lord thy God with all thine heart, with all thy soul, and with all thy might. And these words, which I command thee this day, shall be in thine heart: And thou shalt teach them diligently unto thy children, and thou shalt speak of them when thou sittest in thine house, and when thou walkest by the way, and when thou liest down, and when thou risest up. And thou shalt bind them for a sign upon thine hand, and they shall be for frontlets between thine eyes. And thou shalt write them on the doorposts of thine house, and upon thy gates (Deut. 6:4–7).[4]

Clearly, study itself was a kind of devotion to God, to be done everywhere. This contrasted sharply with sacrifices and other rituals, which were increasingly tied to the one Holy Temple in Jerusalem. Those who could traveled to Jerusalem on festivals and gave their tithes to the priests or burned the first fruit of their flocks and fields on the high altar of God.

For those who could not get there and for everyone between trips, there had to be some way to worship God that was more portable than ark, altar, or Temple. The Teaching, or Torah, filled this need in two ways. First, all of the people were under strict orders to study, interpret, and teach it. This intensified the Jewish obsession with texts. Second, parts of the Torah began to be incorporated into a liturgy, or program of prayer. These sections, recited, chanted, or sung over and over—like the Shema quoted above—would ensure that everyone, even children, would meet the obligation to study Torah. So a parallel religion arose, independent of Temple and priesthood. Far from being tied to a high place, you had to do it sitting in your house, walking by the way, lying down, and rising up. Far from belonging only to great men, the words had to be taught diligently to children. And far from being the property of the pure Temple acolytes, the words were inscribed on the doorposts of every building and in amulets worn by the common man.

If there was so much teaching to be done, who were the teachers? We get some inkling from Jeremiah as he berates the people (8:8–9):

> *But my people paid no heed*
> *To the law of the Lord. . . .*
> *Assuredly, for naught had the pen labored,*
> *For naught the scribes!*
> *The wise shall be put to shame.*[5]

Scribes and wise men, teachers and prophets, were already respected in the time of the First Temple. But in the exile, in the absence of altar and Temple, they became the natural leaders and the source of the people's strength. Their king had been unable to protect his people. The holy priests had fled or were captured, their white robes soiled with the filth of war.

Whatever else they did, they could not continue the Temple religion. They could join the Babylonians in idolatry, which most of them did not. They could weep bitter tears for their broken Temple, which for a time they did. And they could turn to the scrolls a few of their scribes had brought, among the scraps and trappings a defeated, captive people could carry into exile. Then, with utmost grief and love, in hours or minutes stolen from the press of a hard life, they could read, learn, teach, think, and talk to one another about the most important thing in the world, the word of God.

This first great diaspora, in the floodplain of the Tigris and Euphrates Rivers, was, like many things, more complex than the Bible depicts it. It began long before the final destruction of Jerusalem. There were exiles from the defeat of the northern kingdom of Israel, whom the Assyrians had moved to Mesopotamia more than a hundred years before the decisive defeat of Judah. These earlier exiles dispersed in several directions. We know from nonbiblical sources that there were early Jewish communities in Egypt, also probably settled by exiles from northern Israel.[6] Some were Egyptian army recruits. Egypt liked to man its borders with loyal foreign troops, and Jewish soldiers were stationed at Migdol, near Suez, to protect the northern border. They had their families with them, and other Jewish migrants followed, pursuing agriculture, industry, and trade. Archeology shows that Migdol was a fertile, populated area with irrigation, drainage canals, and navigable waters.

Another Jewish community lived at the southern border of Egypt, on Elephantine, an island in the Nile at the edge of Nubian territory. Papyri found there are a treasure trove of records in Aramaic: contracts, memos, legal documents, and copies of letters. They date from 495 to 399, but they also reflect the community's earlier history. At Elephantine as at Migdol, Jewish troops were stationed between the Egyptians and their enemies, and their families and others followed, creating a community. There was even a temple there, and when it was destroyed at the instigation of hostile Egyptian priests, the community rebuilt it. Jedania, the Jewish leader, wrote to officials in both Israel and Judah—those who had stayed behind—to ask for advice and assistance. But the shrine combined the worship of Yahweh with that of Canaanite gods. Reminiscent of Ahab and Jezebel's straying centuries earlier, this kind of syncretism also prevailed in Migdol. It was intolerable to Jeremiah, who condemned the Jews of Egypt, leaving the rebuilding of Jerusalem almost solely to the returning Jews of Babylon.

That exile is one of the greatest Bible stories, on a par for poetry and narrative with the Exodus, the conquest of Canaan, or the life of David. The exquisite literary output from this one event includes the latter parts of Isaiah and Jeremiah, all of Ezekiel and Daniel, Lamentations, and other texts. Psalm 137 is one of the world's most moving poems. In the King James Version,

> *By the rivers of Babylon, there we sat down, yea, we wept, when we remembered Zion.*
> *We hanged our harps upon the willows in the midst thereof.*
> *For there they that carried us away captive required of us a song; and they that wasted us required of us mirth, saying, Sing us one of the songs of Zion.*
> *How shall we sing the Lord's song in a strange land?*
> *If I forget thee, O Jerusalem, let my right hand forget her cunning.*
> *If I do not remember thee, let my tongue cleave to the roof of my mouth; if I prefer not Jerusalem above my chief joy.*

It goes on to express a less meditative sentiment, a cold, murderous rage, ever the offspring of terrible injury:

> *O daughter of Babylon, who art to be destroyed; happy shall he be, that rewardeth thee as thou hast served us.*
> *Happy shall he be, that taketh and dasheth thy little ones against the stones.*

Try to imagine what it must have been like. You see your city's defensive wall demolished, your Holy Temple destroyed, your home burned, your princes slaughtered and their father blinded, your own father, brother, son, or husband killed. Then, having lost all you relied on, hoped for, and believed in, you are carried off in chains to your conqueror's country, never to see your own land again. It seems too much to bear. Yet even the Bible suggests that for most Jews, for most of the exile, the suffering was not so great, and it did not end in rage. Many were imprisoned or enslaved at the outset, but not permanently. Most became tenants of the Babylonian landed aristocracy. Eventually they were allowed to engage in commerce and to accumulate modest wealth. Jeremiah gives us a sense of the conditions, as he paraphrases the first commandment in Genesis, Be fruitful and multiply:

> Thus saith the Lord of hosts, the God of Israel, unto all that are carried away captives, whom I have caused to be carried away from Jerusalem unto Babylon:
> Build ye houses, and dwell in them; and plant gardens, and eat the fruit of them;

Take ye wives, and beget sons and daughters; and take wives
for your sons, and give your daughters to husbands, that they may
bear sons and daughters; that ye may be increased there, and not di-
minished.

This encouraging directive, issued by one of the greatest of prophets, became the model for Jewish diasporas for twenty-five hundred years. But
Jeremiah goes on,

And seek the peace of the city whither I have caused you to be
carried away captives, and pray unto the Lord for it: for in the peace
thereof shall ye have peace.[7]

There could hardly be a more vivid contrast with the close of Psalm 137.
Somehow in Jeremiah's mind the hatred of the conqueror and the desire for
revenge—expressed so vividly in the anguish of the psalmist—are suppressed and even transformed into model citizenship in the empire.

This rule of loyalty was vital. The Babylonians, like most ancient imperial powers, had no interest in confronting conquered peoples in a way that
would make subjugation difficult and loyalty impossible. It was only in situations like the one *preceding* the exile, where religion fostered rebellion,
that religious practices were at risk. This was in marked contrast to the later
situation in Europe, where Judaism itself was viewed as the problem.

For the Babylonians, pragmatism trumped faith and doctrine. Some
Jews were assimilated, but most were not. The impression of a seal dated to
the sixth century exemplifies the tension. It reads, "Belonging to Yehoy-
ishma, daughter of Sawas-sar-usur."[8] The father's name is Babylonian:
"Sun-god-protect-the-king." But the daughter's Hebrew name begins with
a variation on Yahweh: "God will hear," a type of name especially associated
with the Jews of Babylon. Early in the exile, perhaps, an assimilated father
took a Babylonian name, but later gave his daughter a distinctly Hebrew
one. The father is named for a god identified with the sun, the daughter for
the one God who transcends all identities, except for being linked with the
Jewish people.

In Jeremiah's view, the exiled Jews were not forbidden to practice their
religion or carry on their culture and traditions. Their lives included many
occasions for prayer, public and private. They added five annual fast days to
Jewish law, to express their grief and to remember. They may have built
synagogues, but they also held public worship in open spaces. And they developed their knowledge of and devotion to the Law of Moses. However,
not all biblical authors saw the exile as a time of religious freedom. The
Book of Daniel, centuries later, gives a mythic account of religious con-

frontations with the Babylonian, and later with the Persian, king. It has no historical basis, but it reveals much about the collective Jewish memory of the exile.

Nebuchadnezzar builds a gigantic new idol and decrees that all his subjects worship it. Advisers let him know that three leaders of the Jews refuse to obey, so he has them thrown into a "burning fiery furnace." There they stroll around, defying death as they have defied the king's law. The king calls them out, impressed with their God's power. Daniel becomes the king's magician, so respected that he gets away with predicting that his benefactor will be banished and eat grass for seven years. This happens, and then Daniel is not so much in favor with the king's successor Belshazzar. But when Belshazzar sees a human hand appear and write on a plaster wall of his palace, Daniel is the one he calls to consult. He predicts the new king's downfall at the hands of the Medes and Persians, which duly occurs that same night.

⌒⧟⧟⧟⌒

Predicted or not, the downfall did occur. Persia swallowed Babylon whole—not to mention Assyria, Egypt, and what was left of Israel and Judah. Then, like a deus ex machina, the Persian emperor Cyrus let the exiles go home. Indeed—and it did seem almost miraculous—Cyrus decreed that the Jews could return in 539, the same year as his conquest of Babylon. Unlike the Babylonians, the Persians found it expedient to return displaced refugees and allow them to keep their odd local cults. They even granted limited autonomy to local elites, buffers against the enemies of the empire—in the case of the Jews, Egypt.

The Book of Ezra tells us who the returning refugees were—forty-two thousand of them—and what they brought back. We have no good reason to doubt this account, but it seems strange for an exiled, abject, enslaved people to be returning home weighed down with thousands of gold vessels, hundreds of servants, "two hundred singing men and singing women," seven hundred horses, two hundred mules, four hundred camels, and almost seven thousand donkeys. Even if we discount these numbers by half, how do we reconcile this picture with the lament of the psalm? Perhaps the half century in Babylon had gone from horrendous to tolerable and finally ended in wealth. Or perhaps the contradictory views describe the experiences of different groups of Jewish exiles.

In any case, the most important thing the people brought back with them from Babylon was not gold vessels or horses and camels or even singing men, but the scroll of the Law—the Torah—and the learning that came with it. Cut off from the high places, including the Temple in Jerusalem, the people had relied on prayer and study centered on the inspired work they called the Law of Moses. The Bible recounts several waves of repatriation from Babylon, echoing the several waves of exile. Cyrus had decreed not only that the Jews could return, but that they could rebuild the Temple. This took decades, and the full return and integration of the exiles took generations more. But when it was done there was a new realization of Judaism: restored Temple sacrifice side by side with Torah study and liturgy. There was also a new Jewish kingdom centered in Jerusalem, protected by the Persian Empire.

From references to the emperors, we can estimate the dates of certain events. A second wave of exiles returned under Darius in 522, and with the help of a generous imperial grant—and overcoming considerable local opposition—they completed the Temple in 516. Yet many Jews remained in exile. The Book of Daniel is not a history—in fact, it is quite implausible— and it was written three centuries later, but it claims severe oppression for those who remained. For example, Darius forbids Jewish worship, but it is Daniel's practice to pray three times a day in his own home, standing at the window, facing Jerusalem. Daniel's heroism in practicing his faith gets him thrown into the lions' den, where his miraculous survival proves once again the power of the Jewish God. It is hard to reconcile these tales with the generosity of the same regime toward the Jews who returned to their homeland. But they had yearned to return and return they did, bearing a new outlook and a new kind of faith.

A major transformation in Jewish culture occurred after the return of Ezra the scribe from Babylon in 458, and when Nehemiah returned as governor some years later. Ezra was the guardian of the Law, but Nehemiah's role was to rebuild Jerusalem. The Temple was long finished, but the city walls were still in ruins. Nehemiah petitioned the new emperor to let him rebuild, and he mobilized the people and rebuilt them. This was done despite local opponents, including Arabs. "Now the city was large and great: but the people were few therein, and the houses were not builded. And my God put into mine heart to gather together the nobles, and the people."[9] There were thousands of them, listed by family names. Still, Jewish numbers at this time were small, far smaller than those of Israel and Judah at their height centuries earlier. And it took another two or three hundred years before the population recovered to past levels.

Yet what these few people did under Ezra's ministry changed their lives and those of their descendants:

> And all the people gathered themselves together as one man into the street that was before the water gate; and they spake unto Ezra the scribe to bring the book of the law of Moses, which the Lord had commanded to Israel.

> And Ezra the priest brought the law before the congregation of both men and women, and all that could hear with understanding, upon the first day of the seventh month.
>
> And he read therein before the street that was before the water gate, from the morning until mid-day, before the men and the women, and those that could understand; and the ears of all the people were attentive unto the book of the law.
>
> And Ezra the scribe stood upon a pulpit of wood, which they had made for the purpose. . . .
>
> And Ezra opened the book in the sight of all the people; (for he was above all the people;) and when he opened it, all the people stood up:
>
> And Ezra blessed the Lord, the great God. And all the people answered, Amen, Amen, with lifting up their hands: and they bowed their heads, and worshipped the Lord with their faces to the ground.[10]

Ezra did not do this alone, but was surrounded by other leaders, including the priestly Levites. There was no contention here; this was a new but fully realized and legitimate form of worship. The description does seem to have just the slightest flavor of idolatry. But it is not the Torah itself that is being worshiped, it is God. The Torah was the Jews' link to God, and was revered not as an object but as a record of God's word. "So they read in the book in the law of God distinctly," the passage goes on, "and gave the sense, and caused them to understand the reading."

This ceremony, repeated in almost the same way throughout the Jewish world today, contains two key forms of Jewish practice: *avodah,* which refers to either Temple sacrifice, prayer, or keeping the commandments; and Torah, which includes and implies learning.[11] When the scroll is held up, the people rise, bless God, bow, and worship. But then they *read* in the book, in the law of God, "distinctly," giving the sense, so that all can understand. What *was* this book of the law of God, now in Ezra the scribe's hands, held up before the people? It could have been Deuteronomy alone, but it could also have been the combined and edited Torah, the first five books of the Bible. Ezra himself may have put them all together.

In any case, the Torah describes and represents the fundamental faith of the Jews in the word of God and in their covenant with God. The Temple stands, rebuilt and functioning, but the description of this service doesn't mention it. Although the service takes place on Rosh Hashanah, a day when the Temple would be alive with people and sacrifices, this large crowd holds a different kind of worship. It does not by any means signal the end of the Temple's role; that will go on in faith and vigor for half a millennium, until the Second Temple's destruction. But it does establish once and for all two new and different principles in parallel with the old: the Torah read as liturgy, a means to worship God; and the Torah read as law, a means to discern God's will.

༄

What went on in the Temple on those holidays? Rosh Hashanah, then as now, began ten days of repentance. The last was Yom Kippur, a day of fasting, purification, and utmost submission to God's awesome strength and grace. Their non-Jewish Canaanite neighbors held communal fast days, but the Hebrews made the fast a rite of submission to their *one* God. Leviticus 16:

> And this shall be a statute for ever unto you: that in the seventh month, on the tenth day of the month, ye shall afflict your souls, and do no work at all, whether it be one of your own country, or a stranger that sojourneth among you:
>
> For on that day shall the priest make an atonement for you, to cleanse you, that ye may be clean from all your sins before the Lord.
>
> It shall be a sabbath of rest unto you, and ye shall afflict your souls.

Aaron, Moses' brother and the first high priest, has just seen his sons consumed by God's fire because they erred in making a sacrifice. At God's command, Moses teaches Aaron how to approach "the holy place." He must wash and put on the sacred linen garments. Then, for the sins of the people, "he shall take of the congregation of Israel two kids of the goats for a sin offering."[12]

> And Aaron shall cast lots upon the two goats; one lot for the Lord, and the other lot for the scapegoat.
>
> And Aaron shall bring the goat upon which the Lord's lot fell, and offer him for a sin offering.
>
> But the goat, on which the lot fell to be the scapegoat, shall be presented alive before the Lord, to make an atonement with him, and to let him go for a scapegoat into the wilderness.[13]

As if to acknowledge that this is baffling, the text goes on to say,

> And Aaron shall lay both his hands upon the head of the live goat, and confess over him all the iniquities of the children of Israel, and all their transgressions in all their sins, putting them upon the head of the goat. . . .
>
> And the goat shall bear upon him all their iniquities unto a land not inhabited: and he shall let go the goat into the wilderness.[14]

The sins are returned to the wild regions they came from, as if the scapegoat, a domestic animal gone wild, can expiate the people's sins not by dying but by living with them in the wilderness. This central rite of Yom Kippur, the Day of Atonement, was one of many sacrifices and rituals of purity. What did they mean?

Most of Leviticus deals in exquisite detail with purity and sacrifice, which are deeply connected in three ways. First, purity stands in opposition to danger, and indeed its very purpose is defense against danger—real or imagined.[15] Second, sacrifice is not just propitiation of God, but expiation of sin, a ritual of undoing that attempts to cancel impurity out. Third and most important, sacrifice, although it tries to guard against the gravest of all dangers, that of God's wrath, is itself a form of violence—and, paradoxically, a means of expelling violence, that ultimate impurity, from the human heart and community.[16]

The laws of purity in Leviticus reflect related customs in many cultural groups. Human minds love dichotomies—day and night, male and female, left and right, civil and savage, village and wilderness, good and bad, us and them—and we routinely exaggerate the contrasts, suppressing ambiguity with a vengeance. Ambiguity is painful, and although our eyes tell us that there are countless grays, cognitive dissonance urges us to abolish the awkward cases and see the world in black and white. Sacrificial animals must be without blemish, or how could their sacrifice purify anyone? But they must also come from species considered clean or kosher. Thus the laws of sacrifice become the dietary laws; every animal eaten is a kind of sacrifice. Many explanations have been offered for those laws: hygiene, familiarity, separation from neighboring peoples, totemic identification, and the animals' habits, among others. But the common thread among the "abominations" of Leviticus is that they violate intactness, completeness, or wholeness. This is what the Torah often *means* by impurity.[17]

Bodily fluids, including semen and menstrual blood, defile the high priest, the Temple, or the war encampment. Leprosy contaminates until completely cured. There can be no blemishes on the high priest or on a sacrificial animal; such taboos are common in cultures throughout the world. There are prohibitions against mixing wool and flax in garments, planting different kinds of trees in the same orchard, and mixing milk and meat. These mixtures violate the intactness of each kind. The clean animals too are pure, intact kinds: land animals that have cloven hooves and chew their cud; fish that have fins and scales; and insects that, like grasshoppers, crickets, and locusts, have legs above their feet. Clean fowl are those that are not birds of prey. But aside from the birds, the *permitted* animals are defined as a distinct, intact class with clear boundaries. It's not that the animals are clean in their biology or habits, it's that their categories are cleanly, unambiguously defined. Prohibitions deal with boundary violations. Clear boundaries offer psychological safety, a vital need in an uncontrollable world. This was as true for the ancient Hebrews as for the Polynesian peoples who gave us the word *taboo.*

So it is with the purity of sacrifice. Noah, like the pagans, may burn sacrifices because the smell is pleasing in the nostrils of a god, but Israelite sacrifice has more complex goals. Burnt offerings may be pure gifts to God, but sin offerings make the sinner part with something valuable, substituting the animal for himself or his child.[18] At the binding and near-sacrifice of Isaac, a ram appears as a substitute just as the angel stays Abraham's hand. The substitution is made explicit in Exodus (13:11–15), which establishes the custom of Pidyon Ha-ben, the redemption of the firstborn. Because God passed over the firstborn sons of the Israelites while slaying those of the Egyptians, Israelites must bring a firstborn animal for sacrifice, to redeem a firstborn son at thirty days of age.

So as the ancient world relinquished human sacrifice, it embraced animal sacrifice with a whole heart. For the Hebrews, giving the ram for the boy was a transformation close to the core of their identity, and rejection of human sacrifice was, they believed, one of the things that distinguished them from their neighbors. But they had no hesitation in sacrificing large numbers of animals, and for centuries those offerings were the heart of their sacred life. Mass sacrifice on festival days was a very bloody business. Upon completion of the First Temple, Solomon reportedly sacrificed many thousands of sheep and oxen, so that the ground was moist with blood. And the Second Temple had a built-in shaft running down from the altar to carry the blood away. *The Letter of Aristeas,* possibly fictional but close to the realities of the Second Temple, gives what appears to be an eyewitness account:

> All the buildings were characterized by a magnificence and costliness quite unprecedented . . . a pleasant spectacle from which a man could scarcely tear himself away. The construction of the altar was in keeping with the place itself and with the burnt offerings which were consumed by fire upon it, and the approach to it was on a similar scale. There was a gradual slope up to it, conveniently arranged for the purpose of decency, and the ministering priests were robed in linen garments, down to their ankles. . . . The whole of the floor is paved with stones and slopes down to the appointed places, that water may be conveyed to wash away the blood from the sacrifices, for many thousand beasts are sacrificed there on the feast days. . . . There are many openings for water at the base of the altar which are invisible to all except to those who are engaged in the ministration, so that all the blood of the sacrifices which is collected in great quantities is washed away in the twinkling of an eye.[19]

People came from all over Israel and Judah with their sacrificial animals, and at the appointed festivals they must have stood for hours in a
stench like that of a slaughterhouse. Ritual purity notwithstanding, no one
could have doubted that this was a violent process. But it was controlled violence, and that was part of the point. By directing the violence outward to
the sacrificial victim, the dangerous impulse was deflected away from the
community.[20] And in the act of killing the pure victim, sin—including the
sins of rage and vengeance—could somehow be released like pus from a
boil. Like infection, violence is contagious, and epidemics of vengeance are
common. This is especially true in cultures without a strong central authority or an organized system of justice. If human beings have a violent tendency, how much better to take it out on designated ritual victims than to
allow it to spread like plague, destroying the human world.

Of course, for much of the primitive and then the ancient world, sacrificial victims *were* human, and it is the end of such sacrifice that we see in
the rise of Western civilization. The stories we tell in retrospect signify our
struggle to leave human sacrifice behind. Agamemnon sacrifices his daughter Iphigenia to fill the sails of his war-bound ships with wind, but the deed
brings the House of Atreus down on his head. Abraham assents to the sacrifice of Isaac, but God's angel stops him, showing him the ram instead.
And the Christian God sends his only son to become the last and most important sacrificial victim, taking the world's sins on himself and ending ritual sacrifice forever.

ᏬᎠᎠᎪ

By the time of that momentous sacrifice, the Jews had long since built a culture, a new faith and practice in the shadow of the Temple, one that had little or nothing to do with ritual slaughter. A student of Aristotle's wrote of
the Jews that "being philosophers by race, they converse with each other
about the Divine."[21] This was in the fourth or third century B.C.E., not so
long after Ezra's time—perhaps under Alexander the Great. Alexander
conquered Israel, along with the rest of western Asia, in 332, beginning a
centuries-long confrontation between Hellenism and Judaism. Greeks bore
the gifts of art, literature, philosophy, science, architecture, politics, sport,
and war, but the Jews were "philosophers by race," reading and writing
prophecy, steeped in a conversation with and about God.

Between the exile and Alexander, the conversation had produced a
deeper understanding and a new religious culture. Prophecy had blazed hot
for generations but was waning. The Temple and its priesthood stood at the
core of the culture, but Torah study and prayer pervaded it. Scribes took an
ascendant role. Books of the Bible were written, along with nonbiblical
works, and a semiliterate populace read and studied them. This was a

golden age of Jewish history in Israel, in which the shield of the benign Persian Empire fostered peace, prosperity, and religious independence. After Alexander the empire broke apart, but the fragments—Egypt and Syria, for example—remained Hellenized. In Israel the situation became dynamic. The Jewish Bible was finished and the text as a whole canonized. A widespread and vigorous diaspora emerged, where Jews absorbed strong foreign influences yet maintained contact with Jews in Israel, and a contest between Greek and Jewish culture began.

Earlier cultural clashes—the ones with Egypt, Canaan, Babylon, and Persia—had presented their temptations. Some Jews assimilated, and all were influenced. But Greek culture had unprecedented power. The Hebrews and then the Jews had met cultures superior in war, engineering, and architecture, but to these they had opposed their Law, their prophecies, their conversation with God, defining themselves by these spiritual replies to a worldly power they could not resist. With Greece the temptations were subtler and more enticing, the boundaries vaguer, the tidal pull stronger and more inward.[22] Prior empires were not always brutish, but suffering Jews could see them that way. Greece had achieved a life of the mind that at least rivaled their own, and had gone much further in art and science. The Greeks sought a universal culture, and were often influenced by those they conquered. Greek culture was a synthesis, and it partly absorbed the Jews.

Many diaspora Jews primarily spoke Greek, the ancient world's new lingua franca.[23] Only a few inscriptions suggest that these Jews had any knowledge of Hebrew. Even in Israel, many Jews spoke Greek, which coexisted with Hebrew and its sister language, Aramaic. The Torah was translated into Greek, and many new works of literature and philosophy by Jews were composed in Greek.[24] Of course, once Jews had learned it, they could read Homer and Sophocles, Euclid and Archimedes, Plato and Aristotle. Already a people of the mind, how could they resist?

Hellenism's universal appeal persuaded many Jews. They had already expressed universal themes in the Torah—the Ten Commandments, for example, and the injunction to "love thy neighbor as thyself." Indeed, even as the Jews with baffling confidence claimed that their God was the only one, they wanted that God to emerge from a parochial past as their private deity to become the sole and universal God of all the world. This was both arrogant and generous. But the Greeks, despite being polytheists, had carried the universal intellectual life to a much higher plane of abstraction— through Plato and Euclid, for example, whose ideas were accessible equally to every human mind. Their plays depicted human conflict and longing with immense dramatic and poetic power. They were Greek in incident and character, but anyone could experience the emotions.

So Jews showed Greek influence even before Alexander.[25] Proverbs and Ecclesiastes had universal philosophical themes, and Job dramatized them as tragedy. Emerging rabbinical methods of argument reflected Greek legal traditions. Even the word *Sanhedrin,* the highest council of rabbis, comes from *synedrion,* the chief Greek judicial body. And Plato's abstract God, who had nothing in common with the gods of his common compatriots, struck a resonant chord in many Jews. In material terms Jewish culture— or at least the elite part of it—became Greek. Cities were built or rebuilt in Israel on the model of the polis and were run according to Greek political principles. The *gymnasion* and the theater were introduced, while schools, clubs, and associations followed Hellenic leads. Clothing, pottery, architecture, coinage, and art all show strong Greek influence.

This was not new. The First Temple followed Phoenician and Syrian architectural plans, the Jewish liturgy resembles in places the famous hymn to Aton, Proverbs reflects older Egyptian as well as new Greek wisdom, and some exiled Jews took Persian names. But apparently very few Jews *became* Egyptian, Phoenician, or Persian. Greece for the first time presented the Jews with a culture that was open, pervasive, and appealing enough so that the potential for complete assimilation was very great. Yet most Jews resisted the temptation, retaining many traditions and drawing the line at religious faith. People were culturally Hellenized, and yet indelibly Jewish. In the diaspora, Jews spoke Greek and used only a bit of Hebrew, but in Israel Greek was merely a third language—after Hebrew, used for common speech, Scripture, and liturgy, and Aramaic, a literary language and the spoken idiom of the elite. Greek served in foreign trade and secular intellectual discourse, much as German did in eastern Europe in the early twentieth century.

At first there was no problem maintaining the Temple and its independent practices. As under the Persians, the high priest functioned as governor of the province. He protected the priesthood, and the sacrificial rituals and festival observances went on as before. Torah reading and prayer services took place there but also in other locations—early forms of the synagogue. Intense literary activity finalized not only the Tanakh—the Jewish Bible— but also apocryphal works that did not make the canon. Scribes set down or composed these works, and rabbis—the word *rabbi* means "my teacher"— taught and studied them. As was usual in the past, the Jews were allowed their special relationship with their lonely, faceless, insubstantial God.

But again the Jews were caught between two great powers, this time Egypt and Syria.[26] Since Judea was now a subject province, the situation should have been less dangerous than in the distant past, when, as a kingdom, they had dreamed of independence. Yet being the object of a tug-of-war between two powers that fought five major wars in a century was no easy role. Armies were stationed throughout the country, including Jerusalem. The Jewish elite was factionalized, with supporters of Egypt and Syria in conflict. Social inequalities deepened; religious strife was unavoidable.

By the early second century, the province was under Syrian rule. When King Antiochus IV visited, the citizens of Jerusalem welcomed him with a torchlight procession. Around the same time athletic games were held in Tyre, on the Phoenician coast, and Jerusalem sent a delegation. When the Jewish athletes declined to make an offering to the god of the games, they were instead allowed to donate to the support of the city's fleet. But this tolerance did not last. The following year two priests vied for control in Jerusalem, and violence erupted when one robbed the Temple treasury to bribe the emperor. Antiochus eventually quelled the conflict with Syrian troops. He pillaged the Temple, and his troops set the city aflame and massacred many inhabitants. He built a fortress next to the Temple garrisoned with Syrian troops whose pagan cults violated the sanctity of the Holy City.

⟨⟨⟨⟩⟩⟩

Consider one noble, priestly family, the Tobiads, who took part in these events. The Roman-Jewish historian Josephus told their story in *Antiquities of the Jews.*[27] Even granting the inevitable inaccuracies, the family history reveals much about Jewish culture.

A corrupt high priest, Onias, "one of a little soul, and a great lover of money," failed to pay taxes to Egypt, and Ptolemy threatened to seize Jewish land. Onias refused to compromise, but permitted his nephew Joseph to mediate. Joseph gave the ambassador rich gifts, "and feasted him magnificently for many days." The ambassador, "highly pleased with his frank and liberal temper, and with the gravity of his deportment," encouraged Joseph to go to Ptolemy.

He did so, again bearing gifts. In Memphis he found Ptolemy and Cleopatra in their chariot with the very ambassador Joseph had wined and dined in Jerusalem. Brought into the chariot on the ambassador's word, he asked the king to forgive his uncle the priest, "because old men and infants have minds exactly alike." The king, delighted with the young man, took him to Alexandria. Despite opposition Joseph soon ingratiated himself so well with the royal couple—among other things he made Ptolemy laugh— that he was appointed to collect taxes from Judea and other reluctant provinces. This he did faithfully and ruthlessly, with the help of two thousand foot soldiers assigned to him by the king. When the people of Ashkelon refused to pay, he slew twenty of their leaders, and the people of Syria, duly impressed, paid promptly. He became wealthy while meeting his obligations to the king and sending him sumptuous gifts. He had many sons, one born of an incestuous union with his niece—perhaps within the framework of Egyptian custom but not that of Jewish law.

When Ptolemy had a son, Joseph sent his own son, who impressed the king and queen much as his father had—not least because he gave them a hundred boys and a hundred girls he had bought for a talent of silver apiece. Joseph died, having "brought the Jews out of a state of poverty and meanness, to one that was more splendid." By this time power had shifted, with the Syrians ruling Judea after Ptolemy. This was when civil conflicts led Antiochus to occupy Jerusalem, pillage the Temple, and subject religious Jews to every form of abomination. Even if only part of the Tobiad saga is true, it reveals a priestly family devoid of religion and detached from Jewish law. The Tobiads were up to the ancient tricks of Ahab and Jezebel, flaunting God's will as they cozied up to a foreign power. Corruption, bribery, brutality, incest, all these seem acceptable to a family wealthy enough to be above the law.

ᏰᏰᏰ

It is at this point that we meet the countervailing power of the Jewish religious culture. The oppression of Antiochus was unprecedented. People were forced, on pain of death, to eat pork or violate the Sabbath; many were martyred. Second Maccabees tells the story of Hannah, whose seven sons go calmly to their deaths, in order of age, each serving as an example to the next, rather than taste forbidden flesh. But the signal violation of Antiochus was forcing Jews to worship the idols of pagan gods. Previous rulers left conquered peoples to their own beliefs and practices, but most could merge their gods with those of the conquerors. The Jews by this time were deeply opposed to polytheism, and their rituals had long since hardened into law. The Torah, now centuries old, might have different interpretations, but one way or another it told them what the one God wanted.

Then as now, their relationship with God was paradoxical. God was abstract, all-seeing, and omnipotent; but Abraham remonstrated with him, and Moses saw his back, if not his face. God was descended from the Canaanite "most high" god, and kept a distance from human affairs; yet Isaac felt God's presence when he walked out in the field to meditate in the evening. Josiah rent his clothing when the scroll of the Law was found, grieving over his unwitting neglect of God's word. And Daniel, in exile, at grave risk to his life, looked longingly out his window toward Jerusalem to pray and to know God's grace. This was no uninvolved Platonic God. This God's abstractions blended with a kind of divine personhood, a perhaps forbidden yet almost human warmth. This was a God with whom a human being could have that most vital and transcendent of relationships, the one that has been called *I and Thou*.[28]

The Greek phase of Jewish life was not the era of Ahab and Jezebel, nor that of Josiah's idolatrous sons. Then, the cultures of Israel and Judah were forming their religious ideals, struggling to give birth to them in a sea of tempting and confusing competition. This was much later—centuries after Ezra had held the scroll aloft before the people. Their Torah was no abstraction to them, nor were their customs some lightly worn garment that could be shed when a new fashion arrived with a new conqueror. So when Antiochus and his Jewish sycophants built a statue of Zeus in the Temple, bowing down or making an offering was, for a Jew with any faith, not an option. Nor could they violate the other commandments.

Take circumcision, a prominent and galling prohibition. Second Maccabees (6:10) tells us that mothers readily martyred themselves and their sons rather than fail to circumcise them. "For example, two women were brought in for having circumcised their children. They publicly paraded them around the city, with their babies hanging at their breasts, and then they hurled them down headlong from the wall."[29] Equally solemn was the commitment to dietary laws, Sabbath observance, and of course avoidance of idol worship; observant Jews were martyred for keeping any of these commandments. The text goes on optimistically to "urge those who read this book not to be depressed by such calamities." God may discipline the Jews, but will severely punish their enemies, because "he never withdraws his mercy from us."

☙

Among the most cherished Jewish commandments circumcision seems particularly puzzling. Over the centuries it has been viewed as evidence of barbarism and of clever hygiene, as a sign of self-restraint and as a form of self-imposed suffering. It is perhaps all of these; no symbolic act of such importance can have only one meaning. But first of all one needs to understand it from the viewpoint of those who practice it. When an observant Jewish man looks down at himself, he thinks, *Even in my body I belong, in part, to God. Even in my manhood, my most vulnerable place, my connection to normal bodily functions, to pleasure, and to the future, I have been cut and scarred in accordance with God's command.* Circumcision is of the essence of his relationship to God and to his people. It is traced to the ceremony where God commanded Abraham:

> This is my covenant, which ye shall keep, between me and you and thy seed after thee; Every man child among you shall be circumcised.
>
> And ye shall circumcise the flesh of your foreskin; and it shall be a token of the covenant betwixt me and you.
>
> And he that is eight days old shall be circumcised among you, every man child in your generations . . . and my covenant shall be in your flesh for an everlasting covenant.
>
> And the uncircumcised man child whose flesh of his foreskin is not circumcised, that soul shall be cut off from his people; he hath broken my covenant.[30]

The last passage falls like the shadow of an ax across the hope of a human connection, the comfort of belonging to a people. But far more dreadfully, the failure to make this simple, awkward, painful cut cuts through the bond that links God and man. Not to make the commanded cut opens a much worse wound, a lasting, unbridgeable gap between *I* and *Thou*—God and, in this case, man.

Rabbinic legend, or Midrash, has it that God and Abraham, who was ninety-nine at the time, talked a bit about this. Abraham asks, in effect, "To what do I owe this honor?" and God explains that he is the first to deserve it. To the objection that this will not help him bring God's message to the local tribesmen, God replies that it will make him stronger, give him power over his body. But there is a further incentive for Abraham: *Do it,* says God, *or I'll uncreate the world.* This point is persuasive. Abraham circumcises himself and all the men of his household. According to the Midrash, then, the burden this act bears is not just a man's link to his people or even his God. It is the whole weight of creation, the very existence of the world.

◐▨▨◑

The English word *circumcision* describes the act, but the Hebrew word shows no interest in anatomy. It is *brit,* "covenant," the word used repeatedly in Genesis. Even for the Torah, the repetition is impressive. There can be no mistake: It is about the deal, the agreement, the relationship. The removal of the foreskin, perhaps even the wound itself, symbolically connects a man to God. But not *just* symbolically. Symbols are for moderns. Traditional people make no distinction between the religious and the physical, the symbolic and the real. In fact, what we call the symbolic may be more real than real.

The Jews were not the first traditional culture to practice it. It was common among the Semites of the ancient Near East and occurs in cultures throughout the world. It is not always easy to see what it means. As with the ancient Hebrews, you have to work toward the meaning from within.

Among the Ngatatjara of Australia's Gibson Desert, it was done at puberty, in the setting of a dance around a great bonfire, in homage to the sacred Kangaroo. The boy was laid across a "table" formed by friends on their hands and knees, and the foreskin was removed with a stone knife. The operation was a test of the boy's willingness to suffer pain calmly; once endured, it proved his status as a man.

The Ndembu of Zambia did it between ages eight and ten, accompanied by a ritual dance that imitated lions. The circumciser was likened to a lion, and his role was to sever the boy's connection to his mother. The boys, dramatically painted with white clay, entered manhood not just through circumcision, but through a months-long ritual period of healing and instruction.

And the Merina of Madagascar did it much earlier, between ages one and two, in a quiet, dignified ritual among gathered relatives. The ceremony emphasized continuity with the ancestors, and it ensured the little boy ultimate potency and fertility.

Fertility is a common cross-cultural theme in circumcision. Many cultures did it at or before puberty as a rite of passage and a gateway to manhood.[31] African circumcision rites often make the potency and fertility themes explicit. Dances linked to the rite may mime copulation, and medicine may be made from the hard wood of fruit trees, symbolizing the hoped-for hardness of the penis. Circumcision makes the boy a man, potent and fertile, connecting him to his male ancestors.

Genesis says nothing about sex, and holding the rite not at eight or ten or twelve years but at eight days removes the link to emerging manhood. Still, the text stresses fertility; just before the commandment, God says explicitly, "I will make thee exceeding fruitful, and I will make nations of thee, and kings shall come out of thee."[32] Sarah may chuckle skeptically, but even a century-old man and his ninety-year-old wife can be fertile under the covenant.

At the same moment, God gives Abraham his name, changing it from the less fatherly Abram. All subsequent circumcisions symbolize lineal continuity, but this first one *severs* Abraham's ties to his forefathers. His descendants will number the stars, but he must have no ancestors. Forever after, though, the wound will show that all Jewish men trace their lineage back to Abraham. This includes converts, which shows that we are dealing with a different kind of bodily inheritance. And the words "that soul shall be cut off from his people" may mean not just ostracism but sterility, the opposite of God's promise to Abraham, since the childless man is cut off from the *future* of his people. This section of Genesis is by the Priestly author; however old circumcision was, the priesthood wanted it to continue. They also wanted its meaning restricted. It was not to be some sort of pagan magic, but the sign of a covenant with the one true God, who promises endless descendants and commands "the fruitful cut."[33] Still, at eight days the link to sex is concealed, the covenant all-important.

In addition, the usual priestly concern with purity gave the rite another meaning. We have seen that purity can mean intactness or completeness, but in the case of circumcision these two ideas diverge. A human male is not complete if he is intact, but must have his foreskin removed to achieve completeness. This paradox is a key instance of *tikkun olam,* "repairing the world." In this view God has deliberately left the work of creation unfinished, inviting, even requiring human beings to complete it. "Uncircumcised," used metaphorically elsewhere in the Tanakh, refers to incompleteness or immaturity. "Uncircumcised" fruit trees bear inedible fruit. Moses has "uncircumcised lips," denoting a speech defect. And most ominously, one who has not submitted to God's law is said to have an "uncircumcised heart."

Despite its pain and risk, circumcision was always viewed as a joyful event. Circumcision knives with ornately carved or inlaid handles and chairs to sit in while holding the baby for the rite are among the most beautiful artifacts of the Jewish past. Consider the following passage from an anonymous poem of the Middle Ages, framed as a song sung by a baby boy on the eve of his *brit*. It begins, "I will awaken a song of love," and ends,

> *Hear my words and I will sing*
> *The day of my covenant from a watchful night*
> *Tomorrow the red wool goes crimson*
> *The Lord is with me, I shall not fear.*[34]

So prohibiting circumcision alone would have put the Jews on a fast collision course with the Syrians and the Greek ways they imposed. Add to this forcing Jews to eat pork, violate the Sabbath, and worship idols, and you have an unprecedented crisis. Mattathias, a priest from Modi'in, resolved it; he killed a Jew in the act of sacrificing to the idol of Zeus in the Temple. Mattathias and his five sons, led by Judah and called Maccabees, mounted a guerrilla war against a huge army with advanced weapons and training and even battle elephants. Against all odds, they took Jerusalem from the Syrians, restoring the Temple and casting out the idols. This well-known story is the origin of Chanukah, the winter Feast of Lights, which celebrates the victory and commemorates a miracle: a tiny bit of lamp oil found in the defiled and broken Temple burned for eight days and nights.

Miracle or not, the restoration of Jewish power in Jerusalem and the triumph over Syrian tyranny were real. Mattathias's lineage ruled Judea for a century, protecting Jewish faith and practice. But as in David's line, factionalism and conflict tore the fabric of Jewish society, and the Maccabees' triumph was squandered by their descendants. If the Tobiads seemed corrupt, selfish, arrogant, and violent, they were only a hint of what would come.

4

ROMAN RUIN

HOW THE JEWS LOST THEIR LAND

For fourteen years after Judah took Jerusalem, a Syrian fortress loomed over the Temple, manned by foreign troops. But Judah's brother Simon finally laid siege to it, starved the inhabitants, stormed it, and cleansed it of pollution. "The Jews entered it with praise and palm branches, and with harps and cymbals and stringed instruments, and with hymns and songs, because a great enemy had been crushed and removed from Israel."[1] Later they demolished the fortress and even the hill under it, so that nothing stood higher than the Temple.

The joy was short-lived; there was a deep rift among Jews. Allied with the crown were the Sadducees, priests of the Temple faith but also, paradoxically, friends of the Hellenized elite. Their bitter enemies were the Pharisees, fervent champions of Torah learning and liturgy, who had much more in common with the people. This split would last over a century. Sadducees clung to the literal word of the Five Books of Moses, while Pharisees studied more expansively, adding later historical, prophetic, and wisdom writings and taking Torah interpretations seriously as Oral Law. Sadducees avoided any talk of the world to come because the Torah didn't mention it, but Pharisees shared with the common people an interest in resurrection and the end of days.

Against this fractious background, Simon and his son John courted Rome. John expanded Judea, forcing some conquered peoples to convert and be circumcised—a policy that would return to haunt the Jews. As high priest he was hated by the Pharisees but supported by rich merchants and landlords. When John's younger son Jannaeus usurped the throne from his brother, the populist Pharisees ridiculed him as he made sacrifices, pelting him with *etrogs*—the citrus fruit used on the Feast of Booths. Much more dangerously, they tried to depose him, and when they failed he slaughtered the leading Pharisee families. "As he was feasting with his concubines, in

the sight of all the city, he ordered about eight hundred of them to be crucified; and while they were living, he ordered the throats of their children and
wives to be cut before their eyes."[2] This Jewish tyrant had learned his Roman lessons well.

His sons fought bitterly, as civil war in Judea mirrored a much greater
one in Rome. Judea became a Syrian province under Roman rule, but civil
war broke out again, the rebels playing Roman generals against each other.
Julius Caesar became emperor and was generous to the Jews, but his assassination sparked turmoil again, and a new ruler emerged as governor in the
Middle East: Herod, whose family had been among those forced to become
Jewish at sword point.

Challenged by the last of the Maccabean dynasty, Herod convinced the
Romans that he could control Judea. He took the throne and began a career
that was noted for architectural wonders and savage cruelties. Herod—
with the help of a Roman army—took Jerusalem, disbanded the Sanhedrin,
and purged city and Temple of any trace of his predecessors. He named his
puppets to the government and priesthood, surrounding himself with ministers and generals of Greek descent, and brought back Jews from the Hel-
lenistic diaspora and Babylon to replace the native leadership.[3]

This made him popular in the diaspora, but his relationship with Jews
at home was unremittingly hostile. He built Greek cities in Judea as for-
tresses against the Jewish nation itself. He impoverished Jews to enrich
foreigners. He strictly prohibited associations and assemblies and enforced
the prohibitions with an intricate network of spies. Pharisees who refused
to swear loyalty to him were heavily fined. Zealots who removed the eagle
he had suspended above the Temple gate—it was considered a Roman
idol—were put to death. Of his many wives and children, more than a few
ended their lives in the hands of his executioners.

Chaos roiled in his wake. By 6 C.E., a decade after his death, the kingdom disintegrated as his bumbling sons fought over his legacy. Riots destabilized Judea, and it became a province ruled by Rome's proxies, called
procurators. Government moved from Jerusalem to Caesarea on the
Mediterranean coast. Jews could complain to Rome over the procurators'
heads, and only the threat of revolt checked the abuse of power. Pontius Pilate was one procurator in question, and his rule was especially harsh.

⟨∞∞∞⟩

This was a time of intense religious ferment.[4] It was just two generations
before Herod that Jannaeus had crucified the rebellious Pharisees and
slaughtered their wives and children. Yet rebellion continued, along with
large-scale banditry and brigandage, prophetic and messianic movements,
and plain political protest.[5] Popular unrest in these varied forms graded

into civil war. Early in his career Herod, as ruler of Galilee, put down a band of brigands making raids from Jewish territory across the Syrian frontier:

> [F]inding that there was one Hezekias, a captain of a band of robbers, who overran the neighboring parts of Syria with a great troop of them, he seized him and slew him, as well as a great number of the other robbers that were there with him; for which action he was greatly loved by the Syrians.[6]

However, he was not so popular with the mothers of those he had slain, and their protest suggests that Hezekias and his men were not just simple bandits:

> The mothers also of those that had been slain by Herod raised his indignation; for those women continued every day in the temple, persuading the king and the people that Herod might undergo a trial before the *sanhedrin* for what he had done.[7]

This was arranged, but Herod showed up at the trial with an armed guard to intimidate the judges. When it appeared that the death sentence would be pronounced on him anyway, he fled to Damascus and the protection of Rome. Supplied with an army, he led it to the Jerusalem gates; having made his point, he decided not to attack.

It was not till a decade later that Herod made his famous trip to Rome, which sent him back to rule Judea if he could. This entailed, among many other brutalities, routing another large contingent of bandits out of their caves in the Galilee, killing most of them together with their families. Herod and his Roman troops went on to take Jerusalem in a full-scale civil war and to put down various rebellions. This he did efficiently and brutally, his standard throughout his reign.

Herod's death in 4 B.C.E. left an impoverished people with monumental buildings and great social distress. Crowds rioted in Jerusalem demanding lower taxes, release of prisoners, and a new high priest.[8] Herod's son sent troops to attack the demonstrators, slaughtering three thousand. For a few years demonstrators attacked Roman troops in Jerusalem, and there were many revolts throughout the nation. One was led by a shepherd of imposing physical form, another by one of Herod's former slaves. To get a feeling for how the Romans approached such disturbances, consider one general:

> Varus sent a part of his army into the country, to seek out those that had been the authors of the revolt; and when they were discov-

ered he punished some of them that were most guilty, and some he dismissed: now the number of those that were crucified on this account were two thousand.[9]

One might have thought that two thousand crucifixions would discourage rebellion, but it continued. In the year 6 of the Common Era, Rome declared Judea a province, provoking wider revolt. A leader called Judas the Galilean incited resistance. His was a religious as well as political mission, based on a radical reading of the commandment "Thou shalt have no other gods before Me." This, to his mind, precluded serving the "divine" Roman emperor who had supplanted a God-fearing Jewish government. He and his followers believed that God would give them victory.[10] Josephus describes this Judas as a teacher and the founder of a "fourth sect" of Judaism, similar in beliefs to the Pharisees but with "an inviolable attachment to liberty."[11] Their quest for freedom ended badly, with many battle deaths and crucifixions.

Still, ongoing banditry in the countryside, occasional protests in the cities, and new religious movements gave people hope. Pontius Pilate became Judea's fifth procurator in 26 C.E., and his affronts destabilized a precarious situation. He brought Roman troops into Jerusalem in the dead of night, carrying standards with images used in pagan worship. A mob followed him to Caesarea, ready to be killed rather than break the Second Commandment. He removed the standards. Next he confiscated Temple funds to build an aqueduct. Crowds protested at Pilate's next visit to Jerusalem, but this time troops attacked them and they backed down. Finally, in 36, a group of Samaritans—a fundamentalist offshoot of Judaism—followed their prophet to Mount Gerizim, where Moses was believed to have buried sacred vessels. Pilate attacked this peaceful pilgrimage and had the leaders killed. Survivors complained to the Syrian governor, who found them to be in the right, and Pilate was recalled to Rome.

Procurators over the next two decades found the people of Judea accepting of the Roman yoke, as long as their religion was not directly challenged. When a new emperor, a pagan fundamentalist, tried to put a statue of himself in the Temple, protests were peaceful but massive, and the Syrian legate convinced him to reconsider. Rome was prepared to make peaceful Judea a kingdom again, albeit one very firmly under Roman rule. No one knows exactly why the period from 6 to 44 was relatively peaceful, but the memory of the failed rebellions around the turn of the century may have played a restraining role. Two generations is not too long to remember the spectacle of two thousand crucifixions, and they, together with the subsequent suppression of Judas the Galilean, removed potential leaders and chilled rebellious thoughts. As one observer recently suggested, we might think of Caesar as a Stalin or Pol Pot whose program worked.[12]

The peace was deceptive. The suffering in the countryside was great, as peasants and workers in the olive and wine industries were taxed into abject poverty. The pain of their lives, the detachment they must have felt from the Temple religion even at its best, the weakness of all Jews in the face of Roman power, left masses of people yearning for spiritual comfort. Small groups of Jews—the Essenes, for example—had long practiced ascetic and messianic Judaism. Some had been persecuted by mainstream Jews, whether the Sadducees of Temple and literal Torah or the Pharisees of synagogue and study house. Under the Romans splinter groups multiplied as people took refuge in sacred practices, magic, and the dream of divine rescue. Anthropologists call these *revitalization movements* because they energize people brutalized by oppression and make them feel alive again. In Roman Israel, such movements tended to start in the Galilee, where people felt detached from the Jerusalem-centered world. The tradition there began with the miracles and magic attributed to the prophets Elijah and Elisha, and it continued until after the final sack of the Temple.[13]

The Samaritan prophet who led his people to Mount Gerizim was a non-Jewish example; it was likely their messianic fervor that frightened the Roman authorities. A few years later a Jewish prophet named Theudas led masses of people on another pilgrimage, this time to the Jordan River, which he was planning to part for them. This prophecy was never put to the test, since the Roman procurator sent a squadron of cavalry, which surprised them, beheaded Theudas, killed many of his followers, and took many prisoners. Such episodes grew common. The procurator Felix, in the fifties, put down three major incidents. Josephus, as a former Roman-Jewish general, was hostile to such groups regardless of how nonviolent they were. So in his histories he tended to conflate messianic sects with bands of brigands, referring to "impostors and brigands" in one breath—"impostor" being his term for any unconventional religious figure who managed to find followers.[14]

> [T]he country was again filled with robbers and impostors, who deluded the multitude. Yet did Felix catch and put to death many of those impostors every day, together with the robbers.[15]
> ... And now these impostors and deceivers persuaded the multitude to follow them into the wilderness, and pretended that they would exhibit manifest wonders and signs, that should be performed by the providence of God. And many that were prevailed on by them suffered the punishments of their folly; for Felix brought them back, and then punished them.[16]

The punishment was death by crucifixion, the standard Roman method. In his book on the Jewish Wars, for example, Josephus says of Felix that "as to the number of robbers whom he caused to be crucified, and of whom who were caught among them, and those he brought to punishment, they were a multitude not to be enumerated."[17]

Some of these "impostors" *were* robbers, and some of the mobs that followed them looted and burned the homes of the wealthy, even killing some whom they rightly saw as oppressors. But others were completely nonviolent religious leaders; it just suited the Romans to call them criminals. Taken together, violent or not, they were all revolutionaries; a quest for faith, the Romans knew, was also a quest for freedom. The most pacific among them still took people away from their daily work and threatened order. The common people were ready to follow millennial prophets, who inspired them with hope and led them, for a while at least, out of their searing misery.

⟨〰〰⟩

Crucifixion is an exceedingly unpleasant way to die. Nails through the palms, as in the usual depiction, could not have worked, since they would have cut through the tissues of the hands as the victim's weight pulled on them in the days it took to die. So either nails were driven through the wrists or the arms were stretched back, pulled behind the crosspiece, and tied to it, thrusting the chest outward. Death came by suffocation as the pressure on the chest made breathing difficult and, with exhaustion, ultimately impossible. More mercifully, heart failure or shock might intervene. Nails through the feet fixed the legs but also prolonged dying as the victim pushed painfully against the nails, relieving a little the pressure on his chest and making breathing slightly easier. It took days. Corpses were sometimes left to rot on the crosses, attracting buzzards, to teach others. Some birds of prey began their work before death occurred. This was death by torture, but an exceptionally efficient one, since it did not require sustained, individual attention and effort by the torturer.

Events occurring in or shortly after 4 B.C.E., the year of Herod's death, must be thought of as unfolding in the shadow of thousands of such crucifixions. Luke tells of a young couple from Nazareth who had to go down to Judea to enroll in the census decreed by Caesar. This type of census could provoke Jewish riots, since some saw enrollment as apostasy. Perhaps the overwhelming brutality of the government made compliance the better part of valor, or perhaps Joseph was simply the most common kind of Jew, one who went along with things because his goal was to live and to protect those he loved.

In any case, his wife—Miriam, or Mary in biblical Greek—was near term, and gave birth to a boy in a barn in Bethlehem. At eight days he was circumcised and given the name Yeshua, or Jesus, a variant of Joshua. According to the commandment of Pidyon Ha-ben—the redemption of the firstborn—every boy that opened a womb was brought to the Temple and dedicated to God, who had spared firstborn Hebrew sons even as the sons of Egyptians died. This Joseph and Miriam did, in Jerusalem, on the thirtieth day.

The boy grew up in Nazareth, a small village on an east-west range of hills in southern Galilee, halfway from the Mediterranean to the Jordan. Archeology shows that it had been inhabited on and off for over a thousand years, then abandoned for centuries, and finally refounded, probably during the Maccabean expansion. In the first century it was clearly very Jewish, because a majority of the graves have the standard form of the Jewish tomb. There were cisterns, olive oil vats, millstones, and grain silos. There was no major activity other than farming, and there was no hint of wealth.[18]

The hamlet cannot have been important because it is not mentioned outside the Bible, but it was only three or four miles from Sepphoris, a city built by the Greeks after Alexander to try to civilize—Hellenize—the Galilee. Sepphoris was a crossroads of trade and travel, but also a center of rebellion. In the turmoil after Herod, Judas the Galilean seized its royal arsenal, whereupon the Roman proconsul of Syria occupied the city and sold its people into slavery. Mark says that Joseph took his family to Egypt, in flight from Herod's threat to the little boy;[19] certainly the local turmoil could have provoked such a flight.

But Sepphoris, rebuilt and refortified a few years later, was resettled by a Jewish aristocracy staunchly loyal to Rome. Nazareth, settled around a spring in the mountains near the city, was off the beaten path, yet villagers could walk to the city in two hours. With a population of about thirty thousand, Sepphoris had military installations, two markets, courts, a bank, archives, and a theater seating three or four thousand. Jesus and his family must have gone there often. Beyond it, the Lower Galilee was one of the most densely populated areas in the Near East. A major east-west road ran through the city from the Mediterranean to the Sea of Galilee, and a north-south road wound through the mountains to Jerusalem. The region around Nazareth was neither inaccessible, nor backward, nor insulated from Greek culture.[20]

Olives, grapes, and grain flourished on this fertile plain, making oil and wine major exports, and shepherds urged flocks of sheep and goats around the hills. The Sea of Galilee, a large freshwater lake, had an active fishing industry, and was used to transport cargo and passengers. We are told that Joseph and Jesus were carpenters. In a place like Nazareth they probably made yokes for oxen, carts, plows, and other tools and devices for farmers. Perhaps they were sometimes engaged by the wealthy elite of Sepphoris. In any case this family of craftsmen was probably a cut above the local peasants and shepherds, but still very close to them.

At least three first-century synagogues have been found around the lake; this was a religious region. Luke says that Joseph was no stranger to

Jerusalem, going every year at Passover to make the traditional sacrifices. One year, when the boy was twelve, he was missed from among his kin traveling back from Jerusalem, and his parents, searching anxiously, "found him in the Temple, sitting among the teachers, listening to them and asking them questions. And all who heard him were amazed at his understanding and his answers."[21] The boy was surprised at his parents' anxiety, but he returned with them obediently to Nazareth, honoring them and the Fifth Commandment.

Presumably his was a normal village religious life, frequenting synagogues and returning to Jerusalem at least once a year—like many another Jewish boy in the Galilee. But this boy grew to be a man of transcendent religious genius—healer, prophet, visionary, inspired preacher—and a searching, dissident analyst of the Law. Some scholars think his precocious colloquy in the Temple was part of what today would be a Bar Mitzvah. He was close to the age when a child can be called to the Torah to read publicly, deliver an interpretation, and begin to be responsible for his sins. We can perhaps put this Temple foray down to the passionate idealism and intellectual curiosity of a brilliant child entering adolescence—combined with a healthy dose of counterparental rebellion. But the amazement of the teachers tells us that he was a very special boy.

And man. Of the many rebels and visionaries preaching to the Jews under the Romans, Jesus of Nazareth is the only one with followers today—well over a billion of them, a hundred for every practitioner of the faith he was raised in. His followers called him "Rabbi" at times, and a leading Christian theologian of today has called him Rabbi Yeshua Ben Yoseph.[22] But this need not mean a formal certification, since the term was less specific then. It has been suggested that he could have studied with Hillel, the greatest rabbi of the previous generation. Study he did in any case; his knowledge of Torah is evident in his critique of it.[23] Having bested the Sadducees in argument, he debates the Pharisees:

[A]nd one of them, a lawyer, asked him a question, to test him. "Teacher, which commandment in the law is the greatest?" He said to him, "'You shall love the Lord your God with all your heart, and with all your soul, and with all your mind.' This is the greatest and first commandment. And a second is like it: 'You shall love your neighbor as yourself.' On these two commandments hang all the law and the prophets."[24]

The first quote bears a small though significant change from Deuteronomy 6:5, where the last word is "might." The second is Leviticus 9:18. Jesus does not bypass the Law but relies on its authority, as he learned to do in the synagogues of Galilee.

But of course, he has come to challenge the Law and transform it. It is interesting that he finds these two commandments alike. His main message was one of love, and it seems that his love for God was like his love for his neighbor or himself; his was a very intimate relationship to God. It is evident already at twelve when he speaks of "my Father's house." And once he uses the word *abba,* the Hebrew for father, in reference to God. But he uses this intimacy in strange ways. He says to doubting Thomas, "I am the way, and the truth, and the life. No one comes to the Father except through me."[25] This seems to deny others the kind of relationship he himself has with God. For Christians this problem was resolved by a theology that made Jesus a part of God, a part that human beings could *easily* be intimate with. For the Jews, though, this was a permanent problem, because it seemed to them to deny them their cherished, direct, I-and-Thou relationship to the God whom Jesus called Father.

That was not the only problem. Scholars have tried to identify Jesus with one or another branch of first-century Judaism, but he does not fit any of them.[26] Like the Sadducees he was skeptical about Oral Law, but his opposition to Temple practices and his embrace of the poor infuriated them. Like the Pharisees he was allied with common people and concerned with the end of days, but his rejection of divorce and other legal departures made them reject him. Like the Zealots he had a passionate, religious contempt for Roman rule, but his radical nonviolence set him apart from them. Even the Essenes don't fit.[27] Like them, he was ascetic, admired celibacy, opposed divorce, believed in the end of days, and gave himself to God. But they were highly legalistic and segregated themselves from the wider Jewish community, while he disdained legal arguments and immersed himself in the press of human life.

This was his mission and his undoing. We are told that he began by seeking out his cousin John in the desert, where he was baptized and "saw the Spirit of God descending like a dove and alighting on him. And a voice from heaven said, 'This is my Son, the Beloved.'"[28] After fasting for forty days and nights, resisting the devil's temptations, "He left Nazareth and made his home in Capernaum by the sea."[29] There he began his ministry, going "throughout Galilee, teaching in their synagogues and proclaiming the good news of the kingdom and curing every disease and every sickness among the people. So his fame spread. . . ."

People converged on Capernaum—Kfar Nahum in Hebrew—from Judea, Jerusalem, Jordan, and Syria, and he began to speak to them in the way that has transcended many centuries. "Blessed are the meek, for they will inherit the earth. . . . Rejoice and be glad, for your reward is great in heaven." He tells the anxious, yearning people gathered on the hillside, overlooking a wondrous view of the Sea of Galilee, that they are the salt of the earth and the light of the world.

He also begins to preach about the Law. "Do not think that I have come to abolish the law or the prophets; I have come not to abolish but to fulfill. . . . not one letter, not one stroke of a letter, will pass from the law until all is accomplished. Therefore, whoever breaks one of the least of these commandments, and teaches others to do the same, will be called least in the kingdom of heaven."[30] In fact, they must exceed the Law—go the second mile, love their enemies, turn the other cheek. He tells them to give alms and pray not like hypocrites do in the synagogues but privately, without show. And he tells them not to worry about tomorrow.

But his regard for the Law does not extend to those entrusted with the Law. In a later sermon in the Temple itself he says it with painful clarity:

> The scribes and the Pharisees sit on Moses' seat; therefore, do whatever they teach you and follow it; but do not do as they do, for they do not practice what they teach. . . . They do all their deeds to be seen by others; for they make their phylacteries broad and their fringes long. They love to have the place of honor at banquets and the best seats in the synagogues, and to be greeted with respect in the marketplaces, and to have people call them rabbi. . . .
>
> Woe to you, scribes and Pharisees, hypocrites! For you tithe mint, dill, and cummin, and have neglected the weightier matters of the law: justice and mercy and faith. . . . You snakes, you brood of vipers! How can you escape being sentenced to hell?[31]

Such language cannot have endeared him to the Pharisees or their followers.

But for the poor under the fist of totalitarian Rome, longing for help and comfort, it was different. Jesus mingled with peasants and shepherds, rebels and outcasts, thieves and whores as easily as with the learned in synagogues. The poor loved him because he embraced, healed, and taught them, sat them at his table, and, above all, spoke for them. This put him in the line of the Hebrew prophets, who had spoken truth to power—whether king or priest—whenever power strayed from righteousness, ignored the poor, or substituted religious forms for moral substance. Isaiah asks, "To what purpose is the multitude of your sacrifices unto me? saith the Lord: I am full of the burnt offerings . . . and I delight not in the blood of bullocks . . .

> Bring no more vain oblations; incense is an abomination unto me, the new moons and sabbaths, the calling of assemblies . . . it is iniquity. . . .
>
> Learn to do well; seek judgement, relieve the oppressed, judge the fatherless, plead for the widow.
>
> Come now, and let us reason together, saith the Lord: though

your sins be as scarlet, they shall be as white as snow; though they be
red like crimson, they shall be as wool.[32]

Here a Hebrew author writing at least five centuries earlier struck three
of the main Gospel themes: God is not interested in hypocritical practices,
God demands justice for the oppressed, and God welcomes repentance, forgiving sin. Later, Isaiah has the people asking God, "Wherefore have we
fasted . . . and thou seest not?" And God replies with rhetorical questions:
"Is it such a fast that I have chosen? . . . is it to bow down his head as a bul-
rush, and to spread sackcloth and ashes under him?" Clearly not. The fast
has another form and purpose entirely: "Is not this the fast that I have
chosen? to loose the bands of wickedness . . . and to let the oppressed go
free. . . . Is it not to deal thy bread to the hungry, and that thou bring the
poor that are cast out to thy house?"[33]

Isaiah also predicts and invites the "last days," the end time, when an
anointed heir of David will "judge the poor, and reprove with equity for the
meek of the earth." Then, "The wolf also shall dwell with the lamb . . . and
the calf and the young lion . . . and a little child shall lead them."[34] Isaiah and
Micah both predict that God "shall judge among the nations, and shall rebuke many people: and they shall beat their swords into plowshares, and
their spears into pruning hooks: nation shall not lift up sword against nation, neither shall they learn war any more."[35]

Jesus and his disciples, almost all Jews, saw these passages as foretelling
their own time, and brought these Jewish themes to what they saw as a logical next stage of prophecy. Even turning the other cheek has Jewish roots.
The apocryphal book Ecclesiasticus, written two centuries before Jesus, has
this to say:

Forgive your neighbor the wrong he has done,
And then your sins will be pardoned when you pray. . . .
Remember the end of your life, and set enmity aside. . . .
Remember the commandments, and do not be angry with your neighbor.[36]

But Jesus of Nazareth took these urgings to the people in a different
way and time. He has been rightly called a Galilean hasid, a fervently righteous man, but he was also a maggid, an inspirational speaker who, although
well versed in the Torah, touches the heart with insight more than he sways
the mind with argument. But his very uniqueness—his disdain for every
Torah interpretation not his own—ensured that his own people would resist his message. If his first mission was to win Jewish support, it was a failure. But if the goal was to bring the Jewish God to a vastly wider world, to
confront and conquer pagan faiths and replace them with an all-seeing, all-
knowing, strong, just, forgiving, single God, then it was one of the greatest

successes in human history. Despite his failure to win over most Jews, he recruited Jewish disciples who carried his word to the world. He inspired
four Jewish writers of genius who were worthy of his story. And his cause
was taken up by Saul, called Paul, a leader who, as he changed his name,
changed the Christian mission and the world. By the time he got to Damascus, Paul's Jewishness mattered much less, and his pastoral flock was all
humanity.

But for Jesus of Nazareth being a Jew was inescapable, and was of the
essence of his life until the end. It was not just that the contemptuous, ironic
phrase "King of the Jews" was inscribed on the crosspiece of his instrument
of torture. Nor was it merely that the Romans had so effectively used their
divide-and-rule strategy that both those who loved him and those who
mocked him were mostly Jews. It was far more intrinsic than that. All
Christians ever since have come to God through him, but he himself came
to God, and stayed with God, directly, personally, Jewishly, without an intermediary, in the awesome, naked stance of I and Thou.

And when, in the last throes of his dreadful, passionate suffering, he has
only a few words to say, he says them in the Jewish language he learned at
Miriam's knee: *"Eli, Eli, lema sabachthani?"*—"My God, my God, why have
you forsaken me?"[37] The searing poignancy of this simple Jewish question—this bid, with his last breath, to go on wrestling with God—leaves us
with an indelible sense of Jesus the man. Unquestionably, for all of what can
only be called his heresies, the man was a Jew.

⟳∞∞⟲

Who were these Pharisees and scribes for whom Jesus expressed such thoroughgoing contempt?

For ordinary Jews—not the elite, who preferred the priesthood, nor the
fanatics who joined the Essenes or took up arms with the Zealots, nor even
the disenfranchised poor who loved and followed Jesus, but the broad common middle class of Jews—rabbis were leaders, teachers, comforters. They
earned their place through learning, faith, and merit, not by inheritance. It
was they who debated how to apply the Law, passed judgment on a thousand day-to-day uncertainties, and knew the intrinsic sense of the Law, a
sense that the Jews believed was traceable to Moses. It was they to whom
you went to be sure of what to eat or how to pray, or to ask, in the depths of
your suffering, how you might go on another day.

The savage era of Roman rule was bracketed by Hillel and Akiva, two
of the greatest rabbis of all time. It is hard to imagine two more different
men, yet they were linked intrinsically through and in the Law. Hillel lived
under Herod's arbitrary autocracy and through the post-Herod reign of terror. He may have lived long enough to have taught or counseled the young
prodigy, Jesus of Nazareth. Hillel was "Judaism's model human being,"[38]

his teaching the bedrock of all later Jewish thought and practice.[39] He was born in Babylon, but lived and taught in Israel. He came from a wealthy family, but cared about the poor. He was rigorous with himself, but liberal and forgiving in interpreting the Law. He had an exceptional intellect, but simplified the Torah and insisted it be accessible to everyone. His foil was Shammai, the other leading rabbi of the age. Both had students and followers, and it was only in retrospect that Judaism chose Hillel. Shammai's rulings were always the strictest possible reading of the Law; Hillel's were much less unbending.

According to the Talmud, a heathen came to Shammai promising to convert if he could be taught the whole Torah while he stood on one foot; Shammai drove him away with a builder's cubit. He gave the same challenge to Hillel, who said, "What is hateful to you, do not do to your neighbor. The rest is commentary, now go and study." He made many converts. If he did not quite turn the other cheek, he was famously slow to anger. A man lost a large sum betting that he could bait Hillel with a series of stupid questions—Why are the heads of the Babylonians round? Why are the feet of the Africans wide? Hillel calmly answered them.[40]

Justly revered, he was known for his humility. "He who magnifies his name," he said, "destroys it." Yet despite his common touch, he had a rigorous legal mind. He developed seven principles that formed the basis of inference and argument in the Talmud. He resolved a dispute over whether the Passover sacrifices could be made on the Sabbath; they seemed to violate the law against making a fire. Hillel ruled that the offerings took precedence, by a process of reasoning so dazzling that it resulted in his appointment as *nasi,* or "prince" of the Jewish community. And he found a way around the Torah's command to forgive all debts in the seventh year—an initially compassionate law that in Hillel's time was hurting the poor by discouraging all loans to them.

Finally, he was famous for his ethical philosophy, phrased in almost biblical poetry:

> *The more Torah, the more life;*
> *the more study and contemplation, the more wisdom,*
> *the more counsel, the more discernment,*
> *the more charity, the more peace.*
>
> *Do not separate yourself from the community.*
> *Trust not in yourself until the day of your death;*
> *judge not your fellow-man until you have come to his place.*[41]

And in what would be one of the most frequently quoted rabbinical passages for the next two thousand years, he asked, "If I am not for myself, who will be for me? And if I am only for myself, what am I? And if not now, when?"[42]

His injunction to the proselyte was a pre-Christian Golden Rule. But Hillel said, in effect, Do not do unto others what you would not have them do unto you, while Jesus said, Do unto others as you would have them do unto you. Jewish tradition considers the difference significant. Hillel's rule is tantamount to "live and let live," while the Christian rule is more interventional, asking us to take positive action that might be unwelcome. Hillel would have been both impressed and dismayed by Jesus, who read the Law so radically and spoke so bitterly of its rabbinical interpreters, yet touched the hearts of the poor and welcomed them to God. But he would have been more dismayed by the conditions of Roman oppression that made radical movements inevitable. He saw horrors enough while he lived, but he died without seeing the worse ones to come.

Akiva was not so lucky. Born decades after Hillel's death, he would see, as a boy, the entire Jewish revolt and its devastating results—the second leveling of the Temple, the second burning of Jerusalem—the end of Jewish life as Hillel had known it. The first century was already a time of messianic desperation and revolutionary fervor. In the fifties, under the Roman procurator Felix, disturbances widened and thousands died on the cross or, more luckily, at the point of Roman swords.

Akiva in his teens and twenties was completely aloof from Judaism. He later referred to himself at that time as an *am ha-aretz*—one of the "people of the earth," a euphemism for illiterate peasants. He was proud of his ignorance and had thorough contempt for scholars. Of humble origin, he worked as a shepherd for one of the wealthiest men in Jerusalem, until he and the boss's daughter fell in love and married. They were cut off, and according to legend, Rachel had to sell her hair for food, but she knew what she wanted. She had made Torah study a condition of her daring, costly marriage, and Akiva kept his end of the bargain.[43]

It was very late to start studying; he and his son learned the alphabet together. But when he set off for the academy, he never looked back. He is said to have studied twelve years, under the greatest rabbis of the age, before he became a teacher. Yet he is a towering figure of Jewish tradition. He helped build the final canon of the Bible, supervised the translation of the Torah into Greek and Aramaic, and developed methods of exegesis that set the future standard. His central idea was that since the Torah comes from God, everything in it must be meaningful—redundancies, variant spellings, even the tiny crownlets on certain letters, painstakingly copied by the scribes—and our earthly task is to discern its meaning.

He produced an early version of the Mishnah, recording ongoing debates about Oral Law. This would become the core of the Talmud, the great encyclopedic work that guides Jews to the everyday fulfillment of the commandments. Like Hillel before him, he was known for liberal rulings. In debates over the canon, he staked his reputation on including the *Song of Songs*. Akiva and other rabbis saw this group of exquisite love poems, following an ancient Egyptian model, as being exclusively about Israel and God. But it is tempting to guess that, unconsciously at least, Akiva's love for Rachel influenced his judgment.

It was a mystical turn of mind that led him and others to find God in these passionate lines, and that mysticism engaged him for years. This was dangerous. It was said that of four sages who "entered a garden"—delved into mysteries—only Akiva emerged unscathed.[44] But most of his life was spent in argument, attempting to apply the Torah in daily life. Following Hillel, he always took the lenient, compassionate side, making allowance for human weakness. For example, when another rabbi ruled that the evening Shema—the prayer that contains the declaration of faith—could be said only during the first watch of the night, Akiva ruled that it could be said until dawn.[45] This famous tiff is preserved in the Haggadah, the text for the Passover seder.

Another dispute was over the law in Deuteronomy concerning the man who brings home a captive second wife from foreign wars. Rabbi Eliezer, the teacher, who stemmed from the still polygamous patrician class of Jerusalem, claimed the man could marry her after one month. Akiva, the outspoken student—a monogamous plebeian—wanted to spare the first wife's feelings and give her a fighting chance against her rival, so he ruled that three months must pass before the second marriage. And when Eliezer remarked that the proverbial honey of Scripture must be the syrup of dates—which were plentiful in orchards around his upper-class town of Jericho—Akiva countered that it could only mean bees' honey, which was far more plentiful in his own poor hills of Galilee.[46]

❦

These debates took place in Yavneh, where the greatest Torah academy was. The worst had happened, Jerusalem was sacked, the Temple gone, the priesthood scattered, hundreds of thousands of Jews killed, and Roman rule more savage and suffocating than ever. But Israel for a time had pockets of peace. A remnant of the people, under Yochanan ben Zakkai—the mildest and most pacifist of rabbis, smuggled out of Jerusalem on a funeral bier—had made a new life in a town far away. There was trouble enough in the study house, but this was all academic politics, not likely to injure anything but pride. Akiva and others in the populist faction made a sort of palace coup, and after that the more lenient strain dominated Jewish tradition. The Yavneh academy excelled in learning.

But near the end of that calamitous first century, the Romans, perhaps offended by successful Jewish proselytizing, cracked down on the Jews of the city of Rome itself. Akiva and his colleagues, after a mournful visit to the ruins of the Temple, went to Rome to plead for their comrades. They succeeded, and the newly crowned Emperor Nerva struck a coin commemorating the meeting, with his likeness on one side and the words *Fisci Judaici Calumnia Sublata*—"The insult of the Jewish tax has been lifted"—on the other.[47] Returning to Judea, Akiva became the de facto rabbinical leader, founding his own academy, where he preferred to teach outside under a broad-leafed fig tree. Students flocked to him, among them a cobbler, a potter, a tanner, a priest, an Egyptian proselyte, a mystic, and the son of a wealthy patrician who was on intimate terms with the Roman governors. Over the last few decades of his life Akiva codified Hillel's lenient and popular rulings so convincingly and brilliantly that he might as well have carved them in stone.

Yet his liberal view was no abandonment of the Law. He also said, "Whosoever neglects the duty of visiting the sick is guilty of shedding blood," and "It is forbidden to partake of any enjoyment in the world without pronouncing a benediction." His leniency resulted in what is today *Orthodox* Judaism, while the strictness he defeated was so severe that it probably would not have been sustainable. And without his defense of ordinary people, they might not have continued to claim the Torah as their own, in which case there would have been no Judaism at all.

Akiva loved it enough to give his life for it, although at first that did not seem inevitable. The early second century saw unusual Roman tolerance, so much so that people in Judea began to speak of rebuilding the Temple. Following biblical prophecy, this was expected in 119. Sure enough, as that year approached, an imperial pronouncement gave permission for reconstruction, although on a modest scale. Once again it seemed to many a messianic time.

Aged Akiva was caught up in this majestic dream, but there were many opponents. On one side, Christians and Samaritans alike feared a return to ancient Jewish glory. On the other, Jewish nationalists and Zealots had contempt for rebuilding an inadequate, ersatz Temple, when what they wanted was a return to independence with Jerusalem restored to full power. Five years of fruitless negotiations among these rival factions led a perplexed, impatient emperor to shelve the Temple project. The nationalists—repeating the mistake of prior centuries—planned to turn the Parthian Empire against the Romans. Old Eliezer, on his deathbed, told his disciples, "I see fierce anger in the world."[48] For Akiva he foresaw a violent death.

An actual earthquake shook the Roman army, and the Jews took this as a sign. They rioted to the point of insurrection, not just in Judea but in Egypt, Libya, Syria, and Cyprus. The Jews were put down decisively—in Cyprus they were exterminated—and the leaders put on trial. Repression intensified. Over the next decade, the Romans gradually increased restrictions on Jewish practice, forbidding circumcision, worship, sounding the shofar, calibrating the calendar—without which the observance of festivals was impossible—and key functions of Jewish courts. All were practiced surreptitiously, and the whispering of prayer under the breath, as well as other evasive tactics, became permanent Jewish customs.

Akiva, physically weakening, lost most of his disciples to the nationalist cause, and his son and son-in-law, both great scholars, died before him. Discouraged and grieving, he tried to salvage from the all-enveloping chaos one central principle: Judaism is knowledge of the Torah. Nothing could supersede or contradict that. At a national meeting of many Jewish factions, he persuaded them to endorse that principle by majority vote. He also recognized that they were in extremis, and he proposed a radical rule to save lives. To avert martyrdom, violations of the Law would be permitted, with three exceptions: idol worship, murder, and unchastity.

Emperor Hadrian, touring his subject nations in 130, stopped to see the ruined capital of the Jews. Wanting Judea to be productive again, if only for tribute, he granted permission to rebuild Jerusalem. He even agreed to permit a Temple—to Jupiter, in the person of the emperor, whose statue would be worshiped. Then he left the country. Baffled and stricken, the Jews sent ninety-year-old Akiva to beg the emperor to change his mind. Akiva followed Hadrian to Egypt, but Hadrian was not impressed; why this Jewish obstinacy in insisting on their own cult when the rest of the world embraced Rome's?

Hadrian's answer—Akiva's failure—sparked a wildfire of resistance in Judea. People became convinced that they were about to relive the Maccabean revolt, to take back the Temple and rebuild it. Some leaders fell, but a new one—Simeon Bar Kokhba—emerged, and led the ragged bands of nationalistic peasants to a few encouraging victories. His name, portentously, meant "Son of a Star," and people began to see him not as just a new Maccabee, but as the Messiah. Akiva followed them, quoting Numbers 24:17, "The star hath trodden forth out of Jacob." He said of Bar Kokhba, "This is the Messianic King."[49]

The Judean Jews were annihilated. Hundreds of thousands were killed, thousands more enslaved, children dragged out of schools and put to manual labor. One observer characterized the times in a dialogue: Why are you being taken to execution? Because I circumcised my son. Why are you being taken to crucifixion? Because I read the Torah.[50] The Romans built their temples and thoroughly paganized Jerusalem. It was renamed, and Jews were forbidden to live there. Akiva, the erring pacifist, the well-meaning aged man, continued to teach the Torah, in the open, under the old tree. A lifelong opponent warned him that he was baiting death. Akiva answered: The fox told some fish to escape the fishermen by coming onto dry land. The fish replied that if they were in danger in their element, how much worse off would they be out of it! He expanded his teaching and practices, telling one eager pupil, "My son, more than the calf wants to suck, the cow wants to suckle."

He was arrested and sent to a Roman jail in Caesarea, on the other side of the country. He continued to issue rulings on points of law through the window of his cell. He was brought to trial, a frail old man; he had no defense. The Roman judge, a former friend, could not avert the decree. It is said that he was executed by having his skin flayed from his old frame with red-hot iron combs. During this process he recited the Shema—Hear O Israel, the Lord is our God, the Lord is . . . —and he used his last breath to say, One.

❦

Archeologists have unearthed countless treasures in Jerusalem, but among the greatest are two dwellings of the last Temple generation. The first was a mansion or palace that stood from at least Herod's time until the Temple fell. It was a split-level house descending along a gentle slope with a grand view of the nearby Temple. Some walls were almost ten feet high, with sockets for cypress roof-beams near the ceiling. Piles of soot-covered, fallen stones next to the walls recalled the blaze that swept the city. Coins in the palace date the fire precisely; they come from the second and fourth years of the First Jewish Revolt against Rome. The fire raged in the year 70.

The main-floor rooms were built around a flagstone-paved courtyard. On one side were living and guest quarters, two rows of rooms linked by doorways. One suite had a fine mosaic in the vestibule floor—a square frame with an intertwined fret pattern around a rosette and a pomegranate motif in the corners. The cubes of the mosaic had been charred; a thick layer of ash covered everything. On one side of the vestibule was a small room whose walls were covered with expensively painted frescoes—red and yellow panels colored while the plaster was still wet. The style resembled the wall paintings at Pompeii. On the other side was a grand reception hall, thirty-six by twenty-one feet, the walls an elegant white stucco in broad panels simulating polished stone blocks. The ceilings, also stucco, had delicate repeating geometric patterns.

Surprisingly, the wall surface hid a layer of finely painted plaster, with an unusual floral motif. Had someone gotten tired of the flowers? Was there a change of ownership or fashion? The change in this Jerusalem mansion was the opposite of that in Pompeii, where clean white stucco panels were painted over with frescoed plaster. Were the Jerusalem rich deliberately defying Roman fads, or were they just a bit behind in a relentless fashion cycle? In any case, the parties must have been sensational. Across the courtyard was the main living area, where unfortunately only one room survived:

This is a small bathroom paved in colored mosaics with a compass-formed rosette as its only pattern—simple and nice. A low bench in one corner is also covered in mosaics, and there is a sunken sitting-bath at the far end of the room. This was undoubtedly a very pleasant and intimate bath-room and it seems to have been connected with one of the bedrooms in the eastern wing.[51]

The sunken bath is partly protected by a wall, perhaps for privacy. On the lower level were a cistern and two separate sunken baths. The larger had two doors, with a dramatic, vaulted stone archway over them. This may have been a ritual bath with one door for entry and the second for exit after purification. Perhaps the multiple baths served men and women or priests and commoners separately. Here too there were fine mosaics in the floor.

Proof of wealth and Hellenic influence was everywhere: exquisite stone tables, finely worked glass pitchers and bowls signed by a famous craftsman, thirty-five intact clay cooking pots—with shards of hundreds of others thrown into the cistern—and a small, portable sundial carved in soft limestone, decorated with bas-relief rosettes. People in this home marked the passing hours. Whoever they were—a priestly family, powerful Sadducee politicians, wealthy merchants related to the priests—they belonged to the Jerusalem elite. They lived the central Jewish paradox of the age: thoroughgoing cultural Hellenization combined with fundamental, even priestly religiosity, immune to the temptations of pagan faith.

The other house was smaller and even closer to the Temple. A trench sunk near the Western Wall plaza unearthed several layers. The first held fallen building stones discolored by fire. Beneath it was a mixture of earth, charred wood, soot, and ashes. As the excavation exposed the plan of the house, every room was filled with stone debris from collapsed walls, dressed blocks of local limestone, made crumbly and multicolored—white, gray, red, and yellow—by the immense heat of a fire. There were great heaps of charred wood and ashes. "Soot reigned over all," wrote archeologist Nahman Avigad, "clinging to everything.

> It covered the plastered walls, and even the faces of our workmen turned black. There was no doubt that the fire had rampaged here, apparently fed by some highly inflammable material contained in the rooms. It may well have been some oil, which would account for the abundance of soot. The traces were so vivid that one could almost feel the heat and the smell of the fire.[52]

Beneath the ashen mess was a floor strewn with stone vessels, shards of pottery, broken glass, and iron nails. This was the lower floor of the house, evidently a working area. There were several ovens, mortars, cooking pots, and measuring weights and tools. One room was clearly a kitchen. Here archeologists found the skeleton of a young woman's arm and hand, apparently grasping at a step. She had probably tried in vain to flee the fire. In another room a spear stood upright in a corner, carefully set there but never used.

Finally, a stone weight was found, inscribed in Aramaic with the owner's name, Bar Kathros—"son of Kathros." This was the surname of a well-known priestly family complained about, along with other, similar families, in a folk song preserved in the Talmud:

> *Woe is me because of the House of Kathros,*
>   *Woe is me because of their pens.*
> *Woe is me because of the House of Ishmael. . . .*
>   *Woe is me because of their fists.*
> *For they are the high priests, and their sons are treasurers,*
>   *and their sons-in-law are trustees, and their servants*
>   *beat the people with staves.*[53]

Other houses are mentioned, each with fear and loathing, a welling up of popular resentment of a repressive priestly oligarchy by ordinary people just trying to live. Probably the Bar Kathros family had been awarded a lavish Temple contract, and in their basement workshop prepared incense or spices for the priests.

Rich and powerful as they were, it is unlikely that they escaped the fire. The pottery patterns put the building—the "Burnt House"—in the first century. But as with the palace, the inscriptions on the coins again tell a more specific story: "Year Two / The Freedom of Zion"; "Year Three / The Freedom of Zion"; "Year Four / The Redemption of Zion." The series ends just before the destruction of Jerusalem.

Of course, these were the lifestyles of the rich and famous. They bore no resemblance to the lives of the Galilean peasant villagers among whom Jesus and Akiva had grown up. They had little in common with the middle class of artisans and modest landed farmers whom Hillel lived among and Akiva later taught. Those were the small people represented by these great teachers, who unalterably opposed the priestly elite of the Burnt House and the grand mansion.

☙❦❧

Still less did they have in common with a group of ascetic Jews who had withdrawn two centuries earlier to a village called Qumran, near the northern end of the Dead Sea.[54] For two centuries they had set themselves apart from mainstream Judaism, finding grievous fault with Pharisees and Sadducees alike. They viewed themselves as the persecuted, true branch of Judaism, and their leader as the "teacher of righteousness."

They followed the solar instead of the lunar calendar, but otherwise opposed all Hellenization. Although they had followers in many areas of the country, their focus was Qumran, where they led a modest, even monastic life in the desert village. According to their own writings and those of unsympathetic contemporaries, they put new prospective members on probation, organized the sect on strict hierarchical lines, ate communally, and performed endless ablutions. They shared apocalyptic visions of the dawn of the Messianic Age, when "the wicked priest" of Jerusalem would be overthrown. Indeed, they thought they were entering this end time.

They also copied, kept, and studied sacred scrolls, which they stored for safekeeping in clay jars deep in a cave overlooking the Dead Sea. These kept safely for two thousand years, until they were stumbled on by a Bedouin boy poking around the hills. One, the *Halakhic Letter,* is a founding document of the sect. It says that they "have separated from the mainstream of the people and from all their impurities and from mixing in these matters. . . . But you know that there cannot be found in our hands dishonesty, falsehood, or evil."[55]

The Qumran villagers were obsessed with purity, and their two-year initiation was designed as much to keep the impure out as to test an initiate's commitment. Contact with the community's food was particularly restricted. Punishment for infraction of the rules included separation from pure food, reduction of rations, and expulsion. Strict monogamists, they set down many rules of matrimonial purity. Members of the group had to be thoroughly versed in the Torah, but also in the special law, theology, and liturgy of Qumran.

Messianic expectations were central to their lives. In *The Scroll of the War of the Sons of Light against the Sons of Darkness,* they describe a vast worldwide war that will usher in the end of days, destroying all the enemies of the Jews. Such beliefs, shared by apocalyptic zealots of every stripe— some violent, some not—deeply divided the Jews. They were certainly zealous, and their messianic vision had much in common with that of the Zealots (capital Z) who led Jerusalem in revolt. Qumran was eliminated by a Roman garrison in 68, the same year the Zealots took Jerusalem. Some Qumran people may have joined them. Others may have joined the Zealots at Masada, a mountaintop fortress south of Qumran overlooking the Dead Sea.

But most of these links are conjectures. What we do know is that savage Roman tyranny turned many Jews toward holy war. Menacing visions and messianic dreams became in the end self-fulfilling prophecies. Cultivated for generations, these ideas sowed the seeds of apocalyptic war. But the outcome for the Jews was not the one they intended.

⚭

Recall that in the fifties, under Felix, crucifixions and other killings of Jewish "brigands" and "impostors" and their followers were so common that Josephus called them countless. This mass slaughter did not quiet the country for even a few years. Prophecy, zealotry, and brigandage went on unabated. Magic and faith healing swayed many Jewish hearts, as desperate maladies sought desperate remedies. Inevitably, some took up the sword. Freedom fighters, even extremist ones, operated freely in the countryside.[56]

The Romans had practiced divide-and-conquer for over a century, and it worked. The High Priests, or *Kohanim,* fought with the Levites, a second priestly caste, over the distribution of tithe revenues. The Sadducees, identified with the High Priests, despised the Pharisees, but Pharisee popularity limited Sadducee power. Essenes withdrew from both to a monastic rural life. The most radical Pharisees, the Zealots, had so strong a love of liberty that they made it a central religious principle and actively sought clashes with Rome. Submission to the emperor was idolatry, while resistance would help bring about the Kingdom of God. Yet even the Zealots were divided. The Galilean Zealots emphasized social revolution, while the Jerusalem Zealots stressed religion and the reform of the priesthood. In Jerusalem, Sadducees, Pharisees, and Zealots each had some power.

To some extent Hellenization cut across these divisions. Hellenized Jews were the elite of Jericho, Sepphoris, Tiberias, and above all Jerusalem, but Hellenized gentiles were the elite of other cities. In Caesarea, Sebaste, Ashkelon, and Accho, Jews were a persecuted minority. Local gentiles recruited for Jew hatred manned the Roman garrisons. Tension in these mixed towns was great. Anti-Jewish riots, in effect Greek pogroms under the Roman gaze, broke out in several cities—riots against Jews in their homeland. The Jews of Caesarea fled the city. There was ample fuel and tinder for a major conflagration. The spark came from Florus, the procurator, who in the fall of 66 seized seventeen talents of silver from Temple coffers. Jews rioted this time, and Florus put them down in classic, barbarous Roman style. But the Jewish response was not typical: they rose more strongly, and Florus fled the city.[57]

Jewish factions that favored war seized the moment. Eleazar, a revolutionary priest, stopped the required daily sacrifice for the welfare of the emperor. This amounted to a declaration of war, and Jews attacked and destroyed the Roman garrison. But then the priestly rebels were attacked by the Galilean Zealots, rural proletarians who looted wealthy homes and murdered their inhabitants. The leaders of both factions were killed, and the Galileans fled to Herod's mountain fortress at Masada. Revolution spread throughout the country. The Syrian governor brought an army to subdue his restive province, but fearing defeat he backed off from Jerusalem. Jews in the countryside routed his fleeing troops.

Now the emperor had to get serious. He sent Vespasian, one of his most seasoned generals, to Judea with sixty thousand crack troops. Notified of "some commotions in Gaul" that might soon need his attention, Vespasian stepped up the campaign. In less than a year he pacified the Galilee, always the region of fiercest Jewish resistance. The emperor died and Vespasian suspended the war, but the Jews used the respite to resume class warfare, with much slaughter of aristocrats by Zealots, mostly peasants and freed slaves. Large stocks of grain and other staples were destroyed, making the city much more vulnerable to siege.

Meanwhile, Vespasian himself was crowned emperor and sent his son Titus to finish the Jewish war. Troops ringed Jerusalem, cutting off all supplies. Famine followed; there was no route of escape. Sacrifices ceased because there were no lambs. Factional fighting continued. To amuse the Roman soldiers and intimidate the defenders, there were hundreds of crucifixions a day before the city walls, until "their multitude was so great, that room was wanting for the crosses, and crosses wanting for the bodies."[58] Within months the walls were breached and Roman troops surrounded the Temple mount.

It was a rule of ancient warfare to spare temples, but this one had become a fortress. It was set ablaze and razed to the ground. Josephus:

> As for the seditious ... they were everywhere slain ... and as for a great part of the people, they were weak and without arms, and had their throats cut wherever they were caught. Now, round about the altar lay dead bodies heaped one upon another as at the steps going up to it ran a great quantity of their blood.[59]
> ... While the holy house was on fire, everything was plundered that came to hand, and ten thousand of those that were caught were slain; ... children and old men, and profane persons, and priests, were all slain in the same manner ... as well those that made supplication for their lives as those that defended themselves by fighting.[60]

Some days later, with little remaining opposition, the Romans finished the work:

> [S]eeing nobody to oppose them, they stood in doubt what such an unusual solitude could mean. But when they went in numbers into the lanes of the city, with their swords drawn, they slew those

whom they overtook, without mercy, and set fire to the houses whither the Jews were fled, and burnt every soul in them, and laid waste a great many of the rest; and when they were come to the houses to plunder them, they found in them entire families of dead men ... such as died by the famine; they then stood in a horror at this sight, and went out without touching anything. But although they had this commiseration ... yet had they not the same for those that were still alive, but they ran every one through whom they met with, and obstructed the very lanes with their dead bodies, and made the whole city run down with blood, to such a degree that the fire of many of the houses was quenched with these men's blood.[61]

An exaggeration, no doubt. But the excavations of the mansion and the Burnt House in the neighborhood of the Temple mutely testify in support of these claims.

There was yet unfinished business for the Romans after the Jerusalem massacres—Masada, for instance, with its famous mass suicide of Zealots, did not fall until 73, when even that forbidding mountain citadel proved no match for Rome's earthworks and engines of war. But the fall of Jerusalem officially ended the conflict. Vespasian and Titus, father and son, were proud of this accomplishment. Coins were struck, inscribed *"Judea Capta."* Two triumphal arches were erected in the city of Rome. One, the Arch of Titus, still stands at the highest point of the Via Sacra leading to the Forum, carved with this dedication:

> The senate and people of Rome to the emperor Titus ... because with the guidance and plans of his father ... he subdued the Jewish people and destroyed the city of Jerusalem, which all generals, kings and peoples before him had either attacked without success or left entirely unassailed.[62]

This was the most impressive monument to defeat that the Jews had received since the boast-in-stone of Pharaoh Merneptah, thirteen centuries earlier, proclaiming the end of the seed of Israel. But the backhanded compliment was small comfort to the victims of a genocidal war, with their Temple in ashes, their cherished city a heap of stones, their people massively slaughtered, and they themselves enslaved.

5

DIASPORA

Gazing at the bas-relief on the Arch of Titus in Rome, you see a victory parade celebrating the Jewish defeat. Sacred objects from the Temple, honoring the unseen God who did not save them, are carried aloft by the enemy—a golden table, a goblet, a pair of trumpets. But the eye is drawn to the chief shape in the carving, the menorah, poised above the heads of the conquerors. Although the word means simply "lamp," it refers by tradition to the seven-branched lamp in the Holy Temple. Here carved in stone, held high for all to see, it symbolized for Rome as nothing else could the abject, unmitigated defeat of this annoying people. Because the menorah, and not any other object or image, was the oldest and most central symbol of the Jews.

Indeed, the menorah may be older than the Jews, descending from a kind of lamp found in the middle of the second millennium B.C.E., when swords were made of bronze and Israel had not yet been mentioned in any record. This was not a candelabrum but an oil lamp with seven spouts for wicks, which may have symbolized the seven planets known to the ancients, the seven heavenly spheres, the seven days of Creation. According to talmudic legend, God gave Moses explicit instructions on how to craft the lamp, but they were so complex that Moses gave up and God had to finish the job. Jewish mystics later saw in the seven lamps the seven lower emanations of God. In one legend King David carved the seven verses of Psalm 67 on his battle shield in the shape of a menorah. Yet another tradition sees the form of an angel with six wings.

But whatever the echoes of meaning, the menorah became for Jews the symbol of the Holy Temple. The Book of Numbers (8:1–4) gives explicit instructions for its design, and the one on the Arch of Titus corresponds to the Torah's description. The object may have been taken to Rome, but the symbol has echoed through time and space. After the Temple fell, synagogues in the Galilee and a far-flung diaspora used the menorah as the eternal flame, but also as an image in paintings, mosaics, and carvings. In twenty-eight ancient synagogues whose ruins have been studied, the menorah appears three times more often than any other symbol.[1] The Torah said in effect *God is with us,* but the menorah said *The Temple is with us too.*

Remains of synagogues in the Galilee in the first few centuries of the Common Era show the continuous presence of Jews and Jewish communities in spite of partial exile and diaspora. Synagogues were present even in Jerusalem, where they continued Ezra's Torah-reading tradition. Jewish, Christian, and Greek sources all agree that people met in the synagogues, "particularly on their sacred sabbaths when they receive as a body a training in their ancestral philosophy."[2] This quote from Philo, a first-century Alexandrian Jewish philosopher who wrote extensively in Greek, corresponds to Acts 13:14–16: "And on the Sabbath day they went into the synagogue and sat down. After the reading of the Law and the prophets, the rulers of the synagogue sent to them, saying, 'Brethren, if you have any word of exhortation for the people, say it.' So Paul stood up."[3]

A rabbinical source describes the Torah reading on a wooden platform in the center of the synagogue. The hazan, or cantor, stood on the platform holding kerchiefs, and "When one came and took hold of the scroll to read, he would wave the kerchiefs and all the people would answer 'Amen' for each blessing."[4]

According to an inscription on a first-century Jerusalem synagogue: "Theodotus . . . built the synagogue for reading the Law and studying the commandments, and as a hostel with chambers and water installations to provide for the needs of itinerants from abroad."[5] Evidently synagogues were also community centers, as most are today. There is no mention of prayer, and it may be that while the Temple stood, the Jerusalem synagogues left prayer to the priests. But in the wake of the Roman genocide, synagogues in Israel expanded their liturgy and varied their architectural forms.

They also displayed images. Although the menorah was by far the most common, there were four other clearly Jewish symbols.[6] These were images of the shofar or ram's horn, the Torah shrine, and the *lulav* and *etrog*—sacred plants for Sukkot, the Feast of Booths. There were also generic images that might be found anywhere, like eagles, rosettes, wreaths, vines, and lions. Some took on Jewish echoes; to Jews in a synagogue, a lion rampant could be only the Lion of Judah.

In the diaspora, despite much common ground, synagogues had evolved further. One from the first century B.C.E. is on the Aegean isle of Delos, an ancient crossroads for merchants and travelers and, in legend, Apollo's birthplace. Another, in Ostia—the main port of Rome, dense with adherents of many faiths—dates from the first century C.E. Still others are found in Asia Minor and Macedonia.

Perhaps the most famous is at Dura, a remote Syrian city on the eastern rim of the empire.[7] Dura was an ethnically varied caravan crossroads, and Jews had lived there for centuries. The synagogue's fame owes much to a series of wall paintings made not many years before it was destroyed in 256. They astonished scholars because they seemed to flout the second commandment. *A synagogue full of graven images?* Not only that, but the images seem pagan. Yet they are subtly changed to make them Jewish. One panel seems to show Orpheus playing his harp for the animals, as in Greek myth. But he might be that other harpist, David, who would grow up to be king.

Most surprising is Helios, the sun god, who sits enthroned, surrounded by the zodiac, in floor mosaics in several ancient synagogues. Some hymns and dirges also contain the zodiac, and congregants may have stood around the floor mosaics as they intoned:

> *Because of our sins, the Temple was destroyed,*
> *. . . lamentations were heard,*
> *and the host of heaven sounded a dirge. . . .*
> *Ares the ram, first of all, wept bitterly,*
> *for his sheep were being led to the slaughter.*
> *Taurus howled on high.*[8]

So desolate is Judea that even the planets weep. The poem tries to make the zodiac Jewish, but iconography was a pagan narrative mode. Greece and Rome never developed sacred texts, and the Jews never developed sacred icons. For most of history, Jews rejected pictures for words. But briefly in the Roman world, doing as the Romans did, Jews too told their story in pictures.

Still, most of the images are drawn from Jewish texts: in one panel the Israelites leave Egypt and cross the Red Sea, while in another, the Ark of the Covenant sits in the tabernacle in the desert. But even the Jewish icons have a pagan character. Queen Esther and King Ahasuerus closely resemble depictions of a local god and goddess. So diaspora synagogues placed Jewish faith and pagan culture side by side. The communities too were in some ways very Greek, not just in dress and design, but in language and thought. Yet at the core of their deeply religious selves, most of them remained very Jewish.[9]

Diaspora Jews, whether in Greece, Rome, Egypt, or elsewhere, had much in common. Even while the Temple stood, they had lay leaders, not priests. They read the Bible in Greek but kept it at the heart of things; most synagogues had Torah shrines. They circumcised their sons and kept the Sabbath and dietary laws. They buried their dead in separate cemeteries and inscribed gravestones with biblical quotes and Jewish symbols. Last but not least, these communities stayed in touch with each other and with Israel. And the heart of it all was Jerusalem; they put the Ark of the Torah on the wall facing the Temple. Yet diaspora was not the same as exile. Many had gone voluntarily, drifting on currents of commerce, proselytizing, or just seeking a better life than they had in a homeland seething with strife and rebellion.

In these centuries that bracketed the start of the Common Era they were *in* their adopted countries but not completely *of* them. They loved their homeland, yet did not want to go there, except to visit. So they invented the paradoxical Jewish yearning for Jerusalem: a place that you turned toward in prayer or made a pilgrimage to. Not the Jerusalem of corrupt, autocratic priests or contentious Zealot factions, not life in the shadow of Roman crucifixions, but a mythic Jerusalem of transcendent peace and beauty. Of course, it was a real place, and so the almost millennial yearning for a Jerusalem that could not exist was inextricably entwined with the yearning for one that did. But either way, return was an increasingly remote possibility, and in the meantime it would not be bad to accept an easier life among mostly tolerant foreigners.[10]

☙❧

"Mostly" is the key word. There were riots against the Jews from time to time in various places. In the year 41—around the same time the mad Emperor Caligula ordered the Syrian governor to put a colossal statue of him in the Jerusalem Temple—there was a rift between Jews and gentiles in Alexandria. Jews had been there for five centuries and perhaps much longer, given the ancient intimacy of Israel and Egypt. They could practice their own religion and govern themselves in a distinct community, and non-Jewish Alexandrians—"Greeks," but really just Greek speakers—resented their independence, so when the Jews began to demand equal rights and privileges in the city, their neighbors attacked them, desecrating and destroying synagogues, looting homes, and herding the Jews into a ghetto while the Roman governor looked away. The Jews defended themselves, and the Greco-Jewish philosopher Philo, a native of Alexandria, led a delegation to Rome.[11]

Twenty-five years later, with Nero as emperor, another clash had a far worse ending. This was during the first Jewish revolt in Israel, a few years before it was brutally suppressed, Jerusalem was burned, and the Temple was razed. Diaspora cities like Alexandria were *safer,* but they weren't *safe.* According to Josephus, Jews tried to join a town meeting in the amphitheater, but were denounced as spies. In the riot that followed, the Jews fled, but three were captured. They were about to be put to the stake when the Jews returned in force to free them, attacking the amphitheater with stones and torches. The Roman governor prevented them from burning it to the ground and met with Jewish leaders to calm the situation. But someone insulted him, and he promptly ordered his soldiers to kill them and loot their property. The Jews entrenched and resisted in their neighborhood, the

Delta, but five thousand Roman troops arrived from Libya, joined the attack, and slaughtered old and young alike. The governor finally held the troops off, but the citizens went on with the slaughter and had to be dragged away from the Jewish corpses.

Fortunately, the situation of Jews in most of the empire was not so extreme. It is one of the great paradoxes of Jewish history that while the Jews of Israel under Roman domination were experiencing mass crucifixions and even wider mass slaughter, the Jews living elsewhere in the empire were much less likely to be persecuted. Indeed, there were times and places where tolerance was the norm. For example, Jews began to establish communities in the city of Rome itself by the second century b.c.e.[12] Their numbers increased throughout the next century as conquests brought Jewish slaves from Judea and Syria. Some came voluntarily as resident aliens, but they and some Jewish slaves gradually gained freedom and even citizenship.

Except for the Ostia ruins nearby, we know Rome's synagogues indirectly, through gravestone inscriptions or documents. There were four or five synagogues in the city as the Common Era began, some named after tolerant Romans. One honors Augustus, later praised by Philo: "[Augustus] did not expel them from Rome or deprive them of their Roman citizenship because they remembered their Jewish nationality also. He introduced no changes into their synagogues, he did not prevent them from meeting for the exposition of the Law, and he raised no objection to the offering of first fruits."[13] If a distribution of money or food to citizens "happened to be made on the Sabbath . . . he instructed the distributors to reserve the Jews' share . . . until the next day." Another synagogue was named for Agrippa, Augustus's lieutenant and heir, for upholding Jewish privileges in Asia Minor. A third was just "the Synagogue of the Hebrews."

By the end of the first century there were thirteen in all, serving perhaps fifty thousand Jews in and around Rome—most of them poor, Greek-speaking foreigners. They were one of the largest immigrant groups, and although their communities varied, we can make some generalizations.[14] Most lived in a suburb just across the Tiber from the city center. Like today's urban migrants, they were crammed into tenements full of tiny apartments. They were scorned for their poverty—by Martial, Juvenal, and Cicero, among others—and many were slaves. Some of the freedmen in the tenements must have worked on the Tiber's docks nearby. Some Jews were wealthy, some were even slave owners, but most were poor—slaves or former slaves.

The multistory apartment houses were built around inner courtyards with shops on the ground floor. Families that ran the shops might live in them, but some had better-than-average apartments behind them. Small, upper-story, one- and two-room apartments were for poorer families. Latrines were public, privacy rare, and people came out of their confining spaces to socialize. Still, this public social life supported Jewish dietary practices and Sabbath observance, and there were synagogues in the neighborhood.

Marriages were made in or out of Roman law, the groom in his late twenties, the bride in her teens. Bigamy was illegal, but men ruled the roost, and matches were deals between the groom and the bride's father. Many children died before growing up; few families had as many as three surviving. They got Greek or Roman, not biblical, names, which probably helped children fit in, and names derived from pagan gods appear on Jewish tombstones. Extended families were too big for most apartments, but the tenements may have linked individual families to kin. Because of high death and divorce rates, many families must have been blended ones.

For centuries the Jews of Rome were unversed in Latin; their native language was Greek, and they used little Hebrew or Aramaic, even for reading the Torah, even on their tombstones. They arrived in Rome Hellenized and went on adopting Roman law and custom. Where Jewish law was more permissive than Roman—allowing polygamy, for example—they obeyed Roman law. This meant that the family, despite male dominance, was modeled on a monogamous ideal in which, as Philo put it, there was an indissoluble bond of love and kinship.[15] The fact that couples who married as slaves stayed together when they were freed suggests that the bond was real; the fact of divorce shows that it wasn't perfect. These aspects of life were as Roman as they were Jewish.

That assimilation had limits is shown by the views of noble Romans writing about this poverty-stricken, weird, distasteful people. Cicero in 59 B.C.E. referred to Judaism as *"barbara superstitio,"* and wrote of "the odium that is attached to Jewish gold." He continued,

> Even while Jerusalem was standing and the Jews were at peace with us, the practice of their sacred rites was at variance with the glory of our empire, the dignity of our name, the customs of our ancestors. But now it is even more so, when that nation by its armed resistance has shown what it thinks of our rule; how dear it was to the immortal gods is shown by the fact that it has been conquered, let out for taxes, made a slave.[16]

Horace mocked the Jews for proselytizing and credulousness. Livy expressed the common view that the Jews were basically atheists, saying, "They do not state to which deity pertains the temple at Jerusalem, nor is any image found there, since they do not think the God partakes of any figure."[17] Seneca, writing in the sixties c.e., resented them: "Meanwhile the customs of this accursed race have gained such influence that they are now received throughout all the world. The vanquished have given laws to their victors."[18] Quintilian writes of them as "a race which is a curse to others" and berates "the Jewish superstition."[19]

Apion, in a famous anti-Jewish tract, claimed that they worshiped an ass's head; much more dangerously, he delivered the first blood libel. As summarized by Josephus in his answer to Apion,

> The practice was repeated annually at a fixed season. They would kidnap a Greek foreigner, fatten him up for a year, and then convey him to a wood, where they slew him, sacrificed his body with their customary ritual, partook of his flesh, and while immolating the Greek, swore an oath of hostility to the Greeks. The remains of their victim were then thrown into a pit.[20]

This calumny was repeated by Damocritus in *On Jews,* a book known through references by others, showing its influence.

Martial's epigrams make reference to "the lecheries of circumcised Jews" and "the Jew taught by his mother to beg." Plutarch refers to "superstition, such as smearing with mud, wallowing in filth, keeping the Sabbath, casting oneself down with face to the ground, disgraceful besieging of the gods, and uncouth prostrations."[21] He attributes a military defeat to observance: "But the Jews, because it was the Sabbath day, sat in their places immovable, while the enemy were planting ladders against the walls and capturing the defenses, and they did not get up, but remained there, fast bound in the toils of superstition as in one great net." Plutarch at least came by his bigotry honestly:

> My grandfather used to say on every occasion, in derision of the Jews, that what they abstained from was precisely the most legitimate meat. . . . do they abstain from eating pork by reason of some special respect for hogs or from abhorrence of the creature? Their own accounts sound like pure myth, but perhaps they have some serious reasons which they do not publish.

The historian Tacitus displays particular animus:

> To establish his influence over this people for all time, Moses introduced new religious practices, quite opposed to those of all other religions. The Jews regard as profane all that we hold sacred; on the other hand, they permit all that we abhor. . . . They abstain from pork, in recollection of a plague. . . . By frequent fasts even now

they bear witness to the long hunger with which they were once distressed . . . and the unleavened Jewish bread is still employed in memory of the haste with which they seized the grain. . . .

The other customs of the Jews are base and abominable, and owe their persistence to their depravity. . . . the Jews are extremely loyal to one another, and always ready to show compassion, but toward every other people they feel only hate and enmity. They sit apart at meals and they sleep apart, and although as a race, they are prone to lust, they abstain from intercourse with foreign women. . . . They adopted circumcision to distinguish themselves from other peoples . . . and the earliest lesson they receive is to despise the gods, to disown their country, and to regard their parents, children, and brothers as of little account.[22]

The satirist Juvenal issued similar slurs and salvos, but with a grin. He refers, for instance, to "that country where kings celebrate festal sabbaths with bare feet, and where a long-established clemency suffers pigs to attain old age." He conjures up a beggar,

a palsied Jewess . . . an interpreter of the laws of Jerusalem, a high priestess of the tree, a trusty go-between of highest heaven. She too fills her palm . . . for a Jew will tell you dreams of any kind you please for the minutest of coins. Some . . . have had a father who reveres the Sabbath, worships nothing but the clouds, and the divinity of the heavens. . . . Having been wont to flout the laws of Rome, they learn and revere the Jewish law, and all that Moses handed down in his secret tome. . . . For all which the father was to blame, who gave up every seventh day to idleness, keeping it apart from all the concerns of life.[23]

Thus the famous writers of ancient Rome—whose names, at least until recently, were familiar to every educated person—had already concocted all the libels, issued all the slurs, made all the jokes, and promulgated all the misunderstandings that would cause the Jews of Europe twenty centuries of suffering. Every one, that is, except the claim that the Jews killed Christ, and in so doing betrayed and tortured God himself. This durable accusation was a latecomer to anti-Jewish rhetoric. But Roman intellectuals had laid the groundwork for classic European anti-Semitism. The extraordinary virulence of Christian Jew hatred stemmed from grafting the blame of the Gospels onto a trunk and root already thick and deep.

Not surprisingly, pagan bigotry caused riots against Jews in many parts of the empire far from Judea. "Greeks," meaning Greek-speaking non-Jews, had grievances against Jews wherever Jews lived. Some of these grievances were legitimate—lawsuits, contests over resources, unequal treatment by the government, and so on. But almost all were exacerbated by bigotry and resentment. Rome had a vested interest in calm and often protected the Jews against a dangerous majority, but not always. For example, in 115, clashes between Jews and Greeks led to a Jewish revolt against Emperor Trajan.[24] The revolt spread widely, and in several places local villagers joined the Jews; these downtrodden peasants also had many grievances.

Widespread revolt suggests coordination, but may just reflect shared grievances. The revolt was put down, but not before large tracts of Libya and Egypt were laid waste, roads ruined, and many people killed. In Cyprus the Jews, who had lived throughout the island, were exterminated. In Egypt they suffered grave losses and never recovered their prior strength. In many Egyptian districts the Jewish community was destroyed, its institutions ceased to function, and property remained unclaimed. Two centuries passed before Jewish life in Egypt really resumed.

The troubles were serious enough to halt the eastern progress of the empire and to help the Parthians set a geographic limit on Roman rule. The important result was that Jewish life in Babylonia continued beyond Roman reach. But within the empire the Jews had only precarious tolerance, steeped in contempt and punctuated by ravages. Three times in the first century the Jews were expelled from the city of Rome. First Tiberius and the senate banished them, perhaps because their proselytizing had begun to affect the upper classes. But there was general unrest in Rome owing to a failed corn harvest, and in any unrest the Romans expelled untrustworthy groups; they banished worshipers of the goddess Isis the same year. Under Claudius, Jews were banished again, also amid unrest. A Roman author blamed the Jews for the disturbances, which may have had something to do with Christian activity. Still later, under Domitian, "many who drifted into Jewish ways were condemned."[25] Although those born Jewish were not considered criminals, the converts were charged with atheism, and punishments ranged from confiscation of property to death.

Obviously, three such events in a century would leave the Jews uneasy in their adopted city. The pattern established under the Romans was crucial, since it set the balance of bigotry and tense, shaky tolerance that the Jews of Europe lived in for two millennia. But in a deeper sense it did not matter at all what the Romans thought or did, because the mainstream of Jewish history had shifted, and was now flowing between two rivers in Babylon, just beyond the eastern reach of Rome.

☙〰❧

How the Jews got there requires us to return very briefly to the turmoil in Judea under Rome. It was once said that of all Hillel's students, the least of them was Yochanan ben Zakkai. We are not told the reason for this opinion, which may have been a slur against his brainpower or just a reference to his youth. In any case, he did not lack discretion or common sense. He had not supported the first Jewish revolt against Rome, and legend has it that when Jerusalem was under siege, in the process of being destroyed, he had his students smuggle him out of the city in a coffin, supposedly to be buried outside the walls.

After his resurrection, he fled to Yavneh, west of Jerusalem. He began teaching without delay, and for many years the Yavneh academy was the jewel of Torah study in what was left of Judea. In keeping with Yochanan's sly departure from Jerusalem, the Yavneh scholars did not have the slightest interest in confrontation. They wanted to guard the Torah in its largest sense: the tradition of teaching and learning. They opposed messianism and zealotry, and they sat out the second revolt that claimed the life of Akiva.

Still, they could not remain in Yavneh after that conflict; Judea was no place for Jews. So the jewel of Torah learning was reset in the western Galilee, and over the next few centuries it variously graced Tiberias, Sepphoris, and a number of smaller towns. A main determinant was the home of a leading rabbi. But wherever it was, the academy was zealous only in its avoidance of zealotry. If two negatives make a positive, that positive was calm: an atmosphere of safe, unhurried devotion to the Torah, as an object not of fierce passion—although they surely loved it—but serene contemplation, a mystery to be slowly and tenderly unveiled.

What passion there was went into argument. As in the earlier time of Hillel and Shammai, different rabbis had different interpretations of the same commandment or declaration in the Torah, and there was nothing to do but talk it through. Yet even the arguments were calm. It is as if the memories of war—the blaze that devoured Jerusalem not quenched even by a river of blood, the endless stretch of crucifixions planted like trees by the roadsides, the spectacle of Akiva's aged skin torn from his living form— as if these horrific souvenirs of Roman savagery were lurking like ghosts outside the academy, warning against too much fervor. Rabbis had been burned with the Torah wrapped around their bodies, the very thing they loved most embracing them as it killed them.

This was not how the new generation wanted to use the Torah. They would do almost anything to avoid conflict, and they saw this as an absolute obligation. God, they were certain, did not intend the Torah to be a flaming shroud; God gave it to them as a source of life. The liturgy declares, "It is a tree of life to those who lay hold of it, and all who uphold it are happy." *Kiddush Ha'shem*—giving one's life to sanctify God's name—could become an obligation too, but that didn't mean you had to go looking for it. In fact, your first and foremost obligation was to live, and the reason you had to live was to be able to study Torah, both for its own sake and as a guide to life. So the process was recursive: life for Torah, Torah for life.

Whether in Yavneh or Tiberias, the method was the same. The most revered teachers led the school, the advanced students dreamed of succeeding them, and the newcomers or lesser students sat at the benches and tables. Rows of them would listen as a rabbi delivered a *drash*—from the Hebrew for "search"—an interpretation of the Law. At the tables they would pair off and set themselves to intense debate over points of contention large and small. Calm reigned because the bitter infighting of the previous century had cost them too much, but also because the rabbis were having their arguments recorded. Of course, decisions had to be made as to which opinion to follow, and they were made every day, in response to practical questions in the steady march of cases. Judgments became precedents and in time could become law.

Yet defeated opinions survived. More important, reasoning processes survived, and they became the lifeblood of the emerging texts. The debates were not carved in stone, but they were inked on papyrus, and future generations could review them again and again. This was the Mishnah, the Talmud's core, the bedrock of Jewish life for the next nineteen centuries. By Orthodox tradition, this text merely set down what God told Moses at Sinai—an oral supplement to the written Torah. Moses passed it down to Joshua's generation, and it continued to be handed down—accurately, from memory—as the generations turned into centuries. This gives the Mishnah the status of God's word.

In any case, the conversation had begun by Josiah's time, when the rediscovered scroll of the Law made the grief-stricken king rethink Jewish life. In the first Babylonian exile, the debate surely intensified. "What does it mean," we may imagine the scribes asking, "to write the words on the doorpost? Do we really write them on the post, or do we just hang a scroll there? It says we must not seethe a kid in its mother's milk. But suppose the milk comes from a different mother, or from a cow?" Some basic methods were in place by Ezra's time, when the Torah was read out and interpreted for the people. There must have been dueling *drashes* as teachers read the same passage in different ways. Even before the Maccabees there were rabbis with identities, a few of whose names and rulings have come down to us. And generations before the Temple's final destruction Hillel and Shammai established two views of the Torah that would contend for centuries. Tragic, messianic Akiva was a part of it, but so was mild, apolitical Yochanan. These early *tanna'im*—those who study—created the Mishnah, completed in Galilee by the end of the second century.[26] This was the Oral Law, written down in terse, tight, unpoetic Hebrew prose.[27] It begins without a beginning, in anonymity: "From what time do they say the morning Shema?" Opinions are given succinctly, without ceremony, and they do not agree.

If inscribed on a scroll and stretched out, the Mishnah would go on for the length of a football field. Its six books, or orders, are in turn divided into several tractates each, a total of sixty-three. Some are quite abstruse; sacrifices were meticulously debated long after the Temple was gone, no doubt in the hope that it would be restored. Others are as immediate as the cases in small claims court. Suppose my donkey rubs against someone's wall and the wall falls down. Who owes what to whom?

Still others go to the heart of Jewish ethics and philosophy: "Ben Zoma said: Who is wise? He who learns from everyone. Who is strong? He who controls his will. Who is rich? He who is satisfied with his portion. Who is honored? He who honors the community." There is debate about Torah passages, but also about practical situations, and these reflect life in Israel while the rabbis of the Mishnah lived. Much of it is case law; it reflects Jewish life because its purpose was to govern Jewish life, and this exchange between life and text has gone on ever since. Just the titles of the tractates convey an enormous richness of information about people's lives.

The first order's tractates are Seeds, Blessings, Corners of the Field, Doubtful Tithes, Mixtures, Sabbatical Years, Contributions to the Priests, Tithes for the Levites, Other Tithes, Uncircumcised Fruit, and First Fruits.

The second order's deal with Festivals, the Sabbath, Boundaries, Passover, Shekels, the Day of Atonement, the Feast of Booths, Prohibitions on Festivals, New Year's, Fast Days, Scrolls, Minor Festivals, and Festival Offerings.

The third order covers Women, Sisters-in-law, Marriage Contracts, Vows, Nazarites, Adulterous Women, Divorce, and Betrothals.

The fourth handles Damages, Sanhedrin (how to judge crime and assign punishment), Lashes, Oaths, Testimonies, Idolatry, Ethics of the Fathers, and Rulings.

In the fifth order are Holy Things, Animal Sacrifices, Offerings, Kosher Slaughter, Firstlings, Valuations of Temple Vows, Sacrificial Substitutions, Sin- and Guilt-Offerings, Sacrilege, Daily Sacrifices, Temple Dimensions, and Sacrificial Birds.

And in the sixth and last, devoted to purity and pollution, are Purity, Vessels and Utensils, Tents with Corpses, Leprosy, the Red Heifer, Purifications, Ritual Baths, the Menstruating Woman, Food Impurities, Sexual Secretions, Daytime Immersion, Hand-washing, and Impurities of Plants and Fruit.

Finally, there are additional small sections on Ethics, Scribes, Happy Occasions, Brides, Courtesy, Peace, Converts, Samaritans, Slaves, Torah Scrolls, Tefillin, Ritual Fringes, and the Mezuzah.

Every day, people needed to know how to live, moment to moment, now—how to dress, plant, harvest, marry, worship, settle fights, expunge pollution, eat, drink, sacrifice, divorce, atone, celebrate, tithe, and bless; and of course they had to do all this within the framework of the Torah. They could read the Torah, and they could hear interpretations of it, but to follow it faithfully, as they dearly wished to do, they had to understand not just every word but every jot and tittle, every hidden or convoluted or even mystical meaning.

For that they had to ask those who spent their lives and substance studying that Torah from childhood. These men were not authorities by descent—although descent from learned men did matter—but because they had risen through the ranks of Torah learning. This meant decades of intellectual rigor, study, and fiercely competitive debate. A thousand, it is said, can read the Torah, a hundred read the Mishnah, ten devote themselves to study, and only one becomes a teacher. But it was vital to be in the process somewhere, and wherever you were in it you would honor the Torah, and in return it would honor you.

⚭

Apart from guiding religious observance, the rabbis' role in resolving small claims was vital to the Mishnah, and the result reflects daily life. "If he gave to a joiner a box, chest, or cupboard to repair, and the latter spoiled it, he is liable to pay compensation."[28] On the other hand, "The potter who brought his pots into the courtyard of a householder without permission, and the beast of the householder broke them, the householder is exempt."[29]

An ox in a courtyard may be gored by the householder's ox or bitten by his dog, or may fall into the well and pollute the householder's water, but liability depends on the prior agreement between the two. Debates cover ownership of houses, cisterns, trenches, caves, dovecotes, bathhouses, olive presses, irrigated fields, and slaves.[30] Other rulings deal with ovens, stoves, millstones, manure put in a courtyard, chickens brought into a house, gutter spouts, and windows of different sizes. Mistakes in dyeing wool, disputes with storekeepers, fraud, and interest on loans are all grist for the Mishnah's mill. So are disputes over grain stacked on a threshing floor, a basket of grapes, a vat of olives, and balls of potter's clay.

The Mishnah assumes a world of male-headed families living in houses in villages. A divorced woman would return to her father's house, but grave problems arise at moments when a woman moves from one man to another. "A woman whose husband went overseas, and they came and told, 'Your husband has died,' and who remarried, and whose husband afterward returned . . . she requires a writ of divorce from this one and from that one."[31] But "He whose wife went overseas, and whom they came and told, 'Your wife has died,' and who married her sister, and whose wife thereafter came back, she is permitted to come back to him." Despite this and other evidence of gender inequality, at least one woman, Beruryah, was a brilliant Torah scholar.

These opinions came from various courts.[32] The Great Sanhedrin, the highest, consisted of seventy-one rabbis who ruled on matters of state and appointed judges to lower courts. Important Jewish centers each had a small Sanhedrin of twenty-three judges, to mete out criminal punishment. The death penalty was rare; a court that executed someone once in seventy years was called murderous. Small courts of three rabbis dealt with torts and contracts, and below those were three-member arbitration boards, laymen chosen by the disputants. Each picked one, and these two chose a third.

But most governance was left to rabbis. The head of the Sanhedrin was called *nasi*—prince, or governor. Local authorities included synagogue heads and other community leaders. The role of Sanhedrin leadership reached its peak in Rabbi Yehudah ha-Nasi—Judah the Prince—whose wealth and charisma combined with genius to yield a uniquely strong leader.[33] Judah was a correspondent—in a way a colleague—of two Roman emperors, and won their respect for Judaism. He avoided conflict with Rome, focusing his energy on Torah study. But he also fostered settlement of Israel by Jews and organized the Jewish world, not just in Israel but in the diaspora. He emphasized Hebrew, insisting that it, not Aramaic, should be the spoken language of daily life and the only language of prayer. But ever the pragmatist, he was tolerant of Greek.

He had the wealth to live like a prince and did, yet was famous for humility, and he used his wealth to support poorer scholars as well as community projects. Nevertheless, he was contemptuous of the ignorant. "Trouble comes to the world," he said, "only on account of the unlearned." His distaste for Aramaic, the language of people, was inherently elitist. He exempted scholars from taxes, increasing the burden on artisans and farmers, but reversed himself when some rabbis refused to benefit in this way from their knowledge of the Torah. He is best known for finalizing the Mishnah, the basis of all future Jewish life. He did this eclectically, ensuring wide rabbinical support. By the time of his death he was often referred to simply as "Rabbi," and one colleague remarked that "not since the days of Moses were learning and high office combined in one person until Rabbi."

He not only completed the Mishnah but prepared the next stage of the Law, training the best young minds to interpret the Mishnah. As he was the last of the *tanna'im*—students or scholars—they were the first of the *amora'im*—speakers or explainers. As he finished the Mishnah, they began the rest of the Talmud: the Gemara, a large body of commentary and debate about the Mishnah. The rabbis of the Mishnah argued about the Torah, and the rabbis of the Gemara argued about the Mishnah.

Israel itself continued to produce great rabbis, but there was a new center of learning in the Jewish world, and it was in—of all places—Babylon. The place of the first exile, seven centuries earlier, became in the end the most important diaspora. Recall that thousands of Jews trickled back to Israel in the century after they'd gone into exile. They rebuilt the temple in Jerusalem and stood up and sang when Ezra lifted the scroll of the Law. But some Jews never left, and prospering in Babylon under the Persians and other powers, they slowly built a new kind of Jewish life. This life was tied to Jerusalem, but was outside the Roman political sphere. It was filled with yearning for the Holy Land, but free of its tragic politics and messianic dreams. It took its calendar from Israel, but set its own scholarly agenda.

That agenda would now take the lead. Josephus said that the Jews of Babylonia comprised "countless myriads of which none can know the number."[34] Anyway, it was a lot. There were large Babylonian cities populated, maintained, and garrisoned by Jews. They were conscious of their heritage both in Israel and in Babylon, and they were also self-conscious about their purity, resisting intermarriage yet proselytizing in new ways. Indeed, the Talmud compares Babylonian Jewry to "pure sifted flour," even more so than the Jews who remained in Israel.[35] They kept close ties to those Jews, deferring to the Sanhedrin in certain matters of judgment. Some leading rabbis in Israel, such as Hillel, were born in Babylonia, while some leading Babylonian sages "went up" to Israel to die and be buried. Great rabbis in each drew students from the other.

But even in Judah's time, the Jewish Babylon was rapidly in ascendance. His counterpart in Babylon, called the *exilarch* in Greek, was at that time a rabbi of such distinction that Judah supposedly offered to step down as head of the Sanhedrin should he be willing to come to Israel. The exilarch was also by tradition a descendant of King David, adding to his prestige. He had a prominent position among the lords of the Parthian Empire, and their relatively relaxed feudal system enabled him to secure rights and privileges for the Jews.

Most Babylonian Jews were farmers, as they had been during the exile seven centuries earlier. Some were substantial landholders, but most were peasants and tenant farmers. Among their means of livelihood were cultivating Babylonia's famed date palm, growing other fruit trees, poultry farming, and fishing. But many Jews were artisans, merchants, and traders. There were carpenters, blacksmiths, potters, tailors, cobblers, weavers, tanners, builders, goldsmiths, silversmiths, architects, surveyors, doctors and blood-letters.[36] There were of course religious crafts, like making mezuzahs, tefillin, and ritual fringes, and down the social scale were hunters, fishermen, donkey drivers, camel drivers, and sailors. Most teachers were also scribes, and their talents might be used for official secular documents. A few people worked in Jewish courts and synagogues.

And of course, Mesopotamia was a crossroads of world trade, as it had been for millennia—the Silk Route from China went through it, as did Indian spices, fruit, and iron. Jewish participation was natural. As a tolerated, peripheral people, Jews found trading a logical path to success. But far more were petty merchants peddling spices; grocers selling flour, oil, and wine; butchers; ritual slaughterers; or bakers. Some were money changers, but the only important property was land. The Jews paid heavy taxes, and if they could not pay they might lose their deeds and become tenants on their own land. Nevertheless they followed the dictum of one of their leading rabbis, and it would stand for centuries: "The laws of the kingdom are law."[37]

When the doomed Bar Kokhba revolt and the savage repression that followed drove many scholars out of Judea, most joined the community that had stayed in Babylon during the centuries after the exile. Together they established at least two great academies. The one at Sura, on the Euphrates' east bank, had twelve hundred regular students and thousands more who joined for a month in summer and winter during lulls in farming. The one at Pumbedita had a rockier course; it was sacked and rebuilt in the third century, eventually moving to the west bank of the Tigris. The endurance of this tradition was remarkable; both these academies would see the tenth century.

It was here, in an exile-turned-diaspora, that the Babylonian Talmud was written, during the four centuries after the Mishnah was completed. There was a parallel process in Israel, and rivulets joined the two streams. The Jerusalem Talmud, as it was called, although it was made elsewhere in Israel, came to completion first. But the race was not to the swift, and the Babylonian Talmud—more graceful, more detailed, more richly intellectual, and more respectful of argument—became the main permanent source of Jewish Law. It was not a small matter, since they differed in both substance and style. The Jerusalem Talmud was in Hebrew, with some passages in Aramaic and many Greek borrowings; the Babylonian was mainly in eastern Aramaic, with only a few Persian words. The Jerusalem Talmud is spare in discourse, more like an outline of legal conclusions, while the Babylonian is discursive and legalistic, yet somehow more inviting. The Babylonian Talmud spread much more rapidly in the diaspora, and Israel's Jewish community declined while Babylon's grew stronger. Its rabbis carried their Talmud throughout the world and finally took it to Israel as well. Perhaps because the Babylonian Talmud was created in exile—the vast majority of the Jews *were* in exile—but for whatever reason, the Babylonian Talmud became *the* Talmud.

☙〰❧

So what is this Talmud? At its core, literally in the center of each page, are the texts of the Mishnah and Gemara, the debates and rulings from the two great rabbinical eras.[38] As the Mishnah debated the Torah, the Gemara debated the Mishnah. Around this core are later commentaries, notably that of Rashi, a great French eleventh-century rabbi. It is no exaggeration to say that these texts saved the Jews.

When the Second Temple crumbled, ancient Judaism ended. There would be no more sacrifices, priests, tithes, offerings, or rituals of purification, except as remembered abstractions. Torah Judaism was not born in the talmudic age; it was conceived by Josiah and Huldah and born—with Ezra as midwife—after the first exile. It grew to youthful vigor in Second Temple Israel and in the century after the Temple fell. But it came of age as the Talmud was set down, mainly in Babylonia. There Judaism took something like its present form, and from there it won over the Jewish world. The ancient synagogues of Alexandria, Delos, and Rome were already centuries old when they encountered Talmud Judaism, but all succumbed to its spell. It was coherent, smart, and meaningful, and won the hearts and minds of Jews in every land.

Its sages were revered forever after. A recent Orthodox account says, "Each word of our holy Sages was pronounced while the *ruach hakodesh* (Divine spirit) rested upon them." It continues:

> Hillel had eighty disciples. Thirty of them . . . were worthy of having the Divine presence rest upon them as it did upon Moses Our Teacher. Thirty deserved that the sun's orbit should be halted for them as it was for Joshua. Twenty were average. . . . About the least great, Rabbi Yochanan ben Zakkai, it was said that there was no verse of Scripture or of the Talmud he did not know. . . . About the greatest, Yonasan ben Uziel, it was said that while he was studying Torah, the angels would gather around him to listen. As a result of the spiritual fire emanating from them, any bird that flew over Yonasan ben Uziel's head while he was studying would be singed.[39]

These rabbis live in the cultural memory of Orthodox Jews in a place beyond space and time, and the rulings they made were as good as if spoken by God.

In fact, they were better. The story is told of Rabbi Eliezer, who in a certain argument did not win over his colleagues. So sure was he of his rightness that he called upon supernatural aid.

> He said to them, "If the law is in accord with me, let this carob tree prove it."
> The carob tree was uprooted and moved one hundred cubits—and some say four hundred cubits.
> They said to him, "We don't bring proof from a carob tree."
> He then said to them, "If the law agrees with me, let the channel of water prove it."
> The channel of water turned and flowed the other way.
> They said to him, "We don't bring proof from a channel of water."
> Then he said to them, "If the law agrees with me, let the walls of the study house prove it."

The walls of the study house began to fall.

Rabbi Joshua said to them: "If scholars are debating each other about the law, what do you know about it?"

They did not fall down in honor of Rabbi Joshua, but they did not straighten up in honor of Rabbi Eliezer, and they are still standing and leaning.

Then he said to them: "If the law agrees with me, let the proof come from heaven."

A voice came forth and said, "Why do you argue with Rabbi Eliezer? The law always agrees with him."

Rabbi Joshua rose to his feet and said, "It is not in heaven" (Deut. 30:12).

Here the Gemara commentary intervenes in the Mishnah text:

What is the meaning of, "It is not in heaven"?

Rabbi Jeremiah said: "Since the Torah was already given on Mount Sinai, we don't pay attention to voices. For You already wrote in the Torah on Mount Sinai, 'Follow the majority'" (Exod. 23:2).

The Mishnah resumes:

Rabbi Nathan met Elijah the Prophet and said to him, "What did the Holy One, blessed be he, do at that moment?"

Elijah told him, "He smiled and said, 'My sons have defeated me, my sons have defeated me!'"[40]

"Surpassed" may be a better translation, but either way the message is threefold. First, it is fine to argue with God, as Abraham, Jacob, and Moses did; God expects it. Second, the Law is process, not fact. It emerges at the living edge of experience. Third, the Torah was given to humanity at Sinai. After that, forevermore, it belongs to human beings. It contains within itself all we need, provided we understand it. And our minds are granted the power to do just that. The Torah itself says, "It is not in heaven," and "After the majority . . ." God's word enters the mouths of the sages, and when they vote, *that* is the Law.

But debate was just the beginning of enlightenment. The goal of the exercise was to do the right thing by man and God:

How does a man find his Father who is in heaven?
He finds him by good deeds, and study of the Torah.
And the Holy One, blessed be he, finds man

through love, through brotherhood, through respect,
through companionship, through truth, through peace,
through bending the knee, through humility,
through studious session, through commerce lessened,
through the service of the masters, through the
    discussion of students,
through a good heart, through decency,
through No that is really No,
through Yes that is really Yes. [41]

These are the acts that emerge from a life in and of Torah. The passage also implies that God searches for human beings just as they search for God. Recall the passage from Proverbs in the Sabbath morning service: "It is a tree of life to those who lay hold of it, and all who uphold it are happy. Its ways are ways of pleasantness, and all its paths are peace." These claims might astound anyone who knows Jewish history, which seems a trail of tears. Yet the real history is not that of wars and kings, slaughter and exile, but that of the moment-to-moment lives of ordinary people. For them the Talmud's message could not be more clear:

Every place where Israel was exiled, the Divine Presence was with them.
They were exiled to Egypt, the Presence was with them.
They were exiled to Babylon, the Presence was with them. . . .
They were exiled to Rome, the Presence was with them.
And when they shall return, the Presence will be with them. [42]

The Presence is everywhere, its earthly form is the Torah, and the Talmud is nothing less than the Torah's reach into human life.

Part of that reach is through philosophy, the sages' explicit claims about how we should live. The wisdom of ten generations is drawn down into one tractate, "Sayings of the Fathers," the advice of each distilled in a few words. It has been called a talmudic Book of Proverbs. The very first is attributed to Moses, Joshua, and the elders, who "said three things: Be careful in judgement, raise many disciples, and build a fence around the Torah." That fence is the Oral Law: the Torah's command, "Thou shalt not seethe a kid in its mother's milk," repeated three times, leads to a complete separation of milk and meat, including separate sets of dishes, hours elapsed between eating them, and ritual reversal of cross-contamination.

There are many other sayings:

Joshua ben Perahyah says, "Provide yourself with a teacher, get you a comrade, and judge everyone with the scale weighted in his favor."

Shemaiah says, "Love work, hate lordship, and seek no intimacy with the ruling powers."

Abtalyon says, "Sages, watch your words, lest you incur the penalty of exile and be carried off to a place of evil waters, and your disciples who come after you drink thereof and die, and thus the name of heaven be profaned."

Rabban Simeon ben Gamaliel says, "By three things is the world sustained: by truth, by justice, and by peace."[43]

Rabban Gamaliel, the son of Rabbi Judah the Prince, says, "Splendid is the study of the Torah when combined with a worldly occupation, for toil in them both puts sin out of mind; but study not combined with work falls into neglect in the end, and is the cause of sin. . . ."

Rabbi Simeon says, "Be alert in reciting the Shema and the prayer. . . . Do not make of your prayer something automatic, but a plea for compassion, a supplication before God."

Rabbi Tarfon says, "The day is short, the work great, the laborers sluggish, the reward abundant, and the master of the house presses. . . . It is not up to you to finish the task, but neither are you free to desist from it."

Rabbi Hanina ben Dosa used to say, "He whose works exceed his wisdom, his wisdom will endure; but he whose wisdom exceeds his works, his wisdom will not endure."

Ben Azzai used to say, "Despise no man and consider nothing impossible, for there is no man who does not have his hour and there is no thing that does not have its place."

Rabbi Eliezer Ha-Kappar says, "Envy, lust, and a thirst for glory put a man out of the world."[44]

These are just a few of the sayings of the sages, and they have been on the lips of observant Jews ever since.

Yet it is not by philosophy that the good Jewish life is achieved, but by deeds large and small, interpersonal and in covenant with God. In neither realm will philosophy suffice. Not just the spirit of the law, but its letter, must be carried out to the last degree. Declarations of faith do not count for much. Exodus tells us that when God was about to give the Torah to the Jews—the very act that made them the "Chosen People"—they answered in two Hebrew words: Na'aseh v'nishma. It means "We will do and we will hear." The rabbis ask, How can you do before you hear? Well, nishma also means "We will understand." Doing leads to understanding.

Here are some of the doings: dietary laws, Sabbath and festival observance, fast days, circumcision, marriage, burial, charity, kindness, prayer, and Torah study. Hundreds of mitzvot, or commandments—613 in all—the warp and woof of Jewish life, woven tightly and gorgeously in a spiritual shawl that could comfort if not protect through millennia of suffering. This was the Talmud's long reach, inserting the Torah into every person's life, like a loving Jewish mother taking a strong hand in things, to make life sweeter, safer, and better. And of course, the Torah was their covenant with God.

There is another, rather amusing midrash about how the Jews were chosen to be so blessed and burdened. God offered the Torah to the children of Esau, who brazenly asked what was in it. When they heard *Thou shalt not kill,* they respectfully declined, citing the Torah itself, in which Isaac tells Esau "By thy sword shalt thou live" (Gen. 27:40).[45] God went to the children of Ammon and Moab, who asked the same question. When they heard about the adultery clause, they reminded God that their very origin was adulterous, since they stemmed from Lot's forbidden union with his daughters. God went to the children of Ishmael, and *Thou shalt not steal* was the sticking point. In fact, God went to every single nation and in one way or another was turned down flat. If the Jews were the "chosen people" they were chosen by default, because they at last said simply, *We will do and we will hear.*

And so they did, with all their hearts. In two brutal, savage wars, the enemies of the Jews destroyed their homes, land, and Temple, and the public practice of their religion. But the enemies could not break the Jews' bond to the Torah, and out of that they built a far more durable temple in their own minds and bodies. If it was in some sense a new religion, you could easily see its parentage in its face, and hear its forebears in its lyrical, enduring voice. Judea died, it has been aptly said, but she died in childbirth.[46]

6

CROSSED SWORDS

HOW CHRISTIAN POWER
VANQUISHED THE JEWS

The divide-and-conquer policy of totalitarian Rome had no greater or more durable success than turning Jews and Christians against each other.[1] This rift endured for fifteen centuries after the fall of Rome and led to the near-extermination of the European Jews, a grotesque, indelible stain on Christian conscience and memory. But in the first few centuries of the Common Era it seemed little more than a family squabble, a tiff between two sibling Jewish cults neither of which made any sense to Rome.

The deep ambivalence Jesus expressed toward Jewish tradition did not survive his martyrdom by more than a few centuries. His chroniclers, Jewish writers of genius, chose to downplay the overarching role of Roman terror and to emphasize instead the complicity—unquestionably real—of their enemies among their fellow Jews. This was especially true of John, but the other Gospels were interpreted along the same lines. Never mind that thousands of other Jews besides Jesus had been crucified for opposition to Rome. In a manner characteristic of less developed civilizations, the Jews and Christians turned on one another. Rome must have been pleased.

Both religions proselytized throughout the empire in those days, bringing them into conflict with Rome and each other. The Mishnah says nothing about the Christians, although the rabbis of Israel did criticize them, and they are mentioned, not always favorably, elsewhere in the Talmud. For good or ill, they are not any sort of preoccupation in Jewish texts. But the New Testament accuses Jews of being the killers of Jesus (John) or at least complicit in his death (Mark). It depicts Jews as whipping and plotting to kill Paul (Acts 23–35, 2 Cor. 11:24–25). And it condemns those who "say they are Jews, and are not," calling them "the synagogue of Satan" (Rev. 2:9, 3:9).[2] Since Jews in that same calamitous century slaughtered each other over smaller religious differences than those introduced by Jesus, it is quite possible that some Jews supported his crucifixion. He lived and preached as a Jew among Jews, so his supporters and detractors alike were largely Jewish. Nor would it be astounding to find that some Jews opposed Paul.

But there is no doubt that these scriptural passages made Christians hate Jews, exacerbating tensions that inevitably existed. The role of intellectual and spiritual leaders of the early church in fostering this hatred grew as Christians grew in power. The message of Christianity won far more proselytes than the parallel message of Judaism. Both were abject, non-Roman cults routed from their sanctuaries and driven into exile. But Christians were on the rise as Jews were on the wane. The Jews' old temporal power and political aims were completely destroyed. Christianity was new and had no such power to lose. The Jews had to shift their adaptation from that of a nation-state at the heart of a diaspora to that of a diaspora that had lost its homeland. The Christians had never known power, and their tie to Jerusalem was weaker. Having decided, with Paul, that their main mission was not to the Jews but to the gentiles, they put proselytizing at the center of their program.

The message was good and beautiful. Jesus had been sent to earth by God, his father, to bring the good news of heaven, and he was the living path to the one God. By accepting him, by committing yourself to follow in his footsteps, by seeing that he was the last Paschal lamb—the sacrifice to end all sacrifices—you could know and feel that you were cleansed of sin and shielded from the constant threat of pollution. Not only that, but if you followed in his path, if you just tried to emulate him, you would embody decency and peace.

The subject peoples of Rome desperately needed such a message. It told of a future time beyond pain and tyranny even while teaching people how to live in the here and now. Slaves embraced it because it helped them dream of freedom. Noncitizens embraced it because it taught that in the eyes of God they were equal to—no, better than—the haughty elite of Rome. Women embraced it because it undermined the chauvinism and violence of a thoroughly male-dominated empire. And millions found in it the voice of human kindness and the healing hand of peace.

That was at the beginning, when Christians were still weak. In the meantime, Jews too had some success at proselytizing, but consider the obstacles they faced. Their message was one of peace, but also one of accountability. They too talked of God the Father, but you had to face this father directly, without an intermediary, trembling with awe even while hoping for love. Forgiveness was part of the plan, but only with repentance; faith was not enough. To really experience God's grace you had to learn and carry out 613 commandments, one by one. And of course, you had to study Torah to understand God's will. *We will do and we will hear.*

Then too there was the small matter of circumcision. Abraham—recall the midrash—had hinted to God that this would slow conversions. One can imagine competing proselytizers, as there were in Rome at the time. A Christian shows up on the pagan's doorstep with the good news of eternal love and forgiveness in exchange for a genuine declaration of faith and a promise to be good. A Jew shows up the next day talking about hundreds of commandments, including dietary restrictions, prayer schedules, and Sabbath laws, among many others. And, oh, for the men in the family . . . That *both* groups gained converts speaks volumes about Rome's oppression and about the spiritual bankruptcy of its culture. How good it must have been for these discouraged polytheists, tired of trying to take pride in the empire's power, to encounter on an intimate basis one transcendent, loving God. Whether Jewish or Christian, this new God was the God of the oppressed; Isaiah and Jesus spoke with one voice about the abuse of worldly power, and there was no more abusive power than Rome.

So there were converts to both religions, but in the end there was no contest. As Christians saw it, the message spread because it was true. For Jews, it spread because—although there was certainly risk involved in the early years—Christianity was easier to adopt and practice. It was designed to bring the gentiles to God as quickly and easily as possible. Judaism had evolved, over many centuries, as a culture of one people, conscious of its very special history. The concept of chosen-ness did not prevent conversions—if you converted to Judaism, you too were chosen—but it could be a barrier to inclusiveness. Judaism was a universal religion—one God, for everyone—but its historical ambivalence about conversion and intermarriage made proselytizing more complex.

Christianity embraced the world with a whole, open heart. If you wanted to join, you were in, and your status was automatically as good as that of anyone else. Humility before Christ was the rule, and it created a community of equals. From the sect that was a vigorous but minor branch of persecuted Judaism, Christianity became the largest non-Roman religion in the empire. The followers of Christ were fresh, new, passionate, and open to the world. The Jews were an ancient, insular people, just starting to spread their ideas and ideals. Their customs were complex and seemingly bizarre. Of course, they had risen from the ashes of catastrophe, a history full of sorrow. But still, there *was* the catastrophe. This was a people whose God had failed to save them. Why should others now embrace that God?

As if to seal the outcome, talmudic sages at this time were formulating arguments *against* conversion to Judaism. Christians were on the rise, making converts from the lower classes and among some well-to-do women, until they were five or six million strong—perhaps a tenth of the empire. By the end of the second century, their movement had become *the church,* with its seat in the city of Rome and an administrative system that in some ways resembled imperial aegis over the provinces.[3] And Christian authors, codifying the doctrine of their faith just as the rabbis were codifying the Talmud, were crystal clear in denouncing Jews.

The two communities shared much in common. Through the second century Christian and Jewish tombs show so much overlap in style and symbol that they are sometimes indistinguishable. Christians celebrated Easter exactly on Passover, celebrated the Sabbath on Saturday, and with the Eucharist recalled the kiddush over wine and bread.[4] But John had said that the Jews had Jesus' blood on their hands, and this became the dominant view. While great old Rabbi Akiva was being tortured to death in Caesarea, the Christian preacher Marcion was beginning to canonize the New Testament, declaring Jewish Scripture superseded. Jesus replaced the Temple, love replaced Law, and a *new* chosen people replaced the one God had abandoned. The Jewish Bible was retained as prelude, "the Old Testament," succeeded by something better. More important, the idea of *supersession*— the replacement of Jews by Christians and of Judaism by Christianity— became Christian doctrine. The church was now the spiritual Israel.

໐ນນນ໐

In the year 306 the Western emperor died while putting down a revolt in the primitive outlying province of York in England, and his son Constantine, a strapping, charismatic young man, succeeded him. Challenged in Rome, Constantine gathered his armies and besieged the capital, but his troops were exhausted, dispirited, and very far from home. Then Constantine saw a cross blazing out of the night sky over the Tiber, with the Latin legend *In hoc signo vinces* ("In this sign, conquer"). He rallied his troops and won, and in gratitude converted to Christianity. Army and empire followed.

There had been twenty emperors in fifty years in the mid-third century, and for a time the empire was divided. Amid this chaos Rome's end seemed possible. Constantine's goal was stability, Christianity his strategy. Honoring Jesus, he abolished crucifixion, but taught his soldiers to make a cross by tying their knives to their spears. This vivid gesture signified the transformation of the cross from a symbol of abject pain to one of military power.

By 325 Constantine had absolute power in Rome, and convened all the bishops of the empire to the Council of Nicaea. In this and a subsequent council in 381, the doctrine of Christ as God, and as one with God the Father, was made official, followed by that of crucifixion and Resurrection, together the central beliefs of Christian faith. Church merged with empire, assuming the very pomp and power of the state that had not long before thrown its martyrs to the lions. The bishop of Alexandria said, "The power of the cross of Christ has filled the world."[5]

Of course, where there had been two major persecuted cults, there was now only one. The early church fathers did not mince their words. The fourth-century bishop John Chrysostom, today the patron saint of preachers—his name means "golden mouth"—asked in *Homilies against the Jews,* "Of their rapine, their cupidity, their deception of the poor, of thieveries, and huckstering? Indeed a whole day would not suffice to tell all." Jews are the "most miserable of all men . . . lustful, rapacious, greedy, perfidious bandits . . . inveterate murderers, destroyers, men possessed by the devil. . . . They know only one thing, to satisfy their gullets, get drunk, to kill and maim one another. . . . They are impure and impious. . . . they have surpassed the ferocity of wild beasts, for they murder their offspring and immolate them to the devil."

The synagogue? A place of "shame and ridicule . . . the domicile of the devil . . . an assembly of criminals . . . a cavern of devils, an abyss of perdition." Jewish rites are "criminal and impure," Jewish religion "a disease." The Jews are corrupt because of "their odious assassination of Christ." And the bishop adds the un-Christian sentiment that there is "no expiation possible, no indulgence, no pardon." Their punishment is the wrath of God, who has abandoned them. "Flee, then, their assemblies, flee their houses, and far from venerating the synagogue because of the books it contains, hold it in hatred and aversion for the same reason. . . . I hate the synagogue precisely because it has the law and prophets. . . . I hate the Jews also because they outrage the law."[6] Saint John evidently felt the need to explain that in spite of sharing some of the same Scriptures, Christians and Jews have nothing in common; Christians believed in them, Jews betrayed them. Predictably, sermons from "the golden mouth" provoked many assaults on synagogues and Jews.

By this time the church had gone through its first historic split—the Catholics in Rome and the Eastern Orthodox in Constantinople. Perhaps the Orthodox view of the Jews was different? Saint Gregory, an Eastern church father and a contemporary of Saint John's, offered this litany:

> Slayers of the Lord, murderers of the prophets, adversaries of God, haters of God, men who show contempt for the law, foes of grace, enemies of their fathers' faith, advocates of the devil, brood of vipers, slanderers, scoffers, men whose minds are in darkness, leaven of the Pharisees, assembly of demons, sinners, wicked men, stoners, and haters of righteousness.[7]

Saint Jerome, a bit younger than these two men, was a little more subdued: "The Jews . . . seek nothing but to have children, possess riches, and be healthy. They seek all earthly things but think nothing of heavenly things; for this reason are they mercenaries."[8] Saint Augustine, a better mind and a larger soul, took a more subtle and complex view. In *The City of God* he explained that God dispersed the Jews but did not destroy them so that they would be a permanent reminder of the superseded faith, the supplanted Scriptures that, if properly read, predicted the triumph of Christ. The humiliated, defeated Jews showed just what happens to those who reject God's truth.

Still, Augustine took the hard line of the Gospel of John in his description of what happened to Jesus:

> The Jews held him; the Jews bound him, the Jews insulted him, they crowned him with thorns, dishonored him by spitting upon him, they scourged him, they heaped abuses upon him, they hung him upon a tree, they pierced him with a lance.

But even in his *Treatise against the Jews,* he does not rule out forgiveness:

> Let us preach to the Jews, whenever we can, in a spirit of love.... It is not for us to boast over them as branches broken off.... We shall be able to say to them without exulting over them ... "Come, let us walk in the light of the Lord."[9]

Augustine's view, which became canonical, amounted to three things. First, the Jews should not be exterminated; God left them as a reminder of what happens to those who affront him, however much he once may have loved them. Second, they should be made to see the light and brought into the Christian fold. Third, if this famously stiff-necked people remained resistant to the love of the God they had scourged and crucified, of course they deserved to suffer.

For the Jews of the Roman Empire, this Christian triumphalism changed a precarious but tolerable diaspora into a life on the defensive. Where Roman intellectuals had had a distaste for Jews, Roman *Catholic* intellectuals found reason to hate them. Where Roman rule thought it expedient to let this repugnant tribe pursue its own odd practices, Holy Roman rule thought better. The Jews were no longer just a wart on the body politic, they were a thorn in its side that made a festering sore. To have stupidly and scornfully refused to bow down to Zeus, or to a deified emperor, was bad enough; no one liked a scoffer or an atheist. But to have killed Christ, the Son of God—in effect to have murdered God himself—that was something else again.

Augustine's ideology, the *moderate* voice of the early church, placed the Jews at the heart of the pattern. That such an insignificant people should preoccupy Christians even as they came to dominate Europe has puzzled many. Even if the Jews were guilty of that great crime, even if they deserved to be punished until the seventh generation, it was now the tenth generation or so, and one might think that forgiveness was in order. But the vengeful-ness and victimization grew.

One explanation is a sort of sibling rivalry. The rebellious younger brother, however rich or powerful, cannot get over his anger at being sec-ond. He feels he has something to prove every day. Another is Jewish stub-bornness. Jesus preached to them first, and here, centuries later, when scores of millions of gentiles had seen the light, the Jews still turned their backs on it, hiding from it in their cavelike synagogues. Like Muhammad's followers centuries later, Christians were baffled by that stubbornness. The people whose faith gave rise to theirs, the first people taught by their divine prophets, the people who should have been the first to see and know the truth—these very people were the worst and longest holdouts.

Ultimately the simplest explanation may be that Christianity needed the Jews as a pariah group because the Jews were a living embodiment of their history. But of course, that history had to be vulgar and dismal—oth-erwise why would Jesus have rebelled so strongly against it? Why would the Jews have killed him, if not because they saw that his truth would in-evitably destroy their falsehood? And if this interpretation were wrong, why would God have abandoned them? The Jews bore witness to the dreadful past the Christians had won out over; the Jews' suffering proved their guilt and the wrath of a just God.

All the more reason to look the other way when the Jews suffered. And if good Christians added to their suffering, could that not also be a part of God's plan? It is perhaps the greatest irony of Western history that Jesus, who came to teach forgiveness, inadvertently provoked two millennia of vengeance. Little did he realize that the Pharisees and their followers who debated and ridiculed him would one day be as weak and meek as Isaiah's lambs, and that the Christian wolf, far from lying down with them, would track, stalk, pounce, and devour them—victim by victim, village by village, synagogue by synagogue, again and again and again.

༄༅

And yet, between these ravages, the Jews built a life. An old Yiddish story tells of a boy who doesn't understand the purpose of the Sabbath. An angel takes him on a magic-carpet ride around the world, and he gets to see how people who observe the Sabbath get a respite from work for a time, while others never stop their drudgery. The boy is dazzled by the variety in the world, but also impressed by the consistency of the Sabbath, and by the seeming taste of heaven it affords.

Suppose, in imagination, we too were to travel on a magic carpet and survey the Jewish world in, say, the year 600. Flying first—as befits a magic carpet—over the desert sands of Arabia, we would see scattered communities of Jews in the south, now Yemen, and up through the hill country that parallels the Red Sea, including Mecca and Medina. Crossing the Red Sea to Egypt, we would see more than a dozen Jewish settlements, from Alexandria in the Nile Delta all the way upriver beyond Thebes.[10]

Tracing the Fertile Crescent, we would soar over scores of active synagogues and rabbinical academies in Judea and the Galilee, and others in Syria and Lebanon. But the really dense and wealthy populations of Jews, and the most outstanding academies, we would find by veering east over the Tigris and Euphrates. Even farther east along the Asian trade routes we would still find Jewish communities, in such Persian settlements as Susa, Shiraz, and Isfahan.

Retracing our steps into what is now Turkey, we would see Jews in perhaps fifty towns, including Rhodes, Cos, Smyrna, Antioch, Byzantium, and many others. Across the Black Sea in Russia we would glimpse a few settlements along the northern shore, and many more in Greece and the Balkans—Athens, Corinth, Salonika, Sofia, and Sarajevo, to name a few. Italian Jewish communities would be almost as dense and numerous as those in the Holy Land—a legacy of the emigration to Rome, willing and otherwise, but now extending as far north as Milan, Genoa, Ferrara, and Verona.

We would then fly over a number of settlements in Germany (Regensburg, Metz, and Cologne, among others), more in France (Paris—then called Lutetia—Nantes, Bordeaux, Agde, Arles, and Marseilles), and quite a few in Spanish towns like Toledo, Córdoba, Granada, and Valencia. Finally, turning south past Gibraltar, we would begin to pass towns with Jewish neighborhoods dotting the north African coast from Morocco to Libya and back into Egypt.

In all these far-flung places people would have rested on the Sabbath and convened in synagogues or homes to read the Torah and chant the liturgy. Children would have gone to school to learn to read it themselves. Women would have immersed themselves monthly in the ritual bath, and men would have circumcised their eight-day-old sons. They would have avoided pork and shellfish as if their lives depended on it, and kept milk and meat products separate and pure. They would have followed to the hour the ancient calendar of festivals set by the rabbis in Israel. They would have looked to Babylon and the Galilee for the guidance of Torah scholars. And all of them would have prayed toward Jerusalem—at Shiraz turning west, at Mecca north, at Byzantium south, at Rome east—the ancient point of contact with their transcendent, universal, deeply personal God.

In other words, Jews. If we could listen in, we would hear them arguing with that God, and with each other, about what God meant. We would find them exquisitely conscious of their history, their suffering, trying to read God's will into every political event, realizing that they were still, now, *making* history. And on Saturday evening, after they found three stars twinkling in the darkening dusk, we would find them ritually bidding the Sabbath good-bye, as reluctantly and longingly as if they were taking leave of God himself.

But they weren't, not for a moment. God was thanked in dozens of blessings a day and obeyed in scores of mitzvot. The first words of the morning prayer, "How goodly are thy tents, O Jacob!" recalled the man who wrestled with God and won. The fringed garment they draped over themselves and the small leather boxes they strapped to their arms and foreheads met obligations described in the scroll Josiah discovered thirteen hundred years before. They touched the mezuzah on the doorpost, containing words that Ezra had read from the Torah before the people. At meals they blessed God for bringing forth bread from the earth and fruit from the tree. And in the evening prayer they remembered Isaac, who used to go out in the field to meditate in the dusk.

In Israel we would have found a population in slow decline but still attending the synagogues and academies. The office of the *nasi,* or rabbinical prince, had been abolished, and the ruling power was Byzantium—now Greece and Turkey—the eastern branch of the Roman Empire and Church. The political situation would change drastically, but for the moment it was calm. The majority in Israel were Christian because of the church's determined colonization of the Holy Land after Constantine. Strong measures prevented conversion to Judaism and encouraged the reverse. Only the area around the Sea of Galilee and west of it—including Nazareth—stayed Jewish.[11]

Agriculture remained the main livelihood, and the numerous presses found by archeologists attest to still vigorous oil and wine industries. Fishermen still sailed the Sea of Galilee, and trading boats traversed it. Mediterranean commerce and the Far Eastern trade routes were less important than they had been.[12] Most people lived in two-story mud-brick houses in villages of two to five thousand. One found in Kazrin—in the Golan, north of the sea—had indoor and outdoor courtyards, a kitchen with a large oven and a chimney, three outdoor ovens, a sizable living and dining room, a small storeroom, and beds on the upper floor.[13] Taxes supported synagogues, bought Torah scrolls, and paid market inspectors, synagogue sextons, and schoolteachers.

Roman law forbade the building of new synagogues, but some were built anyway, and many older ones remained standing. The Talmud advised scholars to live only in towns that boasted "a prayer-house, a bathhouse, lavatories, a physician, a barber, a scribe, and a teacher of children," as well as five officials to carry out court judgments and five more to collect and distribute charity.[14] Korazim, near Galilee's north shore, appears to have qualified. The main road had a large synagogue on an open plaza, a ritual bath, an oil press, and homes in all directions from these centers. The ongoing discussion of the completed Jerusalem Talmud was the daily work of the Tiberias academy, always in consultation with the Babylonian rabbis. The Law, or *halakhah*—"the way," from the Hebrew verb "go"—was not set in stone, but basic observances were clear. Scholarship was still strong, but by 600 there was political unrest in the eastern empire, and messianic visions had reemerged in the Galilee.[15]

The more ambitious Babylonian Talmud had been completed, and the Law flowed more from the Tigris and Euphrates than from the Jordan. Passing over them, we would find the two great yeshivas of Sura and Pumbedita producing the first post-talmudic rabbinical leaders. They and their students would carry rabbinic Judaism throughout the world, but because the heads of yeshivas were political at this time, few were really great rabbis. Still, thousands still converged on Babylonia for a month of study in early spring and late summer, and these convocations were engines of dissemination of the Law. Questions about exact observance flowed toward Sura and Pumbedita, and responses flowed outward, constantly interpreting the Talmud to preserve the Law in changing conditions. Some diaspora money supported the academies, but most of it came from Babylonian Jewish taxes and real estate. These yeshivas would last four more centuries.

In Arabia we would have found settled tribes of Jewish farmers and craftsmen mingled with the recently ascendant Arab tribes. Jews were influential enough so that they had briefly had, in a sense, their own shared kingdom—Himyar, in what is now Yemen.[16] Himyar was not exactly Jewish, but its Arab elite was tightly allied with Jews. Under their influence—this was *pre*-Islam—Himyar had adopted a clear and unusual monotheism, worshiping one God, "the Merciful One." Himyar had conflicts with Christians and was conquered during the 500s by Christian Ethiopians and then by Persians. But inscriptions show that its pre-Islamic Arab monotheism continued.

Farther north along the Red Sea would be Jews (among others) in a band stretching from Mecca and Medina, through Petra in what is now Jordan, to the Galilee, and on into Syria and Lebanon. In Byzantium, Roman power persisted long after it had waned in Rome, and in effect Byzantium became *the* Roman Empire. The church was very powerful, but the culture remained Greek. In the many synagogues, Jews read the Torah in Greek translation. After the Sabbath, they took up their roles as silk producers, weavers, dyers, tanners—especially in Constantinople, the capital—and other kinds of artisans. But they were kept on society's margins, and conversion was strongly encouraged. There were occasional outbreaks of hostility and persecution instigated by the Orthodox Church—recall Saint

Gregory. As the year 600 approached, Jews were expelled from Antioch and there were anti-Jewish riots in Turkey and Syria. But on the whole, Judaism was more tolerated than in the Roman Catholic West.

Spain, for example—it then included the French towns of Narbonne, Agde, and Béziers—had been ruled for two centuries by the Visigoths. In 600 they had recently become Catholic and were enacting stringent anti-Jewish laws,[17] forbidding them to hold office or hire Christians. Many were forced to convert, yet former Jews were persecuted as Jews. Execution, enslavement, and pulling out of the hair were among the punishments for backsliders.[18] Pope Gregory I supported this program, having himself issued a papal bull that would define the church's relations with Jews for centuries.

But Gregory set limits on persecution, and his actions, particularly in Italy itself, reveal much about Jewish life.[19] In 591 the bishop of Terracina, south of Rome, expelled the Jews from their synagogue for disturbing Christians with Jewish prayers. Gregory ordered an investigation, saying that if the expulsion had indeed occurred, the Jews would have to be given an alternative site for worship. In 598 the bishop of Palermo closed the synagogues and study houses, turning them into churches, but Gregory censured him and ordered him to pay compensation. In Sardinia, a Jewish convert to Christianity desecrated a synagogue; Gregory censured him as well and ordered the crosses removed. In Naples he ordered punishment for Christian zealots who harassed Jews at worship.

On the other hand, he strongly supported "voluntary" conversion, in one instance ordering a group of Sicilian Jews to be baptized immediately and given financial aid before they had time to change their minds. He also supported the severe measures taken against the Jews in more distant locales, like the Spain of the Visigoths. He wanted to convert the Jews voluntarily if possible, but at least to preserve the status quo. This meant no new synagogues, study houses, or other centers of Jewish life.

Moving north, we would find small Jewish communities scattered through France and Germany, living under a similar shadow of grudging, precarious tolerance; still, they lived. There were Jewish merchants in Dijon, Orléans, and other towns north of the Loire. Nearby Troyes was not yet settled by Jews, but in another half millennium it would produce one of the greatest of all rabbis—Rashi, the brilliant Torah commentator whose strange script and striking insights are still studied by every Orthodox Jewish child. Paris was not yet Paris, just an island in the Seine settled by a tribe called the Lutetians, but we have evidence that there were Jews among them.

Finally, still farther north, in the towns between the Meuse and the Rhine, we would have seen tiny settlements that in a far-off future would come to define the dominant culture of the European Jews, and then of most Jews throughout the world. This was Ashkenaz, a Hebrew name that may have been a mistake based on a coincidence—the similarity of "Germania" to "Germanikia," a town in northwestern Syria associated with the biblical and talmudic figure Ashkenaz, son of Gomer.[20] Some scholars hear a similarity between "Ashkenaz" and "Saxons," soon to be the predominant local Germanic tribe. Still others hear a connection to "Scandza" or "Scanzia"—Scandinavia.

Whatever its origin, the word stuck, and soon became the name for the Jews of the Frankish kingdom. For a time the scholars of Regensburg were known as "rabbis of the Rhine," but the common name was Ashkenaz. Consonant with its location in conservative northern Europe, the community was very focused on Torah and Talmud, not noted for the creativity shown by Mediterranean Jews in poetry, art, and mysticism. They would also be known for strictness. Earlier than the Jews of Israel or Babylonia, they had insisted on monogamy. They developed their own method of Torah interpretation, a structure for community autonomy, a distinctive script, and a style of manuscript illumination.

In time they developed a language, a type of Old High German, written in Hebrew characters. It would eventually diverge from the path to modern German, devouring great chunks of Hebrew, Slavic languages, Hungarian, Romanian, even English. But in the year 600 it was just Judeo-German, the patois of small groups of Jews selling luxury goods from the storied, exotic East to the mundane working towns along the Rhine.

The Hebrew poetry of this period was mainly liturgical: requests, laments, and hymns of praise.[21] The poems were called *piyyut* (plural *piyyutim*) from the same Greek root as "poetry." Many originated in Israel itself, were anonymous, and survived as prayers. Form governed and helped to motivate the poems; some had pairs of rhyming lines, each line containing two phrases, each phrase two words. Many were alphabetic acrostics, each line beginning with a successive letter through the Hebrew alphabet, forward or backward.

Moods vary dramatically in these poems. Recall the dirge commemorating the destruction of the Temple, in which all the animals of the zodiac weep—a lament of and for all creation. Ashkenazic Jews still recite it on the Ninth of Av, a fast day on the traditional anniversary of the catastrophe:

> *How long will there be tears in Zion and grieving in Jerusalem?*
> *Take pity on Zion and rebuild the walls of Jerusalem!*

Another *piyyut,* begging for mercy in judgment, is still sung on Yom Kippur, the Day of Atonement.

Then a long ram's horn will wail,
and a soft, gentle voice be heard;
angels will hasten sick and trembling . . .
for in your eyes even they cannot escape judgment. . . .

On New Year's Day it is set down,
on the Fast-Day of Atonement, sealed . . .
who will live and who will die . . .
who by water and who by fire,
who by sword and who by beast,
who by earthquake and who by plague,
who will rest and who stagger,
who will be calm and who harassed,
who will take comfort and who suffer,
who will be raised and who lowered,
who will grow rich, and who poor.

But contrition, prayer, and decency
deflect the bad decree. . . .
For You know their nature:
That they are flesh and blood;
man comes from dust
and goes to dust,
gets food at the risk of his life.
He is like shards of pottery,
like withering grass and fading flowers,
like a fleeting shadow and a driven cloud,
like a puff of wind, like vanishing dust,
like a dream that wafts away.

Another *piyyut,* a prayer for rain, so vital to these farmers, moves from praise . . .

You are pure, untouched by sin,
You are alive, untouched by death,
acquit us for your sake, revive us,
and let us see plentiful water . . .

to reminder . . .

You have no other people like us,
we have no other God like you,

through mystical darkening . . .

> *Your path is in flames of fire,*
> *Your dwelling in streams of water,*
> *You are sanctified by myriad fires . . .*

back to praise and supplication . . .

> *Angels crown You,*
> *princes enthrone You.*
> *Reign in Zion soon,*
> *that we celebrate spring rain.*

But one of the loveliest lyrics bids good-bye to the rain, in a hymn to spring itself:

> *I sing hymns with nightingales,*
> *answering in song:*
> Rain, go in peace. . . .
> *Rain is done, winter past,*
> *and all is kept in beauty:*
> Rain, go in peace.
> *Mandrakes scent the lovers' realm,*
> *and sorrowing is over:*
> Dew, come in peace.
> *Earth's diadem of grain and new wine,*
> *Makes all creation cry out:*
> Rain, go in peace.[22]

Such hymns and prayers were nourished in Israel's soil. Yet as the power of its rabbis waned, it was feared that they would cease to tell the Jewish world when to celebrate its festivals, following the seasons of the Holy Land itself. Since the Jewish calendar was lunar and the rest of the world's solar, this involved some intricate calculations. But as the Jews became more and more far-flung, it seemed wise to set the calendar, accepting the reality of diaspora. This had been done in the fourth century, and the festivals were now predictable without help from the Holy Land. As the poem said, the year began with ten days of repentance, the first being Rosh Hashanah— "the Head of the Year," or New Year's Day—and the tenth being Yom Kippur, the Day of Atonement, both marked with the blast of the ram's horn.

Rosh Hashanah—the first day of Creation and the birthday of the world—was also the day Ezra first read the scroll of the law in rebuilt Jerusalem, and so it has been read ever since, but for two days, not one. Traditionally, the story of Abraham's near-sacrifice of Isaac is one of the Torah texts read. God's salvation is petitioned as a hundred blasts of the ram's horn wake up sinners. It may not be coincidence that Libra is the zodiac sign Rosh Hashanah occurs in, as the balances of justice tilt in God's hand. And bread is cast on flowing water in the late afternoon, an attempt to cast off sin.

But sin was not so easily unloaded. On Yom Kippur Jews denied themselves food, drink, bathing, anointing, sex—the essences of life—dwelling instead on death. As an added memento mori, they prayed in the very shroud they would one day be buried in. Yet it is said that in ancient Israel young women, also dressed in white, danced in the fields in the afternoon, watched by young men trying to find brides. Perhaps this purest day of the year could take courting out of the carnal realm. Then and now *t'shuva*—returning—was the main theme of the day, so the Book of Jonah was read: the tale of a man who returns to God from the very depths in the belly of a whale. Five days after Yom Kippur, at the full moon of Tishri, the Festival of Booths, or Sukkot, began. It lasted eight days, and the ninth was Simchat Torah, the Rejoicing of the Law. On this day men danced with the Torah, celebrating the completion of the annual reading—one portion per Sabbath—followed by its careful rolling back to begin again "In the beginning. . . ."

About two months later, on the twenty-sixth of Kislev, the Chanukah festival began, commemorating the initial victory of the Maccabees and the miracle of the Temple lamp. This was the only Jewish festival other than Rosh Hashanah that occurred at the new moon, and it is no accident that it is known as the Festival of Lights. The new moon comes near the middle of the eight days and nights, and it is almost always the one closest to the winter solstice, making these the eight darkest nights of the year. The lighting of candles, as in many festivals around the world at that time of year, partakes a bit of the ancient pagan protest against the dark and cold of winter, the magical anticipatory invocation of spring.

Intriguingly, one of the things those great rabbinical rivals Hillel and Shammai had debated centuries earlier was whether to go from one candle on the first night to eight on the last, or vice versa. Shammai logically pointed out that going from eight to one would correspond to what happened in the Temple as the oil burned out, lasting for eight miraculous days and nights instead of one. Hillel, always more compassionate, argued that people needed the hope offered by waxing instead of waning light. Hillel's humane stance became law.

Over the next two months there is just one minor holiday, Tu B'Shvat, the "New Year" of the Trees. "Tu" is the alphabetic version of the date, the fifteenth of Shvat; like most agricultural festivals, it is close to the full moon. There is an obligation to plant trees on this date, a planting time in the Land of Israel. One of the rabbis of the Mishnah said that if you are in the midst of planting a tree when you hear that the Messiah has arrived, you should finish the planting first and *then* go meet the Messiah.

Now the architects of the calendar did something really interesting. Since twelve lunar months do not make 365 days—the lunar year is about 11 days short—the difference must be made up with leap years. Otherwise the lunar calendar will drift behind the changes of the seasons, something Muslims allow but Jews do not. However, these leap years do not add just a day but a whole month every second or third year. Seven lunar leap years out of every nineteen mostly synchronize the patterns, so that your lunar birthday coincides with your solar one when you are nineteen, thirty-eight, fifty-seven, and so on.

Given the complexity, it is not surprising that for centuries the High Priests, and then the great rabbis, of Jerusalem met regularly to adjust the calendar. After a highly secretive process they informed the people when to observe the Sabbath and the festivals. But as rabbinical authority shifted to Babylon, the progression of leap years was permanently fixed. Still, astronomical subtleties required ongoing adjustments, and the exact present form of the calendar was achieved in the tenth century.

But for practical purposes it was done by the time of our journey. Jews the world over knew long in advance when a leap year would come, and inserted a second month of Adar in late winter, so that the next holiday would occur in early spring. This was Purim, the festival celebrating one of the happiest and most romantic stories in Jewish tradition. Esther, chosen queen of Persia by a restive, grumbly emperor, has the chance—by virtue of this secret intermarriage—to save the Jews of Persia from a plot to kill them all. She must risk her life, but with the help of her uncle Mordecai, Esther saves the day, and the enemies of the Jews are brought low. Purim occurred at the full moon of Adar, or in the case of a leap year, Adar Bet. It was the only holiday commemorating a diaspora event, and although it was a minor—post-Torah—festival, it was cherished by diaspora Jews. The scroll of Esther was read in the synagogue. People came in costume, and children with noisemakers and stamping feet made a racket every time the name of the villain, Haman, was mentioned. Drinking was encouraged as an aid to merriment, and one rabbi held that you should get drunk enough to mix up Haman and Mordecai.

At the full moon of the next month, Nisan—the first month of spring—Passover begins. This core festival was commanded in the Torah, celebrating the Exodus from slavery in Egypt. Three millennia later, in the 1980s, studies showed it to be the most observed holiday by Jews in both the United States and the Soviet Union. But it was always loved by Jews, religious or not. It was the ultimate liberation, the God-guided transformation of a pathetic mass of slaves into the people Israel.

Also, Passover was celebrated mainly in the home, not the synagogue. Spring cleaning purified the house of leavened bread, which the Israelites did not have time to bake in the desert, and for eight days the only bread eaten was matzo, a flat, crunchy, crackerlike bread baked without yeast in eighteen minutes or less from the moment water is mixed with flour. On the first night in Israel, or the first two nights in the diaspora—outside of Israel you couldn't be sure of precisely observing the right twenty-four hours—seders were held in the home. *Seder* means "order," and in the course of it the story of the Exodus was systematically told. The home became a place of worship, but with an intimacy impossible in the synagogue. This made it one of the most cherished rituals from the time of the Second Temple at least. Today even some Christians are embracing it, as the Jewishness of Jesus—the Last Supper was a seder—increasingly engages them.

On Passover one of the most distinctively agricultural customs begins: the Counting of the Omer. This daily ritual counts the seven weeks to Shavuot, the Feast of Weeks. This, in ancient Israel, was the time of the barley harvest, and the first sheaf—*omer*—of barley was brought as a sacrifice in the Temple on the first day of the seven weeks. On the thirty-third day of the Omer—literally Lag B'Omer—a minor holiday was devoted to Torah study, characterized by a happy mood in which children played outdoors with bows and arrows. It commemorated the initial successes of the Bar Kokhba rebellion, when Akiva and other sages taught their soldier-students in the countryside.

On the fiftieth day of the count, under the waxing moon of Sivan, Shavuot arrived, marking the end of the barley harvest and traditionally celebrated with flowers. More important, it commemorated the giving of the Torah on Mount Sinai. This was the goal and meaning of the Exodus: God chose this people, freed them, and brought them into the desert to give them his Law. As we have seen, legend has it that God offered it to all the other peoples of the world first, but they demanded to know its contents, while the Hebrews *(Fools rush in?)* said, "We will do and we will hear"—obey first and ask questions later. This seems a pretty weak form of chosenness, but it *is* the stuff of legend. It became customary to study all night on Shavuot, and to start teaching children the *aleph-bet* at some time during the holiday.

In each of the next two months there were fast days. The first, in Tammuz, marked the siege of Jerusalem, and the second, Tisha B'Av—the ninth of Av—mourned the destruction of both Temples, which by tradition occurred on the same day centuries apart. The biblical book of Lamentations was read, an exquisite paean to the grief and suffering of the first Babylonian exile. The year's last month, Elul, was devoted to repentance, in preparation for Rosh Hashanah, the nine days of purification, and the awesome Day of Atonement. This ended the annual cycle and began it all again.

More frequent recurring events were no less important. Every month the new moon was blessed, probably in an extension of ancient, pre-Torah Israelite ritual. But Jews made this pagan rite their own, identifying as a people with the moon's constant renewal: "He ordered the moon to renew itself as a gracious crown over those whom he sustained from birth, who likewise will be reborn in the future." The word for "month" shares its root with the word for "new," so renewal is close to the heart of moon-ness. As in many cultures, the new moon was especially sacred to women, and the waxing moon was considered good luck.

At least as important as any festival was Shabbat, Shabbes, the Sabbath, when "all manner of work" ceased, just as God rested from the six long days of Creation. Only Yom Kippur, the "Sabbath of Sabbaths," was deemed more holy than this weekly taste of heaven. The Friday evening dusk was greeted as an arriving queen, and the meal following it was a sacred, joyful family feast, complete with singing, prayer, and the gift of hospitality. Sex between husband and wife was encouraged and blessed. Prayer and Torah reading in the synagogue in the morning was followed by another festive meal, rest, visiting, and study. And the Sabbath's departure at dusk was marked with the rite of Havdalah, separation: the singing of a plaintive scriptural hymn by the light of a braided candle, the taking of a glass of wine, and the smelling of fragrant spices. The newly lit flame, forbidden for twenty-four hours, inaugurated the week of work, while the wine and spices revived the dejected, Sabbath-leaving soul.

⚭

Of course, the year itself had to be numbered, and this was done by reckoning backward through the Bible, adding up the begats of Genesis all the way to the Creation. On this account the world was 3,760 years old at the start of the Common Era. So the Jewish year was just that far ahead of what Christians called the year of the Lord 1040, or 4800, when Rashi was born. Two generations earlier, Christian Europe had been obsessed with the then-approaching millennium, sure of assorted blends of apocalypse and redemption. Two generations later they would create their own apocalypse, at least from the viewpoint of their non-Christian neighbors, in the form of the First Crusade. But at this moment Europe was relatively quiet, and the vindictiveness of Christians toward the seed of the "killers of Christ" was at low tide.

Rashi was born in Troyes, then the capital of Champagne. It was a center for the production of leather goods—parchment included—and a junction of international trade.[23] His maternal uncle wrote prayers and hymns, and his father excelled as a scholar. According to one legend, his mother, pregnant with Rashi, was in mortal danger in a narrow street of the city, and when she pressed herself against a wall, it magically opened a niche where she took refuge. According to another, his father had a jewel that Christians wanted for idolatry, and rather than give it up to them he cast it into the sea, whereupon a voice from heaven foretold the birth of a son whose wisdom would light the world. Righteous parents, an annunciation, a miraculous pregnancy, a child saved from danger—these are themes struck in cultures throughout the world as suffering people relate the birth of a hero.

Growing up in a commercial town in a lush rural region, he understood farming and husbandry as well as trade, banking, and currency. He showed this knowledge in his commentaries, along with crafts like engraving, soldering, weaving, sewing figures into cloth, and embroidering silk with gold. But his magnificent obsession was Torah learning. He was educated in Troyes according to the methods created centuries earlier in Israel and Babylon. When he exhausted his hometown's intellectual resources, he went north to study in Mainz and Worms—Ashkenaz—where the greatest academies in northern Europe then were. He returned home to teach at around age twenty-five, maintaining contact with his German-Jewish masters; he even paid them visits to discuss difficult points of Law. But under his leadership, even before the Crusade, the intellectual center of Ashkenazic Judaism shifted to northern France.

He taught constantly, saying, "We must endeavor to teach even the unintelligent,"[24] and "He who rears his son to be righteous is like an immortal."[25] But this was scarcely a one-sided enterprise, since "Teachers learn from their students' discussions." To students he said, "Be sure to ask your teacher his reasons and his sources"[26] and "Study in joy and good cheer, in accordance with your intelligence and heart's dictates."[27] Like Hillel, he rejected extreme strictness: "It is better to listen to one who is lenient and permits, since anyone can be strict and forbid,"[28] he said, suggesting that leniency demands subtler understanding.

Perhaps it is characteristically Jewish to have a hero who gives his life to interpretation. With great erudition Rashi combined literal reading with that of the midrash, the rabbinic interpretations going back to Mishnah times.[29] He said, "He who meditates over words of the Torah finds ever new meanings in them."[30] For example, in his commentary on Genesis, he points out that Noah walked "with God," showing his willingness to obey, but Abraham walked "before God," showing his independent righteousness. Rashi avoided abstract philosophy, which was central for Spanish Jews but unimportant in Ashkenaz. His style was terse and clear. He readily admitted mistakes; he often wrote, "I do not know what it is." But he also wrote with a tone of unmistakable authority, and this gave students confidence, an anchor in the sea of alternative explanations. Still, he embraced controversy, saying, "A struggle that revolves about the Book ends in love."[31] Rashi's Torah commentary was widely read from the outset. His Talmud commentary replaced all prior ones; it would be in the first printed Talmud and every subsequent one.[32]

Rashi once healed a monk free of charge, saying, "Divided as we may be by religion, we are united by charity."[33] He also believed that "Gentiles of the present age are not heathens."[34] But throughout his life the storm that Jews would call the Unholy Crusades was gathering. There were episodes of local persecution and banishment, even though Rashi's life coincided with an expansion of Ashkenazic Jewry. Mainz, Speyer, Worms, Cologne, Trier, and Metz all had Jewish communities. The Jews of Mainz had been temporarily expelled in 1014 because a bishop converted to Judaism, and there were forced conversions *from* Judaism at various times and places. But on the whole the Jews were protected by bishops and feudal princes, who valued their international mercantile experience, taxed them heavily, and welcomed their lavish gifts. They were often segregated for their own protection and with their consent; in some cities they *asked* for a wall to be built around their neighborhood, shielding them from rioters.

But the church had become steadily more militant, and some orders of monks merged with orders of knights. The ideology of holy war was being taught and was growing. For a time sacred violence was directed against other Christian knights, but since traditional anti-Semitic sermonizing continued, there were spillovers of violence as unruly mobs led by knights in armor moved against Jews. The mood and attitude of the Jewish response is conveyed by this hymn composed in Mainz in the late tenth century, saying that knights

> *Have their fortresses on craggy peaks . . .*
> *Where shields are densely placed*
> *And cuirass and helmet interlaced . . .*
> *Emblems limned and blazoned forth.*
> *They battle with the flashing sword . . .*
> *With gold and silver richly wrought . . .*
> *The horsemen and their neighing steeds . . .*
> *And arrows notched against the string . . .*
> *While we pray to Almighty God,*
> *Who maketh wars to cease.*[35]

So the God of Israel, once mighty in battle on the side of Hebrew warriors, became for the mild, studious Jews of Ashkenaz the God "Who maketh wars to cease."

But even God could not keep this peace. By the time Rashi was fifty the tenuous balance had broken down all over Europe. Official Christian interest in the Holy Land had been growing since Constantine, and preaching against infidels had reached a fever pitch. It was clear to the bishops that sacred rage should be turned against Islam—now a religious worldly power if anything stronger than Christianity—and not be allowed to cause Christian fraternal strife. In 1095 Pope Urban II, then at Clermont in France, called for a Crusade. No kings or princes joined, but knights and feudal dignitaries mobilized masses of common people, provoking a twelfth-century Jewish historian to cite a passage in Proverbs: "The locusts have no king, but go forth all of them together in bands."[36]

The bands were too hungry for crops of infidels to wait till they reached Jerusalem, so they turned along the way to more convenient harvests. Riots struck Rouen first; Crusaders under Volkmar herded the Jews into a synagogue and murdered all who refused to convert. After that France was largely spared, as Volkmar went on to Cologne and then to Prague; he forcibly baptized some, and many others committed suicide or submitted to slaughter to avoid apostasy.

But it was the Rhine valley towns that became the principal objects of this sideshow of sacred Christian rage. Crusaders under William of Melun attacked the Jews in one town after another. Now, there were righteous gentiles even among the bishops and lords who tried to warn and protect the Jews. Most of the Jews of Speyer were saved by Bishop Johann, who sheltered them in his palace. But the Jews of Mainz were not so lucky; many committed suicide as William and his colleague Count Emich were about to baptize them. The holy warriors went on to Würzburg, where 1,100 Jews were killed or committed suicide. In Worms, 800 Jews were massacred in the bishop's palace where they had taken refuge. The Jewish communities of Nürnberg, Regensburg, and probably Cologne suffered similar fates.

With the murders of the Jews of Mainz and Worms, including many scholars, the great academies of Ashkenaz where Rashi had studied were no more, and spiritual leadership for the Jews of the region moved decisively to northern France. Rashi, in keeping with his lifelong devotion to the Torah, was so shocked by these events that he seemed almost to skirt idolatry by composing a beautiful hymn not to God but to the Torah itself, calling on it to intercede with God on behalf of the Jewish people. It is as if he felt, in the wake of this near-genocidal slaughter, an un-Jewish need for an intermediary between himself and God; as if I and Thou had become too awesome a relationship. Or as if, perhaps, a certain mistrust had been introduced.

He almost threatens the personified Torah, warning it not to fail, because "if there be no Israel thy praises to sing, thou art indeed silenced in every mouth and throat." He envisions the Torah as a mother grieving for her children: "Approach in entreaty . . . garbed in black like a widow, demand redress for thy saintly ones . . . at the hands of those who cut down thy students and ripped thy parchment sheets . . . and in their torrential rage destroyed thy habitations." He wants the Torah, not the Crusaders, to win out "in the Holy Land, explain thy lovely words for men to understand, expel . . . the arrogant in blazing wrath, while the offspring of the pious, scholars and students, engage in constant studies there."[37] It is a sweet vision for a scholar, the end of days, but not in war and blood; in ink, on parchment, disclosing the word of God.

Could it be that Rashi addresses the Torah because he is too angry at God? Yet we know that this is a whole nation of God wrestlers, heirs of Jacob, who said to the angel, "I will not let thee go, except thou bless me," and of Abraham, who at Sodom and Gomorrah took it on himself to teach God about justice. So it is not surprising that we have, from some time between the ninth and eleventh centuries, this stunning Hebrew poem, "The Poet's Commandments to God":

> *Thou shalt not ignore the one who cries to Thee from his heart.*
> *Thou shalt not despise the wretch who begs for mercy.*
> *Thou shalt not scorn the lowly poor before Thee.*
> *Thou shalt not drive Thy creature off empty-handed.*
> *Thou shalt not grieve or shame his sin and guilt.*
> *Thou shalt not rage at him when he repents his ways.*
> *Thou shalt not remember his youthful, secret sins.*
> *Thou shalt not demand a pledge to remit his sins.*
> *Thou shalt not banish him who strays but take him back.*
> *Thou shalt not chide him in Thy rage but heal his pain.*
> *Thou shalt not crush the rebel who returns from his way.*
> *Thou shalt not oppress him or repay his evil deeds.*
> *Thou shalt not rage at thy people for generations.*
> *Thou shalt not forsake them, for their suffering is great.*
> *Thou shalt not deliver them always into their enemies' hand.*
> *Thou shalt not leave Thy holy place to void and ruin.*
> *Thou shalt not hurt Thy holy name and let it be profaned.*
> *Thou shalt not shame Thy hope in Israel, who draw near Thee.*
> *Thou shalt not scorn my plea when I stand poor before you.*
> *Thou shalt not recoil from me, my Rock, my God, my refuge.*
> *Thou shalt not forget my trouble, for who can weigh my shame.*
> *Thou shalt not hide when I beg: let my sighs come before Thee![38]*

You could say that this was rank arrogance, yet in essence it merely calls God back to the covenant. But God was not always faithful to these commandments, just as the Jewish people were not always faithful to God's.

7

UNDER THE MINARET

HOW ISLAM (PARTLY) TOLERATED THE JEWS

On the island of Djerba, off the southeast coast of Tunisia, lives a community of Jews who have changed their culture little for perhaps twenty-five hundred years.[1] Some believe that Djerban Jewish life began right after the First Temple's destruction, at the time of the Babylonian exile. The restored Ghriba—"marvelous"—Synagogue, said to be built around fragments from the Temple, attracts thousands of Jewish pilgrims on Lag B'Omer, the spring holiday that commemorates the Jewish rebellion against Rome. This points to another possibility, that the colony was established after the *Second* Temple fell; in this view, some Berbers converted to Judaism, and today's Djerban Jews descend from the union of both peoples.

In any case, the Jews are hard to tell apart from their Muslim neighbors. Men wear calf-length robes or capes in varied subdued colors, scarves draped around their necks or wrapped around their heads, slip-on shoes or sandals, and red, fezlike caps. Under their robes, their trousers are hemmed with a black band, mourning the Temple. Women dress more colorfully, with brightly hued dresses and long black braids poking through their caps or head scarves. Like many Djerban Arabs, some Jews practice the ancient crafts of gold- and silversmithing, but in addition to crafting jewelry they make adornments for the Torah.

Today bicycles vie with pedestrians, sheep, and one-horse buggies on the unpaved streets. Architecture is in the classic North African style: adjoining houses with smooth white facades of plastered stone broken by pretty, fading, blue-painted doors and shutters. Outside, in front of these doors, women pursue homemaking arts, some little changed since biblical times. A man brings a basket of vegetables from market and gives them to his wife and mother. With a little girl sitting and watching, the women clean and slice the carrots, squash, turnips, and greens on straw mats. Then they begin cooking, on ancient fires, in modern pans. In front of another home, two women chat in Judeo-Arabic. One weaves with a hand shuttle on a laptop loom while the other winds sheepskin thread. A third, older but festively dressed, wears silver Star of David earrings dangling among her braids. A pregnant woman mops the street, her husband bringing her pails of water, and a tiny boy, pulling his trousers up, wades uncertainly, ankle-deep in the puddle.

The rabbi, a round-faced, smiling, dignified man, negotiates the wet streets talking with a companion. He arrives to ritually slaughter a chicken, checks the blade of the knife for perfect sharpness, and cuts the bird's throat, inverting it to drip the blood downward. Not far away, a man in his mid-sixties in a red fez plays the *oud*—our word *lute* comes from *al oud*—while a dark-eyed boy looks on intently.

In everyday life one has to listen and look closely to tell them from their Muslim neighbors. Their unique Arabic, peppered with Hebrew and Aramaic words. The black stripe on the trousers. The Star of David earrings. The meticulous kosher slaughter. But in the religious sphere, there is no mistaking who is who. Men go to synagogue three times a day. At the morning service, they put on tefillin, the black leather boxes that hold the words of the Shema, fulfilling the commandment to place them as "a sign upon the hand" and "frontlets between the eyes." All slip their shoes off to pray. Later, most disperse to secular jobs, but some pursue religious crafts. A scribe copies texts by hand; a printer hand-sets ancient Hebrew in metal type.

Schoolchildren study Arabic, French, and other secular subjects, but when school lets out they go to a smaller religious school to study Torah. A beautiful boy with red lips and immense black eyes reads the first passages of B'reshit, Genesis. *"Vayehi mavdil ben mayim lamayim. Vaya'as Elohim et harakiya. . . ."*—"And let it divide water from water. And God made the firmament. . . ."

On Friday a woman makes bread and ornate pastries and sets the table for the Sabbath meal. The shofar, a ram's horn, sounds its plaintive clarion, heralding Shabbat. Ten minutes later it sounds again, and Shabbat begins. The woman covers the set table—bread, meal, and all—with a white cloth, places two candles on top of the mound, lights them, and makes the blessing. She kisses a nearby mezuzah, moves the candles without disturbing the flames, and at last removes the cloth, presenting the meal for her family.

The following morning, people gather in the synagogue, El Ghriba. Shoes crowd a corner. Walls are lined with tiles hand-painted in bold colors, and turquoise pillars prop the ceiling. Men recite the liturgy and read from the Torah. They remove it from the Ark, kiss it, and carry it lovingly around among the worshipers. Finally they uncover it and lay it down on the raised wooden *bima,* the central platform. They unroll it a bit, and—distancing themselves respectfully from the handwritten parchment with a silver pointer tipped with a tiny hand—they intone, in eerie beauty, the ancient story of their people and recite its laws.

☙〰〰❧

Jewish communities dotted the Middle East and North Africa for more than a millennium before the birth of Muhammad and the founding of Islam.[2] The Babylonian exile expanded the Jewish community of Iraq in the early sixth century B.C.E., and they were not the first Jews to go there. The Jewish community at Alexandria in Egypt began not long after that. Surrounding peoples practiced pagan religions—in Egypt, for example, Pharaonic ritual—until some became Christian after the dawn of the Common Era. By the late sixth century there were millennium-old Jewish communities along the Tigris and Euphrates, on the Nile, in Damascus, and all along the coast of North Africa, including Alexandria, Cyrene, Tripoli, Carthage, and Tingis on the Strait of Gibraltar. Jews were also dispersed around the Arabian Peninsula, with communities in Aden, Mecca, and Medina.

These Jews spoke Judeo-Arabic, a language at least as distinct from Arabic as Yiddish is from German. Like their neighbors, rural Jews lived as desert clans and tribes, feuding and shifting alliances. Before Islam, both Jewish and Christian influence grew over the centuries, as pagan peoples responded to the appeal of monotheism. Perhaps the peak of Jewish influence occurred in Yemen, where the king and the royal household practiced Judaism for several years. This short-lived Jewish-Yemenite kingdom was destroyed by an Ethiopian invasion in 525, but it shows the cultural influence of the small Jewish minority.

Muhammad was born around 571, almost six hundred years after the traditional birth of Jesus, and eleven or twelve hundred years after some Jews left Israel to settle in Arab lands. Muhammad's religious genius brought Islam into being in the early 600s, and this new faith, designed to replace both Judaism and Christianity, spread with a speed perhaps unprecedented in the history of major religions. This was partly because of the monotheistic ideal, and partly because Muhammad created an inclusive culture, welcoming all who wanted to join, and defended an ideal of equality among his followers regardless of ethnicity, wealth, or even gender. But unlike Moses, Jesus, or Buddha, Muhammad was not only a religious genius but also a political and military one. He personally conquered and ruled over a large empire, and after his death the aegis of Islam was soon extended until it ranged from Spain and West Africa to Indonesia. Jewish communities in these far-flung lands were engulfed in a human sea that combined fierce faith with immense cultural power.[3]

Even in the birthplace of Islam, the Jews resisted.[4] They were the dominant ethnic group in Medina when Muhammad began preaching, and they were so well integrated into Arabian life that they are properly called Jewish Arabs, and historians have trouble distinguishing them from their non-Jewish neighbors. Yet only a few responded to Muhammad's message. A typical Jew in Medina, passionate in his expectation of the Messiah, said of Muhammad, "This is not the man."[5] Early Islam was not gentle with its opponents. The Qur'an calls again and again for jihad, or holy war, against unbelievers; it refers to Jews and Christians as apes and pigs. It relates that three Jewish tribes were conquered by Muhammad himself around Medina. Two were given the choice of conversion or exile, the third conversion or death. This group, the Banu Qurayza, chose death. Muhammad beheaded the men and distributed the women, children, livestock, and other property among his followers.

Yet the Qur'an also leaves room for tolerance. The Jews of Khaybar, an oasis ninety-five miles from Medina, were defeated by Muhammad but allowed to keep their faith and land as long as they gave half the crop to the Muslims. Fortunately this case, rather than the others, became the model for most future relations with Jews. They were clearly inferior and suffered many humiliating symbols. The Qur'an uses the words *dhull* and *dhilla* to refer to the lowliness and abasement of nonbelievers, and Muslim writers frequently applied them to Jews. From the dawn of Islam to the present, religious edicts have forbidden Jews from building high and ornamented houses, riding horses inside the city, wearing caftans with collars and other costly garments, being massaged or otherwise served by a Muslim, talking loudly to a Muslim, or overtaking a Muslim on a public street. Even paying taxes was a ritualized indignity. A Jew or other non-Muslim was supposed to be treated with disdain by the tax collector, who was encouraged to seize his beard and slap his face. And of course, any statement or act perceived as insulting to Islam, the Qur'an, or Muhammad was punishable by death.

Still, Christianity and Judaism were merely flawed, incomplete, and immature versions of the true faith, not paganism or idolatry. Their adherents were monotheists, at least, and could be tolerated as long as they knew their place. Christians, far more of a threat to Islam, were denigrated often in Muslim writings; Jews, pathetically weak, deserved contempt. Yet, in most times and places under Islam, there was nothing resembling the brew of seething fear and hatred that made Christian anti-Semitism so virulent. Since Muhammad, unlike Jesus, was a victor, not a martyr, the hapless Jews he conquered could be treated with noblesse oblige despite being dogs and pigs.

In Europe Jews were Christ killers, and the enduring fantasy that Jews killed Christian children in rituals re-created this alleged crime of crimes in every generation. As for doctrine, the Trinity was a theological concept Muslims and Jews could unite against, while the notion of Muhammad as a prophet was for Jews a less dangerous leap. Compared to the forced apostasy and massacres of Christendom, second-class citizenship among Muslims was usually the lesser evil.

⟨✿⟩

At times there was a first-class version of this second-class citizenship, and Maimonides, the great rabbi, philosopher, and physician, was a case in point.[6] Known to Jews the world over as "the Rambam," a nickname that stands for Rabbi Moses ben Maimon, he is widely seen as the greatest rabbi to live after talmudic times, as indicated by the affectionate saying "From Moses to Moses there was none like Moses." Late in life he was a renowned physician appointed to the sultan in Cairo. In 1199, at sixty-five, he wrote:

> I must visit him every morning. If he himself or one of his children or harem members is sick, then I may not leave Cairo. I spend most of the day in the sultan's palace. . . . I can come home only in the afternoon. . . . Here, starving as I am, I find the antechamber full of people: Jews and non-Jews, nobles and lowly people, judges and officials, friends and foes, a motley company awaiting me with impatience. I dismount from my horse, wash, and enter the waiting room with the plea that they may not feel offended if I have to make them wait a bit longer while I partake of a hasty light meal, which normally happens only once every twenty-four hours. Then I go out to them again, treat them, and prescribe medicaments on notes. Thus the people go in and out of my home until late in the evening. Sometimes, I swear it on the Torah, it is 2 a.m. or even later before I manage to consume anything. I am then so worn out that I collapse on my bed; I have to say good night, I am totally exhausted and incapable of speaking. Only on the Sabbath can anyone speak to me alone, or can I be alone with myself for even an instant. Then all or most of the members of the community gather in my home after the morning prayer. I indicate what is to be done in the community during the coming week; then they listen to a short lecture until noon, go home, and return in a smaller number. Now a second lecture takes place, between the minkhah and the maariv prayer.
>   Thus do my days go by.[7]

Intimate with the sultan and revered in the community, he ministered to the ills of court and courtyard both. But he was no mere assimilated cosmopolitan trying to pass in the Arab elite. He was already known as the leading Jewish theologian of his day.

He wrote a multivolume abridgment of the Talmud, the *Mishneh*

Torah, making countless durable judgments as to which rabbinical arguments should be viewed as law. He wrote the *Guide for the Perplexed,* a philosophic and theological treatise justifying Jewish belief to its practitioners. He answered countless letters from Jews in many countries asking him about problems of persecution and points of law. He also wrote treatises on medicine, astronomy, and logic, lectured to students, and visited patients in hospitals.

Although the law's details included 613 commandments, Maimonides attempted to lift the minds of average Jews to a more philosophical plane by articulating thirteen articles of faith. These built on eight beliefs articulated by Philo of Alexandria, as well as other lists of the Middle Ages. They are the core Jewish beliefs, derived from ancient texts and traditions, and a guide to Jewish life and thought. To this day Jews recite them during the service on Yom Kippur, the holiest day of the year, beginning each declaration with the same formula:

1. I believe with perfect faith in the existence of God which is perfect and sufficient unto himself and which is the cause of the existence of all other beings.
2. I believe with perfect faith in God's unity, which is unlike all other kinds of unity.
3. I believe with perfect faith that God must not be perceived in bodily terms, and the anthropomorphic expressions applied to God in Scripture have to be understood in a metaphorical sense.
4. I believe with perfect faith that God is eternal.
5. I believe with perfect faith that God alone is to be worshiped and obeyed. There are no mediating powers able freely to grant man's petitions, and intermediaries must not be invoked.
6. I believe with perfect faith in prophecy.
7. I believe with perfect faith that Moses is unsurpassed by any other prophet.
8. I believe with perfect faith that the entire Torah was given to Moses.
9. I believe with perfect faith that Moses' Torah will not be abrogated or superseded by another divine law nor will anything be added to or taken away from it.
10. I believe with perfect faith that God knows the actions of men.
11. I believe with perfect faith that God rewards those who fulfill the commandments of the Torah, and punishes those who transgress them.
12. I believe with perfect faith in the coming of the Messiah.
13. I believe with perfect faith in the resurrection of the dead.

These declarations were never merely academic. Millions lived by them, and many thousands died for them. Articles 2, 3, 5, 7, 9, and 12 made it clear that Jewish faith could not be Christian. Articles 7 and 9 made it equally clear why Jews could not accept Islam. These principles made a Jew a Jew then, and among the Orthodox at least, they still make a Jew a Jew now, as much as any form of practice.

Yet, remarkably, Maimonides wrote them down in Arabic. With the exception of the *Mishneh Torah,* all of his writing, including religious works intended for Jews, was in Arabic, usually written in Hebrew characters—as was the case for most of the important writings of the Jews of Islam until the thirteenth century. Jewish scholars were so steeped in Arab language and culture that they often used the words *Allah* for God, *imam* for the leader of prayer, and *Qur'an* for Torah.[8]

But Maimonides was the ultimate positive product of medieval Muslim-Jewish relations. He was trained in medicine, science, and secular philosophy by Islamic physicians and scholars—unquestionably the greatest of their time in the Western world. (Among countless achievements they invented hospitals, where Maimonides visited some of his patients.) They carried the best of classical Greek and Roman learning forward to the twelfth century, and were the vessels in which that knowledge returned to Europe as the early Renaissance. They also created and added much of their own science and scholarship.

Muslims allowed Maimonides to be not just Jewish but the reigning rabbinical thinker of the age, and yet to lance the boils and treat the digestive ills of Muslim kings and princes. He reflected back to Islam its own respect for learning, and because Muslims allowed him to be what he was, they shared the benefits of his gifts. But the fault lines of his life reveal the underlying tension. He was born in Córdoba in 1135, a time of benign Islamic rule that ended when the boy was thirteen: an attack by Muslim fundamentalists burned the Jewish community to the ground. Although Islamic rule in Spain was generally enlightened, it was often under threat from North Africa. There, fanatic and aggressive Berber sects like the Almohads—today we would call them Islamists—were able to foment rebellion and mount military initiatives even into Spain. In the mid- to late twelfth century they went around destroying wine, musical instruments, churches, synagogues, and, when necessary, Christians and Jews.

The Córdoban Jewish community was put to the torch; homes and synagogues were razed, and their inhabitants killed, forced to convert, or driven away. The boy Maimonides, a rabbi's son, moved with his refugee family from town to town in Spain and ultimately to Fez in Morocco. This should not have been a safe refuge, since Fez Jews had long been fleeing Almohad persecutions *there.* But some stayed, and something about the intellectual ferment in Fez, near the caliph's court, apparently attracted the rabbi father. It proved to be the son's intellectual birthplace, and the place where he developed both a Jewish theology and a philosophy of wider secular influence. In fact, he was in his forties and a highly accomplished philosopher when the death at sea of his much-loved younger brother, a merchant, forced him to practice medicine as a livelihood.

He gained fame in this profession, too, deftly blending theory and practice, and so ended up at the court of Cairo. Never relinquishing his rabbinical role, he became a leader of the Egyptian Jewish community, a great boon to that beleaguered group of people. But the minarets of Spain cast a long shadow. It seems that as a boy, Maimonides had been forcibly converted to Islam, and his continued Jewish faith and practice was apostasy. At the height of his fame in Cairo, a Muslim acquaintance from Spain recognized him and denounced him, demanding the death penalty. Fortunately, the case was heard by his friend and patron at the court, who decreed the forced conversion invalid. Other, less exalted converts from Judaism were not always so fortunate. Some were accepted, but others faced a lifetime of suspicion of continuing Jewish faith and practice. If the charge could be made to stick, the punishment was death.

Two contrasting letters of Maimonides embody the contradictions of Jewish life under Islam. One, to the Jews of Yemen when *they* faced forced conversion, says, "No nation has ever done more harm to Israel. None has matched them in debasing and humiliating us. None has been able to reduce us as they have." The other, to his Hebrew translator in Europe, lauds the richness of the Arabic language and the superiority of Arab science. That such a brilliant mind could hold these seemingly contradictory views points to the complex interplay between the two cultures. But as to the tolerant, cosmopolitan face of Islam, the Rambam's own life is a proof.

◑᙭᙭ᙰᖴ

Much of what we know about medieval Jewry we owe to Benjamin of Tudela, the most famously traveled of all wandering Jews. Leaving his small hometown on the Ebro River in northern Spain in 1159, he traveled through Provence, Italy, Greece, and Anatolia to reach the Holy Land, then held by the Crusaders. He proceeded to Damascus, Baghdad, and the Arabian Peninsula, returning home through Egypt and Sicily. His apparent mission was to document the size and vigor of Jewish communities in all these lands, and he did so admirably, in a text taken very seriously by historians. Although some of it was hearsay and a little merely legend, eyewitness accounts predominate in his narrative.

Benjamin found Jews almost everywhere. Near Constantinople, his first stop outside Europe, he found 2,500 Jews, divided between a majority practicing rabbinical Judaism, based on the Talmud, and a smaller group, called Karaites, who recognized only the Torah:

> No Jews live in the city, for they have been placed behind an inlet of the sea . . . and they are unable to go out except by way of the sea, when they want to do business with the inhabitants. In the Jewish quarter there are about 2,000 Rabbanite Jews and about 500 Karaites, and a fence divides them. Amongst the scholars are several wise men. . . . And amongst them there are artificers in silk and many rich merchants. No Jew there is allowed to ride on horseback. The one exception is R. Solomon Hamitari, who is the king's physician, and through whom the Jews enjoy considerable alleviation of their oppression. For their condition is very low, and there is much hatred against them, which is fostered by the tanners, who throw out their dirty water in the streets before the doors of the Jewish houses and defile the Jews' quarter. . . . So the Greeks hate the Jews, good and bad alike, and subject them to great oppression, and beat them in the streets. . . . Yet the Jews are rich and good, kindly and charitable, and bear their lot with cheerfulness.[9]

In Sidon, on the Mediterranean coast in what is now Lebanon, there were "no resident Jews, but a certain number of handicraftsmen and dyers come among them for the sake of trade, and then return, the people being favorable to the Jews." Just south of there Benjamin stopped at Tyre:

> There is no harbor like this in the whole world. Tyre is a beautiful city. It contains about 500 Jews, some of them scholars of the Talmud, at their head being R. Ephraim of Tyre, the Dayan, R. Meir from Carcassonne, and R. Abraham, head of the congregation. The Jews own sea-going vessels, and there are glass-makers amongst them who make that fine Tyrian glass-ware which is prized in all countries.

After staying among the Jews of Israel for a time he went on to Damascus, "a fair city of large extent surrounded by walls, gardens, and plantations . . . and no district richer in fruit can be seen in all the world." It had an exceptional mosque ("no other building like it in the whole world") and a water supply brought to the city by means of aqueducts. "Three thousand Jews abide in this city, and amongst them are learned and rich men." He saw five thousand Jews in Aleppo, two thousand in Kalat Jabar, seven thousand in Mosul, fifteen thousand in Hadara, ten thousand in Okbara, and so on as he passed from Syria into Babylon, through the Tigris and Euphrates valleys.

In Baghdad "the great city . . . the great king, Al Abbasi the Caliph holds his court, and he is kind unto Israel, and many belonging to the people of Israel are his attendants; he knows all languages, and is well versed in the law of Israel. He reads and writes the holy language (Hebrew)." After detailed descriptions of mosques, gardens, and hospitals, including humane mental asylums, Benjamin says, "The Caliph is a righteous man, and all his actions are for good. In Baghdad there are about 40,000 Jews, and they dwell in security, prosperity, and honor under the great Caliph, and amongst them are great sages, the heads of Academies engaged in the study of the law." The rabbis who headed the ten academies

> do not engage in any other work than communal administration; and all the days of the week they judge the Jews their countrymen, except on the second day of the week, when they all appear before the chief rabbi Samuel. . . . And at the head of them all is Daniel the son of Hisdai, who is styled "Our Lord the Head of the Captivity of all Israel.". . .
>
> . . . And every fifth day when he goes to pay a visit to the great Caliph, horsemen, Gentiles as well as Jews, escort him, and heralds proclaim in advance, "Make way before our Lord, the son of David, as is due unto him.". . . He is mounted on a horse, and is attired in robes of silk and embroidery with a large turban on his head, and from the turban is suspended a long white cloth adorned with a chain upon which the cipher of Mohammed is engraved. Then he appears before the Caliph and kisses his hand, and the Caliph rises and places him on a throne which Mohammed had ordered to be made for him . . . in compliance with the command of Mohammed to give effect to what is written in the law—"The sceptre shall not depart from Judah."

Throughout the caliph's vast empire, the Head of the Captivity—a reference to the original Jewish community of Babylon some seventeen centuries earlier—gave Jews the power to appoint rabbis and ministers, whom he then consecrated and authorized to rule.

> They bring him offerings and gifts from the ends of the earth. He owns hospices, gardens, and plantations in Babylon, and much land inherited from his fathers, and no one can take his possessions from him by force. . . . The man is very rich, and wise in the Scriptures as well as in the Talmud, and many Israelites dine at his table every day.

This was a varied and welcoming place for Jewish life:

In Baghdad there are twenty-eight Jewish synagogues, situated either in the city itself or in Al-Karkh on the other side of the Tigris;
for the river divides the metropolis into two parts. The great synagogue of the Head of the Captivity has columns of marble of various colors overlaid with silver and gold, and on these columns are
sentences of the Psalms in golden letters. And in front of the ark are
about ten steps of marble; on the topmost step are the seats of the
Head of the Captivity and of the Princes of the House of David.

In the Arabian Peninsula alone Benjamin found hundreds of thousands
of Jews, but not all were centralized and rich. Near Teima, in the mountains
of northern Arabia, Jews owned "many large fortified cities" where "the
yoke of the gentiles is not upon them."

They go forth to pillage and to capture booty from distant lands in
conjunction with the Arabs, their neighbors and allies. . . . they give
the tithe of all they possess unto the scholars who sit in the house of
learning, also to poor Israelites and to the recluses, who are the
mourners of Zion and Jerusalem, and who do not eat meat nor taste
wine, and sit clad in garments of black. They dwell in caves or underground houses, and fast each day with the exception of the Sabbaths and Festivals, and implore mercy of the Holy One, blessed be
He, on account of the exile of Israel, praying that he may take pity
upon them, and upon all the Jews.

On the island of Kish, where the Persian Gulf spills into the Indian
Ocean, were many traders, including five hundred Jews. Kish's middlemen
brought Indian spices and exchanged them for cotton, hemp, worked wool,
wheat, barley, millet, rye, lentils, and other farm products from Persia and
the Middle East. At Katif, on the western shore of the gulf, Jews ran an exotic industry of the king's. "On the twenty-fourth of Nisan"—in April, just
after Passover—"rain falls upon the water, upon the surface of which certain small sea-animals float which drink in the rain and then shut themselves up, and sink to the bottom." After Yom Kippur in early fall "men
descend to the bed of the sea by ropes, and collect these shell-fish, then split
them open and extract the pearls." In Libya as in northern Arabia, Jews
were warriors: "The Jews take spoil and booty and retreat to the mountains,
and no man can prevail against them."

Still, for the most part, Benjamin found Jews dwelling in cities as they
did in Europe, attempting to prosper in peace. Urban Jews found safety in
numbers, formed a critical mass to communicate effectively with rulers,
practiced their traditional crafts and traded, and were able to support Jewish learning and collective religious activity. In Cairo, for example—which

Benjamin calls Mizraim, the Hebrew name for Egypt—he found two large
synagogues, "one belonging to the men of the land of Israel and one belonging to the men of the land of Babylon." This suggests that the Cairo
community was split between the distinct groups of descendants. As we
have seen, these two great centers of Jewish learning had, centuries earlier,
produced two slightly different versions of the Talmud.

> Their usage with regard to the portions and sections of the Law is
> not alike; for the men of Babylon are accustomed to read a portion
> every week, as is done in Spain, and is our custom, and to finish the
> Law each year; whilst the men of Palestine do not do so, but divide
> each portion into three sections and finish the Law at the end of
> three years.

But of course, both communities read the Torah, as all good Jews had done
since the first rabbis in Temple times. In a fitting display of unity the two
great congregations of Cairo came together to worship twice a year: once on
Simchat Torah, the Rejoicing of the Law, when religious Jews everywhere
celebrate and dance with the heavy sacred scrolls; and once on Shavuot, the
late-spring holiday that commemorates the giving of the Torah on Mount
Sinai—which, as Benjamin notes in his usual careful way, is just a day's
journey from Egypt's Red Sea.

♒

Fewer than seventy thousand Jews live in Arab countries today, a remnant
of two million or so in the mid-twentieth century. Most became refugees
from violence as the birth of the Jewish state in 1948 heightened already-
existing tensions between Arabs and Jews. Anthropologists have reconstructed those communities, through interviews of those who immigrated
to Israel en masse, retaining much of their culture intact for a generation. These interviews and observations can be blended with documents—
collections of rabbinical responses to questions from congregants, for
example—and at least a few studies of Jewish life in the Arab world before
the mass midcentury exodus.

Take Morocco as a case in point. The Jewish communities there date
from at least the destruction of the Second Temple, and later survived severe persecutions after the rise of Islam.[10] These indigenous Jews were
joined after 1492 by many of those expelled from Spain, but over time
Judeo-Spanish traditions were largely absorbed by Moroccan ones. Religious life rested on a base of rabbinical learning, but folk religious traditions
remained strong and even grew. This decentralized Judaism weakened the
power of leading rabbis, who tended to be of Spanish descent. Many private
synagogues appeared, taking the overflow of an expanding population

away from the large, communal houses of worship controlled by important sages.

Moroccan Jewish life was concentrated in *mellahs,* the Jewish quarters of larger towns. These became crowded and even squalid, with high rates of child mortality, as population grew during the eighteenth and nineteenth centuries. Called to the Torah on Sabbath morning, a man would be given a standard blessing, "The Lord keep his children safe." The blessing frequently failed.

The many craftsmen—silversmiths, sandal makers, tailors, and others—part of a class of elite families in each town, served well-to-do Muslims. But there were thousands of Jewish peddlers selling simple household goods and building materials to Berber tribesmen, the main population of the hinterlands. Some Berbers came to town to trade, but more often the Jewish peddlers went to them, leaving their families for weeks at a time and taking substantial risks. Rabbis had to rule on peddlers' disappearances, the status of their wives, and problems identifying their bodies after attacks by highwaymen. Prayers, letters, and marital disputes that came to judgment show a keen desire to stay close to cities.

Jewish communities were subject to heavy taxes and the ultimate rule of the caliph, but also had considerable autonomy. The official court *(beit din),* the judge, the sage *(hakham),* and the community leader *(nagid,* "governor" or "prince") were crucial, judging disputes, supervising teachers, ritual slaughterers, and other functionaries, and negotiating with the caliph. Within the bounds allowed by Islamic power, law in these communities was Jewish law, and as in talmudic times it pervaded all of life. The sages anchored Jewish life in Morocco as elsewhere since antiquity. These were holy communities *(kehillot kodesh),* and Jewish law governed them.

But of course they were not egalitarian, especially not within families. Grown sons, often in business with their fathers, lived with their wives and children in a multifamily compound around a courtyard. As in most traditional cultures, the nuclear family—husband, wife, children—was ensconced in a larger extended family, and for Moroccan Jews this kin group was patriarchal. Unlike in Europe, there were no matchmakers, but marriages were arranged by the two families, usually after extensive contact. A bride coming into the patriarchal compound was in a very weak position, and proximity to her own kin might be her only protection against unfairness or even abuse. If a husband wanted to move away from the wife's family to further his business, this was often strongly resisted. When not ruled by her husband, a young woman could count on being under the thumb of older women, but even they had little power. Add to this the risk of death in childbirth, and a woman's lot does not seem enviable.

Except in the sexual realm. The laws of menstrual impurity segregated women of childbearing age, and only older women felt comfortable in the synagogue. But because of the strict rabbinical prohibition of contact between husband and wife during the first twelve days of the month, a woman could regulate sexual contact from a position of some power. She had to immerse herself in the *mikvah,* or ritual bath, before he could come to her, and when she did this was largely her choice. This could give her the upper hand.

For Jewish men in Arab lands polygamy was permitted—not always to male advantage, since cooperating co-wives could counter male dominance. Polygamy was less common in urban areas, but could be as high as 15 percent, as it was, for example, in rural Yemen.[11] But Yemenite women did not need co-wives to cooperate, and there was greater gender equality in these rural communities. In Habban, the most remote Jewish community of Yemen, women had much more say in household affairs than in urban Morocco. Women's creative outlets in poetry and song, as well as in the preparation for festivals and rites of passage, gave them a collective sense of control over important parts of their lives and those of their families.

Two disputes in Habban reveal the tensions of gender and risks of family life. In one, a marriage made for love provoked the bride's brothers' anger. They insisted on a divorce, and it was rumored that they might kill their brother-in-law. The couple fled to a still more remote village where he had some tribal protection, and stayed there for several years while tempers cooled. The marriage lasted fifteen years, until the woman died giving birth to their fourth son. In the second, a husband who had converted to Islam returned to reclaim his wife and children. They resisted and fled to another Jewish community, but they could not resist indefinitely. The wife returned and negotiated a divorce, but only by giving up her son to be raised Muslim. The saddened Jewish community quickly married her into a polygamous household to avert a possible change of heart by her ex-husband.

Contact with Muslims was a source of mutual influence. This is evident in wedding customs, which show similarities between Jewish and Muslim practices throughout the Islamic world.[12] In rural Libya, a gift of bride wealth from groom to bride was part of the marriage agreement for both Jews and Muslims, but only Muslims viewed this as a legal transfer of the bride to the husband. In addition, the Jewish marriage contract, or *ketuba,* specified his three basic duties to his wife—food, clothing, and sex—as well as a payment to be made by the groom to the bride in case of divorce. This followed a law in the Mishnah with no exact Muslim parallel.

Celebrations went on for days before the wedding in both cultures, and included sexual symbolism. In a first marriage the bride would let her hair down to show that she was a virgin. Since this practice too is mentioned in the Mishnah it cannot be specifically Islamic, but it may have been widespread for centuries. In another parallel, young men visited the elaborately dressed and made-up bride and touched her hennaed feet with coins, then placed the coins—destined for charity—in a basket on her head, to the eerie tune of ululating women. The groom was among the young men, but was not distinguished in any way. Only later, at the wedding itself—*kiddushin,* or consecration—would the Jewish bride be made sacred to him alone, "by the law of Moses and Israel."

On the "night of the journey," the veiled bride was escorted by two older women in a candle-and-torchlight procession while other women clapped and sang songs composed for her, and men chanted hymns. At the ceremony, the bride was covered in the bridegroom's prayer shawl, another version of the *chupah,* or canopy, seen at Jewish weddings in Europe. And of course, when Jews were wed in Islamic countries, they carried out the essence of *kiddushin* under rabbinic law.[13] The rabbi read the *ketuba* aloud and then made the first of the Seven Blessings, over the wine. The groom and bride were given wine from the cup, and the groom either gave the bride a coin or placed a ring on her right index finger. He had to have bought the ring himself, to not just symbolize but actualize the responsibility of providing for her. The bridegroom repeated after the rabbi, *"Harei at mekuddeshet li be tabba'at zo ke-dat Moshe ve-Yisrael"*—"With this you are made sacred to me by the law of Moses and Israel."

The rabbi then intoned the rest of the Seven Blessings. After the blessing over the wine, three praise God in general terms. The remaining three are the most moving:

> May she who was barren be exceedingly glad and exult, when her children are gathered within her in joy. Blessed art Thou, O Lord, who makes Zion joyful through her children.
>
> O make these loved companions greatly to rejoice, even as of old Thou didst gladden Thy creature in the Garden of Eden. Blessed art Thou, O Lord, who makest bridegroom and bride rejoice.
>
> Blessed art Thou, O Lord, who hast created joy and gladness, bridegroom and bride, mirth and exaltation, pleasure and delight, love, brotherhood, peace, and fellowship. Soon, O Lord, our God, may there be heard in the cities of Judah, and in the streets of Jerusalem, the voice of joy and gladness, the voice of the bridegroom and the voice of the bride, the jubilant voice of bridegrooms from their canopies, and of youths from their feasts of song. Blessed art Thou, O Lord, who makes the bridegroom rejoice with the bride.

Modern Jewish bridegrooms break a glass at the end of the ceremony, and this practice stands in a long line of related, widespread cultural forms. In rural Libya, for example, an egg was thrown and broken against a wall, ostensibly to symbolize the destruction of the Temple. But Libyan Muslims also broke an egg before entering the bridal dwelling. Among Jews in the city of Tripoli, as the newly wedded couple arrived at the groom's house, he went up on the roof with a jug of water and smashed it onto the ground— again said to commemorate the destruction of the Temple. Women ululated, and the bride stepped through the wet, broken shards into the house and threw an egg against the wall of her new home.[14]

In other Jewish communities, a glass of red wine was thrown against a white wall, or even against a white sheet hanging on the wall. This clearly recalls the practice, once widespread in Jewish cultures of North Africa, of examining the bedsheets for blood after the wedding night, for the dual purpose of proving that the bride had been a virgin and that the marriage had been consummated. The symbol of a smashed egg, another irreversible rupture of ripeness, is equally sexual. Yet the custom took on the significance it now has at Jewish weddings—an expression of sorrow at the destruction of the Temple, as well as at the inevitable sadness in every life—as an additional, nonsexual, Jewish meaning.

The ceremony fulfilled all three of the possible methods described in the Mishnah for establishing a marriage: the transfer of wealth, the execution of a contract, and the cohabitation of the bride and groom, each accompanied by a specified blessing. The bride and groom might then have a full day of privacy to fulfill the commandment of rejoicing together. On a Sabbath after the wedding, the groom was escorted from his home to the synagogue by a parade of young men, all taking mincing steps. If the groom took a large step, a friend would needle him, whispering, "Keep your steps slow, have you another day of joy like this?" At the synagogue, accompanied by hymns, he would be called up to bless the Torah, perhaps to read from it. With this central devotional act he would reaffirm his membership in the community of Jewish faith, in his new role as a married man.

ᗧ᙭ᖶᖶᙅ᙭ᗤ

Even though Islam was not marred by the deep anti-Semitism of Christendom, thirteen centuries of contempt prepared the way for a sea change in the twentieth century. This came with the birth of modern Israel, a colossal affront to Islam of precisely the type that had always been forbidden. Jews were to walk rather than ride, build smaller homes, convert if they had any sense, and accept humiliation without resistance or complaint. Now new Jews became a victorious army in Israel and looked down on mosques from a dizzying height. This flew in the face of the patronizing concept of *dhimmi,* or protected people, which had been at the heart of the Muslim treatment of Jews and Christians for fourteen centuries.

Islam from the outset was a vanquishing religion, attached to the military arm of a rapidly growing state. But believers were a pragmatic group of conquerors, recognizing the limits to proselytizing, and this helps explain why Islam spread as fast and far as it did; those who accepted its rule did not always have to choose between conversion and death or exile. The concept of jihad, or holy war, is central and real, but it does not apply in the same way to all non-Muslims. Pagans and polytheists were subject to conquest and forced to accept Islam.

But Jews and Christians were monotheists, regrettably stunted in their growth toward the true faith. They were encouraged to convert, and sometimes forced to, but within limits were allowed their own religious practices. They had to accept constant reminders of their inferiority, remain separate and distinct from Muslims, and never hint at proselytizing, on pain of death. Those who did not accept their inferior status—uppity *dhimmis*—were subject to jihad just like pagans. Certainly, the medieval Crusades were a cause for jihad. Christendom was asserting superiority to Islam, and even regained control of the Holy Land. Although Christians had come from there six centuries before Islam, defeat and expulsion of the Crusaders was a Muslim religious obligation of the highest order, eventually achieved.

As for the Jews, they had been there for at least twelve centuries before Christ, eighteen before Muhammad. But after that they were weak for thirteen centuries, until the arrival of the Zionists—the Jews who settled Israel. During this time it was viewed as Islamic property, so Zionism, from the outset, seemed an insult to Islam. Not a threat—it was far too weak for that—but a very serious insult. As for the Zionists' claim that they were returning home, Muslim leaders never took it seriously.

Yet to see Israel, or even Zionism, as the sole key to deteriorating Muslim-Jewish relations is to miss a century of prior change.[15] The Jews of Islam tolerated their inferior status because they had no choice. But in the eighteenth century Europe was transformed by industrialization and the Enlightenment. The American and French Revolutions sent the message of liberation, and even though that message fell short of the truth, it changed the world. Napoleon's conquests substantially improved the status of Jews in Europe, and many Jewish intellectuals participated in the Enlightenment, including science, reason, cosmopolitanism, and some degree of equality and democracy.

All these trends were good for the Jews, and it was in their interest to spread Enlightenment ideas despite their threat to traditional religion. The Jews of Islam too saw the Enlightenment as liberating, a movement that could end their millennial *dhimmi* status. But modernity was not in the interest of Islam, especially not with a European stamp. So the Enlightenment, and indeed modernity itself, came to Islam as a foreign influence, carried in part by their own inferior Jewish minority. The Jews were a sort of fifth column for the civilization of the future as Europe was defining it. Ironically, this was the same role that Jews had played in Europe centuries earlier, when they brought what was then modernity *from* a much more advanced Islamic world. Now it was to Europe's advantage to use both Christians and Jews as leverage for colonial ambition, but it was also to the *dhimmis'* advantage to play this role.

The Jews had always been multilingual traders, and had moved among many countries due to relentless persecutions. Many had not just coreligionists but relatives in Europe. Restrictions on their economic activity under both Christianity and Islam had made them merchants and traders for centuries, with the overall result that Jews had already achieved the cosmopolitanism that was a vital part of the Enlightenment. And of course, this was always part of the anti-Semitic libel against them: With all those ties to people elsewhere, the accusation went, how could they be loyal to any home country? That they had shown such loyalty from the time of their exile in Babylon had little impact on the libel.

Jewish ties to Christian Europe, Jewish cosmopolitanism, and the Jewish move toward modernity combined to provoke a new kind of Islamic anti-Semitism in the late nineteenth century. Muslims even adopted the blood libel—the horrendous accusation that Jews ritually murdered Christian children—and it gained currency in Turkey, the Middle East, and North Africa. Thus, superimposed on thirteen centuries of Muslim contempt, the anomalous addition of Christian anti-Semitism created a virulent strain.

At around the same time, efforts to expand Jewish life in Israel intensified. European, North African, and other Jews had migrated to Israel in every generation, but now they became a movement. Zionism, accepted by many Jews in the 1890s, mobilized resources, bought land from Arabs, and created settlements. During World War I, the British, having defeated the Turks and become in their place the lords of the Levant, officially granted the Jews their wish of a homeland in Israel. Arab attacks on Jewish settlements increased throughout the first half of the twentieth century, and Jewish reprisals followed. The unprecedented Jew hatred purveyed by the Nazis also took hold in the Arab world, parts of which supported Hitler openly. The Jews' fight for a nation-state in their ancient land intensified. After World War II, in which the Germans murdered more than half the Jews of Europe, a contrite world created the state of Israel.

But anti-Semitism had been building in the Arab world for decades. A leading historian summarizes it this way:

> The earliest specifically anti-Semitic statements in the Middle East occurred among the Christian minorities, and can usually be traced back to European originals. They had limited impact, and at the time for example of the Dreyfus trial in France, when a Jewish officer was unjustly accused and condemned by a hostile court, Muslim commentaries usually favored the persecuted Jew against his Christian persecutors. But the poison continued to spread, and from

1933 Nazi Germany and its various allies made a concerted and on the whole remarkably successful effort to promote and disseminate European style anti-Semitism in the Arab world. The struggle for Palestine greatly facilitated the acceptance of the anti-Semitic interpretation of history, and led some to blame all evil in the Middle East and indeed in the world on secret Jewish plots. This interpretation has pervaded much of the public discourse in the region, including education, the media, and even entertainment.[16]

The creation of Israel by the United Nations exacerbated the process, but the Arabs did not wait for that. In 1945, riots in Tripoli signaled that Jewish life in Muslim Libya was coming to an end.[17] They began on November 4, a few months after the defeat of the Nazis in Europe, a time when the murders of millions of Jews pricked the conscience of the world. Although there had always been tension, relations between Jews and Muslims had not been bad. But nationalist sentiment was rising among Arabs, especially after the British pried Libya away from Italian rule.

Simultaneous riots in several different parts of the city strongly suggested prior planning. There had also been anti-Jewish riots in Alexandria and Cairo on November 2, and activists in Tripoli had been trained in Beirut, Damascus, and Cairo. The Tripoli riots grew more intense over a period of days, including looting, arson, assault, and homicide. Mostly poorer Arab men participated, but the wealthier stood and watched. Women cheered the rioters with high-pitched cries characteristic of festive occasions and celebration of warriors. The frequent shout of the rioters was *"Jihad fil-kuffar"*—"Holy war against the infidels."

Occasionally a Jew met the eyes of a Muslim he knew among the rioters, and that person withdrew. Some Muslims helped Jews. But the result in the end was devastating: thirty-eight Jews were killed in the city of Tripoli alone, ninety-seven more in the neighboring villages. Nine synagogues were burned and thirty-five Torah scrolls ruined. In addition to the killings there were many injuries, and the total property damage ran into hundreds of millions of lire. All observers agreed that the British police did little or nothing to restrain the rioters, obviously a green light for them and their followers. This radically changed the situation of Jews in this ancient community. A year later the director of the Alliance Israélite Universelle schools in Libya expressed their anguish: "An unprecedented blow has been dealt to the Jews' sense of security and any illusions they had for taking initiatives: there is terror, poverty, disease, and suffering, without a glimmer of hope to brighten the dark future. Should they go away? If so, how? And where?"[18]

An answer was soon at hand, as the United Nations created a national homeland for the Jews. But the Arab and Islamic world rejected the UN plan, which would have created a Palestinian and a Jewish state side by side. Six Arab nations sent their armies into Israel and ultimately met defeat. But now life had become untenable for the Jews who had always lived in the Arab world. Denigration turned to persecution, inferiority to danger, isolation to pogrom. They became refugees. The Jews of Libya, for example, began to move en masse to the new state in 1949, as soon as the British allowed emigration. Of perhaps two million Jews living in Islamic lands, all but about seventy thousand emigrated, moving to Israel, France, the United States, and other countries. These nearly two million Jews were refugees from Islamic, especially Arab, persecution. They were driven out of homes they had occupied for centuries, and they never received compensation or apology. Those who made aliyah—went "up" to Israel—created a new life there.[19] The decimated, aging communities left behind continued to dwindle, and Jewish life under Islam, for practical purposes, drew to a close. But Muslim and Arab hatred of Jews did not.

8

SPAIN AND BEYOND

HOW THE SEPHARDIC JEWS FOUND ROMANCE

Desire trumps my fear
And I bound like a deer
To meet my lady's eyes.
But nearing the prize,
I meet up with her mother,
Father, uncle, brother!
I see her and turn quickly,
As if she didn't love me.
They scare me, I'm undone,
And my heart grieves for her
Like that of a mother
Losing her only son.[1]

A century before Maimonides was born, even before Rashi, this poem was composed by Isaac ibn Khalfun, in Córdoba, in the late 900s. In the original it is highly structured and follows a meter-and-rhyme scheme borrowed from Arabic poetry, which in turn probably took it from Spanish folk songs. And although it is said that Spanish is the loving tongue, this small gem was made in Hebrew, and Ibn Khalfun was—not counting the author of the Song of Songs—the first professional secular Hebrew poet. He died not many years before Rashi was born in Jewish northern Europe, but their lives could hardly have been more different. He had a biblical first name but an Arab surname, spoke Arabic and Spanish in common discourse, and was as immersed in Arab and Hispanic culture as Rashi was in Torah and Talmud.

The Jews of Spain, having survived the Christian Visigoths, remained under Muslim rule.[2] But if the predominant culture was Muslim from the heavens down, it was Spanish from the ground up, an exquisite blend of indigenous Iberian folk art and literature with the science, philosophy, and aesthetics of Islamic civilization. Maimonides was more *in* the secular world than Rashi, and was also in the mainstream of Arab philosophy and medicine, steeped in the greatest intellectual achievements of the age. Rashi, a century earlier in Ashkenaz, devoted himself exclusively to the sacred texts, creating a great corpus of permanently influential commentary.

The Jews of Spain were different. They called Spain Sepharad in Hebrew, so they were Sephardim. There on the edge of Islam, they were Middle Eastern and European as well as Jewish. But the rest of Europe was in the Dark Ages, preparing for the Crusades—a futile holy war against a higher civilization. The differences were clear. A German nun who chronicled the era called Córdoba "the ornament of the world," but the phrase could have been used to describe the whole of Muslim Spain.[3]

The Spanish Jews belonged to that civilization, and yet they also belonged to Europe. The great achievements of ancient Greece in science and philosophy survived mainly in the vessel of Islam, and the Spanish Jews drank from that cup, and ultimately shared it with Christian Europe. They were not the sole vehicle of this knowledge, but they were a vanguard of high culture in a still-benighted continent. Centuries before the Renaissance, the Spanish Jews had a renaissance of their own. Among Jews, Sepharad was to Ashkenaz what Islam was to Christianity—an advanced, cosmopolitan culture looking down on an isolated, backward one.

This had not always been so. The accession to the Spanish throne, in 612, of a king who forced the Jews to convert or leave the kingdom was a milestone in Christian persecution. It created the first *conversos,* or *anusim* in Hebrew: Spanish Jews who submitted to baptism but kept some Jewish beliefs and customs. Many generations later there would be scores of thousands, a fixture of Spanish life. But just a century after this began, in 711, the Muslims conquered Spain. The Jews embraced the conquerors, forming economic and military alliances against the Christian natives. This of course confirmed the worst Christian fears about their loyalty, but defection was a result, not a cause, of persecution.

Judaism was far more tolerated under Islam than under Christianity, but the contrast was even greater in Spain than in North Africa or the Middle East. Unlike the Jews of Ashkenaz, the Jews of Spain had military experience and capability, and they were entrusted by the Muslims with the defense of major cities, including Granada, Córdoba, Seville, and Toledo.[4] As long as Islam ruled in Spain, Jewish influence grew.

In the mid-eleventh century, Shmuel Hanagid—Samuel the Prince— became "the defender of Granada." Poet, Talmud scholar, statesman, and warrior, he led the armies of Granada through victorious campaigns, recording his stunning exploits in poems he sent back from the battlefield, in one instance by carrier pigeon, to his son. His poem "The Battle of Al-fuente" commemorates a major victory.[5] "When God came to his aid," it be-gins, "he spoke this song":

> *Then Av, month of ancient woe, left off*
> *and Elul came with its good grace.*
> *Ibn Abbas raised his tents on the hill,*
> *and we pitched ours in the pass,*
> *unfazed by his army as by a passing caravan.*

In this clash of raw power, God is there: "My foe rose—and the Rock rose against him." But human nature is there too, "On such a day of fury, jeal-ousy, and rage," when "Men deem the Prince of Death a princely prize," and nature itself echoes human fury:

> *A dark day thick with fog,*
> *The sun black as my heart.*
> *Tumult like a cloudburst,*
> *A roar of breakers,*
> *Sea swept by storm . . .*

He draws images of the Holy Temple, gone for a thousand years: "Men's blood wet the ground/As rams' blood drowned the altar." Yet his brave men "scorned their lives, sought death." It was Hanagid's first battle, and he won. His own title for the poem was "Shira," "Song," the same as that of Psalm 18.[6] He liked being called the David of his generation, and he pub-lished his war poems in a book called *Son of Psalms*.

But even this Judeo-Spanish David, triumphant in war, did not love it, and later wrote this simple poem:

> *War enters as a beauty*
> *With whom all men gladly play,*
> *But ages and grows ugly,*
> *And all her weeping lovers slip away.*[7]

Other poems were drinking songs, paeans to patrons, cranky com-plaints about same when the allowance failed, and laments over persecution and loss. Biblical themes make some distinctively Jewish, while others echo the Bible in language, imagery, and form. Ironically, the Judeo-Spanish adoption of biblical Hebrew as the language of poetry was inspired by Arab poets' use of the style of the Qur'an.

Even the love poems clearly evoke the imagery of the Song of Songs, although some of them might have made even earthy Rabbi Akiva, who canonized that biblical book, blush crimson.

> *Caress her pretty breasts at night,*
> *And kiss her lips when day is bright!*

"No life," the poet claims, "but with beauty's daughters," who "left Eden to torture us, / And no man lives who doesn't lust!" The only answer, then, is to

> *Plunge your heart into pleasures, revel,*
> *Drain wineskins on the riverbank*
> *To the tunes of lyres, doves, and swifts;*
> *Dance and carouse, clap your hands,*
> *Get drunk, and then . . . pound on the lovely lady's door!*

Thus wrote Moses ibn Ezra, the leading theorist of this literary movement, in Granada, in the late eleventh century. In old age he would rue this message from his misspent youth, but critics have loved it ever since. In another regretted poem, he wrote, "Many denounce me, but I ignore them . . .

> *Come, fawn, and I'll defeat them,*
> *Time will swallow and death keep them.*
> *Come, fawn, and rise to what is fated:*
> *I'll feast on your lips' fruit 'til I am sated. . . .*

Of a young woman's brave dissembling, he wrote,

> *Sick with love, she weeps hot tears at night,*
> *Flooding her cheeks, but laughs with guests*
> *To make them gay, while fire eats her flesh.*

And of every human being, surely approaching death:

> *A quiet passenger on a ship,*
> *He feels at rest, while the ship*
> *Flies on the crest of the wind.*

In old age he wrote poems about God as moving as his love songs. He wrote of God's Talmud,

> *He kindled a lamp in his glory*
> *To light the path of the sage,*
> *And the radiance that lit my youth*
> *Still blazes through my age.*[8]

For his dear friend Judah Halevy, a physician-poet whose genius transformed the liturgy, the metaphor of Israel as God's beloved took center stage. Like Benjamin the traveler, he was born in Tudela, the border of cross and crescent. After years in Granada, where he and Ibn Ezra recorded their friendship in poems, he moved to Toledo as physician to a Christian king. Having seen much death, he gave voice to a mother's grief:

> *There in the underworld I see her wedding day,*
> *How they make her a canopy out of the dust*
> *And sweets from the clods of the grave.*
> *Bitter O bitter for me, my daughter,*
> *Death has come between us.*

But he too wrote love poems:

> *Pity me, you of the hard heart and soft hips,*
> *Pity me, let me bend the knee before you!*
> *... my heart is pure, but my eyes are not!*
> *Grant my eyes the rose-and-lily harvest,*
> *Planted, melded in your cheeks.*[9]

Here he makes light of sacred matters, kowtowing to his beloved as he should before God and mocking the impure mingling of two different flowers. But he also wrote exquisite prayers that entered the permanent liturgy, and his most famous poem, later a wistful, plaintive song, is of Jerusalem:

> *My heart is in the East*
> *But I dwell in the West.*
> *I eat without taste,*
> *Live without joy or rest.*
> *How easy in my eyes to leave*
> *This Spanish life of mine,*
> *Just to see with those same eyes*
> *The dust of the ruined Shrine.*[10]

This longing for Jerusalem would be a theme in Sephardic literature and folklore for almost another millennium.[11] Like many religious Jews of his time, Judah "went up" to the Holy Land in old age, meaning to pray at the Western Wall of that shrine before joining his fathers, but he died on the way to Jerusalem.

Benjamin of Tudela had little to say of his home country, but fortunately others said more. Rabbi Chisdai wrote to the king of the Khazars, the famous Crimean people who had converted en masse to Judaism, introducing himself with near-idolatrous respect: "I, Chisdai, son of Isaac, son of Ezra, belonging to the exiled Jews of Jerusalem, in Spain, a servant of my Lord the King, bow to the earth before him and prostrate myself towards the abode of your Majesty, from a distant land."[12]

The year was 960, and Chisdai had heard of a Jewish kingdom in Asia ruled by a Jewish king. Chisdai Abu-Yusuf, as he was known in Arabic, was physician to the king of Navarre, whom he had cured of obesity and helped reclaim the throne. He had been *nasi* of Judeo-Spanish Córdoba, advancing Jewish interests and Jewish studies.[13] Now he wanted to travel to the one land ruled by Jews, for Jews, but he was stuck in Constantinople and had been strongly advised to turn back. He wrote to Joseph, king of the Khazars, to describe his own country and find out if they could exchange visits.

> Let it be known then, to the King my Lord, that the name of our land in which we dwell is called in the sacred tongue Sefarad, but in the language of the Arabs, the indwellers of the land, Alandalus, the name of the capital of the kingdom, Córdoba. The length of it is 25,000 cubits, the breadth 10,000. . . . Córdoba is eighty miles distant from the shore of the sea which flows into your country.

His account showed immense pride in Andalusia, even though, despite his high position, he was inevitably an outsider:

> The land is rich, abounding in rivers, springs, and aqueducts; a land of corn, oil, and wine, of fruits and all manner of delicacies; it has pleasure-gardens and orchards, fruitful trees of every kind, including the leaves of the tree upon which the silkworm feeds, of which we have great abundance. . . . There are also found among us mountains covered by crocus and with veins of silver, gold, copper, iron, tin, lead, sulfur, porphyry, marble, and crystal. . . .
>
> Merchants congregate in it, and traffickers from the ends of the earth . . . bringing spices, precious stones, splendid wares for kings and princes. . . . Our king has collected very large treasures . . . the greater part of which is derived from the merchants who come hither from various countries and islands; and all their mercantile transactions are placed under my control.[14]

All the great diaspora themes are here. He loves the land he lives in, but longs for Jerusalem and travels half the world to find a Jewish country. He is learned and religious, but also a practical physician, and his king has trusted him enough to put all foreign trade in his hands. King Joseph, the

Jewish Khazar monarch, answered him in kind, describing his own land and urging a meeting, but as far as we know it never took place.

At the start of the tenth century, Córdoba was indeed the capital of Andalusia, and in a sense the capital of Spain.[15] The caliphate's influence extended well up into the Castilian plain when Madrid was a distant outpost of Moorish civilization, occasionally slipping into the hands of the backward Christians. Culturally Córdoba was the capital of Europe. A German nun visiting in the tenth century called it "the majesty and adornment of the world, the wondrous capital."[16] Islam had fostered scientific and literary activity in Baghdad during the eighth and ninth centuries, and both Jews and Jewish converts to Islam had helped render Greek texts into Arabic, the new vessel of mathematics, science, and philosophy.[17] With the Muslim conquest, this mantle of civilization settled on Andalusia, and again Jewish physicians and writers played a role.

Chisdai himself completed the Arabic translation of *Materia Medica,* a great Greek compendium of useful drugs, but scientific and medical writing in Hebrew dated back to the 600s, and continued for centuries more. Unfortunately, then as now, secular civilization under Islam had to contend with fundamentalism. Recall that at the end of the eleventh century, Berber fanatics began an assault on Islamic high culture that would eventually bring an end to Spain's golden age and weaken it until it was lost to the Christians. The Berbers' "lightning push out of the Sahara, through Morocco, and into Spain left a trail of Jewish martyrs and forced converts."[18] The boy Maimonides was driven from Córdoba, together with his family, by a mid-twelfth-century Muslim pogrom. To destroy Islamic high culture as the fanatics were determined to do also meant destroying Jews.

This did not end either civilization. Some Jews, like Maimonides, fled to Egypt and the Middle East, where the Islamic genius went right on, far from the twin fundamentalisms of boorish Christians and fanatic Muslims. Other Jews stayed in Spain, fleeing north to temporarily tolerant Christian towns. Because the Jews had belonged to Islamic civilization, they too were vessels of Greek science, medicine, and philosophy, and because of their cosmopolitan outlook, international trade, forced migrations, and love of learning, many were multilingual. Moving through Europe, they brought both Jewish and secular learning, which coexisted far better under Islam than in Ashkenaz.[19]

There were nodes of scholarship in Toledo, Languedoc, and Provence, where Jews translated Arabic scientific and scholarly works into Latin, Spanish, and French—not only philosophy and medicine, but mathematics, geometry, physics, astronomy, astrology, and magic. Some Arabic works went through Hebrew into Latin.[20] Islam preserved the civilization of ancient Greece, and by giving it to Europe ended the Dark Ages, but Muslims and Christians were enemies, so the gift was brought by Jews.

⟨⟪⟫⟩

These Jews were not the Talmud scholars of Mainz and Worms, yet they too had great centers of Torah learning. The town of Gerona is a gem set in the foothills of the Pyrenees in the eastern corner of Spain, walking distance to the Mediterranean Sea and not far from the French border, where the speech of Pyrenean Spain was once barely distinguishable from that of Languedoc. Among the narrow streets of the Jewish quarter, still called Montjuich, what were once a synagogue and a public ritual bath are dominated by a cathedral and a much higher city wall hundreds of meters long. In the cemetery, then outside the city, tombstones inscribed in Hebrew sketch the lives and thoughts of eleventh- and twelfth-century Jews.

A Torah academy grew up in Gerona under Rabbi Moses ben Nachman, known as the Ramban, an acronym recalling Maimonides, the Rambam, the greatest sage of the previous century. The Ramban referred often to Maimonides and Rashi, but also challenged them. Bitter disputes arose, especially in Montpellier and other towns of Provence, where traditional rabbis disliked the philosophy in Maimonides, with its foreign train of thought. Others began the wholehearted embrace of Maimonides that eventually prevailed. The Ramban tried to mediate and angered both sides.

He was less concerned with details than Rashi and tried to get to the core meaning of a text. He was also frankly mystical, a follower of the emerging school of rabbinical thought in Israel known as kabbala. He founded his own tradition, which strangely enough brought the light of Spanish romanticism into the deepest, most mystical reading of the Torah. But his most dramatic moment was when he was coerced into the Disputation of Barcelona, a debate with a former Jew about the relative merits of their two religions. This managed event was among the first of many, all of which exposed Jews—not just participants, but whole communities—to grave danger. But in this case the Ramban was allowed to speak freely. To critics of particular Talmud passages he explained that the Talmud is a record of arguments, and that no one claim necessarily becomes law. As for Christian claims, he did not see the evidence that Jesus had brought about a messianic time:

> Before they believed in him, Rome ruled over most of the world; indeed, after they accepted the Christian faith they lost many principalities. And now the worshippers of Mohamed have more dominion than you. And likewise the prophet says..."Nation shall not lift sword against nation, neither shall they learn war any more." Yet from the days of Jesus until now the whole world has been filled with violence and pillage. The Christians, moreover, shed more blood than other nations; and how hard it would be for

you, your Majesty . . . and for these knights of yours if they were not
to learn war any more.[21]

This bold logic was prophetic. In the thirteenth century Jews of Gerona
began to participate in the government of the city, and their Hebrew signatures appeared on many documents. But in the same century the priests in
the cathedral began their Easter custom of throwing stones down on the
Jewish quarter from the tower. The king of Aragon objected, but it continued. The Jews helped defend the city from French attacks in 1285, but this
did not prevent persecutions. By century's end they were gone from the city
administration and prohibited from some economic activities; there is no
further record of Jewish land ownership. In 1331 rioters broke into the Jewish quarter.

Meanwhile, there were parallel persecutions elsewhere. In 1190, during
the Third Crusade, the Jews of York had committed mass suicide in a castle where they had taken refuge surrounded by their persecutors. A century
later all Jews were expelled from England and most made a futile move to
France. In 1182 the French king had expelled all Jews from the royal domains, canceled Christian debts to them, and confiscated their property.
They were called back in 1198, but over the next century their situation
worsened. Christian authorities were mounting a coordinated effort to
eliminate Jews from most of western Europe.

Rabbi Jehiel of Paris defended the Talmud on the orders of king and
pope. In this Disputation of Paris, echoed by Barcelona's a generation later,
Jehiel declared that whoever touches the Talmud "touches the apple of our
eye. And if you bring down fury against us—why, we have been flung to
the ends of the earth. This Torah of ours is to be found in Babylon and Media and Greece and Ishmael [Arabia], and among the seventy peoples beyond the Rivers of Ethiopia. . . . Our bodies are indeed in your hands, but
not our souls."[22] Bodies, and books, too: after the debate Christians burned
countless copies of the Talmud, a great setback to Torah study in France. It
is said that a mountain of books was set on fire and that it took two days to
burn all the volumes.[23] But worse would come: in 1288 there was a ritual-
murder trial in Troyes, where Rashi had lived and taught; in 1290 a host-
desecration trial in Paris, where the Talmud had been massively burned;
and in 1306 an expulsion edict, canceling all debts to Jews.[24]

The Dominicans were active against the French Jews, and their reach
extended to Naples, where, in a six-year period in the late 1200s, the ancient
Jewish community of southern Italy was turned to dust.[25] Germany was
more feudal and decentralized but equally threatening. The famed Rabbi
Meir of Rothenberg was arrested in 1286 on his way to Israel and died in
prison. In 1298 gangs of rioters ranged from province to province, destroying 140 Jewish communities.[26] There were more massacres in 1336, and

with the spread of the Black Death Jews were accused of poisoning wells. Even the pope denounced this libel, pointing out that countries without Jews were just as affected by the plague, but to no avail. A contemporary woodcut shows Jews being burned alive en masse.

Conditions were little better in Christian Spain.[27] Periodically, as in other lands, kings encouraged Jewish immigration, seeking their technical and economic expertise. Expulsions might be followed by reinstatement years or decades later. In 1260, for instance, a Spanish Jew—Judah ben Lavi de la Cabaleria—became minister of finance for the kingdom of Aragon. But tolerant views and edicts of kings could not hold back the tide of hate flowing from mobs incited by anti-Semitic priests. There were mass killings in Aragon in the mid-1300s, and twelve thousand Jews were massacred in Toledo. In 1391 mobs went from town to town throughout Castile and Aragon, murdering Jews on an immense scale.[28] All the synagogues of Barcelona were destroyed, and the eight-hundred-year-old Jewish community was eliminated. In all, over the course of a year, an estimated fifty thousand Jews were murdered. Only when rioters turned against other Christians did the authorities quell the disturbances.

By that time tens of thousands of Jews, especially the elite, had converted to Christianity to save their lives and property. Although some conversos had lived in Spain since the Visigoths, this was a population explosion of New Christians. Tens of thousands of others remained in Spain and Portugal as Jews, so the two large communities lived side by side. Public debates staged to humiliate Jewish leaders grew in number, and, as in Barcelona, the prosecutors were often former Jews. Some of these set-piece dramas, despite their inevitable conclusions, had an aspect of fairness about them and resulted in no penalties for the Jews. Others led to riots, destruction of synagogues, book burnings, forced conversions, torture, and mass murder.

Conversions only made things worse. Many conversos sought to prove their Christian loyalty by persecuting Jews. Some were not sincere in their conversions; some, in a weak moment, hoping against hope that they could really be Christian, later longed for Jewish belief and practice. These backsliders, called Marranos—it probably stems from a word for pig, although other derivations have been proposed—were targets of virulent hatred. Conversos continued in their old roles as merchants, administrators, and tax collectors, and this, combined with suspicions about their Christian commitment, led to violence. Anti-converso riots engulfed Toledo and Córdoba.

By this time Isabella of Castile and Ferdinand of Aragon had married and united their two kingdoms. In 1480 they established the Inquisition, an instrument of judgment, torture, and execution directed at Jews and conversos for three and a half centuries. But for more than a hundred thousand Spanish Jews, this particular brand of suffering would soon draw to a close.

After a last, massive effort at forced conversion, the king and queen abolished Judaism on March 31, 1492:

> Therefore, in consultation and agreement with the clergy, the higher and lower nobility in our realm, other men of science and conscience from our Council and having deliberated much on the matter, we have agreed to order the expulsion of all Jews and Jewesses in our kingdoms. Never should any one of them return... and if they are found living in our kingdoms and domains, or come here in any way, they should be put to death, their property being confiscated by our Court and Royal Treasury. These punishments will be inflicted on the basis of the act and law, without trial, verdict and proclamation.[29]

That summer all who did not convert were exiled, ending fifteen centuries of openly Jewish life in Spain. This eyewitness account was by a chronicler usually unsympathetic to the Jews:

> In the first week of July they took the route for quitting their native land, great and small, young and old, on foot or horses, in carts each continuing his journey to his destined port. They experienced great trouble and suffered indescribable misfortunes on the road, some falling, others rising, some dying, others being born, some fainting, others being attacked by illness. There was not a Christian but that pitied them and pleaded with them to be baptized. Some from misery were converted, but they were few.

Yet he also notes that "[t]he rabbis encouraged them and made the young people play on pipes and tambours to enliven them and keep up their spirits and thus they left Castile."[30] Some went to Portugal, where, despite royal promises, they were forced to convert or leave five years later, by persecutions as or more brutal than any in Spain.[31] By the turn of the century Iberia was purged of openly practicing Jews.

☙❦❧

So it happened that, except for Spain itself, Judeo-Spanish was spoken on every Mediterranean shore.[32] It was a form of medieval Spanish written in Hebrew letters, full of Hebrew and Arabic borrowings. For example, Saturday is not *sabado* but *shabbat,* and Sunday is not *domingo* but the Arabic *alhad,* meaning "first day." Because the Jews of Spain were especially close to Muslims, many borrowings from Arabic survived in their speech. In the 1500s the Bible was translated into a stilted form of Judeo-Spanish called

Ladino, strictly faithful to the Hebrew text. Prayer books, the Passover Haggadah, and popular parts of the Talmud like the Sayings of the Fathers also took this form.[33] Ladino is written in Rashi's Hebrew script, and is dominated by Hebrew syntax, foreign to its origins.[34]

But Judeo-Spanish was the language of the people, of conversation, business, romance, lying, begging, castigation, proverb, song, and story. Many people use the terms *Ladino* and *Judeo-Spanish* interchangeably, but this is confusing. *"Muestro español"*—"our Spanish"—was thoroughly Hispanic in syntax and in spirit, but in addition to Hebrew and Arabic, it took words from Portuguese, Turkish, Greek, French, Serbo-Croatian, and Italian, reflecting every realm to which the Jews of Spain were exiled. They and their descendants lived side by side with Jews who had been there since ancient times and spoke the languages of these countries. But the newcomers spoke Judeo-Spanish, and taught it to their children. It persisted. When the Nazis rounded up the Jews of Greece, many of the ancient, Greek-speaking Jewish community survived the war because they passed as Christian Greeks, but they had no trouble finding the ones who spoke Judeo-Spanish.

Yet for four centuries the Jews of Spain lived among other Mediterranean peoples while speaking it and, along with Hebrew, using Ladino versions of Torah and prayer. For example, *I avlo Adonay a Moshe i a Aaron . . . estos son los animals ke komeresh de todas las kuatropias ke estan sovre la tierra,* "And the Lord said to Moses and Aaron . . . These are the living things which ye may eat among all the beasts that are on the earth."[35] But their proverbs and songs also say much about their lives, beliefs, and humor.

Some could come from any people. For example, "He who runs, falls," or "Do, don't brag."[36] Others, even though written in Hebrew characters, have a Spanish flavor: *Asembri mi kampo di preshil i kulantro*—"I sowed my field with parsley and cilantro"—used to apologize for a messy house,[37] and *La madre es madre i lo demas es aire*—"Mother is mother and the rest is air."[38] Still others borrow Greek or Turkish. *Saranda le demandó, peninda le dió*— "He asked for forty, he got fifty"—uses Greek words for the numbers, and *Ken se kema en la shorva, ashopla en el yogurt*—"Who burns himself on the soup blows on the yogurt"—uses the Turkish for both foods.

But the most distinctive use Hebrew. One forgives a fumble, saying *Afilú el hazan se yerra*—"Even the cantor makes mistakes." The Hebrew words here are not just *hazan,* "cantor," but also *afilú,* "even," which appears in the Passover seder's Four Questions. A catchphrase, *la ermozura de Ester amalka*—"the beauty of Queen Esther"—uses the Hebrew for queen.[39] *Estamos en los dayenus*—"We are in the *dayenus*"—refers to a song in the middle of the seder and means we have a long way to go. *Si no yo para mi ken para mi?*—"If I am not for myself, who will be for me?"—is an exact translation of one of Rabbi Hillel's best-known sayings.

Este vende la behora por un plato de lentejos—"This one sells his birthright for a plate of lentils"—refers to the Esau story and uses the Hebrew for birthright. In misfortune one might exaggerate, *Esto es korban de sion*—"This is the destruction of Zion." *Ya torno en teshuva*—"He has repented his sins"—takes the richly resonant Hebrew word *teshuva* for repentance; both *torno* and *teshuva*, in their respective languages, come from the root for turning, giving this spare four-word proverb a deep bilingual echo. And in a moving reference to Maimonides' Thirteen Articles of the Faith, *Este está in sus trejes*—"He is in his thirteens"—is said of someone who under duress is faithful to God and Torah.[40]

But even in Hebrew characters, Spanish is the loving tongue, and sayings like *Ken bien te kere te aze yorar*—"He who loves you makes you weep"—and *Ken se echa kon kriatúra s'alevanta pishado*—"He who does it with a child wakes up pissed-on"—resonate with the sorrows and embarrassments of *amor*.[41] Apart from proverbs, Judeo-Spanish has a repertoire of folk songs about love that is simply spectacular. At once dreamily Spanish and eerily Arabian, the music mesmerizes, and the words tell tales of love:

> *The white girl sailed the high seas*
> *Draped with gold and strings of pearls*
> *On her head a sapphire*
> *Lit the night like the midday sun.*[42]

Some, like the Hebrew poems of Spain, are lovers' plaints:

> *Give me your hand, dove,*
> *To climb up to your nest.*
> *Curse that you sleep alone!*
> *Let me come sleep with you . . .*[43]

and "Open up, my darling, it's almost dawn / I don't sleep nights, thinking of you."[44] Others are more explicit: "O! Your beauty and charm last night" one gushes,

> *In your arms, I felt confident*
> *When your hands squeezed my waist,*
> *So darling, let me hold you,*
> *Let me ease all my passion.*

The seductions of brides by grooms are especially touching. One from Rhodes, "La Galana i su kabayo"—"The Beauty and Her Horse"—boldly symbolizes the bride and her virile groom.[45] It ends, "They go to the bed freshly made. . . . By midnight they have a new game. . . . May it last for years to come!" A subtler one starts with three voices:

Come down, down, gentle bride,
For the roosters sing out at dusk.
I can't, my love, for I am busy
Putting on my silk blouse,
Putting on my wedding coat.
Now our bridegroom comes for kidushim.

The coat is a *sayo,* from the Greek *saias;* it was worn by married women among the Spanish Jews of Salonika. *Kidushim* is Hebrew, denoting the core of the wedding ritual. Such blends pervade the repertoire.

My love's gone to war
I don't know when he will come
If he returns or does not return
I will love him ever more.

Not all are love songs. Some tell stories like that of King Nimrod, a medieval monarch with a magnificent castle on Mount Hermon. He was a hero to the Spanish Jews, but the refrain evokes another hero. The first two and last words are in Hebrew:

Avraham avinu,
Padre ķerido,
Padre bendicho,
Luz de Yisrael.

The merging of two languages, preserved by Jews in a double exile, is in this refrain especially affecting. It is sung again and again in a lilting, nasal Spanish style, a blend of praise and love, memory and longing in the face of martyrdom and exile: "Abraham our father, dear father, blessed father, Light of Israel."

👁

During centuries of relentless persecution, only about half of the Jews of Spain stayed Jewish, but what happened to the others is of no small interest.[46] By the time of the expulsion there were perhaps two hundred thousand of them in Spain, shaping Spanish as well as Jewish history. They are often called New Christians—ironic, since their "newness" as Christians could last for centuries. One denigrating term is Alboraycos, given them by a book meant to indict them—*Libro de Alborayque*—published just before the expulsion in the late 1480s.[47] The image invoked was that of Muhammad's steed, al-Buraq, an animal neither horse nor mule, male nor female. So the New Christians were seen—intolerably ambiguous, violating the universal proscription against mixing. Marranos began as a derogation but became for some a badge of honor, burnished in sarcasm.[48] It refers to the subgroup of converts who continued to feel and in some ways act like Jews. Secret Jews is a respectful designation, but they called themselves "anusim"— Hebrew for "the forced ones."[49]

The most general term is conversos, converts, which covers the range from devout Catholics through uncaring apostates to secretly faithful, cautiously practicing crypto-Jews. Recall that forced conversions began in the early seventh century, but there were scores of thousands after the massacres of 1391, over a hundred thousand more at the time of the expulsion in 1492, and tens of thousands in Portugal after 1497. It is no surprise that many were insincere, but even some of the truest Christians among the converts were persecuted for generations.

Ongoing emigration resulted, provoking Spain and Portugal to prohibit conversos from leaving. Still, they secretly slipped across the border to countries where they could be openly Jewish, or just live as Christians. Those caught backsliding either at home or abroad in Europe were treated savagely. Yet books like Samuel Usque's *Consolation for the Tribulations of Israel* were published, explicitly trying to draw conversos back into Judaism. Large numbers were crypto-Jews, playing a cat-and-mouse game with church authorities while practicing their former faith. Portuguese conversos were so likely to be in this category that by the sixteenth century, as they sought refuge around the world, the word *Portuguese* was almost synonymous with *Jew* in parts of Europe and Latin America.

In the papal lands of Italy conversos were intermittently safe, but the Counter-Reformation produced a pope, Paul IV, who pursued them fiercely. In the spring of 1556, twenty-five "Judaizers" were burned alive and twenty-six others were sent to the galleys. In Ferrara they succeeded for a time, but in the 1580s the duke stopped protecting them. Many were arrested; three were sent to Rome and burned at the stake. Venice alternately expelled and protected them, while conditions in Tuscany attracted them. The duke of Savoy settled Jews in Nice to develop Asian trade, but they were expelled by 1581. In Sicily, Sardinia, and Naples, Secret Jews were systematically purged in the sixteenth and seventeenth centuries.

The Italian Jews were also affected by events unfolding elsewhere. Elia da Montalto was a converso physician who had moved to Venice and there returned to the Jewish fold. On August 15, 1611, he wrote to friends who had recently escaped from Portugal and were living in a village in the south of France: "We have been terrified here by the news about the happenings in Lisbon and Madrid. . . . In these painful tidings we never had nor have now any other consolation than the vivid faith that the Lord, blessed be his Name, guides by the way of such trials those whom He loves."[50] These friends soon began to embrace Christianity more fully, however, and Montalto was moved to write again on May 8, 1612: "I protest incessantly against your following a road which must lead you to the precipice and to the undoing of your soul. . . . May the Lord have pity on your soul and take you away from that blind idolatry."[51]

In France conversos were more tolerated. They had to practice Judaism clandestinely, but could do so for two centuries, despite widespread knowledge of what they were doing. Over time they became less and less Catholic, even giving up church marriage and baptism. In 1730 they were officially allowed to be Jews. In Antwerp, Judaizing was strictly forbidden. Jews sought refuge in newly settled Latin America, where there was much more scope for private Jewish practice, but in time the Inquisition came there, too.

In Muslim and Protestant countries, where people hated Catholics, there was no such persecution. Morocco had long been a haven. In the Ottoman Empire, the sultan at the time of the expulsion ridiculed Ferdinand and Isabella for impoverishing their country by sending away the Jews. Under him and later sultans, Spanish Jews settled safely in Cairo, Damascus, Constantinople, Salonika, Safed, and Jerusalem. In Protestant Hamburg, Jewish settlement was authorized in 1612 and Jewish public worship in 1650. In Episcopal England, forced converts were allowed to practice Judaism but were never officially recognized as Jews. Ordinary Jews won the Crown's protection in 1664, but forced converts and their descendants, now de facto Jews, would lead the community for two centuries.

In Amsterdam, one of the greatest havens Jews have ever had, anusim could be openly Jewish from the beginning. When other Jews fled persecution in France and eastern Europe during the 1600s, many settled in Amsterdam. Some went to Suriname, Curaçao, and other Dutch colonies beginning in 1650, although Peter Stuyvesant barred them from New Amsterdam, later to be New York.

Among anusim it was thought wise for one member of each family to become a priest, who could even keep Hebrew texts with impunity. But many were sincere in their conversions, becoming not only priests but bishops and archbishops. Two—Teresa of Ávila and John of God—were canonized.[52] Others entered into the many public disputations designed to humiliate Jews. Some became the most vicious persecutors of Jews. In 1481 autos-da-fé began. These "acts of faith"—the church's name for publicly burning Secret Jews alive—went on for centuries.

To avoid this Secret Jews did everything but actually give up their faith. They went to mass diligently and made vows and declarations of belief—in fact, the eerie, moving Kol Nidre prayer of Yom Kippur Eve was designed to nullify these vows. They took communion. They named their children Jesús and María. Leaving and coming home, devout Secret Jews would kiss the foot of a statue of the Madonna, knowing that inside it was a tiny Hebrew scroll: *Shema Yisroel*—Hear, O Israel!—"and you shall love the Lord your god with all your heart, and with all your soul, and with all your might." The Madonna's foot was a mezuzah, and the forced converts were carrying out the commandment to "write these words upon your gates."

The church distributed guidelines:

> If you see that your neighbors are wearing clean and fancy clothes on Saturdays, they are Jews.
>
> If they clean houses on Fridays and light candles earlier than usual on that night, they are Jews.
>
> If they fast for a whole day, until nightfall, they are Jews.
>
> If they refer to Queen Esther, they are Jews.
>
> If they eat unleavened bread and begin their meal with celery and lettuce during Holy Week, they are Jews.
>
> If they say prayers facing a wall, bowing back and forth, they are Jews.
>
> If they prepare meat in a special way, draining away its blood and cutting away fat and gristle, they are Jews.
>
> If they avoid eating pork, rabbit, eels, or other scaleless fish, they are Jews.
>
> If you observe them sitting on the floor, eating eggs and olives and throwing morsels of bread into the fire upon the death of a relative, they are Jews.
>
> If they name their children after personages in the Old Testament instead of saints and never say "Glory to the Trinity," they are Jews.[53]

Over time, the Secret Jews became more careful about these things or slowly abandoned them. Still, many were on a collision course with the Inquisition. Add the fact that Christians who denounced their neighbors as Secret Jews got half of the confiscated property, and you have a process as ruthless as any in history. Few tyrants could match the bizarre, inventive cruelty of the Inquisition—nor could any savage practice in the anthropological record. There is no need to speculate on the fate of arrested Secret Jews. The instruments of torture all survive in church museums, and church archives preserve detailed transcripts of many torture sessions.

The Inquisitors routinely extracted confessions by offering an earlier end to torture and an easier death, and the confessions had to include a declaration of faith in Judaism and a rejection of Catholic beliefs. In the complex emotional world of the forced converts, where traditional practices took on a life of their own, this was not always true, but it did bring an end to endless pain. Neither Judaizing converts nor ordinary Jews—guilty by association with backsliders—were the Inquisition's only victims, but they were the great majority in the early years. Some twenty thousand Jews were burned at the stake, most after creative, lengthy tortures.

In some ways the persecution of the conversos was a true instance of racial anti-Semitism, because in Christian eyes the taint of Jewishness remained in the blood even after a thorough and sincere embrace of Christ.[54] Indeed, even at best there seemed something insidious in this Jewish attempt to "pass"—a Christian reaction that prefigured by centuries the worst disaster in Jewish history. Large numbers of Inquisition victims were not Judaizing at all, just tainted by their ancestry. Indeed, it has been forcefully argued that the Inquisition had the cynical goal of ridding Spain of even the most sincere New Christians and robbing them of their property regardless of their faith. Most chilling in this regard were the pre-exilic Spanish laws preventing conversos from holding office, known as *estatutos de limpieza de sangre*—blood-purity statutes.[55] These laws made it clear that Jews were not allowed to become like everyone else even if they embraced Christianity with all their hearts: racial anti-Semitism codified in law.

⟨꧁꧂⟩

In some form the Inquisition was everywhere in Europe. Still, leaving Spain was a watershed for many Secret Jews, the beginning of the end of their grossly inferior status. In each new place economic and social opportunities opened. They rose to the top ranks of merchants, established national banks, minted coins, created insurance companies, and led stock exchanges. They manufactured armaments, built ships, and made crafts, soap, and drugs. They ran the trade in sugar, tobacco, coral, and precious stones, and founded family dynasties. Like exiled Jews before and since, their unintended international experience positioned them for economic activity. Add to this the restrictions against owning and managing land, and you have a set of pressures and opportunities that inevitably drove talented Jews, secret or open, into business. Some attained positions of political influence and leadership.

Anusim, like open Jews, were drawn to intellectual life, becoming scientists, physicians, philosophers, and writers. First Ferrara and Venice, then Amsterdam, Hamburg, and London had important printing presses that helped create converso culture. Some of the works were theological and philosophical, explicitly directed at conversos struggling with the prospect of returning to open Judaism. This kept a wide channel open between the descendants of conversos and the Jewish world.

Consider the experience of three seventeenth-century poets. Juan Pinto Delgado was raised as a Secret Jew, and when he moved from Portugal to France he found a secure Jewish community that made the move to open practice easy. Miguel de Barrios may have had a similar background, but was a military officer and bon vivant who was more aloof from Jewish life in his adopted city of Amsterdam. He ended as a quasi-Christian messianist. Antonio Enríquez Gómez had less Jewish background, but embraced Judaism fully after a crisis at age fifty.

They wrote in Spanish, not Judeo-Spanish or Hebrew, but their works are full of Jewish themes. Delgado's affecting poem on leaving Lisbon calls God's power against his oppressors:

> *You'll beg your gods for help*
> *in vain, O gentile,*
> *If David killed ten thousand,*
> *What then the Lord's hand?*

The same poem takes comfort in "Sacred Jerusalem, / Sweet blessing, sweet remembrance."[56] His "Poem of Queen Esther" brought him fame, and he went on to retell the stories of the Exodus, Ruth, and the Babylonian exile in Spanish verse.

Barrios wrote movingly of his wife's death in a double sonnet, "Memory Renews Pain," which opens, "My kind and gentle wife fell to earth, / and in her fall climbs to heaven." He wrote poems about creation, contrition, God's providence toward Israel, and a defense of the Law, personified as a woman:

> *The three that Lisbon burned alive*
> *Did not fear the pyre*
> *The altar of the Law they loved*
> *Called them to God by fire.*

> *She proves inquisitors false. . . .*
> *She demolishes idols*
> *And those who make them.*

His beloved Torah is with him on fasts and festivals: "She comes on *Kippur* with balances, / On *Pesach* with triumphant songs."

And Gómez wrote about Adam and Eve, Samson, and the Inquisition's victims. He himself was one, but kept his faith:

> *You want me to adore*
> *Three distinct entities*
> *Multiplying deities*
> *With festivals galore. . . .*
> *If He is three gods in one,*
> *The prophets went astray,*

> *For they worshiped One alone,*
> *Not more in any way.*

His monotheistic faith is impassioned as that of the Maccabees: "Only God, says Moses, pardoned you in the desert. . . . Only God, Isaiah says, rules over man. . . . Only God, says David, can redeem his people." This was the faith by which he lived and died.

> *A life devoid of God*
> *I neither seek nor value;*
> *Life's gifts without the Law*
> *I never will consent to.*

Gómez was burned in effigy by the Inquisition in 1660, arrested in 1661, and died while awaiting sentencing.

If Jews are God wrestlers, the anusim and their descendants surely qualify. Many persisted in ambiguity for centuries, and ambiguity itself became the focus of their culture. Hiding meant survival. Some who came to Holland in the 1500s stayed secret for four centuries. In 1920 they became open Jews. Two decades later, almost all of them were murdered by the Nazis, and only a few who had stayed secret survived.[57]

✦✦✦

In the city of Palma on the island of Majorca live the *Chuetas,* the "Catholic Jews." They have distinctive names—Forteza, Aguiló, Martí, and Miró, among others—marry within the community, tend to be silversmiths, and are subjected to strong prejudice. A neighbor said,

> They are Catholics, but to be a true Christian you have to be concerned about something besides money, you have to be something of a romantic. There is nothing romantic about the Chuetas. They are all business like any other Jews. True, they go to church and are good Catholics in that sense; but they have a Jewish psychology, a Jewish way of looking at life. They are dull, unimaginative, and stupid. They are very Jewish looking, too, and their women age rapidly. They are really a rather revolting group.[58]

Prejudices notwithstanding, Chuetas are very good Catholics, some almost too good. But they are aware and mostly proud of being descended from Jews, of once being Inquisition targets, and of being different from their neighbors. The issue of Jewish descent is publicly discussed, especially since World War II, when Spain's Fascist alliance brought Nazi scrutiny of Jewish ancestry. Chuetas are keenly aware of the status of Jews in the world, and are intensely interested in and supportive of Israel. They see it as a potential refuge from persecution, even for them. Twenty-four Chuetas migrated to Israel in the 1960s; all but one returned. Rarely, a Chueta becomes drawn to Judaism. They are thoroughly Majorcan, but one might say they are quasi Jews because they share Jewish vulnerability.

Elsewhere there are people more like the Secret Jews of old. In Recife, in northeastern Brazil, there are many "secret" Jews who now want to be open ones. They want to return to Judaism, not convert to it, and they are being frozen out by the Ashkenazic authorities who dominate Jewish life in Brazil. But they persist, observing Jewish law as well as they can. "There are six hundred thirteen *mitzvot*," said one man about the commandments. "It's better to follow six hundred than none." They are trying to gain acceptance in the Jewish day schools, but in the meantime they follow the tradition of their ancestors in relation to the Christian community. One boy, asked to sing Ave Maria in school, sang the Shema instead.[59]

In the southwestern United States there is a community of 1,500 descendants of anusim. On the surface they are ordinary Hispanic American Catholics, but they have a partly Jewish identity.[60] Their struggles can be intense. One woman found the inscription *Somos Judíos*—"We are Jews"— inscribed in her grandmother's prayer book. A devout Catholic, she felt the book burning her hands and prayed to Jesus that it not be true. But as she learned more about Judaism, Jewish Law appealed to her, especially the strict prohibition of idols. At length she became Jewish, and a few others have done the same. Some visit the cemetery and find their ancestors' tombs facing east, carved with Stars of David or menorahs, pebbles placed on them by unseen visitors. Others recall a grandmother teaching them not to eat meat with milk, having flat, round bread at Easter, and having boys circumcised by a doctor at eight days of age.

Their situation is difficult. As one descendant of an old, distinguished family said,

> Marranos have never been accepted by Jewish communities, anywhere. We are told, "You are not Jews, not *really*." We cry, "What do you mean we're not Jews? We died, were burned at the stake because of our faith!"
>
> At Marrano meetings, one of the main topics is: "When will the Jewish community finally understand us, understand our history? When will they stop shutting us out, when will they stop judging us?" After all those years of being a Marrano, all of us begin to feel like variants, like zebras. The white horse looks at us and sees only the black stripes, and disowns us; the black horse sees only the white

stripes and asks, "Why are you white?" Neither side trusts us, neither side lets us in. They treat us as though we do not exist. But we do exist, whether they like it or not. *Zebras exist!*[61]

But most don't want to be either uncomplicated Catholics or ordinary Jews, and not just because of prejudice. Detested by Catholics, distrusted by Jews, the anusim created a new, third culture of their own, a clandestine world full of mysteries and rituals some of which even they did not understand. In a criminally hostile world, they found comfort in secrecy and felt secure only when they were hiding. After many generations this pattern *was* their tradition, and, in a supreme paradox, they could feel authentic— honor their ancestors—only when they were systematically dissembling. They thought of their forebears as heroes.

〰️

But most anusim who stayed in Spain simply blended into the Spanish fabric over the centuries, while the vast majority of those who left Spain remained Spanish Jews. They are the Sephardim, and it would be difficult to overstate their influence. Shortly before the exile the Jews of Spain and Portugal were more than half the Jews of Europe.[62] They dispersed widely, created new linguistic forms, and had a distinctive culture for centuries. After pioneering this new diaspora, they were joined by a steady trickle of other forced converts who had lingered in Spain and Portugal. The first exiles created havens where their compatriots could become Jewish again, and many did.[63]

Because Inquisition, exile, and genocide greatly reduced their numbers and dispersed their weakened communities, they never regained the status they had had during the early Middle Ages.[64] But their Jewishness flourished and their culture maintained its power and beauty. For example, the great rabbinical scholar Joseph Caro began life in Spain and Portugal but ended in Israel, among the sages of Safed. There in 1555 he published the *Shulkhan Arukh,* "The Set Table," a compilation of talmudic rulings for practical use. A few years later it was adopted by the rabbis of Ashkenaz and published in Cracow with minor modifications whimsically called "The Tablecloth."[65] It largely replaced the earlier *Mishneh Torah* of Maimonides and has been the basic guide to Jewish practice ever since.

For four centuries after the expulsion, most Sephardim lived under Turkish rule because the Ottoman Empire was now the center of Islamic civilization. At its height it extended around the Mediterranean from Algeria to Greece, north into the Caucasus and the Balkans, and east into Arabia and Mesopotamia. The Ottomans, having recently come to power and not sharing Christian prejudices, greeted the Jewish exiles with open arms, realizing that these adept international traders and professionals would strengthen their nation. The sultan who welcomed them, hearing a courtier praise Ferdinand of Aragon, is said to have remarked, "How can you consider intelligent a man who impoverishes his own reign to enrich mine?" He decreed that mistreatment of Jews was punishable by death.[66]

The Jews brought not only international trade but crafts such as glass-blowing, manufacture of silk and other textiles, printing, medicine, even weapons design. Resentment of Christian persecution strengthened their loyalty, and they rose and fell with Ottoman power. Living separately but amicably with the much older Jewish communities known as Romaniot, the exiles kept their language and some of their customs but gradually absorbed Turkish influence in dress, music, and speech. This was also the pattern in Greece, the Balkans, and elsewhere in the empire. But speech, songs, proverbs, foods, children's games, and Bible translations were all Spanish, and remained so until the twentieth century.

As for northern Europe, many of the Sephardim there came from Portugal, and were forced converts returning to Judaism. They spoke mainly Portuguese, although they often knew Judeo-Spanish and Hebrew. Their descendants embraced Judaism strongly, and these born-again Jews played a large role in the expansion of trade during the Age of Exploration. The center of their world was Amsterdam, which had been a Spanish colony and so was a natural destination for the exiles. Indeed, the success of the first anusim in Amsterdam paved the way for Jews generally. Portuguese became the Jewish language of Amsterdam, the Portuguese Synagogue the crown of its Jewish life. Spanish persisted as a more prestigious literary language, but Portuguese continued to be spoken by many Jews in the Low Countries into the nineteenth century.

Jewish intellectual currents in the region did not stop at the boundaries of Judaism, however, and they produced one of the great European philosophers, Baruch Spinoza. Spinoza's skepticism—among other things, he pioneered research on the authorship of the Torah—was expressed with enough genius to threaten the Jewish establishment, and he was excommunicated by Amsterdam's rabbinical authorities in 1656. Another indication of Jewish prosperity in Amsterdam is in Rembrandt's paintings. Not only did he paint many moving scenes drawn from the Torah, but he also depicted well-to-do Dutch Jews. Wealthy Jewish merchants were among his best patrons, and Jewish fees helped sustain him.

But it is thanks to a lesser artist that we can not just imagine but almost see the lives of the Dutch Sephardim. Bernard Picart was a French engraver who settled in Amsterdam and in 1723, after more than a decade there, began documenting the religious lives of Jewish and other communities. Men in classic Dutch dress, with tricornered hats but draped in prayer shawls, sit and stand around the *bima* of a synagogue under a great chandelier burning many candles. On the *bima* a man trumpets a long ram's horn. According to his notes for the engraving, "The horn is sounded on the first day of the year, to tell the Jews that they should listen attentively and humbly to the judgment that God is about to pronounce on sinners. . . . Its curved shape is explained as representing the posture of a man humbling himself."[67] Above the horn, as much elevated as segregated, the women sit in a partly screened balcony. For Yom Kippur, although this time in a German synagogue, Picart depicts a scene of the most serious penitence—weak-looking men in a darkened synagogue, shrouded in capacious prayer shawls:

> We ought to do the Jews that justice which is due to them; they observe everything that may be called the outside of repentance with extreme care. . . . on such occasions the spectator himself can hardly forbear feeling a sharp remorse for his own sins at the sight. . . . Some penitents pass the night and sometimes all the next day standing, without shifting place, perpetually, in prayer and meditation.

Another engraving shows the great Holy Ark of the finest synagogue in Amsterdam, on Simchat Torah, the Rejoicing of the Law, with all doors open, exposing nine or ten sumptuously appointed Torahs, which "after a few prayers . . . are brought out of the ark and carried in procession around the desk."

Still another shows the same synagogue in a wide-angle view of a vast hall, with a forty-foot ceiling on six massive Greek columns. The simple lattice windows flood the hall with light, and the floor is crowded with men, women, and children standing in casual postures but in elegant eighteenth-century dress. Most of the men have prayer shawls draped over their tri-cornered hats. In the exact center of the scene is a *bima,* surrounded by a low rail, with a reader at the table chanting from a prayer book. The occasion is the annual anniversary of the dedication of the synagogue about a century earlier.

But the most touching engraving is that of a much smaller synagogue. Also in prayer shawls but far more modestly dressed, the congregants crowd around a little fenced-in *bima.* The focus is the Torah, spread wide by a pair of strong hands and held high for everyone to see. He "turns it towards the four winds, upon which the congregation say: *Behold the law which Moses gave to the children of Israel.*" The gesture is precisely that of Ezra, two thousand years earlier, holding the scroll of the Law up above the heads of the congregation in Jerusalem.

Speaking of the four winds, Amsterdam, a center of world commerce, became an embarkation point for Jewish migration elsewhere. In some places long-standing Ashkenazic communities were joined by prosperous new Portuguese Jews, reconverted conversos. In London, the tiny converso settlement represented the first return of Jews to England since the brutal expulsion of 1290.[68] They did not keep their culture to the extent that the exiled Spanish Jews did, but they stayed distinct. Traces of Portuguese survive among Jews today in the prayer for the queen in Amsterdam and the announcement of congregational honors in London. The Jews of Britain numbered 150 in 1660, 6,000 in 1734, and 30,000 in 1850.[69] Many were Sephardim, including Benjamin Disraeli, the great Victorian prime minister and novelist, and Sir Moses Montefiore, a banker who established Jewish communities in Israel.

Accompanying the consummate Dutch explorers and being accomplished traders in their own right, Sephardic Jews helped open both the Far East and the Americas to European commerce. Jewish traders brought to the Netherlands wool and furs from eastern Europe, kosher wine from Bordeaux, lemons and oranges from the Middle East, almonds, wax, figs, cork, tin, and grain from North Africa, pepper, cinnamon, ginger, and pearls from Ceylon and India, rice, coffee, teak, and diamonds from the Dutch East Indies, and sugar and spices from the New World.[70] Portuguese-speaking Dutch Jews, mainly anusim, settled in all these places.[71] They came to Goa, the Portuguese colony in India, in 1510, only to be subject to the Inquisition begun there two generations later, with more than thirty burned at the stake. They expanded the Jewish community of Cochin, originally settled by Persian Jews centuries earlier, and built the Paradesi synagogue there in 1568. They joined the Dutch in fighting Portugal for control of the peninsula, and suffered greatly when the Portuguese won.

The Sephardic communities of the Netherlands naturally became the sources of most early Jewish settlement in the New World. They helped the Dutch conquer Brazil in 1624, settling in Recife and elsewhere. Thirty years later, when the Portuguese reconquered Brazil, they moved to Suriname, Martinique, Barbados, Curaçao, Jamaica, and—after initial opposition by Christian authorities—New Amsterdam. In all these places they fostered trade, established plantations, attained high office, and, of course, built synagogues. In Suriname, for example, there were three synagogues by 1685, serving around fifty Jewish-owned plantations. In Spanish and Portuguese colonies, however, the New World was like the old one. Where there were Catholics there were Inquisitors, and Secret Jews were burned at the stake in Peru, Mexico, and Brazil, or sent back to Spain or Portugal to face the same fate.

☙

The most developed and enduring Sephardic culture was nowhere in the Christian world but under the Ottoman Empire, especially in Turkey, Greece, and the Balkans. The sultan who thought the Spanish monarchs fools gained greatly. The exiles brought knowledge, skill, pragmatic imagination, international outreach, money, and prosperity. Through their connections to Jewish traders in Venice alone, they exported linens, woolens, hides, wax, ginger, pepper, lead, and precious stones, in exchange for Venetian silk.[72] Salonika and Safed were textile centers. Guilds of skilled workers and artisans were important economic institutions in Turkey, and during the sixteenth to eighteenth centuries there were specifically Jewish guilds for gold- and silversmiths, silver-button makers, silver-thread makers, weavers, dyers, wool cleaners, butchers, meat-scrap sellers, cheese- and yogurt makers, alehouse owners, druggists and perfumers, musicians and entertainers, dockworkers, fishermen, and boatmen. Some Jews also joined mixed-religion guilds.

The community already had a long history. Benjamin of Tudela, traveling in 1159, had found two thousand Jews and five hundred Karaites near Constantinople, including tanners, artificers in silk, merchants, rabbis, scholars, and the king's physician. By the 1850s, centuries after the Sephardic settlement, a Jewish traveler from Vienna could record the following occupations held by Jews of the city:

> 100 masons, 150 glaziers, 400 nailers, 1,000 tinsmiths, 2 proprietors of hot-houses, 150 manufacturers of mirrors, 2 manufacturers of cotton thread, 100 manufacturers of silk lace, 500 manufacturers of gold and silk lace, 180 dyers of cloth and silk, 100 shoemakers, 500 tailors, 100 furriers, 50 embroiderers in gold and silver, 150 gold and silver-smiths, 1 polisher of jewels, 200 enchasers of rubies and emeralds, 900 fishermen, 100 *restaurateurs,* 550 pastry cooks, 100 sugar-bakers, 200 distillers of brandy, 50 tobacco-cutters, 100 gunsmiths, 300 manufacturers of weights and measures, 1 engineer, 1,000 bookbinders, 20 clerks, 500 physicians, 40 surgeons, 700 barbers, 50 apothecaries, 500 musicians, and 10 rope-dancers.[73]

At the top of the social scale, as early as the sixteenth century, wealthy community leaders like Don Joseph Nasi and Doña Gracia became courtiers and imperial counselors, and Moses Hamon was the personal physician to Süleyman the Magnificent. The first Sephardic printing press in Constantinople was built in 1494, two years into the exile. It published works in Hebrew on Torah and mysticism as well as a flourishing output of formal literature in Ladino.[74] By the early 1500s, just a few years into the exile, Salonika was second only to Safed in Torah studies because of the influx of scholars from Spain.[75] Despite certain Islamic prohibitions, through negotiation and bribery synagogues were built and rebuilt throughout the Ottoman Empire. Their design took varied forms, depending on the community's wealth and place of origin. Aragon, Catalonia, and Toledo were the names of three of them, but others had Hebrew names: Etz Chayim (Tree of Life),

Bikkur Cholim (Visiting the Sick, a major commandment), Shalom, and Talmud Torah.[76]

Finely crafted ornaments graced the Torahs. Wealthier synagogues had ornately carved benches and balconies, beautifully painted ceilings and walls, and Torah ties and Ark curtains sumptuously embroidered in gold and silver thread—including the date of the gift and name of the donor in Hebrew characters. Prayers could be embroidered in a menorah shape, text might cover almost every inch of the curtain, or there might be just one phrase in Hebrew: *Zeh HaSha'ar l'Adonay*—"This is the gate to God"— although God's name would be abbreviated, not written out. Some bore the *hamsa,* or protective hand, common throughout the Islamic world among Muslims and Jews alike. Others had the exclusively Jewish two-handed shape, with Vs between the ring and middle fingers, formed for the ancient priestly blessing.[77]

The *kahal,* or congregation, was the basic communal unit, and for generations each *kahal* reflected the cultural character of the particular Spanish town or region of origin. In Constantinople (today called Istanbul) and Salonika there were dozens of such communities. The leaders were rabbis, assisted by tax assessors, functionaries, and liaisons to the caliphate. Synagogues were educational, social, and political institutions as well as religious ones. The Jewish court (the *beit din,* or house of judgment) handled most cases, but sometimes disputes spilled over into Islamic *shari'a* courts.

This culture changed only slowly for four centuries. In dress, jewelry, and other adornments, Turkish custom gradually supplanted Spanish; except for the required distinguishing marker, it would have been difficult to tell Jewish from Muslim women. Even this distinction was not always enforced, and women of means were dramatically adorned in standard fashion throughout the empire from Bosnia to Jerusalem.[78] The mode was multicolored floor-length dresses covered by fur-trimmed robes, lacy shawls and other head coverings, and several gold necklaces, some made of coins. For men, it was ankle-length solid-colored or striped shirts covered by simple robes, with a tall red fez for a head covering. The poor wore simpler versions of these fashions.

At weddings Islamic customs and Turkish dress mingled with strict observance of Torah Law. Many gorgeously colorful, hand-painted *kettubot* attest to the importance and solemnity of the Jewish marriage contract even while reflecting Turkish decorative style. A particularly beautiful one from Rhodes, in 1843—for Joya, a rabbi's daughter, and her groom, Chayim— repeatedly represents a Turkish-style building with minarets and a bright blue roof shaded by palm trees, and a Hebrew inscription beginning, "In good fortune, blessing, and prosperity. . . ."[79] As in Morocco, the wedding was preceded by a henna night celebration for the bride—a widespread

Muslim tradition—as well as by a strict Jewish ritual immersion. The day after the wedding, the bride was dressed in the robe and headdress of a Turkish married woman, and on the following Sabbath the groom was called to the Torah.[80]

After childbirth, women were lavishly cared for, and mother and child were protected by amulets against the evil eye and against Lilith, the shadowy, sexual demoness who since the time of Eve had menaced Jewish childbirth. If the child was a boy, at eight days he was ritually circumcised; if a firstborn boy, at thirty days he was redeemed. Daughters were ceremoniously named, by a rabbi, in the presence of a minyan, at seven days in Turkey, thirty in Greece. These ceremonies closed the phase of greatest vulnerability and marked the start of a more secure life for the newborn child. As the Sephardic saying went, *Mujer paridera al Satan lo vense*—"The woman who gives birth conquers Satan."[81]

Religious life was equally intense among the Jews of Rhodes, a Greek island off the Turkish shore. Isaac Jack Lévy, a Sephardic scholar who grew up in Rhodes, has vivid memories of weddings and circumcisions, both involving processions through the streets. An eight-day-old boy was carried on a cushion by his grandmother, while "[t]he oriental music of the players, the singing of the people, the laughter, the tossing out Turkish and Greek candy, the carriages decorated with colorful ribbons and flowers, transformed the *judería* [the Jewish neighborhood] in the Old City into a festival. The celebration ended in the home, in the synagogue, or, depending on the wealth of the family, in a large ballroom."[82]

Among the distinctive customs of the Jews of Rhodes were ritually sacrificing a hen and a rooster at each home the day before Yom Kippur and placing a drop of blood on every forehead; parades from synagogue to synagogue on Simchat Torah; oil lamps instead of candles on Chanukah; and the tradition that the trees embrace each other on Tu B'Shvat to celebrate their new year. Like other Mediterranean cultures, the Spanish Jews, far more than their northern European counterparts, made cooking an art form, and elaborate meals prepared from subtle ancient recipes—crowned with pastries and candies—were only one aspect of their gift for enjoying life.

⌒▥▥⌒

As elsewhere around the Mediterranean, Ottoman Jews came under Westernizing influence in the late nineteenth century, partly thanks to the Alliance Israélite Universelle centered in Paris.[83] The First World War and the epidemics of that period led many Jews to emigrate, especially to North America, and those who stayed faced a divided fate. The Jews of Turkey persisted in dwindling numbers.[84] But in Greece and the Balkans, Hitler proved a Satan that even a new mother's magic powers could not vanquish.

His minions arrived in 1941 and gradually began rounding up Jews.[85] Descendants of Spanish exiles still spoke Judeo-Spanish, and were far more easily identified than the Romaniot, Greek-speaking Jews who had been there from ancient times. The vast majority of the Sephardic Jews of Salonika, Rhodes, and other Greek cities were deported to Auschwitz in 1943. The number of Greek Jews murdered approximated sixty thousand, with a similar number in Yugoslavia.[86] It was almost exactly 450 years after the Spanish expulsion of 1492 and effectively ended Judeo-Spanish life in Greece and most of the Balkans. In Bulgaria, however, due to anti-German sentiment and the heroic intervention of a few decent people, transports of Jews to death camps were repeatedly frustrated, and the great majority of the Sephardic Jews there—about fifty thousand—survived.[87]

Sephardim have been called not the Jews *of* Spain, but the Jews *from* Spain, defined as much by their second diaspora as by their centuries-long Spanish sojourn. In a sense these Jews had a double exile. For millennia they had dreamed of an almost otherworldly Jerusalem, and after the expulsion they also longed for an almost mythic life in Spain. They idealized both, and both ideals sustained them. These Jews, at risk of their lives and in forfeit of their property, had refused to convert under the Spanish and Portuguese hammer. Together with large numbers of forced converts, they kept in their hearts the singular God of Israel, the guiding Law of the Torah, and the distant memory of Jerusalem.

But they also held in fond regard the culture of the land of their long sojourn, the language, legend, history, art, poetry, and song of Iberia. The romance of its traditions must have seemed at first not quite Jewish. But perhaps in the end they just embraced the spirit of the Song of Songs along with that of Leviticus, lived a bit more in the mold of King David and King Solomon and not just strictly that of Moses and Aaron. And if—except for the lifeboats of America and Israel—their culture could not survive, then perhaps the Sephardim took comfort in the richness of the tradition they were losing. Some wrote beautiful, heartrending poems about their dreadful experience.[88] Perhaps some, on their way to Auschwitz, even thought of the words of Samuel the Prince, the great Hebrew warrior-bard of medieval Spain:

> *Take heart in time of sorrow,*
> *Though you face death's door.*
> *The candle flares before it dies,*
> *And wounded lions roar.*[89]

9

BRIGHTNESS

HOW JEWISH GENIUS CHANGED AND GREW

The ascent to Safed (Tsfat in Hebrew) today takes fifteen minutes or so in a car. You zig and zag up a steep mountain that juts out of the Galilean plain like a fat pyramidal blob. The climb is dizzying, the views endless, and the feeling, by the time you reach the top—if you are in the least way spiritual—is one of closeness to something bigger, greater, more important than you.

To Joseph Caro in the mid-sixteenth century, having traveled for months from his hometown in Spain, the awe must alternately have burned in his chest and chilled him to the bone. The trip would have taken most of a day and seemed a climb to heaven, the earth easing away beneath and the cares of that world peeling off like so much shed clothing. The air got thinner and cleaner, the spaces vaster, the colors hazier and paler, the vertiginous downward glances more and more unsettling in their bare, sun-washed beauty. Even considering the countless annoyances—the coughs and groans of a balky donkey, the threat of losing what little you had to highway robbers, the overflow of bulky bundles that made you, and especially the donkey, wish you had taken less, the flies and mosquitoes, the ache, itch, smell, and sweat—despite all this, he must have felt that God was *there*.

Caro was born in Spain in 1488, his parents carried him into Portugal four years later, and soon after that they were forced to move to the Balkans. When he made his trip to Safed, he was in the midst of his great compendium of Jewish laws. It was a grand obsession, taking decades, and it has guided Jews ever since. But something else drew Caro to this mountaintop. Safed was growing, from a handful of Jewish families to a town of ten thousand. They manufactured cloth, traded actively with Damascus, learned Torah in yeshivas, and struggled with messianic longings. They composed prayers and poems, of which the most famous is by Caro's friend Solomon Halevi Alkabetz: "L'cha Dodi," "Come, My Beloved," sung in every synagogue on Friday evening. The beloved is Jerusalem, called to arise and meet the Sabbath, personified as the bride for a king descended from David:

> *Come my love and meet the bride,*
> *Welcome the Sabbath soul. . . .*
> *You have lived in the valley of weeping long enough,*
> *In truth God will pity you.*
> *Shake yourself from the dust, arise,*
> *Array yourself in glory. . . .*

Devout Jews came from every outpost of the diaspora, climbed the sacred mountain, and steeped themselves in the sere, mystical spirit of Safed, where fasting scholars assembled at midnight to pray at the graves of sages. One of Caro's students, Moses Cordovero, was commanded by God to devote his life to the Torah, and although he was only twenty, heard the call.

So did Isaac Luria, "the Holy Lion," who embodied everything Jewish. He was born in Jerusalem—his mother Sephardic, his father Ashkenazic. When his father died his mother took him to Egypt along the biblical path of the patriarchs. He studied Talmud and was in business for a while, but found his calling as a mystic. He lived alone for seven years on an island in the Nile, denying himself everything but scraps of food and holy books. The strangest of these—and for him perhaps the holiest—was the Zohar, the Book of Splendor.

This was the crown of thousands of years of hidden, even dangerous thought—the ideas of the most visionary rabbis, the dreams of the holiest prophets. Most of it was composed in Spain in the late 1200s, although its author, Moses de Leon, attributed it to a second-century sage. This sage, Simeon bar-Yohai, was a student of Rabbi Akiva's who fled to a cave in Galilee after the bloody failure of the Bar Kokhba revolt. He and his son, it was said, hid from the Romans for years in a cave near the Dead Sea, lived on spring water and carob fruit, and developed a mystical form of midrash, or Torah interpretation.

But this was only midway through the saga of Jewish mysticism. In the Bible, Saul sought "a woman that hath a familiar spirit," who called up the ghost of the prophet Samuel from the underworld—"I saw gods ascending out of the earth," she told him.[1] Elijah, instead of dying, was picked up by "a chariot of fire, with horses of fire . . . and went up by a whirlwind into heaven,"[2] remaining a messenger between the two worlds ever since. Daniel read the otherworldly writing on the wall, and dreamed wonders: "I saw in my vision by night . . . four great beasts came up from the sea. . . . The first was like a lion, and had eagle's wings." A bear and a leopard appeared in strange guises. Then came "a fourth beast, dreadful and terrible, and strong exceedingly; and it had great iron teeth: it devoured and brake in pieces, and stamped the residue with the feet of it . . . and it had ten horns," and a mouth "speaking great things." He saw "the Ancient of days. . . . his throne was like the fiery flame, and his wheels as burning fire. A fiery stream issued and came forth from before him . . . and ten thousand times ten thousand stood before him."[3]

The Book of Ezekiel too contains strange visions:

> And I looked, and, behold, a whirlwind came out of the north, a great cloud, and a fire infolding itself, and a brightness was about it, and out of the midst thereof as the color of amber, out of the midst of the fire. Also out of the midst thereof came the likeness of four living creatures. . . . And every one had four faces, and every one had four wings.[4]

These extraordinary beings are the harbingers of a message from God: "And when they went, I heard the noise of their wings, like the noise of great waters, as the voice of the Almighty, the voice of speech."[5] Seers and prophets had such visions until the Roman period. But the rise of rabbinical culture put an end to the credibility of overt signs from God.

Some ancient sages flirted with mysticism, but their work was very dangerous. The Mishnah says, "Whoever ponders on four things, it were better for him if he had not come into the world: what is above, what is below, what was before time, and what will be hereafter."[6] Akiva was one of four mystical sages; all "entered a garden" but only he emerged unscathed. The great Hebrew poet Haim Nachman Bialik wrote that Ben Azai "looked and died." At the end of his quest he could not walk upright, but crawled on his belly, with one last plea as he licked the dust: "Could I but look for a moment / Beyond the curtain!" The last, fiftieth gate appeared, and he found the strength to knock:

> Then quenched the torch, and the doors of the gate opened—
> And in he looked,
> And his corpse sank, at its side a smoking ember, and it stretched itself
> On the threshold of the N o t h i n g.[7]

After Akiva's martyrdom at Roman hands, Simeon bar-Yohai, in the long sanctuary and solitude of his cave, wove the fragments in the old, mystical canon into a more coherent vision. In any case, that was the legend: "Rabbi Simeon ben Yohai fled to the desert of Lydda, and lived in a cave with his son, Rabbi Eleazar. A miracle was performed for them, and a carob tree and a water source came into being. . . . Elijah, may he be remembered for good, visited them twice a day, and instructed them, and no one knew where they were."[8] Elijah's lessons privilege the wisdom; he was the greatest of biblical prophets, and his mystical powers came from God. After forty days and nights of fasting and seclusion in the wilderness, God spoke to him: "And behold, the Lord passed by, and a great and strong wind rent the mountains, and brake in pieces the rocks." Yet "the Lord was not in the wind," nor in the earthquake and fire that followed, but "after the fire, a still small voice."[9] Elijah was very close to the angels, yet always a teacher, guardian, and friend of humanity. His visits to Jews great and small at key points in their lives have always been a needed source of hope.

So the mystic tradition continued, but not as direct revelation. God's messages, for the rest of time, could only come through Torah. But the thirst for transcendence was too deep to be ignored. The paradox was resolved by looking into and through the Torah itself to find the visions hidden in the text. This was kabbala—it means "receiving"—and it opened the gates of the Torah to different kinds of religious minds.

The kabbala tried "to make of the traditional Torah . . . a more profound inner experience . . . to transform it from the law of the people of Israel into the inner secret law of the universe, at the same time transforming the Jewish *hasid* or *tzadik* into a man with a vital role in the world."[10] It also was an attempt to grasp the essence of God and of the human soul. In the early 1200s, in the blazing sun of Provence, some of these ideas were set down in an anonymous book, the Bahir, or "Brightness." It defined the distinct aspects of God, known as *sefirot*. If this seemed to skirt polytheism, the Jewish mystics were always careful to stress God's unity. Still, they believed that God had separable characteristics and powers.

These ideas spread to southern Spain and took hold in Gerona, among the stone walks and narrow streets of that graceful walled city. Under the shadow of the cathedral, Rabbi Nachman—the Ramban—and others debated the philosophy of Maimonides and considered the counterclaims of his more parochial enemies. They also read the Bahir, the core of kabbala. And within a century, these visionary Spanish Jews had set the new ideas down much more fully in the Zohar, the largest of the kabbalistic texts. Ezra of Gerona viewed God's essence as "unfathomably profound." God was impenetrable, "a face within a face, an essence within an essence, and a form within a form."[11] Nevertheless, they tried.

The first of the *sefirot*—the "root of roots" in God—is the Ayn Sof, the "No End"; from it all the other features emanate. It sits atop an oft-reprinted diagram, below it an octagon pointed slightly upward, each point of the octagon an attribute of God: Divine Will, Wisdom, Intelligence, Love, Judgment, Endurance, Majesty, and Righteousness are the corners. At their center is a ninth attribute called Beauty or Compassion, and the base of them all is Divine Presence—in Hebrew, Shekhina. In mystical terms, the Shekhina is the feminine aspect of God, and serves to assuage the human longing for an almost maternal side. Some of the *sefirot* are listed every Saturday in a lively, lilting song as the Torah is carried around the congregation, but few who sing it know that they are extolling the *sefirot,* the mystical attributes of God, set down by the mystics eight centuries ago.

Yet the *sefirot* were anything but carved in stone. At the outset of creation the Divine Will made signs in the heavens. Hidden deep in the No End, a dark flame formed like a fog, "neither white nor black, neither red nor green, of no color whatever." But as it took shape it shone with radiant colors that spread from the core of the mystery and descended on all below.[12]

The octagon of attributes is just one way to see them. The *sefirot* are also imagined as a cosmic tree with the No End as its root. Or as God's body: three the head, three the arms and chest, three the legs and genitals, and the tenth the figure's harmony. This was no insult to God; we were made, the Torah says, in God's image. But it meant that not just the form but also the essence of God is reflected in humanity. Another model divided the figure vertically, the left side feminine and the right masculine. Reversing the usual stereotype, the kabbalists put love on the masculine side and judgment on the feminine. Whatever the structure, insights into God's essence were insights into ours. As a great modern scholar put it, "Both man and God encompass within their being the entire cosmos. . . . What exists seminally in God unfolds and develops in man. . . . Man is the perfecting agent in the structure of the cosmos; like all the other created beings, only even more so, he is composed of all ten *Sefirot* and 'of all spiritual things.'"[13]

The *sefirot* were intricately linked. Divine grace pulsed through them, a river out of the infinite, branching into the attributes and flowing into the sea. "This vast basin is divided up into seven channels. . . . Together the source, the current, the sea, and the seven channels make the number ten. If the Creator who made these tubes should choose to break them, then would the waters return to their source, and only broken vessels would remain, dry, without water."[14] This ominous image hints at the dark side of God, something never more than a small step away in kabbala. In fact, human action—human sinfulness—can sometimes tip the balance between light and dark within God, with devastating consequences for the world.[15]

The *sefirot* were vessels, tools, instruments of God. They could be "a candle flickering in the midst of ten mirrors," and the emanation of the *sefirot* from the No End could be like using one candle to light others. As Rabbi Azriel put it, "Even if myriads upon myriads of candles were lit from it, its own light would not diminish."[16] The role of light in the Zohar ("Splendor") and its predecessor the Bahir is pervasive: "The basic and most commonly used symbol in the *Zohar* is . . . light and splendor. It appears in every section of the book. . . . Every link in the chain of the *sefirot* is depicted as a new sparking forth of light; the descent of divine influence is a torrent of light; and the whole world of emanation is a sea of brilliant splendor."[17]

Even God's will is made of hidden flashes of light, and the action of the divine force is likened to a hammer striking sparks. These sparks, even those struck off in the Creation, disperse, persist, and give life to the world.

But God had to deliberately shrink—*tzimtzum* is the word—in order to make room for Creation. Recall that we are God's "perfecting agent"—one of the core concepts in Jewish mysticism, but now mainstream Jewish thought. After all the lights of the *sefirot* had formed, they were given vessels to contain them, vessels themselves made of a sturdier light. But six of them could not contain the brightness and broke, scattering splinters of light. Some became evil influences, reflecting the partly broken nature of creation, and the breakage has been healing ever since—*tikkun,* the process is called. Our role is to follow the Torah and, through good deeds, prayer, and meditation, speed tikkun. Eventually a healed world would bring about final redemption. And today the phrase *tikkun olam*—"healing the world"—may mean one thing more: God left Creation unfinished, so that we could help complete it.[18]

"Come and see" is a common phrase in the Zohar, as it invites us to observe a work of art or the beauty of nature, but ultimately it always means the Torah: "Everyone who studies the Torah sustains the world."[19] God created the world for our sake, and us for the sake of Torah, but he who does not see its deep, mystical meaning must be pitied. "If a man says that a story in the Torah is there simply for the sake of the story, may his spirit depart! For if it were so," it would not be "a Torah of truth."[20] Isaiah 51:16 says, "I have put My words in your mouth, and have covered you in the shadow of My hand, that I may plant heavens and lay the foundations of earth." In their cave sanctuary, hiding from Roman soldiers, Rabbi Eleazar asks about this shadow; his father, Rabbi Simeon, replies:

> When the Torah was being given to Moses, myriads of celestial angels sought to burn him with flames from their mouths. But the Holy One, blessed be He, protected him. And now, when a [new] interpretation ascends, and becomes adorned, and stands before the Holy One, blessed be He, He protects the interpretation and conceals the man, so that [the angels] should not know and become jealous of him, until from that interpretation new heavens and a new earth are made.[21]

Such is the power of a single creative insight into the Torah that it goes, robed in glory like Elijah, directly to God's throne. It wins God's grace and protection for itself and the man who created it, even when he is threatened by jealous angels.

But the Torah is not penetrated easily, and the difficulties are symbolized by some of the Zohar's most evocative pages. Here, the Torah is personified as a desired, mysterious woman who must be approached by her suitor—the earnest, besotted scholar—with indirection, patience, and love:

> She may be compared to a beautiful and stately maiden, who is secluded in an isolated chamber of a palace, and has a lover . . . she alone knows. For love of her he passes by her gate unceasingly, and turns his eyes in all directions to discover her. She is aware that he is forever hovering about the palace. . . . She thrusts open a small door in her secret chamber, for a moment reveals her face to her lover, then quickly withdraws it . . . but he is aware it is from love of him that she has revealed herself to him for that moment, and his heart and his soul and everything within him are drawn to her.

The Zohar goes on to explain the metaphor:

> So it is with the Torah. . . . She knows that whosoever is wise in heart hovers near the gates of her dwelling place day after day. What does she do? From her palace, she shows her face to him, and gives him a signal of love. . . . if he fails, [she] says to her messengers: Go tell that simpleton to come to me, and converse. . . . she commences to speak with him, at first from behind the veil which she has hung before her words. . . . Then she speaks to him behind a filmy veil of finer mesh, she speaks to him in riddles and allegories. . . .
>
> When, finally, he is on near terms with her, she stands disclosed face to face with him, and holds converse with him concerning all of her secret mysteries, and all the secret ways which have been hidden in her heart from immemorial time.[22]

The emotional challenges this passage presents to impressionable young scholars helps explain why they were forbidden to study kabbala until they were forty years old and had mastered the Talmud.

Two other examples suggest the force with which the Zohar reaches into the depths of the human soul, and why it has meant so much to so many. In one of its most moving passages, the Zohar considers children "who still as sucklings are taken from their mothers' breasts." This paradox for the faithful echoes the chilling Torah warning about "visiting the iniquity of the fathers upon the children."[23] For them, the Book of Splendor says,

> the whole world weeps; the tears that come from these babes have no equal, their tears issue from the innermost and farthest places of the heart, and the entire world is perplexed: . . . is it needful that

these unhappy infants should die, who are without sin and without blame? . . .

But . . . the tears shed by these "oppressed ones" act as a petition and protection for the living . . . and by dint of their innocence, in time a place is prepared for them . . . for the Holy One, be blessed, does in reality love these little ones with a unique and outstanding love. He unites them with himself and gets ready for them a place on high close by to him.[24]

Some comfort, perhaps, to the mother of a hopelessly ill child.

Another poignant passage concerns the Tree of Life, which Adam lost because he lived in limbo: "So did Adam move back and forth from one hue to another, from good to evil, from evil to good, from agitation to rest, from judgment to mercy, from life to death; never consistent in any one thing." The consequences are great: "In this wise did he bring about death for himself and all the world."[25] But it is not in the nature of Jewish thought to take away hope, so the passage ends with words of the prophet Isaiah about the time to come: "The days of my people shall be as the days of the Tree," and in the end, "He will swallow up death for ever; and the Lord God will wipe away tears from all faces."[26]

⟨☙⟩

For the rabbis and their disciples, even the mystics, the world was a place of order. No doubt it was frightening at times, incomprehensible at others, occasionally hateful. But God had made a covenant with you, had given you the Torah, with its narrative of suffering and redemption and its rhetoric of uniqueness. You had 613 mitzvot with their countless echoes of meaning and their clear plan for living every moment as if it were holy. You had sages of transcendent judgment, intellect, and purity to interpret God's will and message. If you believed, you would feel God's order, even in the mud pits of Egypt, under the sword of Babylon, on the Roman cross, or in the Inquisition's flames. If you doubted, you had only to continue to practice the laws, to carry out the commandments every hour of every day—*We will do and we will hear*—and faith would undoubtedly come back to you.

For the common people, the salt of the Jewish earth, things were a little more complex. God made the earth and all therein, but some blips and blemishes he didn't seem to control. What were these illnesses that came out of nowhere, and these sudden surges of the oppressor's wild wrath? What were these impulses in your own breast that seemed to reach up and take you by the throat and shake you until God's will became a jumble in your dizzy head? Surely these wacky, inexplicable events were not *all* punishments, or messages, or carefully crafted cogs and wheels in God's great machine. This would be too hard to believe.

Yet explanations were needed, so other beliefs arose. Against the admonitions of their strictest rabbis, the common run of Jews—carpenters and carters, blacksmiths and peddlers, tailors and farmers, store clerks and even synagogue caretakers—lived in a strange world populated by imps, demons, goblins, demiurges, and a host of other unnatural, wondrous, inimical beings and forces.[27] Condemned by the Talmud, beyond the ken of most rabbis—even, God forbid, out of the reach of God—these airy nemeses infested the nooks and crannies of normal life. At best, they spilled milk, caused warts, tripped dignified citizens in the street, made barley moldy, moved keys and pills from the place where one had carefully set them, and strategically stuck the pages of holy books together just where one needed to seek the details of a mitzva. But at worst, they did far greater damage. You could say that these visions were the poor man's kabbala, the mystical dreams of the little people, the *pintele Yidn,* the simple Jews. They were a parallel vision rarely mentioned in Torah or Talmud, ridiculed by some rabbis but both feared and hated by common folk.[28]

Prominent among them was Lilith.[29] Recall the Bible's two tales of the creation of the sexes. One has Eve made from Adam's rib; but there is another account of *one* human creation, the two sexes invented simultaneously: "Male and female," the Torah says, "created he them." A legend arose that this creation produced not Adam and Eve but Adam and Lilith, a fateful error. Lilith, on an equal footing from the start, would have none of Adam's domination, even wanting to be on top in bed. For a patriarchal culture ruled by a patriarchal God, this wouldn't do. So God put Adam to sleep, took one of his ribs, and made a new woman who supposedly knew her place. She didn't, of course. She had a conversation about an apple with a snake, then with Adam, and this ended the idyll. Adam would eat by the sweat of his brow, Eve cry in pain bringing the future to life—pain that was not incidentally a consequence of sex.

But uncreating Lilith did not prove possible. Condemned to the netherworld for her uppity sins, she was not only a woman who felt equal to any man, but also now a woman scorned by God. She did not stay alone long. Men's lustful thoughts at night and the physical impurities of even their deepest sleep gave Lilith a thousand openings to lie with the sons of Adam and make bad use of their seed. In this way she conceived and gave birth to countless demons. Lilith is good at this:

> She dresses herself in finery like an abominable harlot and stands at the corners of streets and highways in order to attract men. When a fool approaches her, she embraces him and kisses him, and mixes her wine lees with snake poison for him. Once he has drunk, he turns aside after her. . . .

[This] is the finery that she uses to seduce mankind: her hair is long, red like a lily; her face is white and pink; six pendants hang at her ears; her bed is made of Egyptian flax; all the ornaments of the East encircle her neck; her mouth is shaped like a tiny door, beautified with cosmetic; her tongue is sharp like a sword; her words smooth as oil; her lips beautiful, red as a lily, sweetened with all the sweetnesses in the world; she is dressed in purple, and attired with thirty-nine items of finery.

If you were not a fool already, you would likely become one after a short chat with this dazzling vision of loveliness. But watch out:

This fool turns after her, and drinks from the cup of wine, and commits harlotry with her, completely enamored of her. What does she do? She leaves him asleep on the bed and ascends to the realms above, accuses him, obtains authority, and descends. The fool wakes up, thinking to sport with her as before, but she takes off her finery, and turns into a fierce warrior, facing him in a garment of flaming fire, a vision of dread, terrifying both body and soul, full of horrific eyes, a sharpened sword in his hand with drops of poison suspended from it. He kills the fool, and throws him into Gehinnom.[30]

Gehinnom is hellfire. But you did not have to be so thoroughly turned aside to meet a bad end. Masturbation, often provoked by Lilith, could be a matter of life and death, and even your wet dreams could father demons.

But demons arose in several ways. According to the Talmud, God was creating them on the first Sabbath eve, but only got as far as their souls when night fell and God stopped to rest, so they were forever bodiless.[31] Others came from Adam's adultery with she-devils after the expulsion from Eden. Still others came from the ranks of the recently dead, especially those who had been wicked in life.

Some rabbis had always acknowledged demons and tried to explain them. In a sense they fit the kabbala's view of a world divided between powerful forces for good and evil. Rashi elaborated on some Talmud passages to set forth categories of demons: some with human forms, some disembodied and formless, some humanlike but with wings.[32] According to both rabbinic and folk traditions, you had to protect yourself against them. A house should not be sealed too tightly or they feel trapped, so a small hole pierced in a door was a good precaution. They inhabited outhouses, so incantations might be made while using them. They also liked moon shadows, which children especially had to avoid. Night in general was dangerous. Storm winds were a favorite demon abode, thunder and lightning salvos in their battles. And since evil spirits could enter the body through any orifice, ritual cleanliness was of the greatest importance.

A famous mystic named Judah the Pious who lived in Germany in the thirteenth century was a counselor for many troubled by demons. He told a barren woman to simulate her own death, having her children place her in a grave and arranging for armed men to scare them away, so that they forgot her at least briefly. She then arose out of the grave, and this symbolic rebirth enabled her to conceive. You could also be possessed by a dybbuk, first mentioned at the dawn of the 1600s. In this instance a young man's body was entered by the spirit of a wicked man who could not find rest after death. He had previously inhabited a cow, but escaped when it was about to be slaughtered. Powerful exorcisms liberated the youth. Some demons popular in talmudic times were no longer feared in the Middle Ages. Shibbeta, who used to strangle children who ate with unwashed hands, no longer had any power, and Keteb Meriri, a heat demon associated with the sun, made only a brief appearance. But Lilith retained full power, and precautions against her were popular.

Isaac Bashevis Singer, the only Yiddish-language writer to win the Nobel Prize—he delivered his Stockholm acceptance speech in Yiddish, declaring that children are the best literary critics—believed in this netherworld and wove it through his stories. In a beautiful tale, "Taibele and Her Demon," there are no actual demons, but there is a wealth of legend about them. Taibele, a small, fair young woman, lost all three of her children in infancy. Prayers, spells, and potions failed to bring her another, and then her husband left her. At thirty-three, she is an *aguna,* a stranded wife, who can neither get a divorce nor prove her husband's death. She can never remarry unless she gets the signatures of a hundred rabbis, implausible for a poor shopkeeper with no means to travel.

One evening, when the town is "as dark as Egypt," Taibele recounts a storybook tale to a group of friends, about a young Jewish woman ravished by a demon who lived with her thereafter. The women are overheard talking and giggling by an impoverished teacher's helper. He soon steals into Taibele's bedroom and threatens to drag her away to the wilderness of the Mount of Darkness, where the earth is iron and the sky copper, roll her in thorns and fire among adders and scorpions, and grind her to dust, unless she does his bidding. He claims he is the nephew of Asmodeus, King of the Demons, and that Lilith has danced for him and bestowed her delights upon him. "Shibtah, the she-devil who stole babies from women in childbed, baked poppyseed cakes for him in Hell's ovens and leavened them with the fat of wizards and black dogs."

He claims that her husband is dead; that he, the demon, has been in love with her for years; and that a black-and-blue mark she once found on her breast was the mark left by one of his surreptitious kisses. Joining threats to seductions, he has his will with her, "and since he was a demon and not a man, Taibele returned his kisses and moistened his beard with her tears. Evil spirit though he was, he treated her kindly."

Over years of twice-weekly visits, he tells her all about the other world—about an imp in hell named Lekish, for instance, who tortures the damned with endless tickling. Taibele's demon has seven other wives, all she-devils: one black as pitch and full of rage, one with the face of a leech who marks you forever, one adorned with jewels and bells who makes the desert ring with her dancing, one who looks and meows like a cat and chews bear's liver during sex, one who robs brides of speech and grooms of potency, one lecherous and unfaithful, and one lone good demoness, who kneads dough for sick women and gives bread to the poor.[33] Such were the denizens of the "middle world," some preserved in folklore for centuries.

The "evil eye" or *ayn hara* was another belief that survived not just through medieval times but into the present day. *Keyn ayn hara*—"no evil eye"—survives as the slurred Yiddishism *kinnahara,* still heard among Ashkenazic Jews in the context of well-wishing or acknowledging good fortune. Any positive event—an honor in the synagogue, a good match, a pretty baby, a brilliant student, or a financial windfall—could bring the evil eye. It came from demonic envy, and some talmudic rabbis believed it had the power to instantly turn you into a heap of bones or make you burst into flames.[34]

Formulaic phrases such as "God forbid!," "God protect you!," and "Health!" ("Gesundheit!") are attempts to invoke religious power against the evil spirits. So is the Yiddish saying *"Zol zokh nisht trefn vi ez ken zokh trefn"*—"It shouldn't happen like it might happen." According to one interpretation, the smelling of spices in the Havdalah service that ends the Sabbath masks the stench from the fires of hell, always rekindled the moment the Sabbath leaves.

The legend of the golem, an inert mass brought to life—a sort of Jewish Frankenstein's monster—is also about protection, although here it is often against worldly persecution. It might be created from clay—some said virgin soil from a mountain where no man has dug—and then brought to life by a powerful rabbi who knew how to inscribe the name of God or the word *emet*—"truth"—on its forehead. Then, if the golem became too dangerous, the *aleph* of *emet* would be removed, the *emet* would turn into *met*—"dead"—and the creature would crumble into dust. The Jews of Prague used to say that the remains of one golem could be found in the attic of the great synagogue, the Altneuschule.

On the other side, curses once believed to invoke the spirit world survived into modern times as stock epithets to express anger against one's enemies. Examples in Yiddish:

Keyn eyn-hore zol im nit oysmaydn!—Let no evil eye avoid him!
Khasene hobn zol er mit malekhamoves tokhter!—He should marry
    the Angel of Death's daughter!
Der fodem zol bay im oysgeyn!—Let his thread run out!
A duner zol im trefn!—A thunder should happen to him!

In addition to particularly Jewish demonology and magic, Jews adopted much of the folklore of surrounding people. For example, Hebrew-Yiddish love magic of the fifteenth century included this recipe:

> Secure an egg laid on a Thursday by a jet-black hen which has never laid an egg before, and on the same day, after sunset, bury it at a crossroads. Leave it there three days; then dig it up after sunset, sell it and purchase with the proceeds a mirror, which you must bury in the same spot in the evening "in Frau Venus namen" ["in the name of Lady Venus"]. . . . Sleep on that spot three nights, then remove the mirror, and whoever looks in it will love you![35]

Another bit of love magic is found in a fifteenth-century work in Hebrew and Yiddish. The prescription, written backward, calls for virgin wax to be molded into a likeness of the beloved—sex organs in plain view—and her name and the names of her parents etched on her breast. You say over it, "May it be Thy will O Lord that so-and-so burn with a mighty passion for me," then bury it in secret. When you later disinter it, dip it three times in water, in the name of the angels Michael, Gabriel, and Raphael, then immerse it in urine, dry it, and pierce its heart with a new needle.[36]

Numerology has power in Torah and kabbala as well as in folk tradition. Like many others, Jews thought the number two unlucky but three a strong positive force. A midrash says that all sevens are beloved, and for a certain kind of fever the Talmud suggests:

> Take seven prickles from seven palm-trees, seven chips from seven beams, seven nails from seven bridges, seven ashes from seven ovens, seven scoops of earth from seven door-sockets, seven pieces of pitch from seven ships, seven handfuls of cumin, and seven hairs from the beard of an old dog, and tie them to the neck-hole of the shirt with a white twisted cord.[37]

The kabbalists advocated the liberal use of salt, as in dipping bread in it after the Friday night blessings, because the numerical value of the Hebrew word is equal to three times that of the name of God.[38] Certain texts, properly inscribed, could serve as amulets, as could certain gemstones, articles of clothing, and religious objects.

But nothing worked better in the war against evil spirits than religious observance, faith in God, and prayer. Another Singer story, "The Last Demon," describes a demon who fears he may be the last of his kind, for two reasons. First, "Why demons, when man himself is a demon? Why persuade to evil someone who is already convinced? I am the last of the persuaders. I board in an attic in Tishevitz and draw my sustenance from a Yiddish storybook, a leftover from the days before the great catastrophe." The "great catastrophe" is the Holocaust, and this passing mention hints at the other reason demons are doomed: there are no Jews left to bewitch, tempt, or trouble.

Before the war, he tried. He'd been banished from Lublin to Tishevitz, "a godforsaken village," where he met a minor imp disguised as a spider, and took on a task that imp had already failed at: to tempt a pious and brilliant young rabbi. He flies through the rabbi's window and tries unsuccessfully to distract him with sexy stories. Then he remembers that "of all the snares we use, there are three that work unfailingly—lust, pride, and avarice," pride being the strongest. The demon presents himself as Elijah and offers to help the rabbi become better known for his brilliance, so he can spread God's word. But first he must shut the Talmud volume he is studying. The rabbi begins to do it but hesitates because of his love of study. "Forgive me, my Lord," he says, "but I require another sign." He asks to see the feet of "Elijah," which ends the ruse, since feet are the one thing demons can't disguise.

Our hapless imp is condemned by Asmodeus himself—King of the Demons, Prince of the Middle World—to stay in Tishevitz for "eternity plus a Wednesday," contemplating his uselessness.

> There are no more Jews, no more demons. The women don't pour out water any longer on the night of the winter solstice. They don't avoid giving things in even numbers. They no longer knock at dawn at the antechamber of the synagogue. They don't warn us before emptying the slops. The rabbi was martyred on a Friday in the month of Nisan. The community was slaughtered, the holy books burned, the cemetery desecrated. . . . Gentiles wash themselves in the ritual bath. Abraham Zalman's chapel has been turned into a pigsty. There is no longer an Angel of Good or an Angel of Evil.

Then his most poignant lament: "Messiah did not come for the Jews, so the Jews went to Messiah." The demons "have also been annihilated. I am the last, a refugee. I can go anywhere I please, but where should a demon like me go? To the murderers?" Absurd—they have already done evil the likes of which no demon could invent; nor were all the charms and amulets, or even prayers and piety in the world strong enough to ward it off.[39]

It is no secret that one of the traditional uses of Jewish genius has been in making money. Money emerged in ancient times, before the Jews, and they learned about it at the feet of the Egyptians, the Babylonians, and the Greeks. But they became very good at it, and that gift helped sustain them.[40] The reasons are simple. Torn from Israel after the First Temple was destroyed, and again after the Second, they fled or were dragged off to other places. Permanent outsiders, an anomalous minority tolerated or persecuted to varying degrees, they were often forbidden to own land, and they typically arrived with little or nothing and had to make a living on the margins.

The Jews were not alone in this. The Chinese and Koreans, first in Southeast Asia and then throughout the world, have played a similar role in their diasporas, as have the Indians in East and South Africa. There are parallels too with the Ibo of Nigeria, sometimes called the Jews of West Africa. This kind of role is for people in the cracks. The big nations that come to foreign lands by conquest can do whatever they want, but the little people who come only by sufferance begin out in the cold with their noses pressed to the glass. Except for those rare societies that forbid entrepreneurship, these little people follow a classic path to success: Find a need and fill it.

We think of the itinerant peddler who gets up before dawn, buys a swath of cloth, cuts it into a few salable pieces, and takes them where people will pay a few pennies (centimos, pfennig, zlotys, groschen) more than he himself paid. Living in severe frugality, wedded to work, he brings his family what they minimally need and still puts a pittance into a sock under a mattress. In a few years he can buy a cart, some years later rent a stall in a market, then lease a little hole-in-the-wall store, then . . .

The cliché is largely true, but it misses two key points. First, the peddler was often a craftsman who created something from the cloth—or the dough, or board, or calfskin, or lump of silver. Such skills, portable across oceans and borders, made Jews valuable to host countries and their rulers. Even more sophisticated skills, like printing and medicine, added to the value of these odd people. Second, the economic health and wealth of nations has depended from ancient times on international trade. The Jews in their many exiles formed a transnational network with a common language, faith, and culture. It was natural for them to enter the import-export business, become seagoing merchants, and invest in international trade.

The resulting wealth has interesting features. Unlike land, money is portable and dynamic. To some extent it can be hidden from those more powerful. Sometimes it can be carried into exile, even if only as swallowed diamonds, and this filthy lucre becomes as life-giving as if it were the nectar of the gods. Some Jews became bankers and moneylenders, with all the resentment those roles can entail. Because Christians were forbidden to lend money at interest—the sin of usury—and because Jews were not allowed to own land in most of Europe, some made loans at interest. As would be true of any ethnic group, not all Jewish moneylenders were decent and honest people, and against a general background of virulent anti-Semitism, any who were not sullied the reputation of all.

Karl Marx, a descendant of rabbis, described the Jews as parasites, continuing a time-honored Christian tradition. But one does have to hate capitalism itself to see merchants and bankers as merely predatory. Did the Jews—and the Chinese, Koreans, Indians, and Ibo—treat their customers from the host people differently from the way they treated their own? Undoubtedly. But none of these outsider minorities could have sustained their success through dishonesty. Few things are as voluntary as opening a purse, and despite inefficiency and corruption, markets serve both buyers and sellers.

Mark Twain made the point best, in his famous essay "Concerning the Jews," published in *Harper's* in June 1899:

> The basis of successful business is honesty; a business cannot thrive where the parties cannot trust each other. In the matter of numbers the Jew counts for little in the overwhelming population of New York; but that his honesty counts for much is guaranteed by the fact that the immense wholesale business of Broadway, from the Battery to Union Square, is substantially in his hands.[41]

From ancient times, Jewish financiers have been chosen by the rulers of the nations where they lived to advise them on their national economies—those of Babylon, Persia, Islamic Spain, Egypt, Turkey, France, India, and the United States, among others. The Jews were clever with money, yes, and they did have international connections, but they also earned the trust of princes. In general it was not the nobility who turned on them, but the masses who resented their relations with the nobles. Princely pragmatists did business with Jews and employed them, but the common people—uneducated, poor, religious, bigoted, angry, and often incited by hostile clergy—smashed the windows of their shops and torched their holy places.

Denied land, they put down roots in bank accounts and books. Talmudic academies served as systems of selection. Whatever we think of what was studied, the process culled the best minds in every generation of Jews for more than a thousand years. Rising stars among these bright young men would board with successful merchants, and matches would be made between them and the merchants' daughters. Thus the smartest, most studious boys would join the wealthiest families, and the children of those unions would staff the stores and trading firms as well as the yeshivas.

Jewish merchants would not have survived the raucous democracy of the marketplace without the votes of countless buyers. But the Catholic

Church created a special niche for Jewish economic activity when it ruled that a Christian could not take interest on loans. This ended Christian lending, which defaulted to the Jews. As Karl Marx later recognized, Jewish merchants and bankers were something like pure capitalists, and if they were not the first, they certainly were a forceful part of the cresting mercantile wave. Jews were prepared for it by a long history of exclusion from everything else and by the international network created by expulsions. They took part in and benefited from the trends toward exploration, colonization, urbanization, manufacturing, and capital investment, and they brought some of these trends from country to country as agents of change.

Were they good at making money? Some were, probably more than would be expected from Jewish numbers. Making money requires intelligence, and the Jews—being, as that student of Aristotle had said, "philosophers by race"—were overrepresented in everything that required intelligence. Among their many adaptations were those that ensured their livelihoods. As Theodor Herzl put it, "We cling to money because onto money we were flung."[42] The Jews in most countries were militarily, politically, and socially weak. They used economic power not as a weapon but as a shield.

They needed one. In central and northern Europe the Crusades faded away and the Inquisition had relatively little influence, but the flames—or at least the pilot light—of hatred burned steadily everywhere. "When the earth shakes, we feel it" is an old Jewish saying, and every ill wind of the Middle Ages—the Black Death, the Thirty Years' War, the Turks' near-conquest of Europe—fanned fires that burned Jews. These conflicts and natural tragedies had nothing to do with the Jews, yet the Jews were always blamed because it was easy to blame them; they were Christ killers, and besides, they had always been blamed before.

Spinoza, the first great secular Jewish thinker of modern times, did something that was then very unusual: he left Judaism without joining another religion. He achieved prominence in a larger, non-Jewish world, and used the traditions of constant debate and questioning, even of arguing with God, to pursue the path of thought to one logical end. He paid for this with excommunication, but he stood by his conclusions. Despite his Jewish origins, his work changed the way the West looked at the world. He contributed to ethics and metaphysics, founded scientific Bible scholarship, and began the thread of modern philosophic inquiry that challenged the claims of theology, an enterprise taken up by philosophers from David Hume to Bertrand Russell. Within mainstream philosophy, theology has retreated ever since.

But Spinoza's genius was only a glimpse of what would come. A century later the great wave of the Enlightenment swept Europe. Before that change, few Jews had the motivation to take up secular philosophy, science, or literature; after it, the floodgates of Jewish creativity opened, not just to Jewish concerns but to the entire intellectual enterprise of the West. The Jewish Enlightenment was called Haskalah, based on a midrashic word that came to mean "rational inquiry."[43] The Talmud had rules for rational discourse, influenced by the ancient Greek philosophers, but these were designed for the Torah framework. Maimonides, perhaps the greatest rabbi since Talmud times, went much further, trying to prove the existence of God and place other aspects of Jewish belief on a base of formal logic. Bitter battles over his methods after his death revealed a tense Orthodox Judaism pulled between reason and faith, and even more so, between those who wanted to reconcile Judaism with secular philosophy and those who viewed this as a fool's errand fraught with risk.

Spinoza no doubt confirmed the worst fears of philosophy's critics, since he followed the path of rational inquiry straight out of Judaism. Looking back after the Haskalah he might be called a *maskil,* a rational thinker; but in his own time he was called an *epikores*—an ancient, contemptuous Jewish term for a follower of Epicurus, the Greek philosopher. The Haskalah's founders indeed courted contempt, but unlike Spinoza, they tried to stay within the Jewish fold. They tended to be teachers, physicians, and court Jews exposed to the Enlightenment in general. The educated classes of Europe were awakening intellectually and politically as the works of Newton, Locke, and Montesquieu were read. But the Haskalah's goal was to join them without leaving Judaism. In 1778 the first Jewish secular school opened in Berlin, teaching Hebrew and Jewish subjects along with general studies; rabbinical opposition was strong.

But Jews were prying open a place for themselves in the secular world. This was especially true of Amsterdam, the Sephardic community that was the center of non-Orthodox Jewish culture, but it was also true of the Americas. In London, the highly cultured Jewish community was prominent in the audiences of George Frideric Handel, whose oratorios on Jewish themes included *Israel in Egypt, Judas Maccabeus, Samson, Esther,* and *Susanna.* But it was in Germany that the Jewish Enlightenment took hold and flourished.

The philosopher Moses Mendelssohn was a founder, and his paradoxical goal was for Jews to stay Jewish while becoming truly German. He translated the Jewish Bible into German written with Hebrew characters, to make it accessible to average Jews. But this was emphatically not Yiddish, which he opposed as degenerate German. (Goethe had called it a "nasal, duck-like quack.")[44] Others, for the first time since Muslim Spain, began to use Hebrew itself for secular purposes, and new periodicals carried secular poetry and social commentary in the ancient holy tongue—an outrage to many rabbis, but the first tentative step toward modern Hebrew.

It is perhaps proof of the risks involved that Mendelssohn's grandson Felix, the great composer, was not Jewish. Following anti-Jewish rioting, his father, the prosperous banker Abraham Mendelssohn, had his children baptized and raised as Protestants. Later he pressured Felix to change his surname to Bartholdy, but the composer insisted on staying Mendelssohn. Always feeling his grandfather's influence, he set Psalm 100 for the Reform temple in Hamburg, wrote the oratorio *Elijah,* and quoted synagogue melodies in some of his secular works. He liked klezmer musicians and their music, and he was a major target of Richard Wagner's anti-Semitic tract on Jews in music. But formally he and his family were no longer Jewish.

Nor was Heinrich Heine, one of the greatest of German poets, born a Jew named Chaim and called Harry. He failed at business and then at law, but entered the pantheon of European poets—not, however, before being baptized as a Lutheran, which enabled him to get his doctorate. His lifelong ambivalence was emblematic.[45] He was active in Jewish affairs as a student and after his baptism made fun of himself for having "crawled toward the cross."[46] Of his conversion he said, "I lack the strength to wear a beard, to let them call 'Ikey Mo' after me on the street. I haven't even the strength to eat *matzoh.*"[47] He joked that the man responsible for his conversion was Napoleon's geography teacher, "who did not tell him that Moscow winters are very cold." That is, if Napoleon had completed his conquest of Europe, Jewish emancipation would have encompassed Düsseldorf, and Heine would not have had to convert.

But he also wrote, "Those who would say Judaism is a religion would say that being a hunchback is a religion. . . . Judaism is not a religion but a misfortune."[48] He soon extended his antireligious views to Christianity as well, but with age and serious illness he returned to his Jewish identity, writing poems he called "Hebrew Melodies." These included a poem in praise of Judah Halevy, the great medieval Hebrew poet, and a long poem about the Sabbath. Just as a prince can be turned into a beast in a folktale, the Jew becomes a dog under the evil magic of oppression, but for one day a week he becomes a prince again, under the transient spell of "Prinzessin Sabbath":

> *Lecho Daudi likras Kalle—*
> *Come, beloved, your bride*
> *Already waits, sends you*
> *Her bashful glance.*

This "silent Princess . . . pearl and blossom of all beauty . . . glances soft as a gazelle, grows lithe as a myrtle." Schiller, according to this poem, would have called *cholent*—the thick twenty-four-hour Sabbath stew—"daughter of Elysium," which is what he called joy itself in his "Ode to Joy" set by

Beethoven. God taught Moses to cook it on Mount Sinai, and compared to this "kosher ambrosia" the nectar of the Greek gods was mere "Devil's Dreck." When the awakened Prince tastes this delicacy, "his eye gleams as if in revelation," and he asks, "Do I not hear the Jordan rushing?" But,

> *Soon the fine day flits away,*
> *The evil hour approaches. . . .*

Sighing, the Prince slowly smells the sweet Havdalah spices in their golden box, and sadly prepares to devolve into a beast again. He drinks his parting glass down to the last drops:

> *He pours them on the table,*
> *Takes a small wax candle,*
> *And dips it in the wetness*
> *So it crackles and goes out.*[49]

Heine wrote many poems on his deathbed, quite a few with Jewish themes, and his collected poems, stories, and writings on Jewish subjects fill a sizable book.[50] He claimed in the end, "I make no secret of my Judaism, to which I have not returned, because I never left it."[51]

Heine became acquainted with the young Karl Marx, first supporting and later opposing his socialist program. But unlike the ambivalent Heine, Marx was a classic self-hating Jew, in the mold of medieval converts who became anti-Semitic bishops. ("What is the secular cult of the Jew?" he wrote. "Huckstering. What is his secular god? Money.")[52] Marx was descended from distinguished rabbis on both sides of his family, but his father converted to Protestantism a year before his birth. Marx saw Jews as among the worst of the hated bourgeoisie, rootless cosmopolitans whose role as money handlers cut them off from social concerns and made them exploiters. He would have abolished Judaism and capitalism alike.

Nevertheless, his grand historical theory, tied as it is to concern for the world's oppressed, recalls in some ways the prophetic books of the Bible. But Marx's reputation stood on an intellectual base, however weak. Indeed Marx, scribbling away at *Das Kapital* in the reading room of the British Library, resembled his studious rabbinical ancestors more than he did the workers and revolutionaries who later revered him. His sense of injustice was also very Jewish; recall that it was the capitalism of Charles Dickens that he was looking at, not ours. As Dickens was moved to create Oliver Twist and David Copperfield, Marx was moved to create a false but intricate economic-historical theory, designed by a born outsider always looking in. He rejected the very foundations of European social life, like dissatisfied

Jews who had preceded him—Moses Hess, Ferdinand Lassalle—and others who followed—Rosa Luxemburg, Leon Trotsky, Emma Goldman, and many more.

Marx was still a college boy when Hess published the first communist work in Germany, *The Sacred History of Humanity by a Disciple of Spinoza.* Hess, who worked with Marx and Engels but never fully embraced their views, later became the first notable Zionist, sealing a bond between Zionism and socialism that would last a century. Lassalle, also more moderate than Marx and Engels, was the founder of social democracy as a European political movement. Luxemburg, firebrand daughter of a Polish-Jewish merchant, cofounded the German Communist Party; she was murdered by army officers on her way to prison. Trotsky, one of the leaders of the Russian Revolution, was a brutal Red Army commander and might have been Lenin's successor, but Stalin edged him out after Lenin's death, and eventually had him killed with an ice pick through the skull as he wrote at his desk. As for "Red Emma" Goldman, she was an anarchist who denounced state, church, and capitalism with equal vigor.

Left-wing Jews played important roles in workers' movements from Communist syndicates to mainstream labor unions. But ironically it was peasants, not workers, who made Communist revolutions, and the societies they created had little in common with Marx's vision. Yet the vision, arrayed for a century against the theoretical claims of capitalism, shaped the twentieth century. In all likelihood, the pressure from Marx's followers, for all the damage they did, made capitalism more humane and decent. This liberal mitigation of "the survival of the fittest"—or "the devil take the hindmost"—is largely responsible for the success of capitalism and the relative stability of the world's economy.

For those in the twentieth century who wanted to change their minds instead of the world, another Jew played the pivotal role. Sigmund Freud was born to a Jewish mother and father in Freiburg, Moravia, and stayed nominally Jewish throughout his life. But the unrelenting scientific gaze he fixed on the human soul left no room for religion and, in contrast to the claims of Enlightenment thinkers, made the quest for reason itself a discouraging uphill fight.

Freud considered himself a Darwinian, so he looked to evolution for the explanation of human nature, not to the claims of religion or the relentless march of history. He put sex and aggression at the center of human experience, and showed how we use reason to deceive ourselves and others about our real motives. Freud was first a physician, neurologist, and brain scientist, so his approach to human suffering was fundamentally medical, one patient at a time. As he embraced psychology, he began to treat certain neurological symptoms with what he called psychoanalysis, the basis of all forms of psychotherapy.

But his work went far beyond medicine, and its influence is as great in the social sciences, philosophy, and humanities as in psychiatry or psychology. It is impossible to understand the twentieth century without reference to Freud's deep skepticism of human reason, just as it is impossible to understand it without perceiving the dishonesty Marx saw in society's order. These two Jewish skeptics shook Western civilization; and some of their followers, if not they themselves, went too far. Marx's dream of a perfect future society killed scores of millions, and destroyed the good life for hundreds of millions more. For some, Freud's demand for examination of every jot and tittle of life can drain life of joy and romance and substitute self-absorption for adventure, giving rise to the half joke that psychoanalysis is the disease of which it purports to be the cure. Nevertheless, a fair backward look from the twenty-first century finds value in both visions. The German-Jewish psychoanalyst Erich Fromm admired the milder, early, non-violent Marx as well as revering Freud, and said that the message of both was "The truth shall make you free."[53]

It seems a big jump from psychoanalysis to physics, but nothing challenged practical reason quite as much as the theory of relativity, presented in 1905 by a German-Jewish patent officer, Albert Einstein. Holding a Ph.D. in physics but unable to get a professorship, he sat at his kitchen table and wrote three papers that changed the world. Galileo had shown that the measurement of velocity depends on where you stand, but Einstein's simple algebra—assuming only the then recently proved constant speed of light—showed that where you stand affects not only the measurement of speed, but those of length, mass, space, time, and gravity. The orderly world described by Galileo and Newton for objects in space, and extended by Faraday and Maxwell for electricity and magnetism, was now a mere approximation. If Einstein was right, then what of the Enlightenment philosophers and social theorists who took Newton's physics as their model? What of the clockwork certainties that science was supposed to discern in every realm of life?

Needless to say, Einstein's vision was resisted. But during the solar eclipse of 1919, the light from a distant star was shown to have bent as it passed through the sun's gravitational field, exactly as predicted by Einstein's equations—accurate to the sixth or seventh decimal place. Two decades later Einstein accompanied his friend, the physicist Leo Szilard, to see President Roosevelt and urge him to use the new physics to design an atomic weapon before the Nazis did it first. Thus Einstein, a famous lifelong pacifist, paradoxically became a midwife of the first nuclear bomb; for better and for worse, this was practical reason indeed.

In another paradox, this lifelong open atheist often used God as a metaphor. "God does not play dice," he would say, in his famous response to quantum theory, which placed uncertainty at the core of the structure of everything in the universe. "God is subtle but not malicious" was another of his sayings, referring to the inexplicable comprehensibility of the world; he often described his work as trying to read God's mind. The idea that we *can* read God's mind—that the world is logical and, through study, can ultimately be understood—has been at the heart of Jewish thought since the first debate over a Torah passage.

Why did Jewish thinkers play a strong role in laying the intellectual foundations of the modern world? First, their ancient tradition of creating and studying texts was one of the oldest on the planet. When other cultures' identities depended on territory, the Jews had to rely on texts. There were always Jews who restricted themselves to holy texts and Jews—Philo, Josephus, the Jewish thinkers of Islam, even Maimonides—who straddled Jewish and secular civilization. Renaissance Europe was no exception, and the Jewish printing presses spreading throughout the Continent and beyond mass-produced sacred texts as well as new secular ones. For centuries Jews had literacy rates several times as high as those of the people around them.

This was evident in eastern Europe. According to the 1897 census of the Russian Empire, there were more than twice as many Jews who could read Yiddish (39 percent, including 49 percent of men and 26 percent of women) as there were Russians literate in *their* language (21 percent).[54] In fact, more Jews than Russians could read *Russian*—their second language, in a different alphabet. These literacy rates were also much higher than historians estimate for classical Greece. Paralleling this grassroots success was another in the academy: Jewish communities found and nurtured, generation after generation, the outstanding scholars in their midst.

With this cultural capital the Jews came seemingly out of nowhere to join the Enlightenment colloquy. Secular thought required intellectual ability, but you also had to think outside the orthodoxies of Europe's culture, to create new forms of thought not beholden to church and king. At great cost to themselves and their families—think of Galileo and Darwin—innovators of all backgrounds cultivated unpleasant doubts about all their civilization held dear.

The Jews were already there, already skeptical of the European order. John Murray Cuddihy, a sociologist who studied the Jewish encounter with modernity, put it this way: "When ghetto walls crumble . . . Jewry—like some wide-eyed anthropologist—enters upon a strange world, to explore a strange people. . . . They examine this world in dismay, with wonder, anger, and punitive objectivity."[55] The only orthodoxy they had to break out of was Orthodox Judaism, and Europe had been urging them to do that all along. With the Haskalah and the limited emancipations of the early 1800s, Jewish thinkers were ready to give up on Orthodoxy even before their admission to the great Enlightenment seminar. In fact, they were frankly embarrassed by their more traditional fellow Jews. They had to persuade non-Jewish Europeans—and, more important, themselves—that they were truly mannered and modern, that they had left the long caftans, swaying prayers, emotional outbursts, and smell of onions behind for good, that they were what the Germans called *salonsfähig*—"fit for the salon."[56]

This was the Jewish "ordeal of civility," a gnawing embarrassment or even shame at the unsuitability of one's origins. It was experienced by other minority groups, and indeed by any upwardly mobile social group in an open society. But the Jews had long cultivated their outsider status, and the Jewish secular thinkers dealt with it by an intellectual counterphobic attack: they criticized and changed the culture even as they attempted to fit into it. For the first time, they had a conversation to join that was outside Judaism yet did not require them to adopt any other religion. Eventually, for many, it would not even require leaving Judaism.

But many did. Isaac Deutscher, a twentieth-century historian with strong left-leaning views, wrote an essay called "The Non-Jewish Jew," containing this striking sentence: "The Jewish heretic who transcends Jewry belongs to a Jewish tradition."[57] He was able to say this with authority. He had been a child prodigy who, at his Bar Mitzvah in 1920, had been virtually ordained. He delivered a discourse at that time that was attended by a hundred rabbis who poured into his small hometown, incidentally ten miles north of Auschwitz. He had already lived through a series of pogroms, hiding terrified in his father's barricaded printing shop.

But he was also already having doubts. He was soon publishing poetry in Polish, slipping into a literature class with the professor's permission—he pinned his sidelocks behind his ears—and organizing a group to discuss literature and philosophy. He dreamed more and more of attending a secular gymnasium, but his father insisted he go to study with a Hasidic rabbi. In protest, and deliberately courting rejection, he took scissors to his sidelocks. His father slapped his face—the only time he was hit—and sent him anyway. But his stay lasted only three weeks before his father relented and brought him home. Poignantly, they began studying secular books together: Goethe, Lessing, Heine, Spinoza, all subjects of heated discussion and argument. His father's feet were firmly planted in Orthodox Judaism, but he strove to understand and admire the great secular works, and he gave his son those same aspirations.

The son, half a century later, reflected on not only Heine and Spinoza but Marx, Freud, and others, representing "the sum and substance of much that is greatest in modern thought":

> I do not believe in the exclusive genius of any race. Yet I think that in some ways they were very Jewish indeed. They had in themselves something of the quintessence of Jewish life and of the Jewish intellect. . . . as Jews they dwelt on the borderlines of various

civilizations, religions, and national cultures. . . . Their mind matured where the most diverse cultural influences crossed and fertil-
ized each other. They lived on the margins or in the nooks and
crannies of their respective nations.[58]

They had dark views of human nature, yet were optimists. They were de-
terminists, but saw the potential to transcend past patterns. They were
skeptical of religion, but believed in a universal human nature and destiny.
And they considered theory to be insufficient, insisting that it be married to
action. They did act, sometimes wrongly, but always in an effort to advance
human welfare—*tikkun olam*—by advancing understanding.

Jews do not have magical minds with special access to the secrets of the
universe. The edifice of modernity rests on discoveries by Copernicus,
Galileo, Newton, Leeuwenhoek, Lavoisier, Boyle, Mendeleyev, Faraday,
Maxwell, Mendel, Pasteur, Koch, and Darwin, none of whom was Jewish.
In the twentieth century Jews did not develop or discover quantum theory,
the enormity of the universe, the nature of chemical bonds, penicillin, the
transistor, heart transplants, or the structure of DNA. But they did develop
or discover relativity, the structure of the atom, quarks, psychotherapy,
streptomycin, polio vaccines, nerve growth factor, the cell's energy cycle,
and the genetic code. Some of these scientists considered themselves Jews
and were proud of it; others couldn't care less. But all were products of a
culture that had revered learning, created texts, and studied them intensely—all with a view toward moral action—for perhaps three thousand
years.

Jews and half Jews, who make up about 0.2 percent of the world's population, have won a total of 155 Nobel Prizes in all fields, 117 in physics,
chemistry, and medicine.[59] Jews have by far the highest number of prizes
per capita of any definable ethnic or national group, with Sweden a distant
second; the ratio of Jewish Nobels per capita to Swedish Nobels per capita
is 17 to 1. Jewish preeminence in Nobel Prizes began as soon as the prize
originated, and long before the advantages of American scientific training.
Opportunities for Jewish American scientists in the United States clinched
the Jewish lead in all fields, not just at the Nobel level but throughout the
structure of science. It is chilling to contemplate what the modern world
would be missing if the Jewish contribution were subtracted. It is interesting to wonder what else we might have if one-third of the world's Jews had
not gone up in smoke. "Jewish physics," the Nazis called relativity. In the
end it was just physics, but a lot of it came from Jews.

It might seem more difficult for Jews to excel in the secular arts—judgments there being more subjective and influence more parochial—but it
would be difficult to write the history of modern creativity without men-
tioning Jews. To name a few, and omitting those who focused mainly on

Jewish themes or wrote in Jewish languages: in music, Mahler, Copland, and Schoenberg; in painting, Pissarro, Modigliani, Rothko, and Lucien Freud; in sculpture, Lipchitz and Nevelson; in photography, Stieglitz, Man Ray, Capa, Eisenstaedt, and Arbus; in fiction, Proust, Kafka, Babel, Pasternak, and Bellow; in playwriting, Ionesco, Hellman, Miller, and Pinter; and in poetry—after Heine—Sassoon, Ginsberg, and Adrienne Rich. Jews have won the Nobel Prize for literature for writing in English, German, French, Russian, Polish, Hungarian, Yiddish, and Hebrew. Great Jewish critics and scholars of the arts include Derrida, Trilling, Bloom, and Berenson; philosophers Bergson, Wittgenstein, and Isaiah Berlin; social scientists Boas, Durkheim, and Lévi-Strauss; and legal scholars Brandeis, Frankfurter, and Ruth Bader Ginsburg, all Supreme Court justices.

The story, perhaps apocryphal, is told of how one major unit of the University of California was planned and founded. The city that was to house it, then small, hired a team of experts to study the likely impact of such a massive institution. They analyzed the effect of the university on the economy, politics, crime, and other aspects of the city's life and submitted a formal report. At the final meeting, the city fathers were cautiously enthusiastic, but there was something else to discuss.

"There is one more thing that goes along with a university," said the experts, "something else that a university always entails."

"What would that be?" asked the city fathers, puzzled that anything could have escaped the thick and thorough report.

"Jews, gentlemen. Jews." The city fathers bit the bullet and built the university.

10

ENDS OF THE EARTH

HOW JEWS THRIVED IN EXOTIC PLACES

According to the Bible, the Queen of Sheba came to visit Solomon, was dazzled and enamored, and duly became prominent among his three hundred wives. According to legend their passionate union, along with the Queen's entourage, became the source of a flourishing Jewish culture high in the Ethiopian hills. Other legends hold that the origins of these hill people are earlier (some Hebrews astray after the Exodus) or later (some drifting tribes of Israel lost after the First Temple's destruction). There is no way to rule these stories out, but there are less romantic, more plausible explanations.

Recall that there was briefly a Jewish kingdom in southern Arabia, now Yemen, around the year 525, indicating a strong Jewish cultural presence there before the birth of Muhammad —as the Qur'an confirms. This community was just across the Red Sea from Ethiopia, and influences may have passed in both directions, but many scholars believe that the conquest of South Arabia by an Ethiopian king forced the movement of thousands of Jewish captives—a pattern known throughout the ancient world. We know that some ethnic groups were in a persistent state of rebellion, and some of those rebels may have been Jews.[1] By the seventh or eighth century, there was probably an autonomous Jewish community in Ethiopia, speaking Agaw, one of numerous unwritten languages in the region. Like the Christians, however, they had a separate language, Ge'ez, for prayer and Scripture. So they followed the pattern of almost all Jewish diaspora groups in having a separate sacred language, but in their case the language was not Hebrew. Still, they clearly had the Jewish Bible early on; a Ge'ez inscription from the early 500s refers to passages from Psalms.[2]

Benjamin of Tudela appears to have passed through Ethiopia (then called Abyssinia or Middle India) on his way back to Spain in the late 1100s. He calls it a Christian kingdom, but writes, "There are many Israelites there, and they are not under the yoke of the Gentiles, but possess cities and castles on the summits of the mountains, from which they make descents into the plain-country. . . . These are the Lybians . . . with whom the Jews are at war. The Jews take spoil and booty and retreat to the mountains, and no man can prevail against them."[3] In the next century, Marco Polo visited and wrote, "There are also Jews in this country; and they have two marks, one on either cheek," distinguishing them from Christians and Muslims.

In later times they would call themselves Beta Israel—"House of Israel"—or simply Israel, but at this time they were simply called *ayhud*—"Jews." Beginning in the 1400s two centuries of war pitted the *ayhud* against their Christian rulers.[4] There were many forced conversions, churches were built, and there was heavy Christian migration into land previously held by *ayhud*. Those refusing to convert had their land confiscated, and were named *falashoch*—"strangers"—by the Christian king. This name stuck to them as Falashas, which they were called for five centuries. One of the king's successors was officially chronicled as the "exterminator of the Jews,"[5] and in this era the *ayhud* were caught up in violent theological conflicts among Christians, as "Jew" became an epithet Christians used against each other.

Not all Jews were converted or killed; some withdrew to more remote areas in northwest Ethiopia. They believed in the Jewish Bible, anticipated the coming of the Messiah, and strictly observed the Sabbath on Saturday; others knew them by their extinction of all fires Friday evening. They observed the Fast of Esther, thus marking the Purim holiday, and had a day of supplication known as *segd*. They cultivated their fields, kept vineyards or cattle herds, or were artisans. Artisanry in time became an emblem of their status; they turned to crafts as their land was taken away. Christians believed they had the evil eye and some were executed for sorcery, but their value in making weapons for the Christians to fight off Muslims helped them survive. Their sacred texts in Ge'ez included the Torah, the rest of the Jewish Bible, some apocryphal books, and a treatise on "Commandments of the Sabbath." They also had prayers in Ge'ez, but these included passages in their ancient vernacular, Agaw.

Centuries of war ended with the complete conquest of the remaining Jews by the Ethiopian state, and many were killed, enslaved, dispersed, or deprived of their land.[6] Still, their value as soldiers and artisans—some were generals in Jewish regiments, others worked as stonemasons building palaces—kept many alive. Wars resumed in the 1500s with yet another Christian push to the northwest, and the odds against the Jews were heavy. In one battle, Kaleb, a Jewish chieftain, "carried out a scorched-earth policy to prevent the king from obtaining provisions:

> When bombarded by cannon and attacked, Kaleb's forces fought back by rolling stones down the hill. But they were overcome and

many were captured. One woman who was tied to her captor threw herself off a cliff, taking him with her to her death. Others followed her example. Even the Ethiopian chronicler, who was an eyewitness, expressed his admiration of Falasha bravery, comparing it to that of the ancient Israelites against the Romans.[7]

Kaleb survived but went mad over the slaughter. Many Jewish women were taken as captives and concubines, including one princess, who became the king's mistress and gave him his only sons.

Gondar, the first city in the Jewish region, was partly built by Jewish masons and carpenters, who became upwardly mobile and might even be granted land. Other Jews stayed poor and landless, working as tenant farmers, blacksmiths, potters, weavers, traders, soldiers, laborers, servants, or slaves. Gradually they began to be a caste.

Once decisively conquered, the Jews, as they had done in other diasporas, allied themselves with their rulers and served them loyally. They prospered while staying separate, with their own prayer houses, priests, and schools. This applied even to Beta Israel warriors. According to one of their own oral traditions, they refused to fight on Saturday in one important battle, praying instead. Their prayers were answered, and the battle was won without them.[8]

Amharic gradually became the Jews' primary language, while Ge'ez remained the language of Scripture, just as they did for Christians. But the Beta Israel's separateness endured for three reasons. They rejected the New Testament and Jesus, hewing strictly to the Orit, the Ge'ez translation of the Jewish Bible. They gradually lost their high-status occupations, retreating to two primary crafts, blacksmithing for men and potting for women. This intensified their castelike status and made them both marginal and dependent. Finally, as elsewhere in the world, anti-Jewish sentiment played a role in making the Beta Israel cohere. In Ethiopia they were called *buda,* or witches. A *buda* could dig up graves, eat cadavers, or morph into a hyena, so that Jews were sometimes called "hyena people."[9] It could enter you and drink your blood or eat your intestines. Perhaps the exclusive mastery of smithing and potting by the Jews, in the region, seemed so mysterious to others that it had to be witchcraft. How could a normal person turn a handful of dirt into a pot or a rock into an iron tool or weapon? Prejudice and separation reinforced each other.

At the same time, they were known for the strictness of their religious practices. They observed the Sabbath, called Sanbat, very rigorously, and washed so frequently that non-Jewish Ethiopians said that they smelled of water—one of the odder complaints ever leveled against Jews. "During the afternoon on Friday, enough food was prepared for that evening and the next day, and then everyone went to a stream to wash, first the men and then the women. They extinguished all fires by sunset Friday. During the Sabbath day, they could not work, light a fire, or draw water; people could leave their houses only to go to the prayer house; they could not cross any rivers or streams and were supposed to speak in soft voices."[10] Even more explicitly than in other Jewish traditions, Sanbat was personified as a female intermediary between God and the people.[11] As one of their sayings has it, "The savior of the Jews is the Sabbath." Their unique religious work, "Commandments of the Sabbath," holds that whoever does not prepare for the Sabbath will die.

The *qes* or *kahen* combined aspects of the roles of priest and rabbi. The Beta Israel ritually marked the new moon and other phases in each moon's cycle—and the main biblical festivals were carefully observed. The observance of Fasika—Passover—began three days early with an exclusive diet of roasted grain. On the eve of Passover itself a lamb was sacrificed according to ancient Hebrew traditions, and only unleavened bread was eaten for the next seven days. The *qes* read aloud from the Torah chapters that specify these commandments, commemorating the Exodus from Egypt. Spring harvest was celebrated fifty days after Passover, with a feast commemorating both the first fruits and the receipt of the Ten Commandments by Moses on Mount Sinai. This was the equivalent of Shavuot, the Feast of Weeks.

To memorialize the destruction of the Temple, not just the Ninth of Av but the first seventeen days of that summer month were observed as a partial fast. The last Saturday of Av was considered Ya Sanbat Sanbat—"the Sabbath of Sabbaths"—a phrase reserved by other Jews for the Day of Atonement. This exceptional Sanbat was marked by repeating the phrase *yeftan*—"open me" or "absolve me"—throughout the day, a request that God recognize their good works of the previous year. In other Jewish traditions the last day of Av begins a month of repentance leading up to the High Holy Days.

The equivalent of Rosh Hashanah was the Feast of Drums, leading into a nine-day partial fast ending in Astasreyo, the Day of Atonement. As among other Jews, the Feast of Booths began five days later. The Beta Israel brought together palm, willow, and cypress branches for it as commanded by Leviticus 23, but without the fourth species, the citron, which they had no way of getting. The *qes* read the relevant chapters from Leviticus as well as Psalms 49–91, and the Beta Israel added to the usual interpretation the belief that they were commemorating the feast Joseph gave his father. Chanukah was absent from their calendar, perhaps because its establishment as a holiday followed their separation from the rest of the Jewish world. Purim was marked not by a feast, and certainly not by drunkenness, but by a three-day Fast of Esther.

One important holiday unique to Beta Israel—and indeed a ceremony of separation from other peoples—was *segd*. Seven weeks were counted from Yom Kippur, and the covenant with God was reaffirmed by a climb to the top of a mountain.

By the late nineteenth century the Ethiopian Jews had split into three groups, one very traditional, one in contact with Europe, and one that became Protestant, a new form of Christianity there. Famine ravaged the country, and the Beta Israel were especially hard hit; a letter in the 1890s described a decline in the number of synagogues from two hundred to thirty: "We are in great misery. Our books have been destroyed; the Dervishes burnt them by fire. We have no longer any schools; they are destroyed."[12] In the late nineteenth century the Jewish linguist Joseph Halevy, followed by his student Jacques Faitlovitch, established continuous contact between the Beta Israel and the rest of the Jewish world. Charity and education increased, and throughout the twentieth century there was growing if grudging acceptance of them as authentic Jews.

A film crew visiting them in the 1970s found them in several hundred villages around Gondar, in many ways typical of rural Ethiopia.[13] They planted cotton and wheat, and threshed it with a team of oxen trampling it under their hooves. The cotton was spun and woven to make most clothes, and others—for example, the infant-carrying sling—were of leather. Homes were small circular huts of bundled vertical sticks. But they held services on Saturday and read from both a recently acquired Hebrew Torah scroll and their three-hundred-year-old large bound-parchment Ge'ez Bible. They obeyed Sabbath and kosher laws and circumcised their sons at eight days. Individuals prayed prostrate on mats, a custom borrowed from Muslims, but the Beta Israel prayed toward Jerusalem, not Mecca. The calendar still blended Ethiopian and Jewish elements, as it had a century earlier.

A wedding showed both similarities to and differences from common Ethiopian practice. The groom sat in a chair, draped in a white robe held from behind by his robed sister. An older man knelt at his feet and laid strips of cloth over his feet, intoning,

> *To earth man is bound and to earth man will return.*
> *But in your loins you have strength*
> *And in man's heart is tenderness, and in his head*
> *Is the wisdom and intelligence that makes him a man.*

At this a narrow headband was placed on the groom's forehead. The bride wore white too, with a Star of David emblazoned on the back of her gown. They made a procession using an umbrella as a wedding canopy. Rhythmic dancing, singing, and clapping followed African traditions, but the *qes* chanted a decidedly non-African blessing:

God took dust from the earth and made Adam after his likeness.
He put him into the garden and then he created Eve,
After taking a rib of his ribs, to be his wife.
Halleluja, Praise God!

A cow was slaughtered as commanded in the Torah, and the tendon on the inside of the thigh was removed, commemorating Jacob's struggle with the angel. A feast of boiled meat was served on large disks of freshly baked flat bread.

The bride and groom went into a seclusion hut for seven days, and then ceremonially emerged and approached the groom's family to get his father's blessing, in the name of "our patriarchs Abel, Abraham, Isaac, Jacob, Moses, Aaron the priest, and the prophets, the children of Aaron, and David, King of Israel. . . . May the God of Israel watch over you and give you happiness. . . . May peace and understanding reign in your house, and may you live to see your children's children and the children of their children."[14]

By the mid-1970s a few thousand Beta Israel had migrated to Israel on foot in horrendous conditions, and their status was uncertain. Chief rabbis in prestate Israel had considered them Jews in official documents dating from 1921, and this was reiterated by the chief rabbi of Israel in 1973. The Beta Israel had long requested mass transfer to Israel as was done with other groups of Jews according to the ancestral promise, but political obstacles in Ethiopia were formidable. They worsened markedly in 1974, when a Communist revolution overthrew the ancient kingdom and war with Somalia ensued. Thirty thousand Beta Israel remained in Ethiopia, down from an estimated two hundred thousand in the nineteenth century. Israeli and other foreign Jewish aid workers were in contact with them, but had no plans for mass transfer.

Still, there was some movement. A Jewish Agency officer who had begun his career by rescuing Jews from the Nazis now applied the same methods to bring an occasional truckload of the Beta Israel out through Sudan. "A policeman can be bribed," he said. "A guard can fall asleep at the right time."[15] C-130 cargo planes stripped of Israeli insignia picked up a truckload of people somewhere in the desert. But this saved only a few half-starved, desperate refugees.

Israeli diplomats involved the United States, and a Jewish American diplomat convinced Sudan to allow an exodus. Millions in American aid were at stake, and the diplomat, keeping a straight face while mouthing anti-Semitic epithets, persuaded a key Sudanese official that because the Jews had so much power in America, aid money would flow more freely if he looked the other way. Rescues became more frequent. Thousands were brought to Israel in Operation Moses, the first mass transfer of Africans by white people to freedom instead of slavery. However, a few press leaks in early 1985 led Sudan to stop the flow for fear of offending Arab allies. Crisis diplomacy intensified. President Reagan approved American involvement, Vice President George Bush intervened, and a concentrated transfer moved thousands more from Sudan to Israel. This operation could have ended very badly, but as the Beta Israel say in Amharic, *"meqseft yasfer-awal"*—"a catastrophe didn't happen."

Fifteen thousand were transferred, but an equal number were still in Ethiopia, and the new immigrants began to demand that their families be brought to them. *"Ad matai?"* was their impatient Hebrew slogan—"Till when?" The second phase, Operation Solomon, took place in 1991.[16] A steady stream of Jewish pilgrims had been walking from remote parts of the country to Addis Ababa, where they camped outside the Israeli embassy and got medical care and Hebrew lessons. Complex negotiations soured when the dictator of Ethiopia went back on the $30 million deal. He was losing a civil war and needed the Jews as a pawn in his international game, but after his fall Israel played the Washington card, getting President Bush to pressure the new regime.

C-130s left Tel Aviv for Addis Ababa at midnight, and by midmorning thousands had crowded around the embassy, some with no real claim to be Jewish. Israeli soldiers dressed as tourists managed the crowd, intervening to help with acute illnesses and lost children. Bribes got people bused to the airport, and they boarded the planes with only their children and the clothes on their back. The flights went on all day and into the night. A woman went into labor. The flight surgeon later said, "I hoped that she would keep the labor till we reached Israel, but she didn't think so." He delivered her tenth child in flight, increasing to 14,087 the number of Beta Israel rescued in Operation Solomon. A pilot said, "This is why I came 40 years ago to Israel. And now I'm fulfilling . . . paying back those who brought me to Israel. Now I'm paying the check back. I brought people to Israel, for their new life." The chief of the mission said, "I think they have changed me more than I have changed them. . . . I have found in them what we have lost maybe, during the generations."[17]

Their adjustment was far from perfect. They were embraced, settled, and supported as many previous groups of immigrants had been, and like previous groups, they were sometimes victims of prejudice. But they had darker skin, they had not used Hebrew texts, their Judaism was pretalmudic, and their status as Jews was still in question. Israel's chief rabbinate demanded that the Beta Israel undergo a partial conversion ceremony: They would have to be immersed in the *mikvah,* or ritual bath, declare acceptance of rabbinic law, and—although all males had been circumcised on the eighth day as the Torah requires—men and boys would have to be symbolically nicked, a ritual recircumcision. Many resisted this indignity, striking and demonstrating to insist that they were already Jewish and needed no conversion. To make matters worse, the rabbinate mistranslated the Hebrew for *mikvah* immersion into the Amharic for baptism. An Israeli writer said, "We have the nerve to call *them* primitive, when the first thing we do when they arrive is to take a drop of blood from their penises!"[18]

Many of these tensions were resolved, and the Beta Israel experience was like that of immigrants in any country. They were brought to Israel and helped, but their dependency could not last long. In this bustling, competitive country, they would have to fight for their share of what was not the world's largest pie. They were looked down upon by those who had come earlier from elsewhere. And if they had a hard time, they did not get unlimited sympathy from people who had drained swamps, fought raiders, had malaria, made the desert bloom, survived the Nazis, and turned back vast invading armies. They were largely on their own, and they largely succeeded.

A crisis occurred in 1996, when an Israeli newspaper revealed that the blood of Ethiopian donors had been discarded for twelve years by blood banks for fear of AIDS. This struck a nerve for people whose traditions emphasized blood and purity. On top of this, there was a series of terrorist attacks that year that led to nationwide calls for blood, and Ethiopian Jews were excluded from this communal experience. Years later the episode remained painful in memory.

But the great melting pot of the army, which has homogenized Israeli society for half a century, had its impact on the younger immigrants. By the year 2000 it was possible to study a group of nineteen Ethiopian-Jewish college students, most at Hebrew University in Jerusalem, Israel's most prestigious institution of higher learning. The strains of various divisions—between the immigrants and the rest of Israeli society, between Amharic and Hebrew, between children and parents, and even within each person—were very much in evidence. All but one said they had experienced some racism in Israeli society, and a large minority saw the blood-discarding as racist. One student said that after the scandal broke, he stopped hanging out with his non-Ethiopian friends: "You want to be with people you are comfortable with, that have a similar background."[19]

Other issues, though, were typical of immigrant families anywhere. An insightful observation was made by a twenty-five-year-old woman:

> In Hebrew I can tell my parents things that I can't tell them in Amharic. If I'm angry, I can be really angry in Hebrew but not in Amharic. In Hebrew I can say "no" to my mother. In Amharic I must respect them. In Amharic I can't tell my parents "I'm going out and don't ask me when I'm coming back." In Hebrew it's more accepted.[20]

For such children the older generation uses the Amharic term "cattle-child," because they wander off like stray cattle, deaf to demands. But after the blood-discarding revelation, she changed her name from Batsheva, which she had been given in Israel, back to Sava, her Ethiopian name. And after her discharge from the army, a time when many young Israelis go to India or America, Sava went to Ethiopia.

Through continued integration, schooling, universal army service, and ultimately intermarriage, the Beta Israel may yet take their rightful place in Israeli society. In April 2002, with Israel under siege again, Azanu Mekonen, a pretty eighteen-year-old, was one of fourteen teenagers chosen to light the torches of Independence Day, a great honor. In 1990, at six, she had left the village of Maure with her family, traveling on foot, horseback, and truck to Addis Ababa. They were among the thousands of squatters near the Israeli embassy, waiting eight months for the airlift. She said, "In our society it was unthinkable that a parent would ever ask a child for assistance, but since we came to Israel, my parents, who can barely speak Hebrew, have to ask even my little sister for help. . . . My mom teaches my Israeli-born sister Amharic and she teaches my mom Hebrew." Azanu started a scout troop for Ethiopian teens, and she participated in Seeds of Peace, which brings young Arabs and Jews together. "The most important part . . . for me was to meet Palestinians and Israeli Arabs and be able to attach a face to all the generalizations. That's often what happens to minorities—they're bunched into one stereotype."[21] Spoken like one who had once been there.

The Beta Israel had an ancient prayer, "Do not separate me, O Lord, from thy chosen, from thy joy, from the light and from the splendor. Let me see, O Lord, the light of Israel, and let me listen to the words of the just."[22] Their courage and persistence over many centuries was at last matched by the resolve of their rescuers, acting on the commandment of *pidyon shevuim,* the redemption of captives. Ironically, this commandment was specified by the Talmud they had not yet accepted. As the chief Sephardic rabbi wrote, citing that talmudic text and accepting the Beta Israel as Jews, to save one soul is to save an entire world.

༄

The Jews of India were far more successful and their lives far less precarious. Their well-documented experience illuminates the trajectory of Jews in a largely benign diaspora. There were three traditional Jewish communities in India: the Cochin Jews, on the Malabar Coast, the western side of the tip of India; the Bene Israel, farther north on that coast; and the Baghdadi Jews of Bombay and Calcutta.[23] The Cochin Jews believed that they came to India in King Solomon's time, but their presence was not recorded until about the year 1000, when copper plates inscribed by the Hindu ruler granted certain privileges to one of them. Benjamin of Tudela and Marco

Polo recorded their presence in the twelfth and thirteenth centuries. Jews fleeing persecution in the Portuguese colony to the north established a new community in the 1500s and built the famous Paradesi synagogue for "foreigners." They were known as the White Jews of Cochin, while the original community, darker in skin color, was called Black Jews. A Dutch presence in Cochin from the late 1600s was a boon to these Jews, and no doubt brought more Jewish merchants and settlers.

The Bene Israel claim to have come in the time of the Maccabees, fleeing Greek and Syrian persecutions in Israel. But they probably arrived later, perhaps in the fifth or sixth century, from Arabia or Persia. More Jews arrived with the Portuguese conquerors, who established a colony in Goa in 1510. These would have been anusim (Secret Jews) and unconverted Jews who hoped to find greater acceptance in this foreign land than they had in Spain or Portugal. But the Inquisition was established there in 1560, and the Paradesi synagogue was partly destroyed soon after. These White Jews found a secure refuge in Cochin because of the tolerance of the raja. Other Bene Israel went north toward Bombay and expanded their contacts with the Dutch. They came to be called "Saturday oil-pressers" because many made coconut oil—a low-caste role—but refused to work on the Sabbath. As in Cochin, White Bene Israel distinguished themselves from their Black co-religionists, re-creating the Hindu caste system in miniature.[24]

The Baghdadi Jews were the most successful, including among others the Sassoon family, "the Rothschilds of the East." They stemmed not just from Baghdad but from many Arab lands, as well as Persia and Afghanistan—wherever in western Asia Jews had been successful. The growth of the British Raj enabled them to trade and settle throughout the empire. They began in Calcutta, the Raj's capital, in the 1700s, and expanded to Bombay, where they joined the much more numerous Bene Israel. In the 1830s persecutions in Baghdad brought many more Jews to Bombay, and they actually were Baghdadis. David Sassoon, former chief treasurer to the Arab governor of Baghdad—the same governor who now drove him away—was among them.

But they were latecomers. The copper plates that establish the Jews' place in Indian history had been inscribed eight centuries earlier in Tamil, and they gave the Cochin Jews the privileges of high-caste Hindus.[25] This included the right to spread a cloth before the bridegroom in a wedding procession or the infant on his way to circumcision, to carry a brass lamp on a chain or a silk umbrella, to wear shoes made of wood and gold, and to ride an elephant or be carried in a palanquin. These privileges of nobility speak volumes about the status of at least some Jews in India a thousand years ago, possibly much earlier. No other country accepted the Jews so thoroughly or continuously over that same period. Ironically, the caste system may have favored this exceptional hospitality; Indians have always considered it natural for identified groups to keep themselves separate and to have distinctive identifying practices.

But the caste system is hierarchical, and for unknown historical reasons the Cochin Jews were treated as a high-caste group. Traditionally they were agriculturalists and international spice merchants, and in centuries past they served the maharajas as interpreters, diplomats, and warriors. The synagogue and the wealthier families owned substantial coconut estates, and landholding was a major criterion of high caste. Their status was also strongly reinforced by their high standard of purity and cleanliness, characteristic of the dominant groups in India.

The Cochin Jews used Hebrew extensively, observed Sabbath and kosher laws, and celebrated all holidays and fasts prescribed in the Talmud, but they also borrowed practices from Brahmans and Nayars, the two highest castes in their region.[26] These were never allowed to violate *halakhah,* Jewish law, but they sometimes intensified it, making it more stringent and ascetic. The Talmud specifies that Passover preparations should begin right after Purim. The Cochin Jews began them when "the Hanukah candles have barely cooled,"[27] under the centuries-long influence of Hindu standards of purity. Houses were whitewashed according to their neighbors' custom in preparation for the Hindu spring festival Holi. Wells were drained and scrubbed to avoid the slightest pollution from even a speck of leavened bread. But because wine was regularly used in Hindu temples to consecrate the gods, no wine touched by a Hindu could be used.

Because of the intensity of the preparations, Cochin Jews gradually withdrew from public life and from normal interaction with their non-Jewish friends before the holiday, and completely separated during the eight-day Passover observance. They were so accustomed to eating with those friends at Brahman restaurants—vegetarian, therefore kosher—that the cessation of that habit for Passover could have caused ill feeling. However, the Hindus seem to have taken this withdrawal as evidence of the Jews' commitment to purity, and thus of their nobility. Periodic ascetic withdrawal was well within the bounds of admired behavior among high-caste Indians. But the caste system presented another problem at Passover: the person who prepares food must be as pure—as high in caste—as the one who eats it. Thus Brahmans could cook for anyone. But the Jews could not eat what they cooked for this one eight-day period, and the possibility of an insult—the implication that Brahman food was not pure enough for them—was always there. Yet in this too the Brahmans extended the canopy of tolerance over their Jewish neighbors.

One Cochini woman reminisced about the exceptional emphasis placed on Simchat Torah in Jew Town, as the Jewish section of Cochin was always called:

These two days are the happiest occasion of the whole Festival season. . . . the scrolls in their silver cases with silver and gold crowns stand out of their usual place. . . . Many gentiles come to see the synagogue specially on the first night. The synagogue is decorated with lights and garlands of Jasmine. All the walls are covered with [curtains] made out of velvet of different colors embroidered with golden thread. A frame of wood in the shape of a cedar tree with oil lights round and round is lighted in front of the synagogue. . . .

On these two days . . . all the men and the ladies, dressed up in gold-embroidered dresses, went from one synagogue to another to kiss the Torah. There were three synagogues in the town, and usually the members of one synagogue did not visit the others except on this occasion. . . . Everyone keeps open house on that day, with tables laden with food and drinks. No invitation is necessary. Drink flows like water. In no other part of the world is this Feast celebrated so grandly as in Cochin.[28]

These trappings of royalty reinforced the feeling that Jews too were of high caste. Women often wore saris and marked their foreheads with *binis,* the striking cosmetic colored dot that completes an Indian woman's formal dress. Of course, the central ritual of the holiday, in Cochin as in Brooklyn, Curaçao, Djerba, or Jerusalem, was the "Rejoicing of the Law," with many processions in and around the synagogues. They had a special songbook with melodies unique to Cochin, along with songs of Moroccan, Iraqi, and Yemenite Jews.

Mayalam, the spoken language of Cochin, is also a language of song. Most happy occasions were celebrated with singing. Men and women would sit on opposite sides of the table, and when the men had finished the Hebrew hymns and blessings after meals, the women sang in Mayalam. Some songs were translated Hebrew hymns with different tunes; others were Mayalam originals. After the naming ceremony for a girl, the baby was given milk and honey, and the women sang,

> *Pleasure and scent shall anoint you,*
> *Honey and milk under your tongue.*
> *For a mother, God created a daughter,*
> *Born perhaps to dearly flow . . .*
> *May blessings and greatness be yours . . .*
> *May the fruits of your womb be full.*[29]

At the end of the Sabbath before a wedding, the groom was accompanied home by a musical band. "Later in that same Saturday evening, the bride is dressed up beautifully in a *lungi* [lower garment] of colored velvet or satin, and a blouse of colored satin or silk, all decorated with tinsel work. People . . . accompany the bride in a procession. . . . they explode fireworks and they sing all kinds of love songs. The bridegroom and the men walk backwards facing the bride, clapping hands and singing in Hebrew."[30]

Seven young married women made raisin wine for the wedding, and in the middle of the night all the women sang Mayalam songs in praise of the bride:

> *Adorned with gold, you songbird,*
> *Shining with diamonds,*
> *Camphor and rose water mixed. . . .*
> *In green silk she is robed,*
> *The woman blessed by God is she. . . .*
> *More than a hundred years may she live.*[31]

At dawn came another procession through the streets, paced by a band with many loud wooden drums. After a wedding everyone had sore throats from shouting over the drummers' din.

On the day itself, revelry ushered the bride from *mikvah* to synagogue, where she kissed the Torah. Then she visited those too infirm to come to the wedding, and they blessed her. After a great party in the afternoon, the women sang the Mayalam wedding song, with echoes of the stories of the patriarchs. As they sang, the groom kissed the hands of the elders of the community, and the men went to the synagogue to pray.

The wedding itself was not conducted by a rabbi, as indeed Jewish law does not require. With yet another musical procession the groom and the veiled bride were brought under the *chupah,* or wedding canopy. The oldest man in the groom's family read the Seven Blessings, and the *ketubah,* or marriage contract, just inked on parchment by a scribe, was chanted in a special tune by a six- or seven-year-old boy. The groom signed it with two witnesses, and it was given to the bride. The wedding ring was placed inside the cup of wine, which the groom blessed and drank, only then giving the bride the ring. He chanted a marriage prayer, and the bride's mother unveiled her before the guests, who sang a Hebrew song, "Beautiful Like the Moon."

They celebrated through the night and the next day, Jews and non-Jews alike, and the women sang a Mayalam song as the gifts were presented. "Multiply, Multiply" is full of innuendo. "When our bride goes for her ritual bath," the song admonishes, the "blessed rain" should not fall:

> *The best women going with her won't get wet. . . .*
> *The finger with the ring won't get wet.*
> *The hair with the garland and the breast won't get wet.*

Then, in what seems a non sequitur except in erotic symbolism, "Who is there to catch the deer? / 'I will catch it, I will catch it,' called out the groom."[32] Next Sabbath this deer catcher was called to the Torah with special songs and read of Abraham sending his servant to find a bride for his son, an object lesson about the right kind of girl. And at yet one more party, the bride sang a Mayalam song—once, it is said, there were 140 stanzas—made up of translations of Torah portions, each repeated by the other women after her.

The Bene Israel, farther north along the coast, were quite different, so much so that at times their Jewishness was questioned. Their cultural history was deeply intertwined with that of the Hindus they had lived among for centuries. They observed dietary laws, circumcision, Sabbath rest, and festivals including Rosh Hashanah, Yom Kippur, Passover, and Purim, reciting the Shema—the most important Jewish prayer and the declaration of monotheistic faith—in Hebrew on these occasions. But they had lost many details of Orthodox practice, and had no Hebrew prayer books, Bible, or Talmud. They spoke Marathi, the local language—there were Jewish journals and a Passover Haggadah in Marathi—and had Indian-sounding names: Samaji for Samuel, Issaji for Isaac. They also adopted some Hindu laws of inheritance and marriage—prohibiting widows from remarrying, for example—some wedding and funeral rituals, and ceremonial food offerings, but these did not interfere with Jewish law or ritual. Since they were farmers and oil pressers, they were considered essentially lower caste, and this taint affected even those who became wealthy. Some of their Hindu customs were apparently adopted to make them seem higher caste.[33]

So we have the Cochin Jews, who were the most ancient and preserved all aspects of Judaism; the Bene Israel, who lost many Jewish practices while retaining their Jewish identity; and the Baghdadis, who were latecomers—basically Orthodox Middle Eastern Jews transplanted eastward—and became rich. All three communities largely emigrated to Israel, which seems paradoxical given the tolerance of the Hindus.[34] The answer lies in a conjunction of historical circumstances.[35] In the 1920s and 1930s the appeal of Zionism affected the middle-class Baghdadi Jews, even while the wealthy ones were attempting to gain more power in British India. They in turn were concerned that they would be lumped together as Jews with the dark-skinned, nonreligious Bene Israel. Underlying the concern was the ferment in Indian society. The British were trying to weaken the caste system by emphasizing ethnic identity in a nonhierarchical arrangement, and more privileged Jews feared they would lose their status.

An even greater concern was the crisis of independence. Muslim and Hindu nationalism were pitted against each other, and the outcome—Gandhi's assassination and the two-state religious separation he had opposed—was anything but reassuring to Jews. Soon after independence they moved to Israel almost en masse. In Israel it seemed for a time that they might lose their special culture completely, but in the end they have maintained some aspects of their Indian identity, returned to India for visits, and preserved ties with family and community members left behind. Israel and India have strong political and economic links, and the old cultural ties to Hindus are now strengthened by a common concern with Muslim fundamentalism. Pilgrimages back to Cochin in particular have helped to prevent complete assimilation to Israeli culture and have exposed a younger generation to an old and beautiful tradition.

☾ இ ☽

In the tenth century there was a silk shortage in China, a crisis for its expanding population.[36] It turned increasingly to cotton, and the merchants who had long traveled the Silk Road from the West had something to offer. Some were experts in weaving, dyeing, and printing designs on cotton fabrics, some were dauntless adventurers who braved the risks of the thousand-mile journey, and some were just rich investors. And some in all three categories were Jews. A Persian business letter in Hebrew script, dated in the year 718, was found in Xinjiang Province, then the farthest western outpost of the Chinese empire. Also, among thousands of Chinese manuscripts, there was a single creased page with a Jewish prayer in block Hebrew letters, probably folded for carrying during travel. Its owner came overland by caravan, but others came by sea with Muslim traders. During a rebellion in the Canton port in 878, scores of thousands of Muslims, Christians, and Jews were reported massacred.

The Jews cannot have been very numerous, and most were transients. But around the time of the silk crisis, a thousand Jews bringing cotton goods from India or Persia were granted permission to settle in Kaifeng, the provincial capital in the Sung Dynasty, about halfway between present-day Shanghai and Beijing. They were called "sinew pluckers" in denigration—Jacob's tendon again—or, with greater respect, "Scripture teachers."[37] They built a synagogue in 1163, attested by the stele inscription giving them permission. Destroyed repeatedly by flood and war, it was repeatedly rebuilt. Its form followed that of Confucian temple architecture, with imposing, brightly colored twin buildings connected by a passageway, and elegant sweeping tiered roofs. Over the centuries Jewish and Chinese culture became intertwined in Kaifeng in other ways as well.

Marco Polo found Jews in China in the 1200s, and in 1300 a dejected Catholic missionary in Fujian Province wrote the Vatican that he had failed to convert even a single Jew. Proclamations during the 1300s further attest to their presence. Like Muslims, they were taxed, drafted, and prohibited from practicing levirate marriage, in which a man marries the widow of his deceased brother; to the Chinese, this was an abomination. In 1342 there was a theological disputation between Christians and Jews in Beijing, but since the Christians had no power there, the stakes were not like those in similar disputes around that time in Europe.[38]

Stone column inscriptions, however, show that the Kaifeng Jews tried hard to persuade others that they were good Confucians. In 1489, carved in stone, we have, "Although there are some minor discrepancies between Confucian doctrine and our own . . . both are exclusively concerned with honoring the Way of Heaven, venerating ancestors, valuing the relations of ruler and subject, obedience to parents, harmony within families, correct ordering of social hierarchies, and good fellowship among friends: nothing more than the 'five cardinal relations' of mankind. Although it differs from Confucian texts in its writing system, if one scrutinizes the basic principles he will find that it is the same, as it contains the Way of constant practice."[39] A 1663 inscription adds that the Jewish sacred texts have the same basic meaning as the "Six Classics," revered Confucian works. And a 1679 one states that Jewish Scriptures support the teachings of Confucius and Mencius. This special pleading, carved in stone over the centuries, could suggest a fear of persecution, but it may merely be a sincere effort to fit into the "correct ordering" central to Chinese society.

The inscriptions also meld characters in the two cultures' narratives. The 1489 column derives the Jews from Adam, placing him nineteen generations before Abraham, but it identifies Adam with Pan Gu, a Confucian progenitor; but since Pan Gu is the creator and Adam merely a creature, the conflation is a stretch. Noah is easily linked to Nüwa, a Chinese mythic figure who is involved in the "repair of Heaven" and the re-creation of humankind after a great flood. But Noah is still a key genealogical link between Adam and Abraham. Abraham's name is depicted in characters suggestive of "sudden enlightenment," while the term *yicileye,* which can be translated as "the one granted joyful domains," may be a gloss of Yisrael—Israel. But the joyful domains in this case are as likely to be the Scriptures themselves as the land of the covenant. The inscription says too that the Scriptures were given because Moses' devotion touched the heart of Heaven—that he was the "master of the law"—and that Ezra made the law shine with renewed brightness.[40]

A 1512 inscription records a concept that requires no stretch to be seen as a common thread of Judaism and Confucianism: condemning idolatry. "For if one fashions it into physical shapes, or traces its image in tangible forms . . . this is tantamount to heresy."[41] It also interprets the Tao—the Way of Heaven—as halakhah, also "the way," and takes pains to cite the Torah as a record of it: "If the Way were not incorporated into scripture it would have no basis for continuing existence; if the scripture were without the Way, it could not be put into practice." Also, "One can never be separated from the Way, even for an instant."[42]

By this time, too, Confucian thought had absorbed enough Taoism and Buddhism to be compatible with monotheism: "He is One, pure and inimitable."[43] "Heaven" is the common way the inscriptions refer to God, and a later inscription, in 1663, describes Sabbath rest and meditation as communing with the mind of the universe. "What is the Dao?" it asks rhetorically. "It means the principles commonly followed by all men, past and present, in the abiding practices of daily life."[44] The same words could define halakhah.

Not all attempts at blending worked as well. Reverence for ancestors is of course no problem for Jews; the Fifth Commandment requires it, the Torah narrative encourages it, and some of the most important prayers— for example, the eighteen silent benedictions at the heart of every service— ring with lavish and repeated praise for Abraham, Isaac, and Jacob. Avotenu—"Our fathers"—is one of the most common words in the prayer book. However, it usually occurs in the phrase "God of our fathers," leaving no room for confusion as to who is being worshiped. Ancestor reverence is one thing, worship another, very close to idolatry in Jewish law. All told, however, the evidence suggests a more or less successful "Jewish-Confucian integration of Kaifeng Judaism."[45]

In Beijing in 1605, a Jesuit priest, Matteo Ricci, met a Kaifeng Jew, Ai Tien, who related some facts about his community. Ricci reported that the Kaifeng Jews had a Torah, practiced circumcision, and refrained from eating pork. They were called the "blue-hatted Westerners" or "blue-turbaned Muslims" to distinguish them from Muslims and Christians.[46] They may have needed to wear this special sign because by this time they looked Chinese. A genealogical register for the community was recorded in the 1660s in both Chinese and Hebrew. In 1663 the best-known drawing of the Kaifeng synagogue was made by missionaries; the view drawn is the one from Sinew-Extracting Lane.[47]

It must have been a pretty and serene place to be. It is thoroughly Chinese in design, and to the Western eye it has echoes, on a much smaller scale, of the Forbidden City: spacious courtyards, multitiered flared roofs, and square columns around the ornate timber buildings. Stone lions stood on either side of the entrance, stylistically Chinese but possibly also Lions of Judah. Three successive gateways led to the worship hall, the path flanked by apartments that may have housed visitors. There were trees and shrubs— some potted—inscribed stone columns, an incense burner, and a well. There were two lecture halls and a kitchen, and finally, toward the back, there were halls to the left and right where incense was burned to Abraham and the other patriarchs, to ancestors of congregation members, and to Confucius.

Between these last two halls was the large main sanctuary. Inside, however, there was no *bima,* or platform characteristic of other synagogues. Instead, the focal point was the Chair of Moses, which was used not as a chair but as a place to read Torah and prayers. The name evoked the chief rabbi of the Sanhedrin, who occupied the Seat of Moses, a place of supreme honor. A red satin umbrella held over the rabbi's head echoed the practice of shielding the head of royalty, and the Kaifeng rabbi may also have served as a judge. In the Western synagogue structure, the Torah was kept in an Ark on the eastern wall, but here worshipers faced *west* toward Jerusalem. A part of Judaism's most important prayer, the Shema ("Hear O Israel, the Lord is our God, the Lord is One"), was inscribed three times in the sanctuary—twice, significantly, above the emperor's name.

The Jesuits also noted services several times a day: "Bowing and kneeling, worship toward one direction, and prayer in bare feet were repeatedly observed. (Barefoot prayer is typical of Jewish worship in the Muslim world and of Muslims in China.) So was the wearing of skull caps (but not prayer shawls), the use of exclusively vocal music, and bathing before or during festivals."[48] By some reports the synagogue complex had the equivalent of a *mikvah,* and was also a place for ritual slaughter according to Torah laws governing kosher food. As in synagogues ancient and modern, other inscriptions honored wealthy Jewish families—the Zhaos were one—who had helped build and support it.

A thriving Jewish communal life centered on this synagogue, but it was destined to decline. China is the world's oldest meritocracy, and the Jews' achievements depended mainly on their performance. They were well integrated into the bureaucratic and merchant classes, and there was little or no anti-Semitism; it has been said that "[t]he Jews of China were simply assimilated out of communal existence."[49] The last rabbi in Kaifeng died around 1800, and Christian missionaries obtained a collection of prayer books from the community in 1850, along with a remarkable Scroll of Esther with illuminations by three different Chinese artists.[50] As they were assimilating, some Kaifeng Jews attained high positions in the provincial government and the army, but they gradually intermarried and adopted Chinese surnames until they were no longer Jewish. At some point, probably early in this process, they were no longer physically distinct from their non-Jewish fellow citizens.

As the twentieth century ended, perhaps two hundred Kaifeng residents traced their ancestry, not without pride, as partly Jewish. A few families insisted on their Jewishness, and valued that identity.[51] One young mother said, "What we pass on to our grandchildren, is that we tell them our ancestors were Jewish. That is what we say to the younger generation. But as for customs in our life, we have none. None. Only that our ancestors were Jews." Yet after experiencing her first traditional Friday night service and dinner, with visiting young American and Israeli Jews, the same woman—after groping for the right pronunciation of "Shabbat"—said,

"We are from different countries, but we are one people, celebrating the Shabbat. My heart is filled with happiness."[52]

Others are more secure in their Jewish identity. Some refuse to eat pork and as such are mistaken for Muslims, but they deny any Muslim identity and claim instead that this one dietary taboo proves their Jewishness—that, and their descent from Jews. In a culture where ancestors are worshiped, this is no small fact of life. The leader of this tiny community is called Moshe, Hebrew for Moses—"a sage's name," he proudly reports—which he says he got from an uncle who told him to remember that he was Jewish. He has taught his young son the story of Israel's enslavement in Egypt and their exodus under his namesake's leadership. He said, "As long as I have known of my Jewish heritage, that my ancestors were Jews, I am very proud. . . . Jews are friendly. They are lovers of life. They are of true character. Real Jews know how to live life. The content of the Jew's life is genuine." For him, Jewishness is not something tied to territory, military success, or even learning, but is a matter of character; he defines it in moral terms. Another man emphasized his family's tradition of charity and good deeds.

Given a certain amount of support from Jewish visitors, along with their natural curiosity, it is possible that Jewish identity among the Kaifeng Jews' descendants will continue or even grow stronger. On one such visit several in the community were called up to the Torah, and a teenage boy repeated the Hebrew blessing "who has chosen us from all peoples." And more, as Moshe explained, "The Jewish history and culture of Kaifeng is part of the history of the world's Jewish people. If Kaifeng's Jewish history is missing, then the Jewish people's history is not complete."[53]

In any case, by this time there were newer Jewish communities in China: thousands of Russian Jews had settled in Harbin, Manchuria, fleeing the pogroms and the rebellion of 1905 and, later, the chaos following 1917. These hardy pioneers numbered around twelve thousand in the 1920s. Shanghai was also settled by Jews, first Baghdadi and British merchants in the 1840s, then an Ashkenazic group that paralleled the flight of the Jews to Manchuria, and finally some twenty thousand refugees from Hitler in the late 1930s.[54] The brutal Japanese occupation made their lives miserable, and most left after the war, but the Shanghai refugee experience stands out in Jewish memory as a beacon of decency and acceptance in a world of hostile nations, which almost uniformly barred the Jews from entering, instead turning them back to be gassed and burned.

᠀ᨆᨆᨆ᠀

The Jews of Ethiopia, India, and China are only three of the many communities Jews have built in unlikely places in every corner of the world. To chronicle the wanderings of Jews or even their pauses on those wanderings would take many volumes, and has. Nevertheless, an overview is illuminating.

The Jews of Yemen, at the south end of the Arabian Peninsula, believe they were there before the destruction of even the First Temple.[55] We know they were there by the third century C.E., and the Himyar Kingdom had Jews sharing power with Arabs at least a century before Islam came to Arabia. Under Islam, the Yemenite Jews had typical *dhimmi* status. Documents found among the thousands in the Cairo Geniza—a storage room full of fragments of Hebrew texts that has been a treasure trove for historians— show that they participated in the bustling trade out of Aden, a crossroads between Europe and the East. Maimonides' letter in the twelfth century commiserates with them for their persecutions, so conditions were not always good. They were oppressed and even expelled but eventually invited back because of their craftsmen and traders.

They lived in thousands of locations throughout the country, most in villages under the protection of the local tribesmen. The variety of dialects, customs, and dress was enormous and dependent on customs of local non-Jews. Many were silversmiths known for their craft, although they were not allowed to carry the weapons they decorated. Others practiced a wide range of valued crafts supplying many of the finer textiles, embroidery, jewelry, and architectural ornamentation used by Muslims. The influence was strongly mutual, however, and to this day the Yemenite Jews in Israel are known for their distinctive dress and jewelry reflecting the style of their wealthier Muslim neighbors back in Yemen. Most impressive is the bridal attire, made famous in Israel some years ago when a Yemenite Jewish rock star wore it at her wedding. Traditionally,

> The bride, who could hardly move under the weight of the decoration, wore a gold brocade coat—the material imported from India—and two undergarments: a simple white dress and a wide reddish dress.... The leggings of her trousers were embroidered with silver and red silk threads forming star motifs, an exclusively Jewish embroidery pattern. Her back and shoulders were covered with a silk scarf, and the high-towering, pearl-embroidered "crown" was framed by fresh fragrant flowers. Branches of rue at the sides of her face and neck and in her hands were believed to ward off the evil eye.[56]

Under the wedding canopy itself the bride and groom were separated by a partition, and after the wedding a goat was slaughtered at their feet. "When a woman gave birth, a ewe lamb was killed in her honor and passed three times over her head." Two days before the circumcision, people were invited to a special ceremony. "An animal skin decorated with colorful illustrations was stretched over a round dish. When the colors on the skin were dry, the preparers would cut around the dish and remove the round-shaped skin, which would serve as a diaper."

Despite these exotic touches, the Yemenite Jews preserved all standard Jewish practices, had an effective system of schooling, and had great rabbis and sages who produced many significant religious works.[57] Persecutions led them to migrate gradually to Israel beginning in the 1880s. But the assassination of a benign imam in 1948 led to worsening conditions. Some fifty thousand were airlifted to Israel in 1949–50 in Operation Magic Carpet, which brought them to Israel "on eagles' wings," fulfilling a biblical prophecy of return to Zion.

The origin of the Jews of Afghanistan is likewise obscure, but they may well have arrived in the late fifth century when persecutions drove many Jews out of Persia.[58] We know they were there at the time of the Silk Route, and Benjamin of Tudela said he saw many thousands, perhaps an exaggeration. In the mid-nineteenth century there were about forty thousand in the country, in two groups: the smaller indistinguishable in language and physique from Afghans, the larger with strong Persian affinities. Their lives were male-dominated in the general Afghan mode: women wore dark blue *burqas* and had little education, while boys studied Torah and Talmud into their teens. Men wore black dome-shaped caps commemorating the destruction of the Temple, and this distinguished them from Muslims. On the Ninth of Av fast day commemorating the same event, cattle and sheep were sacrificed in the synagogue. On Rosh Hashanah each family sacrificed a sheep, in remembrance of the ram that God substituted for Isaac, and the blood was painted on the doorpost.

Older men sought to make a pilgrimage to Israel at least once, and as in the Muslims' hajj to Mecca, they were honored with the name hajji, or pilgrim. Around four thousand Afghan Jews migrated to Israel to stay after 1948, and today there are none left in Afghanistan. A few hundred live in the United States and elsewhere in the diaspora, but almost all are well integrated in Israel. One grew up to be the Israeli consul general for the southeastern United States during the 1980s. As of January 2000, the last Jew in Afghanistan, the rabbi of a community that no longer exists, was still trying to stay, despite having spent forty days in a Taliban jail for cherishing his Torah scroll.[59] Overall, the older Jewish communities of Central Asia are on the wane. The Bukharan Jews of Samarkand and elsewhere in Uzbekistan—a two-thousand-year-old community—have declined to one thousand from ten times that number in 1989.[60] The centuries-old Subbotniks or "Sabbath people" of Armenia have lost most Jewish practices and are dispersing throughout the world.[61] The rugged mountain Jews of Dagestan—they sing of themselves as "Samson warriors" and "Bar Kokhba's heirs"—have mostly moved to Israel, although several thousand may remain.[62] Likewise their brethren, the mountain Jews of Kurdistan, who once lived as Kurds do—they were uneducated but knew many Hebrew prayers by heart—now have a thriving community in Israel where they preserve some of their traditions.[63]

But there are many other, more positive examples. About six hundred Jewish families live in the Brazilian Amazon, descended from traders of animal hides, hardwoods, spices, and rubber who came from Morocco as pioneers during the nineteenth century.[64] Many of them still trade on the great river, and the community's two rabbis help maintain their Jewish identities. Japan has a thousand Jews or so: Yokohama has a Jewish cemetery, and a few families remain from the European Jews who came in the 1860s; Kobe has a synagogue with a dozen families, descended from Sephardi refugees fleeing twentieth-century wars; and over a thousand, mostly businessmen and students, live in Tokyo, where the smallness of the community does not prevent battles over whether men and women should sit separately in the synagogue.[65] Jewish gauchos, some now prosperous ranchers, descend from Ashkenazic Jews who settled in the Argentine pampas in 1889. They still attend their original synagogue in the town of Moises Ville, with its central platform, or *bima,* that looks like a corral.[66] And a single Jew in Angola, descended from a small intermarried group that came there in the early 1900s, takes his family to a little synagogue, maintains his ties to Israel, and is absolutely committed to raising his five children Jewish.[67]

But not all exotic Jewish cultures are far away from us. One observer of the Texas Jewish experience had moved to the state and needed a *mohel,* a ritual circumciser, for his new son, but had to import one from Houston. He saw no *mohel* at the airport, so he paged him. The page was answered by a man striding up in a ten-gallon hat, blue jeans with a silver belt buckle, and boots. "I panicked. 'Are you the mohel?' I asked. 'I am,' he said in a drawl and lifted his ten-gallon hat and showed his yarmulke to me and then pulled out a string of *tsitsit* (ritual fringes)!"[68] Roughly a hundred thousand Jews live in Texas, many descended from new migrants but a few from the small number that came in the nineteenth century. Some were successful in banking, cattle ranching, and retail—Neiman Marcus—but most were of modest means. They fought for the Confederacy in the Civil War, built synagogues, and numbered fifteen thousand at the end of the century. Thousands more were brought in en masse to relieve the pressure of Jewish immigration to the eastern seaboard. They experienced little anti-Semitism and integrated fully with the rest of the population, and while they still maintain a strong Jewish identity, they also cherish their Texan identity, complete with independence, machismo, and ten-gallon hats.

Alaska, the "Last Frontier," has three thousand Jews, about 0.5 percent of the population.[69] Most live in the cities, but the ones in small towns hold a special fascination. A social worker who had grown up in Brooklyn—she went to the Yeshiva of Flatbush—moved to a town of 2,500 with her non-Jewish husband and they built a log home on their own wooded land. As Passover approached she took out an ad in the paper seeking other Jews; she got ten phone calls, they held a seder together, and from then on they were a Jewish community. Even more than the Texans, Alaskan Jews are rugged individualists, yet their small community cannot tolerate divisiveness: there are no other Jewish choices.

In this sense they are like a tiny African or Asian village; tensions may run high, but they need each other too much to allow a break. In this sort of situation self-important people may have undue influence for a time, but compromise usually allows communal ties to survive. One man took the paradoxical position of joining the group and then opposing any steps to give it more identity—for example by starting a Judaica discussion group. He stormed out of one meeting, taking his daughters with him, and most who remained felt that it was more important to keep him in the fold than to institute the discussions. Jews in small towns throughout North America tell similar stories of isolation, community, assimilation, and renewal of Jewish faith in the face of overwhelming odds.[70]

We think of Jews as living in dense urban centers full of other Jews, but this kind of tiny community must have been the pioneering nucleus of countless Jewish groups that settled the diaspora. It may be more prototypical than we think. A handful of Jews went to Egypt and Persia in ancient times, a handful to Spain and Germany later on, a handful to Poland and America still later, and every one of these tiny groups founded a great and lasting Jewish culture. The courage of these kinds of pioneers, clinging to one another and cherishing their traditions in the midst of an often hostile surround, has blazed the path for many of the world's Jewish communities.[71]

11

YIDN

HOW THE JEWS HELPED CREATE
MODERN EUROPE

In the late eighteenth century six out of ten Jews—about 1.5 million—lived in Europe, among some hundred million other Europeans.[1] While western Europe went through the Enlightenment and revolution, more than half the Jews lived in backward parts of Poland and western Russia, within the Pale of Settlement allowed by the czars. In some Polish cities and in Amsterdam they approached 10 percent of the population, but in most countries less than 1 percent. Many were dispersed in rural villages; thousands of hamlets had only one Jewish family each. Half the population was under fifteen, so it was growing very rapidly. Of cities that ultimately would be home to many Jews, Berlin, Vienna, and Paris had very few legal Jewish residents, Kiev and Lodz disallowed them, and Odessa was still a tiny village.

Occupations changed little. Around 1700 in Frankfurt, for instance, 70 percent of the four hundred working Jews were merchants, peddlers, and moneylenders, 10 to 15 percent were professionals, and 10 percent were craftsmen or day laborers. In Cologne a century later, a tiny group of Jews included two teachers, five butchers, one day laborer, and ten merchants. In Alsace, where Jews were prohibited from nearly all other occupations, most were peddlers and moneylenders. "Court Jews" in some capitals were important in banking, and in the Sephardic communities Jews conducted international trade.[2]

In eastern Europe more were artisans. Over a third of the Jews in Vilna, Lithuania, were tailors, furriers, jewelers, and other craftsmen. In Hungary in 1735, half were peddlers and merchants, a third were artisans, and the rest were rabbis, teachers, ritual slaughterers, and other community officials. In Poland Jews could not hold land, but some managed estates for absentee landlords—and so were visible targets of peasants' legitimate grievances. Some operated toll bridges. In Zhitomir, Ukraine, in 1787, 40 percent of the Jews were inn- or tavernkeepers, 25 percent were shopkeepers and tradesmen, 20 percent were artisans, and the rest were maids, servants, and other poor laborers.

The tension between these different worlds—east and west, town and hamlet, rich and poor, educated and ignorant—is felt in this account from the late 1700s:

> My first position as family tutor was an hour's distance from my home. The family was that of a miserable farmer in a still more miserable village.... The poverty, ignorance, and crudeness ... in this house were indescribable. The farmer's ... language was a sort of muttering, intelligible only to the boors with whom he daily associated. Not only was he ignorant of Hebrew, but he could not speak a word of Yiddish; his only language was Russian, the common patois of the peasantry.[3]

The petulant description might have noted that this crude farmer was paying good money to a stuck-up city boy to make his children different from himself. An earlier, mellower writer, Glückel of Hameln, described her rural culture shock more kindly:

> I, a young child brought up in luxury, was taken from parents, friends, and everyone I knew, from a town like Hamburg to a village where only two Jewish families lived. And Hameln is a dull, shabby place. But this did not make me unhappy because of my joy in my father-in-law's piety. Every morning he rose at three and wrapped in *talith* (prayer shawl), he sat in the room next to my chamber studying and chanting Talmud.... Then I forgot Hamburg.[4]

As in the Muslim world, Jewish communities had some autonomy and were expected to police themselves, resolve disputes, take care of their poor, and keep problems from being brought to state authorities. In western Europe pogroms and blood libels had declined, but in the east riots by Cossacks and others posed a continual threat. Still, the population was growing, and Ashkenazic traditions spread in cities, towns, and villages. Poland and Lithuania housed the world's greatest rabbinical academies. Inevitably, growth led to divisions, such as the battles between the religiously innovative Hasidim and their enemies. Still, both produced great rabbis and academies, and both extended the colloquies of ancient scribes and sages.

But the Jewish world was about to collide with modernity, or at least with the Enlightenment, and would be torn by the appeal of both. Although it had happened before in ancient Greece and medieval Spain, it was now both more threatening and more inviting. Spinoza, we have seen, became the first European to leave Judaism without becoming Christian or Muslim. Moses Mendelssohn, whose grandson Felix won fame as a composer, labored a lifetime to reconcile Judaism with the Enlightenment, and for his pains was hated by many Orthodox Jews. A colleague, Naphtali Herz Wessely, wrote a Hebrew essay, "Divrei Shalom ve'Emet"—"Words of Peace and Truth"—expressing the shared goal of Jewish Enlightenment thinkers. He argued that "even though the laws and teachings of God are far superior to 'human knowledge' they are closely correlated to it; where 'human knowledge' ends, the divine teaching begins, instructing us on what is beyond man's power of reason."

But Wessely went on to admonish his fellow Jews: "There is one people in the world alone who are not sufficiently concerned with 'human knowledge' and who have neglected the public instruction of their youth in the laws of etiquette, the sciences and the arts. We, the children of Israel . . . Those among us who dwell in Germany and Poland have been especially negligent."[5] The Orthodox were appalled. Rabbi David ben Nathan of Lissa, a center of Torah learning in Poland, replied forcefully that Wessely was an "imposter" and "a cunning man."

> May God punish this ever so glib tongue—a tongue that renders its master as disgusting as a creeping reptile. . . . Who of the pious students of God's laws . . . is not a tribute to humanity, even if he has not learned etiquette and languages. Can such a man be lacking in human knowledge? . . .
>
> . . . If [Wessely] has raised his hand against these individuals who have consecrated their lives to the service of God, let his hand wither! He has chosen to blaspheme God and those whom He has hallowed merely because they err in the customs of men [and do not] adorn themselves and paint their eyes.

However, the rabbi had hope: "It is a source of great consolation to learn from a reliable report that in Vilna, the great city of God, they have burned Wessely's book in the streets."[6]

These were the first salvos in a war that still rages. But the rabbis, without giving up a jot of halakhah, were in another sense to beat a steady retreat: eventually most would be reconciled with the project of modernity and embrace the results of most scientific research. They would never, of course, embrace the *customs* of the "enlightened," and in any case it was silly to link science with table manners. But the defensiveness of the very Orthodox continued, even as momentous events changed the fate of the Jews.

The French Revolution of 1789 created new conditions, and despite the dreadful outcome of that event, the *liberté* was very good for the Jews. The National Assembly officially emancipated the Jews of France in 1791, and

Napoleon's armies brought this message to much of Europe within a decade. In Padua, for example, the ghetto was abolished on August 28, 1797, with a simple decree: "[I]n the name of the French Republic One and Indivisible, 'First, that the Hebrews are at liberty to live in any street they please; Second, that the barbarous and meaningless name of Ghetto, which designates the street which they have been inhabiting hitherto, shall be substituted by that of Via Libera.'" It was dated "Padua, Fruttidoro 11, year V of the French Republic and year I of Italian Liberty." A month later the government decreed "that the municipal police committee shall carry out the solemn leveling to the ground of the Gates, Arches and simple precinct Walls of the ex-Ghetto in such a manner that no vestige shall remain of the ancient separation from other neighboring streets."[7]

In 1806 Napoleon, almost solely responsible for the spreading wave of Jewish emancipation, convened an Assembly of Jewish Notables. Count Molé, who opposed Jewish rights, nevertheless proposed a remedy for anti-Jewish sentiment: the Jews should assemble a board of rabbis and others responsible for the administration of Jewish life and law. Molé convened the assembly and conveyed a list of questions from the emperor, encapsulating European curiosity about the Jews:

> Is it lawful for the Jews to marry more than one wife? Is divorce allowed by the Jewish religion? . . . Can a Jewess marry a Christian, or a Jew a Christian woman? . . . In the eyes of Jews are Frenchmen considered as brethren or as strangers? . . . Do the Jews born in France, and treated by the law as French citizens, consider France their country? Are they bound to defend it? Are they bound to obey the laws? . . . What kind of police-jurisdiction have the Rabbis among the Jews? What judicial power? . . . Are there professions from which the Jews are excluded by their law? Does the law forbid the Jews from taking usury from their brethren? Does it forbid or does it allow usury toward strangers?[8]

Reasonable questions. If Napoleon was giving the Jews complete rights as citizens, would they accept the obligations of citizenship? And what about conflicts between Jewish and secular law?

The minutes for this session of what would soon be "the Paris Sanhedrin" record great emotion about defending France: "Even to the death!" was their collective exclamation. In their written answer, they informed Napoleon of the Jewish obligation, traceable to the Babylonian exile, of loyalty to the nation that welcomes them. They explained that polygamy had been outlawed by a hundred rabbis meeting in Worms in the eleventh century, that divorce was allowed but not if it conflicted with French law, that intermarriage was permissible but frowned upon, that Jews could practice any profession, and that "[i]n the eyes of Jews Frenchmen are their brethren, and are not strangers."[9] They said that rabbis have no police jurisdiction, and that their religious courts—the *beit din,* or house of judgment, in Jewish communities—could make no decisions contradicting French law. They explained the conflicting rules regarding usury, but said it was forbidden whether the borrower was Jewish or not. However, there were distinct borrowing purposes, and in the normal course of commercial activity lending with interest was accepted. They acknowledged that some Jews grossly violated these laws.

But perhaps the most important thing they had to say was this:

> The love of country is in the heart of Jews a sentiment so natural, so powerful, and so consonant to their religious opinions, that a French Jew considers himself in England, as among strangers, although he may be among Jews; and the case is the same with English Jews in France.
>
> To such a pitch is this sentiment carried among them, that during the last war, French Jews have been seen fighting desperately against other Jews, the subjects of countries then at war with France.
>
> Many of them are covered with honorable wounds, and others have obtained, in the field of honor, the noble rewards of bravery.[10]

Count Molé returned bearing the message that "His Majesty the Emperor and King is satisfied with your answers," and went on to praise them:

> And who could behold without astonishment such a society of enlightened men, chosen among the descendants of the most ancient people in the world?
>
> The Jews, exposed to the contempt of nations, and not unfrequently to the avarice of princes, have never, as yet, been treated with Justice. . . .
>
> His Majesty's intention is, that no plea should be left to those who refuse to become citizens; the free exercise of your religious worship and the full enjoyment of your political rights, are secured to you. But, in return for his gracious protection, His Majesty requires a religious pledge for the strict adherence to the principles contained in your answers.[11]

To ensure this adherence, the emperor called for a governing body that would give these answers "a place near the Talmud." To cut through the "crowd of commentators" that might make Jewish law ambiguous, there had to be a binding decision: "To find in the history of Israel, an assembly capable of attaining the object now in view, we must go back to the Great Sanhedrin, and it is the Great Sanhedrin, which His Majesty this day intends to convene."

Although the Paris Sanhedrin lasted only a few months, it committed the Jews to secular citizenship, with momentous effects. In 1812, as Napoleon retreated from Moscow with an army in tatters, Frederick William III of Prussia issued an emancipation proclamation for the Jews in words resembling Napoleon's and reflecting the answers of the Assembly of Jewish Notables in Paris. With some delays, the nineteenth century saw a steady spread of Jewish emancipation. In one country after another, the Jews were guaranteed most if not all of the rights of citizenship and were subject to its burdens, including conscription and full loyalty to the state.

The Jews met emancipation more than halfway. German Jews established Reform Judaism to modernize religious practice and bring it in line with Protestant decorum. Believing "our newly gained status as citizens . . . a partial fulfillment of our messianic hopes," Reform Jews by 1845 had rejected a return to Palestine. "The hope for a national restoration contradicts our feeling for the fatherland. . . . The wish to return to Palestine in order to create there a political empire for those who are still oppressed because of their religion is superfluous. The wish should rather be for a termination of the oppression."[12] Some Reform Jews held services on Sunday and abandoned prayer in Hebrew, tefillin, prayer shawls, and head coverings. Orthodox Jews were outraged, and a middle-of-the-road movement, Conservative Judaism, arose as a compromise.

But many Jews were leaving religion altogether, seeing less and less need either to practice Judaism or to convert to Christianity as emancipation progressed. It was not until the late nineteenth century—a hundred years after Napoleon's grand gestures—that a small critical mass of Jews decided that emancipation was a failure, assimilation a fool's errand, acceptance a vain dream, and that only a Jewish state would save them. But by then millions of Jews in Europe believed that they were complete citizens of their respective nations, whether or not they had turned their backs on Jewishness. Wearing this conviction as a badge of pride, they would march straight into a blazing furnace of hate.

Consider the family of Gerhard, later Gershom, Scholem, the greatest secular scholar of Jewish mysticism.[13] Growing up in Berlin during World War I—his three older brothers were all in the kaiser's army—he became obsessed with Hebrew and Zionism. He was twelve when this journey began, and his parents hated every step of it. Nominally Jewish, they were essentially German nationalists. They celebrated Christmas, and the year he was fourteen Gerhard found among the piles of presents his lone ironic gift: a framed portrait of Theodor Herzl, the avatar of Zionism. After that year he stayed out of the house on Christmas. His Jewish interests grew, nonreligious but intense; he spent his teenage years in a trance, in love with Hebrew and Israel. One morning when he was nineteen his reverie was interrupted by a registered letter that came for him during breakfast with his parents:

> I have decided to cut off all support to you. Bear in mind the following: you have until the first of March to leave my house, and you will be forbidden to enter it again without my permission. On March first, I will transfer 100 marks to your account so that you will not be left without means. Anything more than this you cannot expect from me. . . . Whether I will agree to finance your further studies after the war depends upon your future behavior.

> Your father, Arthur Scholem[14]

Gershom was fine on his own. After receiving his doctorate he moved to Jerusalem, and in 1925 was a founding faculty member of the Hebrew University. His father did not live to discover what his own status as a patriotic German was worth. His mother, after Hitler's ascent, wrote, "I cannot digest what is happening. . . . I simply can't imagine that there are not 10,000 or 1,000 upright Christians who refuse to go along by raising their voice in protest." In March 1933 she wrote, "It's a real piece of luck that you're out of harm's way! Now, suddenly, I want to see everyone in Palestine! When I only think of the outcry heard among German Jews when Zionism began! Your father and grandfather . . . beat themselves on the breast and said with absolute conviction, 'We are Germans!' And now we're being told that we are *not* Germans after all!"[15] She and two of her sons escaped to Australia; the fourth brother, Werner, was murdered in Buchenwald. Gerhard—Gershom—who had understood at age fourteen that he could never be German, stayed in Israel, one of the leading Jewish scholars of his time.

☙〰❧

In the 1940s, two anthropologists, Mark Zborowski and Elizabeth Herzog, supervised by Ruth Benedict and Margaret Mead, interviewed 128 people who had come from various eastern European shtetls, or towns.[16] Unlike the sophisticated Jewish world of western Europe, these towns would afford the researchers a view of Jewish life at its simplest and most authentic. They wanted to reconstruct an ethnography of the Ashkenazic shtetl as it had been before World War I. While retrospective and composite, it is as close as anyone is likely to come to an anthropological study reflecting the human reality of thousands of Jewish communities, similar in different times and places.

There was unanimity, for example, on the importance of Shabbes, the

Sabbath. A woman began by preparing dough for the baking of challah. At least by dawn on Friday—Erev Shabbes, or Sabbath Eve—she rose, poured water over her fingers, and made the blessings. She fired up the oven, checked the risen dough, and inspected the chicken for flecks of blood or other blemishes, any of which could mean a trip to the rabbi's study or even a wasted chicken. She prepared chopped, or gefilte, fish[17]—"Without fish there is no Sabbath"—and made noodles from scratch. She braided the dough for challah and then attended to the other meaning of challah: the commandment that women throw some dough into the fire, with a blessing. The loaves were glazed with egg white and baked.

Friday was a rush, especially in the winter when it got dark early, and you could insult a disorganized homemaker by saying, "For her every day is Erev Shabbes." The children and the house were scrubbed intensely. Beggars came and were not turned away. The fear that dusk would fall too soon was a palpable driving force. Finally, the shammes, or synagogue caretaker, would walk the streets of the shtetl calling "Jews to the *mikvah*!" reminding the men and boys that it was their turn for immersion, to cleanse their souls for Shabbes. All donned their Sabbath best, and the lady of the house exchanged her kerchief—she had to cover her hair—for a stylish wig.

At a predetermined time before dusk, she lit the candles—the Shabbes *licht*—urging the light toward her with a gentle embracing gesture, and said the blessing, sometimes shedding tears. If she could read, she might chant from the Yiddish prayer book until the men and boys returned from the synagogue. Since hospitality was sacred, they often brought a guest—a strange traveler, a Jewish soldier posted nearby, a rabbinical student—whether they could afford it or not.

All said Git Shabbes, and the father changed his fur-brimmed hat for a yarmulke, a skullcap. He sang "Sholem Aleichem"—"Peace to you, angels of God"—read the "Woman of Valor" prayer in praise of his wife, filled the sacred goblet to the brim and overflowing, and "made kiddush," the blessing on the wine, with the passages from Genesis describing God's rest at the completion of the Creation. Children were formally blessed: "May God bless you and keep you, may he cause his face to shine on you and be gracious to you, may he turn his face to you and bring you peace."

All poured water over their hands three times, said the prayer, and blessed the challah while holding the two loaves together. Bread was broken, dipped in salt, and eaten, all in silence, since there could be no mundane talk between ritual washing and eating. Fish, clear chicken soup with "gold coins"—globules of *schmaltz,* or fat—and the chicken itself made the best meal of the week by far. Dinner conversation might be learned, but in any case was mainly male. Still, the lady of the house was richly praised. One woman said, "I don't remember my mother sitting at the table when we ate, except for Friday night and Saturdays. Those days she even sat on the whole chair. . . . When I was older I asked her why . . . and she said, 'Friday night, on Sabbath Eve, I am a queen, like every Jewish woman. On weekdays I am just a woman.'"[18] At the end of the meal, knives were removed from the table, sacred songs were sung, and the long, plaintive, sweetly melodic blessing after meals was intoned in the candlelight.

So began Shabbes, the sacred day of rest. In the morning the family would leave the house—kissing the mezuzah on the way out—and walk to shul, men and boys a little ahead, carrying embroidered bags with their prayer shawls. This shawl, the tallis, draped a man during prayer, and a boy would be wrapped in it going to school for the first time. It and a prayer book could be carried on Shabbes because of the *eyruv,* a cord or wire surrounding the whole community, within which carrying was permitted.

In the shul women sat in their own section, upstairs from or behind the men. Men sat in benches facing east, leaning forward on reading desks, but standing and swaying while chanting important prayers, so as to pray with all their senses. The core of *avodah,* the service, was the eighteen silent benedictions. A knowledgeable woman led the others in Hebrew prayers, and they might weep on her command. In the center of the space was the *bima,* a railed-off platform where the cantor sang and the Torah was read. A sometimes ornate Ark—it might have carved wood doors and a sumptuous velvet curtain adorned with the Star of David or Lion of Judah—was centered on the eastern wall.

The Torah was removed from it, carried around to songs of praise, laid on the table slightly unrolled, and read in a comforting chant. The reading had to be virtually flawless, but a helper corrected errors. Others were called up to bless each successive section of the reading. But for the congregation this was no time for silence. People came and went, chatted just outside the doors, and generally mixed the sacred and the mundane. At home they ate *cholent,* the thick stew that had simmered untouched since the day before—Heine had called it the ambrosia of the gods—took delicious naps, and woke to talk (not about business), visit with neighbors, study, nibble on cookies, and drink tea kept hot for twenty-four hours.

After a briefer service at the shul and a third, small meal, they made Havdalah, the wistful rite of separation, bringing the Sabbath to a close. A daughter held the braided candle while the father said a prayer over wine, a second over a treasured, possibly silver box of spices; the spices were formally sniffed, and the wine was drunk. As a last gesture, all looked at their fingernails in the candle glow, to show that the light was now usable, no longer holy. The candle was doused in the remaining wine, and with the words *"a gute vokh"*—"a good week"—the Sabbath spell was broken. Now every form of anxiety, misery, toil, and burden could and would come rushing into consciousness as the family prepared for their workaday world. Yet they had just finished blessing God for *making* separations—between light and darkness, between Israel and other nations, between the Sabbath and the days of the week, between the sacred and the everyday. Separations were at the heart of halakhah: kosher and *trayf,* meat and milk, wool and flax; the boundary at the edge of night that determined the time of prayer; the dark new moon that began months, and the Days of Awe that delimited years; the division between menses and sexual possibility; and of course, the gap between Shabbes and *vokh.* In a world full of danger these were certainties.

As for life outside the Sabbath, it left much to be desired. Although perhaps the Jews didn't notice it on Shabbes, peasants' pigs roamed all the streets of town, including theirs, rooting for trash. Contempt for Jews was always in the air. Commerce marked every time and place, and every penny earned in a transaction with a non-Jew was a source of resentment and danger. Despite the tensions, the open market was the main public aspect of daily life, and its varied and colorful stalls, their owners vying to tempt customers, brought Jews and non-Jews raucously together, as buyers and sellers. Transactions with Jews and non-Jews might not be so different, but they carried a different kind of charge. Interactions were mostly civil, but both insulted each other behind their backs. Market days were intense, and dusk often settled on resentments; peasants drinking in town bars might go out to attack Jews. However, there were plenty of frustrating people *among* the Jews, and the less educated were prone to rowdiness and even violence—behavior *nit Yiddish,* "not Jewish."

To be Jewish in the strong sense meant having a Jewish childhood, having parents who saw you as a little prince or princess. Of course, the greater treasures were boys. They were not only celebrated and feted on the eighth day—even as they were cut—but were welcomed into learning with almost as much drama. On the first day of school a boy of three or four would be carried to the *kheder,* the classroom, and immediately introduced to the Hebrew alphabet. As the child pored over the letters, candy and coins mysteriously dropped from above and behind him onto the slate. Honey might be dripped onto the letters and licked off by the child, to make learning sweet. At five or six, when he was fit for Torah study, a ceremony at home marked the transition. Next to a table laden with nuts, cakes, and wine, the tiny boy discussed Torah with his teacher, ringed by relatives and attended by three older boys who blessed him.

Just before the blessings, the teacher asked him if he would like to "say some Torah." The boy replied as prepared, "Of course! That is what I was created for. Although I am not yet worthy to 'say Torah' before you, yet I will say a few words. My teachers and friends . . ." And he would proceed to interpret the first few lines of Genesis. The older boys' formal blessings followed, and women showered them with nuts and candy.

Good students went on to ever-higher levels; others dropped out and became apprentice craftsmen, farmers, laborers, or merchants. Still, the ideal was lifelong study. Adults would set goals for themselves, like mastering a Talmud section, and offer a celebration in the synagogue when they reached the goal. It didn't matter that a laborer's accomplishment might seem trivial to the advanced student; the comparison wasn't made. The goal set was suitable, and when it was reached it was celebrated with all joy and solemnity. But the system had its dark side, especially in the early grades, where teachers were paid a pittance and got no respect from parents. They sometimes responded with punishment, humiliation, even cruelty to pupils. Paradoxically, this ancient system that honored learning and produced not only scholars but widespread general literacy adulterated sweetness with pain, praise with humiliation, and it left some people with lifelong bitter memories.

There was, of course, a philosophy behind shtetl culture: *Yiddishkayt*—"Jewishness." There was a saying in the shtetl that "It is hard to be a Jew and it is good to be a Jew." *Yiddishkayt* carried countless associations on both sides:

The joy of the Sabbath, brightly cleaving the drab world of the week—candles gleaming over a white cloth, the lordly Sabbath loaf, the clean clothes, the holy peace. The ecstasy of the Passover with its springtime purification, the household [and] the soul made new and beautiful. The proud festivity of the boy's Bar Mitzvah, the "pleasure of children" and of family, the warm sense of belonging . . . The "melody of learning," chanted over sacred books whose tattered pages spread back through the centuries . . . to touch all Jews of all time. The gratification of obeying the myriad commandments, of living out the Law that penetrates every humble act . . .

The complement of pain is in it too, "the yoke" that glorifies as it oppresses, the pride of enduring persecution. Bound into the word is also proud pity for those who live without the light and who, in their darkness, fulfill the will of the Most High even as they oppress the children of Israel.

Yiddishkayt also conveys "the veneration of learning, the acceptance of obligations, the inextinguishable hope of ultimate reward. And somewhere between its syllables flickers the wry, ironic acceptance of the price that must be paid for membership . . . a price acknowledged with tears, with groans, and with innumerable quips. . . . a continuity has been maintained through long centuries. . . . The stronger the attack against it, the stronger the resistance that rose to meet it. 'God, Torah, and Israel are one,' says the tradition. That unity is complex and vibrant. Nevertheless, it has held."[19]

✆

As the twentieth century dawned, Jews made one of three responses to the increasingly vicious anti-Semitism around them: prepare for emigration to Israel, go to the United States, or stay in Europe. Each attracted a different sort of person, yet each spanned the spectrum from sacred to secular. Each gave rise to one of the three great Jewish communities of the modern world. Those who went to America were the least ideological, except to the extent that a thirst for freedom and opportunity is ideological. Zionist groups ran the gamut from religious (Mizrachi), through socialist (Hashomer Hatza'ir), to the radical revisionists led by Vladimir Jabotinsky. Still in Poland between the two world wars, they learned and spoke modern Hebrew, sang Israeli songs, taught Jewish history, practiced agriculture, set themselves difficult physical challenges, even organized themselves into ersatz kibbutzim in the Polish countryside. They rejected what they saw as the soft, money-oriented occupations of diaspora Jews in favor of physical labor. They lived in a dream, yet some brought the dream into being.

But the non-Zionists and anti-Zionists were far more numerous. Agudas Israel, or Agudah, a party of rabbis, scholars, merchants, and storekeepers, gave voice to Orthodox anti-Zionists, including many Hasidim and their charismatic rabbis. Some of the wealthiest dynasties housed their rabbis in palaces, yet even this movement was not immune from the changing times; it was *neo*-Orthodox, with innovations like schools for girls. There was also *intellectual* anti-Zionism, led by Simon Dubnow, who spoke of the "myth of territory" and insisted that the real home of the Jews was not Israel but the diaspora; the lives Jews had lived in the countless places where they settled had made the diaspora their home. He considered himself a patriot of the Jewish exile, a *diaspora* nationalist, and believed that the Jews were in essence a spiritual people whose distinctiveness would be ruined by an attachment to any single place. Their home was wherever they were, and they should not look elsewhere. How many Jewish lives were lost because of leadership like this, and because of the naive assimilationists, we will never know.

Probably the largest anti-Zionist group was the Bund—"band," "bond," or "alliance"—a huge, vigorous labor union movement with strong socialist ideals. Its size was a tribute to the expansion of the Jewish working classes, especially factory workers, and the labor activism was part of a worldwide union movement in which Jews in many countries played a part. This movement at its height united hundreds of thousands in various unions— porters, leather workers, textile workers, and so on. It was international in

outlook, naively thinking that nationalism was outmoded, and that transnational ties among workers counted more than unity within borders. "The
International" was sung in Yiddish, as in many other languages. But it was
also very Jewish; the Russian Marxist Georgy Plekhanov once referred to
the Bundists as Zionists with seasickness. As in the United States, union
building was a violent and dangerous enterprise, and underworld thugs
played a role in protecting striking workers from scabs and police. But the
Bund also organized study groups, libraries, periodicals, summer camps,
and other educational and social institutions.

Still, many Jews were just trying to live, and they too felt cultural currents. In a Yiddish popular song an impatient young woman urges her beau
to get with it:[20]

> *You have to learn to dance,*
> *I swear on both our heads,*
> *Or you and I are quits.*
> *Be whatever you like,*
> *A burning Zionist,*
> *A Bundist, who could care?*
> *All the "ists" that exist*
> *Even the Agudah-niks,*
> *Dance the Tango and Charleston.*

These Jews were looking west in an already globalizing popular culture,
and displaying their contempt for any sort of ideology.

But political ferment intensified as anti-Semitism grew. It is simply not
true that no one knew what was coming. Some did. Theodor Herzl had
started the Zionist movement in the 1890s because he believed the Jews had
no future in Europe, that they might well be headed for extermination. All
his followers understood this, from leaders like Chaim Weizmann and
David Ben-Gurion down to the teen in braids scratching the Polish earth
with her hoe, her mind and heart already in Zion. Yet thirty years after
Herzl gave up on Europe, many Jewish leaders vigorously opposed Zionism while defending the diaspora. Soon Europe would give up on them.

Germans did not bring anti-Semitism to Poland.[21] Anti-Semitism in
every country of eastern Europe was at least as old and vicious as in Germany. What the Germans brought to Poland was their intellectual brand of
anti-Semitism, their legendary organizational skills, and their obsessive
commitment to solving "the Jewish question" by murdering every Jew. But
years before the invasion Nazi flags flew all over Poland, and anti-Jewish
laws paralleled German ones. Pogroms became more frequent and destructive. Jewish businesses were boycotted. When kosher slaughtering was outlawed, there was rare unity in the Jewish community; even the most secular

saw this as an attack on all Jews, and differences dissolved in the face of a common enemy.

Very large numbers of Jews now wanted to leave. But by the late 1920s, the United States cut off immigration from Europe completely, Great Britain cut off immigration to both Israel and Britain itself, and almost all European Jews were trapped in Europe. Even the few who managed to leave felt ambivalent about going. Roman Eisner, a former resident of Lodz, reminisced:

> When I was younger, my brother was always trying to get me to go to America.
>
> But I didn't care too much to go to America. I was doing pretty well for myself. . . . I was single and I was happy. . . . But ten years later the Hitler Era was in full bloom, and we wanted to go to America. This was 1938. Before we left we went to the cemetery to say goodbye to our people. It was a custom to do that, because . . . you never really knew if you were ever going to come back here to see them—matter of fact, I never did. And riding the trolley car, there was a gentile fellow says to me, "You see those buildings? Those buildings belong to the Jews, and the street belongs to us. . . . There'll be a time pretty soon, those buildings will belong to us, and you'll be out of the city."[22]

Few had the luck that Eisner had; 3 million of the 3.5 million Jews in Poland would be murdered, the greatest Jewish community in history utterly destroyed.

✺

Blessedly, more than a little of it had already gone to America. Sephardic Jews had done well, and they turned their noses up at the German Jews who followed them, even while they helped them. German Jews did well, and had the same reactions toward the eastern European Jews who followed them. But these vast numbers of new immigrants completely lacked preparation for life in the New World, so they created a massive, vibrant Ashkenazic culture in the United States, centered in New York City, even as they stepped off the boat. It was the mirror image of Jewish life in eastern Europe, centered in Warsaw and Vilna, except that there was little danger. Also, there was little Zionism; these people decisively left Europe, but they went *away* from Israel. Still, they had an enormous number of Yiddish-speaking Jews, reflecting the whole range of Ashkenazic life. First-generation Jews ranged from those reluctant to assimilate to those who wished they could be American yesterday. Second-generation immigrants usually were American, but poverty often prevented them from leaving the Jewish neighborhoods, and a constant resupply of new immigrants kept the community Ashkenazic and largely Yiddish-speaking for decades.

The influx had been huge. In 1870 there were an estimated 60,000 Jews in the United States; by 1910, 1.1 million.[23] The year 1881, when Czar Alexander II was assassinated and Alexander III succeeded, was a turning point almost as significant for the Jews as the destruction of the Second Temple. The flight to America began immediately. One 1882 immigrant, Dr. George Price, kept a diary: "Sympathy for Russia?" he asked rhetorically. "Am I not despised? Am I not urged to leave? Do I not hear the word *zhid* constantly? Can I even think that someone considers me a human being capable of thinking and feeling like others? Do I not rise daily with the fear lest the hungry mob attack me?" This was not a hard puzzle. "It is impossible," he concluded, "that a Jew should regret leaving Russia."[24] Mary Antin, who would leave nine years later, described the ferment in the Russian air:

> America was in everybody's mouth. Businessmen talked of it . . . the market women made up their quarrels that they might discuss it . . . people who had relatives in the famous land went around reading their letters . . . children played at emigrating; old folks shook their heads and prophesied no good for those who braved the terrors of the sea and the foreign goal . . . but scarcely anyone knew one true fact about this magic land.[25]

The Orthodox resisted, fearing complete loss of religion, but masses of other Russians moved.

Other nations followed. In 1899 a famine in Romania triggered a large pogrom led by police; Jews were expelled from their homes by government edict. This produced bands of *fusgeyer*—"foot-goers"—walking West. They were younger, healthier, and less poor than the Russian immigrants, and they earned their way to America by working and performing. Whatever the origins of the immigrants, the journey combined adventure with trauma. Departures were grief-stricken. One immigrant wrote,

> In the evening when we were alone together my mother would make me sit on her footstool, and while her deft fingers manipulated the knitting-needles she would gaze into my eyes as if she tried to absorb enough of me to last her for the coming years of absence. "You will write us, dear?" she kept asking continually. "And if I should die when you are gone, you will remember me in your prayers?"
>
> At the moment of departure, when the train drew into the station, she lost control of her feelings. As she embraced me for the last

time her sobs became violent and father had to separate us. There was a despair in her way of clinging to me which I then could not understand. I understand it now. I never saw her again.[26]

Like all immigrants, these Jews were different from the ones who stayed behind. They were capable of tearing themselves away from ties of love and place, facing an arduous journey, and starting alone in a unknown land. America consists of such people, and Jewish America consists of such Jews.

Some did move with their families, but still the trip was dreadful. The philosopher Morris Raphael Cohen recalled the legendary privations:

> We were huddled together in the steerage literally like cattle—my mother, my sister and I sleeping in the middle tier, people being above us and below us. . . . We could not eat the food of the ship, since it was not kosher. We only asked for hot water into which my mother used to put a little brandy and sugar to give it a taste. To-wards the end of the trip when our bread was beginning to give out we applied to the ship's steward for bread, but the kind he gave us was unbearably soggy.[27]

Filth and disease were inevitable. Collisions too were a real risk, and Cohen's family "escaped a crash only by a hair's breadth."

Lady Liberty was a sight for sore eyes, but her torch first lit the way to Ellis Island, where there were days of waits, questions, medical examinations, more waits, and, not infrequently, rejection. Tuberculosis was called "the Jewish disease." Yet the numbers tell a benign tale: tens of thousands of Jews passed through every year. And not just Jews; Ellis Island processed up to fifteen thousand people a day. Jews were not abandoned at the gate. The United Hebrew Charities helped them get on their feet, and the Hebrew Immigrant Aid Society showed up at Ellis Island with the charity's logo stitched in Yiddish on their small blue caps. They stood between hundreds of thousands of immigrants and an abyss of loneliness and fear.

☙❧

So began the American adventure; but then paths diverged in a thousand ways. Many wanted an immediate change in identity. In his 1917 memoir *An American in the Making,* Marcus Savage lamented them:

> Cut adrift suddenly from their ancient moorings, they were floundering in a sort of moral void. Good manners and good conduct, reverence and religion, had all gone by the board, and the reason was that these things were not American. . . . old age had forfeited its claim to deference because it had thrown away its dig-

nity. Tottering grandfathers had snipped off their white beards and laid aside their skullcaps and their snuffboxes and paraded around the streets of a Saturday afternoon with cigarettes in their mouths, when they should have been lamenting the loss of the Holy City in the study room adjoining the synagogue.[28]

But there *were* synagogues and study houses, and most did not avoid them. Indeed, Morgan Zhurnal recalled that at the turn of the century "there were two or three small synagogues and places of worship on every block; and on the first day of Elul"—the month of preparation for the High Holidays— "every one of them sounded the *shofar* in the early hours of the morning, continuing throughout the month."[29] The effect must have been eerie, a kind of sacred cock-crow ringing down the crowded streets.

These tiny synagogues, or *shtibls,* all had committees to hire cantors, so they could compete in a buyer's market for High Holiday tickets. "Top salary for a cantor was forty dollars, and only if he had a reputation. But the committee bargained . . . 'because a Jew has to pray anyhow.' The cantor just has to sing a little louder than the rest of the congregation. . . . On *Rosh Hashanah* one could really see how the Jewish population had grown; all the big and little synagogues were packed. The back rooms of East Side saloons and empty stores were transformed into prayer halls. . . . Yiddish theaters became synagogues too."[30] On these holidays even Ellis Island had two rooms set aside for Jewish worship, and at the end of Yom Kippur immigrants just off the boat broke the fast with tea and cake from the Hebrew Immigrant Aid Society. Tashlich, the ceremony of casting bread on the waters to rid oneself of sin, was performed on the Brooklyn Bridge.

Theater was pervasive and powerful. In 1903 the daily *Forward*—the largest and longest-lasting Jewish newspaper, still in publication today— asked its readers for their opinions of Yiddish theater in New York. One wrote, "A play should teach us how to behave toward our wives, sweethearts, parents, etc. The *Kreutzer Sonata* can teach young children; *King Lear* can teach older children." Another demurred: "I want entertainment, not education. The critic condemned the play *Aygene Blut* ["Own Blood"] with 'scientific arguments' proving it was not modern, not moral, etc. But there are long lines at the box office. I was deeply moved in the first act when Lydia sang *Kol Nidre* to prove she was a Jewess. The second act was entertaining from beginning to end." Another reader complained, "Yiddish theaters are a potpourri of opera, vaudeville, drama, etc., and don't satisfy those who want specific kinds of entertainment. It must reform. Each theater must devote itself to one kind of show. A play should have action, and no miracles. Also psychological study of good and bad characters."[31]

Playwright Jacob Gordin and actor Jacob P. Adler dominated the Yiddish theater during its golden age, from 1890 to the First World War.

Gordin's Yiddish-language adaptation of *King Lear* was a pinnacle. An old
Jew shuns his favorite daughter and moves to Jerusalem, returning as a beggar when his other daughters refuse to send him any of the money he gave
them. It is melodrama, not tragedy, when the blind old man returns at the
end to his good daughter's loving embrace. But the critic Hutchins Hap-
good, not Jewish but fascinated by Yiddish theater and by the Lower East
Side in general, wrote that Adler's portrayal "would be enjoyed even by
those who understand no word of Yiddish. For great acting is great pan-
tomime, and Mr. Adler, being an actor, knows how to use his whole body,
rather than merely his voice, to express what is going on in his soul."[32]
S. Anski's *The Dybbuk,* the most acclaimed and durable Yiddish play, came
to America soon after its first performance in 1920, and its tale of love and
spirit possession brought high art to the Yiddish stage.

Many Yiddish songs were made in America, but some were made in the
old country *about* America. One poignant lullaby, from a Sholem Aleichem
poem, evokes the great day when mother and son will join *Tateh,* Daddy, in
the Golden Land, *far Yidn a Gan-Eden*—"for Jews a Garden of Eden."
What is this paradise?

> *Dortn est men in der vokhn*
> *Khale, zunenyu,*
> *Yakhelekh vel ikh dir kokhn,*
> *Shlof zhe, lyu-lyu-lyu.*

"There they eat *challah* on weekdays, my son, and I'll cook you chicken
soup, so sleep." Chicken soup and challah on weekdays—that's paradise.
Tateh will send twenty dollars and his picture, and when they arrive in
America he will scoop the boy up in his arms as Mother watches, weeping
silently, trembling with joy.

Alas, not all such dreams came true, and some became the source of sad
stories. Fiction, often serialized in Yiddish newspapers, ran the gamut from
literary classics to romance novels. But Abraham Cahan, the editor of the
Yiddish *Forward,* wrote much of his fiction in English, and dealt with the
conflicts between and within Americanizing Jews. *Yekl,* a classic novella—
later the feature film *Hester Street*—tells of a young man who, despite his
broken English, considers himself thoroughly American.[33] He works in a
cloak shop, dresses nattily, spends his evenings in dance halls, and is generally quite impressed with himself. Unfortunately he has a wife and small
son back in the old country, and when they show up at Ellis Island his life
changes utterly. Gitl is devoutly religious and bound to tradition; worse,
she is the rankest of greenhorns, unable to speak, dress, walk, even breathe
like an American. Yekl, now "Jake," is thoroughly ashamed of her. But she

meets a fine Orthodox man—"a young man of silk who is fit to be a rabbi,"[34] one of her friends says—completely unlike that "rowdy, a sinner of Israel, a *regely loifer*, may no good Jew know him!"[35] And when Jake divorces her to marry one of his dance-hall girls, who is footing the bill—in Jewish law *he* must divorce *her*—Gitl finds happiness with her *beshert*, her destined one, while Jake takes his new bride to city hall, full of misgivings.

Many of the tensions of Lower East Side life are here: Europe or America, tradition or assimilation, Yiddish or English, poverty or getting ahead, religion or secular life. In some ways the novel reflected the turmoil in eastern Europe, with rapidly expanding populations sending more young people for factory work in industrializing cities. But in the United States political freedom gave the union movement a different character. Jews were a much smaller proportion of the American population than in Poland, but they gave local expression to a multiethnic national process.

Many were just trying to get ahead, and the mythic American dream became real for some. Others had no ideology other than Judaism itself. But an overview of the political discourse among Jewish immigrants and their first-generation American children leaves no doubt that it was strongly left-leaning. Before World War I the Bund was active on the Lower East Side, attempting to imbue American-Jewish workers with socialist ideals. Labor unions were less ideological and committed to collective bargaining under the threat of strike. Some unions, like the International Ladies Garment Workers Union, were heavily Jewish, and in this case also heavily female. Strikes were nevertheless the central weapon in the struggle for more pay, shorter hours—a forty-nine- versus fifty-three-hour workweek, for example—and safer working conditions.

By this time scores of thousands of Jewish workers had been organizing and striking for better conditions, which they steadily, bit by bit, did obtain. A massive strike had occurred in the fall of 1909 involving twenty thousand blouse makers, mostly young Jewish women. A young reporter watched the picket line:

> The girls, headed by teen-age Clara Lemlich, described by union organizers as a "pint of trouble for the bosses," began singing Italian and Russian working-class songs as they paced in twos before the factory door. Of a sudden, around the corner came a dozen tough-looking customers, for whom the union label "gorillas" seemed well-chosen.
>
> "Stand fast, girls," called Clara, and then the thugs rushed the line, knocking Clara to her knees, striking at the pickets, opening the way for a group of frightened scabs to slip through the broken line. Fancy ladies from the Allen Street red-light district climbed

out of cabs to cheer on the gorillas. There was a confused melée of scratching, screaming girls and fist-swinging men and then a patrol wagon arrived. The thugs ran off as the cops pushed Clara and two other badly beaten girls into the wagon.

Clara was a firebrand, known for her passionate speeches in Yiddish describing and decrying the horrendous conditions of tenement families. The reporter followed the retreating pickets to the union hall. "There a relief station had been set up where one bottle of milk and a loaf of bread were given to strikers with small children in their families. There, for the first time in my comfortably sheltered, upper West Side life, I saw real hunger on the faces of my fellow Americans in the richest city in the world."[36] The strike went on from November until February, and although there was no formal union recognition, there were substantial improvements in working conditions.

> In the immigrant world, the shirtwaist makers had created indescribable excitement: these were our daughters. The strike came to be called "the uprising of the twenty thousand.". . . New emotions swept the East Side, new perceptions of what immigrants could do, even girls until yesterday mute. *"Unzere vunderbare farbrente meydlekh,"* "our wonderful fervent girls," an old-timer called them.[37]

These young women inspired the men. The male-dominated cloak makers union now struck in force, and completed the triumph of collective bargaining that made the garment workers union impossible to ignore.

Nothing highlighted the need for safety measures more than the Triangle Shirtwaist Company fire of 1911, in which a blouse-making factory burst into flames and 146 workers, mostly Jewish and Italian women, were killed in less than twenty minutes. Most burned to death, but not all:

> [A] young man helped a girl to the window sill on the ninth floor. Then he held her out deliberately, away from the building, and let her drop. He held out a second girl the same way and let her drop. He held out a third girl who did not resist. They were all as unresisting as if he were helping them into a street car instead of into eternity. He saw that a terrible death awaited them in the flames and his was only a terrible chivalry. He brought around another girl to the window. I saw her put her arms around him and kiss him. Then he held her into space—and dropped her. Quick as a flash, he was on the window sill himself. His coat fluttered upwards—the air filled his trouser legs as he came down. I could see he wore tan shoes.[38]

Over the next decade, responding to this and other events, unions grew stronger. By mid-1925, forty thousand cloak makers and dressmakers could assemble in Yankee Stadium; they organized a work stoppage in which thirty thousand left the shops and filled seventeen halls to listen to union speakers. Factionalism was rife in the labor movement—Communists and anticommunists, revolutionaries and liberals, organizers, strikers, and mobsters—but incremental change was real, unions were recognized by employers and by government, and a great step forward was taken in the welfare and status of working people in America. Most Jews moved on to more middle-class occupations, but not before making an enormous contribution to one of the most important advances in the American way of life. And not incidentally, they made it in concert with Italian Americans, Irish Americans, German Americans, and other immigrant groups standing firmly together, insisting that the future must be better than the past.

✐✐✐

But it took a poor, passionate, brilliant Ashkenazic girl to bring this joining of Jews and America to its logical conclusion. "I am a Russian Jewess, a flame—a longing," wrote Anzia Yezierska in *Salome of the Tenements*. "I am the ache of unvoiced dreams, the clamor of suppressed desires. I am the unlived lives of generations stifled in Siberian prisons."[39] She was also the bard of the Lower East Side, a popular spinner of tales that brought to life the suffering, humor, and dignity of Jewish immigrant families. Her best-known novel is *Bread Givers,* another tenement narrative, about Sara, a young girl with three grown sisters and a mother always anxious about their next meal.[40] The father hovers over holy books all day, supported by the pittances earned by the three women. When the landlady comes for the rent, she argues with the father over his failure to work, and then knocks the *Chumash,* the bound-book version of the Torah, out of her father's hand. He slaps her hard on both cheeks, is sued, and wins in court when the lady's shoe matches the muddy print on the book.

But he is no Torah hero. He shouts insults incessantly at his wife and daughters, drives away the decent men two of them are in love with, and forces all three to marry men they *don't* love. One turns out to have lied about being a diamond dealer, the second is rich but a hopeless gambler, and the third is a fifty-six-year-old widowed fishmonger with a house full of wild children. After wrecking his daughters' lives, he blames them: "No wonder it says in the Torah, 'Woe to a man who has females for his offspring'!" "And woe to us women," his wife replies, "who got to live in a Torah-made world that's only for men."[41]

Swindled out of the fishmonger's dowry, the father tries to force Sara into the sweatshop-slave role her older sisters had taken, but she leaves home in a fight with him. He attempts to retrieve her and calls her selfish when she refuses. "All my selfishness is from you," she says. "What have you ever done for your wife and children but crush them and break them? I ran away from home because I hated you. I couldn't bear the sight of you." His typical reply:

> "*Schlang!* [Snake!] Toad! Wild animal! Thing of evil! How came you ever to be my child. I disown you. I curse you. May your name and your memory be blotted out of this earth." He rushed from me, slamming the door, a defeated prophet, a Jeremiah to whom the people would not listen.[42]

She works, studies, becomes a teacher, and, in a storybook ending, reconciles with her father and tends his old age. She has married a school principal, and he asks her father to teach him Hebrew. A broken old man, still arrogant but no longer nasty,

> his eyes grew soft and moist. He looked most gratefully from Hugo toward me. "I thought that in America we were all lost. Jewishness is no Jewishness. Children are no children. Respect for fathers does not exist. And yet my own daughter who is not a Jewess and not a gentile—brings me a young man—and whom? An American. And for what? To learn Hebrew. From whom? From *me*. Lord of the Universe! You never forsake your faithful ones. . . . Even my daughter with the hard heart has come to learn that the words of our Holy Torah are the only words of life."[43]

Yezierska's readers wanted to see the triumph of everything American, even at the price of the Jewish past, yet they loved the fantasy of the thoroughly American Jew coming hat in hand to the aged scholar, asking to study Torah.

Yezierska's own experience was also a kind of prison. She escaped by organizing a cooking class for young ladies—"Miss Hattie Mayer" was her *nom de cuisine*—and, since she knew nothing about cooking, let them teach each other. But she studied to be a real teacher—a *teacherin,* Yiddishizing and feminizing the word—and graduated from Columbia Teachers College in 1904. But her restlessness persisted; she tried acting and began writing stories. A first marriage was annulled and a second produced a daughter, but stifled her despite her husband's kindness. She left, and the little girl stayed with him.

Her daughter would later describe her as "the loneliest person I knew." But she was also "youthful in her reactions . . . as freshly indignant, appreciative, excited as a child." She was, at forty, "an auburn-haired, broadfeatured, radiantly handsome woman, with a white velvet skin, wide, challenging blue eyes, short, broad-hipped, vigorously healthy, dressed always in tailored navy-blue suits . . . but to know her was to be close to an emotional volcano." The daughter, who loved her father, described her parents' marriage as "a devastating collision of expectations."[44]

In 1917, Anzia could not find a steady teaching job to support her writing habit, so she strode into the office of a famous former professor and told him she was being treated unfairly by the board of education. He went downtown to watch her teach and recommended her. But when she showed him one of her best stories—"The Fat of the Land"—he said, "I wish you well, but I don't wish you to be a teacher. Something creative, yes, but a teacher, no." He encouraged her, gave her her first typewriter, even submitted one of her stories to the *New Republic*.[45]

The professor was John Dewey, fifty-eight, one of the most important figures in American philosophy and education, and he was falling in love. Though apparently never consummated—Dewey was in a long, lonely marriage—it was reciprocated, intense, and emblematic of the love affair between the Jews and America. Dewey, as he himself said, was reserved to the point of coldness; his work was his life. An upper-crust New England background, a professorship in a top Ivy League school, and leadership in a dozen liberal causes made him seem unattainable to the passionate, slightly wild Jewish immigrant. Yet she was proof that everyone was educable, that great things could come from someone who was poor, foreign-born, Jewish, and female—in short, that all the prejudices of an America that on the whole was much less liberal than he was could be overthrown. His poems about her, retrieved from his wastebasket by a student, take up most of his small book of collected verse, and they contrast his coldness with her passion. But she unlocked passion in him, and both of them knew how much he needed that:

> *I am overcome by thunder*
> *Of my blood that surges*
> *From my cold heart to my clear head—*
> *So at least she said—*[46]

She would fictionalize this love affair repeatedly, but in 1920 she wrote a vengeful review of a book Dewey had published four years earlier: "Can it be that Professor Dewey, for all his large, social vision, has so choked the feelings in his own heart that he has killed in himself the power to reach the masses of people who think with the heart rather than with the head?"

But Dewey did not need to speak to the masses directly to change their lives for the better. A scion of old America, he knew the country thrived on repeated infusions of irrepressible newcomers full of hope and yearning. East European Jews were not yet really "white." They were still snubbed by uptown German Jews who felt their status threatened by these emotive, uncouth, un-American foreigners. So it is wonderfully ironic that Anzia Yezierska sped past all that prejudice to embrace a man who stood for America itself. Her journey traced the path of immigrant Jewish culture in the United States, and it logically led to the office of America's leading liberal philosopher, himself the reigning viceroy of white Anglo-Saxon Protestant tolerance and dignity. The passion they briefly, secretly shared symbolized the Jewish American bond.

12

MAMEH-LOSHN

HOW THE ASHKENAZIC JEWS
SPOKE AND THOUGHT

The linguist Roman Jacobson said that the difference between a dialect and a language is an army and a navy; Yiddish had neither, but it diverged from German a thousand years ago as both arose from Middle High German.[1] It is written in Hebrew script and has countless borrowings from Hebrew and Aramaic—perhaps as much as 15 percent—as well as from Slavic and other non-Germanic languages;[2] speakers of German cannot understand speakers of Yiddish. Many words are preserved in Yiddish from Middle High German that are lost to modern German, and vice versa. Like Judeo-Spanish, with its own distinguished history, Yiddish had achieved a literary and political status worthy of universal respect. It was spoken by millions, all with ideas of their own. Yiddish not only coexisted with Polish and other eastern European languages, it lived side by side with the cultures of Jews who vainly tried to be *really* German or Polish.

The Jews had been speaking Yiddish since at least the tenth century, and had done well in most walks of life other than politics and landholding. For example, in Poland in 1570 there were three hundred thousand Jews, and their community began to rival that of Turkey in size and vitality. They were craftsmen in silver and other metals, printers, tailors, bakers, distillers of liquor, and innkeepers. They traded grain, timber, cattle, horses, fish, honey, and textiles, and they collected tolls and managed estates. The Polish Empire extended from the Baltic to the Black Sea, and the Jews were well tolerated compared to their status elsewhere. This was a golden age of Torah study, with a yeshiva in every town; a town of fifty somehow supported thirty young scholars. But the empire was cruel and generated rebellion. An oppressed Ukraine revolted violently against Polish rule; under the leadership of Bogdan Chmielnicky—and with the encouragement of priests—Tatars, Cossacks, and peasant mobs rioted against the Jews for a decade. A hundred thousand were killed in the worst Jewish devastation between the Spanish expulsion and the Holocaust.

In the wake of this suffering, false messiahs arose. Shabbatai Zvi, after years of leading Jews astray and toying with their dreams, converted to Islam under threat of death. Jacob Frank, another receptacle of betrayed Jewish hopes, pretended to embrace Christ under pressure from Catholic bishops. His followers burned a Talmud in Lvov, and many were baptized. There were other messiahs, all rejected by faithful Jews, but the tragic events instilled a legitimate hunger for new religious ideas and forms. With their usual adaptability, Jews created them, and they swept across eastern Europe like a welcome storm, the kind that clears the air and leaves freshness, optimism, and calm in its wake. This was Hasidism, meaning "piety" or "righteousness," the first great Yiddish cultural revolution, and it changed Orthodox Judaism forever.

Its first practitioner was Israel ben-Eliezer, later known as the Baal Shem Tov—the "Master of the Good Name"—or Besht, for short. An autodidact of poor and humble origins, he was influenced by his devout and more learned wife, Hannah; like Akiva, he was unlucky in birth but lucky in love. The pair immersed themselves in the ideas of Luria and other kabbalists, but their overall goal was not mysticism. It was to infuse the life of the mind with bright color. "The anecdote, the parable, the metaphor, and the aphorism took the place of *pilpul* (dialectics). . . . To speak of the Baal Shem Tov is to speak in stories and legends that glow like beacons in the darkness."[3] He taught that self-denial is a sin because it weakens the body, which has to be strong in the service of God. He insisted on joy, writing that "our Father in Heaven hates sadness and rejoices when His children are joyful. And when are His children joyful? When they carry out His Commandments."[4] There was no conflict between a joyful life and the Law.

Still, there was a softening. Spontaneous prayer was held to be more important than worshiping at prescribed times. The Besht never castigated people with fantasies of hellfire. "Woe unto those who dare to speak evil of Israel," he said, and claimed that "every Jew, when he utters even a brief prayer at the close of day, is performing a great work before which the very angels in heaven bow down in homage." Forgiveness was central: "God does not look on the evil side, how dare I do so?"[5] His disciple Rabbi Dov Baer said, "He taught me the language of the birds and the trees. He revealed to me the secrets of the sages and the mystical meaning of many things."[6] Believing that Torah study, like prayer, must be filled with passion, he brought Baer into touch with his emotions and taught him to use feelings as aids in interpretation.

Baer's own tombstone described him as "the Divine Eagle, the Holy Light, a Man of Wonder, our Teacher and our Master."[7] Famous for his sermons, he inspired disciples from Galicia throughout Poland and even Lithuania, where strict Orthodoxy reigned. Among those he "converted" was Rabbi Levi Yitzhak, whose passion was legendary. He was also known for his arguments with God. On Yom Kippur, the Day of Atonement, he persuaded the town tailor to speak before the whole congregation:

"I, Yankel, am a poor tailor who, to tell the truth, has not been too honest in his work. I have occasionally kept remnants of cloth that were left over, and I have occasionally missed the afternoon service. But You, O Lord, have taken away infants from their mothers, and mothers from their infants. Let us on this Day of Days, be quits. If you forgive me, then I will forgive you." At this the rabbi sighed, "Oh Yankel, Yankel, why did you let God off so lightly?"[8]

Levi Yitzhak was also known for an ecstatic song, a haunting melody with words in Yiddish based on Psalm 139. It is called "Dudele," a diminutive of *Du*, "You"—"the You Song"—and is full of the mesmerizing refrain "Du, Du, Du." More than two centuries later, it is still recognizable to many:

> *Where I go, You,*
> *Where I stay, You,*
> *Only You, Only You. . . .*
> *When I am happy, You,*
> *When I am sad, You,*
> *You, everywhere You,*
> *You, You, You . . .*

This cherished song encapsulates a central Hasidic belief: God is everywhere, and a Jew should feel God's presence in every moment of life.

Needless to say, Hasidism was vigorously resisted by more conservative rabbis and their followers. They viewed it as heresy, a corruption of Judaism; they cursed and excommunicated its leaders. They brooked no departures from the letter of the Law, saw singing and dancing as sacrilege, and suspected all religious ecstasy of grading into witchcraft. No routes to God but conventional prayer and Torah study; no insights into the Law except through legal debates—*pilpul,* the ancient method of asking and answering questions about the meaning of sacred texts. The Hasidim saw such debates as blocking access to God for many by narrowing the path, of losing the spirit of the Law in a dry, relentless obsession over its letter. It is a tribute to the success of Hasidism that the rest of the Orthodox world is known by the name Mitnagdim—"Opponents."[9]

This doesn't do them justice. The traditionalists overreacted to Hasidic practices, but their contributions to Torah study were great. Not long after the birth of Hasidism Napoleon named Vilna—the center of opposition— "the Jerusalem of Lithuania," and that name was valid until the German mass murders of 1941. The rabbi known as the Vilna Gaon—the Sage of

Vilna—was one of the greatest of Orthodox scholars. Not only a Torah prodigy from childhood, he mastered secular subjects, too, translating Euclid's *Geometry* into Hebrew and authoring treatises on algebra, trigonometry, astronomy, and Hebrew grammar, in addition to dozens of religious books. Like the Hasidim, he was impatient with *pilpul,* favoring a literal reading of the texts: "with a single shaft of the light of truth he would illumine the darkness, and with a single word would overthrow heaps of *pilpulim* hanging by a hair."[10] He also loved kabbala, but beyond this common ground, he and the Hasidim diverged strongly.

He rejected the cult of the tzaddik, or righteous man, which bound Hasidim around their leaders. He detested the passionate swaying, singing, and dancing in their services, favoring an ascetic approach to religion. He was appalled by their laxity with the appointed times for prayer, rejecting the claim that faith and devotion in prayer could make up for lateness. He essentially accused them of Deism in their insistence that God was everywhere—a notion that was literally anathema to him. When an epidemic broke out in Vilna and killed many children, the Gaon and his colleagues blamed the Hasidim. They expelled one rabbi even as he begged for forgiveness, imprisoned another, and burned Hasidic books. The Gaon's views of them were entirely based on hearsay and were invariably biased and distorted. Yet when two leading Hasidic Torah scholars came to explain their position, he refused to meet with them, even leaving town to avoid them. Isolated in his study, his genius became increasingly detached from the hopes and dreams of many Jews.

Some leaders issued excommunications. The Gaon signed the Vilna writ in 1781:

> Because of our many sins, worthless and wanton men who call themselves *hasidim* have deserted the Jewish community. . . . they worship in a most insane fashion. . . . The exaggerations and stories of miracles that are described in their books are particularly transparent and obvious lies. . . . a fire has been kindled in the midst of Jewry. . . .
>
> Therefore, we, the undersigned, are in agreement that every community is most urgently bound to adopt rigorous measures—carrying with them every possible penalty—in order to put into effect all the protective and defensive measures described below.[11]

This included "measures to put an end to the prayer meetings of the heretics in all communities, so that they will be deprived of the means of common assembly," a ban on reading their literature, and a prohibition of pilgrimages to Hasidic rabbis. Their meat was declared unkosher, a devastating insult and a grave economic blow. "No one is to shelter any member of this sect. . . . No community may permit any one of them to hold a position as cantor or rabbi, and it goes without saying that no one of them may teach our children." Faithful Jews were commanded to spy on Hasidim and bring the information to the court.

The rift became so deep that the unthinkable happened: gentile rulers had to intervene to keep order among Jews. In 1800, the civil authorities of Lithuania prohibited anathemas and excommunications and decreed that all Jewish communities could have their own synagogues and choose their own rabbis. These measures enshrined coexistence in law, but it was and is not simple. An uneasy truce has generally held, but there have been outbreaks of violence, and animosity seethes under the surface. Neither the Jewish emancipation of the nineteenth century nor the Nazi devastation of both camps could heal the rift. Both the Vilna Gaon and the Hasidic *wunder-rebbes* ("wonder rabbis") he detested have many intellectual descendants today, and Yiddish is still a primary vehicle of their mutual contempt.

In the early twenty-first century there are twenty-five or thirty Hasidic groups, each numbering from a hundred to five thousand or more families and totaling only half of ultra-Orthodox Jews—the rest being Mitnagdim. Each group centers on a court and its rebbe, who is far more exalted than an ordinary rabbi. His righteousness and wisdom give him special powers, and because he usually has not only a religious but a blood link to the rebbes of the past, he seems anointed. Each sect is in part a cult of personality. Both halves of the ultra-Orthodox world have very large families and so are expanding rapidly. Many thousands of them raise their children in Yiddish; aside from a few academic centers, the future of spoken Yiddish lies with them. But—their visibility notwithstanding—they are a tiny fraction of the Jewish world.

Except for covering bare skin, their style of dress—long black coats and wide-brimmed hats for men, old-fashioned wigs for married women, who are not permitted to show their hair—preserves the style of the eighteenth century in eastern Europe. Some Mitnagdim oppose Israel, believing there should be no Jewish state until the Messiah comes. Some Hasidim actively plan for the Messiah's coming, and one large group, the Lubavitcher Hasidim, believe that their last rebbe—he died at an advanced age in the early 1990s—may soon return as the Messiah. "We Want *Moshiach* Now!" is one of their favorite slogans. The Bratslaver Hasidim, on the other hand—like most such groups, they are named for the town in eastern Europe that gave rise to the sect—have bumper stickers, banners, and crudely lettered signs up all over Israel honoring their founder, Rabbi Nachman. In Brooklyn, conflicts *among* Hasidim have occasionally been violent. As for the overall rift with Mitnagdim, graffiti in certain Jerusalem neighborhoods often condemns Hasidic dance and song.

Hasidic life in America centers on three Brooklyn neighborhoods, although a strong community has arisen farther up the Hudson River in New York State, around Monsey and Monroe Town.[12] Many of the original members were Holocaust refugees, and one famed rebbe was ransomed from the Bergen-Belsen death camp. They have expanded and done well, especially in the diamond, camera, and computer businesses. Successful merchants support communal life. Two groups dominate—the Satmar and Lubavitcher Hasidim—and their rivalry is serious. The Satmar are steeped in the past and insular; the Lubavitchers are open and pursue Jewish outreach. The Satmar not only oppose Zionism but blame it for the Holocaust; the Lubavitchers find this explanation abhorrent, believing that no explanation can be found. The Lubavitchers think that God has often intervened with miracles that saved the state of Israel; the Satmar see *that* view as sacrilege. Among other occasions, serious violence broke out when the Lubavitchers—much in the manner of the Northern Ireland Orangemen—staged a massive Passover march through Satmar streets.

In both groups marriages are arranged, and the sects are endogamous. Women are thoroughly subordinate to their husbands, and young women are also dominated by their mothers and mothers-in-law. Their roles follow the strictest reading of halakhah, and they more or less accept their task: to raise a large family. Troubled women only go to Orthodox psychotherapists, who reinforce their acceptance. Divorce is moderately common, and so is abuse, which occurs at high levels in all cultures where women are subordinated. Not all children stay in the fold, and those who leave often play interesting roles in other parts of the Jewish world.

Lis Harris, a gifted writer who spent a year with Lubavitcher Hasidim, said that on her first visit, on Purim,

> I felt as if I had wandered into a dream. Pale, bearded, black-hatted, dark-suited men, looking remarkably alike, hurried along the sidewalks with downcast eyes, pointedly avoiding eye contact. . . . Every woman under forty-five appeared to be pregnant. . . . high-spirited children hopped like rabbits everywhere. That day the community was celebrating Purim . . . and many of the children wore masks and colorful costumes. Giggling, mustachioed Hamans and gaudily crowned Esthers chased one another up and down the streets.[13]

She describes her first *farbrengen,* the rebbe's Friday evening discourse. "There were about four thousand people crammed into the synagogue—a space that . . . ought to have comfortably sheltered two thousand." She squeezed in upstairs in the women's section. "Below, a black sea of Hasidim swayed back and forth. Above, a tremendous din. Downstairs, little boys raced between the men's legs and around the dais, and small girls drowsed on their fathers' shoulders. Upstairs, innocent-looking teenage girls and delicately powdered old ladies mingled with plump young mothers and innumerable babies. . . . The smell of sour milk and wet diapers was faint but pervasive."[14]

The rebbe's appearance was dramatic, as "a white-bearded figure with a brisk, almost military gait and kindly, penetrating blue eyes entered the room, and, except for the lip-smacking sound of sucking babies, it fell completely silent." Beginning "in the manner of a teacher picking up the threads of a discussion with his students," he spoke for four hours in Yiddish, without notes. His huge audience understood and hung on every word. During brief half-hourly breaks he toasted his flock with a tiny wine-filled Dixie cup and was toasted in return, as the men sang songs and hymns on the themes of the discourse.

Almost a century earlier, another secular Jew had made a journey to the Hasidic world that—partly because he was male—proved more permanent. "One summer's day in 1913," Jeri Langer wrote of his own journey, "a nineteen-year-old youth . . . left Prague inspired by a secret longing." He "set out for the east, for strange countries," for "the empire of the Chassidim." He arrived one Friday as the town of Belz, "the Jewish Rome," approached the Sabbath:

> Small towns in eastern Galicia have all had the same character for centuries. Misery and dirt are their characteristic outward signs. Poorly clad Ukrainian peasant men and women, Jews wearing side-whiskers, in torn caftans, rows of cattle and horses, geese and large pigs grazing the town square . . .
> It is a long summer afternoon. There are still six or seven hours before dusk, when the Sabbath begins. . . . In spite of this, the shops are already shut, the tailors are putting away their needles, and the casual laborers—wearing side-whiskers like the rest—their hoes and spades. The housewives in the cottages are adding the last touches to their preparations for the festival.[15]

He tries to fit in but feels an outsider; bored with Torah study, he returns to Prague. There, one sleepless night, he has a vision:

> Suddenly I am dazzled by a bright light penetrating into my dark bedroom through the half-open door. What is it?—I know that I have put out the lamp, and there is no one in the kitchen. I stare at the light, and in the middle of it a few steps in front of me, I can see quite clearly through the half-open door—*the saint of Belz!* He is sitting in his room at Belz looking fixedly at me. On his expressive

countenance shines that barely recognizable, sublime smile of his, full of wisdom. . . . So I travel to Belz a second time.[16]

This time he stays, becoming one in a long line of secular Jews who return to the fold. *Ba'alei t'shuva,* they are called—"Masters of Return"—and they make up a surprising proportion of Orthodox Jewry now.

But it wasn't just secular Jews who sought out the Hasidim. A favorite story reveals what they thought the Mitnagdim were doing wrong. An abstemious young scholar studies constantly, denying himself to the verge of illness, yet begins having visions of naked, dancing women while immersed in Torah study. He denies himself further, fasting until dusk and sleeping on a board. The visions become more frequent, and someone tells him to seek help from a Hasidic rabbi in a nearby town; this is anathema, but his visions and health get steadily worse.

Finally, desperate, he goes to the Hasid's court. There, amid joyous talk and ecstatic dancing and singing, the frail, withdrawn young man is seen by the rebbe, who orders him to eat, drink, sing, dance, and enjoy life—not to abandon the Law, but to fulfill it in joy. This will banish his visions and restore him to health. But the young man cannot follow this program, and some days later the rebbe's disciples sadly report that the young man has died. Even the rebbe could not save him; he had fallen too far into habits of despair.

⌇⌇⌇

Such was the Yiddish-speaking world of the early nineteenth century, but by the time Hitler rose to power, Yiddish was the vehicle of thousands of newspapers, periodicals, poems, books, plays, songs, and political tracts. Offerings in it ranged from the Lithuanian rabbis' sermons condemning Hasidism as a soft, mystical corruption of Torah Judaism to arguments between Stalinists and Trotskyites over how exactly to make the revolution. Every year, scores of thousands of toddlers drew it out of the air as their first language. Yiddish translations of Darwin and Einstein took their place beside those of Torah and prayer book. It resisted every attempt to stamp it out as degenerate German, and was properly recognized as an independent and very beautiful language.

The sixteenth to eighteenth centuries, a golden age for Polish Jews, saw a great florescence of religious creativity. But in the nineteenth, war, partition, and internal conflict brought grave economic distress, and Jews moved to survive. Many assimilated Jews settled in large cities like Warsaw, Cracow, or Vilna, and some tried to live among Polish Catholic peasants, but most stayed in shtetls. Religious traditions were strong; towns with the means built stately wooden synagogues several stories tall, looming over the neighborhood like a poor man's cathedral.

But in the cities, Jews felt freed from Torah Judaism. The Reform movement had come to Poland, and the wealthier, more assimilated Jews went to temple instead of synagogue; they thought of themselves as Poles of Jewish faith. They gave charity to Orthodox Jews out of affection mingled with contempt. The secular Jewish intelligentsia thought that ethnic divisions no longer mattered, that it was foolish for a Jew in France or Poland to think of himself as anything but French or Polish. But beneath the surface of civil life was something else. George Szabad remembered: "When I as a boy, or a young man . . . would open my mouth and speak my kind of Polish, which classifies a Pole even more than the English classifies an Englishman . . . and the way I was dressed, and the way I looked, the Pole would, if he was a worker, or a janitor, would immediately take off his hat, because it was a highly stratified society. But if he found out in the next three minutes that I was a Jew, he might just spit on me. And I didn't change at all in those three minutes."[17] Many of these Jews spoke Yiddish—the *mameh-loshn* or mother tongue—but Polish was their pass to a wider world.

Poorer Jews—peddlers, jugglers, tailors, and other small craftsmen—*lived* in Yiddish. They hawked their wares and services in the streets, yelling up at the tenement windows in singsong advertising chants. In shtetls much of the pettier commerce took place in the open markets. In the cities, more and more Jews worked in factories; Lodz, for example, attracted many as its textile industry grew. Urban migration intensified with the widespread pogroms in the wake of the First World War. Some Jews did well in the cities. Cosmopolitanism became the faith of many who thought ethnicity was on the way out as a force in human affairs.

World War I did not change their view. Jews fought loyally for every combatant nation and killed each other in sizable numbers. In Poland, patriotism among educated Jews ran very high, and they did their duty and more in the Polish army. After the war there was a growing sense that Jews might actually *be* Poles. Thirteen Jews from Orthodox, Zionist, and Populist parties sat in the new democracy's parliament, and there were scores of Jewish municipal representatives, including mayors. The Christian first president of the Polish Republic was known as "the Jewish president" because of the role played by the Jewish vote.

But the newborn Soviet Union threatened Poland's independence, provoking prolonged war in the 1920s. Jews in the Polish army, fighting for Poland's freedom, were suspected of treason, and all Jewish soldiers were sent to a prison camp. Economic stagnation and poverty followed war, and anti-Semitism flared ominously. Yet the United States closed its doors to east European immigration in 1924, and other nations followed, trapping millions of Jews in a cesspool of primitive anti-Semitism. In 1930, fifty thousand Jews demonstrated in Warsaw in protest against British restrictions on their immigration. By the late thirties a popular movement to get the Jews to emigrate had made this wish official government policy; but they had no place to go.

In the 1920s most of them did not know how trapped they were. Urban Jews in Poland were in an unprecedented flowering of the arts, education, journalism, and politics, a cultural revolution imbued with ferment, excitement, and hope. Many Jews felt liberated from the shtetls and from Orthodox Jewish traditions, which they replaced with an unprecedented variety of personal and political engagements. Yet Orthodoxy in all its branches continued to thrive in shtetls and cities alike.

New schools taught Polish literature in Yiddish, and classic cheders used it to teach Hebrew prayer and Scripture. It was spoken by porters and bagel peddlers in the urban ghettos, rabbis and ritual slaughterers in the shtetls, sweatshop-factory workers appended to textile machines, farm Jews sweeping wheat with scythes, and mountain Jews riding mule-back on dirt roads in the hills. Clock makers, butchers, spinners, weavers, seamstresses, tailors, umbrella makers, water carriers, chair menders, shoemakers, locksmiths, glaziers, housepainters, ferrymen, innkeepers, and musicians all lived, worked, thought, and loved their children in Yiddish.

A quarter of Poland's Jews, three quarters of a million, now lived in five cities: Warsaw (the largest Jewish community in Europe), Vilna (compared by Napoleon to Jerusalem), Lodz ("the Polish Manchester"), Cracow, and Lvov. Vilna had almost a hundred synagogues and prayer houses and was a great rabbinical center until the Germans smashed it; yet it also had fifteen Yiddish theater companies in 1935. Some Jews became factory owners and industrialists, employing large numbers of freed serfs. Most rich Jews were not born to it, but cottage industries could quickly become great manufacturing enterprises. One Jewish textile tycoon in Lodz had begun as a factory clerk. A top tobacco manufacturer had once been a small shopkeeper; he ended up with his own private fire brigade. Poor tailors became rich dressmakers practically overnight. As a sign of the times, a wealthy rabbi built a factory for hand-weavers after mechanization put them out of work.

The traditional system of cheders and yeshivas was complemented in the nineteenth century by an enormous variety of schools. As the Haskalah spread from Germany to Poland, schools combining Torah and secular subjects were founded. The state built a hundred schools for Jews, but some assimilating Jewish families bypassed those to go to regular government schools. Others realized that acceptance had limits, and supported a wide range of Jewish schools. Improved cheders taught Hebrew in Hebrew instead of Yiddish, and Zionist schools did the same with their programs about Israel. Still, Yiddish remained a key mode of instruction, and Yiddish secular schools spread rapidly, supported by Jewish socialist parties. There were Polish-Hebrew and Polish-Yiddish bilingual schools, and trilingual ones that taught all three. The Orthodox ran separate schools for boys, girls, and religious Zionists. Jewish trade schools taught industry, agriculture, crafts, housekeeping, nursing, commerce, administration, communication, and surveying.

None of these schools was funded by the Polish government, all by Jewish charities. Before the twentieth century, Polish universities were closed to Jews, so the path to higher learning led out of Poland. When this changed, Jews soon took 20 percent of the places—twice their level in the general population—until restrictions in the 1930s cut this sharply. Many libraries and scholarly institutions sprang up, including the YIVO Institute for Jewish Research, the Institute for Jewish Studies, and a seminary where rabbis got both religious and secular training.

But the greatest modern flowering of Ashkenazic culture was literary, achieved not only in Yiddish and Hebrew but Polish, Russian, German— all the national languages of the countries Jews lived in. As Heine, one of the greatest of German poets, had been Jewish, so were several eminent Polish writers of the twentieth century: the poet Julian Tuwim, the short-story writer Bruno Schulz, and the novelist Jósef Wittlin. I. L. Peretz, born in 1852, exemplified Jewish ambivalence: he wrote first in Hebrew, then Polish, then Yiddish—especially for fiction about the poor—and then Hebrew again. Sholem Rabinowitz became one of the greatest Yiddish writers, known as the Jewish Mark Twain, but under the name Sholem Aleichem ("Peace Upon You")—which he took to placate his Hebrew-loving father. The first Yiddish-language journal began in 1862 with a Hebrew name: *Kol Mevasser*—"Announcing Voice." By the 1930s there were 250 Jewish journals in many languages.

But Yiddish was the *mameh-loshn* of four out of five Polish Jews, religious or secular. There were about eleven million Yiddish speakers worldwide at that time—seven million in Europe, three million in North America, a million elsewhere. The first Yiddish books had been printed ages before—a Yiddish Haggadah, for the Passover service, appeared in 1526—but the nineteenth century transformed the language and literature.[18] Yiddish writers rejected the pressure to write only holy books, the insistence by some that Yiddish should be replaced by German, or at least German written with Hebrew letters, and the attempt to replace Yiddish with a new, secular Hebrew. They began creating novels, short stories, essays, and polemics in a literary Yiddish that reflected the language of Jewish street and shtetl.

Between the 1880s and World War I, classic Yiddish fiction was created by three writers who still tower over Yiddish language and literature: S. Y. Abramovitsh, Sholem Aleichem, and I. L. Peretz.[19] All were also Hebrew writers, and the mutual influence of the two literary languages passed through them. All were satirists, making fun of Jew and gentile alike. And all were concerned about social justice, and used their biting wit to expose dreadful conditions for the Jewish poor in both eastern Europe and the United States. Abramovitsh's leading creation, Mendele Moykher-Sforim—Mendele the Bookseller—became so identified with his creator that many refer to the author by the character's name. Aleichem's main character, Tevye the Milkman, became one of the most familiar characters not only for Jews but, through *Fiddler on the Roof,* for people throughout the world.

These three men created a literary style as far removed as possible from the romance novels and other potboilers that were already standard fare for Yiddish readers. They did this through satire, which purged romantic sentiments from their stories. To some extent this came at the cost of purging or at least dampening sentiment in general. Mendele and Tevye are endearing bumblers, not heroes. They have real emotions and face tragic situations, but they neither control their fates nor gain much dignity from their tragedies. These stories depict the plight of simple Jews, but they also ridicule them and, in particular, their religious beliefs. It took a subsequent generation of novelists and poets—the Singer brothers, Anski, Sutzkever, Glatstein, Korn, and others—to give Yiddish literature the serious tone and lofty goals of the great tradition of literary art. Peretz, interestingly enough, came closest to this high art by reaching back into folktales and Hasidic stories.

It was where he found his most moving voice. In "If Not Higher," a shtetl rabbi disappears every day as the Days of Awe approach; his congregation believes that he ascends to heaven. A visiting Litvak—a Lithuanian Jew skeptical of Hasidism—undertakes to embarrass the rabbi by following and exposing him. He discovers that every day the rabbi dons peasant garb, chops wood, delivers it to a helpless old woman, and builds a fire for her. After that, when the Litvak is asked whether he believes that the rabbi goes to heaven, he says: "If not higher." In "Bontsche Schveig"—"Bontsche the Silent"—the simplest of poor Jews dies and is brought before the heavenly court to be praised and rewarded for his quiet, enduring faith. He cannot understand what the fuss is about and is too timid to speak even now. But the Throne of Heaven insists that he name his reward, so he asks for a hot roll with fresh butter; the Heavenly Host are shamed by this small man's modest longings. Such tales endow the simplest of Jews with the greatest of dignity.

᠅

Because women were deprived of Hebrew training, they supported an independent literature in Yiddish, including translations of the prayer book, the Book of Psalms, and the *Chumash*—the bound-book version of the Torah, or Five Books of Moses—called in Yiddish the *Taytsh-Khumesh,* or in Yiddishized Hebrew, the *Tseynu u'Reynu*—"Go Out and See." From their gallery high above the synagogue floor, they could follow Shabbes services in Yiddish, and they often comforted themselves in solitude by chanting the psalms in the *mameh-loshn*. A mischievous 1922 poem by Miriam Ulinover evokes the effect of this Yiddish Bible on a young woman set dreaming by the tale of Abraham's servant's search for Isaac's bride.[20] The translation is by Kathryn Hellerstein:

> *Oh, what a nice matchmaker*
> *Eliezer is!*
> *Oh, what gold and silver*
> *He throws at her feet!—*
>
> *No, you've read enough girls,*
> *In the* Taytsh-Khumesh:
> *Something chases me out*
> *Into the night tonight.*
>
> *Longing is so lucid,*
> *The night is ever dim,—*
> *Throw yourselves at happiness, sisters,*
> *Burst into silvery laughter!*
>
> *Suddenly the evening*
> *Arranges shadows verse by verse . . .*
> *Perhaps messengers are waiting*
> *For us, too, in the field!*
>
> *Far away the distance trembles,*
> *Twitches and flashes, and calls,—*
> *I see golden jewelry*
> *Glistening in the air . . .*
>
> *Throw yourselves at happiness, sisters,*
> *Burst into silvery laughter:*
> *Rebecca's star will shine*
> *Throughout the night.*

Another literary response to limits on women tells us something different. This is Isaac Bashevis Singer's novella *Yentl der Yeshiva-Bokher*—"Yentl the Yeshiva-Boy." Yentl was a girl's name, so the title alone would leave readers laughing. But the story is not so funny. Yentl's beloved father, who taught her Torah, dies, and she cannot bear the thought of a woman's life. She cuts her hair, dresses in men's clothes, and—as Anshel—sets out to become a student. She impresses the rabbi and joins the yeshiva. She falls mildly in love with her study partner, Avigdor, who is rejected by the town beauty's father because of Avigdor's brother's suicide. A demon persuades Avigdor and Yentl that *she* should marry the girl, which leads to some hilarious situations. When Yentl reveals her identity to Avigdor the ruse crumbles, but Avigdor—although stunned by the commandments they have broken—is himself now smitten, and proposes. Yentl, however, knows she can't go back, and slips away to find her own path in Torah and in life.

Singer, so far the only Yiddish writer to win the Nobel Prize, grew up on Krochmalna Street in Warsaw, where his rabbi father heard complaints and resolved disputes from dawn to dusk. Singer explained why he stopped writing in Hebrew: "After many trials," he wrote,

> I decided that I could not convey in Hebrew a conversation between a boy and a girl on Krochmalna Street or even the litigants who came to my father's courtroom. I turned to Yiddish, but I soon realized that this language had limitations and peculiarities. . . . Yiddish was never spoken by military men, police, people of power. . . . It was the language of the tailor, the storekeeper, the Talmud teacher, the rabbi, the matchmaker, the servant girl, but never of the engineer. . . . The leitmotif of Yiddish was, that if a day passes without a misfortune it is a miracle from heaven. . . . It is the language of those who are afraid, not of those who arouse fear.[21]

He never stopped writing in Yiddish, describing the fears and foibles of his people with great literary power throughout six decades. When he won the Nobel, he delivered his acceptance speech in Yiddish from the podium in Stockholm, before the king of Sweden and the assembled critics and writers of the world. Yiddish literature had gone from the shtetl street to the Nobel Prize in about a century.

But long before there were distinguished works of literature, there were folktales, songs, and proverbs galore. The Wise Men of Chelm are among the most delightful figures of folklore, and tales of how their love of moonlight led them to capture the moon in a barrel of water, or how they punished a carp that had slapped one of them with its tail by drowning it in the lake, have delighted children of all ages for generations. Once, after they carried down the mountain the logs they needed to build their new synagogue, a passerby from another town pointed out that they could roll them down, so they carried the logs back up and rolled them down.

Jokes in Yiddish laugh at the precariousness of Jewish life. In one, a Jew recommends a wonderful doctor: "He took care of Reb Shulsinger, may he rest in peace, and Mrs. Rabinovits, may she intercede for us in heaven, and Reb Friedman, may his memory be for a blessing." In another, a Jew says to his friend, "You know, Dovid, my grandfather is eighty-five years old!" "You call that old? If my grandfather were living, he would be a hundred and two!"

Folk songs expressed every hope, every longing. In the haunting lullaby "Raisins with Almonds" a widow tells her baby that she will sell their little goat to buy him raisins and almonds—*rozhenkes mit mandlen*. "Oyfn Prip-itchik"—"By a Firelight"—evokes the quintessential scene of Jewish child-hood, a group of children in a small warm room learning the Hebrew alphabet. "Don't be afraid, little children, every beginning is hard. Whoever learns Torah is happy, does a person need more?" In "Yome, Yome," a shy young girl wants something, and her mother guesses: "We need to see the dressmaker? No. The shoemaker? No. The hatmaker? No. Ah, the match-maker! Yes mother, now you understand!" And in the beloved popular song "Tum-Balalayke," a young man trying to decide which bride to choose puts riddles to one of them, who has no trouble at all: "Silly boy! Stone can grow without rain, a heart can yearn without tears, love can burn without being consumed."

Traditional proverbs went to the heart of Ashkenazic life.[22] *A gefalenem helft Got*—"God helps those who fall down"—is a quaint expression of faith, but God was also the target of gentle humor: *"Ata bekhartanu mikol ha'amim"—vos hostu zikh ongezetst oyf undsz?* A classic Hebrew quote, "'You chose us from all the nations,'" is followed in Yiddish by "What did you have against us?" Serious subjects are wisely mocked, as in *Der malekhamoves gefint stendik a terets*—"The angel of death always finds an excuse"—and incorporated into curses: *Heng dir oyf a tsuker shtrikl vestu hobn a zisn toyt*—"Hang yourself with a sugar-sack cord and have a sweet death!" About their situation in life, they would say, *Fun a gemeyner bulbe komt aroys di faynste latke*—"From a poor potato comes the finest pancake." References to Torah and prayer were frequent, even in business. *Er hot gemakht a gesheft vi feter Eysev*—"He made a deal like Old Man Esau"— meant he'd sell his birthright for a bowl of stew, and *Megst dernokh kadish sogn*—"You can say Kaddish over it"—meant you could kiss it good-bye. They were not above vulgarity, sometimes combined with wisdom: *Az der pots shtet, ligt der seykhel in dr'erd*—"When the dick stands up the brain lies down"—is one saying; *Gots vinder—a pots makht kinder*—"God's tricks—a dick makes kids!" is another.

The sense of community is pervasive: *Vos es vet zayn mit kol yisro'el vet zayn mit reb yisro'el*—"What happens to All Israel happens to Mr. Israel"— and *Ganz Ashkenaz iz eyn shtot*—"All Ashkenaz is one town." So too is the sense of Otherness: *Azoy vi es kristelt zokh azoy yidelt zich*—"What Chris-tians do, Jews do too"—and of course the ever-useful *Es iz git far yidn?*—"Is it good for the Jews?" Perhaps the most poignant proverbs deal with war: *A shlekhter sholem iz besser vi a gitte krig*, says one—"A bad peace is better than a good war." *Beser a hund in fridn eyder a zelner in krig,* says another: "Better a dog in peacetime than a soldier in war." These were not the Jews of medieval Spain, heroes tempered in battle; they were the victims of other people's wars. And the most chilling of all in its eerie foreboding: *Er antlayft fun di beren un falt zvishn di velf*—"He escapes the bears and falls among the wolves." By the time Yiddish had added to this folk idiom both literary genius and the force of political rhetoric, the bears had attacked and the wolves were poised and waiting.

Most Yiddish writers did not survive the Holocaust, and it remains to be seen whether Yiddish itself will. But those who lived continued to write in Yiddish, and in this tongue of the murdered millions they tried to understand the catastrophe. In I. B. Singer's novel *The Family Moskat,* the antihero, a typical Singer rake and bumbler, visits old friends and relatives in Poland on the eve of the Shoah. With all that has been written about the Holocaust, the last line of this book may be the most chilling. A friend suggests that this would be the right time for the Messiah to come at last. The answer: "Death is the Messiah."

☙ ⁘ ❧

For better and for worse, Avraham Sutzkever contains within his superb life the whole of twentieth-century Ashkenazic history.[23] And as one of the era's great poets in any language, he gave life to it in words. If he had not been trapped in Yiddish, he would be universally recognized as a leading modern poet, but he would not leave his mother tongue. He was born just before World War I in Smorgon, near Vilna. When German troops burned the town, his family moved to Siberia—not the Siberia of Stalin's gulags, but a strange and wondrous landscape of sun, snow, and ice. Exile, yes, but that was nothing new for Jews. To a small, dreamy boy who had known nothing else, it was magical. Years later, with his poetic gift in full strength, he would write a long poem called "Siberia," later published with drawings by Marc Chagall. "Sunset over blue and icy roads," it opens,

> *My soul filled with sweet and sleepy colours.*
> *Down in the valley a little hut,*
> *Covered with the snow of the sunset, is ablaze with light.*
> *Shadows of trees swing strangely across window-frames,*
> *magic sledges jingle round in circles.*
> *In the tiny loft the cooing doves*
> *spell out my name. Beneath the ice,*
> *sparkling with lightning crystals,*
> *the River Irtish, half-awake, struggles along its course.*
> *In the dome of space, dreamed up from silence,*
> *a child of seven years moves in a world of his own making.*[24]

As Chagall said in his preface, this is "Jewish poetry of a new kind."[25] The gifted translator, Jacob Sonntag, said of the long work, "The poem does not once refer to Jews or specifically Jewish ideas of any kind. Nor, for that matter, is the child's experience burdened with the memory of the war and the flight of his parents."[26]

Yet the poem was written in 1935, in the heart of Jewish Vilna, in the eye of the gathering storm. But Sutzkever took himself out and away from all that to a childhood memory ablaze with light and beauty. The only sad part of the poem is an elegy for his father, who died in Siberia when Sutzkever was nine. The stanza "In a Siberian Wood" calls up a time two years before his father's death:

> . . . I hear my father say: "Come, my child,
> let us go to the forest to cut wood!"
> Our white colt is harnessed to a sledge.
> The day shines bright in the flashing ax
> and the flaming snow is cut with sharpened sun-knives.
> Sparkling dust—our breath! We leave
> through a sunny web, speeding across steppes,
> past sleeping bears, to the sound of clicking hoofs.
> All the stars which yesterday were shaken from the sky,
> rest frozen now on the ground.

His father's death shaped his life, and he continued to write about him:

> A shade takes down the violin from the wall.
> And thin, thin, thin snow-sounds fall upon my head.
> Hush. That's my father playing,
> And the sounds—graved on the air—
> Like bits of silver breath in a frost
> Ranging blue over the snow moonlike glassed.[27]

He said of his father's death, "That moment the poet in me was born."[28] Sutzkever came from a long line of rabbis; his father had been ordained but did not practice. In his memory his father collapsed while playing the violin, the haunting Hasidic melody composed by Rabbi Levi Yitzhak of Berdichev, addressing God with one repeated syllable, *Du, Du, Du*—"You, You, You," the ultimate expression of I and Thou.

This death sent the family back to Vilna, where he lost his much-loved older sister to a fever. He went to a Yiddish school and began to write poetry, first in Hebrew, then Yiddish. But at sixteen he burned his poems and started again with a new commitment. A group of poets, Young Vilna, were crafting a new Yiddish and would enter its literary canon. But Sutzkever was rejected; Siberian snowscapes and peasant romances did not fit the pretensions of urban poets trying to join the mainstream of European literature. Ultimately he would be viewed as one of the greatest Yiddish poets; for now, writing sustained him as the terror closed in.

Another Yiddish poet, Itzik Manger, described him: "A thin slim youngster, tripping along the narrow twisted little Vilna streets. His steps are light. He does not walk. He floats. He floats all over the humps and bumps of the town. In his imagination everything is symmetrically rearranged. Created anew. Not for nothing he tells himself to learn from the Creator of all how to create poems."[29] For the great Yiddish novelist Chaim Grade, part of Young Vilna himself, Sutzkever "put to himself poetic problems like mathematical problems, and he was delighted when he solved them. . . . It was Sutzkever whom Fate put into the Vilna Ghetto, made him live in Hell and come out alive. . . . [He] saw everything he had believed in and had loved trampled under the German jackboot—and he stood the test, came out unbroken, whole."[30]

He married as World War II broke out and the Russians occupied Vilna. He published a book of poems, "the most exquisite crystal of the Yiddish language and, perhaps, the last Yiddish book printed in Europe before the Holocaust."[31] But the German assault crushed Vilna, and about one hundred thousand of the city's Jews were murdered by systematic shooting and buried in mass graves in the dull suburb of Ponar. Lithuanians, staunch aides of the Nazis, took Sutzkever and the Vilna Rav into the hills—they happened to be arrested on the same day—and made them dig their own graves. The Lithuanians cocked their rifles behind the two men—the intense young secular poet and the old bearded rabbi. Sutzkever recalled, "When they ordered us to put our hands over our eyes, I understood that they were going to shoot us. And I remember as if it were now: when I put my fingers on my eyes, I saw birds fluttering . . . I never saw birds flying so slowly, I had a great aesthetic joy in seeing the slow-slow motion of their wings between my fingers."[32] But the Lithuanians fired over their heads and, having tired of the game, took them back to the ghetto.

Sutzkever wrote and wrote, and he and some literary friends risked their lives to save archived Yiddish manuscripts—they claimed they were burning them to heat their freezing rooms. Once he hid in a coffin to elude passing Germans:

> *Or let it be a boat*
> *On stormy waves.*
> *Let it be a cradle . . .*
> *I still sing my word.*[33]

As the Vilna Jews were relentlessly murdered, Sutzkever lost almost everyone he loved. "I went to see my mother. She told me the glad news that my wife had given birth in the Ghetto Hospital. My mother had forgotten Murer's decree that children born in the ghetto must be killed. The next day the child was gone. . . . Unable to compose myself after this calamity with my child another tragedy followed. I went to my mother's home and my mother was gone." She had been taken to Ponar during the night.

Still, his was an indomitable spirit. The poem to his dead baby gives the boy mystical power:

> You—the seed of my every dream . . .
> who came from the earth's ends
> wondrous as an unseen storm,
> to draw, flood two together
> to shape you in delight:—
>
> Why have you darkened creation,
> why have you shut your eyes
> and left me outside begging
> bound to a world swept with snow. . . .

In this cold world he imagines swallowing the tiny boy to warm him, but demurs:

> I don't deserve to be your grave.
> I will let you slip
> into the beckoning snow,
> the snow—my first holiday,
> and you will sink
> a sunset sliver
> into its still and deep
> and bear my greeting up
> into the frosty shoots of grass.[34]

Even then the Siberian landscape comforted him. In "My Mother," he depicted her praying on Friday night, "quivering in the moonlight on the prayer book." His faith kindled, he wrote, "Your devotion is like the warm challah / you prayerfully feed the doves." Her bullet wounds are roses; she blesses him with her last breath. Then, "The shots clatter. / She falls like a dove on the throne of the sun."[35] In another poem, "The Shoe Wagon," he recognizes her best shoes, the ones she wore only on Shabbes, among the thousands of pairs being carted from Ponar to Germany.[36]

Still, writing sustained him. He referred to the poems as "burnt pearls," still reflecting light, the only thing visible in the ashes. "To a Friend" reads in part,

> *Unbroken friend*
> *on the barbed wire,—*
> *you pressed a bit of bread*
> *to your heart.*
> *Forgive me my hunger*
> *and forgive me my brazen nerve,—*
> *I've bitten through your bread*
> *your bread flecked with blood. . . .*
>
> *Quieted comrade,*
> *I take you in and live . . .*
> *If like you I fall*
> *on the barbed wire—*
> *may someone gulp my word*
> *as I your bread.*[37]

Throughout his life words would be like bread to him, and he would go on recording every meaningful experience. He and his wife, Freydke, joined the underground led by the Jewish hero Abba Kovner—also a great poet, but in Hebrew. They planned a ghetto rebellion, but well-organized opposition from Jewish "leaders" who worked with the Nazis prevented the uprising. Sutzkever and others escaped through the sewers to the forest, and attempted to join the partisans. But the Polish underground was slaughtering Jews in the forests; even in Byelorussia the partisan units disarmed Jews and forced them into menial service roles. Sutzkever's poetry was already known in the Soviet Union, however, and the Soviet-Jewish critic Ilya Ehrenburg had praised it highly.

By coincidence, the president of the Moscow-based Lithuanian government-in-exile had once translated Sutzkever into Lithuanian. He arranged for Sutzkever and Freydke to be allowed to travel to Moscow. Repeatedly shot at by Germans and anti-Semitic partisans, walking through a live minefield strewn with human bodies and animal carcasses, they somehow managed to cross the German lines. After the war they returned to Vilna, where they salvaged Jewish cultural treasures and established a museum. It was later closed by the Soviets, but the Sutzkevers managed to get to Israel in 1947. He fought for Israel's independence and defended it in several wars. He wrote poems about picking blackberries at night with the forest fighters, about his first inspiring encounter with Jerusalem, and about the Negev and Sinai Deserts, as eerily beautiful as the snowscapes of Siberia.

Some of his most beautiful poems are about Africa, which he toured for several months in 1950. The collection, called *Elephants at Night,* opens,

> *All rushing, all sounds sleep.*
> *Terror sleeps under seven streams.*
> *And the elephant sleeps so soundly,*
> *You could cut off his tail. . . .*

Many years later, he was still strangely moved by African echoes:

> *Remembering three flamingos at Lake Victoria*
> *That stay for me unaltered in their splendor:*
> *Three strings taut on a wave, as an arc*
> *Curves over them, the great arc of a rainbow.*
>
> *Fiddle or lyre will not bring forth such music:*
> *Such a three-stringed instrument is not known to be.*
> *Its master had an impulse to test his creation,*
> *To play the living strings with his own hand. . . .*

Yet it is the image in his own mind that fascinates him most:

> *. . . They glisten in their unchanging revelatory pose,*
> *On their unchanging wave, like a pink dawn. . . .*
>
> *Once in a lifetime such a gift is given,*
> *Intended to be seen, and to be heard.*[38]

This was written in the 1960s, and almost forty years later his poetic career has not yet ended. Although Hebrew had by then eclipsed Yiddish as the main Jewish language, the reigning Labor Party had a sense of noblesse oblige and supported Sutzkever's periodical, *Di Goldene Keyt* (The Golden Chain) for half a century. He continued to edit it until 1996. He once said that Yiddish and Hebrew are the two eyes of the Jewish people. It is an apt metaphor; you can see out of one eye, but without depth.

13

SMOKE

HOW THE GERMANS GAVE THE
JEWS GRAVES IN THE AIR

It isn't quite true that 6 million Jews were killed in the Holocaust. One widely accepted estimate is 5,933,900.[1] Approximately. Also approximately, this was 67 percent of the total Jewish population of the twenty-four countries of occupied Europe. So, 5.93 million. It's easy to remember: Five for the Books of the Torah, which was used by the Germans to line shoes and wrap fish; nine for the months of pregnancy, which was punishable by death; three for the triune God the Jews could never accept, fostering nineteen centuries of hatred. Adolf Eichmann, who was in charge of the murder operations, claimed 6 million in some conversations—4 million in the killing centers, 2 million in mass shootings and other operations. In more modest moods he gave the figure as 5 million. As the war ended, he summarized his accomplishments: the feeling of having killed 5 million Jews satisfied him so much that he would laughingly jump into the grave with them.[2]

We associate the Holocaust with gas chambers and ovens. This is reasonable, since 4 million of the 6 million were murdered in this way, and since these killing centers or death camps were a historic step forward in the efficiency and scale of mass murder. Tyrants of old razed cities and slaughtered their inhabitants; Rome did it to the Jews, the Crusaders to the Muslims, and the Asian tyrant Tamerlane to everyone. But they never dreamed of mass murder without blood and gore, thousands of deaths a day for years, in a process that owed more to the automobile assembly line than to the sack and slaughter of ancient towns. These operations were carried out in six centers in Poland, "the collecting points for thousands of transports converging from all directions. In three years the incoming traffic reached a total of close to three million Jews. As the transports turned back empty, their passengers disappeared inside. . . . A man would step off a train in the morning, and in the evening his corpse was burned and his clothes were packed away for shipment to Germany. Such an operation was the product of a great deal of planning."[3] And imagination.

Not that the intention to eliminate the Jews was new. In the late nineteenth century, even as their emancipation progressed and their culture became ever richer and more varied, their enemies began to move against them. Houston Stewart Chamberlain, a British historian writing in German, published *Foundations of the Nineteenth Century* and *Race and Nation,* explaining the fall of nations as a result of the influx of Jews and the rise of nations as a result of getting rid of them.[4] This explicitly racial theory was very influential in Germany and Austria, widely discussed among German students from the time it was first published.[5] It was something quite new. Although there was a racist element to the Inquisition's pursuit of formerly Jewish converts, it was never made explicit; officially it was a search for Secret Jews. Now a respectable intellectual movement began to blame the world's troubles on the racial taint of the Jews, and it did so with all the power of "modern" biology.[6]

This meant that even more than Christian Spain, Germany was beginning to detach its hatred of Jews from its contempt for Judaism. The families of Mendelssohn, Heine, and Marx might call themselves Christian, but German anti-Semitism still called them Jews. By the early twentieth century Germany had a culture of anti-Semitism that was deep, pervasive, "scientific," and in some important circles quite respectable.[7] To be sure, the nearly two millennia of explicitly Christian anti-Semitism paved the way for the Nazi movement, which bottled the old wine of ancient hatred in new bottles; it is not for nothing that the swastika is a kind of twisted cross. But something really new was being added in the form of racial theory.

This occurred in the context of a growing interest in the genetics of behavior and in eugenics throughout the civilized world.[8] Long before Hitler, compulsory sterilization laws were passed by the state legislatures of Pennsylvania, Indiana, New Jersey, Iowa, California, and Washington, providing for the "unsexing" of an impressive range of undesirables.[9] Similar ideas became respectable and established in German academic and medical discourse while Hitler was still a child.[10] By 1920 a distinguished jurist, Karl Binding, and a distinguished psychiatrist, Alfred Hoche, published *The Release and Destruction of Lives Devoid of Value,* advocating large-scale, eugenic euthanasia.

Two years later, when Hitler wrote in *Mein Kampf* ("My Struggle") that he wanted to get rid of the Jews, he was no doubt aware of these "scientific" views.[11] He and those around him were clearly aware of the work of Houston Stewart Chamberlain. Alfred Rosenberg, Hitler's adviser during the early years of the Nazi movement, called Chamberlain's work "the strongest positive impulse in my youth," and prepared excerpts of *Foundations of the Nineteenth Century* for Hitler's easy study.[12] Heinrich Himmler, later the head of the SS and a key figure in all concentration and killing operations, read *Race and Nation* in 1921, and wrote of it in his diary: "It is true and one has the impression that it is objective, not just hate-filled anti-Semitism. Because of this it has more effect. These terrible Jews."[13] It was only a small step to defining the Jews as genetic defectives, as lives devoid of value, as a threat to public health.

In 1933 Hitler came to power with the help of the German army and aristocracy, and began his project. "Alle Zehnjährigen in der Hitlerjugend"— "All Ten-year-olds in the Hitler Youth"—read a poster that year, with the führer gazing over the head of a young blond god. These ten-year-olds would be twenty in 1943. Local pogroms, synagogue burnings, beatings, and murders were encouraged. A boycott of Jewish shops intimidated customers. "The Jews of the whole world are trying to destroy Germany," read posters in every city; "German people, defend yourselves! Don't buy from the Jews!"[14] "Jews not wanted" signs were everywhere. Jewish professors, including Nobel laureates Fritz Haber and Albert Einstein, were driven from universities. Jews who had faithfully served Germany in World War I, including decorated war heroes, were arrested and sent to work camps.

In 1935, the Nuremberg Laws set clear restrictions in national law.[15] Jews were defined racially, marriage and sex between Jews and non-Jews were forbidden, offspring of such unions were defined as *mischlinge,* Jews were forbidden to fly the German flag, and "citizen" was redefined as "a national of German or kindred blood." Protecting the blood of the German people from the Jewish taint was of the essence. The *Times* of London said, "Nothing like the complete disinheritance and segregation of Jewish citizens, now announced, has been heard of since medieval times." Two official English visitors to Germany reported that "German policy is clearly to eliminate the Jew from German life, and the Nazis do not mind how this is accomplished."[16]

Many Germans knew the jingle *"Was er glaubt is einerlei / In der Rasse liegt die Schweinerei"*—"It doesn't matter what his faith / the piggishness is in the race."[17] Now it was law, and centuries of forced apostasy ended; religion didn't matter. The public health apparatus of the Reich devoted enormous resources to "racial hygiene," a program of total apartheid and cradle-to-grave education about the genetic inferiority of Jews. This occurred in the context of growing interest in euthanasia for the mentally retarded and other people deemed genetically defective. This was not politics, it was public health; German physicians were the earliest, most numerous, and strongest professional backers of Hitler.[18]

In 1938, Germany annexed Austria and was welcomed with open arms. Elderly Viennese Jews, especially doctors, lawyers, and merchants, were publicly humiliated. "The SS sentries threw out the Chief Rabbi . . . a man of seventy, and he . . . was ordered to brush these pavements. . . . he was thrown out wearing his gown, and with his prayer shawl on."[19] Others were made to put on tefillin and wash unflushed toilets. In September four nations signed the Munich Pact, ceding Czechoslovakian territory to Hitler in a move now synonymous with appeasement. In November an enraged young Jew shot a German official in Paris, and when he died the next day a vast and vicious pogrom engulfed the Reich—Kristallnacht, it was called, but more than glass was broken.[20] Torah scrolls and prayer books, along with secular history, philosophy, and literature, burned in large bonfires in Jewish neighborhoods. Jews were chased, humiliated, and beaten by the thousands. Ninety-one were killed in the street.

In Baden-Baden, Jews were forced to read aloud from *Mein Kampf* on the synagogue steps and beaten if their enthusiasm flagged, while others had to urinate on the walls; in an hour the building was in flames. In the village of Hoengen, the storm troopers who razed the synagogue were cheered by an eager civilian mob. Three men smashed the Holy Ark and threw the Torahs out the front door. "The people caught the Scrolls as if they were amusing themselves with a ball-game—tossing them up into the air again, while other people flung them further back until they reached the street outside. Women tore away the red and blue velvet and everybody tried to snatch some of the silver adornments."[21]

These are just a few examples of the countless similar incidents that took place on one night of centrally planned actions. After the riots, the Jewish community was fined a billion marks to pay for the damage; 20 percent of each person's property was seized. German-Jewish children were barred from German schools. Over thirty thousand, 10 percent of the Jews in Germany, went to concentration camps.

On September 1, 1939, after years of preparation, posturing, bullying, and expansion, the Germans invaded Poland, starting World War II and trapping three million Jews. In November a Polish policeman was shot by a Warsaw Jew, and in reprisal all fifty-three males in his building were executed. Evacuation and forced marches of large numbers of Jews during the Polish campaign were simplified by mass murders. Of 1,800 Jews who were driven out of Hrubieszow, for instance, 1,400 were shot to death. But efficiency was not always a prime consideration. Diaries kept by Jews in Lodz recorded that German soldiers forced Jewish girls to clean latrines with the blouses they were wearing and then wrapped the excrement-soiled blouses around their faces; that a rabbi was told to spit on the Torah or die, and when he had no more saliva the soldier spat in the rabbi's mouth so he could resume spitting; and that German soldiers held entertainments where Jewish couples were made to strip naked and dance to phonograph tunes.

However, those in authority knew there was a real problem to be solved. Hans Frank, governor of Central Poland, wrote in *his* diary that the Jews were "extraordinarily malignant gluttons. We have now approximately 2,500,000 of them . . . and counting half-Jews, perhaps 3,500,000. We cannot shoot 2,500,000 Jews, neither can we poison them. We shall have to take steps, however, designed to extirpate them in some way—and this will be done."[22] Frank lacked imagination, but others were more creative. In the spring of 1940, German forces occupied Norway, Denmark, Belgium, the Netherlands, and France. At this time deportation without murder was still an option; on May 19, Himmler sent Hitler "some thoughts" on this: "I hope that, through the possibility of large-scale emigration of all Jews to Africa or some other colony, the concept of the Jew will have completely disappeared from Europe."[23]

Of course, no one wanted them.[24] Severe restrictions on immigration had been in place in the United States for fifteen years, and other nations had followed the American example. By the late 1930s large numbers of Jews desperately attempted to leave Europe, and this intensified as German hegemony expanded. They were rejected almost everywhere. In one decisive episode in 1939, 1,128 Jewish refugees on a ship called the *St. Louis* attempted to land at various ports in the United States and the Caribbean; almost all were sent back across the Atlantic, and most would in time be murdered.[25]

In June 1941, the Germans invaded the Soviet Union, which would be their undoing but also that of the Jews. From the outset, special killing squads set about murdering very large numbers of Jews. On the first day of the invasion, in the border town of Virbalis, an eyewitness recalled, Jews "were placed alive in anti-tank trenches about two kilometers long and killed by machine guns. Lime was thereupon sprayed upon them and a second row of Jews was made to lie down. They were similarly shot." Seven times, lines of Jews were forced into the trench. "Only the children were not shot. They were caught by their legs, their heads hit against stones and they were thereupon buried alive."[26]

No wasted bullets. This was manageable and the scale was effective, but more was needed. Throughout the East, Germans could rely upon vicious, ancient hatreds to enlist local people, Lithuanians, Latvians, Ukrainians, Poles, and others, making mass murder faster and easier. Whole Jewish communities could be wiped out in a day without the involvement of Nazi soldiers. In the village of Lubiaz, Ukraine, a Jewish group arriving to protect the most vulnerable "found the bodies of twenty children, women, and men without heads, bellies ripped open, legs and arms hacked off."[27] In Jedwabne, Poland, the entire Jewish community was herded into barns and other buildings and burned to death by their Polish neighbors.[28] In nearby Bialystok, eight hundred Jews were locked in the Great Synagogue before it was burned to the ground. In Kishinev, Russia, famed for the murder of around fifty Jews in 1903, German police units and their collaborators now murdered twenty times that number in fourteen days. In Zhitomir, 2,500 were murdered, as observed by a Major Rosler, who commanded the regular German troops there: "I saw nothing like it either in the First World War or during the Civil War in Russia or during the Western campaign. I have seen many unpleasant things . . . but I never saw anything like this." A Polish journalist in Ponar, outside Vilna, Lithuania, kept a diary:

> 1941. July 27, Sunday. Shooting is carried on nearly everyday. Will it go on for ever? . . . People say that about five thousand persons have been killed in the course of this month. It is quite possible, for about two to three hundred people are being driven up here nearly every day. And nobody ever returns. . . .
> 1942. July 30, Friday. About one hundred and fifty persons shot. Most of them were elderly people. The executioners complained about being very tired of their "work," of having aching shoulders from shooting. That is the reason for not finishing the wounded off, so that they are buried half alive.
> August 2, Monday. Shooting of big batches has started once again. Today about four thousand people were driven up . . . shot by eighty executioners. All drunk . . .[29]

In this way, *before* the gas chambers, hundreds of Jewish communities were completely destroyed, and all their inhabitants murdered.

These mass murders by gunshot also continued after the gas chambers were operative, and they were done not just by specially trained SS or Gestapo killers but by ordinary Germans. One well-studied unit was a Reserve Police Battalion made up largely of middle-aged family men—workers, artisans, salesmen, clerks—considered too old for combat service. Without any form of coercion, indeed with a certain amount of enthusiasm, these 500 men murdered about 38,000 Jews by shooting and rounded up 45,000 more for shipment to the killing center at Treblinka.[30]

In May 1941, Field Marshal Hermann Göring informed all German consulates in occupied Europe that Jewish emigration was banned, and made the first reference to the "doubtless imminent final solution"—*Endlösung*—of the Jewish question. In Kalisz, Poland, in October, an ingenious new method was devised to murder Jews on transports. First used on feeble hospital patients, it entailed placing the victims onto a hermetically sealed truck whose exhaust was fed into their cabin through a specially designed pipe. Much ammunition was saved as thousands died on their way to mass graves. Under Hitler's orders, trainloads of Jews from western Europe began moving eastward, and the fates of sophisticated German Jews mingled with those of their traditional eastern brethren. Wherever Gypsies were found, they too were murdered.[31]

Also in the fall of 1941, a German expert who had devised methods for murdering the sick and feebleminded began to design large-scale chambers to administer poison gas. In January 1942, about six weeks after Pearl Harbor, the highest officials of the Reich met in the Berlin suburb Wannsee for a "Plenipotentiary for the Preparation of the Final Solution of the European Jewish Question."[32] It dealt with not only the Jews already under German rule, but all eleven million Jews in Europe, discussed country by country with precision. Yet there was no mention of the forty thousand Jews and Gypsies who had been murdered by gassing in Chelmno alone during the previous six weeks.

The nature of the solution was not preserved in the notes, except indirectly: "Separated by sex, the Jews capable of work will be led into these areas in large labor columns to build roads, whereby doubtless a large part will fall away through natural reduction. The inevitable final remainder which doubtless constitutes the toughest element will have to be dealt with appropriately, since it represents a natural selection which upon liberation is to be regarded as a germ cell of a new Jewish development." The notes said too that "In the course of the practical implementation of the final solution, Europe will be combed from West to East." Construction of the gas chambers had already begun. Ten days later, in a speech to one of his huge, adoring audiences of ordinary Germans, Hitler said clearly, "The result of this war will be the complete annihilation of the Jews."

By late spring, five centers for assembly-line mass murder had been built in Poland, ready to process thousands of people a day. The largest, at Auschwitz-Birkenau, was described by historian Raul Hilberg:

> Originally it had been intended to build crematoria with two furnaces in Birkenau, but . . . five-furnace installations were decided upon. Eventually, two such units were constructed, each containing an underground gas chamber called a *Leichenkeller* (corpse cellar), complete with an electric elevator for hauling up the bodies. Two more units were built, as an economy measure, with two furnaces each and a gas chamber called a *Badeanstalt* (bath house) at the surface. The Leichenkeller were very large (250 square yards), and 2,000 persons could be packed into each of them. The Badeanstalten were somewhat smaller. The hydrogen cyanide, solidified in pellets, was shaken into the Leichenkeller through shafts, into the Badeanstalten through side walls. In the gas chamber the material immediately passed into the gaseous state.[33]

With this simple method the Germans would murder four million Jews in Auschwitz, Treblinka, Majdanek, Belzec, Chelmno, and Sobibor.

But conveying the Auschwitz *experience* demands a different kind of description. Among the most powerful is Elie Wiesel's, in his autobiographical novel, *Night*.[34] He and his family have just left all they owned behind on the train as they stepped off at Auschwitz, and with their belongings, "our illusions. Every two yards or so an SS man held his tommy gun trained on us. Hand in hand we followed the crowd." Then they heard the command, "Men to the left! Women to the right!" from another SS man. He watched his mother and sisters until they disappeared. "My mother was stroking my sister's fair hair, as though to protect her." He went on walking, holding his father's hand. An old man fell behind him, shot by a German soldier. The boy clung to his father's hand, and a Jewish prisoner helping to process the new arrivals asked him his age.

> "I'm not quite fifteen yet."
> "No. Eighteen."
> "But I'm not," I said. "Fifteen."
> "Fool. Listen to what *I* say."

To the same question his father replied, "Fifty," which enraged the man. "No, not fifty. Forty. Do you understand? Eighteen and forty." Another Jewish helper in a more vicious mood said, "You'd have done better to have hanged yourselves where you were than to come here. Didn't you know what was in store for you at Auschwitz? In 1944?" They explained that they had not heard. The reply was almost hysterical:

> "Do you see that chimney over there? See it? Do you see those flames? . . . That's your grave. . . . You dumb bastards, don't you understand anything? You're going to be burned. Frizzled away. Turned into ashes."

A murmur of revolt arose. "We can't go like beasts to the slaughter," someone said. A young man cried, "Let the world learn of the existence of Auschwitz. Let everybody hear about it, while they can still escape." But older, if not wiser, heads prevailed: "You must never lose faith, even when the sword hangs over your head. That's the teaching of our sages."

They marched toward the square. "In the middle stood the notorious Dr. Mengele (a typical SS officer: a cruel face, but not devoid of intelligence, and wearing a monocle); a conductor's baton in his hand, he was standing among other officers. The baton moved unremittingly, sometimes to the right, sometimes to the left."

Mengele asked his age, in an almost paternal tone. He lied as instructed, and also wisely said that he was a farmer instead of a student. The baton directed him to the left, but he first checked to see what would happen to his father. Although they did not know whether right or left was better, he was relieved that they were sent to the same place.

Yet another prisoner told them they were destined for cremation. They were now nearing a ditch ablaze with great flames. A truckload of small children's corpses was delivered into the flames; nearby was another ditch where adults were burned. His father said that it was "a shame that you couldn't have gone with your mother. . . . I saw several boys your age going with their mothers."

The boy reasoned that it could not be true, that humanity would not permit such cruelty in the modern age. His father replied, "'Humanity? Humanity is not concerned with us. Today anything is allowed. Anything is possible, even these crematories . . .' His voice was choking." He told his father that he would throw himself on the wire and be electrocuted rather than die slowly in the flames. His father did not answer, but began weeping and shaking convulsively. Someone was saying kaddish, the prayer that hallows God at the time of death, and his father joined in a whisper. But the son refused to bless God's name. What, he asked himself, did he have to thank God for? The flaming pit was upon them.

The boy stiffened his resolve, planning to throw himself onto the barbed wire. He silently bid his father and the world good-bye, and found himself whispering the Kaddish against his will: *Yisgadal v'yiskadash sh'mei rabba. . . . May his great name be magnified and sanctified.* He felt that his heart was bursting, that he was "face to face with the Angel of Death." Somehow, something held him back. For the time being at least, he was sent to work, not to burn.

This was a single share of the Holocaust, one boy's experience. Like many important Nazi mass murderers, Mengele would live out his normal life span in safe obscurity. Wiesel's faith failed that night, but his life did not end. His gentle mother and fair-haired sister were murdered that first day. His father was dead from slave labor, illness, and beatings—or at least close to death—a few months later when he was thrown into the ovens. But the son would live, against all odds, to tell the world what had happened there. He would write wise and moving books, fighting for life and peace as his enemies had fought for death and slaughter. And one day, half a century later, he would speak boldly to a president of the United States, teaching him the nature of remembrance.

☙〰️❧

To see how the murderous campaign intersected with traditional Jewish life, read *responsa*. These letters from respected rabbis answer questions about halakhah—the Law, the Way. In a sense the Talmud itself was provoked by such questions, but since the great sages could not live forever, lesser ones had to do the best they could. Never were they more challenged than during the Nazi period. A bloody tide was drowning the Jews of Europe, but rabbis still answered questions every day. One of those called upon was Rabbi Ephraim Oshry of Lithuania, who buried his notes in tin cans in the ghetto, retrieved them after the war, and published five volumes of *responsa*.

The first came during the initial roundups and clumsy killing actions in June 1941. A sixteen-year-old boy had survived, hidden by a non-Jewish maid, after both his parents were murdered on one day. As time passed, his brave benefactor became afraid for both their lives and brought him to a priest, who offered to protect him on condition of baptism. But no matter how safe he now was, the boy could not find peace of mind. "Before his eyes he kept seeing the horrors of the murders of his father and his mother . . . even at night his pain did not abate; how could he sleep when he knew that his people were suffering . . . ?"

The boy gathered his courage, left his safe gentile haven, and went back to the Kovno ghetto to share the Jewish fate. Ultimately the boy regretted his baptism and returned to the God of Israel with all his heart. There were three questions. "First: was it permissible to include this boy in a *minyan* of ten? Second: Since the boy was a *kohein,* might he be called to the Torah to the *kohein*'s reading? Third: could he raise his hands in benediction in the tradition of his forefathers?" The boy was, by family tradition, a descendant of the high priests of the ancient Temple, entitled to be called to the Torah first and on occasion to bless the congregation. The rabbi reasoned that the boy was compelled to convert; he said yes to all three questions. Three years later the ghetto was liquidated, and the boy was sent to a death camp. "May G-d recall him along with the rest of the righteous," Rabbi Oshry writes, "when He avenges the blood of His martyred servants."[35]

This was only the beginning. The questions poured in, and every one of them was painful and, in modern times, unprecedented. Rabbi Oshry recorded them faithfully.

> **Question:** On 4 Elul 5701—August 21, 1941—the Germans captured stray dogs and cats and brought them into . . . a house of study in Slobodka . . . where they shot them to death. . . . They proceeded to force a number of Jews to rip apart a Torah scroll with their own hands and to use the sheets of parchment to cover the carcasses of the shot animals.

If a Torah is even dropped in a service, the whole congregation fasts. The rabbi was asked to arrange a program of penitence.

> **Response:** Those who saw the scroll being torn were obligated to rend their garments. . . . Those who were forced to rend the Torah

scroll with their own hands were obligated to fast, even though they had been forced to act at gunpoint. . . . But if they could not fast because of physical weakness due to the hunger and the other sufferings they bore daily in the ghetto, one could not obligate them to fast.[36]

Some time later a thousand men were taken daily to work on an airfield as slave laborers. "One of my students, Reb Yaakov—may G-d avenge his death . . . had the opportunity to work in the kitchen where they cooked the black soup that the Germans supplied the Jewish laborers," but "he would be compelled to work on Shaboss (the Sabbath)." Also, could he eat the soup that he himself had cooked in violation of the Sabbath? . . . I ruled that he was allowed to cook on Shaboss, because the alternative of slave labor in the airfield on Shaboss was no less a desecration. . . . In neither case would he be desecrating the Sabbath willfully. . . . I allowed him to eat the black soup . . . because it is not forbidden to eat the product of Shaboss labor where one eats it to preserve life."[37] The careful reasoning process he applied to these heartrending questions has characterized *responsa* for two thousand years. And there were so many more.

He ruled that a cracked shofar could be blown on Rosh Hashanah if none other was available.

He ruled that critically ill patients were forbidden to fast on Yom Kippur.

He ruled that a sukkah could be built with boards stolen from the Germans, and that *tzitzis,* ritual fringes, could be made from stolen wool.

He ruled that "learning Torah with Nazi murderers" was permissible when they demanded explanations of the Talmud.

He ruled that the garments of martyrs could be worn by survivors.

He ruled that a man the Germans had beaten deaf and dumb could be counted in a minyan, although a deaf-mute is not supposed to be counted. How, though, could the man be called to the Torah? "To uplift his shattered spirit, I suggested that he be called to the Torah together with the reader and, while the reader recited the blessings, that he concentrate on each word. When he read my ruling, his eyes lit up and he wrote, 'Rabbi, you have revived me. May G-d console you and grant you life!'"[38]

He ruled that contraception and abortion were permissible in the ghetto, since pregnancy was punished by death.

He ruled that under extreme constraint one could eat in the presence of a corpse.

He ruled that the daily blessing thanking God "who has not made me a slave" could be recited by slave laborers because the freedom meant was spiritual, not physical.

He ruled that a minyan could be made up of men in hiding who could hear but not see one another.

He ruled that the risk of putting a mezuzah on the doorpost of a ghetto home need not be taken, because the dwellings were temporary.

He ruled that a man whose left arm had been cut off for stealing food could have someone else put tefillin on his right arm.

He ruled that a ghetto prisoner could risk death attempting to join the partisans in the forest.

He ruled that the leaders of the ghetto could make selections in an effort to save a few Jews from the Nazi murder machine.

He ruled that a *kohein* whose testicles had been deliberately crushed—German police had caught him with a crust of bread hidden behind them to take to his starving family—could no longer have sex with his wife, but could still be called to the Torah as the descendant of priests.

He ruled that a Jew could not have a baptismal certificate, even to save his life.

He ruled that children at risk of liquidation could be handed over to non-Jews for care until after the war, even though there was a risk that they would become Christian, but that infants could not be given to priests.

He ruled that a young man from a totally assimilated family—"All their assimilation was to no avail"—who decided to return to the faith of his ancestors could be circumcised by a doctor who didn't keep the Sabbath.

A boy asked him if he might be permitted to don tefillin, although his Bar Mitzvah was three months away, since there was a good chance that the Germans would murder him before that time. "Tears gushed from my eyes. . . . I ruled that that precious child who had such a great desire to merit the privilege of fulfilling this mitzvah because he feared that he might not live to fulfill it if he waited to reach 13, certainly had authorization."[39]

Question: On 6 Marcheshvan 5702—October 27, 1941—two days before the horrifying Black Day of the Kovno Ghetto—when some 10,000 men, women, and children were taken away to be butchered—every one of the ghetto dwellers saw his bitter end coming. At that time of confusion, one of the respected members of the community came to me with tears on his cheeks. . . . He felt that he could not bear to see his wife, children, and grandchildren put to death before his very eyes. For the German sadists . . . would kill the children before the eyes of their parents and the women before the eyes of their husbands. . . . [H]e asked whether he might terminate his own life earlier so as to avoid witnessing the deaths of his loved ones. . . .

Response: Although the man knew he would definitely be subjected to unbearable suffering . . . he still was not allowed to commit suicide. . . . Suicide was viewed as a great desecration of G-d, for it showed that a person had no trust in G-d's capability to save him. . . .

I cite proudly that in the Kovno Ghetto there were only three instances of suicide. . . . The rest of the ghetto dwellers trusted and hoped that G-d would not forsake His People.[40]

Two days later the rabbi himself was among thirty thousand Jews herded into the central plaza for the selections that would take away a third of them. A man asked him, "What is the precise text of the *berocha* [blessing] that sanctifiers of G-d must recite before being put to death?" The man then proposed two alternatives. "He wished to know precisely which text to use to fulfill what might turn out to be the last mitzvah of his life. Besides he wished to tell as many people as possible what blessing to recite if their turn came to die." The rabbi ruled that "the proper blessing was neither of the texts he had mentioned, but . . . '*asher kideshonu bemitzvosov vetzivonu lekadeish shemo borabim,*' the very text that I intended to recite. Reb Eliyahu repeated the text several times, then proceeded to inform other Jews as to its exact phrasing so that they should be prepared when and if their time came to die."[41] The text blesses God "who has sanctified us by thy commandments and commanded us to sanctify his name before many people."

But Rabbi Oshry was spared, to have his ears assaulted by many more questions. Moshe Goldkorn—"may G-d avenge him"—was smuggling flour into the ghetto for Passover: "The flour was hidden in a secret place guarded very carefully so that no harm would come to it. Bit by bit, Goldkorn smuggled in enough flour to bake matzos for nearly 100 Jews, each of whom would receive one olive-sized piece of *matza*. . . . But the happiest of all was Goldkorn, for he had merited the privilege of bringing the flour in." Two days before Passover the German police caught him with a small bag of flour and beat him savagely, breaking most of his teeth, among other injuries. Goldkorn came to the rabbi. "As he spoke, he broke into tears. 'With my broken teeth, how can I fulfill the mitzvah of eating [at least] an olive-sized piece of *matza?*'" He thought the law forbade eating soaked matza, the only kind he could now eat. But the rabbi ruled that the tradition of not eating soaked matza was "a stringency"—a custom beyond the law; Goldkorn ate matza in spite of his broken teeth.[42]

Question: On 20 Iyar 5702—May 8, 1942—the Germans issued the following edict: Every Jewish woman found pregnant will be put to death. That very day a pregnant Jewish woman passed by the ghetto hospital. A German noticed her belly and shot her for violating the German order against reproduction. His bullet penetrated her heart and she fell dead on the spot.

The woman was in the last weeks of pregnancy, and since the rabbi was present and the hospital nearby, he was asked if a cesarean section could be done. The concern was that if the baby was dead the surgery would be a desecration of the mother's body.

> **Response:** It was clear to me that when a doctor who knows his medicine rushes to operate minutes after a woman's death, declaring that the baby can be saved, one must listen to him. . . . To our great sorrow, our hopes were shattered.

Some Germans appeared with their usual diligence to record the name of the murdered woman. "When they found the baby alive their savage fury was unleashed. One of the Germans grabbed the infant and cracked its skull against the wall of the hospital room."[43] This was not unusual. On March 27 and 28, 1944, the Germans carried out the mass murder of the remaining children "by butchering some 1,200 children and infants whom they tore from their mothers' bosoms and shot and burned." The rabbi was asked by the parents if they should say kaddish for their children, and he ruled that this was necessary for any over thirty days of age.

The war ended but the questions did not.

He ruled that a mercy killer who had responded to the request of a suffering fellow Jew was permitted to lead prayers.

He ruled that a scribe who had lived as a Catholic could return to his craft of copying Torah scrolls.

He ruled that gold from the teeth of the dead could not be used.

He ruled that a man whose parents were buried in a cemetery that had been destroyed and plowed under could put up a stone with their names, saying that their graves were somewhere nearby.

He ruled that a woman forced into sexual slavery and tattooed with "Prostitute for Hitler's soldiers" could live with her husband as man and wife, but that she should not remove the tattoo. "On the contrary," he wrote, "let her and her sisters preserve their tattoos and regard them not as signs of shame, but as signs of honor, pride, and courage—proof of what they suffered for the sanctification of G-d."[44]

He ruled that a woman should not remove the concentration-camp number tattooed on her arm, "for by doing so she is fulfilling the wishes of the accursed German evildoers and abetting their effort to have the Holocaust forgotten."[45]

One orphaned boy had not been through the ceremony of the redemption of the firstborn, and now, at thirteen, he wanted to know if he could redeem himself. The rabbi ruled that he could do it after finishing puberty.

A man came to him and explained that his parents, brothers, and sisters had all been killed by the Lithuanian janitor of the apartment house in which they had lived. He wanted to know if he was obligated to find the man and bring him to justice, "a problem faced by many people." The rabbi instructed the man "to make every possible effort to avenge the murder of his family. Several weeks later he returned and told me that he had thrown a hand grenade into the janitor's house, killing him." The rabbi advised him to leave the country.

A gentile woman who had saved a Jewish child and returned him to his relatives fell ill and asked for the Jewish prayer for the sick. The rabbi ruled that this was certainly permissible. Another non-Jewish woman who had saved many Jews died shortly after the liberation, and the Jews she had helped wanted to say kaddish for her. "Not only is it permissible to say *Kaddish* with her in mind, it is a *mitzvah* to do so. May He Who grants bounty to the Jewish people grant bounty to all the generous non-Jews who endangered themselves to save Jews."[46]

A man who had been a Jewish policeman working with the Germans was about to become a cantor. "I ruled that this man was not to be appointed a cantor. . . . everyone knew how he had cursed and beaten his fellow-Jews. No matter how much penance he might claim to have done, he was not to be appointed to any communal position."[47]

A man who had seen an old rabbi forced to burn a Torah decided to keep his own from desecration by letting it sink in the river, but after the war he could not find the place. Did he need to atone for his deed? No, he had acted to preserve the Torah's holiness, but he should donate money for the purchase of another.

In all, the Germans burned some five hundred Torahs in Kovno and nearby towns. "Woe unto the eyes that saw a major Jewish city . . . once filled with sages and scholars, synagogues and study halls, now bereft of Torah! . . . we saw with our own eyes how the non-Jews defiled the Torah scrolls. Many of them ripped the sacred sheets of parchment and turned them into shoes. Torah! Torah! Don sackcloth and mourn your beauty which has been trampled into the earth!"[48]

⟨✿⟩

Although they were few compared to the acts of cruelty, a speck in the vast sea of apathy, some survived, in part through acts of courage and generosity by non-Jews.[49] One man said his survival was "a succession of miracles" and that too rings true.[50] If a handful of people escape a systematic process of mass murder that kills six million, their survival can only have been the result of a succession of improbable events, and their stories will seem hard to believe for that reason. They had been torn out of their lives and could not return to them. The reaction of the handful of survivors from Rhodes upon returning there was typical: "Though still a Paradise in the Aegean Sea, with its vineyards, roses, rolling hills, crystal blue sea, and familiar alleys and courtyards, Rhodes had been drained of Jewish blood. The life was gone. What the shattered souls of the Nazi death camps found was a war-ravaged *judería* whose houses and streets belonged to strangers."[51]

Many said that survival depended on an act of will, an impulse to stay alive to bear witness, to tell their story. Yet most did not tell it for many years. Life took them out of that hell into new worlds, and if they could not keep the memories out of their minds or their dreams, at least they could refuse to succumb, they could keep trying to drive them out with family, joy, work, art, and love. As Viennese survivor Ruth Beker poignantly wrote,

> *Don't.*
> *Don't show me any more pictures*
> *I don't want to know*
> *about children in horse carts*
> *about men in cattle cars*
> *about women being taken away*
> *about mass goodbyes, unearthly cries . . .*
>
> *No. My grandparents were not murdered.*
> *No. My parents were not slaves.*
> *No. My arm has no number . . .*
>
> *Don't show me any more.*
> *Don't tell me any more.*
> *Don't.*[52]

In any case the world did not have much interest. But when a certain number of years had passed and the world did want to hear it, many of them were at last persuaded to tell.[53]

After decades of neglect, the story of the *Shoah*—Hebrew for the Holocaust, and the preferable term—now crowds in on many other Jewish stories.[54] Some Jews study the Holocaust instead of the Torah, discuss the details of mass murder at what should be joyous occasions, visit Auschwitz instead of Israel, and neglect the three-thousand-year saga of their people in favor of twelve years of German terror. Yet it is understandable for a people with the smell of burning human flesh fresh in their nostrils to dwell on the worst of their stories, and, more important, to try to give the destruction meaning.

Recall that Elie Wiesel had come to question God's existence during his stay at Auschwitz. In 1966 the Jewish theologian Richard Rubenstein went

further, finding in the Shoah decisive evidence that God does not participate in human history; to believe otherwise, he argued, one had to think
that Hitler was part of God's divine plan and that the Jews were being punished for their sins.[55] This indeed was the viewpoint of some Orthodox rabbis, who saw it as punishment for secularism and Zionism. For others, the
Shoah was more proof, if indeed proof were needed, that God is not omnipotent, and that God wept along with all decent people in the face of this
ultimate catastrophe.

In an extraordinary attempt to keep God in history while rejecting the
notion that the Holocaust could be a just punishment for anything, Rabbi
David Blumenthal finds in the Jewish mystical tradition an angry, dangerous, even evil part of God, an attribute capable of unmitigated destructive-
ness. In *Facing the Abusing God,* Blumenthal sees the Shoah not as appropriate
but grotesquely exaggerated punishment.[56] Just as an abusive parent's anger
can be out of all proportion to the child's infraction, the sins of erring humanity tipped the balance of God's attributes, triggering the destructive
part and bringing about the worst catastrophe in Jewish history.

It is "a theology of protest and suspicion . . . distrust and challenge."[57]
He sees this as the only remaining viable theology: "To have faith in a post-
holocaust, abuse-sensitive world is, first, to know—to recognize and to ad-
mit—that God is an abusing God, but not always."[58] This is Blumenthal's
unsettling, innovative theology, but "[t]heology is not real unless one can
pray it."[59] So he invents new prayers that can burst out of the heart of a child
who still loves his abusive parent passionately, but who is also angry and
confused.

> May God, Who is our Father and our King,
>   Who injures, destroys, and harms beyond reason,
>   Who also loves graciously, and is compassionate, and cares . . .
> May God share with you His anguish and His shame at His own hateful
>   actions.
> May God bless you, and may you receive His blessing.[60]

A more widely accepted theological consequence of the Shoah is Emil
Fackenheim's 614th commandment.[61] To the 613 mitzvot counted by the
rabbis, Fackenheim added one: Thou shalt not grant Hitler a posthumous
victory. This commandment put peoplehood in the limelight of Jewish
Law, joining religious and secular Jews in a new way. The Jewish people
must survive, in defiance of Hitler's dream. Part of the obligation of this
commandment rests with Holocaust remembrance, but it can go too far.
We can read only so many books, go to so many lectures and seminars. Of
those that have Jewish content, what percentage should be about the
Shoah? Ten? Fifty? At what age should children be taught about these

horrific events? Current practice in Jewish schools introduces them so early that the child cannot really respond to them. This is far from the concern that the child will be traumatized. If the child cannot respond and later feels that she already knows all about it, the impact of remembrance is lost.[62]

But in general, how much should the Shoah be allowed to pervade Jewish life?

A poignant episode: Cantor Isaac Goodfriend—a man with a huge, brilliant bass voice who has sung for seven consecutive American presidents—is the most prominent Holocaust survivor in Atlanta. The large synagogue where he served decided to "twin" Bar and Bat Mitzvahs with Holocaust child victims. That is, the name of a murdered child who never got to have a Bar Mitzvah would be prominently announced at the current occasion. Cantor Goodfriend and his wife, also a survivor, spoke vehemently against this practice, decrying it as an intrusion of victimization and murder into a joyous celebration. These survivors, who had worked throughout their lives on behalf of remembrance, drew a line in the sand. Jewish celebrations, they said, should be free of these terrible memories. Too much Holocaust memory would also grant Hitler a posthumous victory.

But at the other extreme there is, in historian Deborah Lipstadt's words, a "growing assault on truth and memory." Her book on Holocaust denial is chilling to read; it details the efforts of those—including some "respectable" historians—who deny that there were gas chambers, claim that no more than a few thousand Jews were killed, and argue that their fate was no different from those of other ethnic groups throughout the war.[63] Lipstadt was sued by one of the worst offenders, who denied denying the Holocaust and accused her of libeling him. The trial in England, where libel is broadly defined, required Lipstadt to prove that the Holocaust happened. She won, but it cost her years of effort and the Jewish community at least $2 million. What will happen when the last survivor dies?

Simon Wiesenthal, and later Serge and Berta Klarsfeld, have devoted their lives to preserving truth and memory quite differently: bringing Nazi criminals to justice. Poring through archives, knocking on doors, asking questions, they brought hundreds of Nazis to trial and punishment, including Adolf Eichmann, Klaus Barbie, and the SS man who arrested Anne Frank. To understand the character and purpose of this work, consider this episode.

One of the men brought to trial by Wiesenthal was Franz Murer, who had managed the murder of eighty thousand Lithuanian Jews. Murer spent seven years in a Soviet prison, but then was released in an international agreement. Free in Germany for eight years after that, he was finally tried for his crimes, which, however difficult to measure, were certainly worth more than seven years in prison. Wiesenthal attended the trial, and one of the witnesses was Jakob Brodi. Before his testimony, he asked Wiesenthal if it was true that Murer's sons sat in the front row of the courtroom and sneered at the witnesses. It was.

> Brodi said quietly: "They'll stop sneering when I am called to the stand." . . . He opened his waistcoat and pulled out a long knife. . . . "I know that the witness stand is close to where Murer sits. Murer killed my child before my eyes. Now I'm going to kill him before the eyes of his wife and children."

Wiesenthal invoked every conceivable argument to dissuade him, but "Brodi shook his head. 'I am not here for the State of Israel. I am not here for the Jewish people. I am here as the father of my murdered child.' He stared at me out of hard, pitiless eyes." Finally they talked about that child, and then, "I grasped his shoulders. Suddenly Jakob Brodi put his head on my shoulder. I felt a convulsion go through his body. He cried. We stood there for a while, without saying a word. When I left his room a few minutes later, I carried his knife with me." Murer was acquitted. "I met Jakob Brodi in the lobby of a Vienna hotel a few days after Murer's acquittal. He looked through me as if I hadn't been there. I understood. I may have saved Murer's life. It is not a very pleasant thought, but there was nothing else I could have done."[64] As Wiesenthal at eighty summed up his life's work: Justice, not vengeance.[65]

☙※❧

And, of course, there is a Holocaust art. The paintings of Charlotte Salomon, the drawings of Bruno Schulz, the music of the partisans, and the stories of Tadeusz Borowski—*This Way for the Gas, Ladies and Gentlemen* was one of his searingly ironic titles—take their place beside countless expressions of ordinary Jews and other victims in almost every art form known to human creativity.[66] In Theresienstadt, a relatively benign concentration camp that the Nazis built to persuade the world that they weren't monsters, inmates of all ages were encouraged to write, paint, and play and compose music.[67] One boy, Pavel Friedmann, wrote,

> *The last, the very last,*
> *So richly, brightly, dazzlingly yellow.*
> *Perhaps if the sun's tears would sing*
> *against a white stone . . .*
> *. . . Only I never saw another butterfly . . .*[68]

In Auschwitz, where a drawing or a poem might be punished by immediate death, artistic expression—scratched on concrete walls, scribbled on scraps of newspaper and buried, sung in secret gatherings in the dark—still flowed. Children invented and played evocative games dramatizing their plight and mocking their tormentors literally up to the doors of the gas chambers.[69]

Many poems were written in Jewish languages during and after the war. Avraham Sutzkever's *Burnt Pearls* stands out as a masterpiece, but there were many other Yiddish poems of lasting value. Abba Kovner—as we will see in the next chapter a great resistance hero—wrote his poetic account in Hebrew. Violette Mayo Fintz and her sister Sara Menasche, two of about sixty thousand Jews deported to death camps from the island of Rhodes, described their experience in their native Judeo-Spanish. "La vida de los Djudios en 1944" reads in part, "At Auschwitz battered we arrived / The roll calls kept increasing." . . .

> *Weeping night and day,*
> *Shouting constantly, "Mother dear!"*
> *We were told and assured,*
> *That they were consumed in the fire.*[70]

But the two most famous writers of the Holocaust did not write in the languages of the Jews. Primo Levi and Paul Celan were both victims and, for a time, survivors. Each was a literary master trapped in a language of Fascists that echoed endlessly with the mass murder of Jews. Each escaped to write beautifully in that language. Each lived many years after the flames died down, surviving largely through the sustaining power of his writing. And each in the end took his own life.

Primo Levi began his book *Survival in Auschwitz* with the almost scientific distance and calm that characterized his prose:

> It was my good fortune to be deported to Auschwitz only in 1944, that is, after the German Government had decided, owing to the growing scarcity of labour, to lengthen the average life-span of the prisoners destined for elimination; it conceded noticeable improvements in the camp routine and temporarily suspended killings at the whim of individuals.[71]

Levi was born in Turin in 1919, and he was twenty-four when he was sent to Auschwitz. He was captured in the mountains with a group of young people trying to join the Italian partisans, but he was not treated like other partisans; Jews went to death camps. There was nothing Jewish about him except his genetic descent—enough for the Germans.

But he would be chosen to work. For most of his time at Auschwitz he did the typical work of inmates, almost guaranteed—indeed intended—to end in death. "The days all seem alike and it is not easy to count them. For days now we have formed teams of two, from the railway to the store—a hundred yards over thawing ground. To the store, bending underneath the load, back again, arms hanging down one's sides, not speaking. Around us, everything is hostile. Above us, the malevolent clouds chase each other to separate us from the sun; on all sides the squalor of the toiling steel closes in on us. We have never seen its boundaries, but we feel all around us the evil presence of the barbed wire that separates us from the world."[72] He survived because after many months of slave labor he was reassigned to work as a chemist under more humane conditions.

The train taking him home to Italy after the liberation stopped briefly in Munich. "We felt we had something to say, enormous things to say, to every single German, and we felt that every German should have something to do with us. . . . [They had a duty] to learn everything, immediately, from us, from me: I felt the tattooed number on my arm burning like a sore."[73] He did say much to the world in his spare, strong, understated prose, in books written while he continued his career as a chemist. But he suffered from lifelong depressions, which he believed were not connected to Auschwitz. One day in 1987, after picking up the morning mail—it often overwhelmed him, laden as it was with unwelcome requests and obligations—he threw himself over the balcony of the central stairwell of his apartment building, on the fourth floor, just outside his apartment.[74]

Paul Celan was born Paul Antshel and raised in Czernowitz, Romania, where half the hundred thousand residents were Jews.[75] But German was his *Muttersprache,* his mother tongue, and he loved it, although he also spoke Romanian and reluctantly studied Hebrew. German was in fact his mother's language, and he felt close to her but distant from his Orthodox Zionist father. As a teenager in the 1930s he briefly belonged to a left-wing group and raised money for the republicans in the Spanish civil war. But his great love was lyric poetry—Goethe, Schiller, Heine, Verlaine, Rimbaud, and especially Rilke.

In 1938, as anti-Semitism intensified in Romania, he went to study in France. He happened to pass through Berlin on Kristallnacht, and he later wrote of it, "you caught sight of some smoke / that was already from tomorrow."[76] Unluckily, he returned to Czernowitz the following summer. First the Soviets took it over, but with the German invasion the Jews were herded into a ghetto and three thousand were murdered in the first twenty-four hours. Living with many others in a small apartment, Celan wrote "Darkness," which ends, "The east smokes after this night . . . / Only dying / sparkles."[77] He was put to work clearing rubbish, hauling debris, and destroying Russian books. Systematic deportations gradually cleared Czernowitz of Jews; one night Celan came home from work to find the door sealed shut and his mother and father gone. He was later sent east with a labor battalion attached to the Fascist Romanian army, and he spent much time in labor camps. He learned Yiddish there, but continued to write in German. Many poems came from that period, along with translations of Shakespeare, Yeats, Éluard, and others.

In 1942 his father died from typhus and his mother was shot as unfit for work. He wrote,

> *It's falling, Mother, snow in the Ukraine:*
> *The Savior's crown a thousand grains of grief.*
> *Here all my tears reach out to you in vain. . . .*
>
> *What would come, Mother: wakening or wound—*
> *If I too sank in the snows of the Ukraine?*[78]

He would never stop wondering.

As the Red Army pushed west in 1944, Celan escaped and returned to Czernowitz. Not long after he wrote the poem that more than any other is the emblem of the Holocaust. "Todesfuge"—"Deathfugue"—was first published in his own Romanian translation as "Death Tango," which gives it an even more chilling intimacy. The English translation, as for the other Celan lines, is by John Felstiner.[79]

> *Black milk of daybreak we drink it at evening*
> *we drink it at midday and morning we drink it at night*
> *we drink and we drink*
> *we shovel a grave in the air where you won't lie too cramped*
> *A man lives in the house he plays with his vipers . . .*
>
> *he whistles his Jews into rows has them shovel a grave in the ground*
> *he commands us play up for the dance . . .*
>
> *. . . he writes when it grows dark to Deutschland your golden hair Margareta*
> *your ashen hair Shulamith . . .*
> *He shouts jab this earth deeper you lot there you others sing up and play*
> *he grabs for the rod in his belt he swings it his eyes are so blue . . .*
>
> *He shouts play Death more sweetly this Death is a master from Deutschland*
> *he shouts scrape your strings darker you'll rise then as smoke to the sky*
> *you'll have a grave then in the clouds there you won't lie too cramped . . .*

The poem gathers force from repetitions, and Felstiner uses them brilliantly to bring the English reader a small way into the German:

Black milk of daybreak we drink you at night
we drink you at midday Death is a master aus Deutschland
we drink you at evening and morning we drink and we drink
this Death is ein Meister aus Deutschland his eye it is blue
he shoots you with shot made of lead shoots you level and true . . .

In the end we return entirely to the *Muttersprache* for a chilling repeat of the contrast between a German and Jewish woman: "he plays with his vipers and daydreams der Tod is ein Meister aus Deutschland / dein goldenes Haar Margareta / dein aschenes Haar Sulamit."

Celan understood the attraction of Israel, but he could not bring himself to move. In the summer of 1948, as the Jewish state fought for its life, he wrote to one of his relatives there "trying to justify 'my destiny to you, who stand at the very center of Jewish destiny.'" But he also wrote, "There is nothing in this world for which a poet will give up writing, not even when he is a Jew and the language of his poems is German," and "Perhaps I am one of the last who must live out to the end the destiny of the Jewish spirit in Europe."[80]

He would go on writing beautifully for a quarter century, mainly in Paris, a successful poet and translator. Like Avraham Sutzkever, he was once compared to Marc Chagall, but Celan's work, unlike theirs, is suffused with darkness and marked by the wounds of the past. The spare, tense beauty of the poems seems to arise from the forcing of a Jewish spirit, painfully, through the German language, amid the clanging echoes of catastrophe. Jewish themes came into them more and more. He visited Israel several times, and after its triumphal 1967 war began a poem,

Just think:
the Peat-Bog soldier of Masada
makes a homeland for himself, most
ineffaceably,
against
every barb in the wire.[81]

"Peat-Bog soldier" refers to the Jewish partisans and to one of their Yiddish marching songs. Masada is the ancient suicidal city destroyed by the Romans, used, perhaps unwisely, by modern Israel as a symbol of uncompromising resistance. Israeli Jews, he seems to say, make their home in the face of the barbed wire of the death camps, and they will not be removed.

Celan suffered severe depressions and at times was medicated and hospitalized. Around Passover in 1970, he jumped from the Pont Mirabeau into the Seine; his body was found in May. A biography of the German poet Hölderlin was open on his desk to an underlined passage: "Sometimes this genius goes dark and sinks down into the bitter well of his heart..." He had not underlined the rest of the sentence: "but mostly his apocalyptic star glitters wondrously."[82] Celan's star did, and more so after his death. At least seven composers and a dance troupe set works to "Todesfuge," and it was dramatically read in the Bundestag on the fiftieth anniversary of Kristallnacht. Primo Levi quoted it when he wrote the partisans' song in his novel *If Not Now, When?*—their murdered brothers "have dug themselves a grave in the air."[83] He wrote of Celan's poem, "I carry it within me like a graft."[84]

"People have said that Celan took his own life at forty-nine," Felstiner writes, "because valid speech in German was impossible after or about Auschwitz. Yet this was the impossibility that incited him.... And he did speak—more validly than could ever have been imagined."[85] Both Celan and Levi violated Fackenheim's 614th Commandment. But they have to be forgiven; they were victims as much as survivors, and their victimization lasted decades. Their work survives, a reminder of both how low the perpetrators sank and how high their victims rose.

A very different response to the Holocaust was that of Viktor Frankl, whose *Man's Search for Meaning* has inspired millions. It tells the story of this physician and psychoanalyst's stay in Auschwitz, and how this most devastating of human experiences left him with a determination to find meaning in life in the midst of suffering and to help others do the same. He was led to create a new form of psychotherapy, logotherapy. In it, the acceptance of unavoidable suffering and an acknowledgment of the transience of life become the basis for humane and meaningful action to rescue time and life from lack of purpose. One evening in the death camp, 2,500 men on the verge of starvation had been denied even their hopelessly inadequate daily ration because they refused to name the one among them who had stolen a few potatoes. Frankl was asked by another inmate to talk to a group that sat starving in the barracks in the dark.

Overcoming his own pain, he encouraged them. He said that they might live for the sake of a loved one, even a departed one; or for God, if they had faith; or in gratitude for being alive; or because this experience could not be taken away from them; or because it would make them stronger. He told them that he estimated his own chance of survival at one in twenty, but that he would not give up. War and death were unpredictable, and any of them might yet have a future. "But I did not only talk of the future and the veil which was drawn over it. I also mentioned the past; all its joys, and how its light shone even in the present darkness.... Having been is also a kind of being, and perhaps the surest kind. I told my comrades (who lay motionless, although occasionally a sigh could be heard) that human life, under any circumstances, never ceases to have a meaning, and that this infinite meaning of life includes suffering and dying, privation and death."

They were not original or earthshaking sentiments, these words sent into the darkness, nor were they offered as such, yet they found their mark. "When the electric bulb flared up again, I saw the miserable figures of my friends limping toward me to thank me with tears in their eyes." But he also adds, in an honest afterthought, "I have to confess here that only too rarely had I the inner strength to make contact with my companions in suffering and that I must have missed many opportunities for doing so."[86] During half a century as a psychotherapist, author, and teacher after the war, he missed very few.

Unless we humans are stupid enough to exceed it, the Shoah will be the permanent representation of reasoned cruelty, recalled with a painful rush of horror, disgust, and pity, until the last tick of human time. Perhaps it can serve a spiritual purpose for the world, to call ourselves constantly back from the brink of pointless hatred to a decent, thoughtful restraint. No doubt, as Frankl insisted, there is meaning in it. Significantly, though, there was nothing explicitly Jewish in Frankl's life and work, and he proudly refused to make reference to his Jewishness. Universalizing suffering was part of his path to transcendence, but in a sense he denied a central part of the meaning of his life; he was persecuted not as a universal human being but as a Jew. For most survivors, indeed for most Jews, there is neither transcendence nor forgiveness. There is only the image that will last till the end of memory: men, women, and children—fifteen hundred thousand children—dwarfed by hunger, bound in wire, nailed by bullets, choked with gas, martyred by the million on a vast, twisted cross.

14

FIRE

HOW THE JEWS FOUGHT BACK

Of the many debates surrounding the Shoah, the most painful concerns Jewish resistance. There are agendas on both sides. Some rabbis avoid all mention of it because it interferes with their concept of the Shoah as *Kiddush ha'Shem*—the sanctification of God's name. This was from ancient times the last gesture of grace of the Jewish martyr, dying willingly for God and Torah.[1] Some Jewish historians say little on the subject lest ample resistance make the process seem like war, not genocide. And many in Israel, especially in the early days of the state, had a stake in believing that there had been no resistance, since this fit their view that the diaspora destroyed Jewish manhood, even Jewish humanity.

Abraham Foxman, an American Jewish leader, defined resistance broadly, sounding a note that resonated with many:

> Attempting to stay alive another day was resistance. Escaping from the ghetto or hiding in a bunker was resistance. So was giving birth to a child, praying in congregation, singing, studying the Bible or the Talmud, bringing flowers into the ghetto, keeping archives, writing humor under the shadow of death, rescuing Torah scrolls left lying in the streets.[2]

Fair enough; but this was not the kind of resistance that became controversial.

In a comprehensive work composed in effectively cold prose and full of tables and numbers, historian Raul Hilberg recorded the destruction of the Jews meticulously and without emotion. His assessment was that "[t]he reaction pattern of the Jews is characterized by almost complete lack of resistance.... the Jewish victims, caught in the straitjacket of their history, plunged themselves physically and psychologically into catastrophe."[3] The language here does not describe just passivity: the victims plunged *them-*

selves into catastrophe. Hannah Arendt, the German-Jewish philosopher, relied on Hilberg's assessment when, in her book about the Eichmann trial, *The Banality of Evil,* she described the Jews as not merely unresisting—the resistance was "pitifully small, . . . incredibly weak, and essentially harmless"—but aiding in their own destruction.[4]

A related argument had been made much earlier, when the psychoanalyst Bruno Bettelheim described his own concentration camp experience—a year in Dachau and Buchenwald—in "Individual and Mass Behavior in Extreme Situations," published in a psychology journal in 1943. Given later events, his situation was not extreme; he was in a labor camp for a fixed term early in the war. There was no assembly-line murder, but there were many deaths, and the SS guards took time to torture the prisoners, trying to make them hurt each other, curse their God, and accuse their own wives of prostitution. He attempted to answer the question, How did some Jews become part of the camp police and gradually come to resemble their Nazi captors? He answered with a psychological analysis that, if true, might apply broadly beyond the camps themselves.

The phenomenon was real. "Old" prisoners—those there longer than three years—identified with the SS, and "not only in respect to aggressive behavior. They would try to acquire old pieces of SS uniforms. If that was not possible, they tried to sew and mend their uniforms so that they would resemble those of the guards."[5] This was impressive, since it was punished by the SS, but when asked about it these inmates said that "they loved to look like the guards." They expressed hatred of American and British journalists who wrote the truth about the camps. Bettelheim asked more than a hundred old prisoners whether, if he was lucky enough to reach foreign soil, he should support foreign efforts against the Nazi regime. Ninety-eight of them said no; Germany should have its own revolution and solve its own problems. New prisoners tried to sabotage the work they did for the Germans; old prisoners took pride in their work. They felt superior to the newer inmates because of their roles as guards, but they felt inferior to the Germans, whom they sincerely viewed as a superior race.

Bettelheim suggested that the whole of Germany was a kind of concentration camp, and that similar processes were going on outside the camps. In fact, each Jewish community in occupied Europe set up a Jewish council—the *Judenrat*—to manage other Jews for the Nazis. In every community some Jewish leaders accepted this assignment, not always reluctantly. In many communities they made the Germans' job much easier. They helped identify the Jews and herd them into dense, filthy ghettos fraught with plague and famine. They helped suppress resistance and rebellion and countered communication from the camps about what really went on there. They designated Jews for transport to the east, first by hundreds, then thousands, then tens of thousands. The reports of mass murder had to be false, they thought, and if they were true it was better to sacrifice "the few" to save the many. When it became clear that they *were* true and that the numbers were reversed—the many were sent to their deaths so that the few could stay in the ghetto—their behavior remained the same.

In the death camps, Jewish inmates known as *Sonderkommandos* were a vital part of the mass murder process. They met the trains, ushered people off, reassured them, took away their suitcases, supervised the disrobing, cut off the women's hair, described the "disinfection" process they were about to undergo, and guided them into the gas chambers. They removed the bodies, extracted the gold from their teeth, and processed the corpses through the crematoria. Most of them did this work efficiently; their own survival depended on it. They could not of course claim that they didn't know what was going on, but they wanted to live to take revenge on the Germans, or to bear witness to history, or simply to ensure that some Jews survived. Most were eventually killed like the other victims. A few did take revenge or bear witness. A few helped build and fight for the Jewish state. A few just lived.

And some Jews fought back.

How Jewish resistance to the Nazis emerged is one of the great stories of Jewish history, but it is seldom told. Initially, before they realized what they were dealing with, some Jews took strong, desperate action. In 1938 a Jew named Herschel Grynszpan killed a German official in Paris and triggered the vast pogrom of Kristallnacht. Any Jewish action produced a huge retaliation, usually against randomly chosen innocent Jews. One resister considering killing one German could count on triggering the murders of a minimum of fifty Jewish bystanders.

Yet resistance never died. In Berlin, the Baum group started as a secret protest movement of left-wing youth but grew to active resistance.[6] Similar groups emerged in Munich, Dresden, and other German cities, but the Baum group stood out. They recruited among Jewish slave laborers at the Siemens plant. They risked their lives to give out leaflets, posted notices around Berlin, and went out at night with buckets of paint to cover walls with anti-Nazi slogans. To aid refugees with food and false documents, they stole from wealthier Jews. In May 1942 Joseph Goebbels, the propaganda minister of the Reich, put up an anti-Soviet exhibit, an attempt to cover up the failure of the Nazi assault on Moscow. Getting chemical supplies from the German resistance, the Baum group set fire to the exhibit and partly destroyed it. The Nazis suppressed news about the event, but the German underground gained a new respect for the Jews. The Gestapo arrested almost all the group's members, who were tortured to death or executed if they could not kill themselves. They also arrested five hundred randomly chosen innocent Jews; half were killed immediately, the other half sent to the camp at Sachsenhausen.

In the Polish town of Czestochowa, where there were thirty thousand Jews, selections and deportations began in the town square. The Jewish Fighting Organization (ZOB)[7] resisted—one man with a knife, another with bare fists—and its fighters were shot on the spot, along with twenty-five random Jews in the crowd. The ZOB smuggled chemicals into the ghetto and made grenades in secret workshops. A failed train derailment resulted in several fighters' deaths and the murder of twenty-five innocent Jews in reprisal. In June 1943 the Germans assaulted the ZOB "headquarters," and its defenders fought to the death.[8]

In the Warsaw ghetto, jammed with hundreds of thousands of people and overwhelmed with starvation, typhus, tuberculosis, and other diseases, Jewish physicians set up a clandestine medical school that trained five hundred doctors, and there were nursing and pharmacy schools as well.[9] In one crisis, sixty nursing students had to compete for five tickets to avoid deportation to Auschwitz by answering the question "Describe the appropriate nursing care for a patient during the first days following a heart attack."[10] Examination performance was a matter of life and death. This organized response to terror demonstrated the extraordinary resourcefulness of this, the largest Jewish community in Europe.

This community not only made the greatest and most damaging uprising against the Germans, it was the first and for a long while the only such uprising by any ethnic group in any occupied country.[11] In fact, it took less time and thought for the Germans to conquer the French nation than to put down the Warsaw ghetto rebellion. Armed clashes with a vigorous and brave Jewish underground increased in the first few months of 1943, to the point where Himmler decided to liquidate the ghetto. His goal was to finish by April 20, Hitler's birthday, giving his führer the gift of a Warsaw free of Jews. Himmler understood—it must have astounded him—that he would face Jewish resistance. He mobilized 2,000 soldiers and officers, three detachments of artillery and mine sappers, two battalions of German police, 360 Polish police, and 337 Ukrainian and Lett Fascists. In addition to these almost 3,000 troops and police, 7,000 SS men and police were moved to Warsaw as a backup force.

There were about a thousand organized Jewish fighters, but thousands more joined the uprising. They had Molotov cocktails and small amounts of ammunition, but they also had fierce courage and excellent organization. Emmanuel Ringelblum, the ghetto archivist, wrote, "We realized that this was a struggle between a fly and an elephant. But their national dignity dictated that the Jews offer resistance and not allow themselves to be led to the wanton slaughter."[12] On Sunday, April 18, it became apparent that the Germans were preparing to attack the following day. That evening was the first

Passover seder, and it led to an all-night vigil of a kind the ancient rabbis might have been familiar with, given that the Romans were worthy fore-runners of the Nazis.

The following day the first German incursion was a rout that led to a humiliating retreat for their forces, as they were "met by a hail of Molotov cocktails, hand grenades, bombs, and bullets" and forced to leave their dead and wounded behind.[13] Nazi officers were stunned. "All is lost in the ghetto!" said the commander of the action to SS Major General Jürgen Stroop. "We are not in the ghetto! We cannot get into the ghetto! We have wounded and dead!"[14] There were no Jewish losses.

Rejecting the shame of calling for aerial bombardment, General Stroop took over and attacked again under the cover of an artillery barrage. The Jewish fighters retreated with their dead. "Enraged by the Jewish resistance Stroop's forces wreaked their vengeance on the sick. They bombarded and set fire to the ghetto hospital. The soldiers broke into the burning wards. . . . They tossed the sick into the flames. They seized infants and smashed their heads against the walls. In the maternity wards they ripped open the bellies of pregnant women with their bayonets. . . . The Ukrainian Fascists espe-cially distinguished themselves with their sadism."[15]

However, the Germans' troubles were far from over. The Jewish resis-tance stopped the advance and flew two banners over the neighborhood they held. One group was led by Zivia Lubetkin; she detonated mines that killed many German soldiers. In the evening Stroop withdrew again. "Everywhere the mood was one of pride and tension. On that fantastic Passover night Jews sat down in bunkers to celebrate the traditional Seder." Meanwhile, the difficult situation was reported to Berlin. Hitler must have spent at least part of his birthday the following day wondering how long this humiliation at the hands of a swinish slave race could go on.

On the third day Stroop decided to cut his losses by setting the ghetto on fire. Huge flames raged, and still the resistance continued. Mordecai Aniele-vicz, the commandant of the Jewish ranks, wrote to his friend Yitzhak on April 23, accepting their impending doom yet excited about a Polish radio broadcast on the uprising and a non-Jewish Polish resistance action inspired by the Jews. "Be well, dear friend. Maybe we will see each other some day. The main thing: the dream of my life was realized. The Jewish Self-Defense in the Warsaw Ghetto became a fact. The armed Jewish struggle and the revenge became a reality. I am a witness to this grand, heroic battle of the Jewish fighters."[16]

They turned to partisan tactics, the hit-and-run guerrilla methods of the forest fighters, and continued to inflict serious damage. Others made successful escapes. Still others were slaughtered in a stubborn battle as they emerged in a group from the sewers. The battles went on for weeks. On May 8 the Germans stormed the nerve center of the resistance, and

Anielewicz died along with hundreds of others, some by suicide. "On Saturday, May 13th, the twenty-fifth day of the uprising, when the ghetto had been razed to the ground and the Fighting Organization no longer had a high command, SS General Stroop was compelled to note in his report that new fighting flared with fierce stubbornness."[17]

On May 16, Stroop reported that the ghetto no longer existed. Himmler blew up a historic synagogue, a nineteenth-century masterpiece by an Italian architect, in celebration. Still the resistance continued. On May 31, the German general in charge of security for Poland reported that Jewish attacks and assassinations in Warsaw continued. On September 26 some remaining fighters fled the razed ghetto and escaped. Others stayed and exchanged shots with German soldiers. In October a slave labor detail from Auschwitz came to clear the ghetto debris. In one bunker "they found on the table the fresh remains of an unfinished meal and an open volume of Sholem Aleichem's stories."[18]

A more decisive uprising took place in the second-largest mass-murder camp, Treblinka, where eight hundred thousand Jews were killed, including many from Warsaw.[19] In his eyewitness account one of the few survivors, Samuel Rajzman, wrote that he was already undressed for the gas chamber when a Jewish inmate ordered him to get dressed. Rajzman reproached the man for saving him. "I did not save you to keep you alive," was the reply, "but to sell your life at a higher price. You are now a member of a secret organization that is planning an uprising, and you must live."[20]

Three combat units were formed from Warsaw ghetto deportees and others, under the leadership of Dr. Julian Chorazyski, a former Polish army captain. He was captured and swallowed poison, delaying the rebellion for several months, but a Jewish locksmith had made a copy of the key to the arsenal. In May 1943 a physician named Leichert, also a former Polish officer, was brought to the camp and agreed to serve as leader. On August 2 a group of masons entered the arsenal and removed twenty hand grenades, twenty rifles, several handguns, and ammunition, smuggling them out in a wagonload of debris. They were distributed among the combat units.

A disinfector in one of the units sprayed throughout the camp using gasoline instead of disinfectant. At 3:45 a rifle shot from the direction of the Jewish barracks signaled the start of the rebellion. The arsenal exploded and the entire camp was in flames. Yankel Wiernick, a survivor, wrote, "Each group had to fulfill its separate tasks: kill the German and Ukrainian personnel, set fire to the buildings, clear the path for the escapees, etc.

> Everything was prepared for this goal: blunt weapons to kill with, wood for bridges, buckets of gasoline. . . . there were watchtowers on all sides manned by armed guards. At every turn there was either an armed Ukrainian or an armed German. . . . Everyone

who was in our path was killed. . . . In a matter of minutes everything was burning. We carried out our sacred mission in an exem-
plary manner. I armed myself and hacked away at all around me,
right and left. When I saw that everything was burning and the
path was clear I grabbed an ax and a file and escaped.[21]

With that ax, Yankel killed his Ukrainian pursuer. More than twenty Germans were killed. Of the 700 inmates, at least 150 escaped, but even the
great majority of these were killed by pursuing Germans. A non-Jewish
friend of one of the remaining escapees risked his life and those of his family to bring them food. Forty survived. But Treblinka, where the Germans
and Ukrainians had murdered thousands of Jews daily, was completely destroyed and out of use for the rest of the war.

Sobibor was another mass-murder operation, killing fifteen thousand a
day at its peak. It was also the site of the most dramatic death-camp revolution. The camp's destiny changed when Alexander Pechersky, a Russian
prisoner of war who happened to be Jewish, arrived. He learned what the
fires were, and immediately began asserting himself in small but risky ways.
Three days after his arrival he heard the screams of children being torn
from their mothers and decided he must act. That day he passed up a
chance to escape, and began organizing the Jewish inmates and the Soviet
prisoners of war.

After less than three weeks of surreptitious, dangerous effort, his plan
was carried out. Four high-ranking Germans were killed with knives and
hatchets as they synchronously visited a Jewish tailor, a shoemaker, and so
on. In Pechersky's account:

> We stood there listening for a moment. A deadly silence had
> descended on the camp. I ordered Brzecki to give the signal. The si-
> lence was shattered by a piercing whistle. . . . People came streaming
> in from all sides. . . .
>
> "Comrades, Forward!" I called out loud. . . . The slogans rever-
> berated like thunder in the death camp, and united Jews from Rus-
> sia, Poland, Holland, France, Czechoslovakia, and Germany, six
> hundred pain-racked and tormented people, surged forward with a
> wild "hurrah" to life and freedom.[22]

They hacked through the barbed wire, and hundreds ran from the camp in
a hail of German bullets. Many fell in this barrage, many more were shattered in the minefields, but many reached the woods and joined the partisans, guerrilla groups run by non-Jews. Rudolf Hoess, the commander of
Auschwitz, wrote in his memoir that "the Jews . . . were able by force to
achieve a major breakout during which almost all the guard personnel were

wiped out."[23] Some of those who survived severely damaged German troops and supply lines in partisan actions on the eastern front.

As in Treblinka, the Sobibor revolt shut down the camp for the rest of the war. Four days after it, the SS sent a special unit to dismantle the camp. "All the buildings and watchtowers were dynamited. The barbed wire fence posts were pulled out of the ground. The excavators that dug the pits for the ashes of the burned, the transmitters still laden with dead bodies, the diesel motors that propelled the gas into the gas chambers, these were all piled up on the platforms and removed. Even the geese and rabbits were killed on the spot."[24] Most of the German officers had been killed, but the Ukrainian guards eluded punishment until 1963, when eleven of them were tried for treason in Kiev and ten were executed. The lead prosecution witness was Alexander Pechersky.

And in Auschwitz itself during 1944, while twenty thousand Jews a day were being murdered and either cremated or buried there, a rebellion was being planned.[25] Rosa Roborta, an extremely courageous twenty-year-old who worked in the munitions factory, smuggled small buttons of dynamite to the camp's underground, to be made into bombs by a Russian prisoner. These bombs were to be part of a general uprising, and they were in the possession of the *Sonderkommando* in charge of the four crematoria.

But these men learned that they were about to be liquidated and could not wait for the planned uprising. They blew up Crematorium III in a huge explosion, killed several SS men—a particularly sadistic overseer was thrown alive into the flames—and cut the barbed-wire fence. About six hundred escaped, but most were killed by a contingent of SS pursuing them. Crematorium III was destroyed and never rebuilt. Rosa and several other young women from the factory were arrested and tortured, but Rosa gave up no names except that of one man who was already dead. After long, sadistic tortures and savage beatings, the four young women were executed by hanging before the assembled Jewish prisoners left behind.

In the east, there were Jewish rebellions in the ghettos of Bialystok, Marcinkonis, Lachwa, and Tuczyn. Thousands of Jews escaped from the Minsk ghetto to join the partisans. Jewish fighters filled the woods around Bialystok, Vilna, Minsk, and many other eastern European towns, where they sometimes had to contend with deadly anti-Semitism among their non-Jewish supposed partisan comrades. Jews served in the resistance forces in Bulgaria, Belgium, Italy, and France. "In 1942, in occupied France, Jewish resistance groups together created the Jewish Army (l'Armée juive). Its members attacked German military trucks and trains and sabotaged factories where war materials were made. In 1944, a more important movement, the Jewish Combat Organization (l'Organisation juive de combat) took an active part in the liberation of two French towns, Castres and

Mazamet."[26] More than 250 Jewish members of the French resistance were executed by the Germans or the Vichy government during just the six months before D day, but until that time they were actively fighting Germans.

But there is no story more poignant than that of Vilna, the Jerusalem of Lithuania. In the Vilna ghetto, as thousands of Jews were being taken to Ponar, forced into mass graves, and shot, a resistance network formed among young Zionists and socialists. Jacob Gens, the head of the Jewish police, cooperated fully with the Germans, falsely reassuring people that they were being transported to labor camps, calming them, selecting who would go and who would stay. A delegation of rabbis admonished him, citing Maimonides' saying that it is better that all be killed than that one soul of Israel be surrendered. Gens was deaf to these protests, but to a handful of young resisters everything was coming clear.

Abba Kovner, already a noted Hebrew poet, addressed a meeting of the Young Guard in a low-ceilinged candlelit room beneath the *Judenrat*. He was cold, unshaven, in dirty work pants, and trembling. "Our dear ones have been sent to their deaths . . . and yet many still do not see the truth clearly. What is that truth? That our friends and families, those who were deported, are no longer alive. They were taken to Ponar—to death. . . ."[27]

"Is there any chance of rescue? . . . We must give the true answer, cruel though it may be. No. There will be no rescue. Perhaps tens or hundreds of Jews will be saved; but for our people as a whole, for the millions of Jews in the areas of German occupation, there is no chance. Is there any way out? Yes. Revolt and armed self-defense. This is the only way which promises any dignity for our people." To the objection that they were Zionists and should turn their backs on Europe, a young woman named Ruzka Korczak asked, "Will you be able to look into the eyes of a child in Israel when that child asks, 'What did you do?' When that child says, 'What did you do when thousands or millions of our people were murdered?' Will you tell that child, 'I saved myself alone'? . . . What will the coming generations learn from us? How good will they be if their entire history is one of slaughter and extermination? . . . We cannot allow that. It must also have heroic struggles, self-defense, war, even death with honor."[28]

Another man objected that there would be mass reprisals against innocent Jews for every resistance act, and this caused a shouting match until Kovner stopped it. "No matter what we do, we will die. . . . If we are cowardly, we will die. If we are courageous, we will die." A young man named Jacob asked the meaning of this. Kovner answered, "It means we can decide just the one thing. . . . We can decide that, whatever happens, we will not go the way the others went." Jacob objected that he could not know for certain what would happen. "That's right . . . I don't know for sure. And no one will ever know for sure. No. Let me change that. One person will know for sure. When they come to take the last Jew in Europe to Ponar—he will know for sure."

Ruzka stood beside Kovner in resistance, as did others. They gathered intelligence about the ongoing mass murders and told anyone who would listen. They recruited as many fighters as they could, and they began making preparations for attacks. Vitka Kempner became romantically involved with Kovner, and she carried out the first successful mission, setting an explosion on a railroad bridge and sending a German military train into the gorge. More than two hundred soldiers were killed.

Back in the ghetto, while Kovner and his fellow fighters were trying to organize a rebellion, Gens was encouraging cultural activities. His cooperation with the Nazis increased. When the Jews of a nearby town, Oszmania, were rounded up to be murdered, Jewish police in leather jackets and boots, wearing shiny hats emblazoned with Stars of David, participated fully in the action. In the spring of 1943 news came of the Warsaw ghetto uprising, and all that summer the underground steadily worked to organize a similar rebellion. They stole weapons, killed German soldiers, distributed leaflets, and created a network of people prepared to repeat what had happened in Warsaw.

Gens and his Jewish police thwarted them at every turn, spying on them for the SS, confronting them violently, arresting them. The ghetto was now a fraction of its original size, that fraction was continually decimated, and Gens was still making selections, "giving up the few to save the many." The ghetto had started with eighty thousand Jews the previous year, and the last ten thousand were transported to their deaths that fall. Kovner, Kempner, Korczak, and the other surviving ghetto fighters escaped to join the forest partisans, where they continued to be persecuted as Jews, but with great tenacity were able to fight through the war in the east, harassing and killing Germans and destroying trains and installations until the Red Army swept the Germans away. Through exceptional skill and luck the three survived to fight again in Israel, and remained close until their deaths in old age, on a ghetto fighters' kibbutz near the Mediterranean Sea.

Isaac Rudnicki, then seventeen, later recalled the day they left the ghetto: "I had a strange sensation as I went through the fence. Something fateful was taking place in my life. From this moment on my comrades and I were not humiliated Jews under Nazi rule, sentenced to annihilation, but free fighters who had joined the millions fighting the Nazi beasts on all fronts. I touched the revolver hanging at my belt and the grenade in my pocket. I felt great confidence. The ghetto was behind us, the forest and the unknown before us."[29] He would in time become Yitzhak Arad, brigadier general in the Israel Defense Forces, a Ph.D. historian, and director of Yad Vashem, Israel's Holocaust memorial museum.

Kovner himself, fighting terminal cancer at the Memorial Sloan-Kettering Cancer Center in New York more than four decades after the war, would look outside his hospital window and see three chimneys, "a crematorium."[30] He faced painful death courageously again as an old man, and he wrote Hebrew poems as he had done even in the forest, even in the ghetto. A Jew, he believed, has no existence without meaning, and he found meaning in his cancer, which took away his voice before it killed him, in his decades of living in and fighting for Israel, and in his memories of the terrible days when he had fought a savage and seemingly unbeatable foe—a foe worse than cancer.

Yet he could not write about just the pain. He recalled a ghetto fight on the sixteenth of July forty-three years earlier, and he wrote about the partisans:

> And then they searched for lice by the outskirts of the fire
> and roasted potatoes for the evening meal
> in the embers
> and brewed tea with green swamp water . . .
> Every man sitting with his gun. They pass the night
> in burrowed earthen dugouts, well camouflaged,
> young men and women together . . .[31]

And he wrote about Vitka, still beside him at the hospital:

> when you were blond and radiant,
> pulling the wool over German eyes,
> like an imp   of mischief.[32]

Such mischief as hers helped cost the Germans the war. As for Kovner, Leon Wieseltier aptly described him as "one of the most valiant men in Jewish history, one of the most valiant men in modern history."[33]

Why more were not like him is easy to understand; why more did not follow him is another question. A Yiddish saying may help: *A sho gelebt is oikh gelebt*—"An hour lived is also life." Perhaps some had too great a reverence for that hour. There was also a saying at the time, "God forbid that the war last as long as the Jews are capable of enduring."[34] Some Jews were willing to shorten their lives a little on the chance that they could hurt their tormentors, punish their families' murderers, slow, just a little, the pace of the slaughter, or make a little noise that someone in the world might hear. But the great majority did not.

There were many reasons. The Germans knew that the Jews had never been trained to fight, and they used this knowledge to full advantage. They used the improbability of their program to make people believe it wasn't

happening. They murdered fifty, a hundred, a thousand people, razed whole
buildings and towns in reprisal for acts of resistance, so that to rebel one had
to be willing to bring quick and certain death to many others. They routinely tortured resisters and their loved ones. They kept families together
until the end, so that helping one's children to die without being too frightened seemed the only humane imperative.

The Warsaw ghetto uprising detained part of the German army for a
time, humiliating it before the world. The Belsky partisans and the Vilna
ghetto fighters played small but valued roles in the German defeat on the eastern front. The Sobibor rebellion shut that death camp down. Even the
Auschwitz rebellion destroyed two crematoria. If these actions had increased
tenfold, might they have markedly shortened the war? If they had increased
a hundredfold, might they have prevented the Final Solution? These are legitimate questions, and they are not raised just by insensitive philosophers;
they have been on the lips of Jewish schoolchildren, especially in Israel, for
more than half a century. They deserve an answer that goes beyond platitudes.

It is not an insult to the memory of the victims to make distinctions, nor
is it blaming them to try to learn lessons. If we don't distinguish between the
Jewish leaders of Warsaw, who finally supported the rebellion, and those of
most other cities, who efficiently served the deportation machine until there
were no Jews left and they themselves were deported, then what is left of
the moral meaning of leadership? If we look at Abba Kovner and the other
Vilna fighters, who risked everything to fight the Germans any way they
could, and Jacob Gens, the head of the Vilna *Judenrat,* who helped the Nazis
hunt those fighters down like dogs, torture them, and kill them, and say,
"Don't judge, Kovner and Gens were both victims," then how can we hope
to make the right choice tomorrow? Hannah Arendt, known for unpopular views about Jewish complicity, quoted an inmate of Theresienstadt as
her summary of the behavior of the Jews: "The Jewish people as a whole
behaved magnificently. Only the leadership failed."[35]

In the Ghetto Fighters' House, an Israeli museum of Holocaust resistance, there is an attempt to remember, specifically, those who fought.
Yitzhak Zuckerman, one of the museum's founders, said it with simple
force: "We thought that there were lessons to be learned both from the
Holocaust and from the Jewish Resistance. Therefore we established this
house, which will tell the younger generations and those who come after us
what happened, how it happened and how we should continue living." The
partisans had a hymn that they sang in the forest, written by Hirsh Glik:

> *Never say that you are on the final way,*
> *Though leaden skies blot out the blue of day,*
> *The hour for which we yearn will yet appear—*
> *And the drum roll of our feet says—We are here!*

They were indeed. Much has been done in tribute to the six million victims; it cannot dishonor them to give prominence to the memory of a few thousand Jewish heroes.

⚭

The world is intimate with Anne Frank, but far fewer know Hannah Senesh. She was eight when Anne was born; both were Jews from assimilated families, both were spirited, both were good writers, and both were killed by Nazis; but there the resemblance ends. Anne was a child with a luminous spirit and a great writerly gift who recorded her own coming of age but was not allowed to live to grow up. Hannah Senesh came of age before the war began, and after that she made her own choices. Her story deserves attention because it exemplifies the greatest transition in modern Jewish history: from exquisitely perceptive, deeply felt consciousness to bold builder, brave fighter, and legendary hero.

Senesh was born in Hungary to a typical, largely assimilated middle-class Jewish family and grew up in comfort and safety. Her diary, like Anne's, is a tale of emerging womanhood, and like Anne's it flows from touching evocations of mundane school and family life to the cri de coeur of a passionate voice raised against the threatening tide of history.[36] Her playwright father had died young, and the diary opens, "This morning we visited Daddy's grave. How sad that we had to become acquainted with the cemetery so early in life. But I feel that even from beyond the grave Daddy is helping us."[37] It was 1934 and she was thirteen. Another entry:

> This morning there was a lovely celebration, and this afternoon I went to synagogue. Those afternoon services are so odd; it seems one does everything but pray. The girls talk and look down at the boys, and the boys talk and look up at the girls—this is what the entire thing consists of.
>
> I'm glad I've grown lately. . . . I don't believe people think me a particularly pretty girl, but I hope I'll improve.

She worries about her brother: "It's a good thing George is still so young. Even so, God protect us from war. Why, the whole world would be practically wiped out." She is still thirteen, recording her experiences ice-skating, dancing—"I have a lovely pink dress"—and a class ring: "We got our class reunion rings today. We'll meet on May 1, 1945. Ten years from now! What a long time! How many things can happen before then."

"I must improve in French," she writes, and when she begins piano lessons, "I haven't got a very good ear." But she loves the music, and "Sometimes when Mama plays Chopin I feel like crying." She sees no need "to stand before Daddy's grave for a few moments when I'm actually with him in thought every evening, asking whether he is satisfied with me. . . . I can hardly remember Daddy (his face) but just the same I love him very much, and always feel he is with me. . . . I would like to be worthy of him as a writer, too. . . . Perhaps, through writing, I will be able to contribute something towards human happiness." But the world was already intruding on her reverie. October 4, 1935:

> Horrible! Yesterday war broke out between Italy and Abyssinia. . . . The papers are already listing the dead. I can't understand people; how quickly they forget. Don't they know that the whole world is groaning from the curse of the last World War? . . . Why must youth be sacrificed on a bloody scaffold when it could give so much that is good and beautiful to the world. . . . Truly, the ugliest thing in the world is politics.

But politics was not all she had on her mind: "When I began keeping a diary I decided I would write only about beautiful and serious things, and under no circumstances constantly about boys, as most girls do. But it looks as if it's not possible to exclude boys from the life of a fifteen-year-old girl, and for the sake of accuracy . . ." For the sake of accuracy, of course. At fifteen she had become a vegetarian, and "I still long to be a writer. It's my constant wish. . . . And I would like to be a great soul. If God will permit."

She finished *War and Peace* that year—"among the very best I have ever read"—and was an officer of the Bible Society. She wrote a play, read her poems at the Literary Society, even sold a poem. Visiting Italy that summer, she wrote of the Duomo in Milan.

> When I stepped out of the lift, which took me up several hundred feet, my breath caught in my throat. . . . I moved forward towards the lacy, supple Gothic arches, pinnacles and pillars, thinking, if this were music it would be the trills played on the highest notes of violins. The white marble sparkled under the blue sky. . . . This was how I had imagined fairyland to be. . . . How distant the feverish commercial city, the noise of cars and trams from up there, how ridiculous the glitter of the shop windows. . . .
>
> I . . . began climbing the narrow spiral staircase leading to the summit. A new vista at every turn . . . another lacy crenellation—like some sort of frost flower. . . . I stood on the top step . . . feeling as if I had climbed there on Jacob's ladder, in a dream. . . .
>
> I had to turn back. I said goodbye at every step. It hurt so to leave the brilliance, the height, the peacefulness . . . I suddenly knew I was actually taking an everlasting memory—a memory of a great longing for light, for height, for peace.

Peace was a vain dream. Shortly before this trip, she was cautioned that she could not be an officer of the Literary Society because "the person elected must be a Protestant." She reflects, "Only now am I beginning to see what it really means to be a Jew in a Christian society. But I don't mind at all. It is because we have to struggle, because it is more difficult for us to reach our goal, that we develop outstanding qualities." She understands that if she were Christian, all paths would be open to her. Yet, "[u]nder no circumstances would I ever convert to Christianity, not only because of myself, but also because of the children I hope one day to have. I would never force them . . . to deny or be ashamed of their origin. . . ." She rejected the notion that faith is a crutch for the weak, saying that it is exactly what makes you strong. Yet faith for her did not mean strict practice: "It's the Jewish New Year and I wondered whether or not to write on this day. But to my way of thinking this is a prohibition impossible to obey. Religion, in the truest sense, does not consist of such things."

Restrictions on Jews grew. The following spring, politics dominated her writing as Fascism did Europe. "Saturday morning . . . the occupation of Austria began, troops were on the march, and at this moment Austria is entirely under Nazi control." Yet life in Budapest went on: "A gayer and lovelier event was the affair last night at Lily's house. . . . After the usual leisurely beginning, we danced, had a buffet supper, sang, and the atmosphere became delightful and relaxed. I danced a lot, and had a fabulous time."

Her faith wavered: "I would like to be as good as possible to Mother, to wear my Jewishness with pride . . . and I would very much like always to be able to believe and trust in God. There are times I cannot, and at such times I attempt to force myself to believe completely, firmly, with total certainty." A month later she wrote: "I don't know whether I've already mentioned that I've become a Zionist.

> I now consciously and strongly feel I am a Jew, and am proud of it. My primary aim is to go to Palestine, to work for it. . . . Three years ago . . . I vehemently attacked the Zionist Movement. Since then people, events, times, have all brought me closer to the idea, and I am immeasurably happy. . . . I am going to start learning Hebrew. . . . I've become a different person.

A few months later, after the largest synagogue in Budapest was bombed during Friday night services, killing and injuring many, Hannah presented a paper on Zionism to the Bible Society. Noting the mockery and hostility that had greeted Hungarian Zionists just a few years earlier, she described a new movement embraced by once-hostile Jews now convinced that this radical solution might be the only answer. After two thousand years of longing, many thousands of Jews had returned to "this tiny piece of land on the shores of the Mediterranean.... Even today, in its mutilated form, Palestine is big enough to be an island in the sea of seemingly hopeless Jewish destiny, an island upon which we can peacefully build a lighthouse to beam its light into the darkness, a light of everlasting human values, the light of the one God." Later she confided to her diary, "Perhaps I don't exaggerate if I write that the only thing I'm committed to, in which I believe, is Zionism."

March 10, 1939: "I am sending off my application to the Nahalal Girls' Farm" in the Jezreel Valley. "If only they'll accept me!" The application letter, which she wrote in Hebrew, closes, "With cordial Zionist greetings." Her brother in Lyon, also an ardent Zionist, closed a letter to her with Joseph Trumpeldor's famous words as he died from his battle wounds: "It is good to die for our country." By July 17, she could write in Hebrew:

Today is my birthday. I am eighteen. It is so hard for me to see myself as such an "old lady." But I know these are the most beautiful years of my life, and I enjoy my young ideas, my youth. I am happy with my life, with everything that surrounds me. I believe in the future. My ideal fills my entire being.

She was accepted, and in September, as Hitler overran Poland, she left Hungary for her beloved *Eretz*. From her ship, the *Bessarabia*, anchored in Constantinople, she wrote to her mother with her typewriter on her lap: "Life aboard ship is extremely pleasant.... This morning I got up at six because I couldn't stand staying in bed when I saw how beautiful the sunrise was.... The majority of Jewish passengers are from Palestine, returning from visits to relatives... and a lot of children from Palestine who are adorable and speak only Hebrew. There are opportunities to practice my Hebrew with them." A week later she wrote the first entry at Nahalal. She says she must write in Hungarian because she has "so many impressions to record, that I can't possibly cope with them all in Hebrew.... I have been here four days. A little *Sabra* is climbing up the olive tree directly behind me; in front of me are cypress trees, cacti, the Emek Valley.

I am in Nahalal, in Eretz. I am home.... And in a way this is true since, after all, I've always lived among Jews. But not among such free, industrious, calm, and, I think, contented Jews. I know I still see things idealistically, and I know there will be difficult days.

Yesterday, on Yom Kippur Eve, I was very low. I mean spiritually. I made an accounting of what I had left behind.... For a moment I lost sight of the goal.... But even behind the tears I felt I had done the right thing. Here almost every life is the fulfillment of a mission. . . . I would like George to come as soon as possible. And then Mother.

At the kibbutz two years later, she wrote

> *To die . . . so young to die . . . no, no, not I.*
> *I love the warm sunny skies,*
> *Lights, songs, shining eyes,*
> *I want no war, no battle cry—*
> *No, no, not I.*

But if she does have to live "with blood and death on every hand"—even if she herself should die that very day—she is glad to be where she is: "Praised be He for the grace . . . to live . . . upon your soil, my home, my land."

One wants to say, *She met a man, they worked the land, they filled it with children and grandchildren, she died in the fullness of life.* But in 1942 she heard of the mass murders. The rest of the world heard of them too, although most, including most Jews, proved hard of hearing. Senesh heard it clearly. She joined the Haganah, volunteering to train as a paratrooper and drop behind German lines, where she would rescue Allied pilots and Jews and organize resistance. She was captured by the Hungarian police, was tortured severely without giving up information—her mother was arrested and held in the same prison—and, refusing a blindfold, was executed by firing squad, just as thousands of Hungarian Jews were being rounded up for the gas chambers.[38] Like Anne, she left a diary, in addition to poems in Hungarian and Hebrew. But here was someone who escaped the jaws of death, looked back, saw others in them, took a breath, and swam straight back in. In the clear impermanence of her own short life, she left this poem in Hebrew about beauty enduring, now a popular folk song:

> *God, God,*
> *Let them be there:*
> *The sand and the sea,*
> *The water's rush,*
> *The glimmering sky,*
> *A human prayer.*

She wrote it while still at work building the kibbutz, at the seaside near the ruins of Caesarea, where the Romans had imprisoned and tortured Jews in the second century. While with the forest partisans, before crossing into Hungary, she wrote another:

. . . Joyful the flame that glowed secretly in the heart
Joyful the heart that knew how to stop in honor
Joyful the match consumed while kindling flames.

As she once wrote, thinking of dead heroes, "There are stars whose radiance is visible on earth though they have long been extinct. . . . These lights are particularly bright when the night is dark."

⟨❦⟩

Many Jews served in the British army—in all the Allied armies—but not *as Jews,* and the Haganah, the Jewish Defense Force in prestate Israel, called for a specifically Jewish unit within the army.[39] In 1942, as Field Marshal Erwin Rommel, the brilliant German general, advanced through North Africa, it was not clear that the British would hold the line before the Jews were overwhelmed. The Haganah prepared for the complete destruction of the Yishuv—the Jewish community of Israel—planning a retreat to Mount Carmel near Haifa, where they would fight to the last man or woman. The British did hold, but the demand for an official Jewish fighting force persisted.

On September 20, 1944, Winston Churchill, over the protests of the War Office and Colonial Office, told the House of Commons, "It seems to me indeed appropriate that a special Jewish unit, a special unit of that race which has suffered indescribable torment from the Nazis"—as always, he deliberately mispronounced "Nazis" as *Nar-zees,* using a lengthy *a* and a soft *z* to display his complete contempt—"should be represented as a distinct formation amongst the forces gathered for their final overthrow." His Majesty's Jewish Brigade was born.

Five thousand Haganah members quickly enlisted in three battalions. Veteran Ted Arison said many years later, "We started hearing stories about what Hitler is doing, slaughtering Jews in Germany, in Poland, and so on, and we just said that—I just said that I just have to go out there and kill as many Germans as possible. Period."[40] They chose the Star of David as their insignia, but not the traditional blue-and-white motif; a yellow star, like those of the murdered millions. They were allowed to fly their flag, which stayed blue-and-white, and at their opening ceremony in the midst of the British-controlled Egyptian desert, it flew beside the Union Jack, as a chaplain draped in a *tallis* made a blessing.

"We were all gathered in the Western Desert, and we had the first parade, and the Zionist flag was flown for the first time officially. And we all stood there, well armed, well equipped, and that flag in front of us—this was something that moved everybody to tears." The Palestine Symphony Orchestra came to the desert for their send-off. "All around," said Avraham Uzieli, "nothing, nothing, and nothing. And all of a sudden you hear the symphony orchestra . . . and we felt high . . . and this was an opening to our adventure." These men had defended their homes against Arab marauders for decades, but now they were well equipped and going to fight the Germans. Their artillery shells were painted with a small, crude Jewish star, and in Hebrew, *"Shay l'Hitler"*—"A Gift for Hitler."

They were sent to Italy. "We were given the discipline of the British army," said Maxim Kahan. "The British army has been in existence for over 400 years. It's served in sixty, seventy, eighty different countries in the world. So the British army may not be the best in the world, but one thing I can vouch for: It's a bloody *good* army." Still, the Jewish Brigade was not quite British. They flew the Star of David, spoke Hebrew, held Sabbath services, and erected a giant menorah on Chanukah. As they lit it, each man held a child on his shoulders, from a large group of Jewish orphans in Italy.

They knew the German army had defeated far more experienced forces, and they were appropriately afraid. In their most intense battle they had to make an uphill assault on well-fortified German positions. "I told them, 'Up,' and 'Charge!'" Johanan Peltz recalled. "It's a fantastic feeling. A person loses all fear . . . to sort of a communal madness. Something grabs you, and you just can't stop. I have never felt anything like it in my life." He also remembered a German-speaking fellow soldier: "When we broke into the German positions and we started sticking the bastards with bayonets . . . one corporal—his name was Corporal Levy—during the assault, standing on the German bunker, shouted *'Heraus ihr schweine, die Juden sind da!'—Out with you pigs, the Jews are here!'*"

They passed this test but faced another. One brigade officer wanted to kill their German prisoners on the spot, screaming at them in fury, but he was stopped by another, who reminded him that they had orders to bring the prisoners in alive. They were transferred to another part of the Italian front, to face seasoned German paratroops. But they paused on Passover—the Jewish feast of liberation from slavery—to hold a makeshift outdoor seder, and the well-known hymn "Eliahu Ha'navi"—"Elijah the Prophet"—drifted over the war-torn Italian countryside.

The Allied offensive began in earnest, with the Jewish Brigade at the front. Arie Amir, a sniper who could hit his target at six hundred meters, said, "Because I'm Jewish and I got to the front full of hate, I resolved ahead of time to hurt as many Germans as I could. So when I hit my targets, it didn't bother me." In an assault during the big offensive, a brigade soldier stepped on a mine. "And this poor fellow is brought down, so that all of us could see that his foot was completely gone," Kahan remembered, "and he's shouting, *'Chevra, nekama!'*—Revenge! Revenge! Revenge! And I went to the head of the column, and I took them through the minefield—not because I was so bloody clever, because I was so damn lucky."

The overall Allied offensive succeeded, Hitler killed himself, and the

German armed forces surrendered unconditionally; the war in Europe was over. The Jewish Brigade was moved north, supposedly headed for Germany. But they were stopped on the Italian border: the British did not want them in Germany. Peltz and Israel Carmi disobeyed orders and went to the concentration camp at Mathausen. Starving survivors surrounded them; one pointed at the Jewish Star on Carmi's sleeve and asked quite seriously, "You're Jewish angels?"[41]

It was the first of many illegal trips. They began searching for family members; almost none were found. Confronting the loss of their loved ones, learning day by day the full details of the German atrocities, the huge numbers, they began to plot revenge—not in their official capacity as brigade members, but small groups slipping away to act in secret. They simply found SS and Gestapo criminals and killed them. Oly Givon used his fluent German to pose as an SS man in a beer hall and was directed to the house of a Nazi in charge of helping war criminals escape. A secret meeting was arranged. "And I said, 'Okay, we are now alone. I'm a Jew. You act against the Jews. You killed Jews.' And I start to talk with him. And the moment that I was a hundred percent sure that he is the man who killed Jews, then I said, 'In the name of the nation of the Jews, I kill you.' And I killed him."[42] Givon and Peltz captured two SS officers identified by—chilling irony— the blood groups tattooed under their left arms. They drove them to a mountaintop and backed them off a cliff. Givon liked the men to be facing him when he killed them, and he always announced, "In the name of the Jewish people, I sentence you to death."[43] Another Jew, Meir Zorea, preferred strangling SS men with a rope.[44]

In time brigade soldiers began to see the limits of vengeance. "What could we do?" Hanoch Bartov recalled. "We couldn't just walk the street and shoot. What we could do, is to look for Jews."[45] So they searched for refugees. One group was hiding in a bombed-out house. "And we entered . . . and we say 'Shabbat Shalom,' and they are all shocked, and we tell them that we are soldiers . . . from the Jewish Brigade. And this was something which I think, if I live a thousand years, I will not be able to forget. Because their reaction was as if they saw the Messiah. And they jumped, first of all, and then they started physically to touch us . . . if we are *real.* . . . A rumor passed all through Europe, that there *are* soldiers from Palestine. And if we go to them, if we reach them, or if they reach us, there is a future."[46]

◊ⵎⵎ◊

Dr. Moshe Bejski was a teenager freed from a concentration camp in Czechoslovakia on May 9, 1945. As he recalled decades later, he and other survivors crowded around their liberator, a Russian Jewish officer in the Red Army, saying, "Now tell us, where should we go?"

And his answer I will not forget until my last day. He said, "Don't go to the east, because they don't like us there. And don't go to the west, because they don't like us either." . . . The first day of liberation, after five and a half years being in ghettos and camps, and the man who liberated you, he brings you the message that you have no place to go. I decided not to return to Poland . . . because I knew Poland was a big Jewish cemetery.[47]

He and a group of other Jewish refugees walked west until they met a soldier from the Jewish Brigade who fed them and gave them hope.

Rinna Irmay was another of the thousands rescued, at a time when she felt that "nothing actually exists in the world that's worth to fight for and live for. And now you meet suddenly with young people—who weren't born heroes . . . just simple people—and who go and fight for something, they *believe* in something . . . All the young people who still were alive . . . We needed something to hang on."[48] A brigade veteran echoed this: "We were neither saints, nor knights, we were simple Israeli boys who understood that we stand now for the Jewish people."

The Allied high command decreed that all refugees would go back to their country of origin. This was impossible for the Jews, whose special status and vulnerability were not officially recognized. Those who tried to return found nobody, nothing except a gentile who had taken their homes after their deportations. Hundreds of Jews were killed by Poles and Ukrainians after the end of the war. But, said Avram Silberstein, another survivor, "We understood the situation. We understood that Europe—for the Jews—it's finished." But this was not understood by the Allied occupation forces. One camp commander, denying the presence of hundreds of Jews under his supervision, pointed at a chalkboard: "Here we have the names of the countries. You are not a nation, and therefore you don't appear on my board."[49]

The common notion that as the war ended the Jews were liberated and safe is out of touch with reality. Three months after the end of the war, in August 1945, anti-Jewish riots broke out in Cracow, Poland, and gradually spread elsewhere. During the first seven months after the armistice—up to a year after the last German had left Poland—350 Jews were murdered on Polish soil. Jews attempting to return to their homes were murdered by Polish underground groups all over the country—eight in Boleslawiec in October, eleven in Kosow-Lacki in December, four on a train from Lodz to Cracow in February, five dragged out of a car and murdered by shooting on the outskirts of Nowy Targ on Easter Sunday. Poles leaning out of windows laughed loudly at the procession of mourners. Six days later seven more Jews, men and women eighteen to forty-three, were murdered at almost the same spot. Violent incidents occurred in every town in Poland.[50]

The climax came on July 4, 1946, in Kielce, when Jews were accused of kidnapping a boy who had in fact been visiting a family friend. The Polish mob murdered forty-two Jews, including two children, four teenagers preparing to go to Israel, three Jewish officers in the Polish army, and one concentration camp survivor, tattoo number B 2969. The bodies were "neatly stacked like firewood around the fountain in the central square."[51] This final action had the desired effect. One hundred thousand Jews turned their backs on their Polish "homeland" and desperately sought refuge elsewhere. Rabbi Herbert Friedman, an American army chaplain stationed in Germany, was sent to examine the situation in Poland. "We found Poland's small Jewish communities in a state of near-hysteria. People were leaving their shabby homes without even attempting to take belongings, deserting their little shops or stores without locking the doors—just running."[52]

Friedman, a young Reform rabbi fresh from his first pulpit in Denver, had been working with the Jewish Brigade's clandestine operatives to save Jews. Months before, stationed in southern Bavaria between Munich and the Alps, he had roamed the countryside with a convoy of U.S. Army trucks rescuing homeless, traumatized Jews.[53] Remnant German "Edelweiss" units— that part of Bavaria was known as a hiding place for Nazis—sniped at the convoy and murdered many refugees. The children especially were frightened of everyone. Friedman encountered "a boy and girl, walking slowly along a farm road, filthy, clothes in tatters, holding hands, not talking.

> As our truck approached, and they saw we were slowing down, they started to run, jumping off the road into a ditch, he pulling her with all his strength, which wasn't much, across a plowed field, zigging and zagging as though looking for a place to hide. I walked, rather than ran, trying to indicate by stance and gesture that I did not intend to capture them, but was a friend. Gradually the distance between us narrowed, they tired and slowed down, and I overtook them. They held hands again, as though to go together to whatever lay in store.
>
> I told them my name and asked theirs. They did not know. Nor did they know where they were born, how old they were, what camp they had been in, or how long they had been on the road.... Eating the bread I gave them, they followed me back to the truck, to be hugged and kissed by the burly soldier-driver who was crying because these kids reminded him of his own.[54]

Friedman was driving through an Alpine snowstorm when he stopped for the night at an inn he knew. Called to the one phone at the front desk, he heard "a woman's voice, low and inviting." She wanted to know if he was the Ninth Division chaplain who had been bringing refugees to shelter. On whose orders, and with what funds? He bristled, but she asked him to meet her "in Room 203 of the Royal-Monceau Hotel in Paris," at his earliest convenience. He arranged a leave of absence.

> Three days later, I knocked on the mystery-woman's door at the Royal-Monceau. She was middle-aged, plain, somewhat tough-looking, and all business, with the bearing of someone who has seen much in life. . . . She took a deep breath and asked whether I would be willing to work with "them." When I asked who them was, she answered in just one word: *"Haganah." . . .* The question did not permit equivocation. . . . Not knowing what in the world I was getting into, my gut told me to say yes, and I did.
>
> Still holding me at the threshold with a gesture, the woman crossed the salon, knocked on a door at the far end, and escorted me toward a short man with a massive shock of white hair sprouting in all directions from the sides of his large, balding head. He was wearing an old sweater, khaki trousers, and house slippers. When she told him that I would work with "them," he offered me a quick, vigorous handshake and a verbal thank-you, turned, and retired.[55]

The man was David Ben-Gurion, soon to be the first prime minister of Israel, and he appeared to be satisfied. So began Friedman's association with the Haganah and the Jewish Brigade. They would commandeer trucks, smuggle contraband across the snowy mountains, bribe officials, and save scores of thousands of refugees.

At last the Jews were officially exempted from repatriation and moved "temporarily" to the displaced persons camps on Cyprus. After the gas chambers, the mass graves, and the crematoria had been photographed and the pictures published all over the world, it seemed logical to expect that the British would lift their immigration blockade of Palestine, but no; there was no gateway open to these people, except that the door to Israel was very slightly ajar. Prying it open was no small feat. Friedman's bending of the rules of the U.S. Army was difficult enough, but it required really unorthodox methods, said brigade member Maxim Kahan, to "exploit the British Army. We had no alternative. We cheated, we lied, we stole, we crooked— what didn't we do?" Meir Zorea recalled, "We had every facility for every service of life, from the womb to the tomb. We stole blankets, beds, medicine, milk, chocolate." There were five million people moving around Europe, "and we directed *our* streams toward Palestine."[56]

Most brigade members went on with their normal activities, but hundreds of others devoted themselves entirely to clandestine work with refugees. The army loved acronyms, so they made one up: TTG. It stood for Arabic and Yiddish words meaning "Up-My-Ass-Business." They could be stopped twenty times during one transport, flashlights shined on their human cargo, their work ticket checked each time. "You showed it to him with a smile on your face as if you owned the bloody world, you and Churchill are chums. And he says, 'TTG? What's that?' 'You don't know what TTG . . . ?—Huh! He doesn't know what TTG means!' That's all you need."[57]

Shaul Ramati proudly wore the kilt of the Gordon Highlanders, but when he was found to have signed off on illegal transports of Jewish refugees, the military police paid him a visit. "So I said, 'Well yes, that's my signature, alright.' And he said, 'Well, this is not the kind of behavior we expect from a British officer.' . . . And I said, 'Well you should expect something like this, because, you know, my mother was murdered in the Warsaw ghetto, and nearly all my family was destroyed there. And you can't expect me to sit here with folded arms, not even to try and do something to save those who survived.'"[58]

Cooperating with Jews in other British units and in the uniform of the United States, as well as sympathetic non-Jews, the brigade helped the Haganah move thousands upon thousands of people to Mediterranean harbors, where they boarded ships for Palestine. Most were turned back by the British blockade and confined to DP camps again. The Jewish Brigade was eventually punished by being withdrawn from central Europe and sent west. In Holland, they were put in charge of German prisoners; they set the POWs to cleaning the synagogues Germans had desecrated. Meanwhile, the brigade members stole thirty-four trucks to transport even more Jews. They worked without rest.

Their goal was to put a hundred thousand Jews in DP camps and then create overwhelming international pressure on the British to let them into Palestine. They constantly worked with the refugees, teaching them about Israel, practicing Hebrew with them, singing and dancing to the folk melodies of the new Jewish homeland. As for Jewish history, they already knew all they needed to know. Survivor Alex Shore recalled, "When they started singing, when they started dancing with us, we felt, my God, they are different. They're singing the same songs, but they are somehow taller than us. And we straightened up and we started singing like them, with more gusto, with the real Hebrew. We felt suddenly we belonged to our own people, belonged to our own kind, but with pride."[59]

The British would not relent; neither the new *aliyah*—immigration wave—of refugees nor the Jewish state itself would come without a fight. Brigade members began stealing weapons in vast quantities. Their boldness grew by leaps and bounds, and they were now not just running afoul of British policy, they were threatening British rule. All knew that if statehood depended on it, the Haganah would use these stolen weapons against the same British soldiers who had taught them to fight the Germans. The British had an inkling of what was going on but could not conceive its scale.

Finally the British gave up trying to control the Jewish Brigade; they disbanded it and dispatched its soldiers to Britain. But through a stunning ruse a hundred soldiers stayed behind to continue smuggling refugees and arms. They trained a hundred look-alike refugees as their doubles, schooling them in all the details of their lives, and sent these doubles to take their places as the brigade was broken up and transferred. In the end hundreds of thousands of Jewish refugees were rescued from a Europe that remained intensely hostile to them. They were moved to DP camps, and from there many were smuggled into the Yishuv to become part of the new state.

They would soon face new troubles and dangers. But for Bartov, the brigade had proven itself, and was now the core of the new Jewish army. "We had the inner feeling that we are able to do it, that we are able to defend ourselves, that we are able to acquire this piece of land for ourselves and the remnant. Could it *not* have happened? It *could* not have happened—but it did happen, and we are here."[60]

Peltz would summarize the Jewish Brigade's experience this way: "After the Holocaust, after so many million Jews went to their death without fighting, I think this is the most important facet on that Jewish Brigade. We broke a taboo. We proved to the world that we can fight. We proved to ourselves that we can fight. The Jews can fight, and they can win." They needed that assurance. The Haganah had proven for decades its bravery and sacrifice in defense of Jewish settlements. But it was not until the Jewish Brigade that they learned how to fight a regular army. And as veteran David Ben-David recalled, "When the war ended, there was big rejoicing among all the fighting armies. Most soldiers knew that when they finished the war, everybody would go home. But for us, our war was just beginning."[61]

15

THE GOLDEN LAND

HOW THE JEWS HELPED MAKE AMERICA

There were five great golden ages for diaspora Jews in five empires, where the tolerance of the dominant cultures created not just a safe haven but an embrace of friendly alliance and even an honored place. The first was Babylonia, now Iraq, where the main version of the Talmud was created during the first millennium. The community there led the Jewish world for nearly a thousand years until the eclipse of its academies by other centers—Rashi's Torah academy in Troyes, the kabbala school in Girona, Maimonides' oracular voice from Cairo, and the debates over his teachings in Provence and Ashkenaz.

In the second, Muslim Spain, Jews reached the highest ranks of science, scholarship, poetry, statesmanship, and military prowess for centuries, slowly spreading the great achievements of Islamic civilization up into backward Europe. This ended with a Christian return to power, culminating in 1492, when generations of persecution peaked in a vast expulsion and a coerced mass conversion, much of it dubious and temporary.

It was then that the Ottoman emperor said that the Spanish crown's foolishness was his good fortune, and the third Jewish golden age was ushered in with Constantinople at its heart. Four centuries of prosperity and tolerance ended with the immense and still puzzling shift of world leadership from Islam to Christian Europe.[1]

By this time, in parallel, the fourth golden age was established with welcoming Amsterdam as its center, also a consequence of the great Spanish expulsion. Here the ancient Jewish flair for trade and finance reached even greater heights, and the vigorous Dutch exploration of the world had important Jewish participants and backers. Jews found their way to every corner of the empire, settling from Guyana to Suriname.

But the fifth and most radiant of all golden ages was the one in the United States of America. Not that no Jews were persecuted. Christian sects seeking asylum from their enemies in Europe promptly became intolerant themselves. Yet the problem was largely temporary, and by the time of the American Revolution, it was clear that this would be a new kind of country, one where—with the crucial and shameful exceptions of Native Americans and African slaves—all comers would be on an equal footing. Every immigrant was new, none had ancient prior cultural claims, and America's face was turned toward the future, not the past.

At least in theory. Jews or conversos were with Columbus on his maiden voyage, and it is likely that his interpreter, a convert named Luis Torres, was among the first Europeans to set foot on American shores. This occurred at the exact moment of the exile from Spain, and Jewish financiers may have been among Columbus's backers—perhaps in an effort to find a place to go. In addition, the exile to Portugal led to some Jewish participation in Portuguese overseas explorations and, more important, to an even larger role in Dutch seagoing voyages. "Portuguese" Jews accompanied Dutch expeditions throughout the East Indies and the Americas and settled throughout the New World.

This was not always easy. Peter Stuyvesant, the first governor of Dutch New Amsterdam, rejected a group of twenty-three Jews attempting to settle there. They had helped the Dutch take Brazil from the Portuguese, but when the Portuguese took it back, the Jews had to flee. Some sailed to Newport, Rhode Island, others to New Amsterdam. Indeed, one of the earliest documents pertaining to North American Jews is Stuyvesant's letter about them to the Dutch West India Company's Amsterdam office in which he says that although "the Jews who have arrived would almost all like to remain here . . .

> we have, for the benefit of this weak and newly developing place and the land in general, deemed it useful to require them in a friendly way to depart; praying also most seriously in this connection . . . that the deceitful race,—such hateful enemies and blasphemers of the name of Christ,—be not allowed further to infect and trouble this new colony.[2]

New Amsterdam was then a colony of about 750 people of different sects and nations, speaking *eighteen* languages, and immigration was continual. In other words, what would in a decade become New York was already in microcosm what it is today, and a vivid contrast to the monolithically Puritan Massachusetts Bay Colony. Still, Jews were unwelcome.

In a petition the following January, the Jews reminded the company (which controlled the colony) of their sacrifices for the Dutch cause in the New World, that "[y]onder land is extensive and spacious," that the French admitted Jews to Martinique and the British admitted them to Barbados, and, not least, that they would be paying taxes. The company wrote

Stuyvesant in April that in view of the Jews' sacrifices in Brazil and "the large amount of capital which they still have invested in the shares of this company . . .

> after many deliberations we have finally decided and resolved . . . that these people may travel and trade to and in New Netherland and live and remain there, provided the poor among them shall not become a burden to the company or to the community, but be supported by their own nation. You will now govern yourself accordingly.[3]

As always, the Jews combined loyalty, courage, financial power, and force of argument in favor of fairness to attempt to ensure their survival. They faced many restrictions in the ensuing years, but they persisted, and these twenty-three Jews created what would be the greatest Jewish diaspora community in history, while setting the stage for a truly tolerant New World.

Tolerance of Jews began at home. Congregation Shearith Israel in New York had integrated Sephardic and Ashkenazic Jews by 1728; this required that they overcome many tensions, including a prohibition against intermarriage and an attempt by the Sephardic religious authority in Curaçao to prevent the Ashkenazim from joining the synagogue. The Ashkenazim had to recite some prayers in Portuguese, and the Sephardic Jews remained dominant, but some barriers gradually broke down.[4] So one of the first synagogues in the American colonies had to struggle to reduce tensions between different Jewish subcultures.

The story of Jewish settlement in the Georgia colony is also striking. A group of Jews in London, of Portuguese descent, had dwelt for generations in Amsterdam before moving to England. In their search for religious freedom, they believed the rumors of a new world of tolerance across the great sea. They set sail led by the acknowledged head of the community, a physician, and in 1733 arrived at the coast of the Georgia colony, where Governor James Oglethorpe had set up a village called Savannah. He had not built much, but he knew he did not want Jews. They were turned away and were preparing their ocean voyage when Oglethorpe learned that there was a doctor on the ship. There was an epidemic in Savannah at the time, and the governor invited the doctor to disembark; he refused to do so without his co-religionists.

Thus the first Jews in Georgia, admitted just months after the colony was founded. Like almost all the early Jews in the New World, they were Sephardim. Portuguese Jews fleeing Brazil settled not only New Amsterdam but Newport and elsewhere. By the mid-1700s they participated in all aspects of life in the colonies, helping to open the West, fighting on both sides in the French and Indian War, and in the South holding about 2 percent of the slaves, just in proportion to their share of the population. Documents show them, occasionally, stealing from each other. Others reveal every aspect of normal life. In Newport a Jewish social club was founded in 1761, and the rulebook specified the evening for the weekly meetings (Wednesday), the time supper was served ("eight of the clock"), and the fine for betting more than twenty shillings at whist ("four bottles good wine for the use and benefit of the ensuing club night").[5] The same fine was decreed for unruly behavior, swearing, or—remarkably—discussing synagogue affairs; even then synagogue politics could ruin a good evening. In New York in 1771 a *shochet,* or kosher butcher, was temporarily suspended by Congregation Shearith Israel for alleged laxity in ritual slaughter, but he was cleared and reinstated.

Jews participated in the growing resistance to Britain. For example, eleven Jews were among 375 merchants who signed a petition pledging to reject British trade restrictions. Some Jews were Tories, but many joined the Revolution. One, Francis Salvador of South Carolina, an elected member of that colony's Provincial Congress, was killed on August 4, 1776, a month after the Declaration of Independence. His commanding officer reported his death in a battle against Cherokee Indians fighting for the British. At night the enemy "poured a heavy fire upon my men; which, being unexpected, staggered my advanced party," the officer wrote.

> Here, Mr. Salvador received three wounds; and, fell by my side. . . . I desired [Lieutenant Farar] to take care of Mr. Salvador; but, before he could find him in the dark, the enemy unfortunately got his scalp: which, was the only one taken. . . . When I came up to him, after dislodging the enemy, and speaking to him, he asked, whether I had beat the enemy? I told him yes. He said he was glad of it, and shook me by the hand—and bade me farewell—and said, he would die in a few minutes.[6]

Salvador died "about half after two in the morning; forty-five minutes after he received the wounds, sensible to the last."

But most important are the exchanges of letters between several Jewish communities and President George Washington. The Hebrew Congregation of Savannah, writing on May 6, 1789, congratulated him on his unanimous election: "Yet, however exalted the station you now fill, it is still not equal to the merit of your heroic services." They also refer to "our eccentric situation," and thank him pointedly:

> Your unexampled liberality and extensive philanthropy have dispelled that cloud of bigotry and superstition which has long, as a veil, shaded religion. . . . [You have] enfranchised us with all the

privileges and immunities of free citizens, and initiated us into the
grand mass of legislative mechanism. By example, you have taught
us to endure the ravages of war with manly fortitude, and to enjoy
the blessings of peace.

Washington replied with comparable courtesy and characteristic modesty:

I rejoice that a spirit of liberality and philanthropy is much
more prevalent than it formerly was among the enlightened nations
of the earth; and that your brethren will benefit thereby in proportion as it shall become still more extensive.

He closed by invoking the blessing of the God they shared in common:

May the same wonder-working Deity, who long since delivered
the Hebrews from their Egyptian Oppressors planted them in the
promised land—whose providential agency has lately been conspic-
uous in establishing these United States . . . continue to water them
with the dews of Heaven and to make the inhabitants of every de-
nomination participate in the temporal and spiritual blessings of
that people whose God is Jehovah.[7]

Not only did Washington use the central Jewish experience of deliverance
to symbolize the birth of American freedom, he suggested that the United
States would be an example to the world, and that the freedom and equality of the American Jews would set the standard for treatment of all citizens.

Yet even more powerful and pointed was his answer to a letter from the
Newport Congregation after a visit the following year. They began, "Permit the Children of the Stock of Abraham to approach you with the most
cordial affection and esteem," and reflected

with pleasure . . . on those days of difficulty and danger, when the
God of Israel, who delivered David from the peril of the sword—
shielded your head in the day of battle . . . and the same Spirit, who
rested in the bosom of the greatly beloved Daniel, enabling him to
preside over the Babylonish Empire, rests, and ever will rest upon
you, enabling you to discharge the arduous duties of Chief Magistrate in these states.

Deprived as we have hitherto been of the invaluable rights of
free citizens, we now . . . behold a Government . . . which to bigotry
gives no sanction, to persecution no assistance—but generously af-

fording to All liberty of conscience, and immunities of citizenship—deeming every one, of whatever nation, tongue, or language
equal parts of the great governmental machine.

Washington's reply echoed some famous phrases, but added a point of the
utmost importance:

> All possess alike liberty of conscience and immunities of citi-
> zenship. It is now no more that toleration is spoken of, as if it was by
> the indulgence of one class of people, that another enjoyed the exer-
> cise of their inherent natural rights. For happily the government of
> the United States, which gives to bigotry no sanction, to persecution
> no assistance, requires only that they who live under its protection
> shall demean themselves as good citizens.[8]

"It is now no more that toleration is spoken of. . . ." Don't make a mistake,
he is saying, about what this new country stands for. There is no one for you
to thank. Your citizenship is the same as everyone else's. I don't tolerate you
any more or less than you tolerate me.

The value of these words cannot be overstated. This was to be the first
and only diaspora in which Jews did not live by someone else's sufferance.
Jews would stand on American soil with the same firm and confident stance
taken by everyone else, as Washington showed by addressing them as equals:

> It would be inconsistent with the frankness of my character not
> to avow that I am pleased with your favorable opinion of my ad-
> ministration, and fervent wishes for my felicity.
>
> May the children of the Stock of Abraham, who dwell in this
> land, continue to merit and enjoy the good will of the other inhabi-
> tants, while every one shall sit in safety under his own vine and fig-
> tree, and there shall be none to make him afraid.
>
> May the Father of all mercies scatter light and not darkness in
> our paths, and make us all in our several vocations useful here, and
> in his own due time and way everlastingly happy.

Everlastingly happy they may not have been, but better off than ever before
they most certainly were. It is a mark of Washington's genius and character
that when the Jews said *Thank you,* his firm and instructive retort was, *We.*

There were many departures from Washington's principles. But in every
instance, prominent Christians intervened to protect Jews or condemned

their persecution afterward, and over time there grew a body of law and custom admitting Jews to all the protections and opportunities of Americans. Some rights took two centuries to secure, but today the Jews of the United States are blessed with an equality unprecedented in history. Indeed, having proved countless times their ability to survive persecution with their culture more or less intact, they now face what may be a greater challenge: Can Jewish culture survive acceptance?

Jews were always more well-off than Mexican Americans, more integrated than Asian Americans, and on these shores knew no pain remotely comparable to that of African Americans. Still they were hated, feared, mistrusted, and persecuted. The difference was in the balance between parochial persecution and the universal tolerance enshrined in the Constitution. "Not under man but under God and law" has always been an American motto; the Jews provided the first strong tests of that belief, laying the groundwork for the struggles of other minorities.

Jacob Henry served in the North Carolina legislature in 1808 and was reelected the following year, but this time a colleague proposed that his seat be vacated because he did not take the standard oath swearing allegiance to the New as well as the Old Testament. In his defense, Henry pointed out that "the Language of the Bill of Rights is that all men have a natural and unalienable right to worship Almighty God according to the dictates of their own Conscience." He asked his colleagues, "[w]ho among us feels himself so exalted above his fellows, as to have a right to dictate to them their mode of belief? Shall this free Country set an example of Persecution, which even the returning reason of enslaved Europe would not submit to? . . . Will you drive from your shores and from the shelter of your constitutions, all who do not lay their oblations at the same altar, observe the same ritual, and subscribe to the same dogmas?" Sadly, he felt a need to justify Judaism:

> The religion I profess, inculcates every duty which man owes to his fellow men; it enjoins upon its votaries, the practice of every virtue, and the detestation of every vice; it teaches them to hope for the favor of Heaven exactly in proportion as their lives are directed by just, honorable and beneficent maxims—This then Gentlemen is my creed; it was impressed upon my infant mind, it has been the director of my youth, the monitor of my manhood, and will I trust be the Consolation of my old age.[9]

Supported by two prominent Catholics, he kept his seat.

But a later controversy showed that the separation of church and state was not to be complete. The governor of South Carolina declared a day of thanksgiving and undertook to "invite and exhort our Citizens of all denominations to Assemble at their respective places of worship to offer up their devotions to God the Creator, and his Son Jesus Christ, the redeemer of the world."[10] Over a hundred prominent Charleston Jews wrote the governor that his decree excluded them. He replied with regret about any unintended offense, but did not apologize or change the proclamation, "because I suffer little when I am satisfied that I have done no wrong." Considering that the inaugural oath taken by President George W. Bush in the year 2001 was bracketed by two prayers invoking Jesus Christ, it is scarcely surprising that in 1844 the governor stood his ground.[11]

The tradition of Jewish American soldiering begun in the French and Indian War continued. In 1846 Jacob Hirschorn, sixteen, left his mother and sister in Bavaria and moved to New York. As he later wrote, "I . . . was left entirely to myself and I could do as I pleased. I would generally visit the Café de Paris on Broadway, to sit down comfortably to read the *Courier des Etats Unis.* . . . This café was the rendezvous of the best class of French and German, who came there regularly to drink their 'verre de Cognac.'"[12] There Jacob met a French count who chatted with him, murmuring, "Bon garçon." He soon invited the boy to become his "protégé" in the New York Volunteers, raised for the Mexican War. "You will get a position in the army, you will fight for 'Uncle Sam,' and you will see a great deal of the world." Jacob was eager, and the count got around the army's lower age limit.

They soon landed near Vera Cruz, where "quite a respectable fleet of U.S. warships" pounded the city. With the town in flames, "the Mexican flag came down, and the 'Stars and Stripes' were hoisted . . . celebrated by a salute . . . deafening to a novice but nothing unusual to me after hearing that racket for two days." Moving inland, they encountered General Santa Anna, "entrenched on the heights with 20,000 troops and any amount of artillery." After six hours of uphill fighting the Americans prevailed—"the Mexicans fled 'vamoosed' as they call it,"—but when they encamped "about half our force were invalids, some killed and wounded in battle and a great many sick at the hospitals as a result of eating the fruits of the country, which our boys could not stand."

As they ran short of food, Jacob, conversant in English, French, and German, found a role. He was too young to be an officer, "but they would send me out in the country at the head of a company of dragoons or mounted riflemen and six or eight wagons, to scout and forage for anything eatable for man or beast."

After three months their force of twelve thousand marched on Mexico City. Jacob's brigade laid siege in a very difficult battle. The assault on Chapultepec was mounted by a group of volunteers "called the 'Forlorn Hope,' because none expected to return alive.

We advanced two hundred strong. I omitted to say, that I volunteered to join. Under a terrible fire of artillery and muskets from the castle and wall we approached the wall, raised our ladders, and began to climb up. It was a terrible sight to see our brave fellows drop from the ladders, shot. Finally we reached the top of the wall. . . . As soon as the glorious "Stars and Stripes" floated from the wall the Mexican flag came down. The defenders became demoralized and vamoosed.

The U.S. troops "finally entered the city, opposed by the retreating enemy, who defended every foot of ground stubbornly and who were nobly assisted by hundreds of Mexican ladies, who from the tops of their houses . . . were pouring boiling water, boiling oil, rocks, anything they could lay their hands on, upon the very much exposed heads of our boys."

After the war, Jacob shipped to New Orleans with the army. "Here I took sick, with yellow fever, where I was tenderly cared for by the good sisters. An hour or so in the afternoons my nurse would read a little tract to me. I seemingly listened very attentively to her, but inwardly I muttered to myself: 'Geh veg mit Deiner Schabbes Schmues' [Get out of here with your Sabbath shmooze]." After recovering he returned to his unit for discharge. "New York City gave us a splendid and very enthusiastic reception and a silver medal for each soldier. We left New York 1200 strong and we returned about 260."

It is hard to imagine Jews in the Wild West, but they were there.[13] John M. Levy was an Indian agent for the Winnebago Indians, based at La Crosse, Wisconsin, on the Mississippi River. The son of a London cantor, educated in Amsterdam and Paris, he came to St. Louis and there met his future wife, Augusta. He and his partner, Isaac Marks, were traders in La Crosse, and in 1846 he brought his wife and son to live there. The Indians had recently been pacified and requested a chief's council under Levy's auspices. Augusta recalled the event:

Next day about eleven o'clock, a beautiful, bright day, we could see a great way up and down the river, all at once we saw the greatest sight I ever saw. About fifty canoes appeared, filled with all the Indian chiefs, all of them dressed and painted, and with big bunches of feathers on their heads and tomahawks in their hands. They were dressed in their best, and glistened as if a procession all shining with gold and silver was coming down the river. I didn't know anything about their arrangements, so little Willie and I were scared. We feared that they were coming to kill us all, I ran to shut all the windows and lock all the doors.[14]

John calmed Augusta down, and the council was held. The chiefs prevailed on him to write to Washington and try to reverse their impending relocation. ("They liked this country so well they refused to leave till they were taken by force," Augusta had written.) John's letter, "To the President of the U.S. or To the Secretary of Indian Affairs," said that the Winnebago Indians begged to be allowed to move north along the riverbank instead of far from the river, promising peace and protection for their white neighbors and "sworn brotherhood with the Sue nation . . . who are willing to live in unity with them." They also requested an audience with the president. None of these requests was granted.

The Far West was more civilized. By 1860 there were Jewish congregations all over California. In San Francisco alone the Jewish businesses paying heavy taxes in 1865 included fifteen dry-goods jobbers, seven in clothing (including Levi Strauss), five in cigars and tobacco, four in jewelry and watches, three in gents' furnishings, two hat and cap jobbers, two carpet and upholstery jobbers, two in boots and shoes, two wholesale grocers, two insurance men, two merchants, one real-estate man, one banker, one mining-stock broker, one wholesale stationer, one hides and wools jobber, one crockery and glassware dealer, and one willow-ware merchant. Henry Labatt, a Jewish attorney, tried to explain, in an 1861 article in the *True Pacific Messenger,* "the large number of mercantile houses conducted by Israelites":

> Each mining town and city has a large representation, and everywhere you hear of their success and prosperity, which in turn they devote to the improvement of the place. . . .
>
> In all the great fires which have devastated the settlements of California, they have been great sufferers. Year after year, have they seen the hard earnings of their labor swept away by the ruthless conflagration, and yet, with the indomitable energy of their race, have they toiled on.

The racial explanation gives way to more plausible specifics:

> . . . their individual industry dispenses with the necessity for extra clerks. . . . They seldom pay unwarrantable rents. . . . They eschew all display of brilliant fixtures, or other unnecessary expenses. . . . They seem anxious to dispose of their stock in a short time, and at little profit, and you will generally find . . . that their stores are known as "cheap stores." This is a great secret of trade . . . and then, by courtesy and a determination to give satisfaction, success seems inevitable. . . .
>
> Their quick perception gives them an insight into the require-

ments of every branch of trade . . . and the natural sympathy of, and connection with, the other members of their faith, incite them to an emulation, the result of which is a high commercial position in the community. . . . This has had much influence in banishing the shameful prejudices . . . against the Israelites, as a sordid and cunning race.[15]

Even allowing for special pleading, these are insights into the culture of Jewish business, the lessons of thousands of years.

Jews served on both sides in the Civil War. Judah P. Benjamin had been the first Jewish senator from Louisiana before the war, was attorney general, secretary of war and then of state in the Confederacy, and became counsel to the queen of England after the surrender. August Belmont was a German-born Jewish New Yorker who had worked for the Rothschilds and had considerable influence in Britain and continental Europe. Although a Democratic Party stalwart and Lincoln opponent before the war, he rallied to the Union cause and on Lincoln's request made the government's case in Europe.

And Jews were in the rank and file. An anonymous letter from "a Jewish soldier" on the Union side claimed that there were five thousand Jews in the army and little anti-Semitism, but "as a general rule, the Jews do not care to make their religion a matter of notoriety, as it would at once involve them in an intricate controversial disquisition with the Christian Chaplains, for which they do not always feel themselves qualified." He found soldiers religious, the Jews being no exception:

It is quite common for Jewish soldiers belonging to the same company, to meet together for worship on Sabbath, in some secluded spot, and I know a young soldier, who was on Kippore morning, ordered to take part in a skirmish, near Harper's Ferry, which he had to go through, without having tasted food, and as soon as the enemy retreated, he retired to the woods, where he remained until sunset, reading his prayers. . . .

I cannot help reflecting on the remarkable history of our race. Here are the descendants of the Hebrew patriarch who smote the confederated kings near Damascus, the descendants of those who overthrew the colossal hosts of proud Egypt, and conquered the powerful nations of Philistea, who, under the Maccabees, triumphed over the Syrian despot. . . . behold them now in the New World, shedding their blood for the maintenance of the liberties secured to them by this Republic. . . . I feel most solemnly impressed by hearing in these Virginian forests my brethren, utter the *Shymang Israel,* which first our great lawgiver proclaimed in the plains of Arabia.

Some of the Jewish officers and soldiers had fought in European wars, and "not liking the dull routine of a soldier's life in times of peace, they eagerly avail themselves of every opportunity to return to their tents and the battle-field. This was the first time I had ever heard of such a class of military adventurers among our people." He also relates a story he has heard sec-ondhand, but worth telling. A "very religious" Dutch Jewish artilleryman at the Battle of Waterloo shouted "Shema Yisrael" at the top of his voice every time he fired his cannon. This primary Jewish declaration of faith— "Hear O Israel, the Lord is our God, the Lord is One"—seemed odd in this context. Asked to explain, he said, "It may be some Yehudee gets killed by him, and he could never pardon himself, if any one of his brethren should, through him, go out of the world without *Shemos.*"[16]

On the Confederate side, Private Lewis Leon, who with his brother Morris and his friend Aaron Katz fought with the First North Carolina Regiment, kept a diary in which he recorded Jewish holidays as well as bat-tles, including Gettysburg. Captured and imprisoned, he finally "took the cursed oath" of allegiance to the United States, closing his diary with, "I still say our Cause was just, nor do I regret one thing that I have done to cripple the north."[17]

That war saved the Union, but it did not unite Jews and Christians. A celebrated court battle in 1869 dealt with the separation of church and state in schools. The Cincinnati school board decided to stop the reading of the King James Bible in schools. The board had forty members: eighteen Protestants, ten Catholics, assorted Unitarians, Quakers, and atheists, and two Jews, one on each side of the vote. Protestants filed suit to reinstate Bible reading, and the board's attorney, J. B. Stallo, addressed the plaintiffs' claim that the law in general was really Christian. His argument spoke vol-umes about what Jews had already achieved in America.

> I know of no civil right which the Christian holds in preference over the professors of another creed or of no creed. The Jew for in-stance, can hold property. . . . He can sue and be sued. There are the same remedies, civil and criminal, for wrongs inflicted upon a Jew, as for those done to a Christian. The Jew can be a witness in a court of justice, for the Constitution provides, that "no person shall be in-competent to be a witness on account of his religious belief." The Jew has a right to vote. He can hold any office. . . . A Jew may sit upon the bench, and administer justice *"without respect of persons,"* between Christians, as a Jew now sits upon the bench in New York. A Jew may not only administer the law, but help to make it. A Jew sat last winter, in the Ohio Legislature, and there is nothing in the Constitution to hinder that the majority of the Legislature may be Jews—a case which, according to the theory of the plaintiffs, would

present the remarkable anomaly of a body of Jews making Christian laws. . . . Jews have sat in both houses of Congress. A Jew may be President of the United States, if he has the requisite other qualifications and can obtain the requisite number of electoral votes. . . . I might proceed indefinitely . . . but I have gone far enough to show, that there is no particular, definite civil right, which Jews, Christians, and non-believers do not share in common. And in view of this I am not able to see the force of the assertion so frequently and so confidently made, that Christianity is part of the law of the state.[18]

This case was fought against the background of a Presbyterian campaign to amend the Constitution to include "national recognition of God the Lord Jesus Christ, and the Holy Scriptures." The Cincinnati Superior Court found for the plaintiffs, but the Ohio State Supreme Court reversed the decision unanimously, explicitly denying that Christianity is part of the law of the United States. Yet a quarter century later, in 1895, a new school board reinstituted Bible reading and this time was upheld by the courts. By 1933, 85 percent of Ohio schools had the readings, and other states were divided, with twelve requiring it, seven specifically permitting it, seven making it optional to school boards, and eleven prohibiting it. The controversy continues.

⟳〰〰⟲

At the time of the Revolution, America's Sephardic Jews were assimilated and prosperous but few in number.[19] In 1800 there were more Jews in South Carolina than in any other state, and they were about to make a historic transition from Sephardic Orthodoxy to an American version of Reform Judaism. Southern Jewry was already over a century old.[20] An official document penned in an elegant hand, dated May 26, 1697, reads in part, "Greeting: Know you that Simon Valentine Merch[ant]: an Alien of the Jewish Nation . . . hath Taken his oath of Allegiance . . . and is fully and Effectually to all Intents, Constructions and Purposes Qualified and Capacitate to have, use and Enjoy all the Rights, Privileges, Powers, and Immunities Given or Intended to bee given to any Alien then Inhabitant of South Carolina."[21] Within a few years Valentine and his partner Mordecai Nathan had purchased a 350-acre plantation, making them eligible to vote. These were the first Jewish settlers in the colony, and by 1800 their descendants and other Jews had established a life that was culturally rich, economically comfortable, and in touch with other Jewish communities, exchanging goods and marriage partners up and down the eastern seaboard. In 1816, Isaac Harby of Charleston wrote to then Secretary of State James Monroe, echoing Washington's words of a generation earlier, saying that Jews "are by no means to be considered as a Religious sect, tolerated by the government; they constitute a portion of *the People* . . . in every respect, woven in and compacted with the citizens of the Republic . . . one great political family."[22]

Almost all the communities from Newport, Rhode Island, to Savannah, Georgia, were proudly Sephardic in origin. This changed with immigration from Germany and Austro-Hungary beginning in 1820. There were 3,000 Jews in the United States in 1818, 15,000 in 1840, 50,000 in 1850, and 150,000 by 1860. In the 1820s it had already taken on the character of a mass migration; a leading German newspaper reported that whole Jewish communities had left and synagogues were closing. After the failed revolutions of 1848, in which Jews had played some role, the migrations stepped up markedly. Anti-Semitism certainly figured in this process. "It must have been disconcerting for Bavarian Jews to know that shouts of 'Banish the Jews to America!' resounded in the chambers of the Bavarian Diet."[23]

These Ashkenazic German Jews tended to be Orthodox, shocked by the lack of observance among American Jews, and viewed as boors by their established predecessors. The new immigrants were earthy, emotional, and even inclined to fistfights in the synagogue, one of which occurred on Yom Kippur Eve in a dispute over whether "Adon Olam" or "Yigdal" should be the closing hymn. We saw how Shearith Israel, a wealthy Sephardic congregation in New York, tolerated Ashkenazic members as early as 1728. A century later things were different; the membership committee said in 1835 that it was its "imperious duty" to introduce laws "rendering the admission of improper persons as members more difficult than it has heretofore been."[24]

But the situation changed rapidly. The German Jews tended to be entrepreneurs, and they spread both their business and their religion throughout the land. Now the great majority of American Jews, they established synagogues everywhere. There were 160 Jewish communities by 1860. A German-language paper noted in that year, "Many, very many of these beggarly-poor emigrants are nowadays at the head of business concerns that own enormous property, command unlimited credit, and each year amass great fortunes."[25] Temple Emanu-El in New York, which served the rising class of German-Jewish businessmen, was a case in point. In 1845 the impoverished members raised $28.25 for the congregation; in 1868 they dedicated a new building at the corner of Forty-third Street and Fifth Avenue, and the pews were sold for a total of more than $700,000. Rabbi Isaac Meyer Wise, the spiritual leader of the German Jews, had been punched on the pulpit of an insignificant Albany shul in 1850 by the congregation's president, who wanted him out. In 1867 he stood beside Ralph Waldo Emerson in Boston at the first meeting of the Free Religious Association, declaring that man could perfect himself through reason.

With this new status came a disdain for traditional Judaism. Reform Judaism, founded by German Jews, began to influence German-Jewish

Americans, and even before the Civil War they had shortened services and introduced some English. But after the war they attacked traditional forms with a vengeance. Services were shortened much more, prayers for return to Zion were abolished, Hebrew was nearly eliminated, organ music was introduced, and men and women were seated together. Men were prohibited from wearing skullcaps and prayer shawls, and many services were switched from Saturday to Sunday. The Hebrew Union College of Cincinnati was the first rabbinical training school in America, but it was so devotedly Reform that the dinner honoring its first graduating class served shrimp, crabs, oysters, and littleneck clams—all *traif,* or forbidden foods. Orthodox rabbis present rushed from the room, the first major rift in the American Jewish community.

Nevertheless, Jewish American life was complex and thriving. Jews were even making inroads into American letters. In anticipation of the arrival of France's great Centennial gift, the Statue of Liberty, a poetry contest was held, with Emerson—Boston Brahmin, Protestant minister, and American literary giant—as the judge. He chose a sonnet by a Sephardic Jewish woman from New York, Emma Lazarus, which only much later— tragically and ironically, after Jewish immigration had been almost stopped— was engraved in bronze at the statue's base:

> *Not like the brazen giant of Greek fame,*
> *With conquering limbs astride from land to land,*
> *Here at our seawashed, sunset gates shall stand*
> *A mighty woman with a torch. Her flame*
> *Is the imprisoned lightning and her name,*
> *Mother of Exiles. Keep, ancient lands, your*
> *Storied pomp, cries she with silent lips . . .*
> *Give me your tired, your poor,*
> *Your huddled masses yearning to breathe free*
> *The wretched refuse of your teeming shore,*
> *Send these, the homeless, tempest-tost to me,*
> *I lift my lamp beside the golden door.*

But now the tables were turned on the German Jews, and they would experience the same kind of discomfort that they had caused among the Sephardim. The golden door swung open, and by 1880 there were 250,000 Jews in the United States, one in five of whom were from eastern Europe. In 1920 there were 4 million, and the ratio was more than reversed—five out of six were from eastern Europe.[26] Most stopped or at least passed through the Lower East Side of Manhattan, where population densities in the 1890s were double those of the worst slums in London.[27] These added millions changed the character of American-Jewish culture, and American culture, permanently.[28]

The new immigrants peddled, worked in garment industry sweatshops, made cigarettes, joined the building trades. Wages were low, working conditions were dreadful, and the workweek was seventy hours, but most of them considered this a solid stepping-stone. While learning English they continued to speak Yiddish for decades, supporting a flourishing culture in that language—journalism, novels, poems, songs, plays, even movies. The *Forverts,* or *Forward,* was the leading Yiddish daily, and it exposed social injustice even while avoiding ideological commitment. Its most popular feature was "A Bintel Brief"—"A Bundle of Letters"—in which immigrants poured their hearts out to the editors and each other in a language only they could understand. This one came from Chicago in 1910:

> Worthy Editor,
> My husband, ——— [here the name was given], deserted me and our three small children. . . . I was left without a bit of bread for the children, with debts in the grocery store and the butcher's, and last month's rent unpaid.

She explained that she couldn't work because her youngest was six months old, and that the local Jewish Welfare Agencies wouldn't help her because it had been only four months since her husband brought her over from Canada.

> It breaks my heart but I have come to the conclusion that in order to save my innocent children from hunger and cold I have to give them away.
> I will sell my beautiful children to people who will give them a home. I will sell them, not for money, but for bread, for a secure home where they will have enough food and warm clothing for the winter.
> I, the unhappy young mother, am willing to sign a contract, stating that the children belong to the good people who will treat them tenderly. Those who are willing and able to give my children a good home can apply to me.
> Respectfully,
> Mrs. P———

They published her full name and address, along with this answer:

> What kind of society are we living in that forces a mother to such desperate straits that there is no other way out than to sell her three children for a piece of bread? Isn't this enough to kindle a hellish fire of hatred in every human heart for such a system?

The first to be damned is the heartless father, but who knows what's wrong with him? Perhaps he, too, is unhappy. We hope, though, that this letter will reach him and he will return to aid them.

We also ask our friends and readers to take an interest in this unfortunate woman and to help her so that she herself can be a mother to her children.

Lighter notes were struck as well; there was much advice to the lovelorn. A beautiful 1907 letter came from a young woman who had fallen in love while on a trip back to Europe. "He was handsome, clever, educated," loved her dearly, and played a big role in his town, where the young women envied her. When he came to America, her parents embraced him, but her friends made fun of him and of her for loving him: "This greenhorn is your fiancé?" This mockery gradually affected her.

> In short, my love for him is cooling off. . . . I am suffering terribly because my feelings for him are changing. . . . I haven't the courage to tell him. . . . He still loves me with all his heart. . . . I choke it all up inside myself, and I beg you to help me with advice in my desperate situation.

The editor wasted no words:

> The writer would make a grave mistake if she were to separate from her bridegroom now. She must not lose her common sense and be influenced by the foolish opinions of her friends who divided the world into "greenhorns" and real Americans.
>
> We can assure the writer that her bridegroom will learn English quickly. He will know American history and literature as well as her friends do, and be a better American than they. She should be proud of his love and laugh at those who call him "greenhorn."

Few institutions matched the "Bintel Brief" as a source of advice for poor Jews negotiating the treacherous, unknown shoals of immigration.

Most arrived as Orthodox Jews, but families were riven by the strain of assimilation. Parents wanted their children to be American, but then they lost them as the linguistic, religious, and cultural gulf widened. *"A klug zu Columbusn!"*—"A plague on Columbus"—was a remark sometimes heard as the pain and loss of assimilation were felt. To mitigate this loss and hold on to their ancient religion, American Jews produced an unprecedented spectrum of religious adaptations. Solomon Shechter moved to New York from Cambridge University to found the Jewish Theological Seminary, which would ordain thousands of Conservative rabbis. Reform temples, founded by German Jews, expanded greatly, and many more were established, as the demand swelled for a more American Judaism. Yet at the same time Orthodoxy thrived; Orthodox day schools, or yeshivas, multiplied, and in 1897 Yeshiva University was founded.

Ethically and socially conscious, ever willing to protest injustice, these millions of new Jewish Americans joined their non-Jewish counterparts in creating labor unions that transformed work in America. Some Jews became socialists or even communists, but most were just unionists. They followed the lead of Samuel Gompers, a Jewish American immigrant from England who founded the American Federation of Labor in 1886, and whose program of cooperative negotiation with employers became the basis of modern collective bargaining. More militant Jewish labor leaders also made an impact, and strikes, as we have seen, were a valuable instrument of persuasion.

All in all, "Eastern European Jews forged and sustained a unique transitional culture in New York for almost four decades."[29] The new immigrants created a stunning variety of Jewish organizations, including clubs, cultural centers, ideological societies, and federations—immensely successful charitable organizations supporting Jewish causes. At the grassroots level a core institution was the *landsmanshaft,* or "countrymen's society," naturally formed from the ties that bound immigrants from each shtetl or small region of eastern Europe.[30] Coming of age in Jewish Brooklyn as late as the 1950s, one still heard old men say, *"Er iz mein landsman!"*—"He's my countryman!"—with a particular smile of warmth and indulgence.

On a much larger communal scale, a growing national network of Jewish social services steadily reduced the burden these immigrants placed on their adopted country. Nevertheless, anti-Semitism grew as the Jewish population did, and in 1924 the trend culminated in an act of Congress that turned Jewish immigration off, trapping millions in Hitler's web. Not until the late 1930s would Jewish immigration resume, and at only a fraction of former levels. The American-Jewish community, then timid and wary of anti-Semitism, did almost as little as the American government to save Hitler's victims.[31]

✺

But not all Jews were religious or industrious. There were a million recent Jewish immigrants and their families in New York as the twentieth century dawned—impoverished, culture-shocked, and struggling for a foothold—and this created ideal conditions for crime. It happened with every immigrant group, and the Jews were no exception. Not only in New York, but in many other cities where Americanizing Jews numbered scores of thousands, predatory lowlifes and desperately poor wrongdoers emerged from the nooks and crannies of the Jewish American world, and some parlayed their wrongs into vicious little empires.

Human, or at least male, needs were at the heart of the first wave of crime, as prostitution flourished in all the ghetto neighborhoods. Of 581 foreign-born prostitutes brought before the New York City Magistrates Court from November 1908 to March 1909, 154 were French, 64 German, 31 Italian, 29 Irish, and 10 Polish; 225 were Jewish. Many other surveys and sources of evidence show a preponderance of Jewish prostitutes in New York. The Lower East Side had become "one of the infamous red-light zones of the age."[32]

With so many thousands of unattached men in the immigrant populations, prostitution was inevitable, and even some authorities viewed it with compassion. As William McAdoo, a New York police commissioner, wrote in 1906, "The horrors of the sweatshop, the awful sordidness of life in the dismal tenement, the biting, grinding, poverty, the fierce competition, the pitiful wages for long hours of toil under unwholesome conditions, physical depression, and mental unhappiness are all allied with the temptation to join the better-clad, better-fed, and apparently happier people."[33] The great muckraking journalist Lincoln Steffens covered crime on the Lower East Side:

> "Oh, Meester Report!" an old woman wailed one evening. "Come to my house and see my children, my little girls." She seized and pulled me in . . . up the stairs, weeping, into her clean, dark room, one room, where her three little girls were huddled at the one rear window, from which they—and we—could see a prostitute serving a customer. "*Da, sehen Sie,* there they are watching, always they watch. . . . They count the men who come of a night," she said. "Ninety-three one night." (I shall never forget that number.) "My oldest girl says that she will go into that business when she grows up; she says it's a good business, easy, and you can dress and eat and live."[34]

Pimps did a lot of recruiting among women who knew what they were getting into. For example, the many dance halls that filled up as the twelve-hour workdays ended provided a steady supply. As famed reformer Jacob Riis reported even in the 1880s, "young people in Jewtown are inordinately fond of dancing." Belle Lindner Israels, writing in 1900, said, "If you walk along Grand Street on any night in the week during the winter months, the glare of lights and the blare of music strikes you on every side. It might be an esplanade at Dreamland instead of a business street. Columbia Street, Delancey Street, Stanton Street, Allen Street, Houston Street all have their quota of places, good, bad and indifferent. . . . You cannot dance night after night, held in the closest of sensual embraces, with every effort made in the style of dancing to appeal to the worst in you and remain unshaken by it."[35] At a nickel a night, even a lowly shirtmaker could dance.

But pimps cruising dance halls were only the beginning. Entrepreneurs built whorehouse empires. Motche Goldberg turned one girl out in the 1890s, and by 1912 earned four thousand dollars a month (a fortune in today's dollars) from 114 women in eight establishments. He shipped women to the South and West, wherever there were solitary men, and many other Jews shared in this thriving export business. But the darker side was the import business. At a *Jewish* international conference in London in April 1910, it became clear that Jewish white slavery had international scope. Arthur R. Moro reported that "the traffic of Jewesses is almost worldwide."

> In 1901, a Rabbi came from the Transvaal and told me that the amount of Jewish prostitution and traffic in Johannesburg, Pretoria, Lourenço Marques, Beira, and Salisbury are appalling. In later years the same story came from another Rabbi regarding Capetown. . . . In 1903 a Jewish schoolmaster who had spent some time in Egypt said that the traffic by Jews of Jewesses to Alexandria, Cairo, and Port Said was an absolute scandal.
>
> There were Greek, Italian and French prostitutes, but they were far outnumbered by the Jewesses. . . . this awful condition of affairs exists in Calcutta to a large extent, and also all along the free ports of China. . . .
>
> From the Chief Rabbi of Constantinople, from a distinguished Jewish-American scholar, from a prominent London gentleman, and from a schoolmistress in Galata we have had letters during the past six months describing an outrageous condition of affairs in Constantinople where traffic in prostitutes is carried on openly and shamelessly, and where the traffickers have their own Synagogue. . . . They say that in Damascus things are even worse.[36]

Citing Argentine authorities, the conference found that of 199 licensed brothels in Buenos Aires in 1909, 102 had Jewish madams and half the prostitutes were Jews.

One could now begin to speak of Jewish organized crime, and although prostitution was at the heart of it, there was much more. Gambling was another human weakness exploited by fringe entrepreneurs. Card parlors abounded, and off-track betting was institutionalized in poolrooms. At first Lower East Side gambling was run by well-connected Irishmen like Big Tim Sullivan, but he soon had "smart young Jewboys" like Herman Rosenthal and Arnold Rothstein working for him. One of the few Jewish mobsters who did not start life in poverty, Rothstein gambled obsessively from his teens. His politically influential Orthodox father, Abraham, who owned a dry-goods store and processed cotton, was known as Abe the Just. When Arnold brought home a non-Jewish bride, his father covered the mirrors, said kaddish, and disowned his son forever. This "set Arnold free" to break every rule in the book.[37] Although there is no decisive evidence, many believe that Rothstein was the man who fixed the 1919 World Series, by far baseball's greatest scandal.

Rebellion against religiosity—the breakdown of tradition and parental authority—was common among immigrants. Steffens wrote that he "would pass a synagogue where a score or more of boys were sitting hatless in their old clothes, smoking cigarettes on the stoops outside, and their fathers, all dressed in black, with their high hats, uncut beards and temple curls, were going into the synagogue, tearing their hair and rending their garments. . . . Their sons were rebels against the law of Moses; they were lost souls; lost to God, to the family and to the Israel of old." Some young people remained religious, but many did not.

By the turn of the century the Lower East Side was already divided up into networks of thieves, fences, pickpockets, and arsonists that defended their territories viciously. The first major gang was headed by Monk Eastman, a ferocious-looking man with a bullet-shaped head and wild hair who loved violence and freely used blackjacks, brass knuckles, and pistols to pummel his enemies—although women he only hit with his bare hands. He organized other thugs and hired them out to protect gambling operations and whorehouses, branching out into shielding scabs from striking union workers. When he went to prison at Sing Sing, Max Zweibach took over. Better known as Kid Twist, he added a crucial dimension to the gang by hiring large numbers of "repeaters," people who voted over and over again to keep the thugs at Tammany Hall in power. Jewish gangs joined the Irish political mafia that had unquestioned control over New York.

When Twist was killed in 1908, Big Jack Zelig came to the fore, along with his pals Whitey Seidenschnier, Lefty Louie Rosenberg, and Harry "Gyp the Blood" Horowitz, who could break a man's back with his hands. Big Jack rented them out: ten dollars for a knife slash to the cheeks, twenty-five for a bullet in the arm or leg, fifty for throwing a bomb, a hundred dollars for a murder. The trio did in Spanish Louie, a Sephardic Jew who wore black clothes and a sombrero. When Italian gunman Julius Morello came into the Stuyvesant Casino yelling, "Where's that big Yid Zelig? I gotta cook that big Yid!" Big Jack cooked him first. Still, someone shot him dead on a trolley in 1912. Touchingly, jail letters from his three comrades, all awaiting a murder trial, were found on his body.

Dopey Benny Fein was next in line for local power. After a few years in Sing Sing, he had joined Big Jack's gang and specialized in industrial relations. Growing labor unrest in the largely Jewish garment trades called for company goons as well as union thugs, and Dopey Benny hired his mobsters out as both. He franchised some unions to lesser gangs. Furriers and bakers belonged to Joe the Greaser Rosenzweig and his boys, including Little Hymie Bernstein, "Nigger" Benny Snyder, and Tough Jake Heiseman. Yoski "Nigger" Toblinsky's gang (the Jewish Black Hand Association) got the teamsters, and specialized in stealing and poisoning horses. Charley "the Cripple" Vitoffsky got soda and seltzer deliveries, and Johnny Levinsky controlled ice cream.[38]

Needless to say, the "Jewish 400"—rich uptown German Jews—felt soiled by these criminals. This included the Ochs and Sulzberger families of the *New York Times,* the Strausses of Macy's, the Guggenheims, Lehmans, Schiffs, and others. They funded settlement houses to prevent delinquency, redeemed young women from prostitution, and defended eastern European Jews against anti-Semitic attacks in the press. Still, other forces were at work.

World War I drew large numbers of Jewish volunteers, many of them immigrants wanting to prove their loyalty or just find work and get some education. Not all returned, and the American fields of crosses in France are peppered with Stars of David. But many thousands of young men were taken off the streets, and those who returned had more than crime on their minds. Jews were succccding, with two great consequences. First, declining family size meant fewer unemployed. Second, successful younger people left the urban ghettos. Around the turn of the century there were half a million Jews in the Lower East Side; by 1916, the number was three hundred thousand and declining. Brooklyn, the Bronx, and upper Manhattan inherited these increasingly bourgeois Jews. At the same time immigration slowed dramatically, and the most important source of both victims and recruits for organized crime went dry.

Alas, the United States Congress and three-fourths of the states approved the Eighteenth Amendment, prohibiting alcohol, and this called the mob back from the grave. Thugs and gangsters whose power was hopelessly waning were handed their best opportunity, and they took to booze like fish to water. Consider Waxey Gordon, né Irving Wexler, a nasty, thickset *schlammer*—Yiddish for limb breaker—who had fallen on hard times.[39] Then he met Big Maxey Greenberg, just pardoned by President Woodrow Wilson on the request of an Irish gangster-politician. Greenberg saw Prohibition for the vast opportunity it was, and planned to import Scotch from Britain at Montauk Point, Long Island. In 1919 he convinced Arnold Rothstein to stake him to $175,000 for boats, warehouses, trucks, bribes, and gunmen. They started with twenty thousand cases of whiskey, the cornerstone of an empire. By 1930 Gordon was supplying beer to northern New Jersey and eastern Pennsylvania, earning about $1.5 million, on which his tax burden was ten bucks. He was Irving Wexler again, "respectable" businessman and community benefactor.

Because Jews didn't drink a lot, the Jewish gangs had an uphill fight to gain market share among gentiles more logically served by gentile mobsters. To do this they became especially violent. Arthur Flegenheimer of the South Bronx renamed himself Dutch Schultz, or the Dutchman, and used a multiethnic gang to terrorize neighborhoods. In Detroit, Sammy Purple Cohen, the Fleisher brothers, and the Bernstein brothers staked out "Little Jerusalem." The Cleveland Four controlled the Woodland ghetto, and in Minneapolis Kid Cann along with Yiddy and Harry Bloom reigned supreme. In Kansas City it was Solomon "Cutcher-Head-Off" Weissman; in Boston, "King" Solomon and Hyman Abrams; in Newark, Longy Zwillman; in Philadelphia, Boo-Boo Hoff and Nig Rosen. Chicago was rich in opportunity. Buddy and Greener Jacobson, Hershel and Max Miller, Nigger Goldberg and Nails Morton stood tall in the shadow of Bugs Moran and Al Capone.

The anti-Semitism spawned by Jewish organized crime was virulent; it helped to produce immigration restrictions during the 1920s that condemned to Nazi ovens hundreds of thousands of Jews who might, in a different social climate, have been admitted to the United States. Prohibition produced such vast criminal wealth that friendships emerged between Jewish and Italian mobsters. Lucky Luciano had fond memories of a Jewish hatmaker he had worked for who treated him like a son, including him in Friday-night dinners and candle lighting. He later attributed his alliances with Meyer Lansky, Bugsy Siegel, and Dutch Schultz in part to these memories. "When I first started hanging around with Jewish guys like Meyer and Bugsy and Dutch, the old guys . . . used to beef to me about it. They always said that some day the Jews was gonna make me turn and join the synagogue." Frank Costello had similar memories, and married his Jewish childhood sweetheart. At one important meeting Costello brought some Jews, and Vito Genovese yelled, "What the hell is this! What are you trying to do, load us down with a bunch of Hebes?" Wanting to punch him, Costello instead said quietly, "Take it easy, Don Vitone, you're nothin' but a fuckin' foreigner yourself."

This last generation of Jewish gangsters gained the greatest fame. Prohibition gave them a deep vein of easily mined gold, and, more ominously, it blurred the distinction between right and wrong, legal and criminal, in a way that delighted mobsters. If the government knew so little of human nature that it was willing to ban wine and spirits, then maybe some other things it banned—prostitution, bookmaking, corrupt unions, drugs, even gangland wars—weren't so bad either. Prohibition accustomed millions of ordinary people to break the law every day and to rely on vicious criminals as a source of something they wanted. It softened their condemnation of these men, and made life easier for them.

Louis "Lepke" Buchalter, known as Czar Lepke, was a case in point, a thug from Brooklyn who built a protection racket during the lush and wide-open 1920s. He assembled what has been described as "a gang of top-flight Jewish criminals, the most brutal and talented of their breed," Murder Inc.[40] For two decades they protected the furriers and leather businesses of New York from . . . Murder Inc. This expanded to the rest of the garment industry, its workers in the International Ladies' Garment Workers' Union, and eventually the movie studios of Hollywood, each of which paid tens of thousands of dollars a year to a multiethnic mob consortium in which Lepke was a major player. A 1939 Wanted poster offered twenty-five thousand dollars for him, "Dead or Alive," describing him as 5 foot 5½, white, and Jewish. It said, "Eyes, piercing and shifting; nose, large, somewhat blunt at nostrils; ears, prominent and close to head," and added "Frequents baseball games."

Dutch Schultz's gang began by supplying beer and liquor to speakeasies and restaurants and branched out into a lucrative fixed numbers game that sucked millions out of the people of Harlem. But into every life a little rain must fall. Dutch's downpour started when Thomas E. Dewey, assistant United States attorney for New York, decided to destroy organized crime. Al Capone had just been jailed for income tax evasion, and the Treasury men who had put him there joined Dewey in New York and went after Schultz and Waxey Gordon, just then trying to kill each other. Gordon escaped Schultz's gunmen but fell into Dewey's hands.

Dewey detested gangsters and was very brave, but also very ambitious. He prolonged trials and appeals while aggressively courting the press. He humiliated Gordon on the stand, stripping away his pretense of respectability, and got him a ten-year jail term just days before Prohibition ended. Schultz knew he was next, and reasonably proposed that Dewey be assassinated. He had the project evaluated and was convinced it could be done, but wanted approval from New York's syndicate—Lepke, Luciano, Lansky, Costello, and others. They not only turned him down but, fearing that he would betray them when Dewey arrested him, planned his murder. Bugs Workman and Mendy Weiss went into the Palace Chop House in Newark when Schultz's gang was dining late and killed them all—except for the main target. Weiss fled in a hail of dying men's bullets, but Workman found Schultz relieving himself in the men's room and cut him down at the urinal; a few delirious days in the hospital ended the stellar career of Arthur Flegenheimer.

Dewey got Luciano (who on the stand said he needed all those guns to shoot "peasants") and then Lepke, who got the worst of it, because out of his crumbling empire came enough evidence to justify a murder trial. By all accounts the trial was unfair, but Lepke was sentenced to death. Many stays of execution kept both him and Dewey on the front pages, but he was electro- cuted along with two of his cronies in March 1944.

This left Bugsy Siegel and Meyer Lansky. They had started together running thousands of cases of liquor a month from the Bahamas through Charleston, South Carolina, to Brooklyn. Siegel moved to Hollywood with his family, hobnobbed with stars, and ran his rackets from there, while Lan- sky built a crime and gambling empire in Miami and Cuba. As the war ended, Siegel envisioned turning a hick town called Las Vegas into a legal gambling center, and Lansky went along. But Siegel's ambition and possi- ble betrayal ran afoul of Lansky's power, and Siegel was shot dead in the liv- ing room of the gangster moll he had married. Lansky escaped punishment and built a $300 million empire, taking ever greater advantage of the con- vergence of organized crime and legitimate business.

These men may have been scum, but they rejected the inhuman limita- tions of ghetto life. Like the Italian and Irish mobsters who slaughtered or befriended them, they considered themselves superior to the average run of people. They were tough Jews who would not accept a pinched, dismal fate, and they paid for their arrogance with their freedom and their lives.

Once in 1910, Big Jack Zelig and his goons dressed up as Orthodox Jews, surprised an Italian gang that had terrorized Jews, and ran them out of the Lower East Side permanently. They and all their successors were thugs who were only out for themselves, but they were also Jews who did not take insults. Other Jews knew this, and their disapproval was mixed with an ineluctable, grudging admiration. It has been suggested more than once that it would have been interesting to see what would have happened if Adolf Hitler had been put in a room alone with any one of them for, say, twenty minutes. For any Jew who has lived through or after World War II, the image is indelible and redemptive.

⚭

As these Jewish pimps, thugs, con men, and mobsters emerged from their dark holes into a kind of prominence, other Jews were otherwise engaged. We saw that Jews are enormously overrepresented among Nobel Prize winners, but this general phenomenon is even more true in the United States. Albert Michelson, who helped determine the speed of light, became the first Jewish American Nobel laureate in 1907, but there have been dozens of others in all fields, and Jewish immigrants like Albert Einstein have swelled the ranks of American Nobelists. Bernard Baruch advised sev- eral presidents on the American economy, Hank Greenberg and Sandy Koufax made baseball history, Judy Blume guided millions of children through the rocky shoals of growing up, Mark Spitz won seven gold medals for the United States in one Olympics, J. Robert Oppenheimer and Edward

Teller designed the atom and hydrogen bombs, Jonas Salk and Albert Sabin developed two completely different polio vaccines, Admiral Hyman Rickover founded the nuclear-powered navy, Judith Resnick became the first Jewish astronaut and gave her life in the *Challenger* disaster, and sixteen Jews won the Congressional Medal of Honor. But there is no sphere of American life to which Jews have contributed more than entertainment.

Hollywood seems the most American of enterprises, yet almost all the founders of the filmmaking industry were Jewish immigrants.[41] The early heads of Fox Films, Warner Brothers, Universal Pictures, Paramount Pictures, and Metro-Goldwyn-Mayer were without exception impoverished Jewish peddlers or workingmen—really working boys—whose fathers were weak, worthless, or dead. They begged their relatives in Hungary, Russia, or Poland to let them go to America, and they fought their way up from the streets to found retail businesses.

Adolph Zukor, who lived with his rabbi uncle after his father's death, put his earnings from fox furs into an arcade full of peep machines and turned it into Paramount. William Fox, who would spit on his shiftless father's grave, quit school at eleven, peddled his way into a small fortune in the new fad of ready-to-wear clothing, and opened a 150-seat movie theater. Jack Warner, who when punished with a pin stick during a lesson pulled the punitive rabbi's beard, got together with his brothers—a meat packer, a railroad fireman, and a soap salesman—and bought a movie projector: Warner Brothers. Louis B. Mayer, rebelling against his abusive father, left home to become a junkman, saved his money, and turned a broken-down burlesque house into a theater. Many years later, encountering Hollywood, Jewish comedian Eddie Cantor said, "I marveled at this new world of iridescent splendor representing many millions, many romances, many miracles, and it had all come into being through the imagination and the business brains of a former furrier, a former druggist, and a former coronet player."[42]

These men rejected the backgrounds that had hurt them, including the religion of their ancestors. They came from and spoke to a mass of immigrants who wanted to leave the Old World behind forever, and they embraced the fantasy of a perfect new country. They dreamed an America that had never really been, and gave it back to their audiences, themselves imagining a nation full of drama, hope, and courage. Immigrants all, they sat and stared through the dark at a wall dancing with fleeting light, and envisioned real Americans living real American lives—striving, fighting, dancing, falling in love, vigorous, bold, brilliant, and unspeakably beautiful. Or, alternatively, they laughed at idealizations of themselves—poor but kind, bumbling but honest, ignorant but not stupid, down but never, ever out.

The last thing these Jewish moguls wanted was to impose anything on American audiences. Every day their dearest hope was to figure out what audiences—overwhelmingly non-Jewish—wanted to see next. Producers and writers may have been Jews, but actors and directors were mainly "real Americans." It was unusual to find anything Jewish or foreign in the popular films of Hollywood's heyday. In the silent era Jewish themes were more commonly dealt with, under the influence of Yiddish theater and film, culminating in the first "talkie," *The Jazz Singer,* the story of a cantor's son who dreams of fame as a secular singer. In the course of the film he turns his back on everything Jewish, eventually reconciling with his family as he risks his Broadway career to sing Kol Nidre—the central prayer of the Day of Atonement—in the synagogue, taking the place of his dying father.

But *The Jazz Singer* was no trendsetter. Mainstream talkies eventually dealt with Irish Americans, Italian Americans, and African Americans, but rarely and lightly with Jews. In the thirties, as the Nazis made their war against the Jews, themes relating to Jews or anti-Semitism were notably absent from Hollywood's products, even though at least ten times as many films were made then than now. Jewish executives purged any hint of an effort to move Americans toward war. After Pearl Harbor many war films were made, but without Jewish themes. A postwar exception was *Gentleman's Agreement,* but that was made by the only studio now run by a non-Jewish executive (20th Century-Fox), was directed by a Greek American (Elia Kazan), and starred non-Jewish Gregory Peck as a non-Jewish reporter *posing* as a Jew to expose anti-Semitism. This exception proved the rule. It was not until *Exodus* in 1960 that a few films dealt directly with Jewish themes.

Jews stayed way behind the scenes, and what they put forward was the opposite of Jewishness, a vision of "real" Americans—if not always Anglo-Saxon and Protestant, at least white and Christian, meeting a northern European standard of beauty. Jewish movie stars? Sort of. Theodosia Goodman was the "It" girl, the vamp of silent film and the first screen sex symbol, but she had as perfect a face as any girl could dream of, and to millions of star-struck viewers was Theda Bara. Emmanuel Goldenberg terrorized his enemies in mobster roles, but as Edward G. Robinson. Issur Danielovitch starred in *Gunfight at the OK Corral, Spartacus, Lonely Are the Brave,* and *Paths of Glory,* but with the clean good looks and chin dimple of that gorgeous American hero Kirk Douglas. Bernie Schwartz lit up the screen in *Sweet Smell of Success* and *Some Like It Hot,* but the world called this golden boy Tony Curtis. And once when Betty Perske was lunching with director Howard Hawks, he went on about the noisiness of Jews, but she kept silent and remained Lauren Bacall.

The Jewish moguls never depicted anti-Semitism or used their films in any way remotely resembling the manipulations charged by their enemies; they bent far over backward not to do so. By nature they were entrepreneurs who cared most about demand, and so created that most democratic of mechanisms, the box-office voting booth. But they also wanted to be American, to show their adopted country at its best. They were fiercely patriotic, and when it came time to choose between the demagogue Joseph McCarthy and some of their own left-leaning employees, they embraced the McCarthyist cause with embarrassing enthusiasm, blacklisting Hollywood artists who refused to denounce their friends and "name names." There may have been Communists in the lower ranks of the movie business, but the Jewish executives helped deliver them to the authorities. They were always ultra-American, and the claim that they were deliberately changing American values was ludicrous.

Jewish success in other popular arts was also legendary. Many of America's most loved hit songs were by Jews—Irving Berlin, Jerome Kern, the Gershwin brothers, Rodgers and Hammerstein, Frank Loesser, Lerner and Loewe, Stephen Sondheim, and Leonard Bernstein. (Cole Porter, one of the few non-Jews in that company, was an outsider stigmatized for a different reason: he was gay.) All had started life looking in, noses pressed to the glass. "White Christmas," "Easter Parade," and "God Bless America" were all written by a man born in Russia as Isidor Baline and whose only musical training was in the choir of his cantor-father's synagogue, on Cherry Street on the Lower East Side. Irving Berlin lived 102 years, nearly spanning the twentieth century. He wrote three thousand songs that helped define modern America, beginning with the 1911 "Alexander's Ragtime Band" and going on to include "There's No Business Like Show Business," "Anything You Can Do I Can Do Better," and even an occasional Jewish-theme song like "Cohen Owes Me 97 Dollars."

Tin Pan Alley, the songwriters' world was called, and the name seems to derive from the days of peripatetic klezmer musicians. When they played badly in the alleys of the shtetls, displeased residents would lean out of the windows and bang on tin pans. But there were no banging pans for Jerome Kern's "Ol' Man River," George and Ira Gershwin's "I Got Rhythm," Lorenz Hart—a descendant of Heine's[43]—and Richard Rodgers's "My Funny Valentine," Oscar Hammerstein and Rodgers's "You'll Never Walk Alone," Sammy Cahn's "Bei Mir Bist Du Schon," or Harold Arlen's "Over the Rainbow." The Jews did not invent popular song, but they transformed it, and if they invented Hollywood they also created the modern Broadway musical. Kern's 1927 *Showboat* set the standard, and like the men behind the movies, the Jewish inventors of musical theater cared for little else than to give their audiences America.

Rodgers and Hart's *Babes in Arms,* Rodgers and Hammerstein's *Oklahoma!* and *Carousel,* Frank Loesser's *Guys and Dolls,* Lerner and Loewe's *Paint Your Wagon,* and Berlin's *Annie Get Your Gun* all depict a strictly American America, full of tensions—otherwise, what drama?—but reflecting American folk culture. No Jewishness appeared in leading musicals until *Fiddler on the Roof* in 1964, four decades into the life of the genre. The enthusiasm with which Americans embraced this classic Sholem Aleichem saga—persecuted Jews in a Russian shtetl in the Pale, living their own religion and threatened by that of others—proved beyond a doubt that there was a new kind of acceptance of Jews in the United States.

But the Jewish creators of *Fiddler*'s predecessors had no interest in Jewish themes. They treated Irish culture in *Brigadoon* and *Finian's Rainbow,* Italian American culture in *The Most Happy Fella* and *Fiorello,* and Chinese American culture in *Flower Drum Song,* but never the culture that gave them life and set their talent going. Still, *Flower Drum Song* is an example of their attempt to deal with racism and bigotry ("All white men look alike" is a wry line from it), and among the greatest achievements of the musical stage are *Porgy and Bess,* which deals indirectly with the effects of racism in the South, and *West Side Story,* which directly confronts bigotry against Puerto Ricans. In *The King and I* race is never far below the surface, and *South Pacific* addresses the issue explicitly in a song lamenting the fact that we are all brought up to fear "people whose eyes are oddly made / And people whose skin is a different shade." Jews, reluctant to tout their own suffering, expressed it indirectly through the suffering of others.

It was the great Jewish comedians of the 1930s, 1940s, and 1950s—George Jessel, Eddie Cantor, Milton Berle, and others—who dealt with Jewish themes in their stand-up. They had all begun their careers in the Catskill Mountains of New York, where ordinary Jews from the city went for vacations and in the evenings laughed at themselves in the nightclubs of the hotels. The men onstage made good-natured fun of the lives of Jewish immigrants and their children, often focusing on the conflict between them. But this generation of Jewish comics did not make it in movies. The Marx Brothers and Jerry Lewis did, but only through broad slapstick reminiscent of vaudeville—pathetic, endearing, but without a hint of glamour. And of course, without a hint of anything Jewish.

As with movie drama, this changed a bit in the sixties and seventies. Mel Brooks and Woody Allen, who both came to movies from the Catskill circuit via Sid Caesar's live television comedy, *Your Show of Shows,* began creating brilliant feature comedies that hinted at and occasionally depicted Jewish themes. In *Take the Money and Run,* Allen showed the childhood of a petty thief as Brooklyn Jewish, and the depiction of the family was vicious. In a fantasy in *Annie Hall* he became a Hasid—a black-coated, bearded ultra-Orthodox Jew—in full regalia while sitting at his non-Jewish girlfriend's midwestern family dinner table.

Brooks's approach was lighthearted and lacked Allen's anti-Semitic edge. His first great hit, *The Producers,* dealt with two endearingly corrupt, seemingly Jewish Broadway types who make a musical called *Springtime for Hitler,* starring an awful rock musician as the führer. (This makes the playwright apoplectic: "My Führer did not say 'Baby'!") The play is meant to fail, allowing the bumbling antiheroes to pocket invested funds from numerous little old ladies, all enamored of the senior of the pair. But alas, the play succeeds colossally as a parody, and since they have sold shares in it amounting to thousands of percentage points, they go to jail—where they promptly start a new producing scam. In *The History of the World, Part I,* there is a hilariously offensive musical send-up of the Inquisition. In *Blazing Saddles,* a brilliant cowboy-movie parody, a black sheriff and his Jewish deputy fight bigotry in the Wild West, and a couple of Indians speak Yiddish, referring to the sheriff as a *shvartze*—a mildly derogatory Yiddish word for blacks. All of Brooks's films directly confront bigotry and demolish it with humor.

Beginning in 1960, dramatic films overcame their fear of Jewish themes. *Exodus* rode a wave of American admiration for the tough Jews of Israel, the film version of *Fiddler on the Roof* dealt with shtetl Jewish life under bigotry's hammer, and *Judgment at Nuremberg* at last dealt with the Holocaust, although from the distance of courtroom drama. Movie versions of Bernard Malamud's *The Fixer,* Philip Roth's *Goodbye, Columbus,* and Edward Lewis Wallant's *The Pawnbroker*—starring Rod Steiger in perhaps his greatest role—drew smaller audiences. It was not until the 1990s that a Hollywood film depicting the Holocaust directly had a great success, and once again it was an exception that proved the rule. Steven Spielberg's *Schindler's List* was not about Jews but about a heroic German who saved more than a thousand of them. The Jews appear in the background as faceless sufferers and victims, without personalities and certainly without heroism.[44]

◊∾∾◊

If it had chosen to show American Jews, what would Hollywood film in its heyday have depicted? One approach might have been the rags-to-riches story. By the 1930s, the proportion of Jews working in industry had fallen to 20 percent, while that in commerce and public services had more than doubled, to 60 percent. Participation in the professions went from 3 to 15 percent in the same period.[45] There were still quotas in medical and law schools, and no Jews could be found in the upper echelons of old American corporations, but barriers were sinking, inch by inch.

Another genre would have been the Jewish American war story. While World War II was not marked by any specific action against the Holocaust, 550,000 Jews served in the military, of whom 10,500 were killed, 24,000 were wounded, and 36,000 were decorated for bravery. After the war the GI Bill brought many Jews, along with many other veterans, into higher education and the professions. With the liberation of the camps and the revelations of the Nuremberg trials, American Jews at last awoke from their slumber and took a strong Zionist stance. President Harry Truman, for-

merly a haberdasher in Kansas City with an admired Jewish partner, saw
the logic of Zionism in a new way, and the shame of inaction during the war
combined with the refugee problem after it led the United States to support
the creation of a Jewish state.

American Jews, once deeply divided over the Zionist cause, were now
confident enough to be unconcerned about accusations of dual loyalty, and
put Israel near the center of their agenda. Making group "mission" voyages
to the new country, preaching sermons about its survival, and selling Israel
bonds became some of the main sources of solidarity among American
Jews.[46] Not least in importance was the ability to identify with a new breed
of Jewish hero. Israel's initial upset victory over six Arab armies, despite
huge losses, in its war for independence, made American Jews proud, but
that was nothing compared to the triumph of the Six Day War in 1967. Typical was the letter a young woman wrote to the *Village Voice:* "For the first
time in my grown-up life, I really understood what an enemy was. For the
first time, I knew what it was to be us against the killers. Us. Two weeks ago
Israel was they; now Israel is we." Religious scholar Arthur Hertzberg
wrote, "The sense of belonging to the worldwide Jewish people, of which
Israel is the center, is a religious movement, but it seems to persist even
among Jews who regard themselves as secularists or atheists."[47]

The war also changed the gentile mirror in which American Jews saw
themselves. A man pumping gas in south Georgia told an interviewer,
"Them's damn fightin' Jews. I always thought Jews were yaller, but those
Jews, man, they're tough."[48] Another man told a Jewish business associate,
"You Hebes really taught those guys a lesson." American Jews had never
stood taller among their countrymen, and they knew it, even though it was
no accomplishment of their own. Their support for Israel, politically and fi-
nancially, increased enormously as the war approached, and it has never
flagged since—because of anxious solidarity, but also because of gratitude
and pride.

There is a book called *Kissing through Glass,* the title a metaphor for the
relationship of American and Israeli Jews, but this flatters Jewish Americans. Perhaps it applies to those who have moved to Israel and found it hard
to adjust. But the metaphor dignifies the American-Jewish role too much.
American Jews have their lips pressed to the glass well enough, but the Israelis on the other side are going about their business, barely pausing to
smile and wave. The American Jews are spectators, Israelis the idolized
players. The fans yell their lungs out in support and pay a pretty penny for
the front-row seats, but nobody mistakes them for the players. Some Israelis
have little patience for them, and that is perfectly valid; the stakes of this
game are life and death for the players, disappointment—all right, grief—
for the fans. But the Americans can rightly ask: "Would you rather play
without fans?"

Nor has dual loyalty ever become an issue. The oil crisis of the 1970s might have been blamed on the Jews, but it wasn't; Americans on gas lines blamed the Arabs who owned the oil. Menachem Begin was disliked by Americans, and this might have spread to Israel and the Jews, but people had no problem liking Israel while disliking its head of state. After the devastating attack on the United States on September 11, 2001, linked to anti-Israel and anti-Jewish terrorists, Americans might at last have ended their support for Israel and turned against American Jews. On the whole they did none of this, continuing to admire Israel in its complex struggles and accepting little or none of the Arab rhetoric directed against Jews. Instead of condemning Israel for causing their problems, Americans turned to it for advice on how to combat terror.

American Jews have been at home in their country for decades now, and they no longer tiptoe around sensitive issues for fear of anti-Semitism. Jews speak out on the left and right, support Democrats and Republicans, discuss Jewish holidays on television talk shows, and in general identify themselves quite openly as Jews. Rabbi Arnold Goodman of Atlanta, planning an ecumenical Thanksgiving service with Christian colleagues, told his congregation, "If I could have told my grandfather in nineteenth-century Russia that I would someday be a rabbi holding a joint service in a Christian church, and that I would get the minister to agree to cover up the crosses, he would have thought that I had lost my mind." Jews feel free to be fiercely patriotic or unstintingly critical of a country that now truly belongs to them as much as to anyone else. Alan Dershowitz, one of America's leading First Amendment lawyers and a lifelong fighter for the civil rights of all, wrote a book called *Chutzpah*—Yiddish for "boldness," or even "brazenness"—persuasively arguing that after two centuries of American freedom and rule of law, Jews can and should now be out, outspoken, and proud.[49]

And so they are. The American-Jewish saga culminated, in a sense, on April 19, 1985, when Elie Wiesel performed the commandment of "speaking truth to power." He stood in Ronald Reagan's White House, there to accept from the president a Congressional Gold Medal of Achievement. It had been just forty years since Wiesel had been freed from Buchenwald, one skeleton among others on a rack in a famous photograph, one more dispensable Jew inexplicably saved from among millions. He had watched his beloved father go up in the smoke from the ovens, and that was only the start of what he witnessed and experienced. Now, after forty years of writing and lecturing, having become not only a living witness of Jewish suffering but a spokesman for countless other suffering people, he was accorded his adopted nation's highest civilian honor from the most important man in the world.

But there was a catch. Reagan's staff had recently announced that on an impending visit to Germany he would not visit the Dachau concentration

camp as planned, but instead would stop at the military cemetery at Bitburg, to honor the German war dead—including forty-seven SS men. He
had justified skipping Dachau by saying that Germans have "a guilt feeling
that's been imposed on them, and I think it's unnecessary," and that he did
not want to be "reawakening memories and so forth." On behalf of the visit
to Bitburg, he made the astonishing statement that the Nazi soldiers "were
victims, just as surely as the victims in the concentration camps."[50]

A storm of criticism rose quickly in the Congress and the media, but the
president's White House advisers stood firm. They were strongly pro-
Israel, but none of them was Jewish, and unlike most modern presidents,
Reagan had no Jewish friends. Perhaps they just did not understand; also,
they were eagerly courting a new and different Germany. But there, in
anticipation of Reagan's gesture, aging SS men were coming out of the
woodwork, being interviewed by media for the first time and claiming
vindication. Anti-Semitic remarks were once again heard publicly. Wiesel
decided to try to make the Reaganites understand—at the White House, on
live television. Some Jewish community leaders he consulted tried to dissuade him; their complex political agenda might be put in jeopardy. One
said, partly in Yiddish, that you just don't criticize the czar, but another
Yiddish phrase comes to mind: *a shanda fir di goyim*—"a shame before the
gentiles."

This was not, as it turned out, a necessary caution in the United States
of America. Wiesel, displaying the courage of a lifelong moral stance,
went to the White House podium and faced the cameras. He praised
and thanked America, then went on to say gently, "But, Mr. President, I
wouldn't be the person I am, and you wouldn't respect me for what I am, if
I were not to tell you also of the sadness that is in my heart. . . ." And then
the remarkable sentence: "That place, Mr. President, is not your place."[51]

A shanda fir di goyim? Newsweek called it "surely one of the more remarkable moments in the annals of the White House." Almost all media
commentators praised Wiesel's respectful tone. In the House of Representatives 173 Democrats and 84 Republicans signed a letter to German chancel-
lor Helmut Kohl, asking him to withdraw the Bitburg invitation, to give
the president a graceful way out. Republican Majority Leader Robert Dole
and 81 other senators voted for a resolution urging the president not to visit,
Bitburg. In polls of average Americans, about half opposed the Bitburg visit
and a large majority supported Jews' right to protest it.

The visit was made, but in the ensuing weeks leading Republicans
talked a good deal about the damage done to them domestically in exchange
for a small, dubious diplomatic advantage. As for Wiesel, he was not just
forgiven, he was lionized. Once again, a Jew had spoken truth to power—
the phrase harks back to the prophet Nathan's searing reprimand of King
David—and stood up for American ideals, proving that a citizen, if not ex-

actly a common one, could say his piece to the president and walk away unharmed. Once again, a Jew had shown that America is different, that, in Washington's biblical words to the Newport congregation, America is the place where "every one shall sit in safety under his own vine and fig-tree, and there shall be none to make him afraid."

Or stand up and speak in safety, as the case may be.

16

HA'ARETZ

HOW THE JEWS CAME HOME

The facts about the Jews and Israel are quickly told. After living in it from time immemorial and ruling it on and off for a thousand years, the people are driven from their home and dispersed throughout the world, their state and its religion destroyed. A remnant remains continuously on the land, but the great mass must leave. Their religion adapts to exile, but they remain attached to their homeland.

Within a few centuries, Europe becomes politically Christian. Its Jews have a denigrated status—routine persecution interrupted by limited tolerance. A few centuries later the Middle East, North Africa, and Spain become politically Muslim. The Jews there have an inferior but almost respected status—routine tolerance interrupted by persecutions. When Spain becomes Christian again, mass forced conversions end in the expulsion of hundreds of thousands of Jews, who disperse in a second exile.

Diaspora proves permanent, but exile does not. Some Jews in each generation return to their ancient homeland. After eighteen centuries, however, the trickle becomes a movement: first hundreds, then thousands, then tens of thousands of Jews turn their backs to the diaspora and settle in the land that once was Israel. Near the end of the nineteenth century, a substantial minority of Jews throughout the world declare their support for a future Jewish state in that land. This intention is given a name: Zionism.

A century after "emancipation"—Napoleon's welcome but temporary fairness to the Jews—anti-Semitism grows in Europe, based on race and blood instead of religion and culture. It spreads to and through the Islamic world, with riots and pogroms in eastern Europe, the Middle East, and North Africa. Although settlement in Israel is a very arduous path—deaths from malaria and Arab attacks are common—growing threats lead more Jews to choose it. World War I transfers the region from Turkish to British control, and Britain declares that it will help establish a Jewish state in Israel.

For generations Jews accumulate land by buying it from Arabs,[1] creat-

352

ing settlements that range from communal farms to towns. Peaceful coexistence is marred by many attacks from hostile local Arabs, and the Jews defend themselves in an increasingly organized way. Internationally these events are very minor; in the Islamic world, at first, they cause only a modest increase in anti-Semitism.

Independently in Europe, beginning in Germany, anti-Semitism takes an unprecedentedly virulent form, and during World War II more than half the Jews on that continent are cold-bloodedly murdered, a genocide more efficient than any before or since. Not surprisingly, but to the dismay of the British government and the Arab world, many of the remaining Jews of Europe want to move to Israel. Overcoming legal, military, and other obstacles, scores of thousands do.[2]

Having done little to stop the mass murder of Europe's Jews, the world tries to make amends: the United Nations declares a partition of the British territory into a Jewish and an Arab state, a plan accepted by the British and Jews but rejected by the Arabs. As the British withdraw, the armies of Egypt, Jordan, Syria, Lebanon, Iraq, and Saudi Arabia invade Israel. The secretary-general of the Arab League says, "This will be a war of extermination."[3] The spiritual leader of Palestine's Muslims says, "I declare a Holy War, my Muslim brothers! Murder the Jews! Murder them all!"[4]

Hundreds of thousands of Arabs flee during this war, some voluntarily, urged by the invading Arab states to take a temporary exile, and some because of Jewish attacks and threats. Losing 1 percent of its Jewish population—six thousand deaths, almost equal to the combined losses of all its subsequent wars—the newborn state expels the foreign armies and is left with a substantially larger and more defensible territory than it would have had under the UN plan rejected by the Arabs. Arab refugees who fled their homes in the territory that is now Israel are not allowed to return.

In parallel, hundreds of thousands of Jewish refugees are created by Arab countries now hostile to their Jewish citizens. Many go to Israel, leaving everything behind as they flee. For them, as for the Palestinian refugees, there is no prospect of repatriation or reparation, but they are absorbed by tiny, impoverished Israel. Along with the refugees from Europe and hundreds of thousands of Jews residing in Israel before World War II, these Jews build a nation.

Unlike Israel, which accepts all Jewish refugees, Arab nations accept only a fraction of the Palestinian refugees, and grant those accepted only second-class citizenship. Most remain in refugee camps in the West Bank and elsewhere in Jordan or in the Gaza Strip under Egypt's control, a festering sore that the Arab world refuses to heal. For decades, neither these nor any other Arab nations try to absorb these refugees. Of the billions in international assistance provided to them over the years, only a tiny fraction comes from oil-rich Arab states.

In May of 1967 a multinational Arab attack is plainly imminent. Egypt closes the Strait of Tiran to all ships destined for Israel, an act of war, and its president says that in the coming conflict, "Our basic objective will be the destruction of Israel."[5] Iraq's president says, "Our goal is clear—to wipe Israel off the map."[6] Syria and Jordan join forces with Egypt. Israel preemptively strikes the air forces of Egypt and Syria, destroying them on the ground. The war ends six days later with Israeli occupation of the Sinai, the Golan Heights, the West Bank, and the Gaza Strip. Some Israelis predict that this occupation will corrupt Israel's spirit. Others set about establishing Jewish settlements in these territories, with government support.

On Yom Kippur in 1973 Egypt and Syria invade, advancing rapidly. They are turned back in a week, but with 2,500 Israeli deaths, four times the number in 1967. Four years later Egypt's president travels to Jerusalem and addresses the Knesset, Israel's parliament. Two years after that the two countries conclude a peace agreement, the first between Israel and any Arab nation, and Israel withdraws from the Sinai. The army of Israel removes Jewish settlements by force.

After years of rocket attacks from southern Lebanon on northern Israeli communities, Israel invades Lebanon in 1982. Despite a plan to stop about ten miles north of its border, Israel proceeds to Beirut, beginning the only unpopular war in its history. An antiwar movement culminates in demonstrations comprising 7 or 8 percent of the nation, a unique crisis of confidence. Israel withdraws to a buffer zone in southern Lebanon, where it stays for many years.

In the late 1980s Palestinians begin violent protests against the Israeli occupation, and Israel responds by firing rubber bullets and breaking bones. In this uprising or *intifada* there are few deaths. Jordan renounces its claim to the West Bank, leaving its status up to Israel and the Palestine Liberation Organization. This terrorist organization previously dedicated to destroying Israel officially recognizes its right to exist. Five years of talks result in the Oslo peace accords: Israel will withdraw from most of the occupied lands in exchange for peace.

Large parts of the West Bank and Gaza are turned over to the Palestinian Authority, an interim government, which begins to function in some respects like a nation, conducting its own foreign affairs. It is given forty thousand automatic rifles among other weapons to build a police force. Jewish settlements in the occupied territories expand illegally, violating the accords. Still, at the end of the decade peace seems within reach; Israel fully withdraws from southern Lebanon, and an American president uses his last year in office to finalize the agreement between Israel and the Palestinian Authority. The Israeli prime minister meets the Palestinian leader at Camp David, offering more than 95 percent of the territories in exchange for peace. This offer is rejected.

Flanked by a thousand policemen, a right-wing Israeli general visits the Temple Mount, holy to both Jews and Muslims. A second, much bloodier intifada begins. Repeated American attempts to end this violence fail, and in a resounding blow to Israeli doves, the right-wing general is elected prime minister. He too cannot stop the violence.

Some months into this process, young Palestinians begin to blow themselves up in crowded places in Israel, deliberately killing many civilians. They are celebrated as martyrs and their families are paid ten thousand to twenty-five thousand dollars—a large sum for these very poor people—in compensation and aid. After a massacre at a communal Passover seder, Israel reoccupies Palestinian towns, meeting armed resistance. In these battles scores die, including some civilians, and thousands are arrested and detained. A standoff at the Church of the Nativity in Bethlehem, one of Christianity's holiest places, is resolved peacefully. But Palestinian bombings against Israeli civilians become more frequent and take a large toll in lives. Both sides declare the Oslo accords dead. In Europe, populist neo-Nazism combines with anti-Zionism, much of it led by Arab immigrants, to produce a new anti-Semitism. This potent blend spreads rapidly as synagogues, cemeteries, and other Jewish targets are attacked.

Jews have had a continuous presence in Israel since the Bronze Age, but it dwindled during the first few centuries after the second Roman war. Those who remained were scholars, not politicians or warriors, and lived mainly in the Galilee, especially Tiberias and Safed. They produced the Jerusalem Talmud, and some lived in Jerusalem. The Muslim conquerors of Jerusalem found Jews there in the seventh century, as did the Crusaders half a millennium later. Visiting Christian prelates and monks attest to their presence throughout the Middle Ages and Renaissance, one fourteenth-century monk noting "the long established Jewish community at the foot of Mount Zion, in Jerusalem."[7] A rabbi named Petachia left Prague in 1174 and traveled in the Middle East for more than a decade; he found about two hundred Jewish families in Tiberias, and also visited Jewish communities elsewhere in the Galilee, in Acre, and in Jerusalem.[8]

Much later, in 1438, "a rabbi from Italy became the spiritual leader of the Jewish community in Jerusalem, and fifty years afterward, another Italian scholar, Obadiah de Bertinoro, founded the Jerusalem rabbinical school."[9] In 1603 a Jewish visitor to Safed wrote of "a holy community, even a great city before God, with three hundred great rabbis" as well as eighteen yeshivas, twenty-two prayer houses, and a great study house "where about four hundred children and young men are taught by twenty teachers without payment. For there are rich people in Constantinople who provide the salaries."[10] In 1773 a rabbi from Israel visited Suriname, on the Caribbean coast of South America, and wrote critically of the fights between Sephardic and Ashkenazic Jews in that community.[11] In 1839 the British consul in Jerusalem wrote, "The mode of conducting Jewish affairs among themselves . . . is entirely in Hebrew, which ancient custom they are very tenacious of and desirous to maintain."[12]

In addition to this continuously present community, there was always a trickle of visitors and settlers longing for the Holy Land. They would stand on a hilltop and gaze down at the city of their dreams before going to Safed to learn with the great rabbinical masters. Some would have time and energy only to walk through the backstreets of an Arab neighborhood and find a nook where the Western Wall of the Temple Mount was a bit exposed. There they would pray, sway, keen, and weep, conjuring a time many centuries past. Some felt they were not just imagining, but remembering. Some, if they were very old, might only have time to see David's city and die. But they would lie in their sacred land, on the Mount of Olives if possible, so Moshiach, the Messiah, come at last to revive the dead and gather them to Zion, would have no trouble finding them. Those who could not go were buried in the diaspora with a small bag of earth from the Holy Land to pillow their heads eternally, symbolically a burial in Israel.

But the return over the centuries never ceased. There was an *aliyah* movement in the twelfth and thirteenth centuries in which hundreds of rabbis from France and Germany settled in the Holy Land, especially in Acre. Doña Gracia reestablished the Jewish community of Tiberias in the 1560s, and Rabbi Judah Hasid led a thousand pious Jews on a journey toward the Holy Land in 1700.[13] Edmond de Rothschild established the town of Zichron Ya'akov near the Mediterranean Sea in the 1880s and helped establish several other settlements.[14] Recall that the Haskalah—the Jewish Enlightenment—entailed among other things a revival of secular Hebrew. For a century this revival was well-meaning but weak, but then a movement began. Distinguished Yiddish novelists and poets began to write in Hebrew; migrations to Israel grew.

Sir Moses Montefiore was the builder of one of Jerusalem's landmarks, the windmill that never worked, but his life was as effective as his windmill was useless. He was as English as he could be while still being thoroughly Jewish—six feet three with broad shoulders, emanating strength, and a very Jewish face. He was also brilliant, making a fortune on the stock market by age forty and retiring to serve both England and the Jews. An Orthodox Jew, he was active throughout his life in the Spanish and Portuguese Synagogue of London and a firm opponent of the fledgling Reform movement. He took along a *shochet,* a ritual slaughterer, in his entourage during his travels.

He and his wife, Judith, were childless, but by all reports their sixty years of marriage were very happy. They prayed together daily, traveled, and carried out good works, helping Jews in crisis throughout the world. In 1840 Jews in Damascus were absurdly accused of murdering a Capuchin monk and his Muslim servant to use their blood in Passover rites. They were tortured—two died of it—and left in prison to rot. Montefiore headed a delegation to the ruler of Egypt and Syria and then to the Ottoman sultan and rescued the remaining Jews. On two trips to St. Petersburg he took up the cause of Russian Jews with the czars.

In those days of high-risk sea voyages and horse-drawn carriages, he made seven trips to the Holy Land, the last in 1875, when he was ninety-one. After the first visit, in 1829—it took more than five months to get there—the couple came home and put a Hebrew sign over their bed: *Im eshkacheych Yerushalayim* . . . "If I forget thee, O Jerusalem, may my right hand lose its cunning." Judith's diary, dated 18 October, 1836, in Jerusalem, described another visit: "There is no city in the world which can bear com-parison . . . with Jerusalem,—fallen, desolate, and abject even as it ap-pears . . . it is more than probable that not a single relic exists of the city that was the joy of the whole earth. . . . But it depends not for its power . . . on the remains of temples and palaces." Even without certain knowledge of their location,

> it would still be the city toward which every religious and medita-tive mind would turn with the deepest longing. It is with Jerusalem as it would be with the home of our youth, were it leveled with the earth, and we returned after many years and found the spot on which it stood a ploughed field, or a deserted waste: the same thoughts would arise in our hearts as if the building was still before us, and would probably be rendered still more impressive from the very cir-cumstance that the ruin which had taken place was complete.[15]

The entry reveals her piety and bravery, and the couplehood that made her husband's superb life possible:

> I can never be sufficiently thankful to Almighty God for suffer-ing us to reach this city in safety. The obstacles that presented them-selves, the dangers with which we were threatened, the detentions and vexations which had actually to be endured, all rose in my mind as I gave way to the feeling of delight with which I at length saw the fulfillment of my dear husband's long-cherished wish. Nor was my satisfaction a little increased at the recollection that I had strenu-ously urged him to pursue the journey, even when his own ardor

had somewhat abated, and when I had to oppose my counsel to the advice and wishes of our companions.

Without Judith steeling his resolve, they might not have made these trips. Moses was knighted by Queen Victoria in 1837, a year after becoming sheriff of London. The queen wrote in her diary, "I knighted the Sheriffs, one of whom was Mr. Montefiore, a Jew, an excellent man, & I was very glad to be the first to do what I consider quite right."[16]

On his second trip to Israel, in 1839, he recorded his own dream: "By degree I hope to induce the return of thousands of our brethren to the Land of Israel. I am sure they would be happy in the enjoyment of the observance of our holy religion, in a manner which is impossible in Europe." About seven thousand Jews lived there at the time. He founded agricultural settlements near Jaffa and in the Galilee and—with the help of the American-Jewish philanthropist Judah Touro—built the first Jewish community in Jerusalem outside the Old City walls, called Yamin Moshe ("the right hand of Moses") in his memory. There he built the windmill, to provide the poor of Jerusalem with cheap flour. An ad in the *Jewish Chronicle* of London, for February 27, 1857, read, "Wanted, For the Holy City of JERUSALEM, a JEWISH MILLER who thoroughly understands the working of a Windmill with self-acting sweeps, DRESSING the STONES, and the requisite adjustment of a Flour-machine working with a Wired Cylinder and revolving brushes." References "respecting ability, moral and religious character" were requested. But the windmill was not well placed to catch the prevailing winds.

Montefiore's faith in Israel's restoration never dimmed: "I am quite certain of it; it has been my constant dream, and it will be realized the day when I am no more." Sir Moses, whose windmill missed the prevailing winds of Jerusalem, caught the prevailing winds of change in the world, some of which were blowing Jews toward Zion. The assassination of Alexander II in 1881 destroyed the minimal tolerance that made life possible for Jews in the Russian Empire. Mass emigrations to western Europe and the United States began, and what had been a steady historical drip, drip, drip of Jews settling in Israel widened to a rivulet.

This was called the First Aliyah, or "going up"—pioneers determined to return to the land not just in the sense of relocation but in that of physical intimacy. They founded the agricultural villages in which independent farmers cooperated for equipment and marketing. Far less religious than the traditional Jewish immigrants over the centuries, they roughly doubled the population of the *yishuv*—the Jewish community of settlement—to about fifty thousand, at a time when the Arab population was around two hundred thousand.[17] They bought land from Arabs in undesirable locations, fought malaria and hostile neighbors, and frequently failed, yet they were the embryonic heartbeat of a worldwide movement.

Ze'ev Dubnow was part of that movement, and in November 1882 he wrote to his historian brother,

> Do you really think that my sole purpose in coming here was to take care only of my own affairs? . . . No. My ultimate aim, and that of many others, is great, vast, and boundless, but it cannot be said to be beyond reach. The ultimate aim . . . is to take possession of the Land of Israel and to give back to the Jews the political independence of which they have been deprived for 2,000 years. Do not laugh, this is not an empty dream.[18]

That was the year the Russian Empire began its official persecution of Jews, and among these increasingly hopeless people were many new emigrants to Israel.

But the movement needed a leader. In the early 1890s a man born in Budapest completed his legal studies in Vienna.[19] But this young doctor of laws, a completely assimilated, even deracinated, Jew, loved writing too much to bury himself in the law, and soon became both a playwright and a famous journalist. He was the ideal end product of Napoleon's dream of Jewish emancipation and had every advantage any European could have. He knew little of Jewish life beyond the privileged German-speaking middle classes—a world of seemingly infinite possibility. But he was about to learn emancipation's limits.

He was assigned by Vienna's *Neue Freie Presse* to cover Paris, capital of an increasingly free, educated, and thriving western Europe. It was a time of high hopes for peace—only small wars had troubled Europe since Napoleon's campaigns ended in 1815, and many believed that war itself had run its historical course. Science, industry, and capital did wonders, the idea of permanent progress spread, and the ship of universal civilization seemed destined to board all humanity. Spreading wealth and liberty would trump petty hatreds; ethnic walls would melt away.

Theodor Herzl was open to these possibilities and, of all Jews, most likely to achieve them. But he saw in Paris a paradox of "emancipation" that would endure and grow for half a century: as Jews succeeded, they were resented; as they were integrated, they became increasingly suspect. The experience of the conversos in the era of the expulsion was being repeated in central and western Europe, except that this time no one was really interested in conversion. Herzl arrived in Paris to find Jews accused of a scandal involving the Panama Canal; wealthy Jews played a role, but the blame was unfairly fixed on them alone. He reported on a bill—defeated, but gaining

160 votes in the Chamber of Deputies—to bar Jews from public office. And he had to write about a Jewish army officer convicted of treason by the French high command. This convict, Captain Alfred Dreyfus, was sent to Devil's Island to spend the rest of his life alone with his guards, in chains, on the basis of an illegal trial and weak secret evidence. Two years into his sentence, clear proof pinned the treason on a dissipated Polish nobleman who had married a marquis's daughter; the case against Dreyfus was based on forgeries.

But this new evidence was suppressed, and Colonel Marie-Georges Piquart, who found it, was posted to a remote part of Tunisia. New "evidence" against Dreyfus was forged. Piquart went to a lawyer friend with his findings, and for this was court-martialed and imprisoned. But he had pricked a boil, and the stench disgusted decent people, most famously the writers Anatole France and Émile Zola. When the Polish nobleman was acquitted in a manipulated trial, Zola locked himself in his room for twenty-four hours and produced his searing polemic, *J'accuse.* France's greatest living novelist and the bane of unjust rulers, Zola now became the victim of his government and jingoistic French mobs. He was given a year in prison in a grossly unfair trial and barely escaped with his life to England, one step ahead of a savage horde of his formerly adoring fellow countrymen.

This was in 1898, and Dreyfus had been chained to his rock for four years. He would not be rehabilitated until 1906—a thoroughly broken, decrepit, white-haired forty-year-old—when he was reinstated in the army and awarded the Order of the Legion of Honor. He was barely aware of the proceedings. But Dreyfus had been aware enough at the 1894 military ceremony in which he was degraded, surrounded by a Paris mob screaming "Death to the Jews!" So had the young Herzl, watching the mob's wild fury. "Where?" he wrote. "In France. In Republican, modern, civilized France, a hundred years after the Declaration of the Rights of Man."[20] The rights of man no longer included Jews. He emerged from his anguish having abandoned all he had been raised to believe as a citizen of Europe, and became instead a citizen of the nonexistent Jewish state.

In a creative fever exceeding even Zola's he wrote *Der Judenstaat (The Jewish State),* a short book that changed the Jewish world. It claimed a new status for the Jews beyond religion or ethnicity, *nationhood,* running counter to a century of conviction that, given freedom of religion, the Jews could fully integrate into European nations. Herzl was duly opposed by Jews who believed in assimilation, but also by many more who believed in the ancient tradition begun in Babylonia: since Jewishness *was* Judaism, the Jews could and would be loyal to any state that would have them, as long as they could practice their religion. The latter stance was not an option for Herzl, whose dream of integration shattered amid the shrieks of a Paris mob.

Der Judenstaat laid out in eloquent sequence the steps to a Jewish state.

It argued that the needed political, financial, and cultural resources were already in place and could be systematically tapped. In a nationalistic era Jews too must have a nation, and only with that could the Gordian knot of "the Jewish problem" be finally cut. He argued too that the Jews who remained in the diaspora would have their lives normalized by the Jewish state's existence. He could not have been prepared for the reaction.

Herzl was not only brilliant but tall, dark, handsome. His charisma did not always impress the wealthy Jews of his own social class, most of whom thought him naive or dangerous. But to the poor Jews of western Europe, and to the vast, increasingly desperate Jewish masses in the east, who faced vicious pogroms and anti-Semitic laws, he was virtually a messiah. Now, the Jewish masses had had "messiahs" in the past, each of whom had led them into a vale of tears. Bar Kokhba's heroic but hopeless rebellion against the Romans—despite the support of Rabbi Akiva—had led to genocide and millennial exile. Shabbatai Zvi's claims had infected the minds of the helpless Jews of both Europe and Islam in the 1600s, but he ended his campaign as a Muslim apostate, turning his back on millions of grieving followers. Jacob Frank was a similar disappointment, using religion to justify his sexual promiscuity and ultimately becoming a Catholic; there were many others.

Herzl was different. His dream may have been vain, but at least it did not call for divine intervention, just historic human ingenuity. Unless they could get to America, poor Jews had no better offer. Herzl was lionized, and the First Zionist Congress, which he convened at Basel in 1897—he insisted on black tie and tails for the opening meeting—drew Jews from east and west, rich and poor, atheist and ultra-Orthodox, socialists and bankers. Out of this motley crew Herzl built a movement that would not only outlive him—he died in 1904—but realize his dream. He wrote in his diary, "If I were to sum up the Congress in a word—which I shall take care not to publish—it would be this: At Basel I founded the Jewish State. If I said this out loud today I would be greeted by universal laughter. In five years, perhaps, and certainly in fifty years, everyone will perceive it."[21]

It did not, however, include Jewish anti-Zionists, of whom there were millions. Most Jewish groups prefer to forget their anti-Zionist predecessors, but they were powerful and endangered the dream. Many of the ultra-Orthodox considered it sacrilegious to found a Jewish state before the Messiah came. Reform Jews opposed it because they believed in maximum assimilation and insisted that Jewishness meant only Judaism, not peoplehood and certainly not nationhood. The Jews who wanted complete assimilation, even to the point of abandoning Judaism, were of course opposed. Many rich Jews, loath to rock the boat of Jewish capitalism, saw Zionism as a wacky leftist plot. And Jews of all stripes dreaded the accusation of dual loyalty that Zionists provoked in every one of their homelands.

Fortunately, the Jews of the world did not get to vote on the creation of a Jewish state; any time before 1933, they would probably have turned it down. But it was not for them to decide, and the dream became real. The Kishinev pogrom of 1903 was the worst of a series of pogroms in Russia and eastern Europe, and one of the first to be recorded by photojournalists. Children were thrown out of high windows, eyes were gouged out, nails were driven into people's heads. The anti-Jewish riots went on for two days, and the police did nothing. In October 1905, in the wake of a failed revolution, the Russian government itself instigated some fifty pogroms against Jews in a single week. From the outset of modern Jewish settlement in Israel in the 1870s, those settlements had been actively defended.[22] But after the pogroms of the new century Jewish defense forces arose in Europe, and these newly militant Jews allied themselves with the Jewish defenders in Israel.

The specter of Jews murdered by Cossacks just for being Jews made many take their chances with Arabs and malaria. These pogroms accelerated emigration to the United States and started the Second Aliyah, a new wave of migration to Israel. These immigrants were influenced by the growing socialist sentiment in Europe, especially in Russia, and their blend of Zionism and socialism was the core of Israel's culture and character for three generations. Even more than earlier immigrants, they insisted on working the land with their own hands. One pioneer, later the wife of the second president of Israel, came to Israel to do one thing: live. "I crossed the Jezreel Valley on a narrow path," she would later say, "through a haze of swarming mosquitoes. I finally reached Kinneret on the Sea of Galilee, the wasteland which we had begun to restore. It was dead soil. You had to have deep conviction to attempt revitalizing such soil."[23]

After the Kishinev pogrom the British government offered Uganda to the Zionists, and out of fear and exhaustion Herzl and some others argued that the offer should be accepted. It was voted down, however, and the reason became clear to a puzzled Arthur James Balfour, later to declare Britain's commitment to founding Israel, when he called Chaim Weizmann in to see him. Weizmann was a noted chemist, a leading Zionist, and a prominent member of the Jewish community of Manchester. He was also a leading opponent of the Uganda proposal.

> "I said [Weizmann later recalled], 'Mr. Balfour, if you were offered Paris instead of London would you take it?' . . . He looked surprised. He: 'But London is our own!' I said: 'Jerusalem was our own when London was a marsh.'"
> Balfour was profoundly impressed.[24]

David Ben-Gurion was a member of this second wave, and his story is that of the group in microcosm. He was born in Russia and showed courage from the beginning. He helped organize Jewish commando units for self-defense in Warsaw and Plonsk after the Kishinev pogrom. When he went around among the rich Jews of Plonsk to raise funds for the yishuv and its settlements, he dressed in peasant garb. Stuck in his belt was a pistol, which he rested on the table in their well-appointed homes. He wasn't threatening them of course, but . . . In any case, they made donations. He once fired two shots in a study house.[25] Since Turkey ruled the Middle East, he studied law in Istanbul, hoping to use the law to serve the yishuv. But he involved himself actively in both agricultural labor and self-defense. The Arab threat to Jewish life in the Holy Land became a focal point. Against all odds, full of strain, fear, hope, internal dissension, external threat, disease, violence, and almost inhuman work, the yishuv grew.

The immigrants of the Second Aliyah founded the kibbutzim, true collective farms in which all property was held in common, all members contributed equal work, all received equal cost-of-living disbursements and communal benefits, men and women were treated equally, and children were raised in sleep-in communal houses, spending only a few hours daily and a weekend day with their parents. The kibbutz was vital to the yishuv and the state. Its residents staked out the frontier, defended it, dug their hands and tools into the soil, built villages in the most difficult circumstances, died in battles with hostile Arabs, and in general formed the nucleus of the social order of the tough Israeli community. Although a minority, the kibbutzim supplied a disproportionate number of national leaders, and made up the core command of the Jewish army. They were raised for service, teamwork, sacrifice, and courage, and these traits served them well as leaders. Not just their philosophy but their very life was a rupture with the past, and their contempt for the diaspora helped them define themselves in opposition to that past.

The First World War changed everything. The British army, advancing through the Sinai Desert from Egypt, succeeded only with Jewish help. With little Arab support the British and the Jews drove the Turks out of Jerusalem, and eventually out of all of Israel. Meanwhile Weizmann, the immigrant chemist in England, solved the problem of an acetone shortage that was holding back British weapons manufacture—large quantities were needed to make the explosive cordite, and he developed a method for making the acetone from starch. With his adoptive country's gratitude in hand, he negotiated the next great step in the Zionist dream. He persuaded Balfour, whom he had impressed so strongly during the Uganda debates, to make the Jewish homeland official British policy. The cabinet passed this resolution:

His Majesty's Government view with favour the establishment in Palestine of a national home for the Jewish people, and will use their best endeavors to facilitate the achievement of this object, it being clearly understood that nothing shall be done which may prejudice the civil and religious rights of existing non-Jewish communities in Palestine, or the rights and political status enjoyed by Jews in any other country.[26]

The Balfour Declaration and the British triumph over the Turks emboldened the Jews of the yishuv to believe that they might actually be able to stay there. The war had also taught some of them to fight. Joseph Trumpeldor had been an officer in the czar's army and then, with Vladimir "Zev" Jabotinsky, a founder of the Judaean Regiment of the British army—"the largest Jewish military formation since antiquity."[27] He died defending an indefensible settlement against attacking Arabs in 1920. His last words were *"Tov lamut b'ad artzenu,"* "It is good to die for the sake of our homeland." Nine other kibbutz members died in that battle, including two women. In the same year, the nucleus of the Haganah—"Defense"—was formed. The yishuv continued to grow, as individuals and groups purchased land legitimately from Arabs who wanted to sell[28] and fended off attacks by other Arabs who wanted them out.

In 1929 there was an Arab pogrom in Hebron, in which fifty-nine Jews were massacred, but in the late 1930s serious Arab attacks on Jews spread throughout the country. This Arab Revolt targeted the British as well, prompting sympathetic British officers to train Jews to fight. The first large group of Sabras, or native-born Israelis—named for the local fruit that was prickly outside and sweet inside—began to fight in this period, and the kibbutz took on its central role in Jewish defense.[29]

In 1939 the hated British White Paper nullified the Balfour Declaration by blocking further Jewish immigration—an attempt to quell Arab anger. Still, most Jews supported the British against the Nazis. There were thirty-two thousand Palestinian Jews fighting in the British army, four thousand of them women, five thousand under the Star of David in the Jewish Brigade. These young people became the main body of the Israel Defense Force after the war. David Ben-Gurion said, "We will fight the war as if there were no White Paper, and we will fight the White Paper as if there were no war," but it was not clear what exactly that meant in practice. Some critics fault the leadership of the yishuv for giving too little attention to the mass murders in Europe; others say there was nothing more they could have done. What is clear is that at the end of the war millions of Jews who might have come to Israel were dead.

After the war a small radical group, the Irgun, decided that fighting the White Paper knew no bounds. They smuggled large numbers of weapons into Israel not just for defense against Arab attacks but for assault and terror against the British. They and other radical organizations blew up the

British military installation in the King David Hotel in Jerusalem, assassinated a United Nations ambassador, and staged a major prison outbreak from the fortress at Acre. Ben-Gurion sank a ship of theirs, the *Altalena,* as it brought arms and refugees toward the Israeli coast.[30] The mainstream Haganah strategy was to win the world's support for the establishment of a Jewish state; the radicals' strategy was to drive the British out of the country by any means necessary and to take all measures to turn back Arab aggression. Both strategies helped give birth to the state.

Of overriding importance was to import the remaining refugees—a remnant of murdered millions, but still a substantial number. They were confined in displaced persons (DP) camps in Europe and on the island of Cyprus, and the Haganah brought as many of them into the country as they could, the vast majority illegally. Some came a few at a time in small boats. Others came by the hundreds or even thousands in ships that were not seaworthy, were subject to British blockade, and in some cases were sunk. If they could break through the blockade they would anchor offshore and a thousand or more people would don bathing suits and swim to the beach, where tens of thousands of residents would be on the beach in bathing suits waiting for them, ensuring that they would be lost in the crowd as it dispersed throughout the city.

In this way the yishuv community absorbed hundreds of thousands of shattered people, people without hope or confidence, with no choice but to follow dubious leadership to a place where, supposedly, Jews themselves would be in charge. At the time of partition there were six hundred thousand in all, a mere tithe of those murdered a few years earlier, but sufficient in grit and courage to turn back the wrath of many millions. There was absolutely no reason in the world why they should have succeeded, except that they had no choice.

◐▩▩◑

In parallel with these events, spoken Hebrew was reborn. Its revival is unique; there is so far no other instance of a language lying dormant for centuries, used only for religious and literary purposes, brought back to life as the medium of bickering in markets, blathering at family dinners, cursing in street fights, cheering at sports events, murmurs in shadowy lovers' lanes, ecstatic cries between sweaty sheets, and, of course, most astonishing of all, in the mouths of toddlers begging or scolding or wooing their mothers in the only words they know. How this happened is a tribute to human ingenuity and determination that can only be called fierce.

Hebrew was spoken for centuries before it became the language of the Torah, and for many more generations as the rest of the Jewish Bible was written. But it was gradually transformed into the Hebrew of the Mishnah, the core of the Talmud. Mishnaic Hebrew, developed in both Israel and

Babylonia, reflected the influence of Greek and Aramaic, which were common throughout the Middle East and displaced Hebrew for many even before the disastrous Roman wars. For assimilating, ambitious Jews, Greek, then Latin, had taken precedence, and after the exile Jews spoke the language of whatever people welcomed them. Hebrew never died as a written language; in addition to religious texts, the Jews of Spain wrote love poems and war poems, philosophical and scientific treatises, and translations of Greek and Arabic texts. This kept Hebrew not just alive, but flowering, from the tenth to the thirteenth centuries.

The invention of printing in the mid-1400s greatly improved Hebrew literacy.[31] Hebrew presses soon appeared in Avignon, Rome, Lisbon, Salonika, Constantinople, Paris, Prague, Venice, and scholarly, mystical Safed. Throughout this period, as before and since, Hebrew was the main language of Jewish study and prayer,[32] and Hebrew literacy was virtually universal among men.[33] In the 1700s, the Haskalah put Hebrew at or near the core of Jewish culture, although some of its leaders preferred High German, written with Hebrew letters for the masses. Hebrew now became a weapon in the war against Yiddish waged by Jewish intellectuals, who wanted above all to integrate Jews into the European Enlightenment without forcing them to give up being Jewish.

But the golem they created soon became a giant with a mind of its own. In 1853, just a century after the Haskalah began, the first novel in Hebrew—*The Love of Zion,* by Abraham Mapu—told of a visit to the Holy Land in the First Temple Period.[34] In 1856 the first Hebrew newspaper appeared in eastern Prussia, followed by weeklies in Vilna and Odessa in 1860.[35] In 1879, in an obscure Hebrew journal—*Ha-Shahar,* or "The Dawn"—an even more obscure scholar, Eliezer Ben-Yehudah, contributed the article "A Burning Question." This twenty-one-year-old Lithuanian, a medical student and lapsed Orthodox Jew, had concluded not only that Hebrew could be revived as a spoken language, but that it would find its voice in the Land of Israel itself.[36]

Preposterous. But wasn't the world changing with enormous speed?

Ben-Yehudah's idea obsessed his rigorous mind. Giving up his medical studies and moving to Jerusalem in 1881, he informed his family that they would converse only in Hebrew from then on. Later, bringing his elderly mother to Israel, he spoke only Hebrew to her, although she knew not a word of it. He talked to his dog in Hebrew. The first native speaker of Modern Hebrew was his son. Born in 1882, the boy didn't speak until age three, but contrary to some predictions, he was not mentally retarded; he became known in Israel as an orator. His younger sister Dola recalled the family:

> We played among ourselves. The first children were under a
> kind of house arrest. They were not allowed to go out into the street

and speak to strange children. . . . They'd bring home a dog and a cat—a male dog and a female cat. The child could speak to the dog and cat—in the masculine and feminine genders, respectively. . . . These were his first friends, and also the first animals to speak Hebrew for some 2,000 years.[37]

This dream had problems. Orthodox Jews had no love for using the holy tongue to address endearments to a dog. Yiddish writers and politicians and their millions of readers and followers already had a Jewish language, and they were just establishing it as a medium of literary art and scholarly study, overthrowing with great effort the contempt for Yiddish displayed by the Haskalah. And then there was the minor fact that no one had ever revived a dead language before.

But, as Herzl said years later, *"Im tirtzu, ayn zu agadah"*—"If you will it, it is no legend." They willed it with all their hearts. Mendele Moykher Sforim—"Mendele the Bookseller," the Yiddish master born S. Y. Abramovitsh—began to write in Hebrew. Stirring poems and enthralling tales appeared in the transformed ancient tongue, and the first Hebrew daily— *Ha-Yom,* or "The Day"—appeared in St. Petersburg in 1886, with the express goal of creating a simple everyday Hebrew stripped of religious and literary stiffness. In 1905, a primer for learning Hebrew "by the natural method" was published in Warsaw.

One milestone was an intense debate in Haifa in 1913 over whether Hebrew or German would be the language of instruction at the new Technion Institute. Teach future scientists not in German, the world's scientific language, but in . . . Hebrew? Ben-Yehudah won this fight, and the Technion became the fountainhead of engineering genius that transformed the country. In 1922, the British government recognized Hebrew along with Arabic and English as an official language. That year a Hebrew-language board game—something like Scrabble—was invented. By 1926 there was a Hebrew book fair in Tel Aviv.

But the main engine of early Modern Hebrew was not in the cities but in the agricultural settlements, brimming with young pioneers devoted to the revival of Jewish life in a new form. They, like Ben-Yehudah, insisted on speaking Hebrew, and their children grew up in it, often knowing no other language.

But before it became natural, Modern Hebrew had to be created, and Ben-Yehudah set up the Hebrew Language Council to do this.[38] They rejected all borrowings from European languages that were not already in use, and instead shaped the vocabulary by adapting and combining ancient words to describe new things. For example, *kol-noa*—literally "voice-motion"—became the word for cinema. If borrowing could not be avoided, better Arabic than English or French. They chose the Sephardic pronunciation, breaking with the traditions of both the Ashkenazic rabbis and the Haskalah literary lions and making the new language squarely Middle Eastern. Finally, and against Ben-Yehudah's preference for biblical Hebrew, the grammar was based on the Hebrew of the Mishnah, which was a bit more like European grammars.[39]

The battle with the Orthodox was serious. In the 1890s they denounced Ben-Yehudah to the Turkish authorities for alleged seditious activity, and he sat in jail until an appeal freed him.[40] He became discouraged about Israel and, like Herzl, supported an East African homeland at the Zionist Congress of 1903. Fortunately this failed, and Hebrew became the language of Israel as in ancient times. "One Language—One People" was the slogan; an early poster read, "For your sake and the sake of your children . . . Learn Hebrew." The first Hebrew elementary school was founded in Jaffa in 1896. There were ten thousand children in such schools by 1918, and one hundred thousand by 1948. The first volume of Ben Yehudah's dictionary was published in 1908, as was S. Y. Agnon's first Hebrew novel, *Agunot* ("Abandoned Wives"). The first daily, *HaDoar* ("The Post"), was founded in 1910, and its rival, *Ha'aretz* ("The Land"), in 1919. Books in Hebrew rose exponentially.

Hebrew poets were important community leaders, but first they had to get there. Haim Nachman Bialik, Uri Zvi Greenberg, and Nathan Alterman arrived in the 1920s; their nationalist poetry inspired the people and shaped the language. The national theater, Habima ("The Stage"), was founded by Russian Jews in 1928, but they had performed in Hebrew in Moscow for over a decade. Literary achievements have for a century had a much greater significance in Israel than in most nations; not only was literacy always central to the Jews, but they were essentially re-creating their language and literature.[41]

After 1948 the army of Israel became the great melting pot for Jews from every place on earth, and the discipline as well as the exigencies of war shored up the Tower of Babel. You had to communicate, so you did, and Hebrew was the only accepted medium of discourse. From 1949, the *ulpan* program gave immigrants an intense course in spoken Hebrew. Leading Arab Israeli writers like Anton Shammas create literature in both Arabic and Hebrew,[42] and non-Jewish immigrants from Southeast Asia and elsewhere are fluent in the language. A Nobel Prize went to Agnon for his Hebrew fiction, and he once told Saul Bellow, the Jewish American novelist who also won the Nobel, to make sure his books were translated into Hebrew, since in the future it would be the only language.

☾ﻼﻼﻼ☽

From the early twentieth century, the kibbutz was central to the life of the yishuv, and it had an ideology. The young Russian Jews pouring into the land were not just Zionists, they were socialists. Although Martin Buber was the most famous thinker in socialist Zionism, A. D. Gordon was its leading exponent. Gordon got dirt under his fingernails as an act of faith. He and his disciples believed that near the heart of "the Jewish problem" in history was a forced alienation from physical labor and, especially, from labor on the land. He had a Tolstoyan reverence for farming, but spent half his adult life clerking on a baronial estate. He did not move to Israel until he was forty-eight, but he promptly became the grand old man of the nascent movement, helping to found the first kibbutz at Degania. You had to go to "the university of labor" and change your spiritual life before you could change the world. At his death in 1922, he was an awesome figure with a long white beard who worked in the fields all day and led younger kibbutzniks in song and dance at night.

Most kibbutzniks were not communists, but they believed in collective economy on a local scale and lived those beliefs, creating the longest-lasting and most successful communal societies in modern history. There were implications for the yishuv and later for the state, but this ideology focused on face-to-face relationships in tightly knit communities collectively working the land. This was not Marx's communism, but that of earlier thinkers who had tried to found similar small communities based on cooperation, and it had echoes in the hippie communes of the 1960s. Without exception, these experiments failed, most within a few years. The kibbutz succeeded for generations, and in some ways accounts for the success of the Jewish state. Why?

Anthropologist Melford Spiro lived on a kibbutz in the 1950s and again in the 1970s. His first book on the community, which he named "Kiryat Yedidim," was pointedly called *Kibbutz: Venture in Utopia*. The second was *Children of the Kibbutz,* an account of how children were brought up to live in this utopia. He focused on the psychology of Sabras, using methods similar to those he had used years earlier on an exotic South Sea island.

Kiryat Yedidim had been founded by east European Jews in the early 1920s and by the early 1950s had five hundred members. The founders were idealistic young people who settled in a malarial swamp and lived their ideology. They believed intensely in the ideals of brotherhood, equality, and freedom, and attempted to realize these goals in a collectivistic community. They used communal ownership to block the emergence of social classes, and cooperative work to promote brotherhood by muting competition. Foremen and other leaders were merely first among equals, serving at the pleasure of their peers. Despite a labor shortage, no nonmembers were employed by the kibbutz, avoiding social stratification. Kibbutz members—*chaverim,* or friends—did every job themselves. They abolished money as both a medium of exchange and a symbol of wealth, and did away with the profit motive. The necessities of life were distributed according to the principle "from each according to his ability, to each according to his needs," and both abilities and needs were determined collectively at kibbutz meetings. These meetings occurred twice a week, made all decisions democratically, and delegated authority to members elected for temporary terms. Group pressure deterred deviant behavior.

Some kibbutzim introduced manufacturing, but Kiryat Yedidim stuck to the land. They had a dairy, field crops, vegetable gardens, a fishery, fruit orchards, flocks, poultry, and fodder. But a kibbutz was not a peasant village. Mechanized farming left time for books, music, and politics. After work people might attend an English class, a genetics lecture, a concert, play, or debate. Nor was life painfully spare and rustic any longer. Homes were small but tastefully furnished, private gardens lush and individual in character. Household budgets were equal, but people did different things with the money.[43]

They were becoming a sort of landed bourgeoisie, but they would hate this label. They thought of themselves as "the vanguard of man's quest for the ideal society, part of the shock troops in the future social revolution." Equality, community, and cooperation were not just theorized, but practiced. Women and men were equal, married or not. Marriage was based on love and choice and solemnized in only a nonreligious way. Women kept their names, jobs, and status throughout life. Husband and wife stood equal and independent because "domestic services—meals, laundry, mending, and so forth—are provided in the various communal institutions of the kibbutz. Should either become ill, he is assured of complete and continuing economic support. . . . Having a child poses no economic problems. . . . The kibbutz assumes complete responsibility for its economic welfare. In brief, economic factors play no role in cementing the relationship. . . . The marital bond is compounded of emotional, sexual, and social ties exclusively."[44]

Communal child rearing was key. Children spent the bulk of their time in the children's house, from infancy. Parents could visit them during the day if they had time, and Saturdays were family days, but even then the children took their meals with other children. Of fifteen parents interviewed, eleven thought they definitely were *not* the most important influence in their child's life, and none were sure that they *were*. Interviews with the children, however, showed that many parents were wrong; family ties remain most important.

"Kibbutz Har," studied by Paula Rayman, was similar.[45] Established in 1938 on land purchased from Arabs, it was from the beginning an outpost, in the northwest corner of the country near the Lebanese border. It was a key to the Haganah's tower-and-stockade plan for defense, and the famous Scottish Artillery captain Orde Wingate, ever a friend of the Jews, set up training there. There were many Arab attacks during the first months. All members either were Sabras or had been in the country for years.

Decisions were made at town meetings, officials were democratically elected, and there was in principle complete equality. The children's house theoretically enabled women full equality in work and community life. Still, "Key leadership positions were most often held by men," even though "women superficially strived to take on men's roles. They dressed in baggy shorts, refused to wear make-up, and prided themselves on physical strength."[46] Yet they were expected to take on more domestic and service labor than men did. "The pioneer-settler ethos of the kibbutz movement was predicated on masculine norms of physical power and aggressiveness."[47]

Agriculture in this hilly spot was secondary to its strategic value, but after the founding of the state, the kibbutz raised crops farther down in the Jezreel Valley—wheat, grapes, oranges, and cabbages. Many agricultural efforts were unsuccessful. Nevertheless, the kibbutzniks were proudly self-sufficient—crucial when Arab forces cut them off. In the 1940s, as new members arrived with new skills, machine tools were brought in and the kibbutz began to make weapons parts. War took a grave toll, but the kibbutz was a natural source of military leadership: boldness, physical strength, courage, communal responsibility, sacrifice, initiative, flexibility, and resilience were all qualities cultivated in the kibbutz, and all were vital in war.

Industry superseded agriculture, and the kibbutz economy thrived. Social classes emerged as a managerial elite supplanted complete job rotation. Hired laborers ate separately from kibbutz members. There were over 200 members by 1948, 470 by 1975. By this time there was a large communal dining hall with a bomb shelter under it, other community buildings, and an array of one- and two-story housing units all around them. The weapons-parts factory provided twice the income, but bananas, citrus fruit, and cotton were important cash crops. Homes grew a bit and small private gardens bloomed. Standard clothing gave way to individual taste. Women wore dresses. Weddings became relatively lavish and conventional. Yet because of constant tension on the Lebanese border, women at Har received military training not just in the army but on the kibbutz itself. They were not the women of pioneer times, but neither were they like women outside the kibbutz.

A third kibbutz, "Makom," was the subject of an oral history in the late 1970s, when many changes had taken place throughout the movement.[48] Makom was founded in 1928 by seventeen Tel Aviv Jews, soon joined by others. Yehuda, slowed by age, was the only founder still living. He was born in Russia in 1909 and recalled being evacuated from his home during the German advance by Russian soldiers, who burned the town to keep it out of German hands. He and his family became wanderers in the forest, then peripatetic townspeople all over eastern Europe, and finally settlers in Tel Aviv. After a false start in a malarial swamp, they moved to the Jezreel

Valley and created Kibbutz Makom. Many joined them, but many left. Three suicides weighed heavily on the small community.

"When I look back at that period," Yehuda said, "this is how I summarize it: We set out to create a fundamental revolution in our lives, both as Jews and as human beings. We succeeded more or less in doing this. As in life, there is the dream and there is reality." He was critical, but not resigned.

> The kibbutz represents a real hope for us Jews in Israel and for humanity in general. . . . Who knows, we might witness a deterioration of our ideal. But even if that is the case, I believe that eventually our ideas will return with greater force, for the premises of the kibbutz are essential for the future of human society: cooperation and equality. We did manage to create such a society in our lifetime. . . . the whole kibbutz movement has achieved more than anyone thought or expected. There are, however, questions from within, and anxiety is our constant companion.

Yehuda was most anxious about hired labor: "I see manual work, physical labor, as one of our basic principles. . . . This is the Jewish problem: all of the traditional Jewish occupations! And this was our revolution: we wanted to send roots into the soil! And then you see someone, who for twenty or thirty years worked productively . . . suddenly showing his other nature, that of the Diaspora Jew, looking for easy ways of making money, becoming a merchant. We haven't changed his basic identity as much as we thought we had. This is what I am fighting against." He was also distressed by kibbutz members with outside sources of income, and, perhaps most important, by changes in child rearing: "Today many parents aren't very enthusiastic about their son's becoming a cowman, a worker. They want their son to be a doctor—you see, the Diaspora mentality is returning, it's returning. I also would be personally satisfied if my son got a higher education, but first he should be a worker for a while."

Zvi Eisman, a sixty-six-year-old with blue eyes, blue overalls, a pleasant voice, and an easy manner, had founded a family of kibbutz leaders. He was born in 1912 in an upper-middle-class family in a small German-Swiss town. His doctor father was killed fighting for Germany in World War I— there were one hundred thousand Jews in the German ranks, and twelve thousand deaths—but his mother became a Zionist when German anti-Semites discounted the contribution Jews had made in the war. Zvi went to a Catholic school, learned Hebrew from a priest, and was following in his father's footsteps when he discovered two swastikas tattooed on the Jewish cadaver he was dissecting in medical school. This made him a Zionist, and he and his like-minded wife made *aliyah* in the early thirties.

I have been an industrial worker, a gardener, a farmer, a secretary, a cashier, a teacher, and more. I have carried out many functions outside the kibbutz, in the Party or in the Movement's higher-education institutions as well. . . . Whenever I had the choice, I returned to simple labor again.

. . . Years ago I received a large sum of reparation money from the Germans, and handed it all in to the kibbutz, naturally. I receive a monthly pension from the Germans, as well—which goes directly to our cashier; I don't even know how much it is. So I feel I'm a rich man. . . . I do study, though . . . and I travel twice a week to the university and take advanced classes in Judaism, especially in the Talmud. . . . It fascinates me, yet it often aggravates me as well. You see, I'm a Marxist, a left-oriented Socialist and a kibbutznik. . . . To work at integrating my old values with Judaism is not an easy undertaking. But I'm working on it.

I'm content with my life. I think that the kibbutz in its present form has fulfilled my wildest dreams. Actually, reality has surpassed all my youthful fantasies.

Dina, a small sixty-five-year-old woman with pale eyes, was born to a family that had lived in Jerusalem for six generations. She joined Makom in 1934, a couple of years before major Arab riots engulfed the country. Her latest job was supervising the babies' kitchen, but she loved gardening best; while working, she raised four children by the classic kibbutz method. Looking back, she only wished that some of her children and grandchildren were still with her. Her first son, an elite paratrooper, was enticed away to an army career. Her second son moved to the United States. She had doubted he could succeed outside the kibbutz, but he became a successful building contractor and film producer in New York. Her "glamorous" daughter taught modern dance in Israel, and had two daughters of her own. Her third son was studying in Canada.

Of the oldest, she said, "He has participated in so many battles and wars, that it has been a constant nightmare for me. Wherever I have worked I have always run to hear the news broadcasts. I could smell out which news items would be the kind of things in which he participated. . . . I never felt criticized for the fact that none of my children stayed in the kibbutz. The opposite is true. . . . people sympathize with me. . . . It is indeed painful, particularly in the evenings; one walks outside and everywhere one sees grandmothers with children. And on Friday nights and holidays, the big families gathering around the tables in the dining hall . . . so I feel it."

Shlomit, a pretty thirty-two-year-old, was a daughter of one of those large families: "I was born here and have spent all my life here, except for military service. . . . I never thought of leaving. . . . it's always been the most natural choice for me to live here, as my brother and sister do. I feel secure here, in an environment which I know very well. . . . It's my home. . . . I know that if I face any kind of hardship, the *kibbutz,* both the community and the individual members, will always stand by my side and provide all possible help."[49]

Her husband had been killed a few years earlier in the Yom Kippur War. She had been married seven years, "and we had one child, a boy, who was four years old when the war broke out. At that time there were suddenly many widows, as many kibbutz members were killed then. The whole kibbutz was in a state of terrible shock. . . . The way the community rallied to help the families, parents, and widows was really outstanding." Her father had been killed in the 1956 Sinai campaign, and, paradoxically, she considered her mother's lack of resilience to be helpful, "a negative model: I knew what I didn't want to become." She found her new husband, a carpenter, in the kibbutz. "We got married about a year ago and now we have this girl. My son loves him too, so we are a whole family once again."[50]

But things were changing; all the trends in evidence by the 1970s had accelerated. In 1991 there were nearly 130,000 people in 270 kibbutzim, but with a net annual loss averaging over 2,000 a year for five years.[51] Many kibbutzim were in serious debt, and capitalism increasingly asserted itself as the answer, even though the businesses were always collectively owned. Industry, hired labor, and the emergence of a managerial class speeded change. Work outside the kibbutz became the rule, even though on many kibbutzim earnings were still pooled. Individuality emerged in dress, lifestyle, furnishings, and child care.

Women had been in the front line of change. From the beginning, some women resisted adopting male-like roles, and many were uncomfortable with the children's house. These concerns became a very loud chorus by the seventies, with a reassertion of traditional family and child-rearing patterns increasingly apparent.[52] By the late nineties there were no children's houses left, and what had been a collective "family" became a collection of conventional families. Women accepted the impact of ordinary motherhood on their careers and community roles; they wanted their children with them.

Has the kibbutz outlived its usefulness? The question is: usefulness for whom? If the state does not need it as much as it once did, many thousands of individuals still need or want it as a way of life. If its numbers dwindle from 3 percent of the Jewish population to 2, or fewer, it will still serve those who stay. It has been an immensely successful experiment, but kibbutz society has evolved as the country has. Initially it was the vanguard of a fierce pioneering ideology, vital to national defense. Until well after independence, the kibbutz worked in almost ideal ways because the choice was collective action or death. It persists as a model of orderly, relatively selfless communal life, even as it has left behind its ideological commitment to agriculture, even as human nature has asserted itself in patterns of competition, privilege, and family. This tiny segment of Israeli society contributed a huge, disproportionate influence. It is one of the few cases in history of a purely invented communal social form taking root and blossoming. It is impossible to conceive of the Jewish state without the kibbutz at or close to its origins.

As for the feelings of those who created the kibbutz experience, lived it, and died by it, this tribute, from a Hebrew poem by Natan Zach:

> . . . *A breeze blowing from the West brings back*
> *my years of happiness, when I was marching on,*
> *pale, yet with eyes burning,*
> *along the roads of my brave homeland.*
> . . . *I look at my hands, sun-scorched,*
> *fingernails hardened. And I would not trade*
> *this world of yours, never,*
> *not for the best of all possible worlds.*[53]

☙❦❧

Terra nullius is a phrase used by some historians of the Americas to describe a myth cherished by European colonists: that they had found an empty land. But it was not empty, and the suffering of those they took it away from was great. Although the Jews were returning to a place they had once been, and so were not simply colonists, they were part of the mass movement of Europeans into areas that were no match for Europe technologically, that could be subdued with superior force and, theoretically, brought up to the standard of European civilization. In North America and Australia this program was a success, but at the cost of tremendous pain, even genocide, directed against the native residents. In Latin America and on the Indian peninsula, the process was more successful, with the wounds of colonialism gradually healing. In most of the Arab lands, it is too soon to tell what the outcome will be. In Africa the program has been a disaster.

In Israel, with its very different legal and moral foundation, the outcome is nevertheless uncertain. Jewish immigrants never represented a conquering state, and they did not become a nation for three generations. Until 1948 they acquired land almost exclusively by purchase.[54] Although they certainly defended it with weapons, theirs was the inferior, not the superior force. There was no empty land, of course, but still it is instructive to look at the numbers: the Jewish population grew exponentially, mainly through immigration, but so did the Arab population.

In 1880, just before the First Aliyah began, the estimated Arab population between the Jordan River and the Mediterranean and between the Upper Galilee and the Red Sea was 141,000, of whom 25 percent had immigrated during the previous half century under Egyptian rule. The Jewish population at the same time was around 40,000. In the mid-1890s there were more than 250,000 Arabs, a far greater increase than could be explained by an excess of births over deaths. Roughly 80,000 had to have been immigrants.[55] This process continued.

Egypt and Turkey vied for control of Israel, much as Egypt and Babylonia had in ancient times. The territory had neither political legitimacy nor anything resembling independence. People were organized into tribal groups or settled in towns and villages, leadership ranged from the mufti of Jerusalem to marauding Bedouin chieftains, the Arab population was very thin on the ground, and the Jews were thinly distributed among them. Jerusalem was the exception: more than three-fifths of the 45,420 inhabitants in an 1896 census—the year Herzl's *Jewish State* was published—were Jews, with the remainder divided equally between Christians and Muslims.[56]

In most of the country, however, Arabs outnumbered Jews. The Jews did not think too much about the destiny of these people, who would, generations later, come to see themselves as the Palestinian nation. Eliminating them was not considered an option by most Jews, although some were classical racists, and unprovoked attacks on Jewish settlements certainly turned more that way. They were self-consciously building a Jewish state, with the result that any Arabs living in it would necessarily become second-class citizens. However, from the outset Jews acquired land from Arabs by legal purchase, and all the kibbutzim and other early settlements were made on such legally and voluntarily transferred land. Until 1948, there was no transfer of land by force, in contrast to the Americas, Australia, and New Zealand. Until the 1920s, the region's indigenous politics were inchoate, and there were no nation-states. The Ottoman Empire dominated until World War I, when the British won control of it, just as it had changed hands for at least five thousand years.

In the years after World War I, it was victorious Britain's pleasure to carve up the Middle Eastern section of its empire, and, as we have seen, they promised a sliver of it to the Jews. But this promise was not so easily kept. British rule in most of the Middle East officially ended in 1922 as Egypt and Jordan became nations, their unnaturally straight borders drawn arbitrarily with rulers on a map. Iraq was separated from Turkey under the British mandate in 1932, and the French mandates in Lebanon and Syria made similar transitions before or during World War II. These somewhat arbitrary nation-states were all factionalized and turbulent, although there was sometimes a sense of identity in the larger "Arab nation."

Throughout this period, Arab immigration from neighboring countries into Jewish-settled areas of Palestine was one of the dominant trends in the region. It is estimated that about one-third of the immigration to

Jewish-settled areas of Palestine in the 1920s was Arab—immigrants, often illegal, from Egypt, Lebanon, Syria, and Jordan.[57] These migrants sought work in growing Jewish communities. Between 1920 and 1947, "[t]he extent of the settlement of Arab immigrants and the format of their diffusion along the coastal plain and the hills to the east of it parallel the scope and volume of growth in the citrus industry, urban construction and other development processes." In addition, "several times it was economic distress and other events in the adjacent countries which sent streams of immigrants to Palestine. A large wave of immigrants from Southern Syria . . . came in the wake of a drought and changed the complex of the population and the labor market."[58]

So a substantial minority of the Arabs, as well as the vast majority of the Jews, were newcomers to the land. But it was the Jews who had an expansionist ideology that reasserted their ancient claim to the land, fully aware that they would have to succeed at the expense of others' sovereignty.[59] Both populations expanded, the Arabs mainly through birth, the Jews mainly through immigration. In the vicious world of the mid-twentieth century, both peoples were suffering from poverty and persecution, but the Jews were far more limited in their options. To the extent that there was an "Arab nation," Arabs—many of whom were immigrants—living among the Palestinian Jews had other choices. The Jews had nowhere else to go.

It is likely that most Palestinian Arabs were descended from indigenous families, but they were divided over the issue of whether to sell land to the Jews. Those who opposed Jewish immigration pitted themselves against the millennial dream of a shattered, otherwise hopeless people. In the context of European colonial expansion, the Jewish takeover of part of the Holy Land seemed less objectionable than most population movements, since the Jews had a legitimate historical claim. The Arabs had a claim too, but it did not impress the victims of the Russian pogroms of 1882 and 1903, nor those of Arab rioting in 1929 or the late 1930s, nor the hundreds of thousands of Jewish refugees from brutal persecution in Arab lands they had lived in for millennia. Least of all were the survivors of European mass murder inclined to be kind to people whose leaders had been Nazi allies and who, like the Nazis, had sworn to exterminate them.

Melodrama is made up of the conflict of good against evil, but tragedy is the conflict of two goods. The Arab-Israeli conflict has had elements of both, and there is plenty of blame to go around. During the riots of the twenties and thirties, "the Arabs introduced to Palestine the 'pogrom' and its paraphernalia—the knife, the bludgeon, and the fuel-doused rag—as well as . . . the tactics of guerrilla warfare and terrorism. . . . But the Zionists also proved brutally innovative," introducing "what is now the standard equipment of modern terrorism, the camouflaged bomb in the marketplace and bus station, the car- and truck-bomb, and the drive-by shooting with automatic weapons."[60] Although there were other factors, and in many ways the Palestinian Arabs brought tragedy on themselves, the more extreme Zionists used such tactics to get them out.

The massacre of Arabs by Jewish extremists in the village of Deir Yassin was the prime example. "Whole families were riddled with bullets and grenade fragments and buried when houses were blown up on top of them; men, women, and children were mowed down as they emerged from houses; individuals were taken aside and shot."[61] More than a hundred Arabs were killed, many murdered. Of course, Arab massacres of defenseless Jews had been common before Deir Yassin, and the retaliations after it were particularly brutal. But Deir Yassin showed that the Jews, too, could murder civilians, and the impact was profound. Many thousands of terrified Arabs fled the country, and "Deir Yassin" became a rallying cry for Arabs throughout the region.

At least half a million Arabs left Israel during the War for Independence, fully expecting to return to their homes after the Arab victory. Leaders of the attacking Arab nations encouraged them in this mass movement, but they had little use for them after the war, and Israel, having paid a terrible price for victory, had no intention of allowing them to return. Many thousands of them attempted to return by infiltrating the borders during the early 1950s, and they were repulsed or deported, sometimes with great brutality.[62] In relentless sworn hostility to Israel, the "Arab nation"—really six national armies—massed against it again in 1967, and the decisive Jewish victory resulted in further gains in territory. Jewish settlement in these territories began almost immediately and is still expanding. The plight of the Palestinian refugees—rejected by Israel and Arab nations alike—combines with the brazen and illegal expansion of settlements to perpetuate the conflict. However, and this is a crucial point, the great majority of Israelis have for many years favored a peaceful accommodation with the Arabs, and have proven their willingness to trade land for peace, while the great majority of Palestinians want to see the end of Israel. This fact, regardless of the settlements, guarantees permanent war.

The Israeli-Arab controversy is full of paradoxes. The 1.5 million Israeli Arabs are second-class citizens, yet they overwhelmingly say that when a Palestinian state is created, they will stay in Israel. The Palestinians in the West Bank and Gaza tell the world that in this situation the Israelis are the Nazis and *they* are the Jews, but before the year 2000 they had a higher standard of living—lower mortality, higher per capita income, more years of education, and so on—than the people of any Arab nation. The Arab governments have excoriated Israel for more than half a century for refusing to take in Palestinian refugees, but they have also refused to absorb most of them—even though the parents or grandparents of many of those refugees were born in those countries. The same nations demand full compensation and even the right of return to Israel for those refugees while not for a moment considering reparations for the hundreds of thousands of Jews—many there for two or two and a half millennia—whom they drove out during the twentieth century. And they incessantly decry the Israeli treatment of Arabs and other Muslims, which—although not very good— has frequently been better than their own.

This is not ancient history.

In 1982 in the town of Hama, Syrian dictator Hafiz al-Assad slaughtered ten thousand mildly rebellious Muslims. "'The savagery was absolutely fantastic. There was no attempt to hold back,' says a Syrian analyst who . . . asked not to be named. 'It was not only to inflict a punishment, but to inflict a lesson for generations to come.'"[63]

In March 1988 in the town of Halabja, Iraqi dictator Saddam Hussein murdered between fifty thousand and one hundred thousand Kurds—as estimated by Human Rights Watch—with poison gas. "Saddam Hussein's attack on his own citizens marks the only time since the Holocaust that poison gas has been used to exterminate women and children."[64]

By 1994 in Egypt, President Hosni Mubarak had arrested and imprisoned or executed thousands of Muslim opponents. "'No one knows for sure how many political prisoners the Mubarak government holds behind bars,' said Dr. Essam Eryan, the No. 2 man in the Egyptian Doctors Association. . . . He added that while one Egyptian official had said the number might be 10,000, 'We believe it is higher—maybe 50,000.'"[65]

And of course Saudi Arabia routinely beheads women who commit adultery, cuts off the hands of thieves, kidnaps children from their non-Muslim mothers, and uses a savagely repressive and violent form of Islam to straitjacket its people and export terror throughout the world.

Few Arab Israelis would exchange their second-class citizenship for citizenship in any Arab country. Nevertheless, if Israel is to survive in the long run, it must address the problems of its Arab citizens more directly and meaningfully than it has so far. One of the paths to this outcome consists of private attempts to increase trust between Arab and Jewish citizens, and some Jewish Israelis have dedicated themselves to that goal.

Alouph Hareven, a former Israeli army intelligence officer who became an active proponent of better relations between Arabs and Jews in Israel, told this story: "Once, in a lecture, I quoted high security sources in Israel, saying that 99.9 percent of Israeli Arabs have never acted against the state and against its security. A woman teacher about forty years old gets up and speaks very emotionally, saying, '99.9 percent of Israeli Arabs never acted against the state and its security? That's impossible. It's against everything that I feel.' . . . you see here how feelings and facts clash. And often . . . it's the feelings which have the upper hand."[66] Arab Israelis also stereotype Jews and now feel a growing solidarity with Palestinians in the West Bank and Gaza. This conversation between a Jewish girl and an Arab boy was described by a teacher in the program:

> "Are you supporting the PLO terrorist acts?" And he said, "Yes."
> She asked him again, "Are you supporting its political acts toward
> the population?" And he said, "Yes." And she said, "Okay, if you
> heard on the radio that a bomb was put near a central bus stop and
> a girl who was just walking by was hurt, what is your attitude?"
> And he said, "I can understand it." And she asked him again, "Now
> if you heard on the radio that *I* am the girl who was [badly] hurt,
> what is going to be your response?" and he said, "Still, I feel pity,
> but still I understand it." And she started weeping and crying, and
> one of the Arabic girls joined her, and for three minutes all of the
> group—except for the boys—were crying and weeping, trying to
> speak to one another. And he went from one to another, trying
> to speak with them.

In the end the boy said, "I have to reconsider my whole attitude toward the situation. I had my attitudes. I didn't have the opportunity to speak with Jews before. I didn't know other Jews. Now, speaking with Jews, I have to think again about my political attitudes and about those acts."[67] If Arab and Jewish teenagers can weep together over their common tragedy, perhaps there is reason to hope.

෧෨෨෧

For a long time it was the belief of most Israelis that the Holocaust had little to do with the making of the state.[68] Pure pioneers, inspired by socialism, hard work, a fighting spirit, and love of the land created the state out of thin Middle Eastern air imbued with their own dreams, owing nothing to anyone else—least of all to anyone weak and stupid enough to remain in the diaspora. The implausibility of this claim is now increasingly recognized as Israelis confront the reality of their past. Herzl, Weizmann, Jabotinsky, Ben-Gurion, and other Zionists effectively imagined the Holocaust, and were energized by this horrific fantasy; you could say that Auschwitz began to shape the Israeli state half a century before it was built. Flight from Europe during the twenties and thirties by those whose eyes were open greatly expanded the yishuv just at a time when Arab riots put a premium on numbers. Some of these immigrants were brave young pioneers, but many were refugees with no place else to go.

During the war the Jewish Brigade was formed to fight the Nazis, and their training and battle wounds, together with their dreadful days liberating the death camps, combined to make them the fierce, potent, vengeful core of a fighting force that would defeat six Arab armies. The War for Independence could not have been won without the Jewish Brigade and the rest of the twenty-eight thousand men and four thousand women from Jewish Palestine who had fought in the British army.[69] Equally important were the 150,000 or more Holocaust survivors who came to Israel between the end of World War II and the dawn of independence. They swelled the yishuv by a third, and the able-bodied among them, men and women alike, provided the last margin of safety that made victory possible. Many more came, and they defended the borders of the infant nation from the vantage point of their homes in the settlements they founded or joined. Hundreds escaped the Germans only to be killed fighting Arabs.

But these refugees were not the only Holocaust survivors in Israel. The entire founding core of the state was in a sense composed of survivors. They were not in the ovens because they were in the Galilee or the Negev or the Jerusalem hills, and in spite of the fact that they refused for decades to talk about the Holocaust, it pervaded their unconscious lives. How could it not? They have been called "the seventh million."[70]

The Eichmann trial was a first step in dealing publicly with the tragedy, but it was only in the 1980s and 1990s that books, plays, poems, articles, speeches, debates, museums, and death-camp tours began to bring the sons and daughters of the pioneers to terms with what they owed diaspora Jews, dead and living, and especially what they owed Hitler's victims. Chaim Weizmann once said, "A people does not get a country on a silver platter." But Yossi Peled, a child survivor who became a top Israeli general, said, "In fact this country was founded on a silver platter made of six million bodies."[71] Less and less ashamed of the European part of its past, Israel is now almost as Jewish as it is Israeli.

But it is less a melting pot than a potpourri of different kinds of people going in different directions. The rift between the Orthodox and the secular is the widest and deepest, and seems sometimes poised to tear the country apart. The *haredim,* also known as "black-coats," live in a world of their own. Secular Jews call them *"shvartzes,"* an ironic reference to what used to be an impolite Yiddish term for blacks. Some haredim, for their part, call the army of Israel "the national whorehouse," and thousands refuse to serve. A cartoon in *Ha'aretz* showed four sweating soldiers carrying a cheerful haredi man like a prince on a litter. Secular Jews feel that the Orthodox have a stranglehold on marriage and family life, that they are a drain on society, and that they impose their views on others. Some haredim are frankly anti-Zionist. As for the secular Jews, many have no feeling for Judaism, even to the extent of grasping the practical power it has had in creating and sustaining their homeland.

Wave after wave of immigrants for over a century have transformed the country again and again, leaving it intermittently fractious and collegial by turns.[72] Russian Jews have resisted integration more than any previous group, and they brought with them large numbers of non-Jewish relatives through intermarriage who may always remain more Russian than Israeli. Ethiopian Jews have faced a certain amount of discrimination based on skin color, language, and cultural background.[73] Sephardic and Ashkenazic Jews continue their bitter rivalry, with the left-wing Ashkenazic elites increasingly uneasy living with serious Sephardic political power. This large group, always more fundamentally anti-Arab due to persecution in their countries of origin, destabilizes peace efforts made by Israeli doves, and serves as a living reproach for decades of neglect by elitist Ashkenazim. Discrimination continues to burden the lives of Arab Israelis, who are growing increasingly close to their Palestinian cousins, and could become more restive if the Arab-Israeli conflict is not brought to a just close. Many thousands of non-Jewish immigrants from throughout the world have come to Israel to work and live, but neither they nor their children have any hope of obtaining Israeli citizenship.

Finally, several hundred thousand secular Jews have left Israel to settle in the United States and Europe, ironically reversing the Zionist direction of flow.[74] Called *yeridah*—"going down," the reverse of *aliyah*—this path and those who took it at first drew only contempt from those they left behind. But as their numbers mounted and their continued loyalty to Israel was demonstrated—during call-ups for Israel's wars, these émigrés crowded the El Al terminals, desperate to get home to fight—they began to seem as much a resource for Israel's future as a loss. What would be more concerning would be a much larger mass emigration of secular Israelis fed up with the grip the Orthodox have on the country. Some observers have pointed to the possibility of civil war—not between Arab and Jew, but between religious and secular Jews.[75] The assassination of peacemaking prime minister Yitzhak Rabin by an Orthodox Jewish fanatic threatened to tear the country apart.[76]

But it did not. And of course, Israel has survived much worse—indeed, it was created in the face of much worse, in every single decade, for well over a century. Those who think it will fall or fade away in response to current pressures are historically naive or worse; some are anti-Semites, some assimilated Jews. They are modern counterparts of the Jews who opposed the Zionist dream from the outset, who fooled themselves into thinking they could be fully European and still be Jewish, who felt embarrassed by Zionism and later by Israel. Jews paid for their embarrassment with six million deaths. Some critics have essentially no Jewish identity until they "awaken" it for the sole purpose of criticizing Israel. With friends like these, Israel does not need enemies. But their opinion will not affect the mainstream of Jewish history; it has proved irrelevant many times, and it remains so.

Novelist Arthur Koestler understood the reality: "There is no other example in history of a community so persecuted on the face of the earth,
who—between the fires of the Inquisition and the Nazi gas chambers—
continued to pray for rain to fall in the land which their eyes had never be-
held, and to drink a cup of wine with the blessing 'Next Year in Jerusalem'
for two thousand years." Every Saturday for centuries, maybe millennia,
they sang in plaintive voices, "For the law shall go forth from Zion, and the
word of the Lord from Jerusalem." Now they are there, and they will stay
there, if they have to fight to the last man, woman, and child. *New York
Times* columnist Thomas Friedman—ever a critic of Israel as well as of the
Arab world—wrote in 2002, "The Palestinians could never explain why
they were killing Jews to end an occupation that the U.S. and Israel were offering to end through diplomacy. There is only one bumper-sticker phrase
that can explain such behavior: 'Death to Israel.' And if that is their real
strategy, then a war to the death it will be."[77]

Israel will not lose that war. That is not the same as to say that it will
really win; it would be a Pyrrhic victory. There would be such great costs as
to nullify the material effects of having prevailed. But Israel will not lose. If
it comes to an end, then so, in the same sense, will its major enemies. This is
known as the Samson Option.[78] Samson, recall, had his eyes put out and his
hair shorn but slowly regained his great strength. He was on display before
the gathered Philistine elite when he pulled their temple down, killing himself and them. Israel is a fully prepared nuclear power. If it is targeted in a
genocidal attack, it will reduce the major cities of those responsible to piles
of radioactive dust.

If this seems horrific and crazy, consider: it is exactly the same policy
that the United States and NATO had with regard to the Soviet Union for
four decades. Mutually assured destruction, it was called, and MAD it indeed seemed to be. But most knowledgeable observers believed and still believe that it was the only option; in any case, it worked. The Soviet Union
had the destruction of the United States and western Europe literally at its
fingertips, at the touch of a few buttons, for all those years, but it never
pushed the buttons. Nor, for that matter, did NATO attack the Soviet
Union. Israel's hope is that what worked for the cold war rivals will work
in the Middle East.

But the Israeli stance is not just instrumental; it is natural and essential.
The Israelis are Jews with teeth. Lunge at them, they may bite you; strike at
them, and they will certainly do you harm. Hundreds of thousands of Holocaust survivors and their descendants have shaped this little country. But
longing for Jerusalem preceded it by millennia, and this religious impulse
did not need Hitler's impetus. Zionism preceded it by a century, and its ideology was unique and new.

Still, Zionism's leaders anticipated the Holocaust. They knew, generations in advance, that Jewish life in Europe was doomed. The Shoah was long in coming. Its anticipation gave birth to modern Zionism, and its monstrous culmination convinced the world of the need for a Jewish state. Its victims inspired generations of young Israelis to pity and anger. The surviving remnant pervaded Israeli society and helped to create its consciousness. The behavior of the victims became the subject of endless debate. Did Jewish leaders help the Germans? Could they have fought back more? Did they die like sheep? No one can fully answer these questions. But Israelis pose two much more important ones: Will *we* fight back? Will *we* die like sheep? Their lives are in many ways defined by these questions, and their answers are very clear.

At the concentration camp in Dachau there is a stone block memorial inscribed in four languages with one familiar phrase: *Never again.* The Jews of Israel are serious about this. It does not mean, *Never again except if we have to become a flawed, normal country.* It does not mean, *Never again except if the world condemns us.* It does not mean, *Never again except if we have to kill and die to prevent it.* Tragically, it does not even mean, *Never again except if, inadvertently, we sometimes have to harm innocent people.* No nation hinges its survival on contingencies. It means, while Jews have breath to say it and hands to raise in their own defense, quite plainly and simply, *Never again.*

17

WOMEN OF VALOR

HOW JEWISH WOMEN BROKE
THE PATRIARCHAL BONDS

In a Yiddish folk song full of hope and longing, a man asks his rebbe what will happen when the *Moshiach* comes. Ah, says the rebbe, there will be a great banquet. We will eat wild ox and Leviathan, drink seasoned wine, David will play his harp for us, Solomon will speak words of wisdom, Moses will teach Torah, and Miriam, Miriam the Prophet will dance for us. Thus the most ordinary Jewish man could look forward to being entertained in heaven by one of the great women of Jewish history, undulating before his sated eyes.

It is no tribute to the Jews that the contribution of women has been consistently in the background, but in this the Jews were no different from any other traditional culture—and Jews were certainly not the worst. Still, it was not until the twentieth century that women's roles changed, making them fully a part of public history. Yet of course they were vital to every private moment, and these moments woven together added up to real history, however unsung.

It remains the claim of Orthodox Jews not only that men and women have different obligations, but that women's roles are more important than men's. Men have hundreds of commandments to perform that do not apply to women, take all the leadership roles, run the sacred services, read the Torah, wear skullcaps, fringes, and prayer shawls, and learn Hebrew, while women are relegated to a separate, back-row section of the synagogue, walled off by curtains or cagelike bars. A man can have no higher calling than to study Torah and Talmud from dawn till midnight, while a woman may have to run the shop with one hand and keep house with the other. But women are raising the next generation of Jews. They must not be distracted from this central task by the pesky commandments, study, and ritual observances that men do to make themselves feel useful, being unable to bear children.

Or so the argument goes. But no one misses the point that men are in charge of the public sphere, period. Still, there is one way that Jewish practice differs from that of most other male-chauvinist cultures: matrilineal descent. This was and is a patriarchal, mainly patrilineal society, with names and wealth passing from the father to his male heirs. But in one crucial respect descent is through the maternal line. You must have a Jewish mother to be Jewish by birth. The rule is believed to stem from the frequent conquests and occupations of Israel in ancient times, which entailed many rapes; this ties it to Israel's deep history of oppression. But whatever the origin it is the law: your father can be the holiest rabbi who ever lived, but if your mother is not Jewish, you are not Jewish without a conversion. In this sense, the rabbis put their law where their mouth was; they didn't just praise women's childbearing and child-rearing roles, they made the Jewish mother the sine qua non of Jewishness.

We have seen that women played prominent, impassioned roles in the Bible—the names of Eve, Rebecca, Miriam, Deborah, Ruth, and Esther immediately evoke the pivotal position of women in the Bible saga. They lived in a patriarchal world, but they had powerful personalities, showed great courage, and changed the course of Bible history. Their stories have been celebrated for millennia and have inspired girls and women to emulate them. Unfortunately, their forceful participation in events was not easy for women to imitate after biblical times.

In the Greco-Roman world, some synagogues were founded and supported by prominent women, who served as elders or even heads of congregations.[1] This was a crucial moment in Jewish history, when synagogues had to replace the Temple and its religion. Rufina was head of a synagogue in Smyrna in the second or third century, and Sophia that of a Cretan synagogue two centuries later. Tation, daughter of Straton, provided major building expenses for a synagogue in Ionia in the third century, and was given a golden crown as well as the privilege of sitting in the seat of honor—showing that women and men could sit together at some times and places. Among the more lavish women benefactors of these synagogues were converts to Judaism—very numerous at that time—and even some generous non-Jews. Julia Severa, for example, who built a synagogue for the Jewish community of Akmonia (in what is now Turkey) in the mid-first century, may not have been Jewish. Why did she do it? No one knows.

It was probably in talmudic times that the position of Jewish women reached its lowest ebb. Although more than two thousand rabbis are mentioned in the Talmud, and no doubt many of them had helpful wives and mothers—recall Akiva's wife, who drew him from ignorance into learning—only one woman was honored as a scholar. She was Beruryah, a wife and daughter of great rabbis and a highly respected interpreter of the law.[2] She is depicted in the Talmud as defeating men in argument. When her husband, Rabbi Meir, was being harassed by hoodlums, he prayed for them to die. Beruryah rebuked him, quoting Psalm 104: "Let sins cease from the land." This proves, she told him, that sinners do not have to die, just stop sinning. Persuaded, he prayed for them to stop sinning, and they did.[3]

When she heard a student mumbling during Torah study, she rebuked him: "Is it not stated (II Samuel 23:5) 'Ordered in all things, and sure?'—If the Torah be ordered in the two hundred forty-eight organs of your body, it will be sure, and if not, it will not be sure." She could be sharply ironic, tweaking male chauvinism even as she trumped it. She ran into Rabbi Yose while traveling, and when he asked, "By which road shall we travel in order to reach Lydda?," she mocked his wordiness: "Galilean fool! Did not the rabbis say, 'Talk not overmuch with women'? You should have asked: 'How to Lydda?'"[4]

In a final story she applied her wisdom to personal tragedy. She and Meir had two young sons who died on the same Sabbath afternoon, perhaps of pestilence. When Rabbi Meir came home from synagogue he asked about the boys, but Beruryah put him off, keeping the commandment to preserve the Sabbath peace. After the Havdalah ceremony ending the sacred day, she posed a question: "Some time ago, I was given a treasure to guard, and now the owner wants it back. Must I return it?" "Of course," said Meir, surprised she would not know. She then led him into the bedroom to see the boys' bodies. When Meir wept, she gently asked, "Did you not tell me that we must give back what is given on trust? 'The Lord gave, and the Lord hath taken away.'"

Beruryah's reputation was high and pure for a millennium, until it was sullied by none other than Rashi, the Torah and Talmud commentator of medieval France. The slander was so grave that one hesitates to repeat it nine centuries later. Rashi recorded a rumor that Rabbi Meir, angered when Beruryah mocked the adage "Women are lightheaded," engaged one of his students to seduce her; she supposedly succumbed and then hanged herself. This contemptible tale has not only Beruryah but Rabbi Meir and his student guilty of capital crimes. It was transparently concocted by weak, defensive men to discredit the one brilliant woman in the Talmud, and her husband, for letting her study. It is no longer accepted in the rabbinical tradition, but it was used for centuries by the most fanatical Orthodox men to keep women from learning. And it proves that the talmudic rabbis were much wiser than Rashi: slander, they said, is like murder, because both are irreversible. The episode leaves a greater blot on Rashi's reputation than on Meir's or Beruryah's.

The other two thousand sages had definite ideas about the place of women in Jewish life. Aside from conferring Jewishness on her children both biologically and culturally, a woman was specifically assigned only three mitzvot: the law of menstrual purity, the "taking of challah"—removing and burning a small portion of dough from every loaf of bread—and the lighting of Sabbath candles. However, these three precepts were viewed with utmost seriousness. Glückel of Hameln refrained from sharing a last embrace with her dying husband because she was ritually unclean. These laws support Mary Douglas's theory that purity is observed to avert danger, and that separation of clean from unclean—in the kosher laws as well as the ancient sacrifices—is of the essence of Jewish observance. The taking of challah stems from the custom of setting aside dough to bring cakes to the Temple priests, but that may be a holdover from pre-Jewish practices in which women baked cakes for burnt offerings. As for candle lighting, the Talmud says, "The one who is accustomed to buy nice candles for the Sabbath will have children versed in the Torah, for it is written (Proverbs 6:23): 'For the commandment is a lamp, and the teaching (Torah) is light.'" The quote is from the *Shulkhan Arukh,* the code of Jewish Law, which goes on to say that while lighting the candles a woman should pray for her sons to be bright in Torah study.

☙ ❧

Wherever in the world women have entered trade they have done well; countless small markets in Africa and Asia depend on women. But beyond petty capitalism, some women have vaulted the walls of a man's world and succeeded beyond most men's wildest dreams. Jewish women are no exception. Doña Gracia, the doyenne of Judeo-Spanish high society during the Ottoman Empire, was revered in Jewish history for resettling Jews in Tiberias. Born in Lisbon in 1510 to a family of wealthy conversos coerced into Christianity, she was baptized Beatrice de Luna, although at home she was called Gracia. Her father was a high-level silver trader. Her husband came from a family of traders named Mendes—formerly, when they were Jewish, Benveniste.[5] They imported pepper and other spices from Asia and traded in gold, silver, and copper. As the Rothschild family would later do in northern Europe, they relied on their many sons in their trading, and they built one of the first international banks.

This in the face of the Inquisition's growing power. Protection from this mob of torturers lay in the family's special relationship to the royal house, which was heavily in their debt. But as first-generation forced converts, both Gracia's and her husband's families kept secret Jewish practices, and without protection their lives would have been very precarious. The protection ended when Gracia's husband died after a few years of marriage, leaving her alone with an infant daughter, Ana. Alone, that is, except for one of the largest fortunes in Europe, one that could quickly be decimated by mercenary predators with powerful connections and false claims on all of it—not least of all, the Portuguese king.

To defend this fortune and ensure that she and Ana eluded the Inquisition's racks and flames would require firmness and intelligence that few ex-

pected of a woman; she was up to the task. Young and vibrant, she condemned herself to celibacy to keep her status and fortune, but she was not
condemned to passivity. Two years later and still in control, she took Ana
and escaped to Antwerp on a clandestine path taken by thousands of others,
often under her family's protection. A Jewish Underground Railway, it led
by sea via Bristol and London to Calais and then overland to Antwerp, a
leading financial center and to some extent a haven for Portuguese Secret
Jews.

Watched by their enemies, Gracia and her brother-in-law managed
their business interests; aging and suffering various persecutions, he took
her under his wing. At the time of his death—he refused last rites and, like
his brother, died a Jew—he recognized Gracia's gifts and went against all
custom, putting her in charge of everything. He passed over her sister—his
own wife—because she lacked Gracia's ability. Although he provided am-
ply for his wife and daughter, the control he gave Gracia would come back
to haunt her.

But now she was Doña Gracia, and she continued her husband's work
helping escaping anusim, becoming the center of their risky lives. A priest
who spied on Secret Jews wrote, "[She] receives everyone at her home, and
it is said publicly in Antwerp that she has a bank that takes care of those
who come from Portugal."[6] Tolerance was waning. In a city officially ruled
by Holy Roman Emperor Charles V and peppered with Portuguese agents
and Inquisition toadies, she was taking her life in her hands daily with this
converso salon. She was thirty-three years old.

When Ana was fourteen her mother came under severe pressure to
marry her off to a sordid Christian nobleman, an illegitimate descendant of
the Spanish crown. This would bring all the Antwerp Jews *and* their wealth
into the orbit of the emperor, who wrote to his sister, Queen Marie, "As you
can imagine, the loan of the said monies would come at a marvelously pro-
pitious time, given the great need I have of them."[7] Marie, attempting to
sway Doña Gracia, met a wall. Pleading illness, Gracia stalled for time, but
eventually she had to meet the queen.

She told the queen that she would rather see her daughter drown than
make this marriage, and that she was angry because the rejected suitor now
publicly blamed the stepped-up persecution of conversos on her stubbornness. A new law required that all refugees from Portugal be jailed and tried
for heresy, and forty had just been arrested. Gracia pleaded for them, Marie
pleaded for the match, and neither budged. Gracia wrote the nobleman,
and for him this formal rejection by a family of Secret Jews was the ultimate
humiliation. Persecutions intensified, and he helped plan them.

Doña Gracia and her family left Antwerp under a safe conduct from
the authorities in Venice, which resisted the Inquisition and was very protective of commerce. She used the healing waters at Aix-la-Chapelle as a

pretext for travel, and made it a staging point for the rest of the journey. Queen Marie wrote to merchants in various cities asking them not to do business with Gracia or her family, so the privations and dangers of the trip overland by carriage were serious. They reached Venice with most of their fortune, but in much of Europe they were wanted criminals.

The Jews of Venice lived in a crowded ghetto—the first neighborhood to go by that name—but had a thriving Jewish life, with rabbinical academies, synagogues, schools, kosher butchers, and publishers. They did not really accept the converso—"a ship with two rudders," was the resident Jews' epithet—but many berthed in Venice nevertheless. Doña Gracia bought a palazzo near the ghetto, allied herself with a noble Venetian protector, and, through shrewd deal making, soon made the House of Mendes a center of world trade, banking, and venture capital.

Many Sephardic merchants were already established in the Ottoman Empire, and they had a presence in Venice. Gracia did business with them, exporting Venetian glass, paper, tin, and cheese in exchange for silk, hides, tapestry, and caviar. But soon after arriving in Venice, Gracia, consolidating her hold over the family's far-flung enterprise, planned not just to trade with the Ottoman Jews but to join them in Constantinople. Her own sister—wanting to stay in Venice, be a good Christian, and get control of her share of the business—denounced Gracia to the Inquisition as a Secret Jew.

Gracia and her household fled south to the more liberal Ferrara and contacted the sultan of Turkey. Happy to welcome her, her skills, and her wealth into his empire, he sent his personal envoy to escort her to Constantinople. But plague came to Italy, the converted Jews were blamed and terribly persecuted, and Doña Gracia intervened. Public burnings of Hebrew books were staged in Rome and Venice. The sisters' battle for control of the family fortune intensified. Her sister, marshaling the power of anti-Semitism, was able to take over part of the business.

But the gratitude of the Secret Jews was palpable. Four books published in Italy shortly after she left had poignant personal dedications to Gracia, including the Ferrara Bible, an Italian translation, and Samuel Usque's *Consolation for the Tribulations of Israel.* Books of various kinds by Old Christians were also dedicated to her, reflecting her wide-ranging patronage of the arts. In Constantinople her philanthropy increased, and she took back an old family name, Nasi, suggesting a princely heritage. It fit: her position among the Jews of the Ottoman Empire was like that of the *nasi* or prince of old.

Hebrew sources at this time refer to her as *ha-gevirá,* "the Lady," a term of great respect.[8] Rabbi Joshua Soncino of Constantinople accorded her "the headdress of kingship," depicting her as a wise and tireless mediator. The poet Sa'adiah Longo called her "the supreme leader" and said that she "nursed [the Jews] from her breast." She founded a yeshiva, built a synagogue that was open to all—a generous custom she convinced other synagogues to accept—and founded still other synagogues and academies in Salonika and Izmir. She continued to support Hebrew publishing both in Europe and the Ottoman Empire. She devotedly obeyed the commandment of *pidyon shevuyim,* the redemption of captives, paying heavy ransom to pirates and "knights" who had taken Jewish captives. She interceded for Jews with the Inquisition and helped organize a boycott of the city of Ancona after more than fifty conversos were tortured and the twenty-five who refused to repudiate Judaism were burned at the stake.

But her boldest philanthropy was in Tiberias. Safed had attracted thousands of Jews and was a renowned center of rabbinical and mystical study. Nearby Tiberias, the ancient seat of rabbinical government on the Sea of Galilee, held similar promise. Doña Gracia petitioned the sultan for a concession to build up the town. She and one of her nephews sent ships to Europe to bring the most persecuted conversos to Tiberias. They built a perimeter wall, rebuilt ancient buildings, established two yeshivas, and reopened an ancient synagogue on the lakeshore.

On a Friday afternoon in the 1560s a traveler from Yemen visiting that synagogue found "elderly and honorable men" engaged in Torah, Talmud, and mystical studies. "They hurried to the hot springs" to bathe before the Sabbath, then came back to the prayer house for candle lighting. A cantor sang psalms to them from the top of a wooden tower. Some years later a German traveler found "beautiful buildings" being built there "by a wealthy Jewish woman with the permission of the Turkish emperor." Tremendous excitement attended a rumor that Doña Gracia might come to visit or even to live.[9]

She died too soon. Without her support the community could not withstand the hostility of Bedouin marauders and other local Arabs who felt threatened by the Jewish settlement. It lasted less than twenty years. Doña Gracia Street in Tiberias commemorates this great and gifted woman who prefigured the similar, more successful efforts made by Sir Moses Montefiore and Baron Edmond de Rothschild three centuries later. It was the first practical Zionist vision, and the visionary was a woman.

A century later Glückel of Hameln traveled widely in Yiddish-speaking Ashkenaz, visiting fairs and markets in Frankfurt-am-Main and Leipzig, making investments in Danzig, Amsterdam, Copenhagen, Vienna, and Prague. She wrote *Zikhroynes* ("Memories") in Yiddish between 1699 and 1718. For that era it is the single major account of Jewish life and one of the few memoirs by anyone. While it describes economic activity and relations between Jews and other Germans, its main interest lies in its vivid and affecting views of family life.

Glückel had been betrothed at twelve and married at fourteen, and she
and her mother gave birth eight days apart; but that was just the beginning.
"When my daughter Zipporah was two years old, I was brought to bed
again with my son Nathan. The joy my blessed husband had, and the beautiful circumcision feast he gave, cannot be told."[10] There were *ten* others,
and countless stories. "While I lay in childbed with my daughter Mata,
whispers spread that the plague, God shield us! was abroad in Hamburg. . . . It was a time of bitter suffering and desolation. . . . So we resolved
to take our children and go to Hameln, where my father-in-law lived. We
left Hamburg the day after Yom Kippur, and the day before the Feast of
Booths we arrived in Hanover. . . . Since the feast was so near at hand, we
decided to remain there for the week's holy days."[11]

However, a pimple on the forehead of four-year-old Zipporah panicked
the local people, who coerced the family into sending her away for quaran-
tine. "You may know how we loaded the child with farewell blessings, and
the hundreds of tears we shed. The child herself was happy and merry as
only a child can be. But we and those of our own in Hanover wept and
prayed to God, and passed the holy feast-day steeped in woe."[12] Zipporah
did not have plague, and came back after Simchat Torah, nine days later.

Mata's outcome was not as happy. She was three, "and never was there
a lovelier and more charming child. Not only we but everyone who laid
eyes on her or heard her prattle, delighted in the mite. But the Lord delighted in her more . . . and it pleased the good Lord, after the child had suffered four weeks in pain, to recall His share unto Himself and leave ours
lying before us, to the breaking of our hearts. My husband and I grieved beyond all telling, and I greatly fear I sinned in this before the Lord."[13]

But they recovered, the family grew, marriages were arranged. The
first was between Zipporah, then in her early teens, and a very rich man, "a
great prince in Israel."[14]

> Fourteen days before the marriage we set forth "with timbrels
> and with dances," twenty strong, for Cleves, where we were wel-
> comed with all honors. We found ourselves in a house that was
> truly a king's palace, magnificently furnished in every way. The
> livelong day we had no rest for the elegant lords and ladies who
> came to have a peep at the bride. And in truth, my daughter looked
> so beautiful that her like was never seen.

The couple was under the *chupah,* the wedding canopy, ready for the marriage blessings, when they realized that in their excitement they had forgotten to write the *ketubah,* the essential document spelling out a husband's
obligations to his wife. "What was to be done? Nobility and princes were al-

ready at hand and they were all agog to see the ceremony. Whereat Rabbi Meir declared that the groom should appoint a bondsman to write out the contract immediately after the wedding. Then the rabbi read a set-contract from a book. And so the couple were joined."[15] The wedding was attended by prominent Sephardim as well as Ashkenazim, testifying to the spread of Iberian Jews into the heart of the Ashkenazic world.

The business was also a kind of family. When a young traveling trader was shot in the head and killed on the road "less than a Sabbath Day's journey" from his destination—in Jewish law about two miles—she was stricken: "Thus the stout and honest lad came to his early grave; and instead of celebrating wedding feast and honors, he needs must creep into the black of the earth. . . . My God! When I think of it, my hair stands on end. For he was a good, pious, God-fearing child, and had God granted him his life he would have done great things. . . . God knows how my husband and I took it to heart, and our sore grief."[16] They were then trading pearls among European cities, and one of their employees tried to cheat them, leading to a complex lawsuit. "We were young folks, just coming into our own, and we fell into this maze! We had to grope our way." Details of such transactions show that Glückel was an active and equal partner.

Perhaps her greatest grief was her husband's death after thirty years of happy marriage. On his deathbed, "my mother came and flung herself upon him, and kissing him between her tears, she said, 'My son, must you now abandon us?'" A doctor came around midnight, but nothing could be done. "Whereat I said to my husband, 'Dearest heart, shall I embrace you—I am unclean?' For I was then at a time when I dared not touch him. And he said, 'God forbid, my child—it will not be long before you take your cleansing.' But alas, it was then too late."[17] Unwavering piety had sustained them for thirty years, and they would not depart from it now; he died with Shema Yisroel on his lips.

After the thirty days of mourning she auctioned her goods, paid her debts, and set about raising her children and getting them married and settled. One son, an incompetent businessman, was eroding the family wealth, but Glückel took matters in hand.

> At that time I was busied in the merchandise trade. . . . I went twice a year to the Brunswick Fair and each time made my several thousands profit. . . . My business prospered, I procured me wares from Holland, I bought nicely in Hamburg as well, and disposed of the goods in a store of my own. I never spared myself, summer and winter I was out on my travels, and I ran about the city the live-long day.
>
> What is more, I maintained a lively trade in seed pearls. I

bought them from all the Jews, selected and assorted them, and then resold them in towns where I knew they were in good demand.

My credit grew by leaps and bounds. . . . "Yet all this availeth me nothing." I saw my son Loeb, a virtuous young man, pious and skilled in Talmud, going to pieces before my eyes.[18]

She invited him into her business, and he stabilized under her guidance.

At her husband's death, "Many matches were offered me. . . . among them truly the most eminent in all Germany. But . . . the thought of remarriage never once entered my mind."[19] Fourteen years later, when she was fifty-four, her son-in-law proposed a match with a pious, wealthy widower. Wanting to ensure her children's financial future—her youngest, Miriam, was only eleven, and her grown children were not good with money—she married in secrecy; but her husband turned out to be heavily in debt and, like her sons, far less able in business than she was. She remained loyal to him as he became a greater burden to her, and his death left a legacy of debt.

She worked in Metz and Hamburg, trading with merchants from Amsterdam to Prague, and while she built her far-flung financial network, she raised twelve children. But she remained strongly oriented to Israel, and when she faced grave difficulties, she wrote, "[L]eaving behind me the nothingness of this world, I should have taken myself . . . to the Land of Our Fathers. There I might have lived as a good Jewess . . . and there I might have served God with all my heart and soul."[20]

Addressed to her children, the memoir is steeped in piety and laced with Bible and Talmud quotations that show an easy familiarity with the great texts and precepts of Jewish faith. She began it to comfort herself after her husband's death. "In this way I have managed to live through many wakeful nights, and springing from my bed shortened the sleepless hours."[21] Book One opens, "In my great grief and for my heart's ease I begin this book the year of Creation 5451 [1690–91]—God soon rejoice us and send us His redeemer!" Opening Book Six in a meditative, even despondent mood, she repents her sins and praises God: "I write this . . . with trembling hands and hot bitter tears, for it says that we shall serve the Lord with all our heart and all our might. I pray God Almighty to strengthen me . . . that I come not before him in stained garments—as it is said, 'Repent the day before thy death,' but man knows not on what day he may die, therefore, let him repent every day of his life."[22] She will write "no book of morals" since "our sages have already written many." Still, she has messages for her children, and her memoir serves as an ethical will. "The kernel of the Torah is, Thou shalt love thy neighbor as thyself. But in our days we seldom find it so. . . . on the contrary, if a man can contrive to ruin his neighbor, nothing pleases him more." She tells them to "serve God from your heart, without falsehood or sham," not to talk during prayers, and to "put aside a fixed time for the study of the Torah." And she wrote of that great work, "It is like a rope which the great and gracious God has thrown to us as we drown in the stormy sea of life, that we may seize hold of it and be saved."

In contrast to the wealthy and prestigious Doña Gracia and Glückel, Rachel Ashkenazi was a poor rabbi's widow, yet she had realized Gracia and Glückel's dream: she lived in Jerusalem. She wrote to her son Moses—also a rabbi, then living in Cairo—on October 3, 1567, a letter in Yiddish showing concern for his daughter Beile's luckless marriage.

> My dear son, may thy Rock and Redeemer keep thee, I am very much worried because I have not heard from thee for such a long time. I have also been worried by the removal of thy daughter, may she live. . . .
>
> Thy son-in-law is, because of our many sins, heavily indebted to the non-Jews. His house has gone, they have sold all the belongings of Beile so that she, because of our many sins, does not possess any clothes. She has made him two suits from thy silken coat, one for the engagement, the other for the wedding. He has almost torn them already. I cannot describe to thee what foolish things he has done. . . . Therefore, my dear son, be careful that he may not drag thee into his affairs. . . . And be watchful that he may not go away and leave thy daughter destitute, God forbid! I would have preferred her to have stayed here, and would have obtained from him the letter of divorce. But she did not want to do so. So great is her love for him. When everybody told her, "Let not thy goods be taken away! Weep and cry!" she answered: "I wish to let him take everything. If the Lord, may He be praised, helps him, He will change him."[23]

Both Beile and her grandmother had influence. It was Beile's decision, based on her love for her husband; Rachel would have gotten her a divorce. Beile's story was not over, though, nor was she simply her foolish husband's helpmeet: "Thy Beile, may she live, has clever hands; she embroiders very nice things from silver and gold. If thy wife is willing to work she could help her. She is quite reliable, God be praised, and she likes to work, but she was not fond of learning. But I do not want to enlarge upon this." Thus Beile was her grandmother's granddaughter; her industry and skill outweighed not only her husband's foolishness but her mother's reluctance to learn.

The letter is signed, "Thy mother Rachel, who writes in great haste . . . May thy days be prolonged in gladness." But then she adds a rich postscript

nearly as long as the letter. It is partly practical: "I should like to see thee
come hither to take care of thy books. When I, God forbid, close my eyes,
they will take away everything. This must not happen." The dominant
chord is a Jewish mother's love for her son.

> I wished to send thee the candlesticks and the hanging lamp, but
> nobody was prepared to carry them. . . . I have prepared half a mea-
> sure of wine for thee. And let me know fully always about thy
> health. The saying "Out of sight, out of mind" is not always correct.
> For a mother who has experienced pain does not do so. She does not
> forget the pain she suffered with her child.

This "child" is almost a grandfather. But it is not him alone she is thinking
of: "It was my wish to send something for thy child, but, because of our
many sins, I do not possess anything."

Thus the pivotal role of *un*celebrated women, whose skilled hands and
voices constantly saved families. They were not wealthy like Doña Gracia
or Glückel, but they shone just as brightly amid weaker, incompetent
men. Rachel and Beile, like Gracia and Glückel, exemplify the "valorous
woman" section of Proverbs, written two millennia earlier:

> Who can find a woman of worth, of worth far above rubies?
> She does good and not evil all the days of her life. She seeks wool
> and flax, and works them with her hands. Like the merchant ships,
> she brings food from afar. . . . She considers a field and buys it; with
> the fruit of her hands she plants a vineyard. She girds her loins with
> strength, and makes her arms strong; her lamp does not go out at
> night. . . . She stretches out her hand to the poor; she puts forth her
> hand to the needy. . . . Strength and dignity are her clothing, and
> she laughs at the time to come. She opens her mouth with wisdom,
> and the law of loving kindness is on her tongue.
>
> Her children arise up and call her blessed, her husband also,
> and he praises her. Favor is deceitful, beauty is vain, but the mercy
> of the Lord endures. Give her, then, of the fruit of her hands, and let
> her own works praise her in the gates.

☙

As the New World was settled, Jewish women found new roles. Penina
Moise, born in Charleston, South Carolina, in 1797 into an Orthodox community, became a famous poet and pillar of Charleston Jewish life.[24] As the
community turned to the new Reform movement, which seemed to them
more American, Moise wrote many hymns in English. Not only were they
used in temple services in Charleston, but many were added to the Reform

Jewish canon and published in the movement's official hymnal. Never marrying, she was wary of life's pleasures:

> Countless are pleasure's bright decoys,
>   Unwary mortals to ensnare;
> Faith beckons thee from barren joys,
>   And points to her immortal sphere.[25]

But despite their Americanizing ambitions, she and her community remained different:

> Honor and praise to Thee belong,
>   O God of our salvation!
> Who will defend from shame and wrong,
>   Thy first elected nation.[26]

Unique, perhaps, but surely uniquely vulnerable.

Emma Lazarus, whose verses grace the Statue of Liberty, turned her gift not only outward toward the wide world but inward toward the Jews. She wrote many poems on Jewish themes and a remarkable 1883 "Epistle to the Hebrews." A passionate appeal for Jewish renewal, it embraces the Zionist dream just then being born. "Our adversaries are perpetually throwing dust in our eyes with the accusations of materialism and tribalism," she wrote,

> and we, in our pitiable endeavors to conform to the required standard, plead guilty and fall into the trap they set. . . . "Tribal!" This perpetual taunt rings so persistently in our ears . . . in face of the fact that our "tribal God" has become the God of two thirds of the inhabited globe . . . and that as a people we have adapted ourselves to the varying customs and climates of every nation in the world. . . . our national defect is that we are not "tribal" enough; we have not sufficient solidarity to perceive that when the life and property of a Jew in the uttermost provinces of the Caucasus are attacked, the dignity of a Jew in free America is humiliated.[27]

This prominent American writer strongly endorses the need for a worldwide Jewish community despite the largely realized dream of American liberation. But her call becomes more urgent and specific:

> What we need to-day, second only to the necessity of closer union and warmer patriotism, is the building up of our national, physical force. If the new Ezra rose to lead our people to a secure house of

refuge, whence would he recruit the farmers, masons, carpenters, artisans, competent to perform the arduous, practical pioneer work of founding a new nation? We read of the Jews who attempted to rebuild the Temple using the trowel with one hand, while with the other they warded off the blows of the molesting enemy. Where are the warrior-mechanics to-day equal to either feat. . . . For nineteen hundred years we have been living on an idea; our spirit has been abundantly fed, but our body has been starved. . . .

Let our first care to-day be the re-establishment of our physical strength, the reconstruction of our national organism, so that in future, where the respect due to us cannot be won by entreaty, it may be commanded, and where it cannot be commanded, it may be enforced.[28]

This was the scion of a wealthy Sephardic family, a correspondent of Emerson's, a poet, a pampered intellectual. She was free, skilled, smart, and rich, and she could have cut herself off from her far-flung co-religionists as so many American Jews had and would. But she did not. She was a writer of extraordinary vision, and—almost prophetlike—she knew what would come.

It had already begun. Recall that Baron Edmond de Rothschild had established the Jewish settlement of Zichron Ya'akov in 1882—like Emma's essay, a response to the Russian persecutions of 1881. Letters from pioneer women describe the challenge of life in Israel at that time, and the high spirits with which they met it. An 1889 letter reads in part:

So far we have nothing . . . but if God pleases, we will see the time when we will have a lot of possessions. . . . It is absolutely true that after the *Pesach* [Passover] holiday, the Baron will come to visit the colonies. New houses will be built by then. . . . And during the winter, we will be able to live comfortably even in the house in which we are living right now, because it also has a cooking shed, and a large barn built of stones and plaster with mortar both inside and out. . . . Half of the barn we are keeping for the cow and the sheep and the horse, and the other half will be used for living purposes, if the house is too small. . . . Around the house we will make a garden. Our vineyard is far from the house, but it hardly makes a difference. . . .

After all this, I still yearn for Russia. The heat and the *Khamsin* [the desert wind] are very difficult for people from Russia; in the winter it is raining, and this is the best time of the entire year. . . . The winter season here is full of different types of vegetables and fruit which grow on trees.... It is possible to live well here if God grants health and strength!

She mentions the downside almost in passing:

> When I came to town, the change in climate affected me badly, and on the fifth day after my arrival I got sick with malaria, God forbid, and I lay in bed for eight days.... Every foreigner who comes to live here from a faraway land has to drink from this cup, no one is spared.... You mustn't drink water immediately after eating fruit ... because it brings on the fever.

The goal was to produce cash crops, especially wine, and to buy most other supplies from the local Arabs; she boasts that her eldest son is becoming fluent in French and Arabic. "The only thing that's expensive is beer, and it's warm and doesn't taste good. We have here geese, swans, turkeys, pigeons, and various other kinds of poultry, nothing is missing."[29] This pattern was criticized by many later Zionists, whose farming communities strove for complete independence.

Pioneer women were not above boasting about certain luxuries, even though they were due to the baron's largesse.

> Our synagogue is very elegant; it's built like the [progressive] synagogue ... in K[ovno], but has even more paintings and decorations. The *parochet* [the curtain covering the Ark] and the pulpit cloth are made out of red silk, finely made and embroidered with pure gold threads.
>
> We also have a *hazzan* [a cantor] here, who conducts the choir on days of joy and happiness.... The Turkish governor came to visit last week ... accompanied by a large number of soldiers and army officials. He was honored greatly when he came, just like in Russia, when all the Jews would line the streets and greet him with songs and verse. A big banquet was made for him and his men ... and they left the colony very pleased.
>
> My dear, beloved sister-in-law! don't be angry with me because I have made you read such a long letter; when I write, I feel as if we're sitting face to face and talking, because I still haven't forgotten the tears which you shed on the day we parted. Only God knows when we'll be able to see each other again.[30]

A few months later she had learned to speak some Arabic, and her two younger sons were in school, learning to speak French, Arabic, and Hebrew. They had geese, ducks, chickens, pigeons, goats, and a horse of their own. "Eventually we hope that the land will be renewed. In areas where jackals run, railroads will run full of passengers, instead of desolate rocks—there will be hotels for tourists; in places where man does not set foot, people will work and engage in all sorts of handicrafts. . . . My heart pounds inside to think of all these pleasant hopes. If God has revived our precious land . . . we pray that God will also turn all of the scorched and ravaged areas into homes for people, into vineyards and grapevines."[31]

Fifteen years later this dream seemed to be shattered. Another young woman from Russia was attempting to found an agricultural settlement in 1905, and made an assessment of those already in place. "I reached, in 1905, the firm conclusion that the system of agricultural settlement, which the officials of the Baron devised, was bankrupt in every sense of the word. As early as 1881–1882 a pioneering, wonderful, idealistic type of person came to Palestine, capable of minimal independent work. And now, after they spent 25 years in the country, we found them completely reliant on the officials, lacking any faith in their enterprise, and employing Arab workers. They were all bitter and hopeless. They all believed in the Uganda option. Their sons did not continue in the farms and left the country because they could not stand the work regime."[32]

Clearly a new model was needed, and right around this time the first kibbutzim were born, women a vital part of them. There were no more illusions. A woman named Anya wrote this diary entry:

> December 2, 1912
>
> I live in Migdal now. We lead a curious life here. I do the same work every day. It is very boring. In the morning, as soon as I get up, I must stoke the stove, then boil the milk, peel the potatoes for the stew and cook some soup, dairy or *parve*. Then I must do the dishes and sweep the room. And rest for a while. Then the Samovar again, dinner, the dishes, fatigue and sleep. And the next day, it's the same thing all over again. The hands are always dirty. I wash them and feel sad because they are getting so rough. . . . There are eight of us now, six men, one other girl and myself. One of our comrades died last week. He was simple, and gentle and open-eyed. Very sweet and good, alive and practical, a young man of twenty-four or five. We are not yet joined together. There are misunderstandings. We are all so different. I am often ill with Malaria. The climate here is not healthy. I gain weight and then grow thin suddenly. They say one must hope for better times, but I do not believe all this. The entire settlement, the entire region, is infected with Cholera. . . . It is late now. . . . I must get up early tomorrow.[33]

Anya left the country within two years.

Others were different. In 1925 a young woman wrote:

> I am happy to be free, to have regained my energy and warmth, and
> to feel the firm ground under my feet. I believe in Eretz Israel and
> in the people. I am surrounded by people who have faith. . . . I have
> been associated with the kibbutz movement for several years, but I
> only now comprehend its depth, and the beauty of going together
> with other people who believe like me, who strive for a better fu-
> ture. I am not blinded. I can see the negative aspects of our life. . . .
> Is hatred among people necessary? . . . Can anyone exist by him-
> self? . . . I am happy because I love the kibbutz and have such faith
> in its way. . . . I would like to help all those who can understand our
> truth—who can find a way to us.[34]

This dreamy pioneer held reality in her grip; those who would find a way
would number millions.

◔◍◍◍◑

Hannah Senesh was not the first, but she was the most famous of a new
kind of Jewish woman, displaying fierce commitment, exquisite courage,
and a readiness to kill and die for her people. This had become almost common among the women of the yishuv, and the same spirit drove the women
who went to the forests of Europe as partisans. Vitka Kempner, a girl from
western Poland who became a hero of the Vilna ghetto, blew up a German
troop train in July 1942 in the first major act of sabotage in all of occupied
Europe.[35] Sulia Rubin was a teenager when she escaped from the ghetto of
Lida in Belarus to join the forest partisans; she was captured and tortured
for hours but revealed nothing.[36] Lise Magun of Vilna was captured on a
mission outside the ghetto; she was tortured to death without betraying
anyone. Later *Lise Ruft*—"Lise Calls"—became the mobilization signal of
the ghetto fighters.

Niuta Teitelboim of Warsaw, also known as "Little Wanda with the
Braids," was a classic "Aryan" beauty although she came from a Hasidic
family.[37] She was twenty-four but looked a demure sixteen, and when she
smiled, lowered her eyes, and turned her blond head a little, German
guards would let her in to see German officers, whom she would calmly
shoot and kill. With an enormous price on her head, she was eventually captured; she was tortured to death by the Gestapo without revealing anything.
Posthumously, after the war, she was awarded the Polish government's
highest battle medal, the Grunwald Cross.

Women in Israel were equally capable fighters. Before independence, they served side by side with men in combat and sometimes commanded men. Sarah Aaronsohn, one of the settlers of Zichron Ya'akov, led a Jewish espionage network aiding the British in World War I. She was captured by the Turks and tortured, but she managed to take her own life.[38] In 1920 Devorah Drachler and Sarah Chizik were among the ten who died defending Tel Hai. At the peak of fighting in World War II, there were tens of thousands of women in the Haganah—the Jewish Defense Force—and they made up a third of the Palmach—a separate, highly daring commando force.

In the War for Independence, women escorted convoys over besieged roads and defended kibbutzim and other settlements. Dr. Ruth Westheimer, the ebullient, wise, and funny American sex expert, was one of them. Another was Shorika Braverman, a kibbutznik who had parachuted behind Nazi lines, but with better luck than Hannah Senesh: she joined the partisans of Yugoslavia and later took over the training of women soldiers in Israel. In the 1956 war women served on the front lines as radio operators and medics; one piloted a plane that parachuted infantry into the Mitla Pass.

Conscription for two years after high school is nearly universal for unmarried women. Some volunteer to defend outlying settlements. Many are crack shots who train men for combat roles. Some teach tank crews. "This has been known to create initial problems with their 18-year-old trainees, some of whom arrive in the army with macho images—but they are soon overcome as the young women demonstrate total command of their subject and absolute professionalism."[39]

Of course, combat is not the only distinction of Jewish women. Of the ten women who have won Nobel Prizes in science, three were Jewish, as are two of the eight women laureates in literature, three of the thirteen women in the U.S. Senate, and one of the two on the U.S. Supreme Court. But the most neglected aspect of Jewish women's experience is that they have taken up arms to defend their families, people, religion, and honor—even to take revenge; "tough Jews" includes women.

This fact has not been lost on Jewish men, who have had, let us say, an ambivalent view of it. The oddest portrait of this kind of woman is Philip Roth's, in *Portnoy's Complaint,* a hilarious novel about an American-Jewish man hopelessly adrift on the sea of his own roiling lusts. Desire for the Other—shiksa-hunger, in plain Yinglish—is one of the main themes; Portnoy chases one blond bimbo after another, bedding them easily because of their weakness for Jewish men. But it turns out, on a visit to Israel, that Portnoy finds the khaki-clad, Uzi-toting Sabra girls to be Other enough, and seduces one of them. Or does she seduce him? In any case, she is clearly in charge, and he feels so emasculated by her obviously superior fitness, courage, and competence that his one wish is to give her gonorrhea. Powerless to impress a woman who has access to *real* men, he can at least infect her and them with his own flaw.[40]

This escapes being Jewish anti-Semitism because no one emerges un-scathed—the shiksas, for instance, are unbelievably stupid. It is basically good-natured, and comfortably within the Jewish comic tradition. But the depiction of Portnoy's Sabra lover is no less revealing for that, and every non-Israeli Jewish man who is honest with himself feels a twinge of shrink-age at Israel's standard gender roles. So *Portnoy's Complaint* has taken its place in the never-ending saga of Jewish sexual relations.

◈

Although Dr. Ruth is only one of the most recent in a long line of Jewish women who have taught men about sex, countless pronouncements on the subject were made by men—and what a jumble of contradictory dicta they were. Halakhah used the dangers of sex and its associated impurities to jus-tify exclusions of women, but in the Bible, from "In the beginning" onward, sex is a powerful force for good as well as evil. Even if parts of Genesis and Exodus were penned by a woman, it was a three-millennium priestly and rabbinical establishment—100 percent male—that reasoned out their meaning. And for all those centuries the reading of the Bible shaped Jewish concepts of women's sexuality. Two themes dominate: the imperative to re-produce, and the strong, potentially dangerous sexual drive of women.

"*P'ru ur'vu*"—"Be fruitful and multiply"—is the first commandment God gives in the Bible, and urges us to take our urges seriously. Eve's sin is sexual—snake, woman, apple, man—and her punishment is tearing pain in her fruitful place of pleasure. Barrenness is a recurring theme, with Sarah, Rebecca, and Rachel needing divine intervention to fulfill that first com-mandment. Among the matriarchs only Leah, the plain, rejected first wife Jacob is tricked into marrying, has no trouble conceiving. The Torah has no trouble with the idea that Jacob loves Rachel more because she is beautiful; she gets her comeuppance through temporary barrenness.

Both Abraham and Isaac, visiting Egypt, protect themselves by claim-ing their beautiful wives are their sisters, and bring the tempted Pharaohs close to sin. Joseph, in Egypt, is seduced by a lusting princess, and when he rejects her she accuses him of rape. Joseph's older brother Judah and his three sons play out a lusty little subplot that highlights the Torah's fascina-tion with sex and fertility. His eldest is married to Tamar, and when she is widowed he gives her Onan, to fulfill the levirate—the law requiring sur-viving brothers to marry the widow, continuing the line. But Onan spills his seed on the ground instead of doing his duty, giving English a strange "ism." The third son is just a boy, and Judah promises him to Tamar as soon as he is grown.

He breaks the promise, but Tamar, like Eve and Rebecca before her, doesn't take patriarchal rule lightly. Disguised as a prostitute, she beds Ju-dah himself by the roadside, and by keeping his staff and seal proves the resulting twins are his. This gross violation of sexual propriety and law—one of many in the Bible—gets a nod and a wink. Fertility trumps sexual rules almost every time.

Are there any limits? According to the rabbis, Noah is supposed to have been celibate in the ark, but he continues this self-restraint after the flood tide wanes. Where are future generations supposed to come from? Noah is made drunk and seduced by his daughters, and they are more or less condemned, but of course they do have to replenish the earth after the Flood, and we are theoretically all descendants of those incestuous unions. This story repeats after Sodom and Gomorrah burn. Lot's daughters, thinking the world has come to an end *again,* and having seen their mother turned into a pillar of salt, conclude that the future of the whole human race depends on them. They get their father drunk and have sex with him, producing the nations of Ammon and Moab, enemies of Israel. But lowly Moab later returns, through Ruth, another bold woman, to the center stage of Jewish history.

Perhaps the strangest episode in Genesis is the rape of Jacob's daughter Dinah by Shechem, a non-Jew. Shechem follows his violation with tender words of love and a proposal, not an unknown sequence in the ancient world. Jacob accepts, but his sons plan treachery. They agree on condition that all the men of the tribe of Shechem be circumcised. Having thus weakened them, Simeon and Levi murder them all while their brothers sack the town. As for the object of the conflict, "Dinah herself remains silent: the battle over intermarriage is fought by men over her passive body."[41]

The Bible is deeply ambivalent about intermarriage. Of the Canaanites Deuteronomy says, "You shall not intermarry with them" (7:1–3), but Moses himself has already married the daughter of a priest of Midian. Ruth, a Moabite woman—a descendant of Lot's unwitting incest with his daughters—will convert, seduce and marry a prominent Jew, and become the great-grandmother of David, Israel's greatest king, who will in turn give rise to the Messiah. And Esther, the bold beauty who turns the head of a gentile king, marries him without even telling him she is Jewish, and by this forbidden union saves the Jews of Persia.

But the prophet Ezra—the man who raised the Torah to its place beside the Temple after the Babylonian exile—opposed intermarriage vehemently. Other prophets conflated it with harlotry, since Canaanite worship was said to include ritual prostitution. "Others" were impure vessels of lust, and would inevitably lead toward other gods. As we saw in an earlier chapter, one of the hardest things for the Israelites to give up was goddess worship, inherently sexual and intertwined with fertility. Perhaps the Bible's near-obsession with barrenness and God's repeated reversals of it were a way to reassure the people that they did not need the goddess Asherah.[42]

Later in the Bible the fertile saga continues. Hannah is barren, and the High Priest accuses her of drunkenness as she lies prostrate, sobbing, and praying on the Temple steps. But she explains her plight, he gives her God's blessing, and she gives birth to Samuel the Prophet, whom she consecrates to the Lord. Likewise barren is the mother of Samson, who, like many before her, gives birth through God's intervention. He too is consecrated to God, but his bitter downfall comes through lust for Delilah the gentile siren, who robs him of his strength by cutting off his hair and then blinds him.

This is a story of lust gone too far. So is that of Bathsheba, whom David sees after as she bathes on a rooftop near his palace. Although she is married, he seduces her, brushing aside both the Seventh and Tenth Commandments, but it gets worse. Bathsheba is pregnant, so David brings her husband Uriah back from the battlefront and tries to get him to sleep with her, lest he discover the adultery. He refuses; a brilliant and loyal commander, he believes that sex weakens warriors. David, out of options, sends Uriah to the deadliest part of the front, where he is soon killed, and his widow marries the trusted king who cuckolded him.

Now, to be sure, the prophet Nathan excoriates David and curses his lineage, speaking truth to power. And the curses come true: Bathsheba's baby is stillborn, and David's children by his other wives pay a grave price for his dalliance. Amnon rapes his half sister Tamar, for which Absalom, her full brother, kills Amnon. He leads a revolt against his enraged father, and sleeps with David's concubines on a *rooftop* "with the full knowledge of all Israel" (2 Sam. 16:20–22). But Bathsheba gives birth to King Solomon, who will build the Temple, found its religion, subdue Israel's enemies, and, with three hundred wives and seven hundred concubines, almost single-handedly populate the kingdom. Amnon's and Absalom's tragic deaths clear the way for this succession. Lineage and fertility justify unbridled lust, even when it causes covetousness, adultery, and something very close to murder.

Lust is frankly provoked in the Persian king by Esther's careful preparations for a beauty contest. Her uncle and guardian Mordecai, one of Persia's leading Jews, has her conceal her origins even when she marries the king. Because the king delights in her, he stays the hand of the executioner, who has a standing order to cut down any person who crosses the king's threshold without a specific invitation—even one of his many wives. He will grant any request up to half the kingdom. All she wants is for him to come to a banquet with Haman, an evil minister who plans to wipe out the Jews. Haman is already in trouble when the king finds out that she is Jewish. But his fate is sealed when the king comes back in from the garden, where he has gone to cool his temper, only to find Haman "lying prostrate on the couch on which Esther was reclining." He is only begging for his life, but the mere appearance of lust for her inflames the king further, and sends the minister straight to the gallows—together, not incidentally, with all of his ten sons. Not just life for life, but lineage for lineage.

The romance of Ruth is far more touching, but it too uses lust to create a lineage and change history. Ruth has lost her Jewish husband but chooses to follow his mother, Naomi, back to Israel, where they must live off gleanings of dropped grain from the fields of the wealthy Boaz. Coached by Naomi, she steals onto the threshing floor at night, lies down at the feet of the sleeping Boaz, uncovers his legs, and asks him to spread his cloak over her. Naomi and Ruth take the erotic initiative, and the seduction works.[43] The last obstacle is the levirate, Onan's undoing. There is a male relative of Ruth's dead husband who must publicly decline to marry her. This he does by the ancient tradition of handing her his shoe in the city gate, and this last erotic gesture clears the path from a woman's planned seduction in fertile fields at harvesttime to King David and the Messiah.

But the ultimate in Bible sex is the Song of Songs which, although it is held by the Orthodox to be about God's love for Israel, is to secular eyes a collection of sumptuous love poems in the Egyptian lyric tradition. The erotic canvas painted by the imagery has few if any equals in the literature of love. Sex and love are one, separation sweetly agonizing, and longing for union the dominant emotion.

> *Thy breasts are like two fawns, twins of the roe. . . .*
> *Let him kiss me with the kisses of his mouth, for thy love is sweeter than*
>   *wine. . . .*
> *My beloved is mine and I am his, we murmur among the lilies. . . .*

The words are as charged with desire as any ever uttered, and the songs are a dialogue between a man and a woman whose love for each other, for now at least, takes precedence over everything.

But the rabbis could not have such a sexy book in the Bible, so they declared it an allegory of God's love for Israel. This prefigured rabbinical attitudes toward sex for two millennia. Women are dangerous—foreign, mysterious, bloody, polluting, distracting, and hypersexual. They hold within themselves the power to reproduce, and ultimately it is they who control and construe that power. All men know at least unconsciously that they are appendages to the process of life, guardians and servants of it at best. This indelible fact makes all men chronically nervous—call it the anxiety of uselessness. In many, if not most, cultures, men have used their physical power to make them seem far more essential than they are.

Jewish men are no exception, but the Jews of the biblical narrative were explicit about women's power and the realities of the sexual drive, male and female. This changed in talmudic times, and—with the exception of medieval Spain—a certain prudishness has since prevailed in Jewish texts. Worse, women's polluting power has kept them subordinate and separate. But there is more to this separation than meets the eye.

Recall Lis Harris, the gifted writer who lived with Hasidim for a year. Her observations of the twelve days of menstrual abstinence and the *mikvah* experience that ends it are illuminating. One wife and mother believed that marriages are stronger when you don't take physical contact for granted. "In the first place," she explained, "it's a time when couples stress all the other ways that they have of communicating . . . and secondly, most people find that abstinence whets their sexual appetite so that the boredom that many marriages suffer from has no chance to develop."[44] The result for some couples is a small monthly honeymoon.

Harris, a completely secular Jew, visited the *mikvah* herself. Following custom, she went alone. She was not only instructed to bathe *before* immersing herself, but was given a tray full of cleansing implements from Q-tips and dental floss to bleach and alcohol. Absolute cleanliness must precede immersion, lest a speck of dirt or a splinter prevent water from touching skin. All makeup must be removed, every orifice be spotless. Finally the attendant, a kindly woman named Bracha—"Blessing"—took her to the edge.

> I take off the robe and stand expectantly in the chest-deep green water. Bracha tells me to keep my eyes and lips closed but not too tightly and to keep my feet and arms apart, so that the water will touch my whole body. When I go underwater I instantly curl into the fetal position.

She comes up and goes down two more times. "I think of all the generations of people I have not known who have considered the impurities of the world dissolvable. My grandmother floats by, curled up, like me. . . . I look up and see Bracha's smiling face through the water."[45] She emerges feeling good, and finds the outside world intrusive; she will never be a Hasid, but with this feeling she begins to appreciate at last the gentle, protective cocoon, the bracing, guarded, blessedly insular world of halakhah.

༄

In the early twentieth century, Jewish women rose to prominence as political activists in many countries. Rosa Luxemburg the Communist, Emma Goldman the anarchist, and many other Jewish women championed women's rights and embodied women's power. Karl Marx's daughter Eleanor—unlike her father, at peace with her Jewish identity—worked among the poor Jews of London. Rose Schneiderman was a leader of the International Ladies' Garment Workers' Union. Lily Montagu, perhaps the first woman to preach in a European synagogue,[46] was a magistrate and social worker in England, active in progressive causes. Aletta Jacobs, the first woman physician in the Netherlands, was a vocal pacifist and women's rights advocate. Louise Weiss was known as the Susan B. Anthony of France, and Rosika Schwimmer, nominated for the Nobel Peace Prize, played a similar role in Hungary.

In the United States, among poor Jewish immigrants, women's roles were challenged. Because of the Yiddish *Daily Forward*'s left-wing leanings, the "Bintel Brief" advice column formed a cutting edge:

> Since I don't want my conscience to bother me, I ask you whether a married woman has the right to go to school two evenings a week. My husband thinks I have no right to do this. . . . My children and my house are not neglected. . . .
>
> My husband is not pleased and when I come home at night and ring the bell, he lets me stand outside a long time intentionally. . . .
>
> When I am alone with my thoughts, I feel I may not be right. Perhaps I should not go to school.

The answer was decisive. The husband, said the editor, "is scolded severely . . . for wanting to keep his wife so enslaved. Also the opinion is expressed that the wife absolutely has the right to go to school two evenings a week."[47]

But much did not change for decades. The clarion call of late-twentieth-century feminism was Betty Friedan's *The Feminine Mystique,* published in 1963. It spoke of full-time homemaking as a "comfortable concentration camp," and the exclusion of women as "the problem that has no name."[48] She gave it a name, and the name became a movement. As a founding member and first president of the National Organization for Women (NOW), she fought for women's rights, political opportunity, equal pay for equal work, access to abortion, and the Equal Rights Amendment. Born in Peoria in 1921, just after the start of women's suffrage, she lived to see two women on the Supreme Court, a woman vice presidential candidate, a growing number of women in the Senate, and women as CEOs of major multinational corporations.

That some of these women were Jewish—Justice Ruth Bader Ginsburg, Senators Dianne Feinstein and Barbara Boxer—was no doubt also gratifying. Friedan attended a conference on women's rights in Jerusalem in 1984 where "my feminism and my Judaism were converging." For the first time in her life she was invited to help form a minyan, the quorum traditionally made up of ten Jewish men. "It moves me very much . . . to watch Naamah Kelman, an American-born Israeli, daughter of 13 generations of rabbis, in her white prayer shawl, leading us in the ancient rituals only men have been allowed to perform."[49]

I had a related experience two or three years later, at the annual Jewish exposition in San Francisco, seeing, from behind, a figure with waist-length dark hair swaying gently in a prayer shawl. As I walked carefully around to see the davening figure better, I saw first that it was a woman, then that she was also wearing tefillin, and finally that she was about eight months pregnant. Then I knew that things were changing. She was at the booth of the Berkeley Egalitarian Orthodox Minyan, which had cut the Gordian knot of reconciling Orthodoxy with women's rights by just doing it. I reflected that the child in her womb, girl or boy, would grow up in a very different Jewish world than the hundred generations that went before.

Outside Orthodoxy, the pace of change has been much faster, although it was slow to begin. Reform Judaism proclaimed equality in 1845, but the first woman rabbi, Regina Jonas, was ordained in Berlin only in the 1930s, and that was in private, not in a seminary. Sally Preisand became the first woman ordained in the United States in 1972, and in 1984 the Conservative movement followed, as the Jewish Theological Seminary ordained Amy Eilberg. In 1987 women were admitted to the cantorial program there, ending the millennial ban against hearing a woman sing in a synagogue—to the Orthodox, a sexual distraction. The small Reconstructionist movement begun by Rabbi Mordecai Kaplan had been the strongest voice for women's rights in Jewish practice, and Kaplan's daughter Judith became the first Bat Mitzvah—the equivalent of the Jewish boy's accession to manhood—in 1922. In 1973 the Conservative movement ruled that women could be counted for a minyan, which led to Betty Friedan's tearful inclusion.

Deborah Lipstadt, a distinguished historian who is deeply religious, recalls going to a tiny storefront shul near her Los Angeles home to say kaddish on the anniversary of her father's death. This shul blended Orthodox and Conservative customs and, despite mixed seating, counted only men for the prayer quorum. Lipstadt endured the embarrassment of waiting for a tenth man when she was already the tenth adult. The sun was low in the sky, and the time for Minhah, the afternoon prayer, was waning. Then,

> the president of the shul announced, to no one in particular, "in some shuls they now count women." A number of men nodded silently. The sun was disappearing and the time for *Minhah* was rapidly passing. . . . The rabbi glanced at the president and said, "Well, if we are going to say Minhah, we better start right now." I counted heads to make sure I was right. There was a minyan: nine men and one woman.

It was a first not only for Lipstadt, but for nine other Jews as well. She had a dinner date with a friend who was taking her out for her birthday—"And where is it written you can't cry and laugh on the same day?"—and to make it on time she had to leave between the afternoon and evening services.

> I suddenly realized that I had to stay. When I finally arrived at the restaurant I breathlessly explained to my somewhat perturbed friend: "I'm sorry I'm late, but I couldn't leave. I had to stay for *Maariv.*" Then I felt a wonderful wash of warmth and fulfillment fill my body and I smiled a very big smile: "You see, they *needed* me for the minyan."[50]

Rights entail obligations, but in the world of halakhah, obligations are blessings.

The really great flowering of Jewish women's lives and voices has just begun. Like feminism in general, the Jewish women's movement is energized in part by justified anger. Cynthia Ozick, a leading Jewish American novelist, wrote that the loss of Jewish talent caused by the exclusion of women was "numerically greater than a hundred pogroms" and "culturally and intellectually more debilitating than a century of autos-da-fe."[51] This is a gross underestimate. Blu Greenberg, another Jewish writer, recalled feeling erased from Jewish humanity as she sat in the women's section of Orthodox synagogues. "Every single Jew is required to put on tefilin each weekday," said the prayer book in one, as if women were not Jews. "We won't complete the service until every single person here has a *hakafah,*" said the rabbi in another, referring to the honor, restricted by the Orthodox to men, of carrying the Torah around in celebration on Simchat Torah; *person* meant *man.*

Today's Conservative prayer book says "God of our ancestors," not "God of our fathers," women's voices ring out from the pulpits of many synagogues, and almost half the entering classes in Reform and Reconstructionist rabbinical seminaries are women. Women writers and academics are shaping Jewish consciousness. Jewish journals and magazines are focused on women's rights, and changing roles have proliferated, beginning with *Lilith,* a publication as bold if not as racy as its legendary namesake.

As for the Orthodox, in addition to breakaway egalitarian synagogues, there are feminist trends in the mainstream. In one congregation in Jerusalem, women stay separated by a curtain, but behind it they read the Torah for all to hear.[52] More important, perhaps, is the rising participation of Orthodox women in the making of Jewish law. Although restricted so far to the laws of menstrual purity, these women scholars are increasingly empowered to give answers to questions only male rabbis have been allowed to address in the past. At least they are taking control of the law as it relates to their own bodies, and this trend may presage (pun intended) a fuller participation of women in shaping the commandments.[53]

Even the shiksa of song and story is finding a legitimate role in Jewish life, as the unprecedented rate of intermarriage transforms the community and chips away at its margins. When I was a boy the daughter of the family living in the apartment below us married a non-Jewish boy, and her family sat shiva for her, the seven days of mourning for the dead. Thirty years later, the Rabbinical Assembly of the United States, which makes law for Reform Jews, became determined to welcome non-Jewish spouses as "fellow travelers," a role later formalized as *gerim,* the Torah's word for valued strangers. At a meeting of the assembly in 1983 the question arose whether the non-Jewish wife of a Jewish man could legitimately fulfill the mitzva of lighting Sabbath candles while she still believed in Jesus Christ as her Savior. Their answer was yes, the reflection, perhaps, of a fact that genetic studies clearly prove: women have been imported into Jewish communities for centuries.

If the full history of women in Jewish life has yet to be written, that is in part because in some ways it has yet to be lived. This is the most dynamic moment in that history, and except for an extremely Orthodox minority, the Jewish world will be transformed. In a hundred years, the benighted past of the Jewish woman will matter little to the dominant majority. Yet it was always illuminated by bursts of bright light, by countless flickering candles, and by the glow of the warmth that sustained Jewish families for more than three thousand years. Give her, then, of the fruit of her hands, and let her own works praise her in the gates.

18

CONCLUSION: A DROP OF RED WINE

HOW THE JEWS WILL FACE THE FUTURE

Some rabbis, being wholehearted intellectuals, always wanted the Jews to believe more in thought and prayer than in action. In their view of Jewish history, God is at the center, and the Jews do best to follow the commandments, study, pray, wait for the Messiah, and let God take care of things in the meantime. In the most extreme version of this view, modern Israel is a sacrilege because Jews should sit and wait until the Messiah brings them there. Suffering in this world is only supposed to strengthen our faith in the next, and the narrow bridge between the worlds is righteousness, prayer, and study.

The facts are more complex. From the moment David—if not a psalm writer himself, at least a patron of them—pounded a collection of tribes into the semblance or seed of a nation, Jews always had a book in one hand and a sword in the other. Before the Torah, before even the Jewish God, there was a people Israel, and every single day it was fighting for its life. The Pharaoh Merneptah declared it dead and gone in 1207 B.C.E.—3,210 years ago at this writing—and that is the first time it was ever heard of. But the rumor of its demise was greatly exaggerated.

That was the first known instance of unexpected Jewish survival under the hammer of oppression, but there must have been many before that, and by the time King David was a gleam in his father's eye, survival was a habit for the Jews. Perhaps they even had an addiction, not to oppression—certainly not that—but to surviving by the skin of their teeth, the magic trick, the near-miraculous rabbit out of the hat. Winning by force or cunning, triumph whenever possible, but survival no matter what.

God mattered from the outset, and in time the Torah mattered too. Kingdom and Temple were transient, trashed by the Assyrians and then the Babylonians, and the people were dragged away from the ruins in chains. This had happened before with Egypt, and it would happen again with Rome. But in this moment of Babylonian exile, texts had to take the place of land in the people's imagination. Letters inscribed on lambskin scrolls, interpreted by teachers who saw through to meaning. Myth, story, history, wisdom, law, and covenant all leaped out of the letters inked on the scrolls. In the end it was better than land, because it went with you into exile, and it could never be taken away from you, no matter what.

> *I am the Lord, your God, who brought you out of Egypt. . . .*
> *And these words that I command you this day shall be upon your*
> *heart. . . .*
> *We will do, and we will understand. . . .*

A portable temple. Wisdom. Faith. God.

Coming back to the land that first time, they built the Holy Temple again, but it was not the sole center, nor were altars to other gods its only competition. There in the Temple courtyard, held high for all to see, was the unfurled scroll of the Torah, now commanded to be read and explained in the very shadow of the sacrificial altar. It was as if the people had concluded that they could no longer rely exclusively on the Temple or even the land. So for the next five centuries there were two epicenters, revolving around each other like a double star. The priest was high, exalted, pure, but the scribe, teacher, rabbi was not far away. The priest was in charge of the Temple, the scribe in charge of the text. The priest inherited his authority; the scribe earned his. The priest had sacred blood on his hands, the scribe inky fingertips, and in the end ink proved more powerful.

"Not marble, nor the gilded monuments of princes shall outlive this powerful rhyme," one of Shakespeare's sonnets begins. Holding the Torah aloft beside the ruined Second Temple, in the wake of a Roman genocide that would yet come back for a second pass, the rabbis must have had a kindred thought. They had already begun to build their temple of the mind—greater, purer, more gorgeous, far more intimate, and, unlike those stone Temples, destined to last at least 2,500 years. When Yochanan ben Zakkai escaped from Jerusalem in a coffin and went to found his new academy elsewhere in Israel, he embodied the rebirth of a new tradition that was far more important to Jewish survival than land.

From that day to this Jews have spread throughout the world, living by sufferance as second-class citizens in the cultures and societies of others. They were honored guests, they were worse than slaves, they were everything in between. They were forced to live by their wits, in a constant state of anxiety, developing portable skills, portable wealth, portable lives, without land. This meant money, and money meant survival. "We cling to money," Herzl wrote, "because onto money we were flung."[1] Wherever there was a meritocracy, democratic or otherwise, that gave them a halfway decent break in open competition, they thrived. They served their hosts intelligently and loyally as long as it was allowed, and when it was no longer allowed, they went elsewhere. They complained, but nobody took the slightest notice of their complaints.

Wherever they settled they imported and exported people through marriage and conversion, and their imports were better than their exports. For all their protestations, they did not stay pure; that is clear from the genes. But except in a few localities, intermarriage did not make them disappear. It also did not dilute their sense of being *chosen,* nor did it interfere with their success. Their success depended on qualities of mind, temperament, and character that do not seem to have suffered from the softness of the biological boundary.

From ancient times, they were fanatical about learning. The Torah is many things, but one is a device of exceptional power for discovering good minds. Build a study house, collect a few interested people, provide the basics of life, and lay the texts in front of them. Soon you will have a self-perpetuating device for distilling a concentration of brilliant scholars from the Jewish world. Now take the best of them in every generation, those boys with pale faces and glittering eyes ablaze not only with sacred light but also sacred argument, match them with the daughters of the most successful merchants, put their children and grandchildren in the lushest, most pampered, most secure environments a Jew is allowed to have, and you have a recipe for generating intellectual power.

Much as the rabbis wanted to control that power, they could not. Some of it reverted to commerce and finance, and some of it went secular in a thousand other ways. Shmuel Hanagid became the defender of Granada, Maimonides the court physician in Cairo, Doña Gracia the doyenne of Constantinople high society, Spinoza the philosopher who challenged the Jewish God, Karl Marx the theorist of a vast, failed, violent world, Albert Einstein the world's greatest scientist, and Ruth Bader Ginsburg a conscience of the Supreme Court. And they are only the tip of the iceberg. Call it culture, call it genes, call it a combination of both—whatever it is, it is something worthy of note, and of course, something worthy of resentment.

So the Jews are hated because they are successful. But that is not the only reason.

They are hated because they are different, just like other ethnic minorities. They have a certain stamp on their faces, a certain language, a certain religion; they dress, sing, dance, joke, write, and pray differently. Human beings are programmed to fear difference.

They are hated because they claim that they are chosen by God, and because they consider themselves superior.

They are hated because the Gospel of John says that they killed Jesus Christ—a Jew among other Jews who loved him or hated him, one of thousands of Jews crucified by the Romans.

They are hated because they only arrived recently, from elsewhere, and already they have the confidence of the king.

They are hated because they are good with trade and money, the only route to success allowed them for nineteen centuries.

They are hated because they are good at books and schooling, and they seem to have an easy time with mental mysteries and technical abstractions that are difficult for others.

And, strangest of all, they are hated because they are hated, because hating Jews is a habit that is difficult to break. And, logically speaking, if they have been so hated by so many for so long, *surely there must be a good reason?*

✦

"God wrestlers" is a name that has long been applied to Jews, and it has its justifications. Jacob has his name changed after he wrestles with "the angel," an obvious stand-in for God. He seizes hold of his opponent until the man begs to be let go, and Jacob says with astounding arrogance, "I will not let thee go, except thou bless me." The one had the transcendent power to bless, but the other had the power to demand, even compel, the blessing. And that blessing included a new name: Yisrael—Israel—"because you strove with God and men and have prevailed." *Strove-with-God.* It's not just the Jews' résumé. It's their name.

It wasn't the first time, and it wouldn't be the last.[2] According to Genesis, Abraham called God to task for the intention to destroy Sodom and Gomorrah, and he brazenly haggled with God over just how many good people it would take to avert the severe decree, much as you might haggle with a rug merchant in a market in Samarkand. Not only that, but he came within a hairbreadth of accusing God of injustice, of behavior unbecoming of the Sovereign of the Universe. God destroyed the cities, but Abraham won the argument, and it seems God expected him to do that. Indeed, it is said that the reason Noah could not be the first Jew was that when God said *Build an ark, I'm about to destroy the world,* Noah said, *How big?* But Abraham, for the sake of a few thousand strangers, was willing to call God to task. He knew how risky it was: "Oh let not the Lord be angry, and I will speak." And again. And again. And again.

As for Moses, tongue-tied timidity was his prevailing character trait at the time of the burning bush. The closest he came to arguing was some insipid mumbling about how he wasn't worthy, not good enough with words. But God said, *Sorry, you're it,* and sent him down to Egypt to give Pharaoh a hard time. Pharaoh was more than a little annoyed, and increased the people's burden. We are told, too, that God hardened his heart. *God hardened his heart?* God, we might conclude, is waiting for humble Moses to speak up, to *stand* up. And after his paltry stratagems—turning sticks into snakes and other magicians' tricks—backfire with Pharaoh, the people come to Moses and say he has put a sword in the Egyptians' hand to slay them. Aroused at last, Moses returns to God and asks, "Why is it that thou hast sent me? For since I came to Pharaoh to speak in thy name, he hath done evil to this people; neither hast thou delivered thy people at all." Consider going to God and saying, in effect, "Promises, promises. You have not done squat." Unlike Abraham, Moses doesn't even say "Sir."

The next passage is pivotal: "Then the Lord said unto Moses, Now shalt thou see what I will do to Pharaoh: for with a strong hand shall he let them go, and with a strong hand shall he drive them out of his land." Then God repeats the history, the promises, the covenant with Abraham. And then, of course, the plagues put an end to slavery. But it is almost as if Moses has to get angry before God gets serious. A kabbalist might say that Moses has to get angry to kindle God's anger. A simpler explanation is that he has to get angry to earn the mantle of leadership. *Ah, Moses, you have awakened. Welcome to the company of kings. Now you will see what I will do to Pharaoh. . . .*

The Prophets and Writings continue this tradition. Jeremiah famously remonstrates with the people, but doesn't stint in criticizing God: "You will prevail, O Lord, if I bring charges against you, yet will I speak judgments. Why does the way of the wicked prosper?" Psalm 44 reads in part, "Why do you sleep, O Lord? Awaken, do not reject us forever! Why do you hide your face?" Lamentations complains, "You have not forgiven. You have clothed Yourself in anger and pursued us, You have slain without pity. You have screened yourself off with a cloud, that no prayer may pass through." And Job, for all his proverbial patience, is no meek sufferer:

> *I am sick of life.*
> *It is all one; therefore I say,*
> *"He destroys the blameless and the guilty."* (9:21–24)

One of the most paradoxical and moving instances of challenging God is not in the Hebrew Bible but in the Gospels, and it describes a call to God by a unique Jewish prophet. He is Jesus of Nazareth, called Christ, also known as the King of the Jews, but believed by most of his followers to have been the Son of God. In Christian theology Jesus *is* God, or at least an aspect of God, sent to earth in human form as God's own sacrifice for the love and pity of humankind. Jesus of course knows and understands his fate, not merely accepting but welcoming it as the key to human salvation; and yet, according to Matthew, "about the ninth hour Jesus cried with a loud voice, saying, *Eli, Eli, lama sabachthani?* that is to say, My God, my God, why hast thou forsaken me?"

But how can God have forsaken part of God? How can an outcome so plainly predestined evoke a strong protest from the willing sacrificial victim? In Christian theology, this is the human side of Jesus crying out for mercy from the depths of earthly pain. But is it not also a human argument with God? Jesus cries out in the language he learned at his mother Mary's knee—Yeshua, that is, at Miriam's knee—*Eli, Eli, lama sabachthani?* And he is never more Jewish, or more human, than at that tragic moment, when doubt strikes at him as to the justice of God's plan, and he reproaches God for turning away from him.

Recall the Talmud story of the argument in which God's voice came booming down to take one side, and the opposing sage said, "It is not in heaven." Was he struck by lightning? Hardly. The prophet Elijah reported later that God had laughed and said, "My sons have surpassed me."

"The Poet's Commandments to God," that astounding anonymous medieval Hebrew poem, is squarely in this tradition. Its form is a trope that transforms the Ten Commandments. It begins:

> *Thou shalt not ignore whoever cries to Thee from his heart.*
> *Thou shalt not despise the wretch who begs for mercy. . . .*
> *Thou shalt not grieve or shame his sin and guilt.*
> *Thou shalt not rage at him when he repents his ways.*

It goes on and on, one reproach after another, turning the commandments upside down. God is implicitly called to task for past sins, and commanded negatively, in the wording of the Sixth to Tenth Commandments. There are twenty-two, not ten, here, and perhaps the most poignant of all is the last: "Thou shalt not hide when I beg: let my sighs come before Thee." Like all disputes with God, it is in part a petition for a blessing. It was not long after, in the wake of the Crusaders' slaughter, that Rashi petitioned—almost threatened—a personified Torah, demanding that she intercede for the Jews with God, warning that if she fails she will be silenced.

Remember Yankel? He was the little tailor who came before God on the High Holidays in the congregation of one of the great Hasidic rabbis. Speaking on the Day of Atonement in the synagogue of Berditchev, Yankel tries to make a deal with God: *I cut some corners with the cloth, and I sometimes missed the afternoon services—but you take babies away from their mothers and mothers away from their babies. Let's call it quits. You forgive me, and I'll forgive you.* But the rabbi is disappointed. "Oh Yankel, Yankel," he says. "Why did you let God off so lightly?"[3]

Some of the most poignant arguments with God follow the Holocaust, as in Jacob Glatstein's poem in Yiddish "Without Jews."

> *They number millions now,*
> *Our dead skulls.*
> *Stars flicker out around you.*

Recollection of you is dimmed,
Your kingdom will soon be gone.

This is not just a petition, an argument, or a reprimand. It's a threat. Far from assuming God's omnipotence, it predicts God's disappearance: "Without Jews there will be no Jewish God," it opens, yet the poet cannot stop addressing that God.

Who will dream you?
Who remember?
Who will deny you,
who yearn for you?

This is the dark side of the Hasidic rabbi's *Du* song; "You" is still the refrain, but for the Hasid, God was everywhere, while for Glatstein, God may be nowhere. "The last Jewish hour sputters. / Jewish God, you will very soon be gone."

But others saw the Holocaust as a reason to embrace God more fiercely in the endless Jewish wrestling match. We saw how Rabbi David Blumenthal responded in *Facing the Abusing God:* "May God," his prayer begins,

Who injures, destroys, and harms beyond reason,
Who also loves graciously, and is compassionate, and cares—

And in a passionate, paradoxical, almost blasphemous resolution it ends,

May God share with you His anguish and His shame at His own hateful actions.
May God bless you, and may you receive His blessing.[4]

Jacob himself never had God in a tighter hold, nor praised and blamed God through so many tears.

⟶∞⟵

Needless to say, a people known to wrestle God will not be afraid to challenge kings. When Moses is provoked to rebuke God and emerges stronger, Pharaoh should now seem an almost trivial opponent. Despite God's help, the Exodus has widely been interpreted as a kind of rebellion, inspiring revolutionaries throughout the Western tradition. During the English Revolution, in 1643, a sermon in the House of Commons reminded the members that even "meek Moses" had to become a "man of blood."[5] Years later, the day after the execution of Charles I, another preacher addressing the same house decried the people's inability to focus on "their approaching liberty," instead blaming the new government: "Do [the people] lack drink?— Moses is the cause. Do they lack meat?—this Moses would starve them. He would not let them alone by the fleshpots of Egypt; for this they are ready to stone him."[6]

America in its infancy was called "God's new Israel," and this theme pervaded speeches and writings. Tom Paine, in *Common Sense,* saw the Exodus story as proof that "[t]he Almighty hath here entered his protest against monarchical government."[7] Ben Franklin and Thomas Jefferson differed in 1776 about what should be on the great seal of the United States: Franklin wanted Moses, rod aloft, watching the Egyptians drown in the Red Sea; Jefferson wanted the milder image of Israel passing through the parted waters, following God's twin columns of cloud and fire.[8] A preacher in New Haven in 1777, a dark hour of the American Revolution, rhetorically asked his flock, "How soon does our faith fail us, and we begin to murmur against Moses and Aaron and wish ourselves back again in Egypt."[9]

Moses Hess, an early socialist who was Jewish, relied on the story, and Karl Marx, an anti-Semitic Jew, writing shortly after the failed revolutions of 1848, continued to cite it as a source of hope: "The present generation is like the Jews whom Moses led through the wilderness. It has not only a new world to conquer, it must go under in order to make room for men who are able to cope with a new world."[10] Left-wing journalist Lincoln Steffens, in *Moses in Red,* would later use the story to justify Leninist revolution.

In the 1970s Exodus inspired the liberation theology of progressive Latin American Catholic priests, who saw it as a beacon of light for people oppressed by modern dictators. And of course, most intensely and effectively, it inspired the African American slaves as they lost their native religions and adopted—created—their own syncretic Christianity. Negro spirituals are so replete with Jewish imagery—the Exodus, the crossing of the Jordan, the Promised Land—that it is impossible to imagine them without these themes. Given the entire Bible, including the Gospels, by those who brought them to Christian faith, they were drawn powerfully to a few chapters in Exodus about slavery, freedom, covenant, wandering, and redemption. And these resonant themes culminated in the words of the prophet Isaiah that rang out from the Reverend Martin Luther King's makeshift pulpit on the steps of the Lincoln Memorial, during the 1963 March on Washington (Isa. 40:4–5): "I have a dream," he said, "that one day every valley shall be exalted, every hill and mountain shall be made low, the rough places will be made plain, and the crooked places will be made straight, and the glory of the Lord shall be revealed, and all flesh shall see it together."

King would evoke another ancient Hebrew image in 1968, saying, "I've been to the mountaintop," a reference to Moses' climb up Mount Nebo, where he could see the Promised Land he would never enter. Alas, this image proved too true, when King was murdered the following day. But every Sunday in African American churches the halls ring with yearning voices singing of that land beyond the Jordan.

The Jews themselves put this story at the center: *I am the Lord your God who brought you forth from the land of Egypt.* Not only would they never forget, they would never stop seeing this as the pivotal point of their history. Because of God's revolution in Egypt, they could stand up proudly among nations; because of it, they could be given their life-sustaining Torah at Mount Sinai; because of it, they could produce a new generation that would be able to fight and win; because of it, they could gain their Promised Land.

And that wasn't all. Because of it, they would always have a burning sense of injustice that in the end would never fail them even when they failed it. *Love your neighbor as yourself,* their Torah would tell them; and *Do not do unto others as you would not have them do unto you;* and *Justice, justice shalt thou pursue;* and *You shall not oppress the stranger among you, for you were strangers in Egypt.* These are the moral messages of Exodus, and in the story they follow hard upon the revolution and liberation that, for the first time in centuries, had made a truly moral life possible.

These messages of justice are picked up later in the Bible. Samuel reprimands Saul, Nathan castigates David, and so on down the line of Israelite kings as prophets unflinchingly speak truth to power. In the prophetic books the scolding of kings becomes high art. Isaiah urges Israel to become a light unto the nations. More important than Temple sacrifices, he tells them, "Learn to do good. Devote yourselves to justice; aid the wronged. Uphold the rights of the orphan; defend the cause of the widow" (1:17). Amos, speaking for God, is equally clear:

> *I loathe, I spurn your festivals. . . .*
> *If you offer Me burnt offerings . . .*
> *I will not accept them. . . .*
> *Spare me the sound of your hymns. . . .*
> *But let justice well up like water,*
> *Righteousness like an unfailing stream.* (5:21–24)

The prophets stopped short of fomenting rebellion, but there were many bitter battles, and people did fight against unjust Jewish kings. But the greatest rebellions were against imperial colonizers. The Maccabees beat the Syrians, but the Jews were no match for the more brutal and powerful Romans; their vision of liberation was smashed by Roman battering rams. But the people would pick up the pieces. Rabbi Yochanan ben Zakkai, for whom discretion had been the better part of valor, had saved Jewish religious life. His plan—negotiate, withdraw, pray, and study—would guide Jewish life for centuries.

Rebellion resurfaced again in the nineteenth century, in two forms: the always risky and violent return to their native land, and the fight for social justice in the diaspora. The first of these followed Hillel's dictum "If I am not for myself, who will be for me?" But the second fulfilled the second part of the saying: "If I am only for myself, what am I?" And both boldly met the challenge of the third part: "And if not now, when?"

Jews participated in the revolutions of 1848 in Europe, were prominent early leaders of socialist movements, and played critical roles in the labor movement, helping to generate support for child labor laws and safe working conditions. In 1909, Jews were prominent among the few white co-founders of the NAACP. More than any other ethnic group, they vote to the left of their pocketbooks—that is, they vote for liberals far more often than others of similar income. Jews have stood disproportionately for programs benefiting the poor, even when that stand has cost them money.

Throughout the twentieth century, Jews supported liberal causes in every country. They came to South Africa in the early nineteenth century, reaching 24,000 by 1900, but their numbers greatly expanded in the early to mid-twentieth century.[11] They did well for themselves, but they also played a pivotal role in the transformation of South Africa from a vicious apartheid state to a democratic nation. At around the time apartheid ended there were 120,000 Jews in a population of 31 million, including several million whites. With this tiny proportion of the population they led the Progressive Party, the most antiapartheid legal political party in the country. Helen Suzman, the lone representative of the Progressives in Parliament, raised her voice against the apartheid regime for three decades. Jews were prominent among the whites in the African National Congress, Nelson Mandela's banned organization. Jewish lawyers defended blacks unjustly accused and tortured because of their political activities. And when a sweeping arrest of opposition figures was made by the South African police, more than half of the whites arrested were Jews.

In the 1960s they were prominent in America's integration movement, and Abraham Joshua Heschel and other leading rabbis marched beside Martin Luther King, Jr. Jews were the majority of the volunteers in the voter registration drive in Mississippi in 1963, which resulted in three violent deaths: of an African American and two Jews. Jews have no monopoly on social justice, nor is social justice the core idea in Judaism. But it is an ancient priority, and on the whole Jews have practiced it exceptionally seriously.

෬ᨏᨏᨏ෨

The question is, how much longer will their influence continue to matter? The future of the American-Jewish community has come into sharp focus in the last two decades. Serious demographers universally predict a decline of self-identified Jews from about five million at the beginning to between one and two million at the end of the current century. There are three main reasons.

First, half of all Jewish marriages include a non-Jew, which means that about a third of Jews marry out. This is in the neighborhood of ten times the prevailing rate in the mid-twentieth century. Only some of these marriages raise Jewish children. Second, the deeply Jewish past is rapidly receding—the foreign accents and Yiddish or Judeo-Spanish phrases of grandparents, the childhood memories of Sabbath in Jewish neighborhoods, the echoes of Torah learning, the proverbs and Talmud quotes, even the favored family recipes and distinctive aromas all become fainter with every passing year, and for millions of American Jews they are, or were, the main ties to the Jewish world. Last but not least in this triad is pervasive acceptance. Until the late twentieth century Jews could not be found in the top echelons of old American corporations or at the head of Ivy League universities. Now the last barriers are down. Almost nine out of ten non-Jewish Americans now say that they would not mind if their son or daughter married someone Jewish.

This acceptance is both marvelous and threatening. Jews have suffered from persecution, but their culture has also strangely thrived on it. Jews became insular because they had to, and as they closed ranks century after century, they constructed a religious and cultural cocoon. The cocoon could be dented or rent, but it was repaired, to once again comfort those within it. Today in the United States, the cocoon is simply unraveling.

Non-Jews suspect that Jewish insularity is a kind of reverse bigotry, or at least a superiority complex, and for some Jews this is true. But for most who care about Jewish religion and culture, who want to see it survive, it is simply a matter of numbers. Consider: If you let a drop of red liquid—borscht, say, or syrup-sweet Manischewitz wine—fall into a pitcher of water, you can watch it disappear, and after it is gone, the water will seem unchanged. A 50 percent intermarriage rate by Jews would draw off about 1 percent of Christians; even in the extremely unlikely case that all the resulting families became Jewish—fewer than half do—the effect on the Christian community would be negligible. But the loss to the Jewish community is devastating.

The community is aging, and is not being replaced. The Jewish community of Muncie, Indiana, founded in the mid-nineteenth century, has held steady at about two hundred, "but that number included many Jews who downplayed their Jewish identity and/or were unaffiliated. . . . The community lacked a strong central core of Jewishness aside from a small nucleus of committed families. The B'nai B'rith chapter existed in name only. In an age of career women, the temple sisterhood was a shadow organization. . . . The Temple itself continued to function, albeit without a regular rabbi."[12]

A moving and insightful anthropological study of a Jewish senior citizens' center in Venice, California, in the 1960s is a case in point. These elderly American Jews are imbued with a Jewish identity, a sense of social justice, and a love of learning with strong leanings toward Jewish, even Torah, themes. Their graduation ceremony after a period of study was reminiscent of the eastern Europe some of them grew up in. A woman named Rachel said, "Jewish comes up in you from the roots," referring to the kind of family she grew up in.[13] Another woman, Basha, said that they were religious despite not going to shul, because they had God in their hearts.[14] But these lively, intelligent, very Jewish people were on an exit path. "Whose children these days will say *Kaddish*?" asked Nathan, referring to the prayer for the dead.[15] They abandoned most of the religion of their parents, and they certainly didn't pass it on to their children. They were Jewish, to be sure, but most of them were the last generation of Jews in their line.

Another moving study focused on elderly Jews in a synagogue that had survived the destruction of the South Bronx in New York City, one of the poorest and most neglected slums in America. Unlike the Venice seniors, these were practicing Jews who had gone to shul religiously in the same old neighborhood for more than half a century. "Despite congregants' fierce resistance to change and their determination to endure, they are forced to recognize the nearness of death: they observe the constant diminution of the congregation, and they must cope daily with the gradual attrition of their physical selves."[16] But their religion and sense of humor have given them an almost miraculous tenacity, and "remaining in the South Bronx, they have in a sense cheated death."

Stories, both of their own lives and of the history of their people, pull them through. Moishe Sacks, a baker, told the story of Jeremiah laughing while others cried in the ruins of the Temple. He laughed because he had seen a red fox run past, fulfilling a prophecy that wild animals would inhabit the ruins. If this was so, then the prophecy that the Temple would be rebuilt would also have to be true. "So we don't have to go to the ruins of the Temple in Jerusalem. We can look right here at the Intervale Jewish Center to see the prophecy come true. We go to daven, and sure enough we see a furry animal or two come out from where it's hiding in the ruins."[17]

⚭

There are many positive signs, too, and some observers are very optimistic.[18] The United States still surpasses Israel in total number of Jews, and together they have more than 10 of the world's 13 million. Of the eight diaspora cities with the largest Jewish populations, all but the fourth—Paris—are American.

Since the ninth through twelfth are London, Moscow, Toronto, and Buenos Aires, it is clear that the Anglo-Saxon world, including Canada (365,000), Great Britain (280,000), and Australia (100,000) is home to the vast majority of Jews outside Israel, and the United States is the leader of that world.[19]

The Jewish day-school movement has been a great success. When I was a boy the only Jewish day schools were Orthodox yeshivas. Now all three denominations have large networks of schools. To take Atlanta as an example, in the early 1980s there was one real day school, the Hebrew Academy, basically Orthodox but open to others. The Conservative movement's school met in the basement of a synagogue, and the very Orthodox Torah Day School met in a rented store in a strip mall. Now both are in large buildings with hundreds of students, and a new school, associated with the Reform movement, also teaches six grades in a large facility. Two high schools have been founded, one for the Orthodox and one for everyone else. Tuition is expensive in all these schools, yet they teach thousands of students and are comfortably supported by a well-to-do Jewish community of about 100,000.[20]

This story could be repeated for many American cities, and it is justly celebrated in Jewish publications. Overall, the current picture of Jewish America is vibrant, with a marvelous variety of different subcultures. The Hasidim are growing in number and creating new cultural forms.[21] So, in a very different way, are the Jews from the former Soviet Union, who immigrated by the tens of thousands in the late twentieth century; for them even a modestly Jewish life is a strange and wonderful renewal.[22] The Jewish American community is mainly Ashkenazic, but there are about 250,000 Sephardim. Some 30,000 Jews from Aleppo, Syria, some still speaking Judeo-Arabic and others trying to revive it, have lived in Brooklyn, New York, since the early twentieth century, struggling to keep their unique identity in a sea of Yiddish-speaking Ashkenazim.[23] And the mix now includes 300,000 or so immigrants from Israel, who add a brusque, rough-hewn pioneering spirit to the now mostly mild-mannered Jewish American community.[24]

Jews remain primarily urban, with their highest concentration still in the Northeast. New York, northern New Jersey, and Long Island account for a third of all American synagogues, with another 25 percent in the next six largest communities. Reform synagogues slightly edge out Conservative ones, sharing 50 percent of the approximately 3,700 total, while the Orthodox movement alone has 40 percent.[25] The ratio of synagogues to Jews is about the same as it was in the 1930s, 1 to 1,600. Such statistics, combined with those of the day-school revolution, seem encouraging.

But what they omit is the much larger story of the decline in attendance at afternoon religious schools, once the bulwark of American-Jewish education. Synagogue memberships are aging and dying, and they are not being replaced. Fewer and fewer Americans are doing the things that identify them as Jewish—joining synagogues, contributing to Jewish organizations, being married by rabbis, checking the "Jewish" box on religious-affiliation forms, visiting Israel, and so on.

So how can it be that contributions are up? The core of the community is wealthy and committed, and, by all available measures, they are intensifying their own and their children's Jewish identity. This is a great success story. What they are not doing is paying the slightest attention to the hemorrhage at the margins. They have reasoned that it would be throwing good money at an unsolvable problem, and they may be right. But right or wrong, they are writing off millions of Jews.

The National Jewish Population Survey 2000–2001 showed the changing reality of Jewish American numbers:

The number of Jews declined from 5.5 million in 1990 to 5.2 million, a 5.5 percent loss. Jews are now 2 percent of the American population.

Their median age rose from thirty-seven in 1990 to forty-one today. The percentage over sixty-five rose from 15 to 19 percent, while the proportion under seventeen slipped from 21 to 19 percent.

Fifty-two percent of Jewish women aged thirty to thirty-four have no children, up from 42 percent in 1990. This compares with 27 percent in the general population. Jewish women aged forty to forty-four, near the end of their childbearing years, have an average of 1.8 children, below the replacement level of 2.1.

As remarkable as these findings is the response by the Jewish community. An article on the official Web site of the United Jewish Communities was titled "U.S. Jewish Population Fairly Stable over Decade, According to Results of National Jewish Population Survey 2000–01," and referred to "a U.S. Jewish population of 5.2 million, slightly below the 5.5 million found in 1990."[26] Typical of the general media coverage was the *New York Times* article, "A Count of U.S. Jews Sees a Dip; Others Demur."[27] The demurrals come from academics who have done unofficial surveys a fraction of the size of the NJPS, and from Jewish community leaders who explicitly say that even if this is happening, it is better not to publicize it. I call this the Ostrich Syndrome; it will ensure that the trends continue.

Can money and political action alone protect Israel and Jewish communities around the world without that broader base? Can an American-Jewish community numbering two million or fewer hold its own when there are, say, four hundred million Americans—fifty million Hispanic Americans, thirty million African Americans, a vast new Asian American ethnic group, and far more Muslims than Jews? No one knows. What we do know is that, barring a massive increase in birth rate, a revolution in proselytizing, or a mass movement of Jews from somewhere else to here, the American-Jewish community in the year 2100 will be very Jewish, very rich, and very small.

⟨⟩

The story is told in the Midrash (Eicha Raba 3:41) of a Jew who passes the emperor Hadrian and greets him. "Who are you?" asks the emperor. "A Jew." "Does a Jew dare pass the emperor and greet him? Hang him!" A second Jew, watching this, also cannot avoid passing the emperor, and of course he refrains from greeting him. "What?" asks the emperor. "The emperor passes you and you do not greet him? Hang him!" One of the emperor's counselors is puzzled. "We do not understand what you are doing, sire. One man greets you and you kill him, and another man who does not greet you, you also kill?" The emperor's reply is, "Are you trying to teach me how to get rid of my enemies?"

The Jews were killed for keeping their own ways, and they were killed for trying to pass as Greek. They were killed for rejecting Christianity, and when they accepted it they were killed for not embracing it strongly enough. They were killed for being in charge of world capitalism, and they were killed for trying to overthrow it. They were killed for running prostitution rackets and they were killed for helping invent modern physics. They were killed for teaching the Talmud and they were killed for creating a science of the mind. They were killed because they were weak, pathetic, and defenseless, and now they are killed because they are strong, proud, and protected. In the future as in the past, they will be killed for greeting the emperor and they will be killed for not greeting the emperor. Who are you to tell the emperor how to get rid of his enemies?

Well, now the Jews do have something to tell him, and all their other enemies: *You can only kill the Jews at great cost to yourselves.* This is not the same as saying they cannot kill the Jews. Of course they can. It is just that in this millennium, far more than in the last two, the Jews will fight back. In fact, they will fight back massively and dangerously. Those who kill them will, invariably, find cause to weep. Perhaps they will emerge from those experiences thinking that to eliminate the Jews may be more trouble than it is worth. More likely they will not stop trying.

In the meantime, the Jews have a country. You might say that to the age-old rabbinical wisdom, "The God of Israel neither slumbers nor sleeps," the Israelis added another cliché: "God helps those who help themselves." Or in Hillel's words, "If I am not for myself, who will be for me?" Except for its rather remarkable history, Israel is not that special a place. It is certainly not a light unto the nations. In our vicious, war-torn, tyranny-ridden world it is worse than some and better than most. It emerged from a far-from-pure process, but it has much greater claim to legitimacy on historical grounds than, say, the United States, Canada, Australia, New Zealand, or any Latin American nation. The Zionist dream was that the Jews would all come home and that there they would be safe. Of course, not all did, and those that did are not. Some say, "Throughout history the enemies of the Jews have gone to great lengths to identify them, collect them together, and kill them. Israel saves them the trouble of the first two steps." This is true, but there is a difference. Today, if Israel is a light unto the nations, part of the light comes out of the barrel of an Uzi.

The world—especially, in a crowning irony, Europe—would like the Israelis to rely on its protection for their security. To this the Israelis reply, "*You* will protect us? Like you protected the Warsaw ghetto? Like you protected the one and a half million Jewish children who were murdered by the Germans and their countless willing non-German helpers? Like you protected our mothers and fathers when they were stripped, beaten, and gassed? Like you protected the paltry remnant that desperately needed to go to their ancient homeland? Like you protected the handful that got there and were immediately attacked by six enemy armies? Thank you for offering, but we will protect ourselves as best we can. And if we can't, at least we will know that we didn't make the same mistake twice." *If I am not for myself, who will be for me?*

But of course, Rabbi Hillel went on to say, "And if I am only for myself, what am I?" In this historical moment, it is imperative that Israel recognize that others have a legitimate claim to some of the territory between the Jordan River and the Mediterranean Sea. It must walk a tightrope, it is true, between progressive recognition of the legitimate rights of the Palestinians and vulnerability to terror and external attack. But the tightrope may lead toward peace, while the status quo means permanent war.

People move and move again; in the vastness of history most of us, not just Jews, are refugees. The twentieth century alone created scores of millions, and very few will ever go home. Wherever we came from, we have to *be* somewhere. For the Jews, Israel is a better place than most, but another people has a legitimate claim to part of the same small piece of land. Perhaps Palestinians and Israelis must make a bloody separation—two states that cannot keep even a cold peace. If so, Israelis will always be warriors.

In a poem about Jerusalem Yehuda Amichai asks a passerby, "Excuse me, where can I find the Public Forgetter?" Too much remembrance can be deadly. But it is human to remember, even too much; those who lose this capacity through illness are pitiable, not quite human any longer. Jews not only remember but memorialize their suffering. They remember being slaughtered in their ancient land and dispersed throughout the world. They remember being completely at the mercy of whatever power temporarily tolerated their presence, and they remember that this mercy was invariably fickle. They remember the terror of church and mosque, Crusade and jihad, pogrom and ghetto, transport train and gas chamber. And then they remember why they wanted their own country.

⟨image⟩

Repeatedly in 2002 and 2003, Israel's army has made incursions into the West Bank and Gaza and then withdrawn again. Despite the territorial dreams of a vocal minority, Israel as a nation does not want any part of the Palestinian territory beyond what is already occupied by Jews and is necessary to protect those Jews. In fact it wants less than that, discounting many settlements that could be dismantled. This leaves about 5 percent of the territory, which is why the rest was offered to Mr. Arafat at Camp David in the summer of 2000. If the offer was not acceptable—there were legitimate reasons it might not be—then it could have been negotiated. But the Palestinian leader did not negotiate, he left.

A month later, after a provocative but revealing visit to the Temple Mount by Ariel Sharon—soon to run successfully for prime minister—the second intifada began. What it revealed was evident in the common reaction of Israeli Jews: the new intifada, with its widespread public support for savage violence deliberately directed against noncombatants, showed that the Palestinian people were not ready for peace.[28]

Israel did what it has done many times: it braced for war. As dramatic and terrible as the September 11 attacks were for the United States, they do not begin to match the attacks on Israel as a proportion of the population. With a population about one-fiftieth the size of the United States', Israel has had about a fourth as many deaths, a more than tenfold greater preponderance. And of course Israel has none of the geographic protections that we have here. So mobilization began. Regular army training intensified, and reserves were called up, including many mature and decent men who had in civilian life been working toward peace for years.[29] Waiters and bus drivers became national heroes, much like the firefighters of New York City, as they foiled many attempts to kill civilians.[30]

Others got through. After the Sbarro bombing, George Will had a brutally frank piece in the *Washington Post*. "Among reasonable people . . . ," he wrote, "there is a crystallizing consensus: Israel needs a short war and a high wall." He quoted an eyewitness account of the pizzeria bombing by *USA Today*'s Jack Kelley:

> The blast . . . sent flesh flying onto second-story balconies a block away. Three men were blown 30 feet; their heads, separated from their bodies by the blast, rolled down the glass-strewn street. . . . One woman had at least six nails embedded in her neck. . . . A man groaned. . . . His legs were blown off. Blood poured from his torso. . . . A 3-year-old girl, her face covered with glass, walked

among the bodies calling her mother's name.... The mother ... was dead.... One rabbi found a small hand against a white Subaru parked outside the restaurant.[31]

Six of the fifteen killed were children; this has happened again and again. War is hell, we know, but the world expects Israel to act as if it is not at war, as if this were some imperfect form of peace. But as Will noted, the children in this case "were not collateral victims—they were the targets. Abdullah Shami, a senior official of Islamic Jihad, celebrated 'this successful operation' against 'pigs and monkeys.'" Shami's view was "broadcast from the moral cesspool that is the official television station of Yasser Arafat's Palestinian Authority: 'All weapons must be aimed at Jews ... whom the Koran describes as monkeys and pigs.... We will enter Jerusalem as conquerors.... Blessings to he who shot a bullet into the head of a Jew.'"[32]

Thus the perceived need for a wall. But what will the Palestinians do on the other side? Without effective leadership, they will continue to grow their population at prodigious rates, in abject, hopeless poverty, with endemic Islamic fundamentalism and indelible, intensifying anger. They will find their way past the wall and destroy civilian targets within Israel, and they will accumulate weapons with which to shoot over the wall. They and their allies will attack Jewish and American targets far from the wall throughout the world, as terrorists attacked the Jewish Community Center in Buenos Aires, killing eighty-six civilians; the American embassies in Kenya and Tanzania, killing hundreds; the USS *Cole* as it refueled in Yemen, killing seventeen American sailors; and of course the World Trade Center and the Pentagon.

They will find strong allies. Iran, if not stopped, will be able to deliver nuclear warheads to Israel—not to mention chemical and biological weapons—in the near future. Syria is afraid of Israel, but would certainly be emboldened by an international Arab alliance, and for a dictatorship ruling miserable people with an iron fist, there comes a time when war is better than peace. As for Egypt, its population of seventy million or so will nearly double in the next quarter century, and it has built a vast army for which—given that it is at peace with Israel—it can have no plausible defensive need. If the streets of Cairo radicalize in an Islamic fundamentalist revolution, who can predict the consequences for Israel, with its mere five million Jews?

The *New York Times* tries to be fair, but consider the issue of August 21, 2001. On the front page, illustrating a moving story, is a photo of a Palestinian doctor with Israeli soldiers in the background. Her tribulations crossing Israeli checkpoints make it "a daily, dirty obstacle course" to get to her obstetrics hospital in Jerusalem. She is dedicated and attractive, and she stated her opinion that the checkpoints serve no purpose, that "all this is just to put pressure on the people and humiliate them." Terrorists, she believes, easily get around them. One can ask whether a country subject to daily terror attacks can be expected to have unguarded borders. But no one can read this article without sympathizing with the plight of ordinary, nonviolent Palestinians, and it matches what I see and hear from them myself.

Yet far from the front page, where few readers will notice it—buried in the fold in the bottom-right-hand corner of page 6, is a little Reuters squib called "Iraq: Call to Destroy Israel."

> Speaking at an international conference of Islamic clergymen, Izzat Ibrahim, the No. 2 official in Iraq after President Saddam Hussein, said, "We demand from the Islamic and Arab nation to rise quickly to expel the sons of monkeys and pigs, strangers on the land." A conference official, Abdelrazzaq al-Saadi, said participants at the meeting, sponsored by the government, would urge Arab countries to open their borders to volunteers who want to fight Israel.

These views were presented not at a colloquy of terrorists but at an international conference of Islamic clergy. None of these men of the cloth are reported to have risen up in protest at the anti-Semitic epithets, or even to have expressed a differing view.

What is this "Islamic and Arab nation" urged to "expel the sons of monkeys and pigs"? Well, there are twenty-two Arab countries stretching from Morocco to the Persian Gulf, at least six of which have repeatedly attacked Israel in the past, and several others of which have routinely harbored anti-Jewish terrorists and their trainers. As for the Islamic "nation," it circles the globe, comprising between 1.2 billion and 1.5 billion people— more than a hundred times the number of Jews in the world, and more than three hundred times the number in Israel. If of those 1.5 billion people, one in a thousand is willing to fight a holy war, if one in *ten* thousand is inclined to become a terrorist, Israel is doomed.

But what do the Palestinians themselves—not the terrorists but the moderates—really think? Faisal Husseini, a very prominent Palestinian moderate, gave an interview to the Egyptian daily *Al-Arabi* not long before his death in June 2001. Claiming that his goals and strategies were no different from those of the Israelis, he said, "Similarly, if we agree to declare our state over what is now only 22 percent of Palestine, meaning the West Bank and Gaza—our ultimate goal is the liberation of Palestine from the [Jordan] river to the [Mediterranean] sea, even if this means the conflict will last for another thousand years." If this were also Israel's goal, why did it withdraw from much of the West Bank and Gaza during the seven years after the 1993 Oslo agreement? Why did it place forty thousand weapons in the hands of Palestinians and encourage them to train an independent police force? Why did it offer at Camp David to withdraw from almost all of the West Bank and Gaza, setting that part of the land—won by Israel in a fair fight at huge human cost—on the path to full independence?

The notion of parallel strategies makes no sense. Only a minority in Israel claims the whole region "from the river to the sea." There is no Israeli counterpart to Husseini, no leading moderate who has any desire to try to hold that whole territory. All serious Israeli leaders are prepared to trade land for peace. They have done so before, in 1982, giving up the Sinai Peninsula in exchange for peace with Egypt, dismantling a substantial settlement and dragging away Jewish fanatics. But Faisal Husseini, renowned for his enlightened views, said in one of his last public statements that the Palestinian state on the West Bank and Gaza is only a stepping-stone, and that "as a Pan-Arab nationalist . . . as a man who belongs to the Islamic faith . . . and as an ordinary Palestinian" his ultimate goal is to have all the land "from the river to the sea," even at the cost of a thousand years of war."[33]

If you ask me, as an American Jew, what Israel should do now and in the future, I will tell you, as an American Jew, it is not my place to say. Don't charge me with evading the question—I just answered it, after long and careful thought. I haven't fought in Israel's wars and I won't be sending my children to fight. I haven't earned the right to an opinion. But let me give you the answer to a more basic question: Do the Jews, after two thousand years of diaspora, after the most varied and imaginative persecutions by Christians and Muslims in almost every country where they have lived, have a need for and a right to a nation in their own ancient homeland?

That is easy: Yes.

Having answered this simpler, most basic question, I leave it to those Jews who have settled in that homeland—who take the risks, endure the stress, experience the continual threats, go to the wars and send their children to the wars—to decide what they must do to survive. This is no evasion. It is the most important lesson of my seven trips to Israel. It is a main thrust and value of my countless conversations with Israelis from every walk of life and every point on the political spectrum. So far, with a few significant lapses, they have done things that I was able to support, although sometimes reluctantly. It is likely that that will continue.

As for my Palestinian friends, I want them to have their homeland too, and I want them to be secure in it and proud of it. But if the real goal of most Palestinians is to get it all, to get rid of Israel, then they will surely have their thousand years of conflict, and they will never have the lives they say they want. If, however, they are willing to settle for less, for something resembling what they claimed to want in Oslo—a small, independent country, linked to twenty-two stronger, allied Arab lands, in a true détente with a permanent Jewish neighbor—then Israel—little Israel, barely visible on a globe, a life raft for a remnant people drowning in the roiling sea of a vast, hostile world—will offer them a thousand years of peace.

⌒⌘⌒

So what will become of the Jews?

This is the endless question the Jews ask themselves, a conundrum they cannot stop puzzling over even during the rare times when those who want them gone are relatively silent. With their history, who can blame them? Since the outset, except for three bursts of martial competence and national enthusiasm, they have been militarily weak and politically dependent. They have mused intently on their past and on their destiny because large, fierce enemies have often slapped them aside with the back of their hands, enslaving or killing them, sometimes in the millions. For a people that has never had the luxury of counting even tens of millions, the enslavement and death of millions is plausibly close to annihilation.

In the early twenty-first century a new wave of anti-Semitism has swept across Europe, as classic Jew hatred melds with anti-Israel sentiment.[34] Synagogues are burned, gravestones are desecrated, a bus taking boys and girls to school is assaulted, old men and children are taunted in the streets. France is the worst, with a thousand incidents in about a year. Belgium, one Saturday morning, amid widespread anti-Jewish demonstrations, warned Jews to stay home, saying that the government could not protect them. Even Germany, where historical sensitivities make hate crimes not just unwelcome but illegal, has experienced a resurgence of classical anti-Semitism.

Nevertheless, the Jewish communities of western Europe, although modest in size, are relatively strong. They have been somewhat preoccupied with apologies and explanations for the Holocaust, but this concern has been largely eclipsed by the new anti-Semitism. Still, they are stably ensconced in Britain (280,000) and Germany (about 90,000, having tripled in a decade) and holding their own in the Netherlands (30,000) and in Italy (35,000), where the pope finally offered Jews unprecedented acceptance. John Paul II grew up with Jewish friends in prewar Poland, and he refers to Jews as "our older brothers." He is the first pope to set foot inside a synagogue, visiting the main one in Rome in 1985, and the first pope to visit Israel or even mention it by name. He stood at the Wailing Wall in Jerusalem and asked for forgiveness for all the centuries of Christian persecution. These are remarkable steps and hold out the hope of a worldwide diminution of anti-Semitism among the world's hundreds of millions of Catholics.

Even in France, where classic anti-Semitism remains strong and a new pro-Arab sentiment runs high, Jews show no signs of retreat. At 600,000 they make a significant presence, even in a country with 4 million Muslims. The influx of North African immigrants in the late twentieth century included large numbers of Sephardic Jews, and they have risen to prominence in every walk of French life.[35]

Other European Jewish communities (Russia excluded) are relatively small, numbering in the thousands, but are economically vital and have at least some political influence. Israel's ties to these countries, and to their Jewish communities, are significant. Düsseldorf began actively welcoming Jews in the 1990s and several thousand from the former Soviet Union have settled there.[36] At around 6,000, it is the first German city to surpass its pre-Holocaust Jewish population. A synagogue, a Jewish elementary school, a Holocaust museum, and other institutions serve this population, most of whom, having grown up in Communist countries, have to be educated from the *aleph-bet* up. Still, it is a vigorous and optimistic little community, and there are others like it in many German cities.

In eastern Europe, the Jews were effectively eliminated by Nazi murders. A certain nostalgia for the dead Jewish past has recently emerged among Poles, who conveniently no longer have to deal with live Jews. There is no sign that the Jewish communities will recover in any significant way, especially given the deep-seated anti-Semitism that poisons most of Poland, where repeated reductions of 90 percent or more in the size of the Jewish community have left classical Jew hatred more or less intact. Poland proves that to have anti-Semitism you don't need Jews.

In the former Soviet Union, millions of Jews remain, but an exact number is impossible to determine. Close to half a million migrated to Israel between the mid-seventies and the mid-nineties, and they have had an immense impact on Israeli society. But it is unclear what the majority who remained in Russia will do. Judaism is foreign to most of them. Jewish revivals have been strong, with hundreds of independent Jewish organizations emerging in Communism's wake, and with synagogues and Jewish day schools more or less thriving. Given seventy years of complete repression of Jewish affiliation and practice, the revival is remarkable.

Dnepropetrovsk, in Ukraine, is a case in point. Estimates of the number of Jews in this city of 1.3 million range from 10,000 to 75,000, but there are certainly enough to support a Jewish revival. A Hasidic rabbi moved there in 1990 and began building Jewish institutions. About 2,500 Jews crowd into the synagogue to hear the shofar on Yom Kippur, 1,200 students attend Jewish schools, and 1,000 elderly Jews get food delivered to their homes.[37] There have been three hundred Jewish weddings and thousands of Bar and Bat Mitzvahs. Twenty-seven tons of matzo are delivered to thirty-five thousand households on Passover. They have rebuilt the grandest of the forty-three synagogues that used to grace the city, and the rabbi who came from Brooklyn in 1990 now has eighteen other rabbis working under him.

This is a great achievement, but given the millions of Jews whose identity is merging with that of their post-Communist fellow citizens, it does not look so impressive. In Russia alone, estimates of Jewish numbers range from 3 million down to 250,000.[38] The first census since the fall of the Soviet Union is expected to undercount Jews markedly, since most seem to be hesitant to identify themselves. There is certainly anti-Semitism, and if economic conditions deteriorate, a resurgence of classical Jew-baiting is possible. But without that negative pressure—"Jew" on the identity card, "Zhid" on the lips of peasant and politician alike—most of the nominally Jewish people of the FSU will cease to be Jewish within a generation or two, neither moving to Israel nor participating meaningfully in the Jewish revival. Jewish life will persist in a vigorous small way, but 1 million or 2 million Jews will be lost.

Argentina had until recently one of the world's largest Jewish communities, but it has been dwindling owing to persecution at home and emigration to Israel. There are about 200,000 Jews in Argentina, 80 percent in Buenos Aires, down from 300,000 several decades ago. Two major Buenos Aires bombings recently shook that Jewish community—in 1992 the Israel embassy, with thirty-two deaths, and in 1994 the Jewish community headquarters, with more than a hundred.[39] This cut the heart out of the community, destroying the lives of many leaders, a traditional gathering place, and a priceless archive of Argentine Jewish history. Emigration to Israel increased. Iran-funded terrorists are suspected in these bombings, but there has never been an adequate investigation. In 2003 charges were filed, but in the view of the Jewish community it was too little too late.

Nationwide economic problems affected Jews greatly, and accelerated the emigration. This led to understandable resentment on the part of Argentines who had nowhere else to go; less understandable was the surge in anti-Semitism. Nevertheless, there are still seventy Jewish educational institutions in this historically vital community. A recent conference on Yiddish in Buenos Aires drew 1,300 people to a concert of Yiddish folk songs, and included 120 students under twenty-five who are studying the language.[40] Many other countries in Latin America have significant Jewish communities, the largest being Brazil with 110,000 and Mexico with 40,000. In many countries around the world, Jewish life is threatened by assimilation.

As we have seen, in the United States the situation is better but not secure. In the mid-eighties, I heard a Jewish expert on the Middle East say smugly, "When there are fifteen thousand mosques in the United States, then Muslims will have significant influence on American policy"—a reference to the network of synagogues and other Jewish institutions that have enabled American Jews to defend Israel. Well, today there may be as many as twelve thousand mosques in America, and synagogue membership is aging.

Fortunately for Israel, America's affection does not depend on American Jews; as they dwindle, Israel will continue to have strong separate ties to average non-Jewish Americans. Yet these one or two million American Jews will have an intense commitment to Judaism, the Jewish community, and Israel. The community may be a shadow of what it is today, but it will have firmer boundaries, and it will probably still be larger and stronger than all the Jewish communities of Europe put together. Ironically, American Jews, at least in terms of identity, may depend more on Israel than Israel does on them.

As for Israel itself, military questions make prediction more difficult. If prosperity and democracy can take hold in the Arab world, if Arabs can somehow get in touch with their former greatness and emerge from two centuries of stagnation, Israel will be accepted and become a safe haven for the world's largest Jewish community. It will be varied, cosmopolitan, vibrant, unpredictable, and still very Jewish, although the state will have to be more tolerant of non-Jews than it is today. If Arab population growth and increasingly hopeless poverty strengthen the radical Islamic fundamentalism that now seems to be spreading, a state of permanent war would be the best-case scenario, mutual annihilation the worst. Jewish fundamentalism is a serious problem, and the emergence of a radical-right youth movement bent on expanding West Bank settlements is an ominous trend. Still, unpleasant as it is, it is relatively weak; the future depends more on cultural dynamics within the Arab and the wider Islamic world. The worldwide war on terror will have unpredictable consequences for these dynamics, and for the Arab-Israeli conflict.

One thing is clear: the twentieth-century credo of Western intellectuals that religion would fade away—after I lost my faith at seventeen, I shared it—was exceedingly naive. America and Israel both are more religious today than they have been at any time in generations, and fundamentalist movements are alive and well in Judaism, Christianity, and of course Islam. Science, philosophy, psychiatry, prosperity, longevity, capitalism, communism—all were predicted at one time or another to bring the religious impulse, or at least religious forms, to an end. None of them has, except for a few individuals, something that has happened since ancient times. To say that religious faith and practice are part of human nature is not to say that everyone will have them; but it is to say that they will never go away—not for the world, not for the Jews.

From the audience at a conference I once asked Natan Sharansky, the heroic Russian dissident who became an Israeli leader, to explain how the Jews of the Soviet Union could keep their Jewish identity and revive it in force after seventy years of systematic and largely successful suppression. He looked down at me as if I were an idiot, and then explained kindly and patiently that God would not let the Jews go. This belief sustained him in a brutal Soviet prison, and it sustains him now as he navigates the rough seas of Israeli politics. It will sustain him until he dies, as it has most Jews for three millennia.

An old high-school classmate of mine, now an ultra-Orthodox professor of classical Greek in Israel, likes to point out that although the Jewish people lived for nineteen centuries without a state, they have not proved their ability to survive for even a day without the Torah. Plenty of individual Jews have survived without it—not only Jews like Spinoza and Einstein, but ones like Herzl and Ben-Gurion too. Even some whole communities that consider themselves Jewish—Yiddish political and literary culture, socialist Zionist kibbutzim, youthful secular Tel Aviv, middle-aged yuppie Jewish New York—have done just fine without it, thank you, at least for a time. Religious Jews across the spectrum from Reform to ultra-Orthodox consider this kind of secular culture, this Jewishness without Judaism, an exit path. It often is.

But the fact is that since that first diaspora, the Babylonian exile, such Jews have existed. They existed under the Greeks, in Islamic Spain, in Amsterdam, in Poland, in the United States, and in Israel. Philo was a secular philosopher and Josephus a secular historian, but both defended the Jews against their Roman persecutors. Spinoza was excommunicated, but he became the model for Einstein and Freud, secular intellectuals and thorough nonbelievers whom everyone in the Jewish world wants to call Jewish. Herzl, Weizmann, and Ben-Gurion had little patience with Judaism, and they, not religious Jews, founded the state of Israel—now home to five million Jews, thousands of whom sway in passionate prayer at the Western Wall. Isaac Bashevis Singer stopped practicing Judaism but spent his life creating a body of Jewish secular fiction that memorialized for all time a major Jewish culture, and he delivered his Nobel Prize speech in Yiddish. And countless American Jews, rich and poor, large and small, Torah Jews and atheists, defend Israel, vote for candidates who protect it, and send it large numbers of hard-earned American dollars.

Religious Jews have no choice but to accept these paradoxes, which have lasted for twenty-five hundred years, and will continue. However, there is no reason to believe that such a thing as secular Jewish culture can persist without a *relationship* to practitioners of Judaism. None ever has, and none is likely to. Ben-Gurion understood this when he decided to make his peace—some would say his devil's pact—with the Orthodox of Israel, according them privileges that have come back to haunt Ben-Gurion's secular heirs. Socialist Zionism of the type that he espoused was full of passion, but it rested on an ideology that passed. It did inspire the early pioneers, but the worldwide Zionist movement did not arise solely because of secular Jews. It arose through an alliance between them and the equally if not more passionate true believers in Judaism. As Golda Meir said when asked about her faith, "I believe in the Jewish people, and the Jewish people believe in God."

It was not secular Jews who built ancient Jerusalem, twice, and convened the Sanhedrin in Tiberias for centuries after the Second Temple was destroyed. It was not secular Jews who risked everything in the eleventh and twelfth and sixteenth centuries to travel over land and sea to kiss the Wailing Wall and die in the Holy Land. It was not secular Jews who maintained a continuous presence in Israel from the destruction of the Second Temple to the present. It was not secular Jews who funded the settlements at Zichron Ya'akov and Yamin Moshe, although they founded many more in the decades after. It was not secular Jews who viewed Herzl as the Messiah, and followed his prophetic pointing finger from the ends of the earth to Israel. And it is not secular Jews who, throughout the world, aid Israel through political action and funds amounting to billions of dollars annually. Without secular Jews, it is true, there would have been no Israel; more than any other group of Jews, socialist Zionists created the Jewish state. But to think that without religious Jews there could have been an Israel is to ignore the power of symbol, the authority of culture, and the facts of history.

With or without a major resurgence of worldwide anti-Semitism—always a possibility—Jewish life will continue to be strong. Jews, by dint of culture and history, are restless, critical, imaginative, resourceful, ambitious, cooperative, troubled by injustice, and committed to self-defense. They have been an irritant, an itch on the skin of the planet, for three thousand years. They keep saying annoying things like "God is One" and "Thou shalt not kill," "Give me your tired, your poor" and "Workers of all lands unite," "Where there is Id, let Ego be" and "$E = mc^2$," "God Bless America" and "That place, Mr. President, is not your place," "If you will it, it is no dream" and "Never again." These annoying notions in time persuade others, and this will happen again. Some of these outrageous claims were born in secular minds, but all were in some sense descended from the culture of Ezra the Scribe, who first held the Torah aloft in the Temple courtyard; of Hillel, who debated fiercely and lovingly with his rivals in the great Jewish academies of Roman Palestine; of Maimonides, who interrupted his medical work in Cairo to try to reconcile Judaism and philosophy; and of countless rabbis and their students throughout the world throughout the centuries, poring endlessly over texts, arguing incessantly about what God really meant. Echoes of their debates live on in Jewish intellectuals who know nothing of them, even those who hate them and all they lived and fought for. This forgetfulness is normal and will continue. So will the rabbinic debates. So will the distant echoes.

Jews live on the human equivalent of a geological fault line. There have been many earthquakes, large and small. There will be others. Some unknown process opens a gash in the social world, and the support of their fellow human beings, which seemed so solid, is suddenly gone. The place where they were standing now consumes them.

Jewish life is precarious, and Jews are often threatened everywhere in the world. What else is new? They first came on the world stage as their demise was boldly trumpeted, and it has been announced or predicted many times since. We don't know how many Jews there will be a hundred years from now, where and how they will live, or what precisely they will do and be. But it is likely that they will persist both physically and culturally, having survived any future attempts to eliminate them as they have survived all past ones; that the world will be both fascinated by and resentful of their strangeness, their boundaries, and their achievements; that their traditions will make them feel close to their ancestors as well as to their children, and *their* children, and *theirs;* that at their margins there will be losses and gains in faith, commitment, unity, and identity; and that those in the vital core of the community will burn with an exquisite, fervent, bittersweet yearning for People, Torah, and God.

A JEWISH TIME LINE

1800–
1200 B.C.E. Time corresponding to the accounts in the Torah, Joshua, Judges, and Samuel; the Patriarchs, slavery in Egypt, the Exodus, wandering in the desert, the Promised Land.

1207 First mention of Israel: inscription of Pharaoh Merneptah, "Israel is stripped bare, wholly lacking seed."

1200 Iron Age begins; Israel tribal—farming and herding.

900s Possible time of David and Solomon; Israelite kingdom begins.

800s Kingdom splits into Israel and Judah; Israel richer, more advanced and literate.

722 Assyria conquers Israel; Israel's Jews flee south to Judah.

586 Babylon conquers Judah, destroys First Temple; Babylonian exile; scribes and scholars gain importance.

500s Jewish communities in Egypt, Persia, etc.; diaspora extends far beyond Babylon.

500s Gradual return to Israel; Second Temple built; Torah Judaism established.

332 Alexander the Great conquers Israel; Hellenic culture begins.

167 Maccabees retake Jerusalem; Israelite kingdom resumes.

100s First rabbis; debates over Torah; dawn of Talmud Judaism.

63 Roman conquest; brutal rule; political control by crucifixion.

63 B.C.E.–
135 C.E. Time of great unrest; messianism, spiritual healers, zealots, revolutionaries, bandits, violent rivalry among Jews; Jesus of Nazareth preaches, 27–30 C.E.

66–73 First Jewish Revolt; genocidal Roman war.

70 Second Temple destroyed; Jewish slaves taken to Rome; priesthood ends; massive exile; wider diaspora; Torah academies in Israel.

100s Core of Talmud, Mishnah, develops; rabbis become main leaders.

132–135 Second Jewish Revolt led by Bar Kokhba fails; mass slaughter; Rabbi Akiva tortured.

200s Rabbinical Judaism well established through academies in Babylon and Tiberias; synagogues widespread in the Middle East and beyond.

300s Roman Empire becomes officially Christian; persecutions of Jews grow.

400s Second part of Talmud, Gemara, completed; diaspora expands, thrives.

525 Jewish kingdom in southern Arabia; may have brought Judaism to Ethiopia.

600s Muhammad founds Islam; persecutions of Jews, then partial tolerance.

700s Jews thrive in Muslim Spain; Islamic high civilization includes Jews.

718 Jewish business letter written in China, in Persian, but in Hebrew characters.

900s Climax of Babylonian Jewish life; rabbinical leadership waning there. Silk shortage brings Jews to China; 1,000 permitted to settle in Kaifeng.

1000 Cochin Jews well established in India; inscribed copper plates give them high-caste rights.

1000s Rise of Ashkenazic Jewry in France and Germany; life of Rashi; Yiddish language emerges. Rise of Sephardic Jewry in Spain and Portugal; Samuel the Prince defends Granada.

1096 First Crusade; widespread slaughter of Jews in Europe on the way.

1100s Golden Age of Islamic and Sephardic Jewry; life of Maimonides; Hebrew troubadours; Judeo-Arabic and Judeo-Spanish languages emerge.

1163 Jews of Kaifeng, China, build synagogue; inscriptions blend Torah with Confucius.

1165–73 Travelogue of Benjamin of Tudela documents the far-flung Jewish world.

1200s Rise of Jewish mysticism in Gerona, Spain: *Bahir* (Brightness), *Zohar* (Splendor).

1300s Forced mass conversions of Jews in Spain; Secret Jews; Jews blamed for Black Death.

1400s War between Ethiopian Jews and Christians; will last two centuries.

mid-1400s First Hebrew printing press; many more within a century.

1480 Inquisition founded to root out Secret Jews; will last three and a half centuries.

1492 Expulsion of Jews of Spain; second Sephardic diaspora begins.

1497 Expulsion of Jews of Portugal leads to new Jewish era in Amsterdam.

1500s Rise of (Sephardic) Ottoman Jewry; caliph views Spain's loss as his gain; Portuguese Jews build synagogue in India.

1537 Joseph Caro migrates to Safed, Israel; he will publish code of Jewish law in 1555.

1568 Paradesi synagogue; destroyed when Inquisition comes to India.

1560s Doña Gracia, doyenne of Italian and Ottoman Jewry, funds colony in Tiberias.

1600s Sephardic Jews settle the Americas: New Amsterdam, Newport, Curaçao, Recife, etc.

1656 Spinoza, first modern philosopher, excommunicated by Amsterdam rabbis.

1699 Glückel of Hameln begins publishing her diary, moving Yiddish account of family life.

1700s Jewish Enlightenment; rise of secular Hebrew, paralleled by emergence of Hasidism.

1789–90 George Washington's correspondence with Jewish communities: "[E]very one shall sit in safety under his own vine and fig-tree, and there shall be none to make him afraid."

1800s Golden Age of modern Yiddish produces great fiction, poetry, drama, social commentary.

1850s German-Jewish immigrants to U.S. looked down on by Sephardim; later, they became the New York elite.

1861–65 Jews on both sides in U.S. Civil War; Judah P. Benjamin Confederate attorney general, then secretary of war and then secretary of state.

1880–1920 Mass Jewish immigration from eastern Europe to U.S.; Jewish American golden age begins; great cultural achievements, organized crime.

1882 First modern Jewish settlements in Israel; revival of Hebrew continues.

1883 "The New Colossus" written by Emma Lazarus; affixed to the Statue of Liberty's base in 1903: "Send these, the homeless, tempest-tost to me, I lift my lamp beside the golden door."

1894 Dreyfus affair begins; deep French anti-Semitism revealed; Émile Zola defends Jews.

1896–97 Theodor Herzl publishes *The Jewish State;* convenes international Zionist congress; "If you will it," he writes in his diary, "it is no legend."

1900s Jews win more than 150 Nobel Prizes; over 100 in sciences; prize in literature in eight languages.

1917 Balfour Declaration: "His Majesty's Government view with favour . . . a national home for the Jewish people."

1924 IQ tests slow U.S. Jewish immigration to a trickle, trapping Jews in Europe.

1935 Nuremberg Laws in Germany; Jews legally defined as an inferior race.

1938 Kristallnacht, "Night of Breaking Glass"; massive anti-Semitic riots.

1941 Mass murders begin by shooting; mass graves; ordinary German soldiers murder hundreds of thousands of Jews on Eastern Front.

1941–45 America fights Japanese and Germans in World War II; 550,000 Jews serve; 10,500 are killed, 24,000 wounded, 36,000 decorated for bravery.

1942 Gas chambers begin operation; four million Jews will be murdered by this method, as governments, media, and most Jews throughout the world ignore this mass murder.

1943 Warsaw ghetto uprising; Jews resist German army longer than French nation.

1944–45 Jewish Brigade fights Germans in Italy; will help form Israel's army.

1945–48 Jews murdered, robbed, and displaced by Poles, Ukrainians, and other non-Germans; clandestine immigration brings 150,000 displaced persons to Israel.

1947–48 UN creates Israel by partition; Jewish State declared; six Arab armies attack.

1950s Mass immigration of Jews from Arab lands, as Arab persecution creates refugees.

1966 S. Y. Agnon, Israeli novelist writing in Hebrew, wins Nobel Prize in literature.

1967 Arab armies mass against Israel, which conquers West Bank and Gaza; some predict erosion of Jewish values in Israel; American Jews gain new pride.

1969 Golda Meir, raised in Milwaukee after her family fled pogroms, is prime minister of Israel.

1973 Arab armies attack a poorly prepared Israel on Yom Kippur; 2,500 Israeli battle deaths.

1978 Isaac Bashevis Singer wins Nobel Prize in literature; Stockholm speech, like all his works, in Yiddish.

1980s Half a million Soviet Jews emigrate to Israel, with great impact on Israeli society.

1981 Israel destroys Iraqi nuclear plant, blocking nuclear weapons program.

1982 Israel invades Lebanon, in Israel's first controversial war; vast demonstrations, protests.

1985 Writer Elie Wiesel speaks truth to power: "That place, Mr. President, is not your place."

1985, 1991 Mass airlifts of Ethiopian Jews to Israel, where life is much better but still difficult.

1993 Oslo accords; Israeli-Palestinian peace process, the culmination of years of effort; Israel gives Palestinians 40,000 weapons, transfers land to their authority.

1994 Jewish fanatic murders 29 Muslims at prayer in a mosque in Hebron; extremist Jews praise him.

1995 Israeli Prime Minister Yitzhak Rabin assassinated by another Jewish fanatic; some fear civil war among Jews.

2000 Israeli forces leave Lebanon; peace process fails as Palestinian leader Yasir Arafat rejects unprecedented Israeli offer; new intifada begins with riots, shooting.

2000 U.S. Senator Joe Lieberman, an Orthodox Jew, runs for vice president; Americans embrace him.

2001 Suicide bombings in Israel and U.S.; war on terror redraws geopolitical maps.

2003 Ilan Ramon, the first Israeli astronaut, is killed in space shuttle explosion; son of Holocaust survivors takes small Torah and drawing of Earth from space by a boy who did not survive.

2003 U.S. conquers Iraq in attempt to establish democracy and stabilize Middle East; proposes "roadmap" to peace between Palestinians and Israel, which both accept.

NOTES

Chapter 1. Genesis

1. David Rosenberg, trans., *The Book of J,* interpreted by Harold Bloom (New York: Grove Weidenfeld, 1990).
2. Israel Finkelstein and Neil Asher Silberman, *The Bible Unearthed: Archeology's New Vision of Ancient Israel and the Origin of Its Sacred Texts* (New York: Free Press, 2001).
3. Robert B. Coote, *Early Israel: A New Horizon* (Minneapolis: Fortress Press, 1990), p. 73.
4. Ibid., pp. 33–93.
5. Ibid., p. 37.
6. Ibid., p. 18.
7. The calendar is dated around 900 B.C.E., but because the agricultural round changed little in this area for millennia, it describes events in early Israel as well. See Klaas A. D. Smelik, *Writings from Ancient Israel* (Louisville, Ky.: Westminster/John Know Press, 1991), p. 23.
8. Thorkild Jacobsen, "Mesopotamian Religions," in *Religions of Antiquity,* ed. Robert M. Seltzer (New York: Macmillan, 1989), pp. 3–33; Leonard H. Lesko, "Egyptian Religion," in *Religions of Antiquity,* ed. Robert M. Seltzer (New York: Macmillan, 1989), pp. 34–61; Harry A. Hoffner, Jr., "Hittite Religion," in *Religions of Antiquity,* ed. Robert M. Seltzer (New York: Macmillan, 1989), pp. 69–79; Alan M. Cooper, "Canaanite Religion," in *Religions of Antiquity,* ed. Robert M. Seltzer (New York: Macmillan, 1989), pp. 80–95.
9. Finkelstein and Silberman, *The Bible Unearthed.*
10. Ibid., chaps. 3–4.
11. Coote, *Early Israel,* p. 171.

Chapter 2. Kingdom Come

1. Israel Finkelstein and Neil Asher Silberman, *The Bible Unearthed: Archeology's New Vision of Ancient Israel and the Origin of Its Sacred Texts* (New York: Free Press, 2001), chaps. 5–6.
2. Ibid., chap. 7.
3. Amos 5:11–12, Jewish Publication Society, *J.P.S. Hebrew-English Tanakh,* 2nd ed. (Philadelphia: Jewish Publication Society, 1999).
4. Finkelstein and Silberman, *The Bible Unearthed,* chap. 8.
5. Ibid., chap. 9.
6. 2 Kings 23:19–20, Jewish Publication Society, *J.P.S. Hebrew-English Tanakh.*
7. Richard Elliott Friedman, *Who Wrote the Bible?* (New York: Harper & Row, 1989).
8. David Rosenberg, trans., *The Book of J,* interpreted by Harold Bloom (New York: Grove Weidenfeld, 1990).
9. Finkelstein and Silberman,*The Bible Unearthed,* chap. 11.
10. Deut. 1:16–17, Jewish Publication Society, *J.P.S. Hebrew-English Tanakh.*
11. Deut. 7:4–5, ibid.
12. Deut. 10:17–19, ibid.
13. Deut. 15:7–8, ibid.

14. Deut. 15:12–15, ibid.
15. Deut. 24:5, ibid.
16. Deut. 24:14–15, ibid.
17. Deut. 26:5–10, ibid.
18. Deut. 31:24–27, ibid.
19. Gen. 8:21, ibid.
20. Gen. 18:23–33, ibid.
21. Gen. 32:29, ibid.
22. Rosenberg, *The Book of J.*
23. Judg. 5:7, 5:12, author's translation.
24. Judg. 4:21, Jewish Publication Society, *J.P.S. Hebrew-English Tanakh.*
25. Jth. 8:7–8, Bruce M. Metzger and Roland E. Murphy, eds., *The New Oxford Annotated Bible, with the Apocryphal/Deuterocanonical Books: New Revised Standard Edition* (New York: Oxford University Press, 1994), p. 29AP.
26. Jth. 10:3–4, ibid., p. 31AP.
27. Alan M. Cooper, "Canaanite Religion," in *Religions of Antiquity,* ed. Robert M. Seltzer (New York: Macmillan, 1989), pp. 80–95.
28. Gen. 14:18, Jewish Publication Society, *J.P.S. Hebrew-English Tanakh.*
29. Leonard H. Lesko, "Egyptian Religion," in *Religions of Antiquity,* ed. Robert M. Seltzer (New York: Macmillan, 1989), pp. 34–61.
30. Gherardo Gnoli, "Zoroastrianism," in *Religions of Antiquity,* ed. Robert M. Seltzer (New York: Macmillan, 1989), pp. 128–47.
31. Psalm 82:1, Jewish Publication Society, *J.P.S. Hebrew-English Tanakh.*
32. The translation is by John Bowker, quoted in Karen Armstrong, *A History of God* (New York: Ballantine Books, 1994), p. 51.
33. Ibid.

Chapter 3. Babylon

1. Israel Finkelstein and Neil Asher Silberman, *The Bible Unearthed: Archeology's New Vision of Ancient Israel and the Origin of Its Sacred Texts* (New York: Free Press, 2001).
2. Ibid., p. 306.
3. Deut. 31:9–13, Jewish Publication Society, *J.P.S. Hebrew-English Tanakh,* 2nd ed. (Philadelphia: Jewish Publication Society, 1999).
4. King James Version.
5. Jewish Publication Society, *J.P.S. Hebrew-English Tanakh.*
6. James D. Purvis, "Exile and Return: From the Babylonian Destruction to the Reconstruction of the Jewish State," in *Ancient Israel: A Short History from Abraham to the Roman Destruction of the Temple,* ed. Hershel Shanks (Englewood Cliffs, N.J.: Prentice-Hall, 1988), pp. 151–75.
7. Jer. 29:4–7 KJV.
8. Purvis, "Exile and Return," p. 161.
9. Neh. 7:4–5 KJV.
10. Neh. 8:1–6 KJV.
11. According to the Talmud (Tractate Avot), these are two of the three things on which the world stands, the third being *tzedakah,* or righteousness. *Avodah* in modern Hebrew means "work."
12. Lev. 16:3 KJV.
13. Lev. 16:5–10 KJV.
14. Lev. 16:21–22 KJV.
15. Mary Douglas, *Purity and Danger: An Analysis of the Concepts of Pollution and Taboo* (London and New York: Routledge, 1966).
16. René Girard, *Violence and the Sacred,* trans. Patrick Gregory (Baltimore: Johns Hopkins University Press, 1972).
17. Douglas, *Purity and Danger.*
18. Howard Eilberg-Schwartz, *The Savage in Judaism: An Anthropology of Israelite Religion and Ancient Judaism* (Bloomington: Indiana University Press, 1990).
19. R. H. Charles, *The Letter of Aristeas* (Oxford, England: Oxford University Press, 1913).
20. Girard, *Violence and the Sacred.*
21. Purvis, "Exile and Return."
22. Shaye J. D. Cohen, *From the Maccabees to the Mishnah* (Philadelphia: Westminster Press, 1987), chap. 2.

23. John M. G. Barclay, *Jews in the Mediterranean Diaspora: From Alexander to Trajan (323 B.C.E.–117 C.E.)* (Berkeley: University of California Press, 1996).

24. C. D. Yonge, trans., *The Works of Philo,* new updated ed. (Peabody, Mass.: Hendrickson, 1993).

25. John H. Hayes and Sara R. Mandell, *The Jewish People in Classical Antiquity: Alexander to Bar Kochba* (Louisville, Ky.: Westminster John Knox Press, 1998), pp. 19–21.

26. Lee I. A. Levine, "The Age of Hellenism: Alexander the Great and the Rise and Fall of the Hasmonean Kingdom," in *Ancient Israel: A Short History from Abraham to the Roman Destruction of the Temple,* ed. Hershel Shanks (Englewood Cliffs, N.J.: Prentice-Hall, 1988), p. 178.

27. William Whiston, trans., *The Works of Josephus* (Peabody, Mass.: Hendrickson, 1987), pp. 318ff.

28. Martin Buber, *I and Thou,* 2nd ed., trans. Ronald Gregor Smith (New York: Charles Scribner's Sons, 1958).

29. 6:10, Bruce M. Metzger and Roland E. Murphy, eds., *The New Oxford Annotated Bible, with the Apocryphal/Deuterocanonical Books: New Revised Standard Edition* (New York: Oxford University Press, 1994).

30. Gen. 17:9–14 KJV.

31. Eilberg-Schwartz, *The Savage in Judaism,* chap. 6.

32. Gen. 17:6 KJV.

33. Eilberg-Schwartz, p. 141.

34. T. Carmi, ed., *The Penguin Book of Hebrew Verse* (New York: Viking Press, 1981), p. 451.

Chapter 4. Roman Ruin

1. 1 Macc. 13:15, Bruce M. Metzger and Roland E. Murphy, eds., *The New Oxford Annotated Bible, with the Apocryphal/Deuterocanonical Books: New Revised Standard Edition* (New York: Oxford University Press, 1994), p. 221.

2. *Antiquities* 13:380, in William Whiston, trans. *The Works of Josephus* (Peabody, Mass.: Hendrickson, 1987), p. 361.

3. M. Stern, "The Political and Social History of Judea under Roman Rule," in *A History of the Jewish People,* ed. H. H. Ben-Sasson (Cambridge, Mass.: Harvard University Press, 1976), p. 239.

4. Shaye J. D. Cohen, "Roman Domination: The Jewish Revolt and the Destruction of the Second Temple," in *Ancient Israel: A Short History from Abraham to the Roman Destruction of the Temple,* ed. Hershel Shanks (Englewood Cliffs, N.J.: Prentice-Hall, 1988), pp. 205–35.

5. John Dominic Crossan, *The Historical Jesus: The Life of a Mediterranean Jewish Peasant* (San Francisco: HarperCollins, 1991), appendix 2.

6. *Antiquities* 14:159–60, in Whiston, *The Works of Josephus,* p. 376.

7. *Antiquities* 14:168, ibid.

8. David M. Rhoads, *Israel in Revolution, 6–74 C.E.: A Political History Based on the Writings of Josephus* (Philadelphia: Fortress Press, 1976), p. 25.

9. *Antiquities* 17:295, in Whiston, *The Works of Josephus,* p. 471.

10. Crossan, *The Historical Jesus,* p. 194.

11. *Antiquities* 18:23, in Whiston, *The Works of Josephus,* p. 477.

12. James Carroll, *Constantine's Sword: The Church and the Jews: A History* (New York: Houghton Mifflin, 2001), p. 80.

13. Crossan, *The Historical Jesus,* chap. 8.

14. Ibid., p. 162.

15. *Antiquities* 20:160, in Whiston, *The Works of Josephus.*

16. *Antiquities* 20:167–68, ibid., p. 536.

17. *Wars* 2:253, ibid., p. 614.

18. Crossan, *The Historical Jesus,* p. 16.

19. This may have been Herod Antipas instead of Herod the Great.

20. Crossan, *The Historical Jesus,* p. 19.

21. Luke 2:46–47, Metzger and Murphy, eds., *The New Oxford Annotated Bible,* p. 81.

22. Harvey Cox, "Rabbi Yeshua Ben Yoseph: Reflections on Jesus' Jewishness and the Interfaith Dialogue," in *Jesus' Jewishness: Exploring the Place of Jesus within Early Judaism,* ed. James H. Charlesworth (New York: Crossroad Publishing, 1996), pp. 27–62.

23. David Flusser, "Jesus, His Ancestry, and the Commandment of Love," in *Jesus' Jewishness: Exploring the Place of Jesus within Early Judaism,* ed. James H. Charlesworth (New York: Crossroad Publishing, 1996), pp. 153–76.

24. Matt. 22:34–40, Metzger and Murphy, eds., *The New Oxford Annotated Bible,* p. 34.
25. John 14:6, ibid., p. 148.
26. John P. Meier, "Reflections on Jesus-of-History Research Today," in *Jesus' Jewishness: Exploring the Place of Jesus within Early Judaism,* ed. James H. Charlesworth (New York: Crossroad Publishing, 1996), pp. 84–107.
27. James H. Charlesworth, "The Foreground of Christian Origins and the Commencement of Jesus Research," in *Jesus' Jewishness: Exploring the Place of Jesus within Early Judaism,* ed. James H. Charlesworth (New York: Crossroad Publishing, 1996), pp. 63–83.
28. Matt. 3:16–17, Metzger and Murphy, eds., *The New Oxford Annotated Bible,* p. 5.
29. Matt. 4:13, ibid., 5.
30. Matt. 5:3–19, ibid., p. 6.
31. Matt. 23:2–33, ibid., pp. 34–36.
32. Isa. 1:11–19, ibid., p. 868.
33. Isa. 58:3–9 KJV.
34. Isa. 11:4–6, ibid.
35. Isa. 2:4, Mic. 4:3, ibid.
36. Sirach (Ecclesiasticus) 28:2–7, Metzger and Murphy, eds., *The New Oxford Annotated Bible,* p. 124.
37. Matt. 27:46, ibid., p. 44.
38. Joseph Telushkin, *Jewish Literacy: The Most Important Things to Know about the Jewish Religion, Its People, and Its History* (New York: William Morrow, 1991), p. 120.
39. Nahum N. Glatzer, *The Judaic Tradition: Jewish Writings from Antiquity to the Modern Age* (Northvale, N.J.: Jason Aronson, 1987).
40. Ibid., p. 196.
41. Ibid., p. 194.
42. Ibid.
43. Harry Freedman, "Akiva," in *Encyclopedia Judaica* (Jerusalem: Judaica Multimedia, 1972).
44. The Persian-derived Hebrew word is *pardes*—"garden" or "orchard"—and has been interpreted letter by letter to imply hints and secrets. I am indebted to Dr. Shlomit Finkelstein for pointing this out.
45. Louis Finkelstein, *Akiba: Scholar, Saint and Martyr* (Northvale, N.J.: Jason Aronson, 1990), p. 101.
46. Ibid., pp. 101–2.
47. Ibid., p. 153.
48. Ibid., p. 230.
49. Ibid., p. 269.
50. Ibid., p. 270.
51. Nahman Avigad, *Discovering Jerusalem* (Nashville: Thomas Nelson Publishers, 1983), p. 104.
52. Ibid., p. 123.
53. Babylonian Talmud, Pechahim 57, 1 = Tosefta, Minhot 13, 21, as quoted in ibid., p. 130.
54. Ayala Sussman and Ruth Peled, "Treasures from the Judean Desert," in *Scrolls from the Dead Sea: An Exhibition of Scrolls and Archeological Artifacts from the Collections of the Israel Antiquities Authority,* ed. Ayala Sussman and Ruth Peled (Washington, D.C.: Library of Congress/ Archetype Press, 1993).
55. Lawrence H. Schiffman, *Reclaiming the Dead Sea Scrolls* (Philadelphia: Jewish Publication Society, 1994), p. 84.
56. M. Stern, "The Social and Governmental Structure of Judea under the Ptolemies and Seleucids," in *A History of the Jewish People,* ed. H. H. Ben-Sasson (Cambridge, Mass.: Harvard University Press, 1976), p. 259.
57. Cohen, "Roman Domination."
58. *Wars* 5:451, in Whiston, *The Works of Josephus,* p. 720.
59. *Wars* 6:259, ibid., p. 740.
60. *Wars* 6:271–72, ibid., p. 741.
61. *Wars* 6:403–6, ibid., p. 748.
62. Cohen, "Roman Domination," p. 231.

Chapter 5. Diaspora

1. Graydon Snyder, "The Interaction of Jews with Non-Jews in Rome," in *Judaism and Christianity in First-Century Rome,* ed. Karl P. Donfried and Peter Richardson (Grand Rapids, Mich.: William B. Eerdmans, 1998), pp. 69–90.

2. Lee I. Levine, "The Second Temple Synagogue: The Formative Years," in *The Synagogue in Late Antiquity,* ed. Lee I. Levine (Philadelphia: American Schools of Oriental Research, 1987), p. 16.

3. King James Version.

4. Levine, "The Second Temple Synagogue," p. 17.

5. Ibid.

6. Jacob Neusner, *Symbol and Theology in Early Judaism* (Minneapolis, Minn.: Fortress, 1991); Snyder, "The Interaction of Jews with Non-Jews in Rome."

7. A. T. Kraabel, "Unity and Diversity among Diaspora Synagogues," in *The Synagogue in Late Antiquity,* ed. Lee I. Levine (Philadelphia: American Schools of Oriental Research, 1987), p. 50.

8. J. Yahalom, "*Piyyut* as Poetry," in *The Synagogue in Late Antiquity,* ed. Lee I. Levine (Philadelphia: American Schools of Oriental Research, 1987), p. 119.

9. Kraabel, "Unity and Diversity among Diaspora Synagogues," p. 54.

10. From the time of the Mishnah, there have been two expressions: *Yerushalayim shel mala,* or "Jerusalem of the above," and *Yerushalayim shel mata,* "Jerusalem of the below." The distinction remains meaningful.

11. Shaye J. D. Cohen, "Roman Domination: The Jewish Revolt and the Destruction of the Second Temple," in *Ancient Israel: A Short History from Abraham to the Roman Destruction of the Temple,* ed. Hershel Shanks (Englewood Cliffs, N.J.: Prentice-Hall, 1988), p. 213.

12. Peter Richardson, "Augustan-Era Synagogues in Rome," in *Judaism and Christianity in First-Century Rome,* ed. Karl P. Donfried and Peter Richardson (Grand Rapids, Mich.: William B. Eerdmans, 1998), pp. 17–29.

13. Ibid., p. 17.

14. James S. Jeffers, "Jewish and Christian Families in First-Century Rome," in *Judaism and Christianity in First-Century Rome,* ed. Karl P. Donfried and Peter Richardson (Grand Rapids, Mich.: William B. Eerdmans, 1998), pp. 128–50.

15. Ibid., p. 140.

16. Allan Gould, *What Did They Think of the Jews?* (Northvale, N.J.: Jason Aronson, 1991), p. 3.

17. Ibid., p. 6.

18. Ibid., p. 5.

19. Ibid., p. 7.

20. Ibid., p. 8.

21. Ibid., p. 10.

22. Ibid., pp. 13–14.

23. Ibid., p. 15.

24. S. Safrai, "The Lands of the Diaspora," in *A History of the Jewish People,* ed. H. H. Ben-Sasson (Cambridge, Mass.: Harvard University Press, 1976), p. 364.

25. Leonard Victor Rutgers, "Roman Policy toward the Jews: Expulsions from the City of Rome during the First Century C.E.," in *Judaism and Christianity in First-Century Rome,* ed. Karl P. Donfried and Peter Richardson (Grand Rapids, Mich.: William B. Eerdmans, 1998), p. 106.

26. Adin Steinsaltz, *The Essential Talmud,* trans. Chaya Galai (New York: Basic Books, 1976).

27. Adin Steinsaltz, *The Talmud: The Steinsaltz Edition: A Reference Guide,* trans. and ed. Israel V. Berman (New York: Random House, 1989).

28. Jacob Neusner, *The Mishnah: An Introduction* (Northvale, N.J.: Jason Aronson, 1989), Baba Qamma 9:3, p. 67.

29. Ibid., Baba Mesia 5:2, p. 68.

30. Ibid., Baba Batra 3:1–2, p. 72.

31. Ibid., M. Yebamot 10:1, p. 124.

32. Steinsaltz, *The Talmud: The Steinsaltz Edition.*

33. Anonymous, "Judah Ha-Nasi," in *Encyclopedia Judaica* (Jerusalem: Judaica Multimedia, 1972); Meyer Waxman, *A History of Jewish Literature* (London: Thomas Yoseloff, 1960), vol. 1, pp. 69–70.

34. Safrai, "The Lands of the Diaspora."

35. Isaiah Gafni, "Babylonian Rabbinic Culture," in *Cultures of the Jews: A New History,* ed. David Biale (New York: Schocken Books, 2002), p. 232.

36. Steinsaltz, *The Talmud: The Steinsaltz Edition,* p. 16.

37. Safrai, "The Lands of the Diaspora," p. 376.

38. Steinsaltz, *The Talmud: The Steinsaltz Edition.*

39. Moshe Weissman, *The Midrash Says: The Narrative of the Weekly Torah-Portion in the Perspective of Our Sages* (Brooklyn: Benei Yakov Publications, 1980), p. xiii.

40. Adin Steinsaltz, ed., *The Talmud: The Steinsaltz Edition* (New York: Random House, 1990), vol. 3, Tractate Bava Metzia, part 3, pp. 235–37. Translated by the author.

41. Nahum N. Glatzer, ed., *Hammer on the Rock: A Short Midrash Reader* (New York: Schocken Books, 1966), p. 89.

42. Ibid., Mekhilta on 12:51, p. 104.

43. "Rabban" refers to rabbis who were presidents of the Sanhedrin.

44. Judah Goldin, *The Living Talmud: The Wisdom of the Fathers and Its Classical Commentaries* (New York: New American Library, 1957), p. 178.

45. King James Version.

46. Louis Finkelstein, *Akiba: Scholar, Saint and Martyr* (Northvale, N.J.: Jason Aronson, 1990), p. 12.

Chapter 6. Crossed Swords

1. James Carroll, *Constantine's Sword: The Church and the Jews: A History* (New York: Houghton Mifflin, 2001).

2. Bruce M. Metzger and Roland E. Murphy, eds., *The New Oxford Annotated Bible with the Apocryphal/Deuterocanonical Books: New Revised Standard Edition* (New York: Oxford University Press, 1994), p: 368.

3. Carroll, *Constantine's Sword,* p. 166.

4. Ibid., pp. 144–45.

5. Ibid., p. 571.

6. Allan Gould, *What Did They Think of the Jews?* (Northvale, N.J.: Jason Aronson, 1991), pp. 24–25.

7. Ibid., p. 24.

8. Ibid., p. 27.

9. Ibid.

10. Haim Beinart, *Atlas of Medieval Jewish History* (New York: Simon and Schuster, 1992), pp. 14–15.

11. Eli Barnavi, *A Historical Atlas of the Jewish People: From the Time of the Patriarchs to the Present,* trans. Miriam Eliav-Feldon (New York: Schocken Books, 1992), pp. 68–69.

12. Ibid., p. 77.

13. Ibid., p. 66.

14. Ibid., p. 67.

15. Oded Irshai, "Confronting a Christian Empire: Jewish Culture in the World of Byzantium," in *Cultures of the Jews: A New History,* ed. David Biale (New York: Schocken Books, 2002), pp. 181–221.

16. Barnavi, *A Historical Atlas of the Jewish People,* p. 74.

17. Beinart, *Atlas of Medieval Jewish History,* p. 21.

18. H. H. Ben-Sasson, "Effects of Religious Animosity on the Jews," in *A History of the Jewish People,* ed. H. H. Ben-Sasson (Cambridge, Mass.: Harvard University Press, 1976), p. 403.

19. Beinart, *Atlas of Medieval Jewish History,* p. 22.

20. Anonymous, "Ashkenaz," in *Encyclopedia Judaica* (Jerusalem: Judaica Multimedia, 1972).

21. J. Yahalom, "*Piyyut* as Poetry," in *The Synagogue in Late Antiquity,* ed. Lee I. Levine (Philadelphia: American Schools of Oriental Research, 1987), pp. 111–26.

22. T. Carmi, ed., *The Penguin Book of Hebrew Verse* (New York: Viking Press, 1981), p. 207.

23. Aaron Rothkoff, "Rashi: His Life," in *Encyclopedia Judaica* (Jerusalem: Judaica Multimedia, 1972).

24. Joseph L. Baron, ed., *A Treasury of Jewish Quotations* (Northvale, N.J.: Jason Aronson, 1985), p. 98.

25. Ibid., p. 49.

26. Ibid., p. 272.

27. Ibid., p. 480.

28. Ibid., p. 275.

29. Avraham Grossman, "Rashi: Main Characteristics of His Commentary," in *Encyclopedia Judaica* (Jerusalem: Judaica Multimedia, 1972).

30. Baron, ed., *A Treasury of Jewish Quotations,* p. 64.

31. Ibid., p. 66.

32. Jona Fraenkel, "Rashi: Aspects of His Commentary," in *Encyclopedia Judaica* (Jerusalem: Judaica Multimedia, 1972).

33. Baron, ed., *A Treasury of Jewish Quotations,* p. 47.
34. Ibid., p. 139.
35. Ben-Sasson, "Effects of Religious Animosity on the Jews," p. 412.
36. Ibid., p. 413.
37. Ibid., p. 417.
38. Carmi, ed., *The Penguin Book of Hebrew Verse,* pp. 247–48; author's translation.

Chapter 7. Under the Minaret

1. Alain Cohen and Georges Nizan, *The Jews of Djerba* (Teaneck, N.J.: Ergo Media, 1987), video; Ken Blady, *Jewish Communities in Exotic Places* (Northvale, N.J.: Jason Aronson, 2000), pp. 333–43.
2. Haim Beinart, *Atlas of Medieval Jewish History* (New York: Simon and Schuster, 1992).
3. Norman A. Stillman, *The Jews of Arab Lands: A History and Source Book* (Philadelphia: Jewish Publication Society, 1979); Bernard Lewis, *The Jews of Islam* (Princeton, N.J.: Princeton University Press, 1987).
4. Reuven Firestone, "Jewish Culture in the Formative Period of Islam," in *Cultures of the Jews: A New History,* ed. David Biale (New York: Schocken Books, 2002), pp. 266–301.
5. Ibid., p. 284.
6. Abraham J. Heschel, *Maimonides: A Biography,* trans. Joachim Neugroschel (New York: Doubleday, 1991).
7. Ibid., pp. 238–39.
8. Raymond P. Scheindlin, "Merchants and Intellectuals, Rabbis and Poets: Judeo-Arabic Culture in the Golden Age of Islam," in *Cultures of the Jews: A New History,* ed. David Biale (New York: Schocken Books, 2002), p. 327.
9. Benjamin of Tudela, "Benjamin of Tudela (1165–73)," in *Jewish Travelers in the Middle Ages: 19 Firsthand Accounts,* ed. Elkan Nathan Adler (1930; reprint, New York: Dover Publications, 1987), pp. 38–63.
10. Shlomo Deshen, *The Mellah Society: Jewish Community Life in Sherifian Morocco* (Chicago: University of Chicago Press, 1989).
11. Laurence D. Loeb, "Gender, Marriage, and Social Conflict in Habban," in *Sephardi and Middle Eastern Jewries: History and Culture in the Modern Era,* ed. Harvey E. Goldberg (Bloomington: Indiana University Press, 1996), pp. 259–76.
12. Harvey E. Goldberg, *Jewish Life in Muslim Libya: Rivals and Relatives* (Chicago: University of Chicago Press, 1990), chap. 4.
13. Herbert C. Dobrinsky, *A Treasury of Sephardic Laws and Customs* (Hoboken, N.J.: Ktav Publishing House, 1986); Raymond Apple, Raphael Posner, and Reuben Kashani, "Marriage," in *Encyclopedia Judaica,* CD-ROM ed. (Jerusalem: Judaica Multimedia, 1972).
14. Goldberg, *Jewish Life in Muslim Libya,* chap. 4.
15. Norman A. Stillman, "Middle Eastern and North African Jewries Confront Modernity," in *Sephardi and Middle Eastern Jewries: History and Culture in the Modern Era,* ed. Harvey E. Goldberg (Bloomington: Indiana University Press, 1996), pp. 59–72.
16. Bernard Lewis, *What Went Wrong? Western Impact and Middle Eastern Response* (New York: Oxford University Press, 2002), p. 154.
17. Goldberg, *Jewish Life in Muslim Libya,* chap. 7.
18. Ibid., p. 121.
19. Shlomo Deshen and Moshe Shokeid, *The Predicament of Homecoming: Cultural and Social Life of North African Immigrants in Israel* (Ithaca, N.Y.: Cornell University Press, 1974); Harvey E. Goldberg, ed., *Sephardi and Middle Eastern Jewries: History and Culture in the Modern Era* (Bloomington: Indiana University Press, 1996).

Chapter 8. Spain and Beyond

1. T. Carmi, ed., *The Penguin Book of Hebrew Verse* (New York: Viking Press, 1981), p. xx. Author's translation.
2. Jane S. Gerber, *The Jews of Spain: A History of the Sephardic Experience* (New York: Free Press, 1992).
3. Maria Rosa Menocal, *The Ornament of the World: How Muslims, Jews, and Christians Created a Culture of Tolerance in Medieval Spain* (Boston: Little, Brown, 2002), p. 12.

4. Paloma Díaz-Mas, *Sephardim: The Jews from Spain,* trans. George K. Zucker (Chicago: University of Chicago Press, 1992).

5. Carmi, ed., *The Penguin Book of Hebrew Verse,* p. 286. Author's translation.

6. It may be significant that the poem has 149 lines, the same as the total number of the Psalms.

7. Carmi, ed., *The Penguin Book of Hebrew Verse,* p. 291. Author's translation.

8. Ibid., p. 324, L-333. Author's translation.

9. Ibid., pp. 340, 346. Author's translation.

10. Ibid., p. 347. Author's translation.

11. Isaac Jack Lévy, "The Yearning for the Promised Land in Sephardic Literature and Folklore," in *Jewish Culture and the Hispanic World: Essays in Memory of Joseph H. Silverman,* ed. Samuel G. Armistead and Mishael M. Caspi (Newark, Del.: Juan de la Cuesta, 2001), pp. 303–19.

12. R. Chisdai, "The Epistle of R. Chisdai, Son of Isaac (of Blessed Memory) to the King of the Khozars," in *Jewish Travelers in the Middle Ages: 19 Firsthand Accounts,* ed. Elkan Nathan Adler (1930; reprint, New York: Dover Publications, 1987), p. 23. The name sometimes appears as "Hasdai" or other variants.

13. Jesús Peláez del Rosal, "Hasdai Ibn Shaprut in the Court of Abd-Ar-Raman III," in *The Jews in Cordoba (X–XII Centuries),* ed. Jesús Peláez del Rosal (Córdoba, Spain: Ediciones el Almendro, 1991), pp. 61–77.

14. Chisdai, "Epistle," pp. 24–25.

15. Carlos Carrete Parrondo, "The Renovating Legacy Left by the Spanish Jews," in *The Jews in Cordoba (X–XII Centuries),* ed. Jesús Peláez del Rosal (Córdoba, Spain: Ediciones el Almendro, 1991), pp. 29–42.

16. Gerber, *The Jews of Spain,* p. 28.

17. Eli Barnavi, *A Historical Atlas of the Jewish People: From the Time of the Patriarchs to the Present,* trans. Miriam Eliav-Feldon (New York: Schocken Books, 1992), p. 96.

18. Gerber, *The Jews of Spain,* p. 80.

19. Barnavi, *A Historical Atlas of the Jewish People.*

20. Haim Beinart, "The Jews in Spain," in *The Jewish World: History and Culture of the Jewish People,* ed. Elie Kedourie (New York: Harry N. Abrams, 1979), pp. 161–67.

21. H. H. Ben-Sasson, "Social Life and Cultural Achievement," in *A History of the Jewish People,* ed. H. H. Ben-Sasson (Cambridge, Mass.: Harvard University Press, 1976), pp. 558–59.

22. Ibid., p. 558.

23. James Carroll, *Constantine's Sword: The Church and the Jews: A History* (New York: Houghton Mifflin, 2001), p. 309.

24. Robert M. Seltzer, *Jewish People, Jewish Thought: The Jewish Experience in History* (New York: Macmillan, 1980), p. 361.

25. Ben-Sasson, "Social Life and Cultural Achievement," p. 465.

26. Seltzer, *Jewish People, Jewish Thought,* p. 362.

27. B. Netanyahu, *The Marranos of Spain: From the Late Fourteenth to the Early Sixteenth Century, According to Contemporary Hebrew Sources,* 3rd revised and expanded edition (New York: Columbia University Press, 1999); B. Netanyahu, *The Origins of the Inquisition in Fifteenth-Century Spain,* 2nd ed. (New York: New York Review of Books, 2001).

28. Seltzer, *Jewish People, Jewish Thought,* p. 366.

29. Beinart, "The Jews in Spain," p. 83.

30. Gerber, *The Jews of Spain,* p. 140.

31. Ibid., p. 141.

32. Judeo-Spanish is sometimes referred to as Judezmo or, incorrectly, as Ladino.

33. Isaac Benabu, "Judeo-Spanish," in *The Blackwell Companion to Jewish Culture: From the Eighteenth Century to the Present,* ed. Glenda Abramson (Oxford, England: Blackwell Reference, 1989).

34. The font, designed by a printer of the Talmud for Rashi's commentary, is always called "Rashi script."

35. From the Ladino Jewish Bible, *Tora, Neviim, Ketuvim: Ladino,* in Hebrew with Ladino in Hebrew (Rashi) characters on the facing pages. The transliteration is courtesy of Dr. Isaac Jack Lévy, professor emeritus of Romance languages, University of South Carolina. In this and all other Ladino and Judeo-Spanish passages, I try to follow the orthography used by *Aki Yerushalayim,* a leading journal of Sephardic studies. For clarity of pronunciation I have used the Castilian practice of accenting the emphasized last syllable in some words, considered acceptable by many scholars.

36. Marc D. Angel and David Romey, "The Ubiquitous Sephardic Proverb," in *Studies in Sephardic Culture: The David N. Barocas Memorial Volume,* ed. Marc D. Angel (New York: Sepher-Hermon Press, 1980), pp. 57–64.
37. Rebecca Amato Levy, *I Remember Rhodes* (New York: Sepher-Hermon Press, 1987), p. 111.
38. Ibid., p. 91.
39. Ibid., p. 110.
40. Ibid., pp. 110–11.
41. Díaz-Mas, *Sephardim,* p. 113.
42. Levy, *I Remember Rhodes,* p. 129. Author's translation.
43. Ibid., p. 127. Author's translation.
44. Ibid., p. 139. Author's translation.
45. Díaz-Mas, *Sephardim,* p. 123. Author's translation.
46. Netanyahu, *The Origins of the Inquisition;* Netanyahu, *The Marranos of Spain.*
47. Kenneth R. Scholberg, "Alboraycos," in *Encyclopedia Judaica* (Jerusalem: Judaica Multimedia, 1972).
48. Martin A. Cohen, "New Christians," in *Encyclopedia Judaica* (Jerusalem: Judaica Multimedia, 1972).
49. Trudi Alexy, *The Mezuzah in the Madonna's Foot* (New York: Simon and Schuster, 1993), p. 261.
50. Franz Kobler, ed., *Letters of Jews through the Ages: A Self-Portrait of the Jewish People,* vol. 2, *From the Renaissance to the Emancipation* (New York: Hebrew Publishing, 1952), p. 430.
51. Ibid., p. 432.
52. Alexy, *The Mezuzah in the Madonna's Foot,* p. 17.
53. Ibid., p. 268.
54. Netanyahu, *The Origins of the Inquisition.*
55. Timothy Oelman, ed., *Marrano Poets of the Seventeenth Century: An Anthology of the Poetry of João Pinto Delgado, Antonio Enríquez Gómez, and Miguel De Barrios* (London: Fairleigh Dickinson University Press, 1982), p. 16.
56. Ibid., p. 63.
57. Alexy, *The Mezuzah in the Madonna's Foot,* p. 273.
58. Kenneth Moore, *Those of the Street: The Catholic-Jews of Mallorca* (Notre Dame, Ind.: University of Notre Dame Press, 1976), p. 12.
59. James R. Ross, *Fragile Branches: Travels through the Jewish Diaspora* (New York: Riverhead Books, 2000), pp. 164–65.
60. Alexy, *The Mezuzah in the Madonna's Foot.*
61. Ibid., p. 274.
62. Beinart, "The Jews in Spain," p. 82.
63. Ibid., p. 99.
64. Netanyahu, *The Marranos of Spain;* Netanyahu, *The Origins of the Inquisition.*
65. Barnavi, *A Historical Atlas of the Jewish People,* p. 142.
66. Díaz-Mas, *Sephardim,* p. 38.
67. Nicholas de Lange, *Atlas of the Jewish World* (Oxford, England, and New York: Equinox/Facts on File, 1984), p. 49.
68. Beinart, "The Jews in Spain," p. 99.
69. Martin Gilbert, *Atlas of Jewish History,* 3rd ed (New York: Dorset Press/Macmillan, 1977), p. 79.
70. Ibid., pp. 50–51.
71. Haim Beinart, *Atlas of Medieval Jewish History* (New York: Simon and Schuster, 1992), p. 102.
72. Jacob Barnai, "On the History of the Jews in the Ottoman Empire," in *Sephardi Jews in the Ottoman Empire: Aspects of Material Culture,* ed. Esther Juhasz (Jerusalem: Israel Museum, 1990), p. 26.
73. Ibid., p. 30.
74. Ibid., p. 26.
75. Hava Tirosh-Rothschild, *Between Two Worlds: The Life and Thought of Rabbi David Ben Judah Messer Leon* (Albany: State University of New York Press, 1991), p. 81.
76. Esther Juhasz, "Synagogues," in *Sephardi Jews in the Ottoman Empire: Aspects of Material Culture,* ed. Esther Juhasz (Jerusalem: Israel Museum, 1990), p. 37.
77. Esther Juhasz, "Textiles for the Home and Synagogue," in *Sephardi Jews in the Ottoman Empire: Aspects of Material Culture,* ed. Esther Juhasz (Jerusalem: Israel Museum, 1990), pp. 65–119.
78. Esther Juhasz, "Costume," in *Sephardi Jews in the Ottoman Empire: Aspects of Material Culture,* ed. Esther Juhasz (Jerusalem: Israel Museum, 1990), pp. 121–70; Miriam Russo-Katz, "Jew-

elry," in *Sephardi Jews in the Ottoman Empire: Aspects of Material Culture,* ed. Esther Juhasz (Jerusalem: Israel Museum, 1990), pp. 173–95.

79. Shalom Sabar, "Decorated *Kettubot,*" in *Sephardi Jews in the Ottoman Empire: Aspects of Material Culture,* ed. Esther Juhasz (Jerusalem: Israel Museum, 1990), p. 224.
80. Esther Juhasz, "Marriage," in *Sephardi Jews in the Ottoman Empire: Aspects of Material Culture,* ed. Esther Juhasz (Jerusalem: Israel Museum, 1990), pp. 197–217.
81. Miriam Russo-Katz, "Childbirth," in *Sephardi Jews in the Ottoman Empire: Aspects of Material Culture,* ed. Esther Juhasz (Jerusalem: Israel Museum, 1990), pp. 255–70.
82. Isaac Jack Lévy, *Jewish Rhodes: A Lost Culture* (Berkeley, Calif.: Judah L. Magnes Museum, 1989), p. 40.
83. Esther Benbassa and Aron Rodrigue, *Sephardi Jewry: A History of the Judeo-Spanish Community, Fourteenth–Twentieth Centuries* (Berkeley: University of California Press, 2000), pp. 83–89.
84. Ayse Gürsan-Salzmann, *Anyos Munchos I Buenos: Turkey's Sephardim: 1492–1992* (Philadelphia: Blue Flower/Photo Review, 1991).
85. Raul Hilberg, *The Destruction of the European Jews,* revised and definitive edition, 3 vols. (New York and London: Holmes and Meier, 1985), vol. 2, p. 692; Benbassa and Rodrigue, *Sephardi Jewry,* chap. 5. The minions here included the young Kurt Waldheim, who would one day be secretary-general of the United Nations.
86. Hilberg, *The Destruction of the European Jews,* p. 1220; Benbassa and Rodrigue, *Sephardi Jewry,* pp. 256–57.
87. Michael Bar-Zohar, *Beyond Hitler's Grasp: The Heroic Rescue of Bulgaria's Jews* (Holbrook, Mass.: Adams Media, 1998).
88. Isaac Jack Lévy, *And the World Stood Silent: Sephardic Poetry of the Holocaust* (Urbana and Chicago: University of Illinois Press, 1989).
89. Carmi, ed., *The Penguin Book of Hebrew Verse,* p. 296. Author's translation.

Chapter 9. Brightness

1. 1 Sam. 28:7–13, King James Version.
2. 2 Kings 2:11 KJV.
3. Dan. 7:2–11 KJV.
4. Ezek. 1:4–6 KJV.
5. Ezek. 1:24–25 KJV.
6. Gershom Scholem, *Kabbalah* (New York: Dorset Press, 1987), p. 12.
7. Haim Nachman Bialik, *Hetsits Va'met: Looked and Died,* trans. Shlomit Finkelstein and David Ritz Finkelstein (Atlanta: privately published, 1997).
8. Fischel Lachower and Isaiah Tishby, *The Wisdom of the Zohar: An Anthology of Texts,* vol. 1, trans. David Goldstein (London: Oxford University Press, 1989), p. 151.
9. 1 Kings 19:11–12 KJV. Shlomit Finkelstein suggests "a voice out of subtle stillness" as a more precise translation of *kol demamah dakah.*
10. Scholem, *Kabbalah,* p. 5.
11. Ibid., p. 153.
12. Robert M. Seltzer, *Jewish People, Jewish Thought: The Jewish Experience in History* (New York: Macmillan, 1980), p. 430.
13. Scholem, *Kabbalah,* p. 152.
14. Seltzer, *Jewish People, Jewish Thought,* p. 432.
15. David R. Blumenthal, *Facing the Abusing God: A Theology of Protest* (Louisville, Ky.: Westminster, John Knox Press, 1993).
16. Lachower and Tishby, *The Wisdom of the Zohar,* p. 274.
17. Ibid., p. 290.
18. Scholem, *Kabbalah,* p. 164.
19. Isaiah Tishby, *The Wisdom of the Zohar: An Anthology of Texts,* vol. 3, trans. David Goldstein (London: Oxford University Press, 1989), p. 1123.
20. Ibid., p. 1125.
21. Ibid., p. 1129.
22. Gershom Scholem, ed., *Zohar: The Book of Splendor: Basic Readings from the Kabbalah* (New York: Schocken Books, 1949), pp. 63–64.
23. Exod. 20:5 KJV.
24. Scholem, *Zohar,* pp. 68–69.
25. Ibid., p. 93.

26. Isa. 65:22, 25:8, cited ibid., p. 93.
27. Joshua Trachtenberg, *Jewish Magic and Superstition: A Study in Folk Religion* (New York: Atheneum, 1977).
28. Ibid.
29. Aviva Cantor, "The Lilith Question," in *On Being a Jewish Feminist: A Reader,* ed. Susannah Heschel (New York: Schocken Books, 1983), pp. 40–50.
30. Fischel Lachower and Isaiah Tishby, *The Wisdom of the Zohar: An Anthology of Texts,* vol. 2, trans. David Goldstein (London: Oxford University Press, 1989), pp. 538–39.
31. Trachtenberg, *Jewish Magic and Superstition,* p. 29.
32. Ibid., p. 31.
33. Isaac Bashevis Singer, *Collected Stories,* (New York: Farrar, Straus and Giroux, 1982), pp. 131–39.
34. Trachtenberg, *Jewish Magic and Superstition,* p. 55.
35. Ibid., p. 43.
36. Ibid., p. 126.
37. Ibid., p. 119.
38. Ibid., p. 160.
39. Singer, *Collected Stories,* pp. 179–87.
40. Stephen Aris, *The Jews in Business* (London: Cape, 1970).
41. Mark Twain, *Concerning the Jews* (Philadelphia: Running Press, 1985), pp. 14–15.
42. Theodor Herzl, *The Diaries of Theodor Herzl,* ed., trans., and with an introduction by Marvin Lowenthal (New York: Dial Press, Grosset and Dunlap, 1956), p. 9.
43. Uzi Shavit, "Haskalah [Enlightenment]," in *The Blackwell Companion to Jewish Culture: From the Eighteenth Century to the Present,* ed. Glenda Abramson (Oxford, England: Basil Blackwell, 1989), pp. 308–12.
44. Charles E. Silberman, *A Certain People: American Jews and Their Lives Today* (New York: Summit Books, 1985), p. 33.
45. Ritchie Robertson, *Heine* (New York: Grove Press, 1988).
46. Jeffrey L. Sammons, "Heine, Heinrich," in *The Blackwell Companion to Jewish Culture: From the Eighteenth Century to the Present,* ed. Glenda Abramson (Oxford, England: Basil Blackwell, 1989), pp. 325–27.
47. Silberman, *A Certain People,* p. 33.
48. Ibid., p. 31.
49. Heinrich Heine, *Selected Verse,* intro., ed., and trans. Peter Branscombe (Middlesex, England: Penguin Books, 1968), pp. 199–206. Translation by the author.
50. Heinrich Heine, *Judisches Manifest. Eine Auswahl aus seinen Werken, Briefen und Gesprachen Herausgegeben von Hugo Bieber* (New York: Mary S. Rosenberg, 1946).
51. Eli Barnavi, *A Historical Atlas of the Jewish People: From the Time of the Patriarchs to the Present,* trans. Miriam Eliav-Feldon (New York: Schocken Books, 1992), p. 173.
52. Karl Marx, *Selected Writings,* ed. David McLellan (Oxford, England: Oxford University Press, 1977), p. 58.
53. Erich Fromm, *Beyond the Chains of Illusion: My Encounter with Marx and Freud* (New York: Simon and Schuster, Trident Press, 1962).
54. Calvin Goldscheider and Alan S. Zuckerman, *The Transformation of the Jews* (Chicago: University of Chicago, 1984), p. 102.
55. John Murray Cuddihy, *The Ordeal of Civility: Freud, Marx, Lévi-Strauss, and the Jewish Struggle with Modernity* (New York: Dell, 1974), p. 68.
56. Ibid., p. 229.
57. Isaac Deutscher, "The Non-Jewish Jew," in *The Non-Jewish Jew and Other Essays,* ed. Tamara Deutscher (New York: Hill and Wang, Farrar, Straus and Giroux, 1968), p. 26.
58. Ibid., p. 27.
59. "Jewish Nobel Prize Winners." Jewish Virtual Library, division of American-Israeli Cooperative Enterprise. www.us-israel.org/jsource/judaism/nobels.html

Chapter 10. Ends of the Earth

1. James Quirin, *The Evolution of the Ethiopian Jews: A History of the Beta Israel (Falasha) to 1920* (Philadelphia: University of Pennsylvania Press, 1992).
2. Ibid., p. 17.
3. Benjamin of Tudela, "Benjamin of Tudela (1165–73)," in *Jewish Travelers in the Middle Ages: 19*

Firsthand Accounts, ed. Elkan Nathan Adler (1930; reprint, New York: Dover Publications, 1987), p. 60.

4. Quirin, *The Evolution of the Ethiopian Jews,* p. 53.

5. Ibid., p. 58.

6. Ibid., pp. 72–73.

7. Ibid., p. 79.

8. Ibid., p. 119.

9. Hagar Salamon, "Religious Interplay on an African Stage: Ethiopian Jews in Christian Ethiopia," in *Cultures of the Jews: A New History,* ed. David Biale (New York: Schocken Books, 2002), pp. 977–1008; Hagar Salamon, *The Hyena People: Ethiopian Jews in Christian Ethiopia* (Berkeley: University of California Press, 1999).

10. Quirin, *The Evolution of the Ethiopian Jews,* p. 147.

11. The word *Sanbat* suggests a very ancient origin for these Jews, as does their failure to observe Chanukah, but their marking of Purim may suggest a lower limit for separation from the Jewish mainstream of around the fourth century B.C.E.

12. Quirin, *The Evolution of the Ethiopian Jews,* p. 169.

13. Meyer Levin and Larry Frisch, *The Falashas* (Teaneck, N.J.: Ergo Media, 1973), video.

14. Ibid.

15. Claire Safran, *Secret Exodus* (New York: Prentice-Hall, 1987), p. 76.

16. Tom Jarriel, *20/20: Operation Solomon,* ABC Television, May 27, 1991.

17. Ibid.

18. Safran, *Secret Exodus,* p. 169.

19. Adam Chesnick, "'Be Israeli, but Don't Forget Where You Came From': Obstacles to Integration among Ethiopian-Jewish University Students in Israel" (bachelor's thesis, Emory University, 2000), p. 85.

20. Ibid., p. 62.

21. Mitchell Ginsburg, "Brief Encounter: Azanu Mekonen, Lighting a Way Forward for Israel's Ethiopian Jews," *Jerusalem Report,* April 22, 2002, p. 8.

22. Safran, *Secret Exodus,* p. 159.

23. Eli Barnavi, *A Historical Atlas of the Jewish People: From the Time of the Patriarchs to the Present,* trans. Miriam Eliav-Feldon (New York: Schocken Books, 1992), pp. 182–83.

24. Joan G. Roland, *Jews in British India: Identity in a Colonial Era* (Hanover, N.H.: University Press of New England, 1989).

25. Ruby Daniel and Barbara C. Johnson, *Ruby of Cochin: An Indian Jewish Woman Remembers* (Philadelphia: Jewish Publication Society, 1995), p. 8.

26. Nathan Katz and Ellen S. Goldberg, "The Ritual Enactments of the Cochin Jews: The Powers of Purity and Nobility," *Journal of Ritual Studies* 4, no. 2 (1990): 199–238.

27. Nathan Katz and Ellen S. Goldberg, "Asceticism and Caste in the Passover Observances of the Cochin Jews," *Journal of the American Academy of Religion* 57, no. 1 (1989): 53–82.

28. Daniel and Johnson, *Ruby of Cochin,* pp. 171–73.

29. Ibid., p. 178.

30. Ibid., p. 179.

31. Ibid., p. 180.

32. Ibid., p. 188.

33. Roland, *Jews in British India,* p. 13.

34. Nathan Katz and Ellen S. Goldberg, *The Last Jews of Cochin: Jewish Identity in Hindu India* (Columbia: University of South Carolina Press, 1993).

35. Roland, *Jews in British India,* "Conclusion."

36. Rudolf Loewenthal and Editorial Staff, "Kaifeng," in *Encyclopedia Judaica* (Jerusalem: Judaica Multimedia [Israel], 1972).

37. Irene Eber, "Kaifeng Jews: The Sinification of Identity," in *The Jews of China,* vol. 1, *Historical and Comparative Perspectives,* ed. Jonathan Goldstein (Armonk, N.Y., and London: M. E. Sharpe, 1999), pp. 22–35.

38. Barnavi, *A Historical Atlas of the Jewish People.*

39. Andrew H. Plaks, "The Confucianization of the Kaifeng Jews: Interpretations of the Kaifeng Stelae Inscriptions," in *The Jews of China,* vol. 1, *Historical and Comparative Perspectives,* ed. Jonathan Goldstein (Armonk, N.Y., and London: M. E. Sharpe, 1999), p. 38.

40. Eber, "Kaifeng Jews."

41. Plaks, "The Confucianization of the Kaifeng Jews," p. 40.

42. Ibid., p. 42.
43. Ibid., p. 41.
44. Ibid., p. 45.
45. Jonathan Goldstein, "Historical Introduction," in *The Jews of China,* vol. 1, *Historical and Comparative Perspectives,* ed. Jonathan Goldstein (Armonk, N.Y., and London: M. E. Sharpe, 1999), p. xv.
46. Zhou Xun, "Jews in Chinese Culture: Representations and Realities," in *Jewries at the Frontier: Accommodation, Identity, Conflict,* ed. Sander L. Gilman and Milton Shain (Urbana and Chicago: University of Illinois Press, 1999), pp. 225–26; Ken Blady, *Jewish Communities in Exotic Places* (Northvale, N.J., and Jerusalem: Jason Aronson, 2000), pp. 253–84.
47. Nancy Shatzman Steinhardt, "The Synagogue at Kaifeng: Sino-Judaic Architecture of the Diaspora," in *The Jews of China,* vol. 1, *Historical and Comparative Perspectives,* ed. Jonathan Goldstein (Armonk, N.Y., and London: M. E. Sharpe, 1999).
48. Ibid., p. 19.
49. Katz and Goldberg, "Asceticism and Caste," p. 76.
50. Loewenthal and Staff, "Kaifeng."
51. Wendy R. Abraham, "Memories of Kaifeng's Jewish Descendants Today: Historical Significance in Light of Observations by Westerners since 1605," in *The Jews of China,* vol. 1, *Historical and Comparative Perspectives,* ed. Jonathan Goldstein (Armonk, N.Y., and London: M. E. Sharpe, 1999), pp. 71–86.
52. Steven Calcote and Jonathan Shulman, *Minyan in Kaifeng* (New York: Gorp Brothers, Interlock Media, 1999).
53. Ibid.
54. Ernest G. Heppner, *Shanghai Refuge: A Memoir of the World War II Jewish Ghetto* (Lincoln: University of Nebraska Press, 1993).
55. Blady, *Jewish Communities in Exotic Places.*
56. Ester Muchawsky-Schnapper, *The Jews of Yemen: Highlights of the Israel Museum Collection* (Jerusalem: Israel Museum, 1994), p. 60.
57. Yitzhak Zvi Langermann, ed., *Yemenite Midrash: Philosophical Commentaries on the Torah: An Anthology of Writings from the Golden Age of Judaism in the Yemen* (San Francisco: HarperSanFrancisco, 1996); Yosef Tobi, "Challenges to Tradition: Jewish Cultures in Yemen, Iraq, Iran, Afghanistan, and Bukhara," in *Cultures of the Jews: A New History,* ed. David Biale (New York: Schocken Books, 2002), pp. 933–74.
58. Blady, *Jewish Communities in Exotic Places.*
59. Tasgola Karla Bruner, "Home Alone with the Taliban," *Jerusalem Report,* January 3, 2000, p. 25.
60. Ehud Ya'ari, "Twilight Time," *Jerusalem Report,* June 4, 2001, pp. 32–33.
61. Frank Brown, "The Last of the Saturday People," *Jerusalem Report,* November 19, 2001, pp. 72–74.
62. Blady, *Jewish Communities in Exotic Places,* pp. 155–70.
63. Ibid., pp. 91–110; Yona Sahar, ed., *The Folk Literature of the Kurdistani Jews: An Anthology* (New Haven, Conn.: Yale University Press, 1982).
64. Bryan Schwartz, "Down in the Jungle," *Jerusalem Report,* January 28, 2002, pp. 32–33; James R. Ross, *Fragile Branches: Travels through the Jewish Diaspora* (New York: Riverhead Books, 2000), pp. 125–48.
65. Matt Nesviski, "Bagels, Lox and Sushi," *Jerusalem Report,* September 9, 2002, pp. 34–35.
66. Bryan Schwartz, "Moses' Cowboys Ride On," *Jerusalem Report,* April 8, 2002, pp. 36–38.
67. Tibor Krausz, "Matters of Faith," *Jerusalem Report,* December 18, 2000, p. 25.
68. Seth L. Wolitz, "Bifocality in Jewish Identity in Texas-Jewish Experience," in *Jewries at the Frontier: Accommodation, Identity, Conflict,* ed. Sander L. Gilman and Milton Shain (Urbana and Chicago: University of Illinois Press, 1999), pp. 185–208.
69. Bernard Reisman, "Alaskan Jews Discover the Last Frontier," in *Jewries at the Frontier: Accommodation, Identity, Conflict,* ed. Sander L. Gilman and Milton Shain (Urbana and Chicago: University of Illinois Press, 1999), pp. 111–26.
70. Howard V. Epstein, *Jews in Small Towns: Legends and Legacies* (Santa Rosa, Calif.: Vision Books International, 1997).
71. This intriguing model of Jewish history is presented in Sander L. Gilman, "Introduction: The Frontier as a Model for Jewish History," in *Jewries at the Frontier: Accommodation, Identity, Conflict,* ed. Sander L. Gilman and Milton Shain (Urbana and Chicago: University of Illinois Press, 1999), pp. 1–25.

Chapter 11. Yidn

1. Calvin Goldscheider and Alan S. Zuckerman, *The Transformation of the Jews* (Chicago: University of Chicago Press, 1986).
2. Ibid., pp. 16–17.
3. Ibid., p. 20.
4. Ibid.
5. Naphtali Herz (Hartwig) Wessely, "Words of Peace and Truth," in *The Jew in the Modern World: A Documentary History,* ed. Paul R. Mendes-Flohr and Jehuda Reinharz (New York: Oxford University Press, 1980), pp. 62–67.
6. Rabbi Ben Nathan of Lissa, "A Sermon Contra Wessely," in *The Jew in the Modern World: A Documentary History,* ed. Paul R. Mendes-Flohr and Jehuda Reinharz (New York: Oxford University Press, 1980), pp. 67–69.
7. The Central Government of Padua, "Abolition of the Ghetto in Padua (August 28, 1797)" and "Destruction of the Ghetto Walls in Padua (September 15, 1797)," in *The Jew in the Modern World: A Documentary History* (New York: Oxford University Press, 1980), pp. 111–12.
8. Count Louis Mathieu Molé, "Napoleon's Instructions to the Assembly of Jewish Notables (July 29, 1806)," in *The Jew in the Modern World: A Documentary History,* ed. Paul R. Mendes-Flohr and Jehuda Reinharz (New York: Oxford University Press, 1980), pp. 113–14.
9. Assembly of Jewish Notables, "Answers to Napoleon," in *The Jew in the Modern World: A Documentary History,* ed. Paul R. Mendes-Flohr and Jehuda Reinharz (New York: Oxford University Press, 1980), p. 118.
10. Ibid., p. 119.
11. Count Louis Mathieu Molé, "Summons for Convening the Paris Sanhedrin (September 18, 1806)," in *The Jew in the Modern World: A Documentary History,* ed. Paul R. Mendes-Flohr and Jehuda Reinharz (New York: Oxford University Press, 1980), pp. 121–23.
12. Reform Rabbinical Conference at Frankfurt, "The Question of Messianism," in *The Jew in the Modern World: A Documentary History,* ed. Paul R. Mendes-Flohr and Jehuda Reinharz (New York: Oxford University Press, 1980), pp. 163–65.
13. Cynthia Ozick, "The Heretic: The Mythic Passions of Gershom Scholem," *New Yorker,* September 2, 2002, pp. 143–48.
14. Ibid., p. 143.
15. Ibid., p. 147.
16. Mark Zborowski and Elizabeth Herzog, *Life Is with People: The Culture of the Shtetl* (New York: Schocken Books, 1952).
17. *Gefilte* actually means "filled." Traditionally, the flesh was removed from the whole fish, chopped, and combined with spices, then stuffed back into the fish. Recently the word has come to mean just the stuffing shaped into oblong patties.
18. Zborowski and Herzog, *Life Is with People,* p. 131.
19. Ibid., pp. 428–29.
20. Jerome Badanes, *Image Before My Eyes,* ed. Josh Waletzky (Teaneck, N.J./New York: Ergo Media, YIVO Institute for Jewish Research, 1991), film. Author's translation.
21. Decades after the Holocaust, some elderly Polish Jews—or, as they would say it, Poles of Jewish ancestry—still insistently asserted their Polishness, in Polish, denying their Jewish ethnicity.
22. Badanes, *Image Before My Eyes.*
23. Irving Howe, *World of Our Fathers* (New York: Harcourt Brace, 1976), p. xix.
24. Ibid., p. 27.
25. Ibid.
26. Ibid., p. 34.
27. Ibid., p. 40.
28. Irving Howe and Kenneth Libo, *How We Lived: A Documentary History of Immigrant Jews in America, 1880–1930* (New York: Richard Marek, 1979), p. 25.
29. Ibid., p. 116.
30. Ibid., p. 117.
31. Ibid., pp. 246–47.
32. Ibid., p. 253.
33. Abraham Cahan, *Yekl and the Imported Bridegroom and Other Stories of the New York Ghetto* (New York: Dover, 1970).
34. Ibid., p. 88.

35. Ibid., p. 87.
36. Howe, *World of Our Fathers,* pp. 299–300.
37. Ibid., p. 300.
38. Ibid., p. 305.
39. Mary V. Dearborn, *Love in the Promised Land: The Story of Anzia Yezierska and John Dewey* (New York: Free Press, 1988).
40. Anzia Yezierska, *Bread Givers: A Novel* (New York: George Braziller, Venture Books, 1975).
41. Ibid., p. 95.
42. Ibid., pp. 207–8.
43. Ibid., pp. 293–94.
44. Louise Levitas Henriksen, "Afterword about Anzia Yezierska, by Her Daughter," in *The Open Cage: An Anzia Yezierska Collection,* ed. Alice Kessler-Harris (New York: Persea Books, 1979).
45. Dearborn, *Love in the Promised Land.*
46. Ibid., p. 113.

Chapter 12. Mameh-Loshn

1. Uriel Weinreich, *College Yiddish: An Introduction to the Yiddish Language and to Jewish Life and Culture* (New York: YIVO Institute for Jewish Research, 1979), pp. 50–52, 58–60.
2. Weinreich, *College Yiddish,* pp. 66–68.
3. Harry M. Rabinowicz, *Hasidism: The Movement and Its Masters* (Northvale, N.J.: Jason Aronson, 1988), p. 34.
4. Ibid., p. 34.
5. Ibid., p. 36.
6. Ibid., p. 42.
7. Ibid., p. 45.
8. Ibid., p. 65.
9. Allan Nadler, *The Faith of the Mitnagdim: Rabbinic Responses to Hasidic Rapture* (Baltimore: Johns Hopkins University Press, 1997).
10. Rabinowicz, *Hasidism,* p. 70.
11. Ibid., p. 78.
12. Jerome R. Mintz, *Hasidic People: A Place in the New World* (Cambridge, Mass.: Harvard University Press, 1992).
13. Lis Harris, *Holy Days: The World of a Hasidic Family* (New York: Macmillan, 1986), p. 14.
14. Ibid., p. 122 ff.
15. Jeri Langer, "From Prague to Belz," in *The Jew in the Modern World: A Documentary History,* ed. Paul R. Mendes-Flohr and Jehuda Reinharz (New York: Oxford University Press, 1980), p. 248.
16. Ibid., p. 249.
17. Jerome Badanes, *Image Before My Eyes,* ed. Josh Waletzky (Teaneck, N.J./New York: Ergo Media, YIVO Institute for Jewish Research, 1991), film.
18. Weinreich, *College Yiddish,* pp. 103–4.
19. Ken Frieden, *Classic Yiddish Fiction: Abramovitsh, Sholem Aleichem, and Peretz* (New York: State University of New York Press, 1995).
20. Miriam Ulinover, "With the *Taytsh-Khumesh,*" in *Four Centuries of Jewish Women's Spirituality: A Sourcebook,* ed. Ellen M. Umansky and Dianne Ashton (Boston: Beacon Press, 1992), p. 153.
21. Isaac Bashevis Singer, "Yiddish, the Language of Exile," in *Next Year in Jerusalem: Portraits of the Jew in the Twentieth Century,* ed. Douglas Villiers (New York: Viking Press, 1976), p. 60.
22. Shirley Kumove, *Words Like Arrows: A Treasury of Yiddish Folk Sayings* (New York: Warner Books, 1986).
23. Joseph Leftwich, *Abraham Sutzkever: Partisan Poet* (New York and London: Thomas Yoseloff, 1971).
24. Abraham Sutzkever, *Siberia: A Poem by Abraham Sutzkever, with a Letter on the Poem and Drawings by Marc Chagall,* trans. Jacob Sonntag (London and New York: Abelard-Schuman, 1961), p. 17.
25. Ibid., p. 5.
26. Ibid., p. 13.
27. Leftwich, *Abraham Sutzkever,* p. 29.

28. A. Sutzkever, *A. Sutzkever: Selected Poetry and Prose,* trans. Barbara Harshav and Benjamin Harshav (Berkeley: University of California Press, 1991), p. 166.
29. Leftwich, *Abraham Sutzkever,* p. 43.
30. Ibid., p. 42.
31. Benjamin Harshav, "Sutzkever: Life and Poetry," in *A. Sutzkever: Selected Poetry and Prose,* trans. Barbara Harshav and Benjamin Harshav (Berkeley: University of California Press, 1991), p. 16.
32. Ibid., p. 17.
33. Leftwich, *Abraham Sutzkever,* p. 48.
34. Abraham Sutzkever, *Poetishe Verk, Band Eyns: Lider un Poemes fun di Yorn 1934–47* (Tel Aviv: Yovel, 1963), pp. 278–79. Author's translation.
35. Ibid., pp. 265–68. Author's translation.
36. Ibid., pp. 275–76.
37. Abraham Sutzkever, *Di Feshtung: Lider un Poemes Geshribn in Vilner Geto un in Vald, 1941–1944* (New York: Yiddisher Kultur Farband, 1945), p. 50. Author's translation.
38. Abraham Sutzkever, *Tzviling-Brider: Lider fun Togebikh, 1974–85* (Tel Aviv: Farlag Di Goldene Keyt, 1986), p. 129. Author's translation.

Chapter 13. Smoke

1. Lucy S. Davidowicz, *The War against the Jews: 1933–1945* (New York: Bantam Books, 1975), p. 554.
2. Raul Hilberg, *The Destruction of the European Jews,* revised and definitive ed., vol. 3 (New York and London: Holmes and Meier, 1985), p. 987.
3. Ibid., p. 863.
4. Houston Stewart Chamberlain, *Rasse und Nation,* 8. unverand. aufl ed. (Munchen: J. F. Lehmann, 1920); *Foundations of the Nineteenth Century,* trans. John Lees (New York: H. Fertig, 1977).
5. Davidowicz, *The War against the Jews.*
6. Melvin Konner, "Caveat: The Dangers of Behavioral Biology," in *The Tangled Wing: Biological Constraints on the Human Spirit,* ed. Melvin Konner (New York: Holt Books, 2002), pp. 489–96.
7. Daniel Jonah Goldhagen, *Hitler's Willing Executioners: Ordinary Germans and the Holocaust* (New York: Vintage, Random House, 1996).
8. Stephan L. Chorover, *From Genesis to Genocide: The Meaning of Human Nature and the Power of Behavior Control* (Cambridge, Mass.: MIT Press, 1979); Daniel J. Kevles, *In the Name of Eugenics: Genetics and the Uses of Human Heredity* (New York: Knopf, 1985).
9. In upholding the California law, the state's attorney general used the language of biology: "Degeneracy means that certain areas of brain cells or nerve centers of the individual are more highly or imperfectly developed than the other brain cells, and this causes an unstable state of the nerve system, which may manifest itself in insanity, criminality, idiocy, sexual perversion, or inebriety." He went on to include "many of the confirmed inebriates, prostitutes, tramps, and criminals, as well as habitual paupers" in this class, all of whose members were potentially eligible for legal castration. The *Harvard Law Review* of December 1912—by which time all these state laws had been passed—argued that they would be constitutional, but only in the case of "born criminals." Leon J. Kamin, *The Science and Politics of I.Q.* (Potomac, Md.: L. Erlbaum Associates, distributed by Halsted Press, New York, 1974), pp. 11–12.
10. In 1895 Alfred Ploetz, a physician, wrote *The Excellence of Our Race and the Protection of the Weak;* in 1903 Wilhelm Schallmeyer won a national prize (given by the Krupp armaments family) for his *Inheritance and Selection in the Life-History of Nationalities: A Sociopolitical Study Based upon the Newer Biology;* two scholarly journals concerned with eugenics and racial purity, *Politisch-Anthropologische Revue* and *Archiv für Rassen und Gesellschaftsbiologie* (Archive for Racial and Social Biology) began publication in 1902 and 1904.
11. In 1923, a director of health in Zwickau wrote to the German minister of the interior urging the enactment of a program of eugenic sterilization: "What we racial hygienists promote is not at all new or unheard of. In a cultured nation of the first order, the United States of America, that which we strive toward was introduced and tested long ago." Still skeptical, the interior minister pursued the matter through the German Foreign Office, and after receiving an extensive report became convinced. Through the legal and judicial example set by the United States, eugenics became respectable government business in Weimar Germany. Chorover, *From Genesis to Genocide,* p. 98.

12. Davidowicz, *The War against the Jews,* p. 20.

13. Ibid., p. 95.

14. Martin Gilbert, *The Holocaust: A History of the Jews of Europe during the Second World War* (New York: Holt, Rinehart, and Winston, 1985), p. 33.

15. Hilberg, *The Destruction of the European Jews,* vol. 1, p. 72.

16. Gilbert, *The Holocaust,* p. 48.

17. Hilberg, *The Destruction of the European Jews,* vol. 1, p. 65.

18. Robert N. Proctor, *Racial Hygiene: Medicine under the Nazis* (New York: Cambridge University Press, 1988); Robert Jay Lifton, *The Nazi Doctors: Medicalized Killing and the Psychology of Genocide* (1986; reprint, New York: Basic Books, 2000); Michael H. Kater, *Doctors under Hitler* (Chapel Hill and London: University of North Carolina Press, 1989).

19. Gilbert, *The Holocaust,* p. 60.

20. Anthony Read and David Fisher, *Kristallnacht: The Unleashing of the Holocaust* (New York: Peter Bedrick Books, 1989).

21. Gilbert, *The Holocaust,* p. 71.

22. Ibid., p. 106.

23. Ibid., p. 119.

24. Beginning in the mid-1920s, psychologists armed with IQ tests had played a central role in keeping Jews out of the United States. Kamin, *The Science and Politics of I.Q.*

25. Overall, the inaction of the United States in the face of the destruction of the Jews of Europe was disgraceful. This was especially true of the State Department, the elite national press, and the American Jewish leadership. See David S. Wyman, *The Abandonment of the Jews: America and the Holocaust, 1941–1945* (New York: Pantheon Books, 1985); Deborah Lipstadt, *Beyond Belief: The American Press and the Coming of the Holocaust, 1933–1945* (New York: Free Press, 1986); Rafael Medoff, *The Deafening Silence: American Jewish Leaders and the Holocaust* (New York: Shapolsky Publishers, 1987).

26. Gilbert, *The Holocaust,* p. 155.

27. Ibid., p. 157.

28. Jan T. Gross, *Neighbors: The Destruction of the Jewish Community in Jedwabne, Poland* (Princeton, N.J.: Princeton University Press, 2001).

29. Gilbert, *The Holocaust,* pp. 176–77.

30. Christopher R. Browning, *Ordinary Men: Reserve Police Battalion 101 and the Final Solution in Poland* (New York: HarperCollins, 1992). Based on interviews of 210 of the men in the battalion, this is one of the most remarkable of all Holocaust histories; it shows how ordinary men became mass murderers.

31. Jiri Lipa, "The Fate of Gypsies in Czechoslovakia under Nazi Domination," in *A Mosaic of Victims: Non-Jews Persecuted and Murdered by the Nazis,* ed. Michael Berenbaum (New York: New York University Press, 1990), pp. 207–15.

32. Gilbert, *The Holocaust,* p. 280.

33. Hilberg, *The Destruction of the European Jews,* vol. 3, pp. 883–85.

34. Elie Wiesel, *Night. Dawn. Day* (Northvale, N.J.: Jason Aronson, 1987), pp. 38–43.

35. Rabbi Ephraim Oshry, *Responsa from the Holocaust, Selected and Translated by the Author from "Sh'eilos Utshuvos Mima'akim"* (New York: Judaica Press, 1983), pp. 3–4.

36. Ibid., pp. 9–10.

37. Ibid., p. 13.

38. Ibid., pp. 74–75.

39. Ibid., p. 114.

40. Ibid., pp. 34–35.

41. Ibid., pp. 36–37.

42. Ibid., pp. 51–53.

43. Ibid., pp. 72–73.

44. Ibid., p. 195.

45. Ibid., p. 196.

46. Ibid., p. 165.

47. Ibid., p. 206.

48. Ibid., pp. 173–74.

49. Eva Fogelman, *Conscience and Courage: Rescuers of Jews during the Holocaust* (New York: Anchor Books, Doubleday, 1994); Saul Friedlander, *When Memory Comes,* trans. Helen R. Lane (New York: Farrar, Straus and Giroux, 1979); Philip Hallie, *Lest Innocent Blood Be Shed: The*

Story of the Village of Le Chambon and How Goodness Happened There (New York: Harper Torchbooks, 1985); Samuel P. Oliner and Pearl M. Oliner, *The Altruistic Personality: Rescuers of Jews in Nazi Europe* (New York: Free Press, 1988).

50. Leo Bretholtz, "Leap into Darkness: Speech at Howard Community College, Columbia, Maryland, March 16, 2002," in *C-SPAN Booknotes* (West Lafayette, Ind.: C-SPAN Archives, 2002); Leo Bretholtz and Michael Olesker, *Leap into Darkness: Seven Years on the Run in Wartime Europe* (New York: Anchor Books, 1998).

51. Isaac Jack Lévy, *Jewish Rhodes: A Lost Culture* (Berkeley: Judah L. Magnes Museum, 1989), p. 83.

52. Ruth Beker, "Don't Show Me," in *Voices within the Ark,* ed. Howard Schwartz and Anthony Rudolf (New York: Avon Books, 1980), pp. 772–73. I thank Isaac Lévy for this reference.

53. Sylvia Rothchild, ed., *Voices from the Holocaust* (New York: New American Library, 1981).

54. The word *Holocaust* means sacrifice in the traditional, ritual sense—a burnt offering. Judaism rejects the notion that Hitler's victims were such a sacrifice. *Shoah* means destruction.

55. Richard L. Rubenstein, *After Auschwitz: History, Theology, and Contemporary Judaism,* 2nd ed. (Baltimore: Johns Hopkins University Press, 1992). "Because of the *Shoah,* some of us enter the synagogue . . . struck dumb by words we can no longer honestly utter. All that we can offer is our reverent and attentive silence before the Divine" (p. 200).

56. David R. Blumenthal, *Facing the Abusing God: A Theology of Protest* (Louisville, Ky.: Westminster, John Knox Press, 1993).

57. Ibid., p. xix.

58. Ibid., p. 248.

59. Ibid., p. 284.

60. Ibid., p. 285.

61. Emil L. Fackenheim, *To Mend the World: Foundations of Post-Holocaust Jewish Thought* (Bloomington: Indiana University Press, 1994).

62. I thank Barbara Rosenblit for bringing this point home to me.

63. Deborah Lipstadt, *Denying the Holocaust: The Growing Assault on Truth and Memory* (New York: Free Press, 1993).

64. Simon Wiesenthal, *The Murderers among Us: The Simon Wiesenthal Memoirs,* ed. Joseph Wechsberg (New York: Bantam Books, 1967), pp. 70–75.

65. Simon Wiesenthal, *Justice, Not Vengeance* (New York: Grove and Weidenfeld, 1989).

66. Tadeusz Borowski, *This Way for the Gas, Ladies and Gentlemen,* sel. and trans. Barbara Vedder (New York: Penguin Books, 1976); Judith C. E. Belinfante, Christine Fischer-Defoy, Ad Petersen, and Norman Rosenthal, *Charlotte Salomon: Life? Or Theatre?* (Amsterdam: Jewish Historical Museum, Waanders Publishers, 1998); Jerzy Ficowski, ed., *The Drawings of Bruno Schulz* (Evanston, Ill.: Northwestern University Press, 1990); Lawrence L. Langer, ed., *Art from the Ashes: A Holocaust Anthology* (New York and Oxford: Oxford University Press, 1995).

67. Gerald Green, *The Artists of Terezin: Illustrations by the Inmates of Terezin* (New York: Hawthorn Books, 1978), p. 175; Norbert Troller, *Theresienstadt: Hitler's Gift to the Jews,* trans. Susan E. Cernyak-Spatz (Chapel Hill and London: University of North Carolina Press, 1991).

68. Hana Volavkova, ed., *I Never Saw Another Butterfly: Children's Drawings and Poems from Terezin Concentration Camp, 1942–1944* (New York: Schocken Books, Random House, 1993).

69. George Eisen, *Children and Play in the Holocaust: Games among the Shadows* (Amherst and Boston: University of Massachusetts Press, 1990).

70. Isaac Jack Lévy, *And the World Stood Silent: Sephardic Poetry of the Holocaust* (Urbana and Chicago: University of Illinois Press, 1989), p. 87. The translation is by Lévy.

71. Primo Levi, *Survival in Auschwitz: The Nazi Assault on Humanity,* trans. Stuart Woolf (New York: Macmillan, 1961), p. 5.

72. Ibid., p. 37.

73. Levi, quoted in Alexander Stille, "Secrets of Primo Levi," *New York Review,* August 15, 2002, p. 32.

74. Although Levi believed there was no connection between his mood disorder and Auschwitz, and at least one of his biographers has accepted this, it is implausible given what we know now about post-traumatic stress disorder. Levi no doubt had a preexisting vulnerability to depression, but much evidence suggests that anyone who has been through such an extreme experience will have added vulnerability attributable to the stress.

75. John Felstiner, *Paul Celan: Poet, Survivor, Jew* (New Haven, Conn.: Yale University Press, 1995).

76. Ibid., p. 11.

77. Ibid., p. 13.

78. Ibid., p. 17. The similarity of the snow imagery to that used by Avraham Sutzkever (p. 265, this volume) at around the same time is striking. They could not have read each other's poems using this imagery.

79. Ibid., pp. 31–32.

80. Ibid., pp. 56–57.

81. Ibid., p. 287.

82. Ibid., p. 287.

83. Ibid., p. 289.

84. Ibid., p. 331.

85. Ibid., p. 287.

86. Viktor E. Frankl, *Man's Search for Meaning,* revised and updated (New York: Washington Square Press, Pocket Books, 1984), pp. 104–5.

Chapter 14. Fire

1. Shimon Huberband, *Kiddush Hashem: Jewish Religious and Cultural Life in Poland during the Holocaust,* ed. Jeffrey S. Gurock and Robert S. Hirt, trans. David E. Fishman (New York: Yeshiva University Press, 1987); Martin Cohen, "Culture and Remembrance: Jewish Ambivalence and Antipathy in the History of Resistance," in *Resisting the Holocaust,* ed. Ruby Rohrlich (Oxford and New York: Berg, 1998).

2. Abraham Foxman, "On Jewish Resistance," *ADL Bulletin,* April 1974.

3. Raul Hilberg, *The Destruction of the European Jews* (New York: Franklin Watts, 1973), pp. 62, 69.

4. Hannah Arendt, *Eichmann in Jerusalem: A Report on the Banality of Evil,* revised and enlarged ed. (New York: Penguin Books, 1964), p. 122.

5. Bruno Bettelheim, "Individual and Mass Behavior in Extreme Situations," *Journal of Abnormal and Social Psychology* 38 (1943): 417–52. Reprinted in Bruno Bettelheim, *Surviving and Other Essays* (New York: Knopf, 1979), p. 79.

6. Ber Mark, "The Herbert Baum Group: Jewish Resistance in Germany in the Years 1937–1942," in *They Fought Back,* ed. Yuri Suhl (New York: Paperback Library, 1967), pp. 62–66.

7. Zydowska Organizacja Bojowa.

8. Dr. William Glicksman, "The Story of Jewish Resistance in the Ghetto of Czestochowa," in *They Fought Back,* ed. Yuri Suhl (New York: Paperback Library, 1967), pp. 81–88.

9. Charles G. Roland, *Courage, Disease, and Death in the Warsaw Ghetto* (New York: Oxford University Press, 1992), chap. 10.

10. Ibid., p. 74.

11. Ber Mark, "The Warsaw Ghetto Uprising," in *They Fought Back,* ed. Yuri Suhl (New York: Paperback Library, 1967), pp. 104–42.

12. Ibid., p. 107.

13. Ibid., p. 109.

14. Ibid., p. 111.

15. Ibid., pp. 112–13.

16. Ibid., p. 122.

17. Ibid., p. 127.

18. Ibid., p. 128.

19. Jean-François Steiner, *Treblinka: The Extraordinary Story of Jewish Resistance in the Notorious Nazi Death Camp,* trans. Helen Weaver (London: Weidenfeld and Nicolson, 1966).

20. Samuel Rajzman, "Uprising in Treblinka," in *They Fought Back,* ed. Yuri Suhl (New York: Paperback Library, 1967), p. 144.

21. Ibid., p. 148.

22. Alexander Pechersky, "Revolt in Sobibor," in *They Fought Back,* ed. Yuri Suhl (New York: Paperback Library, 1967), p. 50.

23. Yuri Suhl, "Editor's Postscript to 'Revolt in Sobibor,'" in *They Fought Back,* ed. Yuri Suhl (New York: Paperback Library, 1967), p. 57.

24. Ibid.

25. Yuri Suhl, "Rosa Roborta—Heroine of the Auschwitz Underground," in *They Fought Back,* ed. Yuri Suhl (New York: Paperback Library, 1967), pp. 237–44.

26. Martin Gilbert, *Jamais Plus: Une Histoire de la Shoah,* trans. Marie-Brunette Spire (Paris: Editions Tallandier, 2001), p. 108. Translation from the French by the author.

27. Rich Cohen, *The Avengers: A Jewish War Story* (New York: Alfred A. Knopf, 2000), p. 45.
28. Ibid., p. 47.
29. Yitzhak Arad, *The Partisan: From the Valley of Death to Mount Zion* (New York: Holocaust Library, 1979), p. 95.
30. Abba Kovner, *Sloan-Kettering: Poems,* trans. Eddie Levenston, foreword by Leon Wieseltier (New York: Schocken Books, 2002), p. 7.
31 Ibid., p. 80.
32. Ibid., frontispiece.
33. Ibid., p. xii.
34. Huberband, *Kiddush Hashem,* p. 117.
35. Arendt, *Eichmann in Jerusalem,* p. 284.
36. Hannah Senesh, *Her Life and Diary,* trans. Marta Cohn (New York: Schocken Books, 1972); Peter Hay, *Ordinary Heroes: Chana Szenes and the Dream of Zion* (New York: G. P. Putnam's Sons, 1986).
37. Senesh, *Her Life and Diary,* p. 14.
38. Judith Tydor Baumel, "The 'Parachutists' Mission' from a Gender Perspective," in *Resisting the Holocaust,* ed. Ruby Rohrlich (Oxford and New York: Berg. 2000), pp. 95–113.
39. Howard Blum, *The Brigade: An Epic Story of Vengeance, Salvation, and World War II* (New York: HarperCollins, 2001).
40. Chuck Olin and Matthew Palm, *In Our Own Hands: The Hidden Story of the Jewish Brigade in World War II* (Chicago and San Francisco: Chuck Olin Associates, KQED, 1998).
41. Blum, *The Brigade,* p. 162.
42. Olin and Palm, *In Our Own Hands.*
43. Blum, *The Brigade,* p. 201.
44. Ibid., p. 198.
45. Olin and Palm, *In Our Own Hands.*
46. Ibid.
47. Ibid.
48 Ibid.
49. Ibid.
50. Martin Gilbert, *The Holocaust: A History of the Jews of Europe During the Second World War* (New York: Holt, Rinehart, and Winston, 1985), pp. 817–18.
51. Herbert A. Friedman, *Roots of the Future* (Jerusalem: Gefen, 1999), p. 81.
52. Ibid.
53. Friedman praises the U.S. Army for its lenient attitudes toward the Jewish refugees, but on September 15, 1945, General George S. Patton, the commander of the Third Army, wrote in his diary that others "believe that the Displaced Person is a human being which he is not, and this applies particularly to the Jews who are lower than animals." J. W. Bendersky, *The "Jewish Threat": Anti-Semitic Politics of the U.S. Army* (New York: Basic Books, 2000), p. 35. See also Paul Johnson, *A History of the Jews* (New York: Harper & Row, 1987), p. 513.
54. Friedman, *Roots of the Future,* pp. 55–56.
55. Ibid., pp. 58–59.
56. Olin and Palm, *In Our Own Hands.*
57. Ibid.
58. Ibid.
59. Ibid.
60. Ibid.
61. Ibid.

Chapter 15. The Golden Land

1. Bernard Lewis, *What Went Wrong? Western Impact and Middle Eastern Response* (New York: Oxford University Press, 2002).
2. Morris U. Schappes, ed., *A Documentary History of the Jews in the United States, 1654–1875,* 3rd ed. (New York: Schocken Books, 1971), p. 1.
3. Ibid., pp. 4–5.
4. Eli Faber, *A Time for Planting: The First Migration, 1654–1820,* vol. 1 of *The Jewish People in America,* ed. Henry L. Feingold (Baltimore: Johns Hopkins University Press, 1992), pp. 62 ff.
5. Schappes, ed., *A Documentary History,* p. 38.
6. Ibid., pp. 46–47.

7. Ibid., pp. 77–78.

8. Ibid., pp. 78–80.

9. Ibid., pp. 123–25.

10. Ibid., pp. 236–37.

11. The opening prayer was delivered by the Reverend Franklin Graham, and ended with the words "We pray this in the name of the Father, and of the Son—the Lord Jesus Christ—and of the Holy Spirit. Amen." The closing prayer, delivered by Reverend Kirbyjon Caldwell, ended with, "We respectfully submit this humble prayer in the name that is above all other names, Jesus the Christ. Let all who agree, say Amen." Kelly J. Coghlan, "Those Dangerous Student Prayers," *St. Mary's Law Journal* 32, no. 4 (2001): 9, n. 19. http://www.schoolprayer.net/pdfs/law_review_02.PDF.

12. Schappes, ed., *A Documentary History,* p. 246 ff.

13. Irving Howe, *We Lived There Too: In Their Own Words and Pictures—Pioneer Jews and the Westward Movement of America, 1630–1930* (New York: St. Martin's/Marek, 1984).

14. Schappes, ed., *A Documentary History,* p. 282.

15. Ibid., p. 441 ff.

16. Ibid., p. 466 ff.

17. Ibid., p. 481.

18. Ibid., pp. 526–27.

19. Charles E. Silberman, *A Certain People: American Jews and Their Lives Today* (New York: Summit Books, 1985).

20. Theodore Rosengarten and Dale Rosengarten, eds., *A Portion of the People: Three Hundred Years of Southern Jewish Life* (Columbia: University of South Carolina Press, 2002). This richly illustrated account accompanies a traveling exhibit of the same name sponsored by the McKissick Museum of the University of South Carolina.

21. Ibid., p. 76.

22. Ibid., p. 75.

23. Hasia R. Diner, *A Time for Gathering: The Second Migration, 1820–1880,* vol. 2 of *The Jewish People in America,* ed. Henry L. Feingold (Baltimore: Johns Hopkins University Press, 1992).

24. Silberman, *A Certain People,* p. 43.

25. Ibid., p. 44.

26. Eli Barnavi, *A Historical Atlas of the Jewish People: From the Time of the Patriarchs to the Present,* trans. Miriam Eliav-Feldon (New York: Schocken Books, 1992), p. 204.

27. Silberman, *A Certain People,* p. 49.

28. Irving Howe, *World of Our Fathers* (New York: Harcourt Brace, 1976).

29. Gerald Sorin, *A Time for Building: The Third Migration, 1880–1920,* vol. 3 of *The Jewish People in America,* ed. Henry L. Feingold (Baltimore: Johns Hopkins University Press, 1992), p. 69.

30. Michael R. Weisser, *A Brotherhood of Memory: Jewish Landsmanshaftn in the New World* (Ithaca, N.Y.: Cornell University Press, 1985).

31. Rafael Medoff, *The Deafening Silence: American Jewish Leaders and the Holocaust* (New York: Shapolsky Publishers, 1987); David S. Wyman, *The Abandonment of the Jews: America and the Holocaust, 1941–1945* (New York: Pantheon Books, 1985).

32. Albert Fried, *The Rise and Fall of the Jewish Gangster in America* (New York: Holt, Rinehart, and Winston, 1980), p. 9.

33. Ibid., pp. 9–10.

34. Ibid., p. 13.

35. Ibid., p. 17.

36. Ibid., pp. 70–71.

37. Rich Cohen, *Tough Jews: Fathers, Sons, and Gangster Dreams* (New York: Vintage, 1998), p. 47.

38. Fried, *The Rise and Fall of the Jewish Gangster in America,* pp. 28–35.

39. Ibid., p. 94 ff.

40. Ibid., p. 143.

41. Neal Gabler, *An Empire of Their Own: How the Jews Invented Hollywood* (New York: Crown Publishers, 1988).

42. Ibid., p. 250.

43. John Lahr, "Walking Alone: Richard Rodgers's Disappearing Act," *New Yorker,* July 1, 2002, pp. 82–87.

44. The positive public impact of the film, as well as Spielberg's generous support of the cause of Holocaust remembrance, can be separated from the deep flaws that have made the film distasteful, even offensive, to many Jews, especially in Israel. See the chapters by Sara R.

Horowitz, Judith E. Doneson, Haim Bresheeth, and Bryan Cheyette in Yosefa Loshitzky, ed., *Spielberg's Holocaust: Critical Perspectives on* Schindler's List (Bloomington: University of Indiana Press, 1997).

45. Barnavi, *A Historical Atlas of the Jewish People,* p. 218.
46. Herbert A. Friedman, *Roots of the Future* (Jerusalem: Gefen, 1999).
47. Silberman, *A Certain People,* p. 201.
48. Ibid., p. 202.
49. Alan M. Dershowitz, *Chutzpah* (Boston: Little, Brown, 1991).
50. Silberman, *A Certain People,* p. 361.
51. Ibid., p. 360.

Chapter 16. Ha'aretz

1. Kenneth W. Stein, *The Land Question in Palestine, 1917–1939* (Chapel Hill: University of North Carolina Press, 1984).
2. For the impressive story of how Israeli agents and American Jews pooled effort and money to make this great migration possible, see Tad Szulc, *The Secret Alliance: The Extraordinary Story of the Rescue of the Jews since World War II* (New York: Farrar, Straus, and Giroux, 1991).
3. Paul Johnson, *A History of the Jews* (New York: Harper & Row, 1987), p. 526.
4. Haj Amin al-Husseini, Grand Mufti of Jerusalem, 1947; http://www.palestinefacts.org/pf_independence_un_arabrejection.php
5. The quote is from President Gamel Abdel Nasser, May 27, 1967; http://news.bbc.co.uk/onthisday/hi/dates/stories/may/30/newsid_2493000/2493177.stm
6. The quote is from a radio address by President Abdur Rahman Aref, May 31, 1967; Bruce Herschensohn, "Ten Mistakes in the Middle East," *The World & I Online Magazine,* 2001. http://www.worldandi.com/public/2001/september/mideast.html
7. Joan Peters, *From Time Immemorial: The Origins of the Arab-Jewish Conflict over Palestine* (New York: Harper & Row, 1984), pp. 84–85.
8. Franz Kobler, ed., *From the Renaissance to the Emancipation,* vol. 2 of *Letters of Jews through the Ages: A Self-Portrait of the Jewish People* (New York: Hebrew Publishing, 1952), pp. 86–87.
9. Peters, *From Time Immemorial,* p. 85.
10. Kobler, ed., *From the Renaissance to the Emancipation,* pp. 394–95.
11. Eli Faber, *A Time for Planting: The First Migration, 1654–1820,* vol. 1 of *The Jewish People in America,* ed. Henry L. Feingold (Baltimore: Johns Hopkins University Press, 1992), p. 62.
12. Quoted in Peters, *From Time Immemorial,* p. 80.
13. Paul R. Mendes-Flohr and Jehuda Reinharz, eds., *The Jew in the Modern World: A Documentary History* (New York: Oxford University Press, 1980), p. 4.
14. Paul Johnson, *A History of the Jews* (New York: Harper & Row, 1987), p. 432.
15. Judith Lady Montefiore, "From Her Private Journal of a Visit to Egypt and Palestine," in *Four Centuries of Jewish Women's Spirituality: A Sourcebook,* ed. Ellen M. Umansky and Dianne Ashton (Boston: Beacon Press, 1992), p. 76.
16. The remaining quotations in this section are from the museum exhibit on the life of Moses Montefiore, in the windmill, Yamin Moshe, Jerusalem.
17. Peters, *From Time Immemorial,* pp. 244–45.
18. Yigal Lossin, *Pillar of Fire: The Rebirth of Israel—a Visual History* (Jerusalem: Shikmona Publishing, in cooperation with the Israel Broadcasting Authority, 1983), p. 22.
19. Ernst Pawel, *The Labyrinth of Exile: A Life of Theodor Herzl* (New York: Farrar, Straus and Giroux, 1989).
20. Ibid., p. 209.
21. Theodor Herzl, *The Diaries of Theodor Herzl,* ed. trans., and with an intro. by Marvin Lowenthal (New York: Dial Press, Grosset and Dunlap, 1956), p. 224.
22. Ze'ev Schiff, *A History of the Israeli Army: 1874 to the Present* (New York: Macmillan, 1985).
23. Lossin, *Pillar of Fire,* p. 37.
24. Conor Cruise O'Brien, *The Siege: The Saga of Israel and Zionism* (New York: Simon and Schuster, 1986), p. 30.
25. Shabtai Teveth, *Ben-Gurion: The Burning Ground, 1886–1948* (Boston: Houghton Mifflin, 1987), p. 81.
26. James Balfour, "The Balfour Declaration," in *The Jew in the Modern World: A Documentary History,* ed. Paul R. Mendes-Flohr and Jehuda Reinharz (New York: Oxford University Press, 1980), p. 458.

27. Schiff, *A History of the Israeli Army,* p. 4.
28. Stein, *The Land Question in Palestine.*
29. For an interesting account of the symbolic meaning of *Sabra,* originally an Arabic word, and of the invention of the native Israeli, see Tsili Doleve-Gandelman, "The Symbolic Inscription of Zionist Ideology in the Space of Eretz Israel: Why the Native Israeli Is Called *Tsabar,*" in *Judaism Viewed from Within and from Without: Anthropological Studies,* ed. Harvey E. Goldberg (Albany: State University of New York Press, 1987).
30. For an affecting account of the *Altalena* episode by a Holocaust survivor who had been one of its young passengers, see Saul Friedlander, *When Memory Comes,* trans. Helen R. Lane (New York: Farrar, Straus, and Giroux, 1979).
31. Martin Gilbert, *Atlas of Jewish History,* 3rd ed. (Dorset, England: Dorset Press, 1977), p. 44.
32. Lewis Glinert, ed., *Hebrew in Ashkenaz: A Language in Exile* (New York: Oxford University Press, 1993).
33. Shaul Stampfer, "What Did 'Knowing Hebrew' Mean in Eastern Europe?" in *Hebrew in Ashkenaz: A Language in Exile,* ed. Lewis Glinert (New York: Oxford University Press, 1993), pp. 129–40.
34. Eli Barnavi, *A Historical Atlas of the Jewish People: From the Time of the Patriarchs to the Present,* trans. Miriam Eliav-Feldon (New York: Schocken Books, 1992), p. 201.
35. Gilbert, *Atlas of Jewish History,* p. 44.
36. George Mandel, "Why Did Ben-Yehuda Suggest the Revival of Spoken Hebrew?" in *Hebrew in Ashkenaz: A Language in Exile,* ed. Lewis Glinert (New York: Oxford University Press, 1993), pp. 193–207.
37. Lossin, *Pillar of Fire,* p. 41.
38. Angel Saenz-Badillos, *A History of the Hebrew Language,* trans. John Elwolde (Cambridge, England: Cambridge University Press, 1993), chap. 8.
39. Shelomo Morag, "The Emergence of Modern Hebrew: Some Sociolinguistic Perspectives," in *Hebrew in Ashkenaz: A Language in Exile,* ed. Lewis Glinert (New York: Oxford University Press, 1993), pp. 208–21.
40. The Orthodox Jews who denounced Ben-Yehudah not only broke but stood on its head one of the most important commandments: *pidyon shevuyim,* the redemption of captives.
41. Ariel Hirschfeld, "Locus and Language: Hebrew Culture in Israel, 1890–1990," in *Cultures of the Jews: A New History,* ed. David Biale (New York: Schocken Books, 2002), pp. 1011–60.
42. Anton Shammas, *Arabesques: A Novel,* trans. Vivian Eden (New York: Harper & Row, 1988).
43. Melford E. Spiro, *Kibbutz: Venture in Utopia* (Cambridge, Mass.: Harvard University Press, 1956). The three kibbutz names were invented by the respective authors.
44. Melford E. Spiro, *Children of the Kibbutz* (New York: Schocken Books, 1965), pp. 6–7.
45. Paula Rayman, *The Kibbutz Community and Nation Building* (Princeton, N.J.: Princeton University Press, 1981).
46. Ibid., p. 53.
47. Ibid., p. 55.
48. Amia Lieblich, *Kibbutz Makom: Report from an Israeli Kibbutz,* Pantheon Village Series (New York: Pantheon Books, 1981).
49. Ibid., p. 225.
50. Ibid., p. 227.
51. Eliezer Ben-Rafael, *Crisis and Transformation: The Kibbutz at Century's End* (Albany: State University of New York Press, 1997), pp. 29–30.
52. Lionel Tiger and Joseph Shepher, *Women in the Kibbutz* (New York: Harcourt Brace, 1975); Melford E. Spiro, *Gender and Culture: Kibbutz Women Revisited* (Durham, N.C.: Duke University Press, 1979).
53. Lieblich, *Kibbutz Makom.*
54. Stein, *The Land Question in Palestine;* Peters, *From Time Immemorial.*
55. Peters, *From Time Immemorial,* p. 245.
56. Lossin, *Pillar of Fire,* p. 21.
57. Peters, *From Time Immemorial,* p. 263.
58. Ibid., p. 265.
59. Benny Morris, *Righteous Victims: A History of the Zionist-Arab Conflict, with a New Final Chapter* (New York: Vintage Books, 2001).
60. Ibid., p. 681.
61. Ibid., p. 208.
62. Ibid., p. 274.

63. Scott Peterson, "How Syria's Brutal Past Colors Its Future," *Christian Science Monitor,* June 20, 2000.

64. Jeffrey Goldberg, "The Great Terror," *New Yorker,* March 25, 2002, p. 52.

65. Grace Halsell, "In Egypt the Real Struggle Is between Mubarak and the Muslim Brotherhood," *Washington Report on Middle East Affairs,* January 1996, pp. 18, 70.

66. David K. Shipler, *Arab and Jew: Wounded Spirits in a Promised Land,* ed. Robert Gardner (Washington, D.C.: Quartet International, Public Broadcasting Service, 1989), film.

67. Ibid.

68. Tom Segev, *The Seventh Million: The Israelis and the Holocaust* (New York: Farrar, Straus and Giroux, Hill and Wang, 1993).

69. Schiff, *A History of the Israeli Army,* p. 16.

70. Segev, *The Seventh Million.*

71. Ibid., p. 513.

72. Dvora Hacohen, "Mass Immigration and the Demographic Revolution in Israel," in *Israel: The First Hundred Years,* vol. 3, *Israeli Politics and Society since 1948: Problems of Collective Identity,* ed. Efraim Karsh (London: Frank Cass, 2002), pp. 177–90.

73. Adam Chesnick, "'Be Israeli, but Don't Forget Where You Came From': Obstacles to Integration among Ethiopian-Jewish University Students in Israel" (bachelor's thesis, Emory University, 2000).

74. Moshe Shokeid, *Children of Circumstances: Israeli Emigrants in New York* (Ithaca, N.Y.: Cornell University Press, 1988).

75. Yoram Peri, "Introduction: The Writing Was on the Wall," in *The Assassination of Yitzhak Rabin,* ed. Yoram Peri (Stanford, Calif.: Stanford University Press, 2000), pp. 1–21.

76. Yoram Peri, ed., *The Assassination of Yitzhak Rabin* (Stanford, Calif.: Stanford University Press, 2000).

77. Thomas L. Friedman, "Fog of War," *New York Times,* August 18, 2002, p. 13.

78. Seymour M. Hersh, *The Samson Option: Israel's Nuclear Arsenal and American Foreign Policy* (New York: Random House, 1991).

Chapter 17. Women of Valor

1. Ross Shepard Kraemer, *Her Share of the Blessings: Women's Religions among Pagans, Jews, and Christians in the Greco-Roman World* (New York: Oxford University Press, 1992), pp. 117 ff. Among other sources, Kraemer cites Bernadette J. Brooten, *Women Leaders in the Ancient Synagogue,* vol. 36, *Brown Judaic Studies* (Chico, Calif.: Scholars Press, 1982).

2. Sondra Henry and Emily Taitz, *Written Out of History: Our Jewish Foremothers,* 2nd rev. ed. (Fresh Meadows, N.Y.: Biblio Press, 1983), pp. 54–58.

3. Joseph Telushkin, *Jewish Literacy: The Most Important Things to Know about the Jewish Religion, Its People, and Its History* (New York: William Morrow, 1991), p. 147.

4. Zvi Kaplan, "Beruryah," in *Encyclopedia Judaica* (Jerusalem: Judaica Multimedia [Israel], 1972).

5. Andree Aelion Brooks, *The Woman Who Defied Kings: The Life and Times of Doña Gracia Nasi—a Jewish Leader during the Renaissance* (St. Paul, Minn.: Paragon House, 2002). According to economic historian Fernand Braudel, this family had achieved "success on a colossal scale," p. 52.

6. Ibid., p. 165.

7. Ibid., p. 175.

8. Ibid., p. 421.

9. Ibid., p. 444.

10. Glückel of Hameln, *The Memoirs of Glückel of Hameln,* trans. Marvin Lowenthal (New York: Schocken Books, 1977), p. 39.

11. Ibid., pp. 47–48.

12. Ibid., p. 53.

13. Ibid., pp. 86–87.

14. Ibid., p. 95.

15. Ibid., pp. 97–98.

16. Ibid., pp. 42–43.

17. Ibid., pp. 150–51.

18. Ibid., p. 179.

19. Ibid., p. 222.

20. Ibid., p. 224.
21. Ibid., p. 1.
22. Ibid., p. 223.
23. Rachel Susman Ashkenazi, "A Yiddish Letter to Her Son Moses in Cairo," in *Four Centuries of Jewish Women's Spirituality: A Sourcebook,* ed. Ellen M. Umansky and Dianne Ashton (Boston: Beacon Press, 1992), p. 39.
24. Theodore Rosengarten and Dale Rosengarten, eds., *A Portion of the People: Three Hundred Years of Southern Jewish Life* (Columbia: University of South Carolina Press, 2002).
25. Penina Moise, "Piety," in *Four Centuries of Jewish Women's Spirituality: A Sourcebook,* ed. Ellen M. Umansky and Dianne Ashton (Boston: Beacon Press, 1992), p. 89.
26. Penina Moise, "Hymn," in *Four Centuries of Jewish Women's Spirituality: A Sourcebook,* ed. Ellen M. Umansky and Dianne Ashton (Boston: Beacon Press, 1992), p. 88.
27. Emma Lazarus, "From 'An Epistle to the Hebrews,'" in *Four Centuries of Jewish Women's Spirituality: A Sourcebook,* ed. Ellen M. Umansky and Dianne Ashton (Boston: Beacon Press, 1992), p. 102.
28. Ibid., pp. 102–3.
29. Ran Aaronsohn, "Through the Eyes of a Settler's Wife: Letters from the *Moshava,*" in *Pioneers and Homemakers,* ed. Deborah S. Bernstein (New York: State University of New York Press, 1992), pp. 34–35.
30. Aaronsohn, "Through the Eyes," pp. 35–36.
31. Ibid., pp. 40–41.
32. Shulamit Reinharz, "Manya Wilbushewitz-Shohat and the Winding Road to Sejera," in *Pioneers and Homemakers,* ed. Deborah S. Bernstein (New York: State University of New York Press, 1992), p. 100.
33. Deborah S. Bernstein and Musia Lipman, "Fragments of Life: From the Diaries of Two Young Women," in *Pioneers and Homemakers,* ed. Deborah S. Bernstein (New York: State University of New York Press, 1992), p. 149.
34. Ibid., pp. 161–62.
35. Rich Cohen, *The Avengers: A Jewish War Story* (New York: Alfred A. Knopf, 2000), p. 63.
36. Nechama Tec, *Defiance: The Bielski Partisans* (New York: Oxford University Press, 1993), p. 54.
37. Yuri Suhl, "Little Wanda with the Braids," in *They Fought Back,* ed. Yuri Suhl (New York: Paperback Library, 1967), pp. 62–66.
38. Ze'ev Schiff, *A History of the Israeli Army: 1874 to the Present* (New York: Macmillan, 1985).
39. Louie Williams, *Israel Defense Forces: A People's Army* (Tel Aviv: Ministry of Defense Publishing House, 1989), p. 335.
40. David Biale, *Eros and the Jews: From Biblical Israel to Contemporary America* (New York: Basic Books, 1992).
41. Ibid., p. 23.
42. Ibid., pp. 23–28.
43. Ibid., p. 15.
44. Lis Harris, *Holy Days: The World of a Hasidic Family* (New York: Macmillan, 1986), p. 139.
45. Ibid., pp. 147–48.
46. Lily H. Montagu, "For Reform Synagogue, Berlin," in *Four Centuries of Jewish Women's Spirituality: A Sourcebook,* ed. Ellen M. Umansky and Dianne Ashton (Boston: Beacon Press, 1992), p. 156.
47. Isaac Metzker, ed., *A Bintel Brief: Sixty Years of Letters from the Lower East Side to the* Jewish Daily Forward (New York: Schocken Books, 1971), pp. 109–10.
48. Betty Friedan, *The Feminine Mystique* (New York: Random House, 1963).
49. Charles E. Silberman, *A Certain People: American Jews and Their Lives Today* (New York: Summit Books, 1985), p. 264.
50. Deborah E. Lipstadt, "And Deborah Made Ten," in *On Being a Jewish Feminist: A Reader,* ed. Susannah Heschel (New York: Schocken Books, 1983), pp. 208–9.
51. Silberman, *A Certain People,* p. 262.
52. Netty C. Gross, "A Year since the Revolution," *Jerusalem Report,* June 4, 2003, pp. 24–25.
53. Netty C. Gross, "Our Bodies, Ourselves," *Jerusalem Report,* June 4, 2001, pp. 18–20.

Chapter 18. Conclusion: A Drop of Red Wine

1. Theodor Herzl, *The Diaries of Theodor Herzl,* ed., trans., and with an intro. by Marvin Lowenthal (New York: Dial Press, Grosset and Dunlap, 1956), p. 9.

2. Anson Laytner, *Arguing with God: A Jewish Tradition* (Northvale, N.J.: Jason Aronson, 1990). Many of the examples come from Laytner's book.

3. Harry M. Rabinowicz, *Hasidism: The Movement and Its Masters* (Northvale, N.J.: Jason Aronson, 1988), p. 65.

4. David R. Blumenthal, *Facing the Abusing God: A Theology of Protest* (Louisville, Ky.: Westminster, John Knox Press, 1993), p. 285.

5. Michael Walzer, *Exodus and Revolution* (New York: Basic Books, 1985), p. 64.

6. Ibid., p. 51.

7. Ibid., p. 128.

8. Ibid., p. 6.

9. Ibid., p. 52.

10. Ibid., p. 54.

11. Gideon Shimoni, "From One Frontier to Another: Jewish Identity and Political Orientation in Lithuania and South Africa, 1890–1939," in *Jewries at the Frontier: Accommodation, Identity, Conflict,* ed. Sander L. Gilman and Milton Shain (Urbana and Chicago: University of Illinois Press, 1999).

12. Dan Rottenberg, *Middletown Jews: The Tenuous Survival of an American Jewish Community* (Bloomington: Indiana University Press, 1997), pp. 135–36.

13. Barbara Myerhoff, *Number Our Days: A Triumph of Continuity among Jewish Old People in an Urban Ghetto* (New York: Simon and Schuster, Touchstone, 1978), p. 234.

14. Ibid., p. 249.

15. Ibid., p. 195.

16. Jack Kugelmass, *The Miracle of Intervale Avenue: The Story of a Jewish Congregation in the South Bronx* (New York: Schocken Books, 1987), p. 214.

17. Ibid., p. 212.

18. Charles E. Silberman, *A Certain People: American Jews and Their Lives Today* (New York: Summit Books, 1985).

19. These figures are from the Web site of the World Jewish Congress, "Jewish Communities of the World: World Jewry," http://www.wjc.org.il/communities/jewish_communities_of_the_world/chartmap.html. The data on the United States precede the National Jewish Population Survey 2000–2001.

20. Larry Tye, *Home Lands: Portraits of the New Jewish Diaspora* (New York: Henry Holt, 2001), chap. 7.

21. Shifra Epstein, "Drama on a Table: The Bobover Hasidim Perimshpiyl," in *Judaism Viewed from Within and from Without: Anthropological Studies,* ed. Harvey E. Goldberg (Albany: State University of New York Press, 1987), pp. 195–233.

22. Sylvia Rothchild, *A Special Legacy: An Oral History of Soviet Jewish Emigrés in the United States* (New York: Simon and Schuster, 1985); Fran Markowitz, "A Bat Mitzvah among Russian Jews in America," in *The Life of Judaism,* ed. Harvey E. Goldberg (Berkeley: University of California Press, 2001), pp. 121–25.

23. Joseph A. D. Sutton, *Aleppo Chronicles: The Story of the Unique Sephardeem of the Ancient Near East—in Their Own Words* (New York: Thayer-Jacoby, 1988); Joseph A. D. Sutton, *Magic Carpet: Aleppo-in-Flatbush: The Story of a Unique Ethnic Jewish Community* (New York: Thayer-Jacoby, 1986).

24. Moshe Shokeid, *Children of Circumstances: Israeli Emigrants in New York* (Ithaca, N.Y.: Cornell University Press, 1988).

25. "Synagogues Flourish in America," *American Jewish Committee Journal,* September 2002, pp. 6–7.

26. http://www.ujc.org/content_display.html?ArticleID=60654.

27. Daniel J. Wakin, "A Count of U.S. Jews Sees a Dip; Others Demur," *New York Times,* October 9, 2002, A23.

28. Rightward-Leaning Jews said in effect, *I told you so.* For a sample of their reactions, see Neal Kozodoy, ed., *The Mideast Peace Process: An Autopsy* (San Francisco: Encounter Books, 2002).

29. Scott Anderson, "An Impossible Occupation," *New York Times Magazine,* May 12, 2002, pp. 34–69.

30. Fiamma Nirenstein, "Israel's Last Line of Defense," *Commentary,* January 2003, pp. 23–27.

31. Jack Kelley, "Explosion, Then Arms, Legs Rain Down," *USA Today,* August 10, 2001.

32. George Will, "A War and Then a Wall," *Washington Post,* August 17, 2001.

33. Faisal al-Husseini, "Interview," *Al-Arabi,* June 24, 2001.

34. Eric Silver, "Target: Jews. Anti-Semitism Sweeps across Europe," *Jerusalem Report*, May 6, 2002, pp. 32–36.
35. Tye, *Home Lands*, chap. 6.
36. Ibid., p. 31.
37. Ibid., p. 76.
38. Lev Krichevsky, "Russian Jews Fear Undercount in New Census," *Atlanta Jewish Times/Jewish Telegraphic Agency*, October 18, 2002, p. 26.
39. Rebecca Weiner, *The Virtual Jewish History Tour: Argentina* [Web site]. Jewish Virtual Library, 2003 [cited March 6, 2003]. Available from http://www.us-israel.org/jsource/vjw/Argentina.html#present.
40. "Historic Yiddish-Symposium in South America," *Forvertz*, November 2, 2001, p. 1.

FOR FURTHER READING

One of the best ways to approach the Jews is through books by non-Jews. Paul Johnson's sweeping *A History of the Jews* is an excellent overview, although Thomas Cahill's *The Gifts of the Jews* is a simpler entry point. Father Edward Flannery's *The Anguish of the Jews: Twenty-three Centuries of Anti-Semitism* is a moving account of Jewish persecutions, and James Carroll's magisterial *Constantine's Sword* recounts the sad history of the Catholic church's relations with Jews. Although nearly two decades old, Conor Cruise O'Brien's *The Siege* is still the best history of Zionism and Israel.

To pursue in greater depth the range of Jewish cultures in time and space, two volumes are especially valuable. Eli Barnavi's *A Historical Atlas of the Jewish People: From the Time of the Patriarchs to the Present* is a lavishly illustrated account of Jewish cultural history, and *Cultures of the Jews: A New History,* edited by David Biale, has up-to-date and authoritative essays on every significant Jewish culture. Harvey Goldberg, the dean of Jewish anthropology, has edited three volumes that bring together the best and most original writing in this burgeoning field: *Judaism Viewed from Within and from Without, Sephardi and Middle Eastern Jewries: History and Culture in the Modern Era*, and *The Life of Judaism*. Everything you always wanted to know about the Jews but were afraid to ask is at your fingertips in Joseph Telushkin's lively encyclopedia *Jewish Literacy.*

Introductions to Israeli archeology independent of biblical accounts include *The Bible Unearthed: Archeology's New Vision of Ancient Israel and the Origin of Its Sacred Texts,* by Israel Finkelstein and Neal Asher Silberman, and Robert B. Coote's *Early Israel: A New Horizon*. Nahman Avigad's *Discovering Jerusalem* takes a similar approach. The works of Josephus, although not always trustworthy, are a sweeping account of late Second Temple Judaism. Adin Steinsaltz's *The Essential Talmud* is a good short introduction to this foundational work of rabbinical Judaism, but there is no substitute in English for dipping into his magnificent multivolume version,

The Talmud: The Steinsaltz Edition. On the Jewishness of Jesus, John Dominic Crossan's *The Historical Jesus: The Life of a Mediterranean Jewish Peasant* is thorough and respectful, and *Jesus' Jewishness: Exploring the Place of Jesus within Early Judaism,* edited by James H. Charlesworth, is a fascinating collection of expert essays.

Robert M. Seltzer's *Jewish People, Jewish Thought: The Jewish Experience in History* is a comprehensive intellectual history. *The Jews of Islam,* by Bernard Lewis, is a brief overview of one great branch of the Jewish people, while Norman Stillman's *The Jews of Arab Lands: A History and Source Book* treats the subject in greater depth. Harvey Goldberg's *Jewish Life in Muslim Libya: Rivals and Relatives* is an indispensable ethnography.

Of the many books about the Spanish Jews, I have found three especially illuminating: *Sephardim: The Jews from Spain,* by Paloma Díaz-Mas, is an elegant brief introduction; Isaac Lévy's *Jewish Rhodes: A Lost Culture* is a vivid ethnography of a great Sephardic center; and Rebecca Amato Levy's *I Remember Rhodes* offers a touching personal view of that center, along with a collection of songs and proverbs.

For the Jews of Ethiopia, an authoritative account is James Quirin's *The Evolution of the Ethiopian Jews: A History of the Beta Israel (Falasha) to 1920.* Joan G. Roland's *Jews in British India* serves a similar function for that community, while Ruby Daniel and Barbara C. Johnson's *Ruby of Cochin: An Indian Jewish Woman Remembers* provides an engaging personal view. The definitive work on the easternmost Jewish community is Jonathan Goldstein's fine collection *The Jews of China: Historical and Comparative Perspectives.*

A superb retrospective ethnography of the Jews of eastern Europe is Mark Zborowski and Elizabeth Herzog's *Life Is with People: The Culture of the Shtetl,* although even it doesn't match the evocative power of Isaac Bashevis Singer's novels and stories. *Image Before My Eyes: A Photographic History of Jewish Life in Poland, 1864–1939,* by Lucjan Dobroszycki and Barbara Kirshenblatt-Gimblett, along with the film of the same name, provides an indispensable window into the destroyed Jewish communities of Poland.

The most readable one-volume history of the Shoah is Martin Gilbert's *The Holocaust: A History of the Jews of Europe during the Second World War,* but Raul Hilberg's *The Destruction of the European Jews* (revised and definitive edition, three volumes) is indeed definitive (with the important omission of resistance). Dramatic accounts of resistance include *They Fought Back,* edited by Yuri Suhl; *The Brigade: An Epic Story of Vengeance, Salvation, and World War II,* by Howard Blum; *The Avengers: A Jewish War Story,* by Rich Cohen; *Treblinka: The Extraordinary Story of Jewish Resistance in the Notorious Nazi Death Camp* by Jean-François Steiner; and the magnificent film *In Our Own Hands: The Hidden Story of the Jewish Brigade in World War II,* edited by Chuck Olin and Matthew Palm.

The best overview of the Jews of modern Europe is *The Jew in the Modern World: A Documentary History,* edited by Paul R. Mendes-Flohr and Jehuda Reinharz, and the corresponding banquet of information on the United States is *A Documentary History of the Jews in the United States, 1654–1875,* edited by Morris Schappes. *World of Our Fathers,* by Irving Howe, is the standard reference on Jewish immigrants from eastern Europe. Neal Gabler's *An Empire of Their Own: How the Jews Invented Hollywood,* Albert Fried's *The Rise and Fall of the Jewish Gangster in America,* Kenneth Libo and Irving Howe's *We Lived There Too: In Their Own Words and Pictures—Pioneer Jews and the Westward Movement of America, 1630–1930,* and Theodore and Dale Rosengarten's *A Portion of the People: Three Hundred Years of Southern Jewish Life* are fascinating windows on the Jewish American past. Sad yet uplifting ethnographies of older Jews include Barbara Myerhoff's *Number Our Days: A Triumph of Continuity among Jewish Old People in an Urban Ghetto* and Jack Kugelmass's *The Miracle of Intervale Avenue: The Story of a Jewish Congregation in the South Bronx.*

O'Brien's *The Siege* remains the best overview of Zionism and Israel, and the *Diaries* of Theodor Herzl are well worth reading even today. *Pillar of Fire: The Rebirth of Israel—A Visual History,* by Yigal Lossin, and the accompanying film series tell the story in unforgettable images. Melford Spiro's *Kibbutz: Venture in Utopia* is the classic ethnography of this great human experiment. Benny Morris's *Righteous Victims: A History of the Zionist-Arab Conflict* is about as fair as any book can be about this seemingly endless human tragedy.

Glückel of Hameln, Anne Frank, and Hannah Senesh left memoirs of Jewish womanhood that will always be read. *Four Centuries of Jewish Women's Spirituality: A Sourcebook,* edited by Ellen Umansky and Dianne Ashton, opens a new window on Jewish history. *Pioneers and Homemakers,* edited by Deborah Bernstein, gives eyewitness accounts of women's lives in early modern Israel. And David Biale's *Eros and the Jews: From Biblical Israel to Contemporary America* is a fascinating account of how Jewish writers, mainly men, have construed sex and gender.

Jews have written lasting verse in many languages, but the poetic treasures in Hebrew are best experienced in T. Carmi's *The Penguin Book of Hebrew Verse.* The best Yiddish collection is Ruth Whitman's *An Anthology of Modern Yiddish Poetry,* and a moving collection of poems by Sephardim about the Holocaust is Isaac Lévy's *And the World Stood Silent.* Recent personal memoirs that I have found especially moving are Julius Lester's *Lovesong: Becoming a Jew,* Sana Hassan's *Enemy in the Promised Land: An Egyptian Woman's Journey into Israel,* Saul Friedlander's *When Memory Comes,* and Leslie Hazleton's *Jerusalem, Jerusalem.*

No one can understand the Jews without the sacred texts. The Jewish Bible—the Torah, Prophetic Books, and Writings, known to Christians as the Old Testament—is central. The Jewish Publication Society translation is widely accepted today, although there is no literary match for the King James Version. The Talmud is most accessible in the Steinsaltz edition cited above, but its cherished philosophic and ethical essence is contained in the much briefer *The Sayings of the Fathers*. The standard edition of the core Jewish mystical work is that of Fischel Lachower and Isaiah Tishby, *The Wisdom of the Zohar: An Anthology of Texts* (three volumes). There are many Jewish prayer books, but a good one for study purposes is the richly annotated *Hertz Siddur*. For respected interpretations representing the four great movements, see Rabbi Joseph Soleveitchik's *Halakhic Man* (Orthodox), Rabbi Abraham Joshua Heschel's *God in Search of Man: A Philosophy of Judaism* (Conservative), Rabbi David Wolpe's *The Healer of Shattered Hearts* (Reform), and Rabbi Mordecai Kaplan's *Judaism as a Civilization: Toward a Reconstruction of American Jewish Life* (Reconstructionist). Another kind of religiosity in Judaism is summarized in Aaron Laytner's *Arguing with God: A Jewish Tradition* and given new expression in Rabbi David Blumenthal's *Facing the Abusing God: A Theology of Protest*. Even in anger the Jews embrace God.

INDEX

Aaron, 25, 36, 46
Aaronsohn, Sarah, 402
Abraham
  arguing with God, 29, 415
  biblical story of, 13, 15
  circumcision commanded of, 54, 55, 56, 104–5
  claiming his wife is his sister, 403
  and Egypt, 16
  external evidence for, 3
  Kaifeng Jews on, 215
  as monotheist, 32, 34
  name changed, 56
  near sacrifice of Isaac, 48, 49, 117
  Rashi on, 121
  smashing his father's idols, 12, 36
  and Sodom and Gomorrah, 29, 415
Abramovitsh, S. Y. (Mendele Moykher Sforim), 367
Abrams, Hyman, 340
Absalom, 405
abstractions, Jewish concern with, 1, 38
academies
  Babylonian, 97
  of diaspora, 110, 112
  in Germany, 121, 123
  Doña Gracia Nasi building, 391
  in Poland and Lithuania, 224, 247, 256
  scholars nurtured in, 196
  as selection system, 189
  at Yavneh, 72, 91
Adam, 30, 181, 182, 183, 215
Adler, Jacob P., 239–40
Afghanistan, 220
Africa
  Ethiopian Jews, 200–208, 382
  South Africa, 421
  Uganda offered to Zionists, 362
  See also North Africa

African National Congress, 421
afternoon religious schools, 424–25
Agamemnon, 49
Agnon, S. Y., 368
Agudah (Agudas Israel), 234
Ahab, 18, 19, 21
Ahura Masda, 35
Akhenaton, 34, 35
Akiva, 71–72
  academy of, 73
  and Bar Kokhba revolt, 74, 119, 361
  execution of, 75, 91, 106
  and Hadrian, 74
  Hillel compared with, 69
  Jerusalem aristocrats contrasted with, 77
  liberal rulings of, 72, 73
  mysticism of, 176
  and Simeon bar-Yohai, 175
  on Torah, 74, 92
  wife of, 71, 386
Alaska, 221–22
Aleichem, Sholem, 240, 257–58, 298, 346
Alexander III (czar), 237
Alexander the Great, 49, 50
Alexandria (Egypt), 85, 127, 143, 337
aliyah
  First Aliyah, 358–59
  Second Aliyah, 362–63
  in twelfth and thirteenth centuries, 356
  yeridah contrasted with, 382
Alkabetz, Solomon Halevi, 174–75
Allen, Woody, 346
Alliance Israélite Universelle (Paris), 172
alphabetic scripts, 22–23
Alterman, Nathan, 368
American Federation of Labor, 335
American Jewish Committee, xxi

477

women in, 388
of Yemenite Jews, 219
trade schools, 257
Trajan (Roman emperor), 90
Treatise against the Jews (Augustine), 108
Treblinka, 273, 274, 298–99
Tree of Life, 181
Triangle Shirtwaist Company, 242
Tripoli, 127, 143
Trotsky, Leon, 194
Truman, Harry, 347–48
Trumpeldor, Joseph, 308, 364
t'shuva, 117
Tu B'Shvat, 117–18
Turkey
    anti-Jewish riots in, 113
    blood libel accusations in, 142
    British drive Turks out of Jerusalem, 363, 376
    Constantinople, 112–13, 132–33, 160, 170, 171, 318, 337
    diaspora Jewish communities in, 110
    golden age of diaspora Jews in, 318
    Doña Gracia Nasi, 390–91
    Spanish Jews settling in Ottoman Empire, 160, 166–67, 169–72
    vying for control of Israel, 376
Tuwim, Julian, 257
Twain, Mark, 189
Tyre, 133
tzaddik, 250

Uganda, 362
Ukraine, 247, 272, 433
Ulinover, Miriam, 259
ulpan program, 368
ultra-Orthodoxy, 251, 361
union movement, 241–44, 339
United Hebrew Charities, 238
United Jewish Communities, 425
United States
    civil rights movement, 421
    compulsory sterilization in, 269
    as example to the world, 322
    as "God's new Israel," 419
    See also American Jews
Universal Pictures, 343
Urban II (pope), 123
Uriah, 405
Usque, Samuel, 159, 390
Uzbekistan, 220
Uzieli, Avraham, 310–11

Valentine, Simon, 330
Venice (California), 423
Venice (Italy), 170, 390
Vespasian (Roman emperor), 80, 81
Victoria, Queen, 358

Vienna, 223, 270
Vilna
    destruction of Jews of, 264–66
    Hasidism opposed in, 249–50
    Hebrew newspaper in, 366
    as "Jerusalem of Lithuania," 249
    Jewish artisans in, 223
    Jewish resistance to Nazis in, 301–3, 304, 401
    Jews settling in, 254, 256
    Wessely's books burned in, 225
    Young Vilna, 263–64
Vilna Gaon, 240–50, 251
Vitoffsky, Charley "the Cripple," 339

Wagner, Richard, 192
Wallant, Edward Lewis, 347
Wannsee conference, 274
Warner, Jack, 343
Warner Brothers, 343
Warsaw
    ghetto uprising, 296–98, 302, 304
    Jews settling in, 254, 256
Washington, George, 321–23, 351
weddings, 138–39, 171–72, 204–5, 211–13, 219–20
Weiss, Louise, 408
Weiss, Mendy, 341
Weissman, Solomon "Cutcher-Head-Off," 340
Weizmann, Chaim, 235, 362, 363–64, 381, 436
Wessely, Naphtali Herz, 225
West Bank
    expansion of Jewish settlements in, 435
    Israeli incursions into, 428
    Israeli occupation of, 354
    Israeli withdrawal from, 430–31
    Jordan renounces claim on, 354
    Palestinian Authority takes control of, 354
    refugee camps in, 353
    standard of living in, 378
Western Wall, 356
Westheimer, Ruth, 402, 403
Wexner Heritage Foundation, xxii
white slavery, 337
Wiernick, Yankel, 298–99
Wiesel, Elie, 275–76, 283, 349–51
Wieseltier, Leon, 303
Wiesenthal, Simon, 285–86
Will, George, 428–29
William of Melun, 123
Wingate, Oren, 370
Wise, Isaac Meyer, 331
"Without Jews" (Glatstein), 417–18
Wittlin, Jósef, 257
women
    Christianity embraced by, 104, 105
    in trade, 388
    See also Jewish women
Workman, Bugs, 341

World Series of 1919, 338
World War I, 255, 270, 339, 363
World War II
    American Jews in, 347
    beginning of, 271
    Jewish women fighters in, 401
    war films, 344
    See also Holocaust
Worms, 121, 122, 123
writing, 22–23

Yad Vashem, 302
Yahwist, 2–3, 24
Yamin Moshe, 358, 437
Yankel the Tailor, 249, 417
Yavneh academy, 72, 91
Yehuda ha-Nasi, Rabbi, 95
Yekl (Cahan), 240–41
Yemen
    diaspora Jewish communities in, 110, 219–20
    forced conversion in, 132
    Jewish Kingdom in, 112, 127, 200, 219
    polygamy in, 138
"Yentl the Yeshiva-Boy" (Singer), 259–60
yeshivas. *See* academies
Yeshiva University, 335
Yezierska, Anzia, 243–46
Yiddishkayt, 233–34
Yiddish language, 247
    in Ashkenazic culture, xviii, 114, 255, 256–57
    Buenos Aires conference on, 434
    curses in, 185–86
    fiction, 257–60
    folk songs, 261
    Hasidim using, 251
    Haskalah on, 366, 367
    jokes, 260–61
    journals in, 257
    Mendelssohn on, 191
    number of speakers in 1930s, 257
    poetry, 257, 262–67
    proverbs, 261–62
    range of publications in, 254
    Singer writing in, 184, 436
    theater, 239–40, 256, 344
    in United States, 236, 237, 239–41, 333
Yochanan ben Zakkai, 72, 90–91, 92, 413, 420–21
Yocheved, 30
Yom Kippur
    dwelling on death on, 117
    as fast day, 46
    in Jewish calendar, 116, 119

Kol Nidre prayer, 160, 239, 344
    Picart depicting, 168
    piyyut sung on, 114–15
    reciting Maimonides' articles of the faith on, 130
    as Sabbath of Sabbaths, 120
    sacrifice on, 47
Yom Kippur War (1973), 354, 374
York, 153
Young Vilna, 263–64

Zach, Natan, 375
Zborowski, Mark, 229
Zealots
    aristocrats killed by, 80
    divisions among, 79
    Essenes compared with, 78
    Jesus compared with, 66
    on rebuilding Temple, 73
    Roman rule opposed by, 59, 69, 79
    suicide at Masada, 81
Zedekiah, 22, 37
Zelig, Big Jack, 338, 342
Zhitomir, 223–24, 272–73
Zhurnal, Morgan, 239
Zichron Ya'akov, 356, 398, 437
Zikhroynes (Glückel of Hameln), 391, 394–95
Zionism
    American Jews adopt, 347–48
    anti-Semitism in establishment of, 235
    anti-Zionists, 234–35, 361, 381
    becoming a movement, 142, 352
    Britain offers Uganda to, 362
    Hasidim opposing, 234, 252
    Holocaust anticipated by, 380, 384
    Holocaust seen as punishment for, 284
    Muslim leaders not taking seriously, 141
    range of groups in, 234
    Scholem adopting, 228, 229
    Senesh on, 307–8
    socialist, 362, 369, 380, 436–37
    terrorism by, 377–78
ZOB (Jewish Fighting Organization), 296, 298
Zohar, 175, 178, 180–81
Zola, Émile, 360
Zorea, Meir, 312, 315
Zoroastrianism, 35
Zuckerman, Yitzhak, 304
Zukor, Adolph, 343
Zweibach, Max, 338
Zwillman, Longy, 340

Grateful acknowledgment is made for permission to reprint the following copyrighted works:

Excerpt from "Don't Show Me" by Ruth Beker. Used by permission of Ruth Beker.

Selections by Paul Celan translated by John Felstiner from *Paul Celan: Poet, Survivor, Jew* by John Felstiner (Yale University Press, 1995). By permission of John Felstiner.

Selection from *Early Israel: A New Horizon* by Robert B. Coote (Fortress Press, 1990). By permission of the author.

Selection from *Ruby of Cochin* by Ruby Daniel and Barbara C. Johnson. Copyright © 1995 The Jewish Publication Society. Reprinted by permission of The Jewish Publication Society.

Excerpt from "Autumn" from *The Poems of John Dewey,* edited by Jo Ann Boydston. © 1977 by Southern Illinois University Press. Reprinted by permission of the publisher.

Excerpt from "I Never Saw Another Butterfly" by Pavel Friedmann from *I Never Saw Another Butterfly* by the United States Holocaust Memorial Museum, edited by Hana Volavkova. Copyright © 1978, 1993 by Artia, Prague. Compilation copyright © 1993 by Schocken Books. Used by permission of Schocken Books, a division of Random House, Inc.

Selection from *Hammer on the Rock: A Short Midrash Reader* edited by Nahum N. Glatzer (Schocken, 1962). By permission of Judith Glatzer Wechsler.

Selections from *Sloan-Kettering: Poems* by Abba Kovner, translated by Eddie Levenston. Copyright © 2002 by the Estate of Abba Kovner. Used by permission of Schocken Books, a division of Random House, Inc.

Excerpts from *Siberia: A Poem* by Abraham Sutzkever, translated by Jacob Sonntag (Abelard-Schuman, 1961). Used by permission of Abraham Sutzkever.

Selections by Abraham Sutzkever from *Abraham Sutzkever: Partisan Poet* by Joseph Leftwich. By permission of Associated University Presses.

"With the Taytsh-Khumesh" by Miriam Ulinover, translated by Kathryn Hellerstein. Translation copyright Kathryn Hellerstein. First published in *Four Centuries of Jewish Women's Spirituality* edited by Ellen M. Umansky and Dianne Ashton (Beacon Press, 1992). By permission of Kathryn Hellerstein.

Excerpt from a poem by Natan Zach from *Kibbutz Makom: Report from an Israeli Kibbutz* by Amia Lieblich. Copyright © 1981 by Amia Lieblich. Used by permission of Pantheon Books, a division of Random House, Inc.